Exploring GenderSpeak
Personal Effectiveness in Gender Communication

Exploring GenderSpeak

Personal Effectiveness in Gender Communication

Diana K. Ivy
North Carolina State University

Phil Backlund
Central Washington University

McGraw-Hill, Inc.

New York St. Louis San Francisco Auckland Bogotá Caracas Lisbon
London Madrid Mexico City Milan Montreal New Delhi
San Juan Singapore Sydney Tokyo Toronto

This book was set in Palatino by ComCom, Inc.
The editors were Hilary Jackson and Jean Akers;
the production supervisor was Leroy A. Young.
The cover was designed by Carol A. Couch.
The photo editor was Elyse Rieder.
R. R. Donnelley & Sons Company was printer and binder.

Cover photo credit: Andre Baranowski

Photo Credits

1: *Comstock;* **2:** *Roger Dollarhide/Monkmeyer;* **3:** *Arvind Garg/Photo Researchers;*
4: *Photofest;* **Fig. 4.1:** *Outdoor Advertising Association of America;*
5: *Lawrence Migdale/Stock, Boston;* **6:** *Sven Martson/Comstock;*
7: *Nancy Durrell McKenna/Photo Researchers;* **8:** *Sven Martson/Comstock;*
9: *Rob Lang/FPG International;* **10:** *Joel Gordon;* **11:** *Jim Pickerell/Stock, Boston;*
12: *Joel Gordon.*

EXPLORING GENDERSPEAK
Personal Effectiveness in Gender Communication

This book is printed on recycled, acid-free paper containing a minimum of 50% total recycled fiber with 10% postconsumer de-inked fiber.

1 2 3 4 5 6 7 8 9 0 DOC DOC 9 0 9 8 7 6 5 4 3

ISBN 0-07-032292-9

Library of Congress Cataloging-in-Publication Data

Ivy, Diana K.
  Exploring GenderSpeak: personal effectiveness in gender
communication / Diana K. Ivy, Phil Backlund.
    p.   cm.
  Includes index.
  ISBN 0-07-032292-9
  1. Communication—Sex differences.   I. Backlund, Phil.
  II. Title.
  P96.S48I96   1994
  305.3—dc20   93-28041

About the Authors

DIANA K. IVY received her undergraduate degree in speech communication and theater from Texas Wesleyan College in her hometown of Fort Worth, Texas. After serving Wesleyan for four years as Assistant Director of Admissions, Ivy pursued graduate education and became a teaching assistant in the Department of Communication at the University of Oklahoma. Concentrating on instructional and interpersonal communication there, she received her M.A. in 1984 and her Ph.D. in 1987. Dr. Ivy's first faculty position was in the Department of Speech Communication at Southwest Texas State University, where she received the Professor of the Year Award from the Nontraditional Student Organization and the departmental Outstanding Teacher Award. She is currently an assistant professor in the Department of Communication at North Carolina State University, where she conducts research on gender, interpersonal, and instructional communication.

PHIL BACKLUND received a bachelor's degree in business administration and a Master's degree in speech communication from Humboldt State University near where he grew up in northern California. He then taught for two years at the University of Alaska before pursuing his Ph.D. at the University of Denver. His first faculty position after the doctoral degree was at Utica College in New York. He currently is a professor of speech communication and Associate Dean of the College of Letters, Arts, and Sciences at Central Washington University. He has a great time as a husband and father, and during his leisure time he can usually be found engaging in family activities or windsurfing.

To Important Women
Hazel, Carol, and Karen
DKI

To My Family
Judy, Shane, Ryan, and Matt
PB

Contents

Part Two
INFLUENCES ON OUR CHOICES

Part Three
LET'S TALK: INITIATING AND DEVELOPING
RELATIONSHIPS

Part Four
THE CONTEXTS FOR OUR RELATIONSHIPS:
PERSONAL EFFECTIVENESS IN ACTION

Preface

When we first discussed with our friends and colleagues the idea of writing a textbook on the topic of gender communication, many responded, "I really hope you write it, because I could do well to read a book on that topic." This common reaction convinced us of something we had detected in our own gender communication classes: in increasing numbers, people are coming to realize just how complex yet pervasive communication between women and men is in our professional and personal lives. One can rarely tune into a television talk show or open a newspaper without being bombarded by the topic. Traditionally male-dominated businesses and institutions are attempting to diversify their workforce to parallel the diversity in our society. Since the roles for women and men, as well as the rules that govern their behavior, have changed dramatically and continue to change, an understanding of the complexity that gender brings to communication becomes increasingly important. Anticipating how men and women will think, talk, and respond in a variety of situations represents one of our most challenging activities.

Exploring GenderSpeak: Personal Effectiveness in Gender Communication goes beyond a description of how men and women are communicatively alike and how they are different. It encourages students to consider the myriad of influences—from physiology to culture to media—that affect their communication with women and men. Most important, as students explore the information presented in the text, they are challenged to learn about themselves, in terms of attitudes, gender-role identity, and communication ability in their relationships.

In our own teaching of a variety of communication courses, we find that students seem to be searching for the concrete, the applicable, the reality based. If your students are like ours, they are cognizant of the fact that they need a theoretical, research-driven background on a given topic. But what they really seek is a translation of that information into a recognizeable, useful form. For example, an interesting discussion developed in one of Ivy's gender communication classes surrounding proactive versus reactive approaches to communication and relationships. While students understood theoretically the notion of proactively communicating to have an effect on other people, rather than assuming a pattern of reactivity, they wondered how this notion would actually work, in terms of initiating dating or romantic relationships. Did this mean that everyone should aggressively initiate relationships, rather than hoping that "Mr. or Ms. Right would find them"? Or was it more a philosophy or way of viewing relationships than an actual style of communication? The class came to realize how proactive communication, stereotypically associated with masculinity, and reactive communication, stereotypically associated with femininity, are translated into ingrained, socialized roles that people tend to assume in their relationships.

From this example and many others, it has become obvious to us that, in the area of gender communication especially, students continually seek empowerment. They seek ways they can use what they learn to more effectively establish and improve their relationships with others. Often textbooks merely report research results without offering a possible interpretation of the findings or an application of the information. The result of this practice is that the reader or you, the instructor, must act as an interpreter, making sense of research findings that are often contradictory and providing avenues for practical application to daily life. One of the things we have tried to do in *Exploring GenderSpeak* is to transfer the classroom discussion of the kind we described above onto the page. We have attempted to depict realistic events in the lives of students, to offer explanations for those events via cutting-edge research, and then to provide a range of communicative options students may employ for enhanced personal effectiveness in their interactions and relationships. We view this approach as a real strength of the text.

We also attempt in the text to speak to college students, using language and examples that they will find provocative. Our rationale is that if students are going to embrace this content and allow it to challenge their relational lives, they will be much more likely to do so if the language is accessible, current, and engaging. The text has been written primarily for college undergraduates enrolled in courses focusing on the effects of gender on the communication process. Such courses may be represented in university curricula as upper-division courses, while at community colleges, for example, they may be more introductory in nature. We believe that this text is appropriate for both these levels. While some prior exposure to basic concepts and theories of interpersonal communication will serve the reader well, we do not view this exposure as requisite to an understanding of the content of this text.

Organization of the Book

Exploring GenderSpeak is organized into twelve chapters within four major sections, with a logical progression from section to section. Part One, "Communication, Gender, and Effectiveness" contains a brief overview of the communication process, including our emphasis on the receiver of communication. We then explore key terminology related to the topic, such as the difference between *sex* and *gender*. The opening chapter concludes with a description of the various components within the personal effectiveness approach.

Part Two, "Influences on Our Choices," encourages readers to explore the many influences that shape their identities, attitudes, expectations, and communication as women and men. This section is based on an assumption that students must first understand what is influencing them—in terms of choices they make about themselves and about communication—before they can work to improve their communication skills and their relationships. Specific topics of discussion include the "nature versus nurture" argument (how biology and society shape one's perception of gender), sexism in language, and communication about the sexes via media. Our approach to the media chapter represents a departure from most gender texts in that we present media as an *influence on* behavior rather than as a *context for* behavior. Other texts tend to offer a treatment of gender communication within the mediated context, along with other contextual chapters such as the workplace. The media chapter in *Exploring GenderSpeak* details ways in which advertising, prime-time television programming, soap operas, talk shows, film, song lyrics, and music videos affect our perceptions of who men and women should be and how they should communicate.

"Let's Talk: Initiating and Developing Relationships" is the title of Part Three, one of the most unique aspects of the text. When we have taught gender communication courses in the past and used other texts, we have detected an oversight in content—content representing a primary interest of college students. Students continually want to know about relationships of all sorts: how to initiate them, how to establish the type of relationship each person wants, how to move a friendship into a romance, how to change a romance back into a friendship, how to know if a romantic partner is "marriage potential," and so on. Most gender communication texts currently on the market omit or slight a discussion of the "nuts and bolts" of how gender communication operates relationally. These texts tend to jump too quickly to discussions of how gender affects communication in specific contexts, such as the workplace or the classroom. In contrast, the first chapter in this section of *Exploring GenderSpeak* offers a discussion of how women and men tend to communicate for different purposes and to use language differently—both important relational components. The two remaining chapters focus on the role of gender in the initiation and development of interpersonal relationships.

Once the building blocks of gender communication and relationship development are conveyed, students proceed into the final section of the text. In Part Four, entitled "The Contexts for Our Relationships: Personal Effectiveness in Action," five chapters explore ways in which gender communication affects and is affected by the following contexts or life-situations: friendships (same-sex versus cross-sex), intimate or romantic relationships, the marriage and family context, the workplace, and educational setting. Suggestions for personally effective communication within each context, given the complex effects of gender, are provided.

Pedagogical Features and Resources for Instructors

Each chapter contains six pedagogical features to serve as aids for instructors and students alike. A *Case Study* appears at the beginning of each chapter. In most instances, these case studies represent actual events that occurred within the gender communication classrooms of the authors. The case study device is used not only to gain attention from readers as they delve into a new topic, but to orient or alert the reader to the nature of the discussion that lies in the next pages. Case studies also operate as realistic illustrations of gender communication in various contexts.

The *Overview* section within each chapter contains bulleted phrases that serve as topical outlines of chapter content. Students can check these phrases against *Key Terms* sections at the end of each chapter, as a means of studying for exams or simply checking their understanding of chapter content. *What If?* boxes within each chapter are designed to provoke student thought, to cause students to envision something commonplace or ordinary in a completely different way, or to spark class discussion about a controversial idea or topic. Many of the topics for the What If? boxes stem from our in-class discussions that encourage students to challenge basic assumptions and expectations about the sexes. A series of *Discussion Starters* appear following the listing of Key Terms for each chapter. Instructors may use these questions as a means of generating class discussion over chapter content, as actual assignments, or as thought provokers for students to consider on their own time. Finally, complete *References* to research cited within the text appear at the end of each chapter. Students may find these references useful as they prepare assignments and/or conduct their own research projects. Instructors may use the references to gather additional material for their own research or to supplement instruction.

An *Instructor's Manual* accompanying *Exploring GenderSpeak* provides the following:

- Sample syllabi and schedules for both a quarter- and a semester-long course
- Perforated outlines of chapter content (which can be used as class lecture notes)
- Suggested activities and exercises that spark discussion and illustrate concepts in the text
- Information regarding potential areas of controversy, termed "Paths of Resistance"
- A comprehensive test item file with computer software for test generation

Acknowledgments

This project has certainly been a "team effort"; thus there are many people to acknowledge and thank. First and foremost, the authors wish to thank Hilary Jackson, "editor extraordinaire," for her enthusiasm about this project when it was only in the mind of one of the authors, her instruction and advice with regard to translating random thoughts into reality, her patience with the "new kids on the block," and her constant support throughout the entire process, from conception to birth.

We express gratitude to our colleagues in the field of communication whose advice and encouragement throughout the review process for this text were invaluable. They include: Elizabeth Altman, University of Southern California; Janis Andersen, San Diego State University; Cynthia Begnal, Pennsylvania State University (whose enthusiasm continually encouraged us); Cynthia Berryman-Fink, University of Cincinnati; Dan Cavanaugh, Southwest Texas State University; Judith Dallinger, Western Illinois University (whose detailed reviewing over the course of the project contributed greatly to the outcome); Pamela Dunkin, Southern Oregon State University; Karen Foss, Humboldt State University; Meredith Moore, Washburn University; Anthony Mulac, University of California, Santa Barbara; Robert Smith, University of Tennessee, Martin; Helen Sterk, Marquette University; and Julia Wood, University of North Carolina, Chapel Hill.

Special thanks also go to: our faculty colleagues in the Departments of Communication at North Carolina State University and Central Washington University, for expecting to hear about this project whenever they saw us in the halls; the various campus offices who provided assistance and support for this project; Em Griffin, Wheaton College, and Steve Beebe, Southwest Texas State University, for their advice, empathy, and encouragement of fellow authors; and Karen Black and the staff of Irving Bible Church for coming through in a pinch.

No project for the benefit of college students has probably ever succeeded without the help of college students. We have many to thank for their participation in the research-gathering process and for being sources of inspiration for the creation of this textbook. In general, students of gender communication at both North Carolina State and Central Washington deserve our thanks for providing the motivation to write this text and the "fuel" for a good deal of its content. Specifically, we greatly appreciate the Independent Study students at North Carolina State who helped in the initiation, development, and refinement of this project. Their constant support and good humor contributed greatly to the mental well-being and determination of the authors. Finally, we thank our families and friends for their listening ears, thought-provoking questions, lively arguments, and persistent belief in this book and its authors.

Diana K. Ivy
Phil Backlund

PART ONE

Communication, Gender, and Effectiveness

Talking the Talk: Gender Jargon, the Communication Process, and Personal Effectiveness

*W*hy *should you read this chapter?* Not just because it was assigned by your instructor, but because this chapter lays the foundation for the rest of the text. Throughout the text, we refer to the basic ideas and information explained in this chapter, including such topics as:

- What gender communication is and why one should study it
- How notions of gender are constructed from our culture
- How such terms as *sex, gender, gender-role identity, sexual orientation, empowerment,* and *power* have distinct meanings
- How something can be sexist but not sexual, and vice versa
- What *feminism, chauvinism,* and *patriarchy* mean today
- How uncertainty affects gender communication and motivates us in relationships
- Communicating from a receiver orientation
- What it means to be personally effective in communication with women and men
- How values are associated with the kind of gender communication that leads to successful and satisfying relationships

OVERVIEW

You can hardly open a magazine or newspaper or turn on the television these days without coming across someone discussing the "problems that plague the sexes." It is easy to find current articles describing the societal issues dividing women and men, whether they involve situations of professional communication between coworkers of opposite sexes, confusion over interpersonal signals, competing messages of homemaking versus careerism, or verbal exchanges that result in violence. Virtually any day you can turn on the television and catch a talk show devoted to yet another sex difference that puzzles society. One thing is for certain: Communication between women and men is a popular topic of conversation, study, and research—more now than ever, it seems.

So just what *is* gender communication? Why do *you* want to study it? Why do *we* want to write about it? In the next few pages, we address these questions and explain why we think gender communication is one of life's most fascinating and challenging experiences. Next we offer our definitions and perspectives of terms you'll need to understand before we go any further. Then we talk about the communication process, with specific regard for how gender affects that process. Finally, we lay out the personal effectiveness approach and some values to go with it, as they pertain to gender communication. As you read this chapter, think about your current relationships and the kind of communication you have within those relationships. Then compare those thoughts with the ideas in this chapter.

INTRODUCTION

What exactly is gender communication? First you need to understand that we're putting the words *gender* and *communication* together to form a modern label for an ancient phenomenon. We have come to believe that gender communication is a unique, fascinating subset of the larger phenomenon known as communication. From our perspective, not all communication is gender communication. (If it were, this text would be a hundred times longer—and you wouldn't like that.) But we must point out that some scholars believe that because gender is an all-encompassing designation, communication cannot escape the effects of gender. In this view, all communication is "gendered" (Spender, 1985; Thorne, Kramarae, & Henley, 1983; Wilson Schaef, 1981). We do not see these viewpoints as necessarily in dramatic opposition with one another. In other words, we believe that the information in this text can be applicable whether one views gender communication as a specific form of communication, or whether one believes that all communication is gendered. The essence of what we mean here is that there is no "right" conceptualization of the relationship between gender and communication; it's too complicated a topic to merely suggest a right or wrong approach.

Here's a simple way to understand our perspective on gender communication in this text. **Gender communication is communication *about* and *between* men and women.** This is an easy statement to remember, but the meaning behind it is more complicated. The front part of the statement—the "about" aspect—involves how the sexes are discussed, referred to, or depicted, both verbally and nonverbally. The back part of the definition—the "between" aspect—is the interpersonal dimension of gender communication, and it's a bit harder to understand.

We believe that communication becomes gendered when sex or gender begins to influence your choices of what you say and how you relate to others. For example, two students could be talking about a project for class. The students could both be male, both be female, or be of opposite sexes. The sex composition of the communicators doesn't matter in a judgment of whether gender communication is going on or not. Thus far, in our view, the conversation about the class project doesn't necessarily involve gender communication. But what happens if the conversation topic shifts to a discussion of political issues that specifically address women's concerns, or of who the interactants are dating, or of opinions regarding birth-control responsibilities? For topics such as these, the awareness of one's own and/or the other person's gender may come into play; thus gender communication is occurring. Notice that we said may come into play, because the topic doesn't always dictate whether or not gender communication is occurring.

Take another example. You may be talking with someone about a totally inane thing, like the weather or some minor current event. The topic isn't related to gender, but as the conversation progresses you find you are becoming attracted to the other person. You become acutely aware of your own and the other person's gender. Now we would say that gender communication is happening. Let's look at a situation that doesn't involve attraction. What if you merely become aware, during a conversation, that you are presenting sort of a "male view" of something and are seeking a "female view," or vice versa? That sounds like playing into stereotypes, but in some situations you may become aware that your own slant on something is overtly affected by your gender. See the difference between these two examples and the first example of classmates discussing a project? When gender becomes an overt factor in your communication, when you become conscious of your own or another person's gender, then gender communication is operating. The remaining chapters of this text deal with both the "about" and the "between" aspects of gender communication.

Earlier we asked, why study gender communication? Our answer to that question is because it is provocative, pervasive, problematic, and unpredictable, just for starters.

Gender communication is **provocative** because we are all interested in how we are perceived, how we communicate with other human beings, and how others respond to us. We are all especially interested in communication with the opposite sex for several reasons, the most obvious being that we cannot experience the other sex firsthand. We cannot "walk in each other's shoes," so it intrigues us to learn about each other. Also, we are all very interested in the possible rewards that may result from successful gender communication.

Gender communication is **pervasive,** meaning that interaction with women and men occurs frequently, every day, every hour. Because of the sheer number of contacts we have with members of the opposite sex, interest in the effects of gender on the communication process becomes heightened. When those contacts affect us in profound ways, such as in work relationships and career opportunities, or in committed, romantic relationships, the importance of these relationships and the pervasiveness of our interactions with significant people further necessitates a greater understanding of gender communication.

Saying that gender communication is **problematic** doesn't mean that all gender communication centers around problems, but that it is complicated. Communication itself is complex; it's not a simple process that can be accomplished just because we're human beings who learned language at some early age or because we've been talking all our lives. When you add gender into the communication process, you expand the complexity because now there is more than one way of looking at or talking about something. Any form of diversity— racial, regional, ethnic, cultural, religious, sexual orientation, age—adds a degree of complexity to communication. We believe that one of the most basic forms of diversity is gender; thus gender is a definite point of complication.

Gender communication is **unpredictable** in that societal norms, rules, and roles have changed. In fact, it seems that they are changing every day. For example, often college students in our classes are bothered by seemingly simple rituals, such as dating etiquette. Male students complain, "If I open the car door for my date, she'll think I don't respect her as a competent, liberated woman who can take care of herself. But if I don't open the car door, she'll think I was raised by wolves and have no manners at all." In this situation and countless others, lessons learned while growing up come into conflict with changes in society, leaving confusion as to what is appropriate behavior.

If you have reason to believe that communication between men and women is so confusing that attempts to improve it are worthless, so you'll just stumble along until the "right" person automatically understands what you say, think, and feel, we have a better suggestion. Amid the mounds of material out there about communication and the sexes is some worthwhile, helpful, and research-based information. By research based, we mean that some people have been so intrigued by the nature of gender communication that they have purposefully studied it from a variety of viewpoints, using various research techniques. The result is a body of information from which to draw—information that we summarize in this text along with offering practical suggestions as to how to apply this knowledge to your life's experiences. As authors of this textbook, we want you to not only *know* the current information on gender communication, but we want you to be able to *use* the information to enhance your communication skills and to enrich your relationships. We hope to help you work through any confusion you might be experiencing in order to help you increase your personal effectiveness in gender communication. Let's begin with some basic, critical terminology.

GENDER JARGON

For us to communicate effectively with you as a reader of this complicated topic, we need to share our perspectives on some key terms related to gender communication. We've discovered that many gender-related terms are given different meanings, primarily by the media. We also realize that your own experience may cause you to adopt meanings that differ from ours for some of the terms. We are not suggesting that our definitions are the "right" ones, but by defining these terms, at least you as a reader will understand them from our viewpoints as authors. These terms are critical to your understanding of the personal effectiveness approach to gender communication that is outlined in a subsequent section of this chapter, as well as to your comprehension of the ideas throughout the whole text. But beyond mere understanding, these terms should become a part of your everyday vocabulary. Granted, some words are more commonplace than others. But becoming more skilled in your communication with men and women begins with the use of current, sensitive, accurate language.

Sex and Gender

You've probably already read or heard the terms *sex* and *gender* used inter-changeably. For clarity's sake, we use them in this text with exclusive meanings, even though some people think the terms overlap in meaning. For our purposes, when we use the term *sex*, we mean the biological and physiological charac-teristics that make us female or male. At some points in this text, we use the term *sex* to refer to sexual activity between men and women, but it will be clear to you whether we are using the term to mean a categorization of persons or an activity.

The term we use most often in this text is *gender*. Most narrowly, gender refers to psychological and emotional characteristics of individuals. You may understand these characteristics to be masculine, feminine, or androgynous (a blend of feminine and masculine traits). But *gender*, in our use of the term, encompasses more than this. Defined broadly, *gender* includes such aspects as personality traits but also involves psychological makeup, attitudes, beliefs, and values as well as sexual orientation and gender-role identity (terms we define and use later).

We believe that gender is "constructed," meaning that one's maleness or femaleness is more extensive than the fact of being born anatomically female or male. What is *attached* or *related* to that anatomy is taught to you through our culture, virtually from the time you are born. In their book on gender and society, Thorne, Kramarae, and Henley (1983) explain, "Gender is not a unitary, or 'natural' fact, but takes shape in concrete, historically changing social relationships" (p. 16). Culture, with its evolving customs, rules, and expectations for behavior, has the power to affect your perception of gender. For example, if you were raised in the Middle East, it is likely that your views regarding the status and role of women in society would be vastly different than if you were raised in the United States. Perhaps you grew up with strict rules for appropriate male-female behavior, such as "men ask women out on dates; women do not call men for dates." If you experience members of another culture (or your own culture, for that matter) who do not behave according to clearly drawn gender lines or rules, or who operate from rules different from your own, then the notable difference may either reinforce your original conception of gender or cause it to change.

We think it more worthwhile, when studying communication about and between women and men, to define *sex* as a biological determination and *gender* as something that is culturally construed or constructed. Thus you'll see references in this text to the "other sex," meaning a comparison between male and female. If you understand the notion of gender as a broad-based, multifaceted concept, then you understand why we do not use the reference, "other gender."

When you view gender as a culturally constructed designation, you can see that conceptions of gender can be changed or "reconstructed." This is a powerful idea. For example, the way you see the gender of male/masculine or female/feminine is not the way you *have* to see it. You can learn to see it differently and more broadly if you discover new information. We discuss this much more thoroughly in Chapter 2, but for now here are a couple of examples to clarify. What if a guy discovers that "being a man" doesn't mean that he has always to be competitive? He might decide that he's tired of competing, that he'd rather help others do well instead. Conversely, a woman might decide that she'd like a crack at being the best, rather than being more concerned with everyone else's success. Do these discoveries alter one's vision of gender? Yes, but these people don't merely replace one stereotypical trait with another; they expand their options and find new ways of seeing themselves in relation to others. That's one of the goals of this text—to give you different ways of seeing things, including gender.

Here's an example to help clarify the notion of "gender as constructed." What is the first question most people ask when they hear that a baby has been born? Generally, the first reaction is, "Is it a boy or a girl?" Imagine if you asked a new mother, "Is it a boy or a girl?" and the answer was, "Yes." That's not the usual response, so you might conclude that the new mother must still be suffering the effects of childbirth! Once we find out the biological sex of the child, different sets of expectations, attitudes, and treatments—what can be termed stereotypical gender "baggage"—are called up in our brains and displayed. Thus we see friends presenting the proud parents with a baseball mitt for a male baby and a doll for a female baby. We see people talking to girl babies quite differently than to boy babies. If gender were not societally induced or constructed, we would not feel the need to align the sex of a child with a particular object, or to alter our style of communication.

One of the more provocative illustrations of these ideas comes from the story "X: A Fabulous Child's Story" written by Lois Gould (1972). Gould offers a fictional account of a child named X whose parents participated in an experimental study by not revealing to anyone the biological sex of the child. The story progresses from infancy through childhood, as X plays with other children, goes to school and deals with sex-specific bathrooms, and gets pronounced mentally healthy by a psychiatrist. What is most fascinating in this story is people's reactions to X. Adults and children alike have extreme difficulty in coping with not knowing the child's sex. It is as if they did not know how to behave with no gender information to guide them.

Sex-typed gift-giving is only one small indication of how gender becomes constructed, and right now it may strike you as unimportant or arbitrary. But it's not so arbitrary when you look down the road and foresee a future full of sex-typed treatment that is culturally induced and, in reality, limiting in opportunities that are afforded men and women. We explore this notion of societally induced versions of gender more fully in Chapter 2, in a discussion of biological versus sociocultural explanations for gender differences. Suffice it at this point to understand that while we may have no control over the sex of a newborn child, we have much to do with the development or construction of the child's gender.

Sexist versus Sexual

You may hear the term *sexism* quite often, and you will see the term frequently in this textbook, so clarification is warranted. This time, the term *sex*-ism as opposed to *gender*-ism is a correct usage. Usually if someone is a victim of sexist treatment, that treatment is generated because of stereotypes and preconceptions based on biological sex, not gender. Remember that gender encompasses a broader, more complex array of variables than sex. Typically, sexist treatment does not delve far enough or personally enough within an individual to reflect impressions of gender.

Often these days when you read the word sexism or hear someone called a sexist, those references most likely correspond to unfair, unequal treatment of women. Women's differential treatment, compared to that afforded men, has been an interesting and controversial topic for decades, one that we explore at several points in this text. But *sexism* simply means the denigration of one sex and the exaltation of the other, or, stated another way, valuing one sex over the other. Thus sexism does not refer exclusively to devaluing women, just as racism does not refer exclusively to the denigration of one specific race to the preference of another. Given this definition of sexism, there can be no such thing as "reverse sexism," even though some have used this term in specific reference to the unequal treatment of men.

Just what is the difference, then, between the designations sexist and sexual? This is a tricky issue. What seems harmless and sexual to one person may be interpreted as harmful and sexist by another. Calling something sexist rather than sexual is a determination derived within each of us, given our own values, beliefs, and standards, but here are a couple of thoughts that might help you determine your own point of separation between the two terms. Stemming from the definition of sexism as delineated in the previous paragraph, a stimulus may be sexual but not necessarily sexist. For example, a scene in a movie might be considered sexually stimulating, but the portrayal is not deemed sexist by those viewing it, meaning that one sex is not demeaned for the sake of the other. Conversely, something may be considered sexist, such as a governmental or corporate policy limiting opportunities for one sex while expanding or protecting opportunities for the other, but the policy does not involve sexuality. When a stimulus is sexual, it arouses primal instincts or urges within a human being; it involves one's sexuality. When the stimulus is sexist, someone has perceived it as devaluing to one sex or the other.

Gender-Role Identity and Sexual Orientation

In this text, we use the term *gender-role identity* as a subset of gender. Specifically, it refers to the way you view yourself, how you see yourself relative to stereotypically feminine or masculine traits. Your self-esteem may be connected, in part, to your gender-role identity, meaning that sometimes people's self-esteem is affected when they compare themselves to some ideal or stereotype of what a woman or man is supposed to be.

Associated with this "measure" of masculinity or femininity is your general perception of appropriate roles for women and men in the society of which you are a member. The term gender-role identity thus encompasses not only your vision of self but your vision of the roles or functions for human beings within a given culture. We offer more detail on the development of gender-role identity in Chapter 2. But for now, realize that while your gender-role identity is affected by your sex and your gender, it is within your control to change this identity. Control and choice are themes that reappear throughout this text. But what about a remaining element within the broad-based view of gender—an element over which you have no control?

At certain points in this text, we discuss the topic of sexual orientation as it affects communication between women and men. To use the term *sexual preference* to designate a person as heterosexual, homosexual, or bisexual is to use outdated terminology. The word *preference* implies that a person *chooses* his or her sexuality, or that one can make a conscious decision as to which sex (or both) to be attracted to in a sexual sense. Members of the gay and lesbian community have led individuals outside this community to a fairly recent realization: Sexuality or the sex of persons to whom one is attracted is not a preference or a decision that is within a person's power to make. While controversy has arisen over this issue, the predominant belief of homosexuals is that they were born gay, not shaped into homosexuality by life's experiences or societal factors. Thus, in an effort to be inclusive, sensitive, and contemporary in our use of language, in this text we refer to a person's sexuality as an "orientation," not a "preference."

Other aspects related to sexual orientation have bearing on gender communication and are explored in later chapters. For now, a basic understanding of some terminology will help you talk intelligently about orientation. Discriminatory attitudes or actions toward homosexuals can be termed *heterosexist.* This term can be applied to behavior that communicates one's belief that heterosexuality is in some way a superior orientation to homosexuality or bisexuality. The reverse of this term and its corresponding behavior can be termed *homosexism.*

Some measure of confusion surrounds the term *homophobic.* To date, we have discovered three uses of this term: (1) The term *homophobic* can refer to a general fear of persons who are homosexual in sexual orientation. (2) The term may also describe the fear of being labeled a homosexual. (3) Within homosexual communities, the term *homophobic* is used to mean behavior or attitudes that indicate a self-hatred or severe loss of self-esteem. In these cases, the homosexual individual, out of anger or hatred for her or his orientation, acts or thinks in ways that inflict that anger onto the self. As is the case with all gender-related terminology, choosing to use current, clear communication will likely minimize the opportunity for misunderstanding.

Feminism and Chauvinism in a Patriarchal Society

Individuals have a wide range of options within their gender communication behavior. This relatively new development stems from changing roles, revised rules for "appropriate" behavior, and increased opportunities for both men and women. Many of the changes in societal expectations, opportunities, and relational patterns can be traced to the work of feminists. Since some of the terminology related to these changes appear repeatedly in this text, it is appropriate to give you our viewpoint on these terms and concepts.

When you saw the term *feminism* in the title of this section, what thoughts or images came to your mind? Did you react with an attitude or emotion that said, "Oh no, this stuff again"? Did you equate feminism with the women's liberation movement of the 1960s and 1970s? As teachers and textbook authors, we are interested in what people, especially college students, are thinking about feminism these days. As we said in the previous paragraph, feminists have played and continue to play a major role in effecting the changes in gender communication that you now are experiencing. As you read this section, think about your initial reaction to the term and what it means, then think about how you may have benefited from the progress of feminists.

A colleague recently referred to the term *feminist* as the new "F-word" (DeFrancisco, 1992). When we ask students in our gender communication classes, "Do you believe that women and men should receive equal opportunities and treatment in all facets of life?" students reply with a confident, hearty affirmative. When we ask, "Are you a feminist?" the response is much more convoluted; the prevalent response is, "Well, no, I wouldn't call myself a feminist." People may believe in equality, yet they are resistant (borderline hostile) to apply the feminist label to themselves, much less have someone call them this F-word.

Time magazine reporter Claudia Wallis (1989) describes a trend for women under the age of 30 to recoil at the thought of being taken for feminists. However, at the same time, they adopt feminist ideals and take advantage of some of the breakthroughs feminists have fought to obtain, such as being able to combine a career with marriage and child rearing. Feminist scholar Victoria DeFrancisco (1992) concludes: "Young women and men quickly reject the term feminism, but when I ask what feminism is, or what feminist theory and methods refer to, it is clear they really do not know what they are rejecting" (p. 1).

In its most basic sense, the term feminist describes a person—male or female—who believes in equality, especially gender equality. Susan Faludi, in her best-selling book *Backlash: The Undeclared War Against American Women* (1991), states that "feminism remains a pretty simple concept, despite repeated— and enormously effective—efforts to dress it up in greasepaint and turn its proponents into gargoyles" (p. xxiii). She continues: "Feminism's agenda is basic:

It asks that women not be forced to 'choose' between public justice and private happiness. It asks that women be free to define themselves—instead of having their identity defined for them, time and again, by their culture and their men" (p. xxiii).

In a more specific sense, feminism involves a reaction to power imposed by a male-dominated system, or "patriarchy" (derived from a Greek word meaning "of the fathers"). Noted gender researcher Dale Spender (1985) describes patriarchy as a self-perpetuating society "based on the belief that the male is the superior sex" (p. 1). In reaction to patriarchy, as communication researchers Pearce and Rossi (1984) point out, feminism "claims that women have been unfairly and/or unwisely limited in their range of activities and perceived capabilities by gender-linked stereotypes, and calls for the development of new social practices and conceptions which are not so constricting" (p. 278).

Maybe you believe that our society is not male-dominated or that patriarchy is okay, because "that's just the way it is." Maybe you feel that no opportunities have been denied and no particular suffering has been endured by either sex during your lifetime. But we challenge you to stop and think, on not only a personal but a global level: Which sex is the most represented among decision makers, such as political leaders and judges, and among highly paid corporate executives? According to a *Time* magazine national survey (Wallis, 1989), who earns 66 cents to the other's dollar of wages? Which sex is the most represented among low-paying jobs and welfare recipients? Conversely, which parent is most often denied child custody in divorce proceedings, simply because of the parent's sex? Perhaps you haven't yet seen any overt instances of sex discrimination in your personal life, but what about missed opportunities—those jobs, benefits and rewards, or relationships that did not come your way, merely because someone held a limited view of which sex or gender is best suited for a certain circumstance?

We contend that subtle, insidious forms of sexism affect women's and men's lives in profound ways, maybe even more than obvious instances of disparity, such as pay differentials and hiring practices. The intent here is not to lay blame, because blaming does not accomplish desired outcomes. It only intensifies and solidifies barriers between men and women. The intent is merely to expose existing inequities and to make you aware of the potential for sex discrimination in our society, so that we can all work harder to counter them.

Another descriptor to arise from women's activism in the 1960s and 1970s is *chauvinist*—a term assigned to an individual who holds attitudes that are discriminatory or who behaves in a discriminatory manner regarding gender. While the term can reasonably apply to both women and men, typically *chauvinistic* has been used as a male descriptor. Interestingly enough, the term *chauvinist* and its derivatives "male chauvinist" and "chauvinist pig" have virtually disappeared from usage today; however, some exceptions linger. With the current societal backlash against feminism, some men are bragging that they are, indeed, male chauvinists, as though that were an acceptable posture. What is even more alarming is to hear women boast about their relational partners who exhibit male chauvinistic tendencies in their behavior with women.

Why has the image of feminism deteriorated or become distorted, so that angry, radical, bra-burning, masculine women storming out of the headquarters of the National Organization for Women (NOW), proclaiming superiority over men, have become the stereotype of feminists? While this is not your textbook authors' vision of a feminist, variations of these images are reported regularly to us by our students. These negative connotations have in large part been cultivated by selective images transmitted to the mass audience by the media. For example, did you know that there are no documented accounts of actual bra-burning episodes among "women's libbers" in the late 1960s? Only one incident was remotely connected—a protest of the 1968 Miss America pageant, where protesters threw their bras into a trash can (Wallis, 1989). Yet the bra-burning images of feminists made headlines (and made money for the media). In some ways, these images still operate to marginalize feminists from mainstream culture, thus reducing their potential threat to alter the status quo.

We do not wish to give a false impression that feminism means the same thing to all feminists. Different strains of feminism exist, ranging from persons who want to see women included within mainstream culture on the same level as men, to those who see inclusion as becoming a "member of an undesirable club." However, a core concept within all strains of feminism is empowerment, feminists' unique view of power.

Empowerment versus Power

Women's movements throughout history have been reactions to female power-lessness within patriarchal societies. However, feminism has adopted a perspective of power that does not reflect the traditional use of the term. As Thorne, Kramarae, and Henley (1983) explain, "A feminist definition of power—power as energy, effective interaction, or empowerment—contrasts with and challenges the assumption of power as domination or control" (p. 19). Gender scholar Barbara Bate (1988) offers a definition that helps clarify this idea: "Empowerment means becoming powerful to accomplish your own goals and spreading the power you possess so that other people become able to accomplish their goals as well" (p. 39). Thus, in the view that feminists adopt, the preferred kind of power is not the typical "power over," which implies dominance and suppression, but empowerment of self and others—the "power to."

One of the goals we have as textbook authors is to "empower" you; we are interested in women and men developing greater "power to" be effective in gender communication. To delve further into what that means, we ask you to think about your own relational life. Do you believe that you can influence the degree of satisfaction you experience in relationships of all kinds? Do you feel you can guide the outcome of a relationship? One component of self-esteem is the belief that you can affect others and the world around you. Everyone has experienced the frustration of feeling that "no matter what I do, it won't make any difference." Perhaps you have felt that way in male-female relationships. However, we believe that you can use verbal and nonverbal communication to empower yourself and others. Contrary to what you may believe, relationships are not out of your control; you can influence the course of their development, depth, and duration.

Some people have a fatalistic view of relationships, believing that "if it is meant to happen, it will happen." While there is some validity to letting nature take its course, that is also a very passive or reactive approach. It won't lead to an increased level of effectiveness or help you achieve your goals. We suggest a more active, empowering approach—one by which you can proact, rather than merely react, to influence the rate of change in relationships. A fundamental idea in this text is the belief that you can communicate to increase the chances of a relationship working out, of developing mutually satisfying relationships, and of deriving more personal satisfaction from them. Empowerment is central to this belief.

COMMUNICATION: A COMPLEX HUMAN PROCESS

Communication is a word that you hear frequently, especially since technology has become so sophisticated that we can easily and quickly talk around the world. As the channels for communicating have expanded, so have the meanings of the term *communication*. In fact, two communication theorists back in the 1970s isolated 126 definitions of communication (Dance & Larson, 1976). Our point in this section is not to exhaustively review perspectives on human communication; other courses and textbooks do that quite well. We present to you a fairly basic perspective of communication, and because it appears throughout this text, you need to thoroughly understand it.

Human communication is not static; it is an ongoing and dynamic process of sending and receiving messages for the purpose of sharing meaning. To accomplish this purpose, people use both verbal and nonverbal communication (e.g., body movement, physical appearance, facial expression, touch, tone of voice). Communication flows back and forth simultaneously, both verbally and nonverbally, in a transactional fashion (DeVito, 1988; Taylor, Meyer, Rosegrant, & Samples, 1989). We believe the transactional model of communication to be the most descriptive and thorough of the existing communication models. However, it can be helpful for analysis purposes to pare down the complex process into a basic conversation between two people in which one interactant, possibly the person who initiated the conversation, is the sender and the other is the receiver or listener.

For example, in the comic strip on the opposite page, depicting a conversation between Nancy and Sluggo, Nancy can first be labeled the sender and Sluggo the receiver. While both interactants are transacting communication, meaning that they are both sending and receiving verbal and nonverbal messages simultaneously, we can analyze the conversation from a sending-receiving perspective. Nancy initiates a conversation by asking Sluggo a question. Sluggo receives the message and responds verbally and nonverbally. Note Nancy's confused nonverbal reaction in the second frame of the cartoon. The conversation continues, as messages are exchanged between sender and re-

NANCY reprinted by permission of UFS, Inc.

ceiver. The point of the cartoon is that even though messages have been transmitted between sender and receiver, effective communication may not be the end result.

Now that you have a better understanding of our view of the basic communication process, there are two additional, related components within this perspective: uncertainty reduction and the receiver orientation to communication. These components have direct bearing on the success of your communication with women and men.

Reducing Our Uncertainty about Others

In the introductory paragraphs of this chapter, we mentioned unpredictability as one of the factors in gender communication. Let's explore this unpredictability notion a bit further. Humans like to be able to form expectations and to predict how others will behave. These expectations and predictions are comforting; thus they are powerful motivators in human interaction. Based on their past and ever-expanding experiences, people strive to anticipate a situation, predict how certain behaviors will lead to certain reactions from others, act accordingly, and reap positive rewards from the situation. Berger and his colleagues have contributed a significant amount of research about the topic of uncertainty reduction. According to these researchers, when people cannot form adequate expectations and are unable to predict what will happen in situations, they experience uncertainty (Berger & Bradac, 1982; Berger & Calabrese, 1975). One reaction to this discomfort is to communicate to gain information and reduce uncertainty.

Can you imagine how the notion of uncertainty reduction applies to communication between women and men? Can you see it operating in your own communication? As we said earlier, communication between genders has changed dramatically and is still changing. The factors contributing to the changes are contributing to uncertainty, too. The world has become a smaller place, in that we have more of a global community now with almost instant access to other people and other cultures. The likelihood is ever increasing that you will become friends in college with someone from a culture vastly different from your own and that you will travel abroad or use technology to communicate with people worldwide. As advanced technology, greater mobility, and easier access have also resulted in greater diversity within our own culture, the complexity of communication has compounded. These factors significantly increase our uncertainty about how to communicate effectively.

Consider this example of a male-female encounter. At a party, Mary sees Paul across the room and is attracted to him. From watching him at a distance, she thinks he may have come to the party alone, but she feels uncertain. She doesn't know Paul and doesn't know if he's dating someone steadily or even if he's married, for that matter! Mary's uncertainty is high, but not high enough to keep her from learning some information about Paul. She finds out from Peter, the party host, that Paul is single, but Peter doesn't know if Paul came with a date or not. Now Mary's uncertainty is somewhat reduced, so she decides to try a more direct method. She strikes up a conversation with Paul, showing that she finds him interesting, and learns that he came to the party alone. While her uncertainty about Paul hasn't completely disappeared, it has been significantly reduced through communication. This Peter, Paul, and Mary example may not fit your experience, but do you get the general idea about how uncertainty reduction works in human communication?

Reducing uncertainty and increasing predictability about communication with others are perplexing tasks. Sex roles in our society have shifted dramatically. For example, today, unlike in past generations, many men and women alike are waiting until later in life to marry—if they make the decision to marry at all. More women are entering the work force and more men are actively involving themselves in child rearing, so that even the basic roles of breadwinner, homemaker, childcare-giver, and the like, have changed. As these roles evolve, and as the rules governing people's behavior fall by the societal wayside, you may experience high uncertainty, low predictability, and resulting confusion, possibly even disillusionment. This often generates a "take your best guess" mentality. If your best guess fails, you are once again reminded of the unpredictable nature of gender communication. One goal of this text is to help you reduce uncertainty and increase predictability both for you and for your relationships.

Becoming Receiver Oriented in Your Communication

While the roles of sender and receiver are both important in the communication process, we believe the receiver's interpretation of the sender's message makes the difference between shared meaning and misunderstanding. This approach is therefore termed the *receiver orientation* to the communication process. What the sender *intends* to convey is important, but it is less important than what the receiver *thinks is being conveyed,* or how the receiver interprets the message. You may clearly understand your intentions in what you say, but a listener takes your message in a different way than you originally intended. The result of not taking a receiver orientation can sound like this: "What do you *mean*, I'm late in calling you?! I said I'd call you *around* five o'clock. Six-thirty *is* around five o'clock!" In an instance like this, obviously the sender intended something different from the receiver's interpretation. Taking a receiver orientation—stopping *before* you say something to think about how your message will be understood by a listener—can greatly enhance your skill as a communicator.

When one is misunderstood, a typical response is to think that the receiver is at fault for not understanding the message. This reaction becomes particularly relevant to gender communication when you consider how frequently women report that they do not understand men because they expect them to react like women. And men get frustrated with women when they do not communicate or interpret communication like men. Here's our proposition to you:

> If people would spend more time figuring out how a listener will best hear, accept, understand, and retain a message and less time figuring out how they want to say something to please themselves, then their communication with others would vastly improve.

This sounds like the "golden rule of communication," doesn't it? Have you considered this receiver orientation to communication before? Do you currently communicate from this perspective, even though you didn't know what to call it? Think of it this way: If you talk, but no one is there to listen or receive what you say, has communication occurred? Some will say yes, at the very least the sender has communicated with the self. But others will argue that without a listener, communication does not occur, making the receiver the most necessary link for the communication process to work. Again, this is part of the receiver orientation to communication.

If communication breaks down (as it seems to regularly), whose fault is it? Rarely are breakdowns completely the sender's fault. Sometimes the best forethought, insight, experience, and skill applied to a situation still lead to misunderstanding on the part of a receiver. But in a receiver-oriented view of communication, the sender is responsible for communicating in a manner that will be most easily understood by the receiver; the receiver's responsibility is to attempt to understand the intent of the sender.

Human action theory supports this emphasis on the receiver of communication. According to communication theorists Intante, Rancer, and Womack (1990), a conversation cannot be assessed without understanding an individual's (the receiver) perception or interpretation of that conversation. The reality or "way of knowing" exists within the subjective experience of the receiver (p. 71). Human action theorists propose that perceptions of an event or a message actually become the reality. Here is an example to more vividly illustrate this notion of taking a receiver orientation to communication.

Say, for instance, Bonnie sees Clyde outside of class and wants to start a conversation with him. She says, "Hey, Clyde, that was pretty funny in class today when the professor called on you just as you were about to nod off to sleep!" Clyde, feeling self-conscious and embarrassed, replies angrily, "Oh, so everybody got a big laugh out of that, huh?" You can see that this conversation is not going the way Bonnie intended; she just meant to lightly tease Clyde to get a conversation going. Clyde took Bonnie's statement as criticism, as though she were making fun of him. Obviously, in this situation, message intended and sent did not equal message received. Who would you say is most responsible for the miscommunication in this situation?

From a receiver orientation to communication, we could say that the sender, in this case Bonnie, should have used more caution in her message to Clyde. If she'd thought about the effect her humorous line might have had on Clyde, she might have considered a different approach, one that wouldn't appear to Clyde as though she was poking fun at his expense. Perhaps she could have merely made a general funny comment about class, rather than one that involved Clyde personally. Now, if you are saying to yourself, "Boy, that Clyde must be one touchy character; he really overreacted and missed the boat," then you are adopting a sender orientation to communication. Again, you are emphasizing what was *said* rather than how it was *taken*. Let's consider a more serious example, one involving gender communication that has more dire consequences than Bonnie and Clyde's misunderstanding.

Before a board meeting at a local corporation, a few executives are milling about, drinking coffee and talking about the upcoming meeting. Maria says good morning to her boss, Jerry, as he comes up to her on her way to the boardroom. He says, as he puts his arm around her waist, "You know, you are a breath of fresh air in this joint, because I sure like a little perfume and soft skin next to me in the morning. Makes the workday go a lot easier, don't you think? Why don't you sit by me at this meeting?" Maria is so taken aback that she cannot respond, except to extract herself from Jerry's grasp, collect her wits, and get ready for the board meeting. Maria views Jerry's comments as a form of sexual harassment—unprofessional talk and inappropriate power play in the workplace. But that's probably not how Jerry intended it. Perhaps he believes that he was complimenting Maria, trying to make her feel more comfortable before the meeting started, or merely offering some harmless teasing to break the tension of the morning.

While we recognize that this sexual harassment example is rather dramatic, and maybe you reacted strongly to it, we offer it here for a reason. Instances of sexual harassment constitute prime illustrations of what we mean by taking a receiver orientation to communication. Whether or not a sender of a message intends to be harassing is not the issue; what matters is how the target or receiver of the message interprets it. In human action theory terms, the subjective interpretation of the receiver of a message constitutes the reality. The topic of sexual harassment will be dealt with fully in Chapter 11 on workplace communication between women and men. Just realize for now that in most situations, instead of defending your intentions when you communicate poorly or inappropriately, you can learn lessons for the next time. Considering in advance how a receiver will take or interpret your message will go a long way toward improving your skills as a communicator. This is an especially critical stance to assume for gender communication because of its increased complexity. It's advisable in every situation, as depicted by our Bonnie and Clyde example, to focus on the receiver of your message *before, during,* and *after* you communicate. Given how gender complicates the process, as depicted in the harassment example, it's even more advisable to consider the receiver's point of view as most important.

You will see the receiver orientation to communication reiterated throughout this textbook, so comprehending this perspective is a key to understanding the remaining chapters. But we want you to recognize that the receiver orientation is only one perspective within the communication discipline; there are several other ways to view the process. In fact, some scholars believe that a receiver orientation to communication is already a gendered approach, meaning that women have traditionally been more receiver oriented and that approach hasn't elevated their status in society. We find validity in that viewpoint, but we still advocate the receiver orientation; if we didn't, would our recourse be to advocate a more sender-oriented, power/control, "masculine" stance as an approach to communication? We don't believe that a sender orientation leads to greater success or that the power or status men hold in our society completely correlates with a masculine or power-based communication approach. Thus we are firmly committed to the belief that a receiver orientation is the most fruitful, especially when the communication process is complicated by the effects of gender. This orientation, together with a focus on uncertainty reduction, forms the basis of our perspective of gender communication. We further your understanding of this perspective as we explore in the next section of this chapter what is meant by personal effectiveness in communication with women and men.

THE PERSONAL EFFECTIVENESS APPROACH TO GENDER COMMUNICATION

Have you ever had a problem communicating with someone of the opposite sex? Sure, everyone has. Have you wished that you were better at it, and what does "better" mean? Everyone struggles with this problem and a majority of questions from students of all ages in our classes center around trying to figure out how to become more successful in communicating with members of the opposite sex.

To be a bit more systematic about students' questions, we conducted a recent survey at our universities to better understand college undergraduates' concerns about gender communication. Admittedly, we surveyed a moderately sized, nonrandom sample of students, but we believe that their responses represent typical concerns. Here are a few of the male students' questions and concerns:

"In a conversation with a woman, when a problem's solved, why does the woman still want to continue the conversation?"

"My wife says that men don't listen. I think that women listen too much."

"In a serious situation, would women rather that guys get emotional and get everyone else upset, or not show emotion and risk getting someone else upset later?"

From the female respondents to our survey, we received questions like:

"When guys say 'I'll call you,' what do they really mean?"

"Why is it that men find it so difficult to say what they mean if there are emotional aspects involved? Is it that they are afraid of what other men will say? Or is it because they feel they will be viewed as less of a man?"

"Guys usually want sex from women. So, after a woman goes to bed with you, why do you talk as though you no longer respect her?"

There is no lack of advice from the popular press or lack of personal opinions on gender communication problems. Through our classroom experience and research, we have developed our own point of view—the *personal effectiveness approach.* Getting "better" in your gender communication depends on becoming a more personally effective communicator.

Why this approach? Each of us will have many different relationships in our lives. Each relationship consists of three things: the self, the other person, and the situation. Which of these three things do you have the most direct control over? Clearly, it is yourself. You can exert some control over the situation, and now and then you can influence another person. But with some self-awareness, learning, and skill, you can almost always control your own communication behavior. Becoming more personally effective means that you will develop greater control over your own communication behavior and will develop a greater ability to influence the development of relationships. "Control" means that you can take charge of your behavior and manage it, rather than letting your communication be ruled by other people and circumstances.

You already control your own communication behavior to some degree. However, you may not do it as well as you would like. Did you ever find yourself saying or doing something (especially with the other sex!) and thinking, "Where did *that* come from?" It was almost like something else made you behave that way. We all occasionally feel we have no control of things around us. But at other times we do plan something and it does work. So you already do have some control and you already know some things about communication and gender. You've experienced some level of success as well, but you've also had some failures.

To use a sports analogy, a baseball or softball player might have a batting average of .300. That's considered quite good, but it means that the player was successful only three out of every ten times at bat. You have what could be called a "batting average" in relationships. You've been successful some of the time, and not so successful other times. How can you improve your relational batting average? If you will use the information in this text—learning about the factors that influence your gender communication, noting the examples of skills that help increase success, and exploring the different contexts that you might face as you move through life—it is highly likely that your relational batting average will improve. At least, if it doesn't improve, maybe you'll know why. Let's now turn to a fuller description of what it means to be personally effective—an approach that involves both communication competence and goal attainment.

Communication Competence

What does it mean to be a competent communicator? There are several conceptualizations of communication competence within the communication discipline (Larson, Backlund, Redmond, & Barbour, 1978; McCroskey, 1984, 1985; Rubin, 1990; Spitzberg & Cupach, 1984; Wiemann & Backlund, 1980). But, basically, competence begins with knowledge of yourself and your own tendencies, extends to your knowledge of the "rules" of society, and includes your knowledge of the communication process. It also involves judgments that other people make about you. But let's examine these components one at a time.

Communication Competence: Your Own Perspective

At various times, you may have looked at how some people communicate and thought, "They are good at this, I wish I was that good." You probably looked at others and thought, "They need some help." No one can be successful all the time, but each of us can be successful *more* of the time. The following four dimensions of competence reflect ways to help you be more successful more of the time.

1. *Repertoire.* You have been communicating for a number of years and have developed patterns of communication that feel natural to you. Within these patterns are communication behaviors that you frequently use. Some work most of the time, some don't, and sometimes you may not know what to do. One of the goals of communication competence is an expanded range of behaviors at one's disposal or, said another way, an expanded communicative "bag of tricks" (Rubin, 1990). We hope to guide your attempts to expand your behaviors into a greater "repertoire" from which to choose when you confront various communication situations. The expanded repertoire is especially helpful in those uncomfortable situations that often involve the opposite sex.
2. *Selection.* Once you have expanded your repertoire, you need to know which behavior to choose (Spitzberg & Cupach, 1984). In subsequent chapters, we talk about selecting the most appropriate behavior for various circumstances. For now, just realize that the selection depends on an analysis of your goals, the other person's goals, and the situation. Decisions are also based on what you might value. At the end of this chapter, we outline some values and suggest that they be applied to selecting your communication behaviors for female-male relationships in particular.
3. *Skill.* To be competent, you also need the skill to perform a behavior so that another person accepts your behavior and responds positively (Rubin, 1982). We spend a good deal of time in this text discussing the skills component of communication competence, as it applies to various situations you may encounter. We also encourage you to develop and practice your communication skills, so that you enhance your view of self and your relationships.

4. *Evaluation.* The last part of this sequence is your ability to judge your own success. You need to be able to see if your efforts have been successful in the way you wanted them to be, and then use this information to adapt your behavior the next time. If you don't evaluate, you won't know what to change for next time and you might continue to make the same mistake over and over.

These four aspects are central to communication competence. You will be more successful in gender communication if you (1) develop a wider range of communication behaviors from which to choose, (2) know how to analyze a situation and select the most appropriate behaviors from your repertoire, (3) perform those behaviors with skill, and (4) carefully evaluate the result. As we said at the beginning of this section, communication competence starts with a perception of the self. But it also includes the view that others may have of you as an individual. The next section describes competence as a social judgment.

Communication Competence: Others' Perspectives

People look at each other and make judgments about communication competence. If you think about it for a minute, you've probably been involved in conversations from which you walked away thinking, "So much for *that.*" Or, for another example, say you ask a person "What time is it?" and he or she responds "Tuesday." You are likely to call into question her or his overall communication competence. On the other hand, if you converse with that person and things go smoothly, you are likely to judge him or her as "pretty good at this." Our point here is that only part of the judgment of competence comes from your viewpoint; the remainder rests within the person who receives your communication.

This means that one fundamental aspect of becoming more effective is to increase the number of times you are considered competent by the people who communicate with you, especially those of the opposite sex. In this case, competence is connected to a determination of "appropriateness." People will judge you as competent if you behave in ways that are consistent with the expectations of the situation and the people in it. We borrow an example from a well-known commentator on social communication, Neil Postman (1976), to clarify this point.

Fred and Ginger have just spent a pleasant, relaxing day on the beach in Hawaii and are watching the sun drop slowly from the sky into the golden sea. Ginger, beginning to stir with romantic feelings, turns to Fred and says, "Isn't the sunset beautiful?" Fred replies, "Well, strictly speaking, the sun doesn't set. You see, the earth's rotation just makes it appear that the sun is setting. It would be more accurate to say that the earth is rising." Now, that's not a bad statement if you're in a high school science class. But it's a lousy one on a beach in Hawaii. We can guess Ginger's judgment of Fred's communication competence. So the judgment of competence is based on the demands of the situation and based on the interpretation of the receiver. It is possible that a different person on that beach might have judged Fred's response as appropriate.

Here's an interesting system for judging the competence of another person; it describes four categories of persons.

1. *The Unconscious Incompetent.* This person doesn't know something, but doesn't know that he or she doesn't know. Ever met someone like that? One of our biggest challenges as teachers is getting unconscious incompetents to realize that they have something to learn. Many aspects of this book may help you realize areas in which you are an "unconscious incompetent."

2. *The Conscious Incompetent.* This second category represents the beginning of real learning. Here, people are aware of what they do not know and are taking steps to correct the discrepancy.

3. *The Conscious Competent.* In this stage, persons have learned a new skill but need to think about it while they do it. Ever learn to snow ski? Someone who is just learning will ski down the mountain constantly thinking about what is going on: "Are my knees bent? Am I keeping the ski tips up? I'll plant my pole for a turn." Learning a new communication skill is like that. It feels awkward for a while and it requires conscious thought to make changes, but when the changes are made, people progress to stage 4.

4. *The Unconscious Competent.* At this stage, persons have integrated the new skill so well that they can perform it without conscious planning. It takes time and effort to get to this point, but it's worth it.

So, one goal is to work on your development of a repertoire of skills that allow you to communicate in ways that others will judge situationally appropriate. If you achieve that goal, you will be seen as more competent. But that's not all it takes; there's one more component to the personal effectiveness approach—goal attainment.

Goal Attainment and Communication

The achievement of personal goals in short means: Do you get what you want? (Diez, 1984; Parks, 1985; Wiemann, 1977). But before you get too excited about that definition, there's another essential element. People who just try to get their goals met all the time will find themselves friendless. To achieve your own goals, you need to be able to help the other person meet his or hers. If goals aren't balanced, the relationship will be unsatisfying in the long run and perhaps in the short run as well. Let's consider two concepts related to this notion of personal goal attainment: intentionality and decentering.

Intentionality

This part of goal attainment asks: What do you intend to communicate? Do you communicate things unintentionally? For example, recall the first day of a new class. What did you do? If you are like most students, you came in, sat down, and started to check people out. You looked around to see if you already knew somebody in the class, and then to see who might be interesting, who wasn't, who you might want to talk to, and who you might want to avoid. While you were doing this, were you also aware that you were being checked out by other people in the class? Think about what you were communicating to them. Were you communicating anything intentionally? Were you trying to look cool or trying to appear serious and studious? Were you trying to act as though you weren't checking anyone else out?

Earlier in this chapter, we talked about gaining more control over our communication behavior. Gaining control means becoming more intentional about your behavior (Parks, 1985). Being more intentional also means that you will plan more of your behavior, particularly with the opposite sex. Plans involve the ability to set clear and specific goals. We are not saying that all of your communication should be planned, but the more important the situation and the relationship are to you, the more helpful it will be to plan your communication behavior. Throughout this text, we give examples of how to plan your behavior to increase the likelihood of achieving your goals. For now, here's a real-life example to help you understand this whole notion; put yourself in the student's situation and see if it sounds familiar.

Dennis, a student in one of our classes some time ago, complained about his inability to talk to women. To analyze this problem, the line of questioning went like this:

TEACHER: How do you feel during these conversations?

DENNIS: Bad; I just feel really awkward.

T: When does this happen?

D: Every time I talk to a woman.

T: Well, I saw you talking with Marci yesterday. You looked like you were doing fine.

D: I guess I was, but Marci is a friend. I don't have any trouble talking to her.

T: So it's not all women, is that right?

D: Yeah, I guess I just have trouble talking to women I'm interested in dating.

T: Let's go back to what happens. Can you describe what happens to make you feel awkward?

D: Well, there are these long pauses, and I get so nervous.

T: Okay, anything else?

D: Because I'm so nervous, I can't look at her; I just stare at the floor. And sometimes I can't finish the sentences I start.

T: Dennis, I think we're getting somewhere. We started with the general problem of your inability to talk to women, and have narrowed it down to some specific behaviors, such as eye contact, pauses, and sentences. Here's what I would like you to do. Work on those three things as goals. Next time you talk with a woman you're interested in, work to maintain eye contact about half the time, have some questions or comments ready so that pauses no longer than a few seconds go by, and finish every sentence you start!

We are glad to report that Dennis is now happily married with three kids (just kidding). The point here is that to feel more personally effective, you need to be able to pinpoint the kind of behaviors that you want to change. In essence, you need to be able to set goals and make plans, even for how you want to communicate with others. Most people are like Dennis; all they can do is generate some abstract feeling ("I feel bad."). You need to take that feeling and turn it into specific behaviors. A second component of effectiveness will help you do just that.

Decentering

A useful but slightly complicated concept is the notion of "decentering." Decentering describes our ability to step outside of ourselves and talk about ourselves as another person might (Dance & Larson, 1972). You can decenter at any moment—when you are alone and pondering your own communication style, or before, during, and after you engage someone in conversation. For example, if you would like to have more of a social life but don't seem to be having much success, then decentering might be helpful to you. First, take some time out and think about those aspects of your personality that your friends find likable. Then replay a past encounter with a person you'd like to date. Do you detect those same personality traits emerging in this conversation? Can you put yourself into the other person's "mind's eye" to envision how this potential date views you? It is often helpful to pull out of ourselves, to attempt to visualize how we are coming across to others. We get a view of ourselves that is closer to reality, so that we begin to learn what communication skills we need to improve.

Decentering is valuable to you in at least three ways. First, you can begin to see yourself as others see you. Second, you can more clearly analyze your own behavior and modify it. Third, you can more clearly understand situations around you. The ability to decenter is best developed by asking yourself questions: What am I trying to accomplish? What things might keep me from achieving my goal? How do I have to adapt my efforts to meet the situation? What about the other person, what is she or he trying to accomplish? Does my goal complement or conflict with the other person's? How will the other person respond? What does the situation suggest as to how I should act? Questions like these help you analyze the situation and your role in it, as well as how you are affecting the other person. Answers to these questions go a long way toward increasing your personal communication effectiveness.

Our point in talking about the personal effectiveness approach to gender communication is that you are likely to change while taking this course and reading this text. We are not suggesting that you merely learn to "figure people out" only to get more of what you want. We are suggesting that you develop yourself, that you change your behaviors for the better. If you want to be personally effective, you may need to communicate differently than you do now. Ideally, you will feel more empowered by what you read in this textbook. We hope you will be more competent, since you will have an increased repertoire of communication behaviors and will know when and how to use it. You will have more of an ability to analyze what is going on and to set goals that will help you (and other persons) achieve those goals. As a result, we propose that you'll find your communication with men and women more satisfying. But there are a few cautions or guidelines in using all this information; the last section of this chapter discusses some values related to making wise choices in gender communication.

VALUES

The previous two major sections in this chapter dealt with communication competence and goal attainment as components of the personal effectiveness approach. Think one step further to consider this: People can be effective in communication without being competent. There are examples in history of highly effective people who used their communication skill for inappropriate purposes. Hitler is an excellent example of a person who was highly skilled in communicating with people, but think of the consequences of that skill. Con artists and others who deceive and trick people may also be quite good at communication. They can talk with people, draw them into their confidence, and take advantage of their trust. We are not interested in these kinds of communicators. This means that we have some *values* associated with the way we teach communication, values related to competence and goal attainment. While some of these values apply to any communicative relationship, we focus mainly on their application to communication within female-male relationships. Here are six values related to long-term effectiveness in gender communication.

Value 1: Equality of Power

There are those relationships which function rather successfully with an uneven distribution of power (e.g., parent-child, mentor-protégé, employer-employee), although abuses of the power imbalance exist within these relationships as well as within other types. However, when an imbalance of power isn't necessarily a societally induced or appropriate expectation for a relationship, such as in marriage, dating and romantic relationships, colleague or work relationships, and friendships, we believe that an ideal and a goal to work for is an even distribution of power or control. This shared power or control capitalizes on the strengths of each relational partner. You've already learned this concept from earlier information about empowerment in this chapter. But let's get more concrete: Think of standard jokes about a henpecked husband or the cruel reality of abusive relationships in which one partner completely dominates the other. There are dozens of examples of imbalanced control in a relationship. We believe that you, as an individual, should try to achieve and maintain a balance of influence, control, or power in your relationships. In later chapters we talk more specifically about how that is done, but we use this value (and others) to guide our suggestions for how to be more communicatively competent and to attain goals.

Value 2: Talking About It Makes It Better

We profoundly believe in the power of communication to help solve the problems we face. Take a stereotypic view of male-female communication for a moment. The stereotypic male doesn't express his feelings, while the stereotypic female is passive and submissive. An approach based on either stereotype is not particularly successful. We have all heard of the trend for children who have difficulty expressing anger and frustration to wind up using physical violence as a means of solving problems. Let's face it, this is a fairly typical male reaction. Think of the last time you saw two guys start to fight, and then one says to the other, "Say, we're having an interpersonal conflict; let's sit down and talk this out." It just doesn't happen that way too often, does it? Our point or value is that talking it over is absolutely critical to success. The willingness and ability to sit down and talk about the topic at hand, the relationship, each other's feelings, and possible solutions to problems are critical to personal effectiveness.

Value 3: Confirmation and Acceptance

Research suggests that a basic dimension within every communication situation is the feeling of acceptance or rejection (Cissna, 1987; Cissna, Garvin, & Kennedy, 1990; Dance & Larson, 1972; Lifshitz & Shulman, 1983; Rosenfeld, 1983; Sieburg, 1969). When we talk with someone, we can go away and say, "That person accepted me and what I had to say." Or we can say that our point of view was rejected. The communication of acceptance is a very important part of establishing satisfying relationships, since relationships don't progress if someone feels rejected. This acceptance is conveyed through a set of communication behaviors called confirmation, described more fully in Chapter 6. For now, simply recognize the value of a basic communicated acceptance of another person as fundamental to effective female-male relationships.

Value 4: Freedom of Choice

When we talk about the ability to direct the course of a relationship, we include the possibility that you will influence or persuade someone else. Many of our communication efforts are designed to get people to do what we want. If you are to be more successful, that means that you must have a greater impact on others. With that possibility comes more responsibility. A value we hold central to this process is the freedom of the other person to choose his or her own line of action. If someone walks up to you with a gun and says, "Your money or your life," that person is severely restricting your freedom of choice. As a more subtle example, people often manipulate the emotions of their partners to get what they want. Even this case depicts the restriction of someone's freedom to choose. We hope that you value the right of each person in a relationship to choose her or his own response to attempts at persuasion. This means that you will need to be able to say to someone, "I tried to persuade you, but you made your own choice and I respect that." This is not easy to do, but it is critical to long-term success in relationships. While the information in this text will help you become more persuasive in male-female relationships, you should also use these persuasive skills in a manner that respects the other person's freedom of choice.

Value 5: Treating Another Person as an Individual

Stereotyping is hard to avoid. Can you imagine starting from scratch with every person you meet, meaning that you can't use past experiences as clues to what to expect? Consider for a minute how you expect college professors to do certain things when they walk into a classroom. You expect salespersons to behave in certain ways when you enter a store. You may have some stereotypical views of people from other cultures. In some ways, stereotypes help to reduce our uncertainty and increase our ability to predict what will happen. But sometimes those stereotypes seriously limit the range of possibilities. For example, what if you applied an inaccurate stereotype to a person from another culture, only to discover that you misjudged the person and possibly lost out on a unique friendship? In your experience, what negative consequences have you encountered when you have treated someone as a stereotype?

Be even more specific. In your relationships, should you stereotype women and men based on their sex? We suggest not—not just because there are so many differences between people, but because no one likes to be treated as a stereotype. A man doesn't like to be told that he is just another unfeeling, inexpressive male. No woman likes to be told that "all women are too emotional." No people like to be told that they "are just like everyone else." In the first place, we are all different and our differences need to be recognized and celebrated. Second, actions based on stereotypes do nothing to advance a relationship. And third, stereotypes can negatively affect someone's self-esteem. When possible, treat people as individuals—as subjects, not objects.

Value 6: Being Open-Minded and Willing to Change

Have you ever talked with persons who are completely closed minded? It's frustrating, and frequently we have a reaction like, "Oh, what's the use? They'll never change their minds anyway, so there's no point in even talking." That's not a desirable reaction in effective communication. A basic dimension of competence is the belief on the part of other people that we are open to change. For example, if our students believe that we can be persuaded if sufficient reasoning is given, they are more likely to attempt to ask us to postpone the next exam. In a relationship, the more each person believes that the other person can be influenced, the more they are both likely to communicate. So we are suggesting that you be open to persuasion. We are not suggesting that you believe everything people tell you or do everything people ask of you, but if there is sufficient cause, it's okay to change your mind. Open-mindedness and the ability to change are positive values for all relationships.

CONCLUSION

In this opening chapter we have offered a definition of gender communication and have described it as provocative, pervasive, problematic, and unpredictable. We have also included brief descriptions of key terms so that you more fully understand the gender jargon that appears throughout the remainder of this textbook. Finally, we have explained our basic perspective of the communication process, including the components of uncertainty reduction, the receiver orientation, communication competence, and goal attainment. One of our aims in this text is to help you develop your sense of personal effectiveness so that you understand more of what is happening when women and men communicate. At the same time, we want you to understand your own communication behavior more fully so that you can predict the potential impact of certain communication behaviors on other people. If you can do that, you will be better at selecting the best option from your repertoire of communication behaviors. And finally, we want to develop your ability to explain why things worked out the way they did, because knowing "why" is the first step in changing things. Information enables people to understand what is happening, to explain why it is happening, and to predict what will happen in the future. The next section of this text presents information to help you understand the many factors that influence your attitudes and beliefs, the choices that you make about relationships, and your communication patterns with men and women.

Key Terms

gender communication	homophobia	repertoire
sex	feminism	selection
gender	patriarchy	skill
sexist	chauvinism	evaluation
sexual	empowerment	goal attainment
gender-role identity	power	intentionality
sexual orientation	uncertainty reduction	decentering
sexual preference	receiver orientation	values
heterosexism	personal effectiveness	confirmation
homosexism	communication competence	stereotyping

Discussion Starters

1. Think about how the *roles* and *rules* have changed for men and women in our society. What kinds of *roles* did your parents model for you when you were growing up? What kinds of attitudes have you developed, regarding appropriate roles for women and men to assume in our society? What are some of the *rules* for behavior that operated during your parents' or grandparents' generation? Do these rules seem outdated to you today? Are there some rules that are unchangeable?

2. Now that you have a clearer understanding of what sexism is, think of something you consider to be really sexist. It could be a policy or practice, or something that you saw, read, or heard. What was your reaction to this sexist stimulus at the time? What is your reaction now? If your reactions are different, why are they different?

3. What comes to mind when you hear the phrase *women's liberation movement?* What comes to mind when you hear the term *feminism?* What is your own response to feminism? Do you consider yourself a feminist? Why or why not?

4. Consider the difference between empowerment and power. Can you think of examples of individuals who communicate from a power base, as in a "power over" manner? Now think of individuals who communicate out of the empowerment, or "power to," motivation. What are the main differences in these two communication styles or approaches?

5. Recall a situation in which your interpretation of a message (as the receiver) did not match a person's intentions (as the sender). It could be something simple like a miscommunication over the time or place you were supposed to meet someone. Or it could be something more serious, like in a class when you were listening to an instructor's explanation of an upcoming assignment. Analyze that situation: Was it a same-sex or opposite-sex conversation? What do you think the sender of the message intended to communicate? How did you, as the receiver, interpret the message? What was said (or done, nonverbally) during the conversation that was the primary cause of misunderstanding? How was the situation resolved? Using a receiver orientation to communication, what could the *sender* in the conversation have done to make the situation better? How could the *receiver* have reduced the potential for misunderstanding?

6. Consider the communication behavior repertoire, or "bag of tricks," explained in this chapter. Then think about communication situations (especially with the opposite sex) that give you the most trouble. What communication behaviors could you add to your repertoire that would improve your future success in these kinds of situations?

7. Think of two very different relationships that you have currently with members of each sex. Now step outside of yourself, or decenter, and imagine how those two people see you. What makes having a relationship with you important to each of them? How do they view your communication ability? Are their views different? Do you think that gender has an impact on these persons' views of your communication ability? If so, why so?

8. How are your values reflected in your communication? Consider the six values presented in this chapter. Which of these values are already consistent with yours? Which ones represent new ideas for you? Are there values that you would add to our list?

References

BATE, B. (1988). *Communication and the sexes.* New York: Harper & Row.

BERGER, C. R., & BRADAC, J. J. (1982). *Language and social knowledge: Uncertainty in interpersonal relationships.* London: Edward Arnold.

BERGER, C. R., & CALABRESE, R. J. (1975). Some explorations in initial interaction and beyond: Toward a developmental theory of interpersonal communication. *Human Communication Research, 1,* 99–112.

CISSNA, K. N. (1987, April). *Advances in the analysis of confirming and disconfirming behaviors.* Paper presented at the joint meeting of the Southern Speech Communication Association and Central States Speech Association, St. Louis, MO.

CISSNA, K. N., GARVIN, B. J., & KENNEDY, C. W. (1990). Reliability in coding social interaction: A study of confirmation. *Communication Reports, 3,* 58–69.

DANCE, F. E. X., & LARSON, C. E. (1972). *Speech communication: Concepts and behavior.* New York: Holt, Rinehart & Winston.

DANCE, F. E. X., & LARSON, C. E. (1976). *The functions of human communication.* New York: Holt, Rinehart & Winston.

DeFrancisco, V. (1992, March). *Position statement: How can feminist scholars create a feminist future in the academic environment?* Paper presented at the Tenth Annual Conference on Research in Gender and Communication, Roanoke, VA.

DeVito, J. A. (1988). *Human communication: The basic course* (4th ed.). New York: Harper & Row

Diez, M. E. (1984). Communicative competence: An interactive approach. In R. N. Bostrom (Ed.), *Communication yearbook 8* (pp. 56–79). Beverly Hills, CA: Sage.

Faludi, S. (1991). *Backlash: The undeclared war against American women.* New York: Crown.

Gould, L. (1972, December). X: A fabulous child's story. *Ms. Magazine,* pp. 105–106.

Infante, D. A., Rancer, A. S., & Womack, D. F. (1990). *Building communication theory.* Prospect Heights, IL: Waveland Press.

Larson, C., Backlund, P., Redmond, M., & Barbour, A. (1978). *Assessing functional communication.* Falls Church, VA: Speech Communication Association and ERIC.

Lifshitz, P., & Shulman, G. M. (1983). The effect of perceived similarity/dissimilarity on confirmation/disconfirmation behaviors: Reciprocity or compensation? *Communication Quarterly, 31,* 85–94.

McCroskey, J. C. (1984). Communication competence: The elusive construct. In R. N. Bostrom (Ed.), *Competence in communication: A multidisciplinary approach* (pp. 259–268). Beverly Hills, CA: Sage.

McCroskey, J. C. (1985, May). *A trait perspective on communication competence.* Paper presented at the annual meeting of the International Communication Association, Honolulu, HI.

Parks, M. R. (1985). Interpersonal communication and the quest for personal competence. In M. Knapp (Ed.), *Handbook of interpersonal communication* (pp. 171–201). Beverly Hills, CA: Sage.

Pearce, W. B., & Rossi, S. M. (1984). The problematic practices of "feminism": An interpretive and critical analysis. *Communication Quarterly, 32,* 277–286.

Postman, N. (1976). *Crazy talk, stupid talk.* New York: Delacorte Press.

Rosenfeld, L. B. (1983). Communication climate and coping mechanisms in the college classroom. *Communication Education, 32,* 167–174.

Rubin, R. B. (1982). Assessing speaking and listening competence at the college level: The Communication Competency Assessment Instrument. *Communication Education, 31,* 19–32.

Rubin, R. B. (1990, June). *Perspectives on communication competence.* Paper presented at the annual meeting of the International Communication Association, Dublin, Ireland.

Sieburg, E. (1969). *Dysfunctional communication and interpersonal responsiveness in small groups.* Unpublished doctoral dissertation, University of Denver, Denver, CO.

Spender, D. (1985). *Man made language* (2nd ed.). London: Routledge & Kegan Paul.

Spitzberg, B. H., & Cupach, W. R. (1984). *Interpersonal communication competence.* Beverly Hills, CA: Sage.

Taylor, A., Meyer, A., Rosegrant, T., & Samples, B. T. (1989). *Communicating* (5th ed.). Englewood Cliffs, NJ: Prentice-Hall.

Thorne, B., Kramarae, C., & Henley, N. (1983). Language, gender, and society: Opening a second decade of research. In B. Thorne, C. Kramarae, & N. Henley (Eds.), *Language, gender, and society* (pp. 7–24). Rowley, MA: Newbury House.

Wallis, C. (1989, December 4). Onward, women! *Time,* pp. 80–89.

Wiemann, J. M. (1977). Explication and test of a model of communicative competence. *Human Communication Research, 3,* 195–213.

Wiemann, J. M., & Backlund, P. (1980). Current theory and research in communicative competence. *Review of Educational Research, 50,* 185–199.

Wilson Schaef, A. (1981). *Women's reality: An emerging female system in the white male society.* Minneapolis: Winston Press.

PART TWO

Influences on Our Choices

CHAPTER 2

Nature or Nurture? Biological and Social Influences on Gender

Just looking at the title of this chapter should make you want to read it, but if that's not enough, take a look at the case study. We suspect that you'll want to read the rest.

CASE STUDY

Here's an account of a discussion that happened in a gender communication class taught by the female co-author of this text. The topic for Ivy's class that day was explanations of how women and men are similar and different, biologically as well as psychologically. The discussion started with contributions from various students around the room, intermixed with instructor comments and questions. But soon the conversation narrowed to an exchange between one male and one female student, Jenny and Marcus.

To understand Marcus and Jenny's disagreement, you have to trace the discussion back a bit. Ivy posed a question to the class: What physical or biological attributes of the opposite sex seem the most mystifying to you? Immediately the men in the room began to answer, "PMS!" "Yeah, that PMS is the weirdest thing." "If you know your girlfriend's got it, better get out of her way!" Other male students expressed difficulty in relating to a condition that could, in their words, turn some women into virtual "monsters" for a few days each month. Some of the female students simply chuckled during this part of the discussion, while others voiced the opinion that PMS was "talked about too much." It was a terrible problem for lots of women, but others didn't even have it. A couple of these women agreed that while PMS was real, it was sometimes exaggerated so that society could deem women unstable and weaker than men. Any chuckling or lightheartedness in the room stopped when Jenny said that she believed men had a type of monthly cycle similar to women's menstrual cycles.

Most of the class sort of stared at Jenny, until Marcus spoke up: "That's nonsense. Men don't have periods; that's just something you women want us to believe, so that we won't joke so much about PMS. You just want to get back at us because we don't have to deal with what you have every month."

At this point the instructor intervened, asking Jenny to clarify her statement. Jenny explained, "The other day I read this article in a magazine that talked about men having cycles, just like women do. There's nothing physical or outward like there is for women, but they go through regular emotional upheavals caused by their hormones." Classmates weren't talking; they were too busy thinking about Jenny's remarks and watching for Marcus's next response.

Jenny continued: "I think it's true; I see it in my own boyfriend. At about the same time almost every month, my boyfriend Scott just gets weird! He starts acting really jealous, and gets really irritated with the least little thing I do. I've learned that it's not *me;* he's just having his 'time.' So, I just cut out then, so we won't get into fights. After a few days, he's back to his old self again. I never really considered it a 'period' until I read this article."

Marcus fired back at Jenny: "Wait a minute, you notice this every month, at about the same time every month? I don't believe it. Guys don't have periods. That's just ridiculous." Then Jenny asked Marcus, "Why is it so ridiculous? Do you have trouble thinking of a guy having a few un-macho days each month? Why is okay for women be on these supposed hormonal roller coasters, but men can't experience anything like that? Do they have to be in control all the time?"

Needless to say, Ivy (the instructor) had to intervene again to keep the discussion at a "friendly disagreement" level. While this could have been an irretrievable moment in the class, she saw it as an opportunity. She capitalized on this opportunity by guiding the class into a discussion of how biological differences can take on social meanings that often increase misunderstanding between the sexes. It was also an opportunity to get female and male students talking to one another about topics that don't normally get discussed. It's not only important in a gender communication course to learn about how men and women communicate; it's good to get a chance to talk to each other, in the relatively low-threat environment of the classroom.

What if this discussion had arisen in *your* gender communication class? Would you have agreed with Jenny or with Marcus? Have you ever considered the possibility of a male cycle? This is only one issue—one that always generates lively exchange. But it's one topic of several embedded within contemporary arguments about biological sex, social influences, and psychological responses.

OVERVIEW

As we said in Chapter 1, one of our goals in this text is to teach you about gender communication so that you become more personally effective and improve your relationships. To attain that goal, we begin by examining the internal and external factors that influence the process of communicating with the opposite sex. Of the many influences, biological and social factors have a profound, if sometimes subconscious, psychological effect. In this chapter, we ask you to examine how these factors affect your self-identity and your gender communication. When you read this information, think about the following things:

1. The extent to which your biological sex (being male or female) is a part of your self-identity
2. How you have been shaped by social interpretations of biology, as well as other influences, such as your family relationships, friendships, education, and experiences
3. Your psychological response to these first two things, in terms of how you have formed your self-identity
4. How you communicate your self-identity to others

Some people believe that because biological differences between women and men are natural and uniquely human, they are something to be appreciated, not downplayed or resented. These biological properties "make the world go 'round," so why be concerned about them? Others believe that biological sex differences are fairly insignificant; the real issue is the social interpretation of those differences. Sometimes the interpretation is that the sexes are more biologically alike than different. But at other times, society uses biological differences as a disguise or excuse for perpetuating a power differential between the sexes.

Social influences complicate the picture. We all know that we don't live in a vacuum; we are significantly affected by the environment in which we live, especially by the people closest to us. In their book on sex roles, researchers Stockard and Johnson (1980) conclude: "Biology by no means fully determines what happens to individuals or groups. While physiological variables may prompt individuals to move in certain directions, the social situation, including economic factors, cultural, or individual desires, may overrule or drastically alter these biological predilections" (p. 116). Social factors affect how we come to understand our own maleness or femaleness. The combination of biological and social factors forms an individual's internal, psychological response—what we term *gender-role identity*. This identity is what we communicate to others. Since this may sound like a fairly complex process, we try to simplify it by studying one part of the process at a time. Here's what you'll read about in the following pages:

- Social interpretations of anatomical sex differences
- How sex differences in hormonal functioning can lead to stereotypes
- Biological cycles in women and men
- Recent findings on sex differences in brain functioning and cognitive ability
- How social influences affect the development of gender-role identity
- How androgyny, masculinity, and femininity relate to gender-role identity
- Gender-role transcendence and the expanded communication repertoire
- How your biological, social, and psychological selves affect gender communication

One simple warning about this chapter: Don't expect any clear-cut, simple answers to difficult questions. Where heredity ends and environment begins is an excellent topic for one of those late-night-in-the-dorm, "What is reality?"–type discussions. We present the most current information around, but right now the evidence is still being collected and it's raising more questions than answers.

INTRODUCTION

Remember the discussion of values and effective gender communication in Chapter 1? Value 5 was "treating another person as an individual." Have you ever been talked to or treated a certain way merely because of your sex? (Notice that we didn't say "gender," because that's a more informed, in-depth designation than biological sex.) Can you recall a situation when someone sized you up, because you were a woman or a man, and then talked to you based on a stereotype or limited vision of what your sex was supposed to be?

Here are some common examples. It seems that people assume that all men, by virtue of the higher concentration of muscle mass in male bodies, can lift all kinds of heavy things. They always get called on to help people move, help rearrange bulky furniture, or lift heavy boxes and objects. Many men have strained their backs or, worse, developed hernias and detached retinas from all of the lifting they are "supposed" to be able to do. Why assume that a guy always has the strength or, for that matter, *wants* to do physical labor?

On the woman's side, ever take your car to a service center for repairs and be treated by the mechanic as though you don't speak English? (Of course men get treated this way too, but there seems to be some expectation that men can understand car maintenance "talk" better than women.) Ever go into a hardware store and ask a clerk for a specific, fancy tool? If you're a woman, watch the clerk's reaction. In these instances, people who know nothing about you may assume a lot about you, by simple virtue of your sex. And we all know of more serious examples of sexual stereotyping and discriminatory treatment than these.

In Chapter 1 we discussed uncertainty reduction as a motivation to communicate. When people are uncertain and don't know you as an individual, they communicate with you based on extremely limited information—your sex and other physical attributes that can be perceived with the basic senses. In the absence of more extensive information, people tend to rely on socially learned stereotypes because they provide some basis for how to proceed. Reducing uncertainty by using the senses first and stereotypes second is natural and understandable, to a point. But if someone always stops there—evoking a stereotype without exploring what makes you a unique person—you may find you do not like that kind of treatment.

For example, take a biological property of the sexes, such as men's higher level of muscle mass and physical strength, and attach to that an expectation that men shouldn't cry or express their emotions. As another example, assume that since women have a monthly cycle that affects their bodies, they can't make decisions because they are emotionally unstable, flighty, and unreliable. Assume that certain personality traits or communication behaviors are decidedly masculine or decidedly feminine. Can you begin to see how conceptions of biological sex differences become intertwined with social influences, embedded within one's culture? What kind of psychological response emerges? What kind of communication results? Granted, this is fairly complex, but if you are beginning to grasp these ideas, then you find yourself at the center of the nature-nurture dialogue.

You may be asking, why focus on *differences,* as opposed to *similarities* between women and men? This is an excellent question. One answer simply relates to human nature. While people don't intend to widen any kind of gender gap, it seems that they are more interested in learning how their sex differs from the opposite one. We are all curious as to what makes us unique and individual, so it doesn't seem as captivating to talk only about similarities between people. A second, more important reason is this: Exposing sex and gender differences so that people understand them increases cooperation between men and women, rather than adding to the mystery or suspicion that may tend to divide us. If you know that someone is different from you but don't know why or don't care to find out what those differences are all about, then you have separated yourself from that person. But if you recognize a difference and communicate your understanding and acceptance of that difference, then you can get along better and celebrate the individuality—yours and the other person's.

BIOLOGICAL SEX AND SOCIAL INTERPRETATIONS

Biological differences between men and women continue to be hot topics these days. Accounts of the latest study on brain functioning, hormonal effects, or anatomical abnormalities can be found on magazine shelves and television talk shows. The major headline on the cover of one 1992 issue of *Time* magazine reads, "Why Are Men and Women Different?" That attention-getter is followed by the lines, "It isn't just upbringing. New studies show they are born that way." In the cover picture, a little boy is flexing his upper arm muscles for a little girl, whose facial expression indicates either admiration or complete boredom, depending on your point of view.

As authors of your textbook, we want to provide you with current, reliable information about biological sex differences and their social interpretations because we believe that they influence communication between women and men. Before you learn more of the specifics of gender communication, you have to understand what is *influencing* your choices and behavior. However, while we want to inform you about biological sex differences, they are neither the central focus of this chapter nor critical to our approach to gender communication. We don't want to make too much out of biological differences because we've seen that they sometimes become a "copout." In other words, it is easy to chalk up a discussion of gender to biological differences and leave it at that, without exploring more deeply the ramifications or consequences of those differences. It is easy to say that "men and women are just naturally different, so stop trying to understand it or fight it. Just let nature take its course." This comment implies that somehow biology gives us permission to behave in a certain way. For all of us who are interested in gender communication, this is not a workable stance. It is also not our intent to suggest that one sex is somehow physically superior to the other. As you will see, there are biological trade-offs for the sexes and in many ways they are more similar than different. Keep in mind that we are most interested in how communication is affected by social translations of biology.

Anatomical Differences and Social Interpretations

We begin this section by discussing three divergent anatomical properties of men and women: differences in sexual organs, reproductive functions, and physical strength. Some of the biological findings that we describe here may be quite familiar to you; some may be new enough to surprise you. But we challenge you to think about the social interpretations of the biology in ways that you might not have thought of before. We challenge you to think also about how those interpretations are reflected in communication between women and men.

Sexual Organs

Since your first class in human biology, you have known that the combination of XX chromosomes creates a female fetus and the XY combination creates a male, in the majority of instances. (There are some exceptions, but we'll leave that to the biologists to explain.) Early on, human embryos develop both male and female sex organs, but the presence of the extra X or the Y chromosome causes the secretion of hormones and the differentiation of sex organs. The fetus starts to form internal female or external male genitalia at around three or four months into development (Devor, 1989; Unger & Crawford, 1992).

Think for a moment about the consequences of that simple differentiation of genitalia. It is not our intent to be crude or to shock you here, but men's and women's anatomy (especially sexual anatomy) is hardly a taboo topic of discussion these days, especially in the media. The sexual dynamic between women and men should not be omitted from discussion, since throughout history it has profoundly influenced how we behave toward one another.

Consider the interesting parallel between the sexes' genitalia and their roles in society. For centuries the male penis has been viewed as a symbol of virility—an external, outward sign of men's strength and their ability to assert themselves in the world. The externality of men's sexual organs has been interpreted socially to identify men as the actors, doers, leaders, and decision makers in many aspects of life—in the home, in relationships, in work, politics, and so on. In contrast, the internal genitalia of women is paralleled with the more passive, submissive profiles that women have traditionally assumed—profiles endorsed by men, and often by society in general. The social interpretations of women's sexual organs identify women as reactors, receivers, followers, and beneficiaries of men's decisions.

Maybe you have never considered these parallels before; maybe your reaction to these ideas is: "The world has changed; these depictions of women and men are past history, so why draw the parallel to sexuality?" If that's what you're thinking, then congratulate yourself. We agree that for many people these profiles no longer apply, thus the biological parallel doesn't apply either. But at times you may be painfully reminded that within many institutions in our society—business, education, political arenas—there exist more than mere echoes of this "historical" view of women and men.

Reproductive Functions

While the sexual organs represent the more obvious anatomical sex differences, perhaps the most profound difference rests in the sexes' reproductive functions. Researchers Bermant and Davidson (1974) define biological sex as "separateness: a division of reproductive labor into specialized cells, organs, and organisms. The sexes of a species are the classes of reproductively incomplete individuals" (p. 9). We know that it takes both eggs and sperm to rectify this "incompleteness," so this is not the differentiating reproductive function to which we refer. What makes the female system so different from the male's in this instance is the woman's capacity to carry a developing fetus for nine months, give birth, and nurse an infant. These tasks have long been

The "Bizarro" cartoon by Dan Piraro is reproduced by permission of Chronicle Features, San Francisco, California.

protected, even to the extent that turn of the century medical information warned women against excessive thinking or exercise, which, it was said, would divert blood away from their reproductive systems (McLoughlin, Shryer, Goode, & McAuliffe, 1988).

Many men believe that the reproductive, nurturing function is the single most enviable aspect of womanhood. What's humorous is that no matter how envious they are, very few of these men would readily offer to change places with women regarding this function. However, they are mystified by the changes in a woman's system as she accommodates to a new life growing inside of her. (Most women are mystified, too.) The reproductive capabilities of men and women have more profound social translations than any other.

To better explain that last statement, allow us to recreate for you a segment of a rather lively discussion that occurred at a recent gathering of some friends. We were all talking about the various topics to be included in this text, when the subject of biological sex differences arose. One of the men commented that sex differences exist in their current form because of centuries of hunter-gatherer cultures—societies that have been studied by anthropologists and with which you are probably familiar (Brown, 1980; Coward, 1983). In these cultures, the men combed the land, hunted the food, and protected their families from danger, while the women had the birthing and child-rearing duties and developed tools to gather and carry the food. This formed the basis of a social structure that worked very well; thus it continued into modern times, in the opinion of our friend at the party. But more important than a mere anthropological lesson, the point in this explanation of sex differences is that because of simple biology, whole societal structures were set in place. Did you ever think that so much might rest on the capacity to reproduce? This is a prime example of what we mean by biological factors contributing to a wide range of social norms and expectations.

Now, granted, our friend had a valid point; in historic times and in some cultures today, women's roles are defined by their biology. Men's roles in these cultures seem balanced with women's roles of child maintenance. (We say "in some cultures" because renowned anthropologist Margaret Mead documented cultures in which the sex roles are reversed and are not based on reproductive capabilities.) The rationale is that because women have birthing and nursing capabilities (and because of their hormonal profile, discussed in a later section), they are more innately nurturing. Thus they are the more likely candidates to hold primary childcare roles within families and society. Further, men, because of their biological makeup, are not physically bound to infants, so they are the more likely candidates to provide economic sustenance for the family. You can understand this explanation for the origin of the wife as mother/husband as breadwinner dichotomy.

But did you ever stop to consider how arbitrary the decision might have been—the decision for women to be the baby-birthers? Whether you believe that the decision was made by a divine entity or occurred as a fluke of evolution is not the focus of our discussion here. However you believe it occurred, what if the reverse decision had been made? Have you ever thought about what kind of world we'd be living in if the conception, pregnancy, birthing, and nursing tasks were biological capabilities of men? Would men still be seen as actors, doers, and decision makers, and women as reactors, receivers, and decision followers? Would the power structure that accompanies going out into the world and making a living versus staying at home with children be reversed as well? How would communication between men and women be affected?

Come out of the "what if" mode now to consider our contemporary society. Medical knowledge and technology have progressed to the point at which women, in particular, can benefit from alternatives to their own biology—alternatives that are changing our social structure. Although still able to carry and give birth to babies, women now have several methods of preventing conception. If they do become pregnant, they do not necessarily have to be the biologically designated, primary child-care-givers once the baby is born. Many women are free to return to work or to pursue other endeavors if they so choose and are economically able to do so. These choices affect how the sexes view each other, as well as how they communicate. So, since modern families are beginning to make nontraditional decisions regarding child rearing, are we witnessing the breakdown of the hunter-gatherer approach to family life?

Not so fast—maybe we're not as far from the hunter-gatherer model as we might think. What would be the social reaction if the father of a newborn baby chose to take time away from his job to be the primary caregiver? You may think that the likelihood of this happening isn't great, but this exact situation was the subject of a recent ABC *Nightline* television program. The main guest on the program was describing his unique situation in the law firm where he worked. The firm negotiated a paternity leave for him, so that his wife could resume her successful career and he could take care of the baby. How did people react to his decision? One guest on *Nightline* applauded the family's decision and the "revolutionary" option created by the law firm, encouraging other businesses and institutions to initiate similar policies. However, most of the program's guests were not so optimistic. While they didn't discredit the spirit of the paternity leave, they felt that reality would prove this to be an unwise decision. They anticipated that the man's colleagues would ridicule and devalue his decision, that eventually he would be viewed as anything but a "team player" like other lawyers in the firm, and that his career would suffer dramatically.

What are the social backlashes for women who don't follow the more traditional path of motherhood? Have you heard criticism leveled at women who choose not to have children, or who return to their careers while their babies are still quite young? If a man chose not to father any children or not to become the primary caregiver for a newborn because it would disrupt his career goals, do you think he would receive as much criticism as women who make the same choices? Most often decisions like these are seen by many as "rocking the biological boat," although, like other aspects related to gender, things are beginning to change. The changing roles described in the preceding paragraphs may seem startling now, but probably they will become more commonplace with time.

Physical Strength

When the subject of biological sex differences is introduced, students are quick to comment about issues surrounding physical strength and endurance. Heightened by Secretary of Defense Les Aspin's announcement in 1993 that women would be allowed to pilot jets in combat missions, the topic of biological attributes and women in frontline military action generates provocative discussion. The general drift of these discussions is that women, by virtue of the higher fat–lower muscle composition of their bodies in comparison to men's, are less equipped with the strength and endurance necessary for combat or sustained military action. The counterargument is that if women are able to endure childbirth, they ought to be able to handle combat. But remember that at the beginning of this section, we said that it was not our intent to imply that one sex was physically superior to the other. In that spirit, let's review what some experts say about muscle versus fat composition, strength, and sex differences.

Fitness experts Covert Bailey and Lea Bishop in their 1989 book *The Fit-or-Fat Woman* discuss the varying fat levels of women and men. According to these authors, by age 20 a woman's fat level averages around 22 percent, while a man's is around 10 percent. Scientists attribute this discrepant fat level of the sexes mostly to the female body's function of protecting a fetus. This inclination toward a genetic, biologically fatty body that serves to insulate potential babies has given more than one woman grief. Besides men's higher concentrations of muscle, four other factors give men more natural strength than women: a greater oxygen-carrying capacity; a lower resting heart rate; higher blood pressure; and more efficient methods of recovering from physical exertion (Stockard & Johnson, 1980). Because of these characteristics, men have long been thought of as the stronger sex, women the weaker sex. But let's take a closer look at determinations of strength.

Webster's defines strength as force, invulnerability, or the capacity for exertion and endurance. If you examine strength from a vulnerability angle, then the sex-typed strength argument breaks down a bit. In psychologist Carol Jacklin's (1989) discussion of biology and behavior, this issue is explained: "One important biological fact that distinguishes the sexes is that males are more physically vulnerable than females. This differential vulnerability is particularly pronounced at the beginning and end of the life span" (p. 128). Jacklin documents how male fetuses experience many more developmental difficulties and birth defects, average an hour longer to deliver, and have a higher death rate than female fetuses. Men average shorter life spans (72 years) in comparison to women (79 years) (McLoughlin et al., 1988). Another aspect of the vulnerability angle relates to the sexual organs. In ordinary circumstances, men's external sexual organs are more readily injured than women's. (Several athletic clothing manufacturers have made fortunes off this very fact.) This is not to say that women cannot be injured, but that the internality of female sex organs make them less accessible to injury than men's. Thus, from these examples, if strength equates to invulnerability, the stereotype of a stronger sex doesn't quite work.

Could it be that the notion of male strength has more to do with social interpretations than biological fact? The answer to that question is no if you equate strength with higher muscle mass, and yes if you equate it with vulnerability. You may be wondering, "Why do we *need* to label a stronger and a weaker sex?" If so, you're again right on track, because arguments over who is the fairer sex or the stronger sex can be quite defeating and a waste of time. Most often a determination of strength depends on the individual, not the sex. Probably we've all seen some women who were much stronger (in terms of muscle strength) than some men, and vice versa. But you also have to realize how many social expectations and stereotypes are steeped in the basic biology.

As an example of a social interpretation of the "strength" issue, how many men reading this text can recall being told, "Boys are supposed to be strong; boys don't cry"? Can you remember a time when you or a male friend didn't *feel* very strong but were reminded to hide that feeling, so as to appear strong to everyone else? Sometimes instances like this occur during crisis or trauma, when men are expected to be the "strong ones," so that everyone else can fall apart. If you've ever been in a hospital waiting room when a man revealed his emotions about a sick loved one, did you notice other people's reactions or do you recall your own? Many times people are so completely stunned by a male emotional display they don't know how to react.

What about situations that aren't related to crisis or trauma, such as more commonplace instances of disappointment, depression, or a bad case of the blues? Many men feel that they are programmed to be strong, to mask or at least downplay what they are feeling, so they react emotionally only when they are alone—if they react outwardly at all. Because of this pressure to "stay strong," sometimes the emotion gets released through physical exertion or in destructive ways. Men explain that although women say they want men to be more emotional, to demonstrate their feelings rather than internalize them, when these men have let their emotions show, the women "freak." On the one hand, women are telling men that they should be more open with their emotions, that it's okay to cry about something if that's what one is feeling. Yet many women don't expect a male outpouring of emotion and have had little experience with it, so they are ill-equipped to respond to it. Thus their negative reactions reinforce the "be strong, don't cry" mentality.

This is not to say that all women react negatively to male emotion, or that women always show their emotions. Some women were taught just like men to "buck up" and put a rein on their emotions. But the pressure to be "strong" just isn't the same for them, in most cases. Does emotional display make women the "weaker" sex? Why do we often equate strength and weakness with an honest demonstration of human emotion? Why do we sometimes communicate with each other based on these stereotypes and expectations?

Biological designations can have profound, far-reaching social implications that can seriously influence your choices. We say "choices" because you do have the opportunity to *choose* how you wish to communicate with others. A more personally effective way to communicate with men and women is free from the limitations of stereotypes and expectations—communicating with each person as an individual, not as a part of some larger group identity. We're not suggesting that it's easy to rid yourself of past "programming," that is, patterns established early in life. It doesn't simply happen because you read this text or take a course in gender communication. It takes a commitment to the belief that communication unencumbered by sex-role stereotypes and expectations is preferable to its converse. Communication like this also takes sincere attempts to change one's patterns and monitor one's behavior, but we contend that the attempt is worth the effort.

Hormonal Differences and Social Interpretations

Another biological designation of significant influence is hormonal functioning in men and women. According to Jacklin (1989), hormonal differences "are among the most common biological causes given for behavioral sex-related differences" (p. 129). However, as hormonal studies are becoming more frequent and are utilizing more sophisticated methods, they are producing inconsistent results. We still do not know exactly the effect that hormones have on human behavior. Some of the complexity results from not knowing where the genetics end and the environment begins. Even more problematic are some researchers' conclusions about their results—conclusions that translate into social interpretations that then dictate "appropriate" sex roles and behavior (Bleier, 1984).

You may already be aware that the three main groups of hormones (androgens, estrogens, and progestogens) are contained within all humans, just at varying levels. For simplicity's sake, we have chosen here to explore those hormones most associated with masculinity (androgens or, more specificially, testosterone) and femininity (estrogens). We've pared some complex information down to three key elements: hormonal effects on nurturance, aggression, and cycles or mood shifts. These functions are the most distinctive for the sexes and have the most significant social interpretations.

Nurturance

Stereotypically, nurturance is associated with women's mothering roles, but it is defined as the "giving of aid and comfort to others" (Maccoby & Jacklin, 1974, pp. 214–215). Research by Anke Ehrhardt has determined a relationship between female hormones and the inclination to nurture. Ehrhardt and colleagues (1980, 1984) examined young girls who had been prenatally "masculinized" by receiving large doses of androgens (male hormones) from drugs prescribed for their mothers. Subjects rarely fantasized or daydreamed about marriage and pregnancy, nor did they show much interest in caring for small children. They more often gave career a higher priority than marriage in discussions of future plans, generally liked to play and associate with boys more than girls, and were more likely to exhibit high levels of physical energy. These studies and other evidence have led researchers to link hormones and nurturance.

But many researchers argue that the ability to nurture goes beyond biology. Stockard and Johnson (1980) caution that "hormonal influence helps prompt the appearance of and interest in nurturing behavior, but social situations and interactions also exert an influence, making it possible for males as well as females to nurture" (p. 137). Such experiences as participation in childbirth, early contact between parents and infants, and even whether one has had experience with younger siblings may affect one's ability to nurture. Given this information, why does society tend to readily associate femininity with the ability to nurture and comfort, as though men were incapable of this? Granted, the association between motherhood and nurturance is deeply ingrained in our culture; thus it is a reasonable connection. But does it have to be the only connection?

If a man finds he has a nurturing tendency as strong as or stronger than his wife or partner, should his masculinity be threatened? Think about why, until only recently, mothers were almost always awarded custody of children in divorce proceedings, regardless of which parent was actually the better nurturer. Conversely, if a woman isn't particularly fond of children and isn't at all interested in motherhood, does this mean that she has a hormonal deficit, or that she is somehow less feminine than women who want to bear children? We suspect that you are beginning to see how hormonal functioning can lead to labels and stereotypes for the sexes—labels that affect our opportunities and influence our choices in terms of how to communicate.

Aggression

Hyde (1986), a noted gender psychologist, states that "gender differences in aggression are generally considered to be a reliable phenomenon" (p. 51). Sex-role researchers Stockard and Johnson (1980) assert that in all known societies, men behave more aggressively than women. These researchers admit that this aggressive behavior may be learned, but they provide evidence to indicate that hormones influence aggressive behavior. However, another gender psychologist, Marie Richmond-Abbott (1992), believes that "it is difficult to characterize aggression as a sex difference because even defining aggression presents a problem" (p. 52). Aggression can be displayed verbally or physically, but it is not always clear whether a certain behavior is aggressive, assertive, coercive, energetic, persuasive, dominant, competitive, violent, and so on. Despite definitional problems, aggressiveness is often discussed as a male characteristic related to androgens, while passivity relates to the female system's lack of androgens.

Stockard and Johnson (1980) reviewed investigations of boys and girls who received high dosages of androgens (male hormones) before birth. In these studies, both male and female subjects had higher energy levels than control group subjects and preferred games, toys, sports, and activities traditionally associated with boys. Female subjects exhibited "tomboy" characteristics and behaviors and were more likely to start family fights than control group female subjects. Internationally noted sex-role scholars Maccoby and Jacklin (1980) reported that male aggression related to hormonal functioning was a conclusive, demonstrable sex difference. However, gender researcher Anne Fausto-Sterling (1985) discovered that approximately half the most recent studies attempting to link male aggression and testosterone levels produced results that contradicted studies reviewed by Maccoby and Jacklin. Thus it appears that the verdict is still out, in terms of determining a cause-and-effect relationship between male hormonal levels and resulting aggressive behavior. Why then do we still tend to associate masculinity with aggressive behavior, femininity with passive behavior? Could it again be the case that judgments about aggression and the sexes have more to do with social influences than biological fact?

A few examples will help us try to answer those questions. First, think again about the messages that lots of little boys receive—messages from their mothers and fathers, siblings, peers, the media, and so on. In addition to those messages about strength that we discussed in an earlier section, boys are warned not to "act like a sissy" and are chastised for anything resembling feminine behavior. One of the worst insults one can level at a boy or a man is to call him a girl or a woman. You see fathers, uncles, and older brothers teaching young boys to stick up for themselves, to develop aggressive attitudes by playing contact sports, and to rough-and-tumble with the best of them. Granted, things are changing and not all parents raise their male children in this manner, but the male-as-aggressor stereotype is still around for some reason.

As another example, some men are verbally aggressive in their jobs. Perhaps they have been in situations where going along or hanging back didn't get them very far, so they come to believe that verbal aggression can enhance success on the job. That aggressive behavior might take the form of emphatic sales pitches, interruptions of subordinates, or fevered attempts to persuade colleagues. Quite often this aggressive behavior in men on the job is expected, tolerated, and rewarded. As a result of positive reinforcement, we might say that these displays of aggression are due to social factors rather than "raging hormones."

We're not certain that men are particularly proud of the legacy of aggression; in fact, many of them are working hard to turn this legacy around. Many men are of the opinion that the expectation to be strong and aggressive constitutes a burden they'd rather not carry. They have begun to resent the implication that being a "real man" means being aggressive, competitive, emotionally aloof or detached, and in control all the time. They have begun to seek alternatives to aggressive behavior. Where do you stand on this issue?

Now consider the sexual flip side of aggression. What happens when girls carry tomboyish behaviors into adulthood? How do most people react when women exhibit aggressive behavior? Many people react negatively, as though a woman who expresses this stereotypically masculine trait is experiencing hormonal imbalance or behaving inappropriately. Occasionally, off-base, derogatory insinuations about sexual orientation are made. Some men are threatened or put off by "aggressive" women, because they don't look forward to yet another context for competition. Some women are put off by unexpected, aggressive behavior in women, too.

Here's an example. As more and more women enter the work force and begin to achieve higher rank, they realize that in some situations passive, "don't rock the boat" communication isn't the best professional strategy. When women demonstrate their expanded repertoire of communication behaviors for professional encounters, how do people react? Have people's reactions to female aggressive behavior changed with the times? If a female manager were to argue aggressively with her coworkers or boss, interrupt the verbal contributions of colleagues, or aggressively strive to achieve a promotion, think about whether she would be viewed through the same lens as a man behaving similarly. In most cases we believe not, but it is more likely today than in times past for female aggressive behavior to be accepted—a reflection of how society is evolving regarding its expectations of appropriate behavior for women and men.

Most of our students believe that reactions to unstereotypical behavior from the sexes have changed with the times—somewhat. They add the "somewhat" because they still see instances where men and women are viewed negatively for not behaving "as expected." Just as one example, male and female students alike are extremely competitive for grades. But we've witnessed situations in educational settings where female students will act in what could be called unstereotypically aggressive ways—either arguing vehemently with professors about grades, or talking about assignments and tests as though they were competitions. Some women in our classes admit that they try to "psych out" their classmates before major presentations, because they feel in competition for the best evaluations. What is interesting is how some of the other students and their professors are taken aback by this unstereotypical behavior.

As a final example for this section, think about one more context in which aggressive behavior is viewed differently for the sexes—sports. Acting out

---

What If ?

What if the signifying color for girls was blue and for boys was pink? Have you ever wondered how the tradition of assigning colors to sex got started? Two reports of folklore reveal somewhat contradictory origins of these traditions. In his book about social customs and traditions, Brash (1965) explains that in Middle Eastern tradition, evil demons were thought to hover over the nursery. Since these demons were considered allergic to certain colors, including blue, parents would paint the doors of their homes blue to ward off the evil spirits. Brash states that "girl babies were regarded as vastly inferior to boy babies and it was assumed that evil spirits would not be interested in them. That is why blue was reserved for boys. Any distinctive colour for girls was deemed unnecessary" (p. 23). Brash also cites European folklore suggesting that boy babies were born under blue-colored cabbages while baby girls were found inside pink roses; thus the designation of the colors. We've heard other explanations, such as one view that claims that in early American history the colors actually were reversed, but they evolved into the boy/blue–girl/pink distinctions that we have now. This bit of history is interesting, but so what? Well, what is interesting is what people associate with the colors, right? *What if* the color pink was connected with boys? Would the color still connote passive, gentle, and sweet personality traits and behavior? *What if* the color blue designated female? Would the assertive, rambunctious, action-oriented behavior still go with the color? Have you ever thought that even simple colors might add to the stereotypes about men and women?

aggression on the football field, the hockey rink, or the boxing ring is encouraged, expected, and rewarded in men. But as more women's sports gain attention and respectability, how do people view female athletic aggression? Most people encourage female verbal and physical aggression in the sporting context, as long as that aggression isn't aimed at male competitors. Maybe you think that statement is harsh, but can you think of any major league or collegiate sports that involve direct, physical competition between women and men? No contact sports on these levels, such as football, basketball, soccer, rugby, wrestling, or hockey, place the sexes in direct competition with each other. Neither do noncontact sports, with the exception of mixed doubles matches in tennis. Men and women don't even bowl against each other on these levels.

In most contexts, stereotypical notions about aggression, like nurturance, do seem to be changing. As stereotypical notions become outdated, people try to find new ways to communicate. For example, if you alter your expectation that "men don't cry" (if you ever held that expectation), then your communication with a man who is expressing his emotions will likely change to reflect your broader set of sex-role expectations. If your communication evolves along with your expectations, then you are becoming more personally effective.

Cycles or Mood Shifts

When we think of cycles or mood shifts, we typically associate them with women's biology. This biological attribute represents one of the more radical contrasts in social perceptions of men and women. Lately, with all of the popular (and often inaccurate) information about cycles and syndromes, we tend to assume biological causes for behavioral effects, rather than considering other possibilities. You or someone you know may have already experienced a negative consequence of the social interpretations of cycles. Since premenstrual syndrome (PMS) is what comes to most people's minds when they hear the term "cycles," let's focus on that one before tackling the possibility of a male cycle.

In Ramey's (1976) groundbreaking research on PMS, 60 percent of subjects reported experiencing menstrual discomfort. More recent sources estimate the percentage of women who suffer from PMS as ranging from 25 to 100 percent (Laws, 1983). Two decades ago, the medical profession largely chalked up women's menstrual discomfort (e.g., irritability, headaches, cramps, bloating, and mood swings) to hypochondria. When enough women reported their problems over time, the medical community researched the malady, reversed their position, and declared PMS a disease (Richmond-Abbott, 1992). Some scholars believe that labeling PMS a disease has added credibility to the condition, but it has also reinforced an old stereotype. Dramatic accounts of outlandish, overemotional, even violent behavior, as well as exaggerated images of women unable to meet their responsibilities, have been attributed to PMS. There's even a T-shirt sporting the message "I Have PMS and ESP. That Makes Me a Bitch Who Knows It All." In their book on women's psychology, Unger and Crawford (1992) state: "The view that their reproductive cycle makes women vulnerable to psychological problems helps to limit women, to define them as dangerous and deviant, and to exclude them from a role in society equal to that of men" (pp. 581–582). So, at the same time that diagnosing the condition legitimizes women's complaints and brings folklore into reality, it can give society more impetus to question women's abilities. Just how does that happen?

One example highlighted by recent events is women's ability to participate with men in life-threatening combat, a topic that we mentioned earlier with regard to the physical strength of the sexes. Some of the arguments about the effects of women's cycles on mental functioning keep women relegated to background or support positions in times of conflict (not just in military conflict). Accusations are made that because women's bodies cycle and their hormones "rage," they cannot be trusted to pilot F-16s, to withhold information if captured, or to make decisions as to when weapons should be fired. Please realize that it is not our intent here to attempt to convince you of some stance on women in combat. The point is to make you aware that social interpretations of women's cyclical biology negates or questions their ability in many contexts.

This issue is most frequently framed as a warning: "Would you want the hand of a woman with PMS on the button to detonate a nuclear bomb?" (Kleiman, 1992, p. 2E). If you accept the perspective that biology rules other functions, then the direct translation of this question is that women cannot be trusted with presidential decision making (or any other decision making, from the most extreme viewpoint). This question implies that women are such victims of their own biology that they could not possibly be relied on in critical situations. What is most interesting here is that the same argument could be made about men's levels of testosterone and resulting aggressive behavior. Do men's hormonal functioning and bent toward aggression better equip them to have "the finger on the button"? If that statement seems comical to you, it's likely because that kind of argument is hardly ever made. While society is quick to link female hormonal functioning with debilitation, the same cannot be said for men.

Like other physical aspects, there are social uses and abuses of PMS. Communication between women and men can be affected by PMS, in that some women use PMS as a justification for communicating hostility or aggression. At other times, PMS can be the excuse for a woman who doesn't want to examine her own behavior. Comedians and comic strips joke about PMS, as though it empowered women or allowed them behavior otherwise considered inappropriate. Some men use PMS as a justification for avoiding communication with women or for discounting what women say.

But what about the notion of a male cycle, which we mentioned in the opening case study? The male cycle is more than a mere notion, according to recent research. Tracking back a bit, researchers in the mid-1970s began to investigate male hormonal functioning as evidence of a male cycle responsible for mood swings in ways that reproductive cycles affect some women. Ramey (1976) found that men displayed regular variations in emotions over each 24-hour period within a 6-week time frame. Ramey also detected a 30-day cycle of men's hormonal functioning. During these cycles, men's physical strength, emotionality, and intellectual functioning were affected.

More recently, Doreen Kimura's (1987) internationally noted research determined a tentative link between seasons of the year and men's cognitive functioning. According to Kimura, when testosterone levels are lower in the spring, men's mathematical and analytic skills are enhanced. These abilities decrease in the fall when testosterone levels are higher. The popular press has picked up on this research, having fun comparing women's monthly periods to what they call men's seasonal "commas" (Kleiman, 1992, p. 1E). This research is in such a tentative stage that caution must be taken in too quickly translating the findings into fact. But let's pretend for a moment.

What if, a few years from now, evidence overwhelmingly documents the existence of a male cycle? What would be the social reaction to such news? Do you think that jobs, opportunities, responsibilities, and social roles would change to reflect this biological "instability" in men? Could this alter communication between women and men in some way? We don't know the answers to these questions, but if this scenario becomes reality, it is likely that the social interpretations of the biology will be far more interesting than the biology itself.

Brain Functioning, Cognitive Ability, and Social Interpretations

Current information regarding sex differences and brain functioning have caused more than mild controversy. Brain functions are extremely complex, tied into hormonal functioning, and related to cognitive abilities. This is not meant to be an introductory physiology lesson, so we review only the primary research findings, emphasizing their social interpretations.

Brain Functioning

We know that the brain has two hemispheres that house various human capabilities. The left hemisphere is primarily responsible for the production of language; the right hemisphere manages spatial ability. Research has attempted to find a relationship between hemisphere dominance and sex, hypothesizing that hormones cause women's and men's brains to develop differently. It has long been thought that men perform better on tests of spatial skills while women excel on tests of verbal ability, as a result of this hormonal and brain functioning (Kimura, 1987).

Some scientists report such findings as the male brain being 15 percent larger than the female brain (Halpern, 1986). But others conclude that while differences in the sexes' brain anatomy and functioning create controversy and reinforce the nature versus nurture argument, the differences are utter nonsense (Bleier, 1984; Gibbons, 1991). Since most of the social interpretations of the information on brain functioning relate to cognitive abilities, let's explore this area before considering interpretations.

Cognitive Abilities

Almost anything you read about sex differences in cognitive ability begins with a review of psychologists Benbow and Stanley's (1980) report of years of research on math abilities in gifted girls and boys. A constant pattern has emerged over two decades of conducting this research: Boys outscore girls on the math portions of the SAT. This finding led to the conclusion that male dominance in math is related to hemispheric specialization in the brain; that is, the right hemisphere is more fully developed in men than in women.

However, other information has emerged to challenge these findings. In Benbow and Stanley's research, among those students scoring in the highest percentile of math ability, boys significantly outscored girls. The differences were minimal and inconsistent in lower percentiles. Other major criticisms surround biases inherent in the SAT and Benbow and Stanley's use of gifted children as subject samples, as well as criticisms stemming from the "nurture" side of the nature-nurture argument. Social scientists insist that attitudes about sex roles affect the picture. They suggest that since boys are expected to excel in math, they are encouraged and coached by parents and teachers. Taking more advanced math courses in school and participating in athletics improves boys' math and spatial abilities as well, while mothers' attitudes and anxiety about the difficulty of math inhibit girls' achievement (Eccles, 1989; Linn & Petersen, 1986).

Concerning verbal ability, the general opinion for decades has been that females outperformed males in such capacities as language acquisition, vocabulary, spelling, writing, and verbal expressiveness (Unger & Crawford, 1992). But, again, recent research challenges this trend. Researchers now believe that if there once was a gap in verbal and math/spatial ability between the sexes due to brain differences and hormonal functioning, this gap has all but disappeared (Hall, 1987; Holden, 1991; Hyde & Linn, 1988). If the human brain hasn't changed, then what are the explanations for the sexes performing more similarly than in times past?

One explanation relates to changing times and changing parents. Perhaps more parents have backed off the old stereotypes, believing now that female and male children can do anything, given encouragement, support, and education (Shapiro, 1990). Another explanation regards teaching. If teachers demonstrate sex bias in their instruction, such as coaching boys in math while sending messages to girls that say "you probably won't be good at this," these biases have ways of becoming eventualities. Teachers who refrain from sex-biased behaviors are helping students maximize their potential, regardless of expectations for their sex (Ehrenreich, 1992). In sum, societal shifts are affecting students' visions of what they can accomplish, and the gender gap in cognitive ability is narrowing.

That's a hopeful trend in that it will affect the way we think about the sexes' abilities. Maybe the stereotype that women talk too much—a myth that most people don't connect with biologically superior verbal ability—will die a well-deserved death. Maybe the image of the strong, silent type of man will deservedly fade away, too. Maybe male-dominated fields related to math and spatial skills, such as engineering, science, and technology, will open up even further to women. Maybe men will feel more comfortable in fields traditionally filled with women, such as teaching or other helping professions that rely heavily on verbal abilities. These are a lot of maybe's, but the thought that things are changing, stereotypes are fading, and past expectations are loosening should give you a feeling of relief and a sense of freedom. Does this information make you feel that way? If it doesn't, if the changes feel threatening, what might cause your concern? Think about answers to these questions, then plunge into the last major section of this chapter—the section on internal reactions to the influences we've discussed. Remember that biology doesn't have to be the default option; as we said before, it's sometimes used as a copout. Understand that, as adults, we can be influenced by biological sex differences, but we can also make choices in how we interpret the biology and communicate as a result.

SOCIAL INFLUENCES ON PSYCHOLOGICAL GENDER

In the first major section of this chapter we talked about biological *sex* differences; note here that we have switched terms to psychological variables, or *gender*-role identity. In quick review, recall from Chapter 1 what we described as the main distinctions between sex and gender. The term *sex* is generally used to refer to maleness and femaleness based on biology, while *gender* is a much broader construct. The view we take in this text is that gender is socially constructed out of psychological characteristics related to androgyny, femininity, and masculinity. Gender also contains attitudes and beliefs, sexual orientation, and perceptions of appropriate roles for women and men in society. First, let's focus on one subject within the larger concept of gender—gender-role identity.

Gender-Role Identity

The process of developing gender-role identity involves acquiring information about social norms and roles for men and women (a social function), then adjusting one's view of self, one's role in society, and one's behavior in response to those norms (a psychological function). Some prefer to call this "socialization," defined by sociologists Davidson and Gordon (1979) as the "process by which people learn attitudes, motivations, and behaviors commonly considered appropriate to their social positions" (p. 9). However, socialization recurs throughout the life cycle and includes gender-role development as only one facet. For example, a person can experience socialization upon moving to another state or country, changing jobs, or encountering new relationships. For our purposes in this discussion, focusing on gender-role identity within the larger framework of socialization helps us understand how we come to develop our sense of self, our own vision of appropriate roles and behavior for women and men, and our patterns in gender communication.

Theories of Gender-Role Identity Development

A few theories have been generated to explain the phenomenon of gender-role identity development. We summarize some of the more prominent ones, then explore the connection between gender-role identity and gender communication.

Social Learning Theories

Social psychologists Mischel (1966) and Bandura (1971) are noted for their research on social learning theory as an explanation for human development. This theory suggests that children learn gender-related behavior from their social contacts, primarily their parents and peers. Through a process known as identification, children model the thoughts, emotions, and actions of others. This role modeling has a powerful effect on how children see themselves, how they form gender-role identities.

A related practice involves a sort of trial-and-error method in which children learn what behaviors are expected of each sex. Some behaviors in little girls and boys are rewarded by parents, teachers, peers, and other agents of socialization; the same behaviors enacted by the opposite sex are punished. As children continue to receive positive and negative responses to their behaviors, they generalize to other situations and come to develop sex identities as girls or boys.

One problem with this theory is the suggestion that children develop according to sex-role stereotypes, which is considered by some theorists to be a limited or confining view of human development. For example, what if a little girl rejects "girlish" stereotypical behavior, because she likes the status or acceptance she sees little boys receiving? When she wants to model their behavior in order to gain that status, it may not work for her the same way it does for boys. She might be labeled a tomboy, perhaps gaining her some acceptance, but also occasional ridicule. If she patterns her behavior after same-sex models, it is possible that she will not receive the respect, power, and status she wants. If a little boy is surrounded predominantly by models of the opposite sex, like his mother and most of his preschool and elementary school teachers, what happens if he closely models their behavior? He may be chastised, ostracized, and labeled effeminate or "a sissy." These examples illustrate what some consider to be a weakness in the theory—its emphasis on sex-role stereotypes as guides for behavior and identity development.

However, we know that our sense of identity is affected by how we imitated or learned from our parents. Think about who you modeled your behavior after; was it your mom or your dad, or some of both? Did you pattern more after a same-sex parent or an opposite-sex parent? Maybe an important model for you was a sibling, a grandparent, or other significant person when you were growing up. Maybe you didn't grow up with two parents. As our own culture continues to diversify, the numbers of single-parent families are growing. If you've experienced this last kind of family profile, what effect do you think the focus on one parent had on your view of sex roles?

An example illustrates this idea of modeling your behavior after that of your parents. This story has been around awhile, but it's a good one. A woman describes how she always followed in her mother's footsteps, especially in the kitchen. It seems that she recalled her mother always cutting one end off a ham before putting it in a pan to bake. That was the way her mother did it, so that was the proper way to bake a ham. She prepared hams this way in her own home and taught her daughter to do so as well. One holiday when the three women (we'll call them the grandmother, the mother, and the daughter) were gathered in the kitchen preparing the holiday meal, the grandmother saw the granddaughter religiously cut off one end of the ham before putting it in a pan to bake. The granddaughter thought nothing of it; that's just the way you cooked a ham. As the grandmother kept watching, she began to burst with laughter, finally realizing what the granddaughter was doing. The granddaughter responded to the laughter by insisting that her mother had taught her that this was how you baked a ham. Wasn't it "Grandma's way"? When the grandmother explained that the only reason she lopped off one end of the ham was because back then she didn't own a pan big enough to fit a large ham, these women laughed at themselves for years of misguided tradition.

Sometimes we don't realize that we've taken on the traits, mannerisms, or communication behaviors of a role model until someone points that out to us. Has anyone ever told you that you sound like or talk like one of your parents? This realization can be a point of pride. It can also be quite maddening—no matter how much you love your family—to discover that you mirror them in many ways. But that doesn't mean that you don't form your own sense of individuality and your own ideas about the roles of men and women, especially since social roles have changed so much over time. We aren't just mirror images of our parents; we can make choices about who we are and who we want to be.

But we are definitely affected or socialized by the gender roles that were enacted in our families. Because of the influence parents have on children's understanding of gender, many modern parents are trying a nongendered approach. They are giving children gender-neutral toys, games, and books in efforts to avoid the more traditional items that often perpetuate stereotypes (like Barbie, GI Joe, and traditional fairy tales). We address the effects of family influence, the role that friendships play in gender identity development, and teachers as role models in subsequent chapters. But for now, think about those people and experiences that had the most influence on you. Who or what is most connected to your gender-role identity today?

Cognitive Development Theory

One of the more prominent gender-role identity theories results primarily from the work of Lawrence Kohlberg. According to Kohlberg (1966), as children's minds mature, they gain an understanding of gender roles and self-identity without external reinforcement (in contrast to suggestions of social learning theory). This theory essentially suggests that children socialize themselves into feminine or masculine identities as they progress through four stages of mental ability. In stage 1, very young children are beginning to recognize sex distinctions, but they cannot attach a sex identity to a person. They are likely to say such things as "Daddy is a girl." In stage 2, children learn their own sexual identity, as well as how to correctly attach sex-identifying labels to others (Ruble, Balaban, & Cooper, 1981). They understand that their own maleness or femaleness is unchangeable. In stage 3, children learn that there are sex-role "ground rules," or guidelines for sex-typed appropriate behavior, that stem from one's culture. Children become motivated to behave in accordance with those rules, persuading others to conform, too. For example, girls want to wear ruffly, "girly" clothing, while boys are appalled at the thought of playing with dolls. At this point, children begin to value and imitate those behaviors associated with their own sex more than opposite-sex behaviors.

This progress continues into stage 4, when children separate their identities from those of their primary caregivers (typically their mothers). For boys, the importance of their fathers' identity and behavior is compounded. But because female children cannot separate themselves from the mother's female identity, they remain at stage 3, unlike their male counterparts who progress through all four stages. In essence, a girl's development is stunted because her sex identity is the same as her mother's. Can you anticipate any problems with this theory? One of the major criticisms of this theory surrounds its use of a male model of development that is then generalized to all humans. The model suggests that girls' development is somehow less complete or less advanced than boys'.

Gilligan's Approach to Gender Identity Development

Carol Gilligan (1982) challenged human development theorists in her groundbreaking book *In a Different Voice: Psychological Theory and Women's Development*. Gilligan's approach expands previous views of human development to account for both female and male paths to gender identity. In a nutshell (which does not do justice to this theory), the core of identity development rests within the mother-child relationship. The female child connects and finds gender identity with the mother, but the male child must find identity by separating himself from this female caregiver. Thus, unlike male development, which stresses separation and independence, female identity revolves around interconnectedness and relationship. As communication researchers Wood and Lenze (1991) explain, "This results in a critical distinction in the fundamental basis of identity learned by the genders. For men, the development of personal identity precedes intimacy with others, while for females, intimacy with others, especially within the formative relationship with the mother, is fused with development of personal identity: the two are interwoven processes" (p. 5). Gilligan's theory offers insight into how men and women function. But Gilligan's critics claim that the theory focuses too heavily on female development, that it implies an advantage for females who can identify with a same-sex caregiver while merely drawing occasional comparisons to how the process works for males. How, then, does one make sense of all of these theories? Does a "best" theory of gender-role identity exist?

While the theories just described significantly contribute to our understanding, they tend to dichotomize or focus heavily on maleness and femaleness. From our point of view, this focus depletes the broader concept of gender; it relegates it to an "either-or" discussion of sex. Another problem is that each theory tends to focus primarily on childhood development or how children discover gender and corresponding social expectations. What we believe to be more interesting for our discussion of gender communication is a model that begins with how we experience gender as children, then shifts to how we progress or "transcend" that experience later in life. A theory of transcendence would offer real insight into how adults negotiate and renegotiate their gender-role identities over time and given experiences and education.

The theory that we believe best serves our purpose in this text is termed "gender-role transcendence." Besides being contemporary and interesting, this theory is empowering. It gives us real hope in terms of understanding one another, improving our gender communication and our relationships with one another, and lessening the divisiveness that accompanies the female-male dichotomy.

Gender-Role Transcendence

Several researchers have developed, expanded, and refined a theory of gender-role identity development called gender-role transcendence. However, we focus our discussion around the notable contributions of sex-role psychologists Joseph Pleck and Sandra Bem. Let's explore this theory by contrasting the major elements of traditional sex-role identity development with the notion of gender-role transcendence.

In traditional views of development, the term "sex role" is defined as "the psychological traits and the social responsibilities that individuals have and feel are appropriate for them because they are male or female" (Pleck, 1977, p. 182). The emphasis here is on the two designations masculine and feminine. Masculinity involves instrumental or task-oriented competence; it includes such traits as assertiveness, self-expansion, self-protection, and a general orientation of self *against* the world. Femininity is viewed as expressive or relationship-oriented competence, with corresponding traits that include nurturance and concern for others, emphasis on relationships and the expression of feelings, and a general orientation of self *within* the world (Eccles, 1987; Parsons & Bales, 1955).

Critics of traditional views of gender-role development believe that the prevailing theories perpetuate the male-female dichotomy and limit individuals' options in terms of variations of identities. Gender-role transcendence theory responds to this criticism. Within transcendence theory, Pleck (1975) envisions a three-stage sequence of gender identity development. The first two stages resemble Kohlberg's (1966) cognitive development model. However, stage 3 represents the departure point of this theory from the more traditional ones. Stage 3 occurs when individuals experience difficulty because the rules of behavior no longer seem to make sense, or because individuals begin to suspect that they possess both expressive (feminine) and instrumental (masculine) abilities (Eccles, 1987).

At this point, individuals may "transcend" their understanding of the norms and expectations of gender to develop "psychological androgyny in accordance with their inner needs and temperaments" (Pleck, 1975, p. 172). *Androgyny* is a term made popular by gender scholar Sandra Bem (1974); the term is derived from the Greek "andros" meaning man and "gyne" meaning woman. Persons who transcend traditional role definitions no longer rely on those definitions when determining their own behavior or when assessing the behavior of others. When this occurs, the "individual heads toward a resolution . . . , which in terms of gender-role development involves the integration of one's masculine and feminine selves into self-defined gender-role identity" (Eccles, 1987, p. 232).

Like other theories of gender-role identity development, transcendence theory begins with a discussion of child development. However, it emphasizes adolescence as a period when traditional definitions of what is male and female are likely to be challenged for the first time. The theory then tracks into adulthood as changing values, social pressures, and life events (e.g., marriage, new jobs, parenting, retirement) cause adults to reevaluate their gender-role identities. Transcendence, then, may occur in adolescence and adulthood; however, it does not occur in everyone. Some people continue throughout adulthood to adhere to traditional roles and definitions of what is male and female.

Let's explore this androgyny concept within gender-role transcendence a bit further. It may make the concept more understandable if you envision a continuum with masculinity placed toward one end, femininity toward the

FIGURE 2.1. Continuum of Gender-Role Transcendence

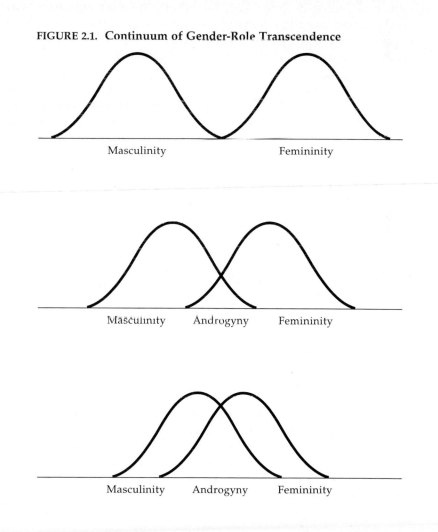

other end, and androgyny in the middle. You don't lose masculine traits or behaviors if you become androgynous, or somehow become masculine if you move away from the feminine pole. Androgyny is an intermix of the feminine and the masculine. Some androgynous individuals may have more masculine than feminine traits, and vice versa.

Perhaps a couple of diagrams will clarify further (see Figure 2.1). The first diagram depicts two bell curves, one labeled masculine and one labeled feminine. If you adopt a traditional view of sex roles, then you fit under one of the two curves in this diagram, depending on your sex. In the second diagram, you see that the bell curves have merged somewhat, with the overlap in the middle representing androgyny. As individuals continue to challenge traditional sex-typed roles and to experience gender-role transcendence, they widen their identities to include male and female traits and behaviors. Over time, the androgynous identity continues to widen, as depicted in the expanded androgynous area of the third diagram.

All this information is compelling, but what's the most important reason for a gender communication textbook to value the gender transcendence perspective over others? While the identity expands, we believe that androgynous individuals also *expand their repertoire of communication behavior.* This should sound familiar, since it is fundamental to the personal effectiveness approach to gender communication. In Chapter 1, we explained how communicatively competent individuals develop a wider range of communication behaviors from which to choose, know how to analyze a situation and select the best behaviors from their repertoire, enact those behaviors, and evaluate the results. Because the process of gender-role transcendence causes an individual to incorporate feminine and masculine traits into a unique blend, that individual chooses to behave in ways that aren't confined by traditional, stereotypical notions of how men and women are *supposed* to behave. For example, an androgynous male may be more likely than a masculine-typed male to talk about and openly express an emotion of sadness, because he does not buy into the notion that revealing one's emotions is "unmasculine." Androgynous individuals readily expand their repertoires of behavior; they are more comfortable with communicative options—options that become extremely helpful in the complicated realm of gender communication.

Another advantage of an androgynous orientation involves how you see and respond to others—an important component of the receiver orientation to communication. To be your most receiver sensitive or listener oriented, you need to be able to accept people for what makes them unique. Because androgynous individuals have expanded views of sex roles and corresponding behavior, they tend to be more generally accepting and less judgmental of those whose behavior deviates from social expectations for the sexes. We use tentative language in that last statement, because what we describe may not always be the case. For some androgynous individuals, accepting their own androgynous behavior is easier than accepting nontraditional behavior in others.

Let's expand previous examples to explain this more clearly. What would be an androgynous person's reaction to a man who is sobbing and "out of control," or to a professional woman who engages in aggressive communication with coworkers? While we can't know for sure, we can make an educated, experienced guess. We believe that the androgynous person is less likely to form rigid expectations, to be shocked at a nontraditional display, and to deem behavior inappropriate than someone who adheres more closely to traditional gender lines. Because androgyny embodies elements of both femininity and masculinity, individuals who have experienced gender transcendence are often better able to understand and accept many variations of sex roles and behavior.

What is your reaction to the theory of gender-role transcendence and the concept of androgyny? Some of you may be thinking that the theory reduces the importance of masculinity or femininity, that it waters down unique, important properties of being female or male. If you have these thoughts, you're not alone. The trick is to view androgyny as you would a glass that is half full rather than half empty. Rather than taking away from the distinctiveness of the sexes, androgyny is a way of recognizing and celebrating qualities of the masculine and the feminine—a way of making these qualities *human,* rather than options for one sex but not the other.

Wouldn't it be great, for instance, for a guy to be able to communicate in a nurturing, caring fashion to women and men alike, without risking rejection or embarrassment for being unmasculine? Wouldn't it be great if women could act assertively (even aggressively) without the risk of being perceived as a threat, without being called masculine, or worse? Wouldn't it be a relief if the only thing differentiating the sexes was biology, so that other judgments were based on *individual* qualities, not gender? Do you get the feeling that we believe this transcendence or androgynous orientation is preferable to traditional ways of developing gender-role identity? If so, you're right, and other researchers think so, too.

In their book on social influences and gender, Davidson and Gordon (1979) reviewed uses of a scale that Bem developed to measure androgyny (Bem Sex-Role Inventory [BSRI], 1974). From these findings, they deduced that "androgynous individuals exist in larger proportions than stereotypes would lead us to imagine and that they fare better than nonandrogynous individuals in the ability to behave appropriately in a wide range of sex-typed situations" (p. 16). Bem (1987), Pleck (1975), and other theorists agree that androgyny through gender role transcendence is a more psychologically mature orientation than enactment of traditional gender roles. Noted gender psychologist Jacquelynne Eccles (1987) calls it a "'higher' level of development than gender-role adherence" (p. 239). From an insightful study of androgynous individuals in interpersonal contexts, Kelly, O'Brien, and Hosford (1981) determined that because androgynous women and men were able to integrate those behaviors commonly seen as sex-specific, they proved to be highly effective in interpersonal situations.

We've made a case for gender-role transcendence and androgyny, but of course there are some cautions regarding this information. First, while we believe that androgyny and repertoire expansion fit together logically, we don't mean to suggest that the *only* way to expand the communication repertoire is to adopt an androgynous gender-role identity. A person who aligns himself or herself with a traditionally feminine or masculine gender-role identity may still expand the communication repertoire. In many situations, this individual may behave appropriately and be viewed as an effective communicator. For example, imagine a man who defines himself by traditionally masculine traits and behaviors, such as aggressive communication, competitiveness, or independence. When the man has a great idea for a project at work but a colleague strongly argues against it, perhaps he will call upon masculine traits to allow him to function successfully in this situation. Here he functions as effectively as an androgynous person who would rely on the same traits and behaviors. But what happens when a situation demands something a little different, a bit "nontraditional"? What about when a friend comes to him for comfort or to share an emotional reaction to a problem? If the man aggressively communicates by attempting to solve the friend's problem rather than by empathizing with how the friend is feeling, is this the best behavior for the situation? (We can't really know, because we aren't there—the situation is hypothetical. But we can take an educated guess.) Assuming an aggressive stance in this situation will probably not achieve the desired outcome and will likely be perceived by the other person as a sign of insensitivity. An androgynous person might choose to draw on masculine traits and behaviors for the first situation but could also draw on traditionally feminine behaviors that might be more successful for the second situation. Therefore, keep in mind that it is more likely that an androgynous person will develop a greater repertoire than a traditionally sex-typed person, but this is a trend, not a hard-and-fast rule.

The second caution is sort of a reverse of the first. We don't mean to insinuate that *all* androgynous people, just because they embody masculine and feminine traits and behaviors, are *automatically* effective communicators in *all* situations. As you are becoming aware, there are no easy answers or quick fixes in gender communication. We believe that gender-role transcendence broadens your approach and enhances your repertoire, and that it is a desirable position from which to communicate with others, but it offers no guarantees.

Here's a final caution. Assuming an androgynous gender-role identity does not erase the power differential in our society. Remember that androgyny is an internal psychological response to biological and social influences; it is not detectable on the outside. Ours is a system that still limits opportunities on the basis of such designations as sex, race, age, and sexual orientation. We have a distance to go before our society rewards both sexes equally on all fronts. But we see evidence that things are changing. We believe that gender-role transcendence can lead to greater understanding between the sexes and can put a big dent in the power differential.

CONCLUSION

Part Two of the text is about influences on your choices. Biological influences discussed in this chapter affect your view of self. Social influences, as well as your own attitudes about appropriate roles for others to assume in society, shape your view of self. Out of these biological and social influences, you form a psychological response—your gender-role identity. That gender-role identity is expressed in your communication with others. Personal effectiveness in gender communication starts with this view of self or gender-role identity. As you learn more about the effects of gender on the communication process, your identity may begin to change. Or you may become more comfortable with your current view of self, so that it solidifies. We challenge you to answer the following questions for yourself, after reading this chapter or this text, or after taking a course in gender communication: What is your current gender-role identity? What aspects of your biology most affect this identity? What social influences most shaped your identity? Are you in the process of changing your gender-role identity? How does your communication (particularly with members of the opposite sex) "clue" people about your gender-role identity? How can you become more personally effective in communicating who you are to others? One frequently overlooked way to enhance your personal effectiveness is to "watch your language." We explain just what we mean by this simple statement in the next chapter.

Key Terms

nature	physical strength	socialization
nurture	vulnerability	social learning
biological sex	hormonal functioning	modeling
stereotypes	nurturance	cognitive development
dichotomy	aggression cycles	theory
social interpretations	premenstrual syndrome	gender-role transcendence
sexual organs/genitalia	brain functioning	androgyny
reproductive functioning	hemispheres	communication repertoire
hunter-gatherer cultures	cognitive ability	
paternity	gender-role identity	

Discussion Starters

1. On a sheet of paper, list ten of the most common adjectives describing women; then list ten for men. Discuss in class whether these adjectives reflect stereotypes or "real" traits. Have people's stereotypes for the sexes changed? In what ways?
2. Think about the reproductive capabilities of women. What if someday science and technology were to progress to the point where men could carry a fetus and give birth? It sounds crazy now, but what if they could someday? Would they still be "men"? After all, what is the real definition of a man? A woman?
3. How are men currently able to show their nurturing sides? Are there some ways that are more acceptable or expected than others? What does it take to make a man feel comfortable enough to show his nurturing capabilities?
4. What's the difference between assertive and aggressive behavior? Are women suspected of acting aggressively when they think they are only acting assertively? What does "aggressive" communication sound like? "Assertive" communication? "Passive" communication?
5. What if more research continued to document the existence of a male cycle and the medical community labeled it TS for testosterone syndrome? Do you think the

existence of a male hormonal cycle is possible? Thinking specifically, how would a male cycle affect perceptions of women and men in society? How would it affect gender communication?

6. Consider the various theories of gender-role identity development that were discussed in this chapter. What are the main strengths of social learning theory, cognitive development theory, and Gilligan's theory? Their main weaknesses?

7. How does an androgynous person's communication differ from that of a traditionally masculine or feminine person? Are there any immediately detectable differences? Is androgyny reflected more in attitude or identity than in communication style?

8. How does knowledge of biological, social, and psychological influences enhance your personal effectiveness in gender communication? Take this question apart. If you understand female and male biological functioning, can that knowledge make you a more effective communicator? If you recognize how social structures are influencing your view of sex roles, as well as your view of yourself within society, can that recognition affect your communication? How is your psychological response to these influences—your gender-role identity—related to your communication with others?

References

BAILEY, C., & BISHOP, L. (1989). *The fit-or-fat woman*. Boston: Houghton Mifflin.

BANDURA, A. (1971). Social-learning theory of identificatory processes. In D. A. Goslin (Ed.), *Handbook of socialization theory and research*. Chicago: Rand McNally.

BEM, S. L. (1974). The measurement of psychological androgyny. *Journal of Consulting and Clinical Psychology, 42*, 155–162.

BEM, S. L. (1987). Masculinity and femininity exist only in the mind of the perceiver. In J. M. Reinisch, L. A. Rosenblum, & S. A. Sanders (Eds.), *Masculinity/femininity: Basic perspectives* (pp. 304–311). New York: Oxford University Press.

BENBOW, C. P., & STANLEY, J. C. (1980). Sex differences in mathematical ability: Fact or artifact? *Science, 210*, 1262–1264.

BERMANT, G., & DAVIDSON, J. M. (1974). *Biological bases of sexual behavior*. New York: Harper & Row.

BLEIER, R. (1984). *Science and gender: A critique of biology and its theories on women*. New York: Pergamon Press.

BRASH, R. (1965). *How did it begin?* New York: David McKay.

BROWN, J. K. (1980). A note on the division of labor by sex. *American Anthropologist, 72*, 1074.

COWARD, R. (1983). *Patriarchal precedents*. London: Routledge & Kegan Paul.

DAVIDSON, L., & GORDON, L. (1979). *The sociology of gender*. Chicago: Rand McNally.

DEVOR, H. (1989). *Gender blending: Confronting the limits of duality*. Bloomington: Indiana University Press.

ECCLES, J. S. (1987). Adolescence: Gateway to gender-role transcendence. In D. B. Carter (Ed.), *Current conceptions of sex roles and sex typing* (pp. 225–241). New York: Praeger.

ECCLES, J. S. (1989). Bringing young women to math and science. In M. Crawford & M. Gentry (Eds.), *Gender and thought: Psychological perspectives* (pp. 36–58). New York: Springer.

EHRENREICH, B. (1992, January 20). Making sense of la difference. *Time*, p. 51.

EHRHARDT, A. A. (1984). Gender differences: A biosocial perspective. In T. B. Sonderegger (Ed.), *Psychology and gender* (pp. 37–57). Lincoln: University of Nebraska Press.

EHRHARDT, A. A., & MEYER-BEHLBURG, H. (1980). Prenatal sex hormones and the developing brain: Effects on psycho-sexual differentiation and cognitive functions. *Annual Progress in Child Psychology and Child Development*, 177–191.

FAUSTO-STERLING, A. (1985). *Myths of gender: Biological theories about women and men*. New York: Basic Books.

GIBBONS, A. (1991). The brain as "sexual organ." *Science, 253*, 957–959.

GILLIGAN, C. (1982). *In a different voice: Psychological theory and women's development*. Cambridge, MA: Harvard University Press.

HALL, E. (1987, November). All in the family. *Psychology Today,* pp. 54–60.

HALPERN, D. (1986). *Sex differences in cognitive abilities.* Hillside, NJ: Lawrence Erlbaum Associates.

HOLDEN, C. (1991). Is the "gender gap" narrowing? *Science, 253,* 959–960.

HYDE, J. S. (1986). Gender differences in aggression. In J. S. Hyde & M. C. Linn (Eds.), *The psychology of gender: Advances through meta-analysis* (pp. 51–66). Baltimore: Johns Hopkins University Press.

HYDE, J. S., & LINN, M. C. (1988). Gender differences in verbal ability: A meta-analysis. *Psychological Bulletin, 104,* 53–69.

JACKLIN, C. N. (1989). Female and male: Issues of gender. *The American Psychologist, 44,* 127–134.

KELLY, J. A., O'BRIEN, G. G., & HOSFORD, R. (1981). Sex roles and social skills in considerations for interpersonal adjustment. *Psychology of Women Quarterly, 5,* 758–766.

KIMURA, D. (1987). Are men's and women's brains really different? *Canadian Psychology, 28,* 133–147.

KLEIMAN, C. (1992, January 23). Males and their raging hormones. *The Raleigh News and Observer,* pp. 1–2E.

KOHLBERG, L. (1966). A cognitive-developmental analysis of children's sex-role concepts and attitudes. In E. E. Maccoby (Ed.), *The development of sex differences* (pp. 82–173). Stanford, CA: Stanford University Press.

LAWS, S. (1983). The sexual politics of premenstrual tension. *Women's Studies International Forum, 6,* 19–31.

LINN, M. C., & PETERSEN, A. C. (1986). A meta-analysis of gender differences in spatial ability: Implications for mathematics and science achievement. In J. S. Hyde & M. C. Linn (Eds.), *The psychology of gender: Advances through meta-analysis* (pp. 67–101). Baltimore: Johns Hopkins University Press.

MACCOBY, E. E., & JACKLIN, C. (1974). *The psychology of sex differences.* Stanford, CA: Stanford University Press.

MACCOBY, E. E., & JACKLIN, C. (1980). Sex differences in aggression: A rejoinder and reprise. *Child Development, 5,* 964–980.

MCLOUGHLIN, M., SHRYER, T. L., GOODE, E. E., & MCAULIFFE, K. (1988, August 8). Men vs. women. *U.S. News & World Report,* pp. 50–56.

MISCHEL, W. (1966). A social learning view of sex differences in behavior. In E. E. Maccoby (Ed.), *The development of sex differences* (pp. 56–81). Stanford, CA: Stanford University Press.

PARSONS, T., & BALES, R. (1955). *Family, socialization, and interaction process.* New York: Free Press.

PLECK, J. H. (1975). Masculinity-femininity: Current and alternative paradigms. *Sex Roles, 1,* 161–178.

PLECK, J. H. (1977). The psychology of sex roles: Traditional and new views. In L. A. Cater, A. F. Scott, & W. Martyna (Eds.), *Women and men: Changing roles, relationships, and perceptions* (pp. 181–199). New York: Praeger.

RAMEY, E. (1976). Men's cycles (They have them too you know). In A. Kaplan & J. Bean (Eds.), *Beyond sex-role stereotypes.* Boston: Little, Brown.

RICHMOND-ABBOTT, M. (1992). *Masculine and feminine: Gender roles over the life cycle.* New York: McGraw-Hill.

RUBLE, D. N., BALABAN, T., & COOPER, J. (1981). Gender constancy and the effects of sex-typed televised toy commercials. *Child Development, 52,* 667–673.

SHAPIRO, L. (1990, May 28). Guns and dolls. *Newsweek,* pp. 56–65.

STOCKARD, J., & JOHNSON, M. (1980). *Sex roles.* Englewood Cliffs, NJ: Prentice-Hall.

UNGER, R., & CRAWFORD, M. (1992). *Women and gender; A feminist psychology,* New York: McGraw-Hill.

WOOD, J. T., & LENZE, L. F. (1991). Gender and the development of self: Inclusive pedagogy in interpersonal communication. *Women's Studies in Communication, 14,* 1–23.

CHAPTER 3

He/She/They Said . . . : The Language of Gender Communication

What did you think when you saw the word "language" in the title of this chapter? Did it spark your curiosity, or did it conjure up less than fond memories of early schooling? If you had negative thoughts, don't give in to them because this is not your typical chapter on language. This chapter won't warn you about dangling your participles or splitting your infinitives. You'll start to see what we mean when you read the case study.

CASE STUDY

"Probably in our lifetime we're going to see a woman elected to the presidency. So what do we call her? Lady President?" Michael, a student in one of our recent gender communication classes, raised this issue during a session on sexist language. The instructor explained that day that one of the more subtle forms of sexist language involved placing a sex-identifying adjective in front of a noun to designate the reference as somehow different or deviant from the norm. Examples of this practice include *woman doctor, male secretary, female boss, male nurse,* and *lady lawyer.* Sara, one of the students in the class, claimed that she didn't see anything sexist in this practice; to her, it was a way of being specific so that a listener would get an accurate picture of what's being talked about. The teacher asked Sara if she was as precise when talking about a male doctor or female nurse; in other words, did she "mark" the noun with a gender-related term when the sex of the person was in line with what she was accustomed to? Sara replied that she didn't, because everyone would just assume the "right" sex and there would be no misunderstanding. In essence, she believed that there was no need to be explicit unless someone of the "unexpected" sex held a certain position.

Another student in the class, Yolanda, then began to describe how this kind of practice affected her personally. She recalled how bothered she was when she overheard some students from another class refer to her as "the black girl in our class." Yolanda explained: "It's demeaning to say that kind of thing, whether it's racist or sexist. You don't hear anybody say 'that white guy in my class,' so why do you feel the need to designate me by my color? Is it because there are thirty white faces and only a couple of black faces in class, so you're the norm and I'm what's different? What comes across—intended or not—is that I'm the misfit or the exception to the rule, so you feel you have to spell that out when you talk to other people."

The class was fairly quiet by this point, because Yolanda's comments had hit home. Most of the students had never considered how condescending or isolating this kind of speech really was. Getting the class back onto the topic of sex-identifying terms, the instructor made the point that even though people may think they're merely being precise, the sexism is in the implication that certain jobs or positions belong to certain sexes, with the higher status, higher paying ones traditionally held by men. When a woman has one of these jobs, people see this as an exception; thus they feel the need to point it out with their language.

Often in classrooms someone will interject an "off-the-wall" comment to lighten things up. In this instance, it was Michael who chimed in to repeat his now famous question, "So, okay, what *will* we call the first woman elected president?" The instructor suggested *Madam President* as an alternative to *Mr. President*. The class thought that *Mrs. President* or *Ms. President* sounded weird but might not be so weird in a few years. Michael then asked, "What do we call the husband of this female president, assuming that the president is married?" Lots of laughs greeted the awkward-sounding options: *First Gentleman*, the *First Person*, and so on. Another student suggested, "Why don't we just call her *President So-and-So* or whatever her last name is, rather than *Madam President*? The word *Madam* has negative connotations for women, too. The press can address her husband as *Mr. So-and-So*. We can get rid of this *President and First Lady* stuff. Why is a president's wife the *first* lady anyway? Where did *that* come from?" You can probably tell how the rest of the class session went.

This kind of discussion is common when you talk about language and sexism—one topic or example leads to another, and to another, and so on. Sometimes people disagree, sometimes the discussion gets tense, and most of the time people realize that they just haven't thought much about their own use of language. Once you start to take a hard look at language, many practices seem archaic and the sexism becomes more obvious.

OVERVIEW

This part of the text examines influences on your choices—choices about how you develop and change your gender-role identity, how you communicate, with whom you communicate, and how you function in relationships. In Chapter 2 we explored how social and cultural influences, coupled with the biological aspects of being a woman or a man, shape your view of self and affect your gender communication. In this chapter we investigate another influence—one that has significant impact on how you are perceived by others, as well as on your communication with men and women. Understanding how language affects you is empowering; this understanding will help you become a more sensitive, personally effective communicator.

Students sometimes suggest that people should concentrate on issues that have more serious consequences on people's lives—like equal pay for equal work and reproductive and family rights—rather than wasting time talking about language. We agree that equal opportunity, wage gaps, or other political and economic issues affecting the sexes are extremely important. But politics and economics aren't the focus of this text; gender communication *is*. Think about it this way: If language is at the very base of our culture, and if that language is flawed (in this case, sexist), then that flawed language is what we use to communicate about so-called bigger issues. Why not address problems that are rampant in the very language that underlies reality? We do that in this chapter by exploring:

- How language influences and empowers us
- What actually constitutes sexist language
- The interrelationship between language and thought
- Problems with using generic pronouns, man-linked terms, and feminine suffixes
- Animal, food, and plant terms for women and men that can be demeaning
- The male-dominated imagery within religious language
- Sexual language and what it communicates about men and women
- How such practices as married names, titles, salutations, and insults can be sexist
- Reasons for using nonsexist language in your gender communication

INTRODUCTION

In Chapter 1 we explained that gender communication includes communication *about* as well as *between* women and men. We then clarified some of the more obvious terms related to gender communication before delving further into the subject. You could probably say that those terms represent the more overt forms of language that are linked to the topic of this text and your course. However, in this chapter we put language under the microscope to examine its more subtle dimensions. As you'll come to see, these subtleties have a profound, far-reaching influence on how you communicate. In a later chapter we deal with language again, but from the *between* standpoint, in terms of how gender affects the way you communicate with others. For now, we discuss language that is used to communicate *about* the sexes—language that is used by others to communicate about you, as well as language that you might be using to communicate about others. A lot of people use language by default—they use it the way they've always used it, simply *because* they've always used it. These people never think about the influence of language on their view of self, their relationships, and their gender communication. If you read this chapter, maybe you won't be one of these people.

You've probably heard before that language is powerful, but exactly how is it powerful? In this day and age, what actually constitutes sexist language?

Responses to these questions appear in the next few pages. We then provide a section detailing various forms of sexist language as well as sexist linguistic practices. Some of you on reading this section may react with: "Oh, *that* stuff again." The information may be somewhat familiar to you, particularly if you are not a sexist person and you try to avoid sexist language. If this description fits you, we applaud you. But we have a sneaking suspicion that some of this information will surprise you because the more subtle, sexist aspects of the English language have likely eluded your education up to this point. In teaching classes in gender communication, this has proven to be the case. Let's begin by investigating how language influences us.

THE INFLUENCE OF LANGUAGE

In the case study presented at the beginning of this chapter, the class discussion began with simple confusion over the label for a female president. Like many other things, we don't always think about how we use language until we become confused or confined by it or realize that there are no good words for what we want to communicate. Language is basic to our lives, but it has real power and influence. In order to understand that influence, we first address what language is in general, then what sexist language is, in specific.

What Is Language?

Because *language* is one of those terms that everyone understands, you may think there's no need for a definition. But if you try to define it, you'll find that's not a simple process. Here's our clinical definition: A language is a system of symbols (words, vocabulary) governed by rules (grammar) and patterns (syntax) common to a community of people. But, like other topics in this text, a simple definition doesn't do the term justice.

   In their book on gender and language, Graddol and Swann (1989) suggest that "language, like gravity, is one of those things with which everyone is familiar but few can adequately describe and explain. This is a surprising fact considering the intimate part that it plays in our lives" (p. 4). These researchers go on to say that language is both personal and social, that it is both a "vehicle of our internal thoughts" and a "public resource" (pp. 4–5). Our thoughts take form when they are translated into language, but sometimes language is inadequate to truly express our thoughts or, particularly, our emotions. Have you ever seen or felt something that you just could not put into words? This isn't all that frustrating when you are only struggling to find a word for an internal thought, but it is really frustrating when you can't find the words to communicate your thoughts to others. When you want to extend yourself to someone else, to communicate who you are and what you think and feel to another person, language becomes increasingly important. In sum, we use language in our private thinking, but also to establish a link with others. If language can accomplish these two things, then wouldn't you agree that language is fairly powerful?

Gender researcher Dale Spender (1985) describes language as "our means of ordering, classifying and manipulating the world. It is through language that we become members of a human community, that the world becomes comprehensible and meaningful, that we bring into existence the world in which we live" (p. 3). In this way, language has power because it allows us to make sense out of reality. But the power of language to determine reality can also be constraining. If you don't have a word for something, can you think about it? We described the situation of feeling or thinking about something but not being able to apply words to it. What do we do in these situations? We usually find some way to talk about what we feel or think, often by stringing several related words together and using qualifiers such as "it was kind of like. . . ." But did you ever consider the possibility that your thinking is limited by your language? There might be a whole host of "realities" that you have never thought of because there are no words within your language to describe them.

Well-known researchers who investigated this notion were Edward Sapir and his student Benjamin Lee Whorf. They developed what has come to be called the Whorfian Hypothesis (referred to in some treatments as the Sapir-Whorf Hypothesis), which suggests an interrelationship between language and thought. Whorf (1956) hypothesized that "the forms of a person's thoughts are controlled by inexorable laws of pattern of which he [or she] is unconscious" (p. 252). In this view, human thought is so affected by or rooted in language that language may actually control what you can think about. As language and gender scholar Julia Penelope (1990) put it, "What we say *is* who we are" (p. 202).

The Whorfian Hypothesis has an interesting connection to gender communication, but one that we will wait to explore in a later section of this chapter, "Why Use Nonsexist Language?" While the hypothesis is provocative, it has fallen into disrepute in past decades. Linguists have criticized the lack of evidence supporting the hypothesis, as well as the fact that this kind of linguistic determinism offers a limited profile of human functioning. Questions about the thinking of infants or children prior to their acquisition of language, coupled with confusion about human reactions and emotions that seem to be unaffected by language, have fostered disagreement with Sapir and Whorf's premise. Another troubling question is: If language determines thought, if we cannot think without using language, then how did a given language get developed in the first place? This discussion may frustrate you a bit, because it's kind of a "chicken or egg" argument, translated into "Which came first, language or thought?" We're not sure how someone would go about testing the Whorfian Hypothesis (which may explain why it was criticized and dismissed by some for its lack of research support). But whether one can actually resolve the argument isn't really the point. The point is that there is an interesting relationship between thought and language. In this text, we adopt the view that thought and language are interrelated, but that humans are not limited in how they think or what they feel by what a given language affords.

From these competing viewpoints, what is most important to know about language thus far? Language is a powerful tool in two ways: it affects how you think, shaping your reality; and it allows you to verbally communicate what you think and feel, to convey who you are to others. But keep an emphasis on the word *tool* when you think about language. Language may control some human beings, but it need not control you. Language is not some mystical entity that cannot be studied or changed. Humans made it, we use it, and we can change it if we so decide. That capacity to change language will become more important to you as you read further into this chapter. So think of language as something that has tremendous influence on us, but we can *choose* how to use it and how to influence *it*.

What Is Sexist Language?

To address this question, we can turn to the discussion of sexism in Chapter 1, where we defined sexism as attitudes and/or behavior that denigrated one sex to the exaltation of the other. From this description, it follows that sexist language would be verbal communication that conveys those differential attitudes or behaviors. It's fairly easy to define sexist language, but it's tougher to label something said or written as sexist. It's tougher still to rid your own language of possible hidden or subtle sexist elements. For example, sexist

"JUST DON'T **LISTEN** TO THEM, JOEY. WE'RE **NOT** PLAYING COWPERSONS AND NATIVE AMERICANS!"

DENNIS THE MENACE ® used by permission of Hank Ketcham and © by North America Syndicate.

language may involve something as subtle as referring to a person's sex when sex or gender is really irrelevant. As we describe in this chapter the various aspects of language that are sexist, we also describe the many efforts that individuals have made to reform the sexism in our language. Some of these reforms you have already learned; they may even make it seem as though there had never been another way to speak.

Before we get more specific, we need to emphasize one point about sexist language in general. One underlying assumption of the English language must be understood: English is a patriarchal language. Recall our discussion in Chapter 1 of patriarchy as a system rooted in the belief that male is the superior sex. Our language and linguistic practices reflect this belief in many ways, for example, in titles for the sexes (i.e., women's titles, like *Mrs.* and *Miss,* are designed to reveal women's relationships to men); in the designation of the masculine form of many generic nouns as the norm, while the feminine form is derived from the male term; in the legal mandate that wives take their husbands' last names and abandon their own; and so on through many other patriarchal practices that we discuss a few pages down the road. Keep in mind this critical point: You did not invent this male-dominated language, you inherited it. Referring to language as patriarchal and sexist is not blaming men, particularly any male readers of this text, for the sexism inherent in our language. It also doesn't blame women with some contrived charge that they have failed to successfully challenge the patriarchy in language. It's nobody's fault (nobody alive anyway) that we have a language that favors one sex over the other, but it's also not something that we just "have to live with."

SEXIST LANGUAGE: FORMS, PRACTICES, AND ALTERNATIVES

There are more ways to communicate a sexist attitude than you probably imagined, ranging from very overt to very subtle. As we said earlier in this chapter, you may just inherently agree with the information in this section, responding with a, "Hey; I've been doing it the right way all along and didn't even know there was a wrong way!" Or you may just downright disagree with some of this information, meaning that your response will be, "No way; that's not a form of sexist language." We anticipate the latter, but we ask that you maintain an open mind when you read, realizing that this content isn't merely the opinion of the authors of your textbook; research supports the information.

This section is divided into two main parts: forms of sexist language and sexist practices that involve language. The first designation refers to language that is sexist in and of itself; the second designation refers to linguistic practices that are sexist. In the second aspect, it's not the words themselves, but the traditions inherent in how we *use* language that are sexist. For example, it's not necessarily sexist for a man to refer to a woman as a "lamb" or his "honey," but a pattern of referring to women in animal or food terms becomes a sexist practice. In the latter half of this section, when we explain each sexist form or practice, we also offer a nonsexist alternative. So, as you work through this information, take inventory of your own communication habits, asking yourself, "Does my communication contain any of these sexist language forms or practices?" If you find that it does, then you might want to consider changing your language to include more of the nonsexist alternatives. Let's explore some forms of sexist language first, not because they are more obvious but because it's more likely that you already know or have been taught something about them.

Forms of Sexist Language

The Pronoun Problem

Think about what you were taught regarding generic pronouns. If you were taught that the generic masculine pronoun *he* (and its derivatives his, him, and himself) was perfectly acceptable as a term for all persons, both female and male, then you got an outdated lesson. Research since the 1970s has shown us convincing evidence that the generic *he* just isn't generic at all; it's masculine and conjures up masculine images (Cole, Hill, & Dayley, 1983; Hamilton, 1988; MacKay, 1980; Moulton, Robinson, & Elias, 1978; Todd-Mancillas, 1981). Let's review some evidence that pertains most specifically to college students' language, then discuss solutions to the pronoun problem.

One of the most illuminating studies on this topic was conducted by gender psychologist Wendy Martyna. Martyna (1978) investigated college students' use of pronouns by asking them to complete sentence fragments, both orally and in writing. In these fragments, pronouns were required to refer to sex-indefinite antecedents (subjects), as in the statement, "Before a judge can give a final ruling, _____." Fragments depicting typically male occupations or roles included such terms as doctor, lawyer, engineer, and judge; feminine referents included nurses, librarians, and teachers; neutral fragments used such nouns as persons, individuals, and students. Then subjects were asked to reveal what particular image or idea came to mind as they chose a certain pronoun to complete a sentence.

In a nutshell, college students in Martyna's research continually read sex into the subjects of sentence fragments and responded with sex-specific pronouns. The nurses, librarians, teachers, and babysitters were predominantly *she*'s, while the doctors, lawyers, engineers, and judges were *he*'s. The neutral subjects most often received the pronoun *they*, which is a common choice, even if it is nongrammatical (i.e., single subject, plural pronoun). If the pronoun *he* had truly been a term indicating all persons, then *he* would have been the pronoun of choice no matter what role the sentence depicted. When Martyna questioned her students as to what images came to mind when reading certain sentence fragments, their answers supported their pronoun choices.

Martyna's results underscore something we said before: People can hardly function without knowing the sex of a person. If they aren't told the sex, they generally assign one based on stereotypes and, granted, based on the numbers of persons in our society who hold the majority of certain positions and roles. So if you argue that when you say *he* you are including everyone and that neither sex is insinuated, your listeners might tell you otherwise. They may tell you that you are referring to men only and excluding women completely. Further, your language implies that male is the standard; if this were not the case, then why didn't you use *she?* From a receiver orientation to communication, your listeners have a point.

If you think that Martyna's study is so dated that the results couldn't apply to today's college students, think again. At an east coast and a west coast university, we recently conducted a replication and extension of Martyna's study into sex-related pronouns (Ivy, Bullis-Moore, Norvell, Backlund, & Javidi, 1993). In the first part of the study, we repeated Martyna's sentence-fragment procedures, hoping to find that college students in the 1990s were attuned to the problem of sexist pronouns. On the contrary, the results were virtually the same—almost 15 years later. For terms like lawyer, judge, and engineer, students responded predominantly with masculine pronouns. Students did not connect librarians, teachers, and babysitters with feminine pronouns as often as they connected "masculine" roles with male pronouns. Most of the students' imagery was sex-typed, too, meaning that many of them reported thinking of women when they saw or heard the term librarian and men when they saw the term lawyer.

In the second part of our study, we extended Martyna's research by taking a measure of psychological attitudes toward appropriate sex roles and by asking subjects about their exposure to sexist language instruction in both high school and college. Neither attitudes nor education had any bearing on students' use of language. We did discover, however, that students had received mixed messages regarding pronoun usage in both their high school and college education. For every lesson that taught them to use inclusive, nonsexist pronouns, students recalled a counterlesson telling them that the pronoun *he* was perfectly acceptable as a substitute for all persons. Here's what we concluded from the results of our study: People aren't getting a clear message about nonsexist language. If you are among the few who have been taught something about this topic, what you have been taught is probably contradictory and confusing. That contradiction may lead people to rely on stereotypes in their language, especially when selecting a term to stand for everyone.

Besides the fact that generic masculine pronouns aren't really generic, other negative consequences of using exclusive language have emerged from research. These have to do with the perceptions or attitudes that are reinforced by such language. Research shows that exclusive pronoun usage does the following (Briere & Lanktree, 1983; Brooks, 1983; Ivy, 1986; Stericker, 1981):

1. It maintains sex-biased perceptions.
2. It shapes people's attitudes about careers that are "appropriate" for one sex but not the other.
3. It causes some women to believe that certain jobs and roles aren't attainable.
4. It contributes to the belief that men deserve higher status in society than women do.

The Pronoun Solution

Is there a pronoun that can stand for everyone? No, not unless you are speaking about more than one person, when the pronoun *they* may be appropriate. Some scholars have attempted to introduce new words, or *neologisms* into the language primarily for the purpose of inclusivity. Such neologisms as *gen, tey, co, herm,* and *heris* are interesting, but they haven't met with much success in being adopted into common usage.

If you want to refer to one person—*any* person of either sex—the grammatical, nonsexist way to do that is to use *she or he*. Sometimes *he/she* or *s/he* may be acceptable. We know what you're thinking: It gets tiresome to say all of those words, so why can't you just use *he* and let people assume that you're including everyone and being nonsexist? We've heard this argument before and our response is, it just doesn't work that way. Most people simply do not hear the term *he* and think of everyone; they think masculine. Many women in particular do not envision themselves being included or represented by the term. Using *she or he* makes it clear that you are referring to persons of both sexes (Kennedy, 1992).

Other ways to avoid excluding any portion of the population in your communication are to omit a pronoun altogether, either rewording a message or substituting an article *(a, an, or the)* for the pronoun; to use *you;* or to use variations of the indefinite pronoun *one* (Maggio, 1988). But it's wise to avoid overusing these terms because they can become a hindrance, as in, "If one wants

---

What If?

What if the term that stood for all persons was *womankind? Could* you relate to that term, or does it seem too ludicrous to even consider? Does the very thought make you laugh? *What if* one of your teachers said in class, "We're all in this life together; we're all a part of womankind"? How would you react? You'd probably look at your teacher like she or he was out of control or had consumed a few beers before class. But think about it for a minute. If you are a female reader of this text, how does the term *womankind* sound to you? Does it represent kind of a fun thought, to think that all humans might be subsumed in a term that was traditionally connected only to femininity? Does it elevate womanhood in some way? If you are a male reader of this text, how does the term *womankind* instead of *mankind* strike you? Can you imagine yourself being a part of or included in that term? Most men react negatively; they make a face, shrug, and say that the term doesn't relate to their experience, thus it doesn't fit them. When women explain that they get the same feelings from the assumption that they are included in *mankind,* then we have some breakthroughs of understanding. Consider other terms like this—terms that you may have accepted because they are traditionally used, although they really don't speak to your experience or apply to you. *What if* you started ridding your own communication of these forms of language? *What if* you had an effect on others' language? *What* would happen *if,* the next time you heard a person use the term *mankind,* you (gently) explained the problem with that term?

to better oneself, then one must learn all one can and seek one's own path." One form that readily emerges in conversation is use of the pronoun *they* in reference to a singular subject, such as in the statement, "If a person wants to better themselves [or themself], then they must learn all they can and seek their own path." According to most grammarians and style manuals, a singular subject of a sentence followed by a plural pronoun is a nongrammatical construction. Pluralizing statements is often the simplest option, as in "If persons want to better themselves, then they must learn all they can and seek their own path."

We encourage you to work more of the options we've described into your communication. Remember in Chapter 1 when we described the "conscious competent" communicator? For a while, omitting *he* and using inclusive pronouns will take a conscious attempt at competent communication. But in time anyone can become "unconsciously competent" at using inclusive, nonsexist language.

Man-Linked Terminology

Man-linked terminology is the use of the words or phrases that include *man* in them, as though these terms should operate as generics. One form is the use of the term *man* or its derivative *mankind* to mean all persons, similar to the problematic usage of *he.* (Even more confusing is the term *he-man!*) Ambiguity and confusion arise when one doesn't know whether the term refers to a set of male persons or to all persons in general (Graddol & Swann, 1989). This confusion led the National Council of Teachers of English to conclude, "Although 'man' in its original sense carried the dual meaning of adult human and adult male, its meaning has come to be so closely identified with adult male that the generic use of 'man' and other words with masculine markers should be avoided whenever possible" (NCTE, 1975, p. 2).

Originally, *man* was derived from a truly generic form, similar to the term *human.* The terms for female-men *(wifmann)* and male-men *(wermann)* developed when the culture decided that it needed differentiating terms for the sexes (McConnell-Ginet, 1980). Linguist Rosalie Maggio (1988) published *The Nonsexist Word Finder,* an illuminating book of information that includes a dictionary of gender-free terminology. Included in this dictionary are the Greek, Latin, and Old English terms for human, woman, and man. In Greek, the terms are *anthropos, gyne,* and *aner,* the Latin terms are *homo, femina,* and *vir,* while Old English terms are *man, female,* and *wer* (pp. 176–177). The problem is that *man* has developed into a designation for *male* persons, not *all* persons. As Maggio insists, "The distinctions have become blurred, and we expect one word ('man') to do double duty" (p. 177). As it did for masculine pronouns, research shows that masculine mental images arise when the term *man* is used. Again, not only does this term exclude women and make them invisible, but it reinforces the male-as-standard problem (Cameron, 1985). As Spender (1985) suggests, "By promoting the use of the symbol *man* at the expense of *woman* it is clear that the visibility and primacy of males is supported. We learn to see the male as the worthier, more comprehensive and superior sex, and we divide and organize the world along these lines" (p. 153).

FIGURE 3.1. Man-linked Terms and Alternatives

Term	Alternatives
adman	advertising executive; ad executive
airman	aviator; pilot
anchorman	anchor; newscaster
bail/bondsman	bail or bond agent
bogeyman	bogey; bogey monster
base man	base player
bellman/bellboy	attendant; luggage handler; bellperson
businessman	businessperson; business executive or leader
cameraman	camera operator
cattleman	rancher; cattle owner
caveman	prehistoric person; neanderthal
chairman	chair; chairperson
churchman	churchgoer
committeeman	committee member
congressman	senator; representative; legislator; member of Congress
con man	con artist
councilman	council member
doorman	doorkeeper; porter
everyman	common person; typical or ordinary person
fisherman	fisher
foreman	supervisor
Frenchman (other nations)	French (or other nations') native
freshman	first-year student
frontiersman	pioneer; settler
garbageman/trashman	garbage or trash collector; sanitation worker
G-man	government or federal agent
groomsman	wedding or groom's attendant
gunman	killer; assassin; sniper
handyman	maintenance worker; repairer
hit man	hired killer; hired gun
layman	layperson; laity; nonspecialist
mailman/postman	mail carrier; postal worker
man	human; humans; persons; people
man about town	worldly person; socialite; jet-setter
man a post	fill a post
maneating	flesh eating; carnivorous
man for all seasons	all-around expert; Renaissance person
manhandle	mistreat; rough up
manhole	sewer; utility hole
manhood	pride; strength
man-hours	staff-hours
manhunt	chase; fugitive search
man in the moon	face in the moon
mankind	humankind; humanity
man-made	artificial; handmade; synthetic
manned space flight	space flight
man of few words	silent type
man of the house	homeowner
man of the world	sophisticate
man-of-war	warship
man on the street	average person; common person
man overboard	overboard; person overboard
manpower	staff power; work force
manservant	servant; butler; valet; maid
man the phones	answer the phones
man-to-man	one-to-one; person-to-person
man your battle stations/positions	assume your battle stations; go to your positions
marksman/rifleman	sharpshooter
may the best man win	may the best person win
men working	workers
modern man	modern people; modern civilization
no-man's-land	limbo; dead zone; void
one-upmanship	going one better; one-up tendency; dominance
patrolman	patroller; patrol officer; trooper
penmanship	handwriting
policeman	police officer
Renaissance man	Renaissance person; all-around expert
repairman	repairer; servicer; technician
salesman	salesclerk; clerk; salesperson
self-made man	independent person; self-made person; entrepreneur
serviceman (military)	soldier; member of the armed forces
snowman	snow figure/person
spaceman	astronaut
spokesman	spokesperson; speaker; representative
sportsman	sports enthusiast; athlete; good sport
statesman	politician; citizen; patriot
stunt man	stunt person; stunt performer; daredevil
under/upperclassman	undergraduate; first-year student; sophomore, etc.
unman	unnerve; frighten; disarm
unmanned	unstaffed; uninhabited
unsportsmanlike	unsporting; unfair
watchman	guard; security guard; sentry
workman	worker
workmanship	work; handiwork; artisanry

There are several alternatives to man, the simplest being *humans* (and derivatives human beings, humanity, and humankind). Even though the word human contains *man* in it, it is derived from the Latin *homo* meaning all persons. The term *human* does not connote masculine-only imagery like the term *man* does (Graddol & Swann, 1989; Maggio, 1988). Other substitutes include people, persons, and individuals.

Man-linked terms include expressions like *man the phones* or *manned space flight.* They also include numerous words that have *man* attached to or embedded within them, thus converting the term into a role, position, or action that an individual can assume or make. One example is the term *repairman,* which takes either the verb *to repair* or the noun, as in *a repair,* and makes it into a description of a person who repairs. Unfortunately, people see the masculine part of the term and form perceptions that the word describes something masculine only. If you are thinking, "People make too big a deal of this 'mailman, fireman, policeman' thing," then check out our list in Figure 3.1 just to see how many man-linked terms there are. The abundance of terms that exclude women is unsettling. And this list is incomplete, because we included only terms that we considered to be mainstream usage. Maggio (1988) cautions, however, that not all words containing man or men are sexist. Some of the examples that she provides include *amen, emancipate, manager, maneuver, manipulate, ottoman,* and *menstruation* (p. 183). In these words, *men* or *man* is not modified to create a job, position, or role from another term.

Our language is filled with many other expressions that are masculine in derivation; thus it's wise to avoid using them as generics. One such term is *master.* The female equivalent term for master is *mistress,* but how often do you use or hear mistress in everyday language, especially with its negative connotation of adulterer? You may hear, "He's a master at the game!" but do you hear, "She's a mistress at the game!"? Again, master is a masculine term that people use as a generic, when actually it evokes masculine imagery and applies more to men than women. Think about the frequency of expressions like master a skill, master bedroom (where's the mistress bedroom?), master switch, master plan, mastermind, a painting is a masterpiece, a problem is handled masterfully (Maggio, 1988).

The alternatives to masculine terms are also listed in Figure 3.1. Notice in this list that only a few of the alternatives call for the addition of "person" to the front part of the term. This change unfortunately has come to stand for a feminine form of a word rather than a generic term (Aldrich, 1985). We wish that were not the case, but some people hear a term like *chairperson,* for example, and think that the –person term signifies a woman. Figure 3.1 lists the many alternatives to the masculine form or the –person form. Some of the alternatives may seem awkward to you and even ridiculous, but over time you will probably come to wonder how anyone could argue with such simple changes. We realize that it takes time and effort to incorporate these terms into your language. It's harder to use them when talking than when writing, because writing is generally a more purposeful task than talking. But, again, an attitude that says "this is important," accompanied by a willingness to apply new forms, is the key to ridding one's language of exclusive, sexist terminology.

Feminine Suffixes

Adding a suffix like -ette, -ess, -enne, or -trix to form a feminine version of a supposed male term is another form of sexist language, whether or not these terms are intended to be demeaning (Blaubergs, 1978). Like other forms, the suffix "perpetuates the notion that the male is the norm and the female is a subset, a deviation, a secondary classification. In other words, men are 'the real thing' and women are sort of like them" (Maggio, 1988, p. 178). Does it really matter if the person waiting tables at a restaurant is female or male? Does someone who is admired need to be called a *hero* or a *heroine?* Again, the point here is that designation of sex when it is irrelevant indicates that one is making a person's sex too important, revealing that one needs to know the sex to determine how to behave or what to expect. That kind of thinking perpetuates sexual stereotypes and heightens misunderstanding between men and women.

How can sexist suffixes be avoided? Figure 3.2 lists words with feminine endings and their appropriate alternatives. One can simply use the original term and omit the suffix. If there is a legitimate reason for sex to be specified, a pronoun can be used for this purpose. An example is, "The actor was performing her monologue beautifully, when someone's watch alarm sounded off in the theater." Again, this may sound like a lot of work, but we encourage you to try it. See how it sounds to other people: Do they react when you omit this language

FIGURE 3.2.   Feminine Terms and Alternatives

actress	actor
adulteress	adulterer
ambassadress	ambassador
authoress	author
aviatrix; aviatress	aviator; pilot
bachelorette	bachelor; single person
comedienne	comedian
equestrienne	equestrian
goddess	god
governess	governor
heiress	heir
heroine	hero
hostess	host
justess	justice
majorette	major
murderess	murderer
poetess	poet
sculptress	sculptor
songstress	singer
starlet	star
stewardess	flight attendant; steward
suffragette	suffragist
usherette	usher
waitress	waiter

from your communication? See if it changes your own attitudes about sex roles and language, as well.

Animal, Food, and Plant Terms for Persons

We all know that there are many derogatory terms for human beings, unfortunately. But did you know that using animal, food, and plant terms as labels for men and women can be interpreted as demeaning and sexist? Figure 3.3 lists such terms. There are more terms for women than for men, because these kinds of references are used more often to demean and make objects out of women than men (Lakoff & Johnson, 1981). Research has also shown that terms like these for women are perceived as significantly more negative than the terms for men (Kleinke, 1974; Nilsen, 1972). One important point: This is one of those categories of language usage that is especially connected to the context of the communication as well as to the relationship between the person doing the naming and person being named. To clarify what we mean, here's an

FIGURE 3.3. Animal, Food, and Plant Terms for Persons

ANIMAL TERMS		FOOD TERMS		PLANT TERMS	
Women	**Men**	**Women**	**Men**	**Women**	**Men**
fox or vixen	fox	honey	honey	rose/rosebud	pansy
pig	pig	sugar	sugar	clinging vine	
lamb	lamb	cookie	cookie	buttercup	
dog	dog	pumpkin	pumpkin	sweet pea	
tiger	tiger	honey bun	honey bun	petunia	
chicken	chicken	cutey pie	cutey pie	honeysuckle	
pussy	pussy	cupcake	cupcake	daisy	
dumb ox	big ox	muffin	stud muffin	violet	
silly goose	gorilla	pudding	candy ass		
old mare	cat or tomcat	tart	beefcake		
cow	ass or jackass	sugar lips	top banana		
bird	buck	tomato	hot dog		
heifer	snake in the	jelly roll	meathead		
kitty	grass	brown sugar	big cheese		
chick	rat	candy			
beaver	stud	baby cakes			
filly	weasel	cheesecake			
bitch	cock	love/lamb chop			
black widow	turkey	peach			
mouse	teddy bear	dish			
hog	worm	marshmallow			
bunny	old goat	cherry			
sow	bull				
broad (pregnant	wolf				
cow)	bear				
chickadee	stag (party)				
sex kitten					
cat ("cat					
fight")					
hen (as in "he's					
henpecked")					
shrew (mouse-					
like mammal)					

example that occurred at the university where one of your textbook authors teaches.

On a day when a couple of groups were to give their final presentations for a class, students were nervously congregating in the hallway outside the classroom. They were nicely dressed (wanting to create that ever-important favorable impression on the teacher) and were going over their notes together one last time before the presentation. When a male classmate came down the hall, he saw one of the female presenters and said, "Wow, you look like a delicious piece of cheesecake today." Needless to say, that comment did not feel like a compliment to the woman who received it; it made her flustered, embarrassed, even more nervous before her presentation, and, later, quite angry. When she finally confronted the male student with her feelings about his comment, he explained that he had no intention of offending her—just the opposite. He meant to compliment her and had no idea that his words would make her feel bad. How does this example strike you? Was the guy a victim of circumstance, a complete jerk, or just an ignorant boob? Was he at fault with his timing, but not his words, because he meant to be nice? Maybe she was just nervous and didn't take him the "right" way?

From a receiver orientation to communication, her interpretation carried more weight than his intentions. The reason the male student was at fault was not because he was complimenting a woman, but because his language objec-tified her and communicated inappropriate sexual overtones—comparing a woman to something soft, sweet, and edible. His "cheesecake" comparison reduced a person who was intelligent, competent, worthy of respect, and concerned about her class assignment, to something trivial. Not only did these two people not have a sexual or romantic relationship, but the educational context and the woman's already nervous state made the comment extremely insensitive and inappropriate. If you deem this example exaggerated, look again at the terms listed in Figure 3.3 and imagine that these terms were being used in comments directed at someone you love, either a woman or a man. Is it easier now to envision how these terms could be demeaning?

As Maggio (1988) points out, "Using animal names to refer to people is neither sensitive nor very socially attractive. Names of foods are also used for people, and while many of them purport to be positive, ultimately they are belittling, trivializing, and make objects of people" (pp. 182–183). Feminist scholars Thorne, Kramarae, and Henley (1983) state their opposition more strongly: "Men's extensive labeling of women as parts of body, fruit, or animals and as mindless, or like children—labels with no real parallel for men—reflects men's derision of women and helps maintain gender hierarchy and con-trol" (p. 9). Only in certain contexts and within certain relationships—those in which two people's feelings and regard for each other are mutually understood—might animal, food, and plant terms for persons be construed as endearments.

Religious Language

The understatement of the year would be to say that the topic of sexism in religious language is sticky. It is not our intent here to uproot your religious beliefs or to assume that you have religious beliefs that need uprooting. Our intent is merely to make readers aware of the perpetuation of patriarchy through religious language. Miller and Swift (1976), in their book about language and women, include a chapter on the language of religion. They state: "Since the major Western religions all originated in patriarchal societies and continue to defend a patriarchal world view, the metaphors used to express their insights are by tradition and habit overwhelmingly male-oriented" (p. 64). These authors explain that within the Christian tradition, religious scholars for centuries have insisted that the translation of such an abstract concept as a deity into a symbol or into language need not involve a designation of sex. According to Miller and Swift, "The symbolization of a male God must not be taken to mean that God really is 'male'. In fact, it must be understood that God has no sex at all" (p. 64). Quoting a dean of the Harvard Divinity School, masculine language about God is "a cultural and linguistic accident" (Stendahl, as quoted in Miller & Swift, 1976, p. 67).

The problem, at least for religions relying on biblical teachings, is that translations of scriptures from the ancient Hebrew language into Old English rendered masculine images of deity (Kramarae, 1981). Thus the literature is dominated by the pronoun "he" and by such terms as father, son, and kingdom. Linguistic scholars contend that much of the original female imagery was lost in modern translation or was omitted from consideration by the canonizers of the Bible (Miller & Swift, 1976; Spender, 1985). After reviewing Old Testament lists of sons who were begat by their fathers, feminist scholar Julia Penelope (1990) suggests, "The women and daughters who must have participated remain nameless and invisible" (p. 191). The Old Testament says that humans were created in God's image—both male and female. Does it make sense that we have come to connect only masculinity with religious images and terms?

Are you uncomfortable enough at this point in your reading to say to yourself, "Come on now; you're messing with religion. Enough is enough"? We understand your discomfort, if indeed that is what you're feeling, because religion is a deeply personal thing. It's something that a lot of us grew up with; thus its images and teachings are so ingrained that we don't often question them or stop to consider where some of the traditions originated. However, questioning the language of religion doesn't mean that one is questioning his or her faith. Again, it's an issue of inclusion, a matter of allowing everyone to "image" themselves in what is being talked about, heard, or read.

Several sects within the Christian religion have begun to lessen male dominance in their forms of communication. The masculinity and femininity of God are beginning to receive equal emphasis, as in one version of the Apostles' Creed which begins with, "I believe in God the Father and Mother almighty, maker of heaven and earth." These kinds of attempts are interesting and increasing in number, but they unnerve many people. Probably nowhere are people more resistant to change than in the area of religious imagery and language. The root of the problem that once again surfaces is humans' need for dichotomizing, for designating everything—even God—as masculine or feminine. Even if you envision some form of deity as a spiritual entity without femininity or masculinity, it is likely very difficult to talk about that spiritual entity, given the sex-typed language that confines you.

We understand that this may represent radically new information for you that possibly you'd rather not deal with at present. While we want you to know current information about language, we also value your right to choose. We encourage you to keep an open mind while you think about *all* of your language and how it may affect others with whom you communicate.

Sexual Language

This section deals with language that is used in a sexist manner to identify persons as sexual partners and to describe sexual acts between women and men. (We purposefully put this section *after* the one on religious language, in case any of our readers need resuscitation.) By exploring the language used to describe sexual partners and acts between women and men, we do not mean to insinuate that heterosexual relations are the only form or are the preferred form of relations. We have simply chosen here to talk about this topic via depictions of heterosexual activity. However, a good portion of the information—particularly the first section on sexual language that is used to identify partners—applies to persons of any sexual orientation.

Sexual language profoundly affects how women and men perceive the sexes, as well as how they communicate with one another. The fact is that this language exists because some people use it. We know that many of you do not use this kind of language, so don't think that we're assuming all college students use this kind of language every day. If something in this section strikes you as crude or insensitive, we apologize for that up front. But if you approach this content with an open mind, more clinically than personally, we suspect you'll learn something.

It will probably come as no surprise to you at this point to learn that sexual language is also sexist, for the most part. We defer a good deal here to the work of linguist Robert Baker (1981), who contends that the following categories of terms are recognized as "more or less interchangeable with 'woman'" (p. 167):

1. Neutral terms, such as *lady, gal,* and *girl*
2. Animal terms
3. Words that describe playthings or toys, such as *babe, baby, doll,* and *cuddly*
4. Clothing terms, such as *skirt* or *hem*
5. A wide range of sexual terms

Baker's college students suggest that the most frequently used female terms fall into the neutral and animal categories; terms used least often are sexual. But frequency of usage is only one aspect. We contend that sexual terms, whenever they are used, are more personally devastating than terms in other categories.

Baker does not offer categories for men, primarily because he is most interested in "how women are conceived of in our culture" (p. 166). We suggest that male categories are less necessary because significantly fewer terms—particularly sexual terms—are used to identify men than women. Evidence for this stems from Julia Penelope Stanley's (1977) research, which uncovered 220 terms for sexually promiscuous women and only 22 terms for sexually promiscuous men.

Most of us know that reducing a human being down to her or his sexual organs is a loathsome, disrespectful practice. While most of us refrain from this practice altogether, particularly to a person's face, think about how many times a group of people will see someone walk by and the comments that follow turn the person into an object by reducing him or her to mere sexuality. One attempt to justify this behavior is the claim, "We were just admiring her [or him]." Most of us would rather be deprived of this kind of admiration. Language that reduces people to sexual functioning objectifies, stereotypes, and degrades.

Granted, in certain circumstances where the relationship between two people is intact and mutually understood, using sexual terms as descriptors may be interpreted as harmless kidding. But those instances are the exceptions. Think of how many terms in our language are based on women's and men's anatomy but may actually be used to describe the whole person. Some of the less graphic terms that describe women's anatomy or sexual behavior, or are interchangeable with the word *woman,* include snatch, twat, pussy, beaver, cherry, a piece, box, easy, some (as in "getting some"), slut, whore, and a screw or lay. Now consider some male sexual lingo: prick, cock, male member, dick, tool, and a screw or lay. There are more terms than these, but we leave those to your imagination rather than putting them in print.

Baker (1981) contends that only men use what he calls nonneutral terms or terms falling into his categories 2 through 5 mentioned previously. His answer to the question of how men conceive of or think about women is as follows: "Clearly they [men] think that women share certain properties with certain types of animals, toys, and playthings; . . . they conceive of women in terms of those parts of their anatomy associated with sexual intercourse" (p. 168). We disagree that only men use sexually demeaning terminology in reference to women. We've heard women call or refer to other women by a few of the terms listed previously, but typically just the ones that imply sexual promiscuity (slut, easy, etc.). But do you agree that thinking about or conceiving of people in terms related to their sexuality is demeaning? And since evidence and experience indicate that women more often than men are thought of, talked about, and communicated to in this way, do you see how this form of language is sexist?

Another form of sexual language is that which describes sexual activity between men and women. The main emphasis is on verbs and their effect on the roles that women and men assume during sexual activity. Here are some of the terms that Baker (1981) provides as synonyms for having had sexual intercourse: screwed, laid, had, did it, banged, slept with, humped, and made love to. Feminist theorist Deborah Cameron's (1985) discussion of sexual language adds the verb *poked* to the list. Students offer such contemporary references as "hooked up with," "got some from," "made [someone]," "took," and even "mated."

The sexism arises when you note the placement of subjects that precede some of the verbs and the objects that follow them. According to Baker (1981), sentences like "Dick screwed Jane" and "Dick banged Jane" describe men as the doers of sexual activity, while women are almost always the recipients. When a female subject of a sentence appears, the verb form changes into a passive rather than an active construction, as in "Jane was screwed by Dick" and "Jane was banged by Dick"—making the woman still the recipient (pp. 175–176). If you question this, then reverse the names in the four statements and note the unreality. Baker calls the argument that the male/active, female/passive linguistic trend is a consequence of the outward nature of men's genitalia and the inward nature of women's "inadequate" (p. 177). If our culture expected active sexual roles from women, Baker contends that the verb "to engulf" would be in common usage. Cameron (1985) proposes that the term *penetration* as a synonym for the sexual act suggests male origins; if a woman had set the term, it might have been *enclosure* (p. 81).

Students report that they believe that the dichotomy of male/active–female/passive sexuality is rapidly changing, as is the language. They offer a few relatively new, active constructions for women's sexual behavior. However, they admit that there are more negative judgments communicated about women who behave actively or dominantly in intercourse than there are about men who behave submissively. We agree that changes are taking place in the sexual arena, but language just hasn't kept pace. If the very language that describes sexual intercourse still predominantly portrays men in dominant, active roles and women in submissive, passive roles, then that parallels the sexism in society. The current language still reinforces stereotypes for the most part, so ignoring the power of language to communicate to us how we are supposed to act is a "head in the sand" reaction.

The bottom line here is awareness of the terms that identify persons according to sexuality and describe sexual acts. Moreover, awareness includes how this terminology perpetuates inappropriate, outdated sex-role stereotypes and promotes disparity between the sexes. We encourage you to take stock of your own communicative behavior. Do you use any of the sexual language that we have exposed here as being sexist, exclusive, and insensitive? If you used it unknowingly, have you started to think about changing this usage?

Sexist Linguistic Practices

Now that you've become aware of forms of sexist language, we move on to consider some linguistic practices that are sexist. By practices, we're referring not to the words themselves but to how language is used in a sexist manner.

The Order of Terms

Upon reading this subheading, did you think of the traditional saying "ladies first"? Many people still operate by this standard, in things like opening doors or letting a woman pass in front of a man. What's interesting is that the ladies-first pattern isn't predominant in the language, nor should it be. Our point, again, is that treatment and references to the sexes should be equal. When you put language under the microscope, you find that male terms are almost always first, female terms second. Three exceptions include the traditional greeting, Ladies and gentlemen; reference to the bride and groom; and one that has a less established pattern, reference to someone's mother and father, as in, "How are your mom and dad doing?" Think about how many times the male-female order occurs, as in the following examples: he or she; his and hers; boys and girls; boyfriend/girlfriend (as in "they are boyfriend/girlfriend"); guys and gals (or dolls); men and women; men, women, and children; male and female; husband and wife (or the more sexist version, man and wife); Mr. and Mrs. Smith; the Duke and Duchess of Windsor; king and queen; prince and princess; lord and lady; president and first lady; brothers and sisters; and host and hostess.

Granted, an isolated instance isn't a big problem, but when you realize how many times this pattern occurs in our language, and especially when you see a parallel in society, then it's easy to see that the ordering of terms contributes to the greater problem. Always putting the masculine term first is a subtle indication of precedence given to men (Frank & Treichler, 1989; Miller & Swift, 1988). So it's advisable to try to alternate the order in which you say or write such terms when you have one of these constructions in your communication. If you're sharp, you'll have noticed that we've been doing this very thing in this text. For every "women and men" and "he or she," a "men and women" and "she or he" appears. It's a simple process which may escape notice at first. But we contend that it will make your communication more gender-sensitive and that it will affect your attitudes as well as the attitudes of persons who *do* notice.

Parallel Construction

This involves the use of symmetry in language; more specifically, it refers to the use of gender-fair, parallel terms when referring to the sexes. Maggio (1988) cites three ways in which terms are asymmetrical and sexist. The first involves instances in which words may appear parallel, although in actuality they are not parallel or equal. An example that seems to be on its rightful way out is this dreaded statement: "I now pronounce you man and wife." If you don't see anything wrong with that statement, look closer. The man is still a man, but the woman is now a wife, the connotation being that she is relegated to that one role while he maintains a complete identity.

A second violation of parallel usage applies to terms that may have originally been constructed as parallel but that have undergone changes in meaning through common usage and time. Unfortunately, the change usually involves the feminine form taking a less positive connotation. Examples include governor/governess, master/mistress, sir/madam, and bachelor/spinster or old maid. In the first example, a man who governs is a governor, but a governess has come to mean a woman who takes care of someone else's children. You can certainly see the gap between meanings in the second and third examples, with *mistress* and *madam* taking on negative connotations, while the masculine forms still imply power and authority. The last example is dramatic, in that as people grow older and stay single, men remain *bachelors* while women degenerate into *spinsters* and *old maids* (Lakoff, 1975). This trend is changing, yet the tendency in our culture to compliment a man for his ability to stay single, while ridiculing a woman for being an old maid, is still quite real.

A final category of parallel construction involves acceptable words used in a way that alters the equality (Blaubergs, 1978; Lakoff, 1975; Maggio, 1988). A prime example comes from how journalists referred to American soldiers taken hostage in the Persian Gulf War. The first news reports explained that "a small number of American soldiers were taken captive by the enemy; one of the prisoners is believed to be a woman." Granted, this may have been the first time in America's military history that a female soldier was a POW—the first time on record, anyway. But do you see how that news report depicted the female prisoner as though men were the norm and she was the aberration? While the origin of this statement may be understandable, the practice is a sexist one nonetheless. Maggio (1988) offers a similar example in the statement, "Seventy people were killed in the derailment yesterday including fourteen women" (p. 169). The next time you come across a statement like this in a newspaper or on television, remember this discussion and see if the statement strikes you differently as a result.

Married Names

When we talk about this topic in class, almost all of our students are aware that this practice has changed, but they aren't sure why. Only in the past three or so decades have women readily chosen to retain their own last names when marrying, rather than adopting their husbands' last names, a choice that has caused some degree of discomfort. We imagine that an argument probably arose back in history somewhere, when Mrs. Sam Cavalry wanted to keep her last name and state law said that she couldn't. Basically, a lot of people—women and men alike—believe that parts of their identities are connected to the names they've had all their lives. So why should a woman be expected to give up her last name, a part of her identity, to adopt her husband's? To some people, assuming the husband's last name identifies a woman as property (Spender, 1985).

Objections are constantly raised to the changes in married-name practices. Some people don't understand why taking a man's last name could be considered sexist. The practice isn't necessarily sexist, but what is sexist is the expectation that a woman is *supposed* to or *has* to take a man's last name, that somehow this is the "norm." If you're a female reader, what would happen if you asked your future husband to take *your* last name as a new family name? If you're a male reader, what would happen if your future wife asked you to take *her* last name rather than her taking yours? Does it seem strange to think of taking someone else's name, as though you'd lose some identity? Did you know that some men have done this—taken their wives' last names?

When you delve even further into this problem, you realize that *all* last names in our culture are male since a woman's birth name is, almost without exception, the last name of her father. For example, Betty's parents gave her the last name of Boop, her father's family name. But what if Betty's parents divorced before she was born? If her mother gives Betty her maiden name, Coop, Betty's last name of Coop is still based on the last name of her mother's father. Confusing, isn't it? The whole naming process is one aspect of patriarchy that sets feminists on their collective ear. As Maggio (1988) puts it, "Ever since the apocalyptic naming of Eve by Adam, human beings have recognized that there is power in naming" (p. 171). The power is abused, as Miller and Swift (1976) comment, when the "'Me, Tarzan, you Jane'" statement is translated into "'Me species, you subspecies'" (p. 87).

Again, there's no point in blaming, but doesn't it seem a bit arrogant to think that names for all persons in the world should stem from male heritage? Many people now think so, and attempts are being made to alter this process. Feminist author Julia Penelope used to be Julia Stanley, but she dropped her last name "Stanley" and began using her middle name "Penelope" as a last name, to give herself an autonomous identity (Spender, 1985). The naming game can get really tense when a married couple with different last names negotiate a last name for their children. Some couples have innovatively put their two last names together or hyphenated them, as in "Smithmartin" or "Smith-Martin." This name becomes the family name, one that reflects both family heritages in their children's identities. This doesn't eradicate the male-name dominance altogether, since the last name of the wife in the example (either Smith or Martin) was derived from her father's family name, but it does launch a new family name for the children to pass on.

Granted, this is a complicated process that can cause marital and family stress. One of our former students revealed that she and her husband had a significant, tense discussion about this very subject. She decided to hyphenate his last name onto hers when they got married, but when they were considering starting a family, her husband just assumed that their children would be given his last name. The couple compromised by using the hyphenated version, reflecting both of their family birth names. Clearly, even among so-called modern or liberated couples, problems still arise. There are no easy answers or rules to guide your decision making in these situations. Because it's complex, it may cause you to once again declare this topic as "making too big a deal out of nothing." We understand that reaction, but we continue to encourage you to explore new options, to keep an open mind, and to work to understand other people's points of view—whether traditional or nontraditional—on even basic names for one another.

References to Relationships

A practice related to the marital naming problem is one of referring to a person according to his or her relationship with someone else. Research tells us that women more often than men are identified, introduced, and talked to based on their connections to men (Lakoff, 1975; Maggio, 1988; Thorne, Kramarae, & Henley, 1983). The predominant connection is to a husband, but connections are also made to a woman's sons or father. Maggio (1988) believes that "one of the most sexist maneuvers in the language is the way we oblige women to label themselves in relationship to a man" (p. 171).

A reference is often made, for example, to "Mary, John's wife," or the introducer may say, "This is Mary, John's wife." Less often do you hear "This is John, Mary's husband." Equally disconcerting is the tendency for wives to be asked "What does your husband do?" more often than husbands are asked "What does your wife do?" (Lakoff, 1975, p. 31). We realize that in situations like introductions, the construction may be reliant on whose company or circle of friends the couple is in. For example, if Mary and John are at her office party, then people might be more likely to introduce John as Mary's husband since they know Mary. But when the situation is neutral, belonging to both or neither person in a couple, the likelihood that the woman will be introduced and addressed relevant to her relationship to the man is greater than the reverse. If you want to avoid statements like, "This is Sandy, Wayne's girlfriend of two years," try the nonsexist phrasing, "This is Sandy; she and Wayne have been together (or dating) for two years." Another way to avoid this problem is to simply introduce Sandy as herself, without any reference to Wayne at all.

Yet another related practice is most obvious in newspaper wedding announcements. Quite often the bride is identified as the "daughter of Mr. and Mrs. So-and-So," while the groom is identified by where he went to school and by his profession. There are some indications that this practice is changing, though. A quick glance at wedding pages of newspapers shows that more grooms' and brides' occupations are both being mentioned, but the identification of a bride via her parents (father first) doesn't seem to be changing much, even with the high incidence of divorce. A similar practice involves referring to Mary Smith as "Jimmy's mother" and Jimmy's father as "Mr. Smith." While practices like this seem to be changing, we still see a lot of evidence that these usages are common. More serious is our perception that few people understand why these practices are limiting, demeaning, and sexist, especially to women.

Titles and Salutations

For a long time, women bought the notion that men's lives and identities were more worthy than their own, so they adopted the conventions of being identified by and talked about via their relationships with men. But as Miller and Swift (1976) explain, "Once enough wives, daughters, sisters, and mothers began to say 'I have my own identity,' new wheels were set in motion, new life-styles began to appear, and new linguistic symbols emerged to describe them. All of which can be seen in the recent history of women's social titles" (p. 88).

Let's take a close look at the titles for women—*Miss, Mrs.,* and *Ms.*—and the title for men—*Mr.* What differentiates the first two female titles is marital status, but that's only a fairly recent usage. Until the nineteenth century, the terms merely distinguished female children and young women from older, more mature women (Spender, 1985). History isn't clear about why the titles changed function, but some scholars link it to the beginning of the industrial revolution when women began working outside the home. Supposedly, that working status obscured a woman's tie to the home, so the titles reinforced the connection (Miller & Swift, 1976).

BORN LOSER reprinted by permission of NEA, Inc.

Note that the title *Mr.* doesn't reflect a man's marital status. Mr. Joe Schmoe can be married, single, widowed, or divorced. The patriarchal nature of language deemed it necessary for people to be able to identify whether a woman was married, but it was not necessary to know a man's relationship to a woman. As Spender describes it, "The practice of labelling women as married or single also serves supremely sexist ends. It conveniently signals who is 'fair game' from the male point of view" (p. 27).

To counter this practice, women began to use the title *Ms.* a few decades ago, although the term has existed as a title of courtesy since the 1940s (Miller & Swift, 1976). According to Miller and Swift, the 1972 *American Heritage School Dictionary* was the first to include *Ms.* in its listing. People of both sexes have resisted the use of *Ms.*, claiming that it is hard to pronounce. But is it any harder to pronounce than *Mrs.* or *Mr.*? Some women choose not to use the new title because it links them with feminists—a connection they consider undesirable. Others use *Ms.* just exactly for that reason—its link with feminism and to establish their identities apart from men. Students report that *Ms.* is well accepted by people their age; they've become accustomed to it. Most of our male students don't seem bothered by the fact that the title doesn't reveal marital status, so this practice is indeed changing for the better.

We often hear students' concerns about written salutations and greetings. In the past, the standard salutation in a letter to someone you didn't know (and didn't know the sex of) was "Dear Sir" (or Sirs), or "Gentlemen." If someone knew only the last name of a person in an address or if the first name did not reveal the sex of the person, the default salutation was "Dear Mr. So-and-So." When in doubt, why use the masculine form? The terms *Sirs* and *Gentlemen* no more include women than the pronoun *he* or the term *mankind*. But what are your nonsexist options in these situations?

Sometimes a simple phone call to the organization you are contacting will enable you to specify the salutation. An easier way to fix this problem is to use terms that don't imply sex, such as (Dear) *Officers, Staff Member, Personnel, Members of the Department, Managers, Resident, Subscriber, Directors, Executives,* or *Professional Persons.* It may seem awkward the first time you use terminology like this. If it is more comfortable for you to use a sex-identified reference, then use such inclusive identifiers as "Ms./Mr.," "Sir or Madam," and "Madams and

Sirs." We suspect that a man's reaction to "Dear Madam or Sir" won't be as negative as that of a woman who sees "Dear Sir" in a letter addressed to her.

Alternatively, you can omit a personal salutation altogether, opting for an opening line that says "Greetings!" or "Hello!" (Maggio, 1988, p. 184). Or you can structure a letter like a memo, beginning with "To the Director" or "Regarding Your Memo of 9/7" or "TO: Friends of the Library." We caution against using "To Whom It May Concern" mainly because it is overused, but also because it may indicate that you are at a loss for how to start your letter. As is the case for all forms and practices of language, it is generally better to omit any reference to a person's sex. If you do refer to a person's sex, it's wise to make the reference one that represents women and men in a sensitive, equal manner.

Euphemisms, Metaphors, and Insults

The English language contains numerous expressions about the sexes that seemingly go unnoticed but that form subtly sexist patterns. These are usually in the form of metaphors or euphemisms—more comfortable substitutes for other terms. Concerning euphemisms for the sexes, Maggio (1988) states, "As is true of the rest of the language, these phrases are dominated by male images" (p. 179). Let's start with the one set of euphemisms that seems to raise more disagreement than others.

One of the most influential authors in the area of language and the sexes is Robin Lakoff, whom we've cited throughout this chapter. Lakoff's (1975) discussion of *lady* and *girl* as euphemisms for the word *woman* is especially insightful. Lakeoff contends that if the terms *woman* and *lady* are used interchangeably in a sentence, use of the latter "tends to trivialize the subject matter under discussion, often subtly ridiculing the woman involved" (p. 23). Adjectives that may be negatively connoted by the term *lady* include frivolous, scatterbrained, frail, sugary sweet, fluttery, insincere, demure, hyperpolite, helpless, flatterable, immature, and frigid (sexually repressed or inactive). Many people think of *lady* as a term of respect that communicates dignity and puts a woman on a pedestal, rather than suggesting negative qualities. If you're a female reader of this text, maybe you can recall instances in which your mother, father, or other authority figure warned you to "act like a lady!" Did you know what that meant, and then how to act?

The term *girl* isn't problematic until it's used to refer to an adult woman; then it's patronizing. It sends her back to the sandbox and negates the process of growing into womanhood. It also communicates innocence, immaturity, and childishness—something most women don't want thought of them. We get lots of flak from our students about this one, the main reason being that there's no acceptable female equivalent term for *guy*—the term most people use for college-aged males. When males are called guys, females are called girls rather than gals or dolls (like the movie). While older, nontraditional students generally don't have this problem, we continually see in traditionally aged students an awkwardness and reluctance to use the terms *woman* and *man* to refer to themselves and their peers. They associate those terms with older people (and

FIGURE 3.4. Masculine Expressions and Alternatives

boy	guy or man
to lord something over someone	to outpower someone
one's fellow classmates	one's classmates
one's fellow man	one's companions; other people
winning a fellowship	winning a student endowment
wanting fellowship with others	wanting togetherness or camaraderie
receiving your bachelor's degree	receiving your undergraduate degree
our forefathers or founding fathers	our founders or forebears
like father, like son	in one's image; following in one's footsteps
the brotherhood of man	humanity; the human collective
I am not my brother's keeper	it's none of my business; I don't know
the little girls' or little boys' room	restroom or bathroom
a Johnny-come-lately	newcomer; new arrival
charley horse	muscle cramp
like a David and Goliath	an uneven contest or mismatch; an upset
that's my Achilles' heel	that's my main weakness
receiving a Dear John letter	receiving a breakup letter; getting dumped
someone is a doubting Thomas	someone is skeptical or disbelieving
someone is a Don Juan	someone is a romantic lover
your average Tom, Dick, or Harry	your average person; a so-and-so
a good Joe	a good or helpful person
having the Midas touch	making something out of nothing
a Jekyll and Hyde	a two-faced person; a split personality
signing your John Hancock	signing your name
having Montezuma's revenge	being sick to your stomach
a Mickey Mouse operation	a slipshod or small-time operation
a peeping Tom	a voyeur or peeper
raising Cain	raising hell; causing a ruckus
say uncle	give up; say when
"Well, I'll be monkey's uncle!"	"Well, I'll be!"
don't be a Scrooge	don't be cheap or tight
borrow from Peter to pay Paul	juggle the bills/money
a gentleman's agreement	an informal agreement or promise
Father Time	time
wearing the pants in the family	heading the household
sugar daddy	bankroller
old as Methusaleh	old as the hills; old as time
king of the hill	big shot; hot shot; big wheel; winner
the patience of Job	tremendous patience; long-suffering
Jack Frost	frost; winter
tomfoolery	foolishness; nonsense
spend money like a "drunken sailor"	throw money around
curse or talk like a sailor	curse; have a trash mouth
the king's English	correct English; perfect language
a mama's boy	a spoiled, privileged, or immature person

FIGURE 3.5. Feminine Expressions and Alternatives

lady; girl; gal; or doll	woman
the queen's English	correct English; perfect language
a daddy's girl	a spoiled, privileged, or immature person
using a lazy Susan	using a revolving dish
an Amazon	a tall, strong, or belligerent person
a Jezebel	an evil influence
Mother Earth or Mother Nature	earth or nature
matrimony	marriage
a patsy	a dupe; a sucker
the mother tongue	native tongue or language
acting like a mother hen	being protective
a nervous Nellie	worrywart; worrier; nervous person
a Pollyanna	an eternal optimist; an idealist
opening Pandora's box	opening a can of worms; causing problems
a dumb blonde	an unintelligent person

it hurts when they view "older" as thirties and forties). As Miller and Swift (1988) suggest, the female terms have "psychic overtones; of immaturity and dependence in the case of 'girl:' of conformity and decorum in the case of 'lady:' of sexuality and reproduction in the case of both 'female' and 'woman'" (p. 67). Interestingly, these feminine substitutes defy the original value of a euphemism, which is, as Lakoff (1975) says, to "put a better face on something people find uncomfortable" (p. 24). For most adult women, female euphemisms do not serve as "better faces" for them.

Think about what would happen if you were to say to a group of men, "Good morning, boys!" Many people won't use this term, recognizing that it is a derogatory, condescending euphemism for men. So if most men resent being called boys, then most women understandably resent being called girls. Don't get the idea that we believe that only men call women girls or ladies. We know that women call themselves and each other these names, in contrast to men, who would hardly dare call themselves or other men boys (except for an occasional reference to a "night out with the boys"). But, for equality purposes, we encourage you to refer to an adult, including yourself, as a man or a woman.

Masculine and feminine expressions that are best avoided, as well as their nonsexist equivalents, are listed in Figures 3.4 and 3.5. Consider how often your communication contains sexist or exclusive terminology; then think about whether that's how you want to communicate yourself to others. If you decide to make some changes, we've given you the options for how to do so.

One final type of expression needs to be discussed—terms used for the specific purpose of demeaning or insulting another person (i.e., name-calling). In Chapter 2 we said that one of the worst insults that can be directed at a man is to reference him by a feminine term. Let's examine some of the main derogatory terms used for men: bastard, son of a bitch, motherfucker, queer, fag or faggot, fairy, and queen. Why are these seen as male terms when they all have to do with women? A *bastard* by definition, describes a child who doesn't know who his or her father is. The implication of the term is that the mother was possibly unmarried and likely someone who "slept around." Granted, this term doesn't put fatherhood in the best light either, but the clinical interpretation of the term implies that the mother figure is really the person at fault. If a man is called a "son of a bitch," it can be more of an indictment of the mother than the son, because the term *bitch* is used more often to demean a woman than to describe a female dog. The worst term in this category, according to our students, is *motherfucker*. There could hardly be a more disgusting term with more taboo imagery than one that accuses someone of having had intercourse with his or her mother.

The remaining terms in the list are derogatory, first, because they are negative terms for homosexuals, primarily homosexual men. Second, they are terms for women which become derogatory when applied to men. Exceptions are the terms *fag*, which actually means to become tired, and *faggot*, defined in the dictionary as a bundle of sticks. Occasionally, terms that imply masculinity are derogatory when leveled at women, such as *bull dyke* or *butch*. But most of the name-calling that is directed at women is done via terms that demean their anatomy or exaggerate their sexuality. The point here is not to determine whether name-calling has its place but to note that the predominance of names used in name-calling are sexist.

Thus far we've discussed various practices and forms of sexist language, so that you would understand the nature and scope of this problem. We've also provided nonsexist options or alternatives to these practices. In the final section of this chapter, we examine some reasons for using nonsexist linguistic patterns of communication.

WHY USE NONSEXIST LANGUAGE?

Reason 1: Nonsexist Language Reflects Nonsexist Attitudes

To understand this reason, think back to Sapir and Whorf, who hypothesized about language and thought. Even though we aren't sure about the exact relationship between language and thought, we feel certain that a relationship exists. So if you communicate in a sexist manner—whether or not you are aware that a particular usage is sexist and regardless of your intentions—it is possible that you hold some form of sexist attitudes. If our thoughts are indeed influenced by our language, and if our language affects the quality of our thought, then sexist language may be linked to sexist thoughts. Stop and think for a moment: Now that you have a fuller understanding of what constitutes sexist language, can you say that your communication—both oral and written—is free from such usage? The tougher question is: If you use this form of sexist communication, could someone claim that you hold sexist attitudes?

That's a valid claim if you buy the premise that language and thought are interconnected. As Bobbye Sorrels (1983), author of *The Nonsexist Communicator*, explains: "With an English language that portrays males as the norm and females as abnormal or subnormal, those who analyze and practice the language must believe that females have less value than males" (p. 2). It's a difficult notion to accept, especially when dealing with forms of language that aren't the more overt indications typically associated with sexism. But using sexist language, even the more subtle forms, may convey sexist attitudes, whether intended or not. Thus the point of Reason 1 is that eliminating sexist language and practices from communication is an initial step in the process of freeing the mind from remnant sexist attitudes.

Reason 2: Nonsexist Language Is Basic to the Receiver Orientation

We're repeated the principles behind adopting a receiver orientation to communication a few times already in this text; thus we feel fairly safe in assuming that you know what it means, even if you are not yet able to incorporate it into your communicative life. Hardly any other topic that we discuss in this text pertains more to the principles of receiver orientation than the topic of sexist language. How does it pertain? Very simply. If, in a given situation, a listener perceives your language to be sexist, then the receiver orientation to communication deems that your language in that situation is sexist. Moreover, the listener is likely to judge *you* as sexist, just by your remarks.

For example, if you say, "If a person needs help, he should feel that he can call on me to be his friend," a listener may interpret your comments as sexist because you are insinuating (1) that only men are persons, and (2) that only male friends can call on you for help. If your message is interpreted to be sexist, then you're going to have a tough time explaining to the listener how it wasn't sexist, or how you didn't intend to come across that way. You may not have meant anything sexist or demeaning in your message, but once it's been said and interpreted by a listener, you can't erase it, can you? The communication is *out there,* and undoing it or convincing a listener that you meant otherwise takes ten times as long as if you'd applied a little forethought. So, if you want to embody the respect and concern for others that is an underlying principle of the receiver orientation to communication, eliminating sexism—and other demeaning "isms," like racism, classism, heterosexism, and ageism—from your communication will go a long way toward that goal.

Reason 3: Nonsexist Language Is Contemporary

One set of goals within higher education is that upon graduation, students will be able to think, write, and converse with the world in a manner befitting an educated person. Using outdated, sexist language undermines the profile of an educated person. It also suggests that a person is "in the dark" rather than "in the know" about the world in which she or he lives. Sorrels (1983) suggests: "Whereas in the past society virtually restricted males to certain roles and females to others, such restrictions no longer exist. Therefore, communication symbols based on past roles simply do not portray current conditions properly. Instead, they distort reality" (p. 2). The reality is that the roles that women and men can fulfill have changed with the times. More women are pursuing occupational paths once reserved for men, and vice versa. More men feel able to assume the roles and behaviors that were long expected only of women. Since these changes have occurred, and are likely to keep occurring, language should accurately reflect these changes to more clearly match what is going on in society.

Besides wanting to be up-to-date and to project a current image to others, there is another angle to Reason 3. Did you realize that publication standards are explicit on the matter of using nonsexist language? As early as the 1970s, publishing houses and style specialists began to specify nonsexist language policies for all publications. In 1977, the American Psychological Association included "Guidelines for Nonsexist Language in APA Journals" in its style manual. This means that something rarely gets into print if it violates current standards regarding nonsexist language. Probably some of your college professors—maybe even your high school teachers—have instructed you in nonsexist language practices for your writing. Maybe they talked to you about eliminating sexism from your speaking as well. We encourage you to start working on this area of communication now, if you haven't already. This kind of work projects an image of being educated, sensitive, and contemporary.

Reason 4: Nonsexist Language Is Unambiguous

Identify the sex of the person being referred to in the following statement: "If a person wants to be treated as an adult, he must earn the respect worthy of such treatment." Is the "person" a particular man, a particular woman, a human being of either sex, or all human beings? Compare this first statement with the following one: "If a person wants to be treated as an adult, she must earn the respect worthy of such treatment." Has the meaning of the statement now changed? Are we talking about one person—a woman—or all persons? Some interpretations might say that the second statement leaves men out completely. These statements illustrate the kind of confusion sexist language causes. How can the term *man* mean one male person, while at the same time it means all persons? The problem is knowing which meaning of the term is being used—a specific, narrow meaning or a broad, generic one. Avoiding such terms reduces ambiguity and confusion in spoken and written communication.

Reason 5: Nonsexist Language Strengthens Expression

Another benefit of nonsexist language usage is an enhanced writing style. Maggio (1988) suggests: "One of the most rewarding—and, for many people, the most unexpected—side effects of breaking away from traditional, sexist patterns of language is a dramatic improvement in writing style. As you examine sexist words from the standpoint of good writing you will notice that they fail the test nearly every time" (p. 164). Maggio describes several ways that writing is enhanced by avoiding sexist linguistic practices, such as the replacement of fuzzy generalizations with precise terminology, the substitution of clichés by explicit wording, and the use of concrete examples instead of "one-word-fits-all descriptions" (p. 164).

Many of our students balk at our suggestion that they rid their talk of even the most subtle forms of sexism. They often hold the belief that nonsexist language is cumbersome, that it "junks up" one's speaking and writing with a "bunch of extra words," just to "include everybody." However, once they begin to practice the many simple methods of avoiding sexist, exclusive means of expression, they readily admit that it does make their communication more clear, contemporary, dynamic, and persuasive. They find that they are quite able to say what they want to say without the use of insensitive, exclusive terminology.

Reason 6: Nonsexist Language Demonstrates Sensitivity to Others

This seems like an obvious reason for using nonsexist language, but it may be more obvious in spirit than in practice. What we mean is that while you may hold a basic philosophy that variations among people are worthy of respect, you may communicate in a manner that negates your philosophy—out of either ignorance (because you just didn't know any better) or nonchalance (thinking that some forms of sexist communication are "just no big deal"). Maybe you simply feel that some of the subtler forms of sexist language that have developed into habits will take too much time and energy to change, and that people will realize that you didn't intend to be insensitive in something you said, that's just how you talk. Maybe you believe that if people get the wrong impression of you from your language, they'll take the time to learn differently; if not, they weren't worth your energy in the first place. Do any of these statements echo your own thoughts? Or do they may remind you of someone else whose communication is anything but sensitive?

Spoken and written communication are ways of extending oneself into the world, of getting to know others and being known by them. If you desire to present yourself as a caring, sensitive individual who believes in a basic system of fairness for all persons, then doesn't it seem logical that your language reflect that desire? This is yet another dimension of developing personal effectiveness as a communicator. As Sorrels (1983) puts it, "A basic sense of fairness requires the equal treatment of men and women in the communication symbols that so define the lives of the people who use them. Sexist communication limits and devalues all humans" (pp. 2–3). Acknowledging differences, then accepting and enjoying them begins as an internal process, a process of establishing, evaluating, and reworking your attitudes. The next step is to convey those attitudes through language that avoids "isms."

Reason 7: Nonsexist Language Empowers Others

How can nonsexist language empower other people? First, it makes people feel good about themselves when language is used to include them, to address their experiences, and to convey an attitude of equality. Second, nonsexist language can make people think about themselves in ways they might not have otherwise considered. For example, when we teach communication courses to students, we are careful to use nonsexist language. We especially avoid using masculine forms of language to represent all persons. We have noticed (and have received direct comments on the fact) that students pick up on this language and the reasons behind it. We structure statements to make both male and female students feel that they are being spoken to: "A good student will start working on her or his paper early—at least the night before it's due!" equally includes women and men in our vision of a "good student." We feel certain that if we used only *he* in a sentence like the one above or, more dramatically, if we used only *she,* some of our students would feel left out, and some of them would communicate that omission to us. Language is powerful; nonsexist language is empowering.

CONCLUSION

We suspect that this chapter has given you more than a few things to think about, because when you put something under a microscope, you see it in a new way. While we hope that the information hasn't offended you, we're glad if it has overwhelmed you. We hope that you understand the full extent of this problem and can help continue to change things for the better. However, we realize that we cannot control your response to this information, nor do we want to. Since we value and emphasize choice in this text, we affirm your choice of how to respond to this material. Granted, some readers may respond by saying, "This is too much trouble," "There's too much to worry about," or "This is too big a deal about nothing." Others might respond with something as basic as being more careful in their writing. Or you might decide to rid both your written and oral communication of *some* forms of sexist language—overt instances that could most detract from your personal effectiveness. You might decide to "jump on the nonsexist-language bandwagon" full force, ridding your communication of virtually all practices and forms of sexist language. You might then carefully and competently encourage others to examine their language usage as well. Again, the focus of this section of the text is influences—those influences that exist externally in your world and internally within your body and mind that profoundly affect your gender communication. You first have to understand how you are influenced before you can choose to lessen or negate the influence.

Key Terms

language
Whorfian Hypothesis
sexist language
generic pronouns
inclusive language
exclusive language
neologisms

indefinite pronouns
man-linked terminology
feminine suffixes
nonneutral terms
parallel construction
titles
salutations

euphemisms
metaphors
insults
receiver orientation
empowerment

Discussion Starters

1. What were you taught in junior high or high school about sexist language? Do you remember any reactions you had at the time to what you were being taught? If you received no instruction on the use of nonsexist language, why do you think this information wasn't included in your education?

2. Why do you think our language contains so many ways to identify a person's sex? Do you think that it is necessary to know the sex of an individual? Do you think our culture places too much emphasis on gender? If so, in what ways?

3. Think again about the receiver orientation to communication. Do you believe that adopting a receiver orientation to communication puts more pressure on people to be nonsexist? If so, do you believe that this pressure is a good thing, or that it may have a negative effect on communication?

4. Why do you think a neologism like *Ms.* made its way through the language when nonsexist pronouns like *tey, gen,* and *herm* did not? What does it take, in your opinion, for a new term to be accepted in society? If you wanted to introduce new words into the language, how would you go about it?

5. Imagine that you are in a conversation with someone about nonsexist language. The other person argues that changing the language is "making too much out of nothing" and that "people should concentrate on more important issues that affect the sexes than language." Having read this chapter, how would you respond to this person? Would you agree or disagree? What are your opinions regarding the areas of sexist language usage that are discussed in this chapter?

6. Sexism in religious language is one of the more difficult topics to explore and discuss. For some people, it is an affront to put the language used to convey their deeply personal religious beliefs under the microscope. What are your views on this subject? Do you think that sexist, male-dominated aspects of religious language should be examined? Do you think religious language should be an exception within the larger topic of sexist language?

7. We all know that names are important parts of our self-identities. Assuming that you are single now, if you get married, how will you deal with the "name-taking" practice within our culture? If you are male, have you always wanted your future wife to take your last name? Have you always assumed that a woman you would marry would want to take your last name? What if your bride insists on keeping her last name? How will you react? If you are female, what do you think about women keeping their last names upon marriage? If you become engaged, what will you say to your future husband regarding the taking of his last name? Does it seem too "radical" to suggest that you hyphenate your two last names? What about the suggestion that he take *your* last name?

References

ALDRICH, P. G. (1985, December). Skirting sexism. *Nation's Business,* pp. 34–35.

AMERICAN PSYCHOLOGICAL ASSOCIATION. (1983). *Publication manual of the American Psychological Association* (3rd ed). Washington, DC: Author.

BAKER, R. (1981). "Pricks" and "chicks": A plea for "persons." In M. Vetterling-Braggin (Ed.), *Sexist language: A modern philosophical analysis* (pp. 161–182). New York: Rowman and Littlefield.

BLAUBERGS, M. S. (1978). Changing the sexist language: The theory behind the practice. *Psychology of Women Quarterly, 2,* 244–261.

BRIERE, J., & LANKTREE, C. (1983). Sex-role related effects of sex bias in language. *Sex Roles, 9,* 625–632.

BROOKS, L. (1983). Sexist language in occupational information: Does it make a difference? *Journal of Vocational Behavior, 23,* 227–232.

CAMERON, D. (1985). *Feminism and linguistic theory.* New York: St. Martin's Press.

COLE, C. M., HILL, F. A., & DAYLEY, L. J. (1983). Do masculine pronouns used generically lead to thoughts of men? *Sex Roles, 9,* 737–750.

FRANK, F. W., & TREICHLER, P. A. (1989). *Language, gender, and professional writing: Theoretical approaches and guidelines for non-sexist usage.* New York: Modern Language Association.

GRADDOL, D., & SWANN, J. (1989). *Gender voices.* Cambridge, MA: Basil Blackwell.

HAMILTON, L. C. (1988). Using masculine generics: Does generic "he" increase male bias in the user's imagery? *Sex Roles, 19,* 785–799.

IVY, D. K. (1986, February). *Who's the boss?: He, he/she, or they?* Paper presented at the annual meeting of the Western States Communication Association, Tucson, AZ.

IVY, D. K., BULLIS-MOORE, L., NORVELL, K., BACKLUND, P., & JAVIDI, M. (1993, February). *The lawyer, the babysitter, and the student: Nonsexist language usage and instruction.* Paper presented at the annual meeting of the Western States Communication Association, Albuquerque, NM.

KENNEDY, D. (1992). Review essay: She or he in textbooks? *Women and Language, 15,* 46–49.

KLEINKE, C. L. (1974). Knowledge and familiarity of descriptive sex names for males and females. *Perceptual and Motor Skills, 39,* 419–422.

KRAMARAE, C. (1981). *Women and men speaking.* Rowley, MA: Newbury House.

LAKOFF, G., & JOHNSON, M. (1981). *Metaphors we live by.* Chicago: University of Chicago Press.

LAKOFF, R. (1975). *Language and woman's place.* New York: Harper & Row.

MACKAY, D. G. (1980). Psychology, prescriptive grammar, and the pronoun problem. *American Psychologist, 35,* 444–449.

MAGGIO, R. (1988). *The nonsexist word finder: A dictionary of gender-free usage.* Boston: Beacon Press.

MARTYNA, W. (1978). What does "he" mean? Use of the generic masculine. *Journal of Communication, 28,* 131–138.

McCONNELL-GINET, S. (1980). Linguistics and the feminist challenge. In S. Mcconnell-Ginet, R. Borker, & N. Furman (Eds.), *Women and language in literature and society* (pp. 3–25). New York: Praeger.

MILLER, C., & SWIFT, K. (1976). *Words and women: New language in new times.* Garden City, NY: Doubleday.

MILLER, C., & SWIFT, K. (1988). *The handbook of nonsexist writing* (2nd ed.). New York: Harper & Row.

MOULTON, J., ROBINSON, G. M., & ELIAS, C. (1978). Sex bias in language use: "Neutral" pronouns that aren't. *American Psychologist, 33,* 1032–1036.

NATIONAL COUNCIL OF TEACHERS OF ENGLISH. (1975). *Guidelines for nonsexist use of language in NCTE publications.* Urbana, IL: Author.

NILSEN, A. P. (1972). Sexism in English: A feminist view. In N. Hoffman, C. Secor, & A. Tinsley (Eds.), *Female studies VI,* Old Westbury, NY: Feminist Press.

PENELOPE, J. (1990). *Speaking freely: Unlearning the lies of the fathers' tongues.* New York: Pergamon Press.

SORRELS, B. D. (1983). *The nonsexist communicator.* Englewood Cliffs, NJ: Prentice-Hall.

SPENDER, D. (1985). *Man made language* (2nd ed.). London: Routledge & Kegan Paul.

STANLEY, J. P. (1977). Paradigmatic woman: The prostitute. In D. L. Shores (Ed.), *Papers in language variation.* Birmingham: University of Alabama Press.

STERICKER, A. (1981). Does this "he or she" business really make a difference? The effect of masculine pronouns as generics on job attitudes. *Sex Roles, 7,* 637–641.

THORNE, B., KRAMARAE, C., & HENLEY, N. (Eds.). (1983). *Language, gender and society.* Rowley, MA: Newbury House.

TODD-MANCILLAS, W. R. (1981). Masculine generics = sexist language: A review of literature and implications for speech communication professionals. *Communication Quarterly, 29,* 107–115.

WHORF, B. L. (1956). Science and linguistics. In J. B. Carroll (Ed.), *Language, thought, and reality.* Cambridge, MA: MIT Press.

CHAPTER 4

The Sell, the Screen, and the Sound: Women and Men in Mass Media

*T*urn off that television, turn down the CD player, put away that magazine, and read this chapter, because you might get a better understanding of what you're watching, listening to, and flipping through. But first, another case study.

CASE STUDY

About six months before the 1992 presidential election and just a few days after the Los Angeles riots in reaction to the decision in the first case against the officers charged with beating Rodney King, then–vice president Dan Quayle made a speech about the "poverty of values" in the country. In this speech, Quayle described decaying family values and the problems of "bearing babies irresponsibly" as well as "failing to support children one has fathered" (Quayle, as cited in Rosenthal, 1992, p. 6D). Whether one agrees or disagrees with Quayle's views about decaying family values is not the purpose of our discussion. What is pertinent about Quayle's speech was his choice of examples to support his claims.

Explaining what he meant by "bearing babies irresponsibly," Quayle elaborated, "It doesn't help matters when prime-time television has Murphy Brown—a character who supposedly epitomizes today's intelligent, highly paid professional woman—mocking the importance of fathers by bearing a child alone and calling it just another 'lifestyle choice.'" A news reporter commenting on the speech felt compelled to remind the vice president, as well as the newspaper's readership, that "Murphy Brown is not a real person" (Rosenthal, 1992, p. 6D). It's an understatement to say that this was an interesting moment—a real-life, high-ranking political figure using in a national speech a fictional television character as his main illustration of irresponsible parenting. This probably isn't the first time in history this kind of thing has happened, but Quayle's event likely received more media coverage than other such instances in the past.

Quayle's reference to the lead character in the popular television sitcom *Murphy Brown* can be viewed as exemplifying the blurred line between fantasy and reality. The pervasiveness of media in our lives is underscored by the fact that an unmarried television mother was seen as a more recognizable supporting example for a speech than a statistic about the country's rising rates of single motherhood or an example drawn from real life. This was an fascinating occurrence, but aren't these kinds of references made a lot in daily life? Consider how often you hear someone refer to something on television, such as, "I just don't trust that guy I went out with last night; he reminds me of Arnie Becker on *LA Law*," "My wife and I have arguments kind of like that couple on *Home Improvement*," or "I felt like I was in a commercial for Hallmark cards."

Think about how often you compare real life—your work, your family life, your relationships with significant people—to how these things are depicted in the movies, on television, or in song lyrics and music videos. Some people argue that technology has made it easy for us to escape reality, meaning that high-tech communication media have allowed us to avoid connecting with one another. The claim is that movies, television, computerized networks, and music for many people take the place of a social life, substituting for a roommate or spouse a companion that can be turned off with just the click of a switch. What do you think about that claim? Do various forms of media act as substitutes for something in your life?

OVERVIEW

"Influences on Our Choices" is the title of Part Two of the text. Having just immersed yourself in the chapter on language, your thinking has probably been energized, regarding the number of things that can affect a person's view of self, of men and women, and of the gender communication necessary to make relationships function. After you read this chapter, we'll add media effects to your ever-expanding list of agents of influence.

Probably no force, with the possible exception of language, influences our daily lives more than media. Media are highly influential in how they communicate messages *about* women and men. Perhaps your parents' teachings and your family background—that is, how you were raised—have more to do with shaping your gender attitudes and patterns of communication about the sexes than exposure to media. But did you ever think about how your family and social environment might have been influenced by media, making it difficult, if not impossible, to separate out what force had what effect?

Do you know, for example, if your parents' viewing of Katherine Hepburn–Spencer Tracy movies had an impact on their marital relationship? Did Elvis Presley's "Love Me Tender" affect your parents' dating relationship? Could they have been influenced by parental figures on such television programs as *Leave It to Beaver* and *Father Knows Best*? Might your children be affected by your viewing a top-ranked sitcom like *Roseanne?* This chapter explores how different forms of media communicate various messages *about* men and women; specifically, we examine the following topics:

- How theories of mass communication help explain media influence
- The impact of depictions of women and men in advertisements on attitudes about the sexes

- Gender instruction in prime-time television shows and social issues programming
- Communication about the sexes via daytime soap operas and talk shows
- Gender-bending in film, or how men's and women's film roles influence viewers
- Song lyrics and portrayals of the sexes
- Music videos as communication about women and men

INTRODUCTION

The term *mass communication* encompasses an ever-widening range of outlets for information—so many that we had to be selective with what we could cover in this chapter. Before we address some specific forms of media and what they communicate about the sexes, here are some terms related to mass communication, as well as some theories about media effects on consumers.

A General Definition and Discussion of Mass Communication

Mass media expert John Bittner (1989) defines mass communication as "messages communicated through a mass medium to a large number of people" (p. 11). He contrasts interpersonal communication, which typically occurs between persons in a face-to-face situation, with mass communication, which needs an "intermediate transmitter of information" to reach a large audience (p. 10). Among other defining characteristics of mass communication Bittner discusses is the fact that mass communication is primarily an impersonal channel, that it requires a person or sponsoring agency, termed a "gatekeeper," to carry the message, and that it offers delayed rather than instant feedback (p. 12). Examples of gatekeepers include a reporter who presents a story on the nightly news and a newspaper editor who decides what information reaches print.

Media Infiltration into Our Lives

You are literally bombarded with forms of mass communication every day and the effects of this bombardment are dramatic, as several research efforts have documented (Cathcart & Gumpert, 1986; Comstock & Strzyzewski, 1990; Dambrot, Reep, & Bell, 1988; Jensen, 1987; Lindlof, 1987, 1991; Press, 1991a). Think about how many hours you spend listening to tapes, CDs, and records; watching television sitcoms, soap operas, talk shows, and music videos; listening to the radio; going to movies; reading billboards and signs while you drive; watching videotapes; reading books, newspapers, magazines, and other forms of print journalism; and maybe even logging on to your PC to interface with a national computer network. Your modern existence is jammed full of mass communication from sunrise to sunset, every day, but just how are you affected by it? We don't tackle that whole question or every form of media in this chapter, but we do focus attention on how media exposure and consumption affect the way you communicate *about* and *with* men and women in your various relationships.

As a college-educated person, you are probably an above-average critical consumer of mass communication, meaning that you consciously select mediated messages to take in and to filter out. However, a great deal of mediated information is absorbed unconsciously, even by the most critical consumers. Few of us have time in our busy lives to focus attention on all the mediated messages we receive at given moments in a typical day, so that we make conscious decisions about their effects. This critical thinking process becomes a skill we use less frequently as we take in more and more mediated information. Just how this absorption affects us has been the subject of a good deal of attention among media researchers.

Explanations for the Effects of Media Consumption

Media and gender scholar Gaye Tuchman (1979) describes how, as mass media grew "exponentially" during the years between World War II and the beginning of the 1980s, "so did study of the media" (p. 528). Several theories have emerged that attempt to explain how media affect consumers.

The Hypodermic Needle or Direct-Effects Theory

This was an early theory of media effects, which viewed the mass audience as individuals who directly consumed mass messages. The imagery was that of a hypodermic needle that "injected" mass communication directly into the veins of its consumers. This theory offered a fairly inadequate explanation of media effects because it ignored how friends, coworkers, family members, and others might influence the process (Dominick, 1993). For example, this theory suggests that a person watching a televised portrayal of marital interaction would be directly affected by that portrayal, discarding the possible effects of the person's own experiences or how her or his parents interacted.

Uses and Gratifications Theory

Bittner (1989) describes the uses and gratifications approach as a functional theory that has more to do with the question "What do people do *with* media?" compared to "What do the media do *to* people?" (p. 378). Basically, research from this perspective focuses on how consumers use various media and what gains, rewards, or gratifications they receive from such consumption (Palmgreen & Rayburn, 1985; Rubin, 1986). Media researchers have employed uses and gratifications theory to better understand what uses people make of television news or commercial advertising, or why people are such loyal watchers of soap operas, for instance (Rayburn, Palmgreen, & Acker, 1984). Studies using this theory have determined that people follow soaps for various reasons: to attain approval for their own lives, out of habit, for relaxation or entertainment purposes, to seek models for male and female behavior, and so on (Allen, 1985; Compesi, 1980; Lemish, 1985).

Agenda-Setting Theory

This theory proposes that the media do not merely report, reflect, or dramatize what is important in society; media actually guide our thinking in terms of what's important. As Bittner (1989) explains the theory, "The media create an *agenda* for our thoughts and influence us in what seems important" (p. 382). For an example of how this theory applies to gender concerns, consider daytime talk shows. Many consumers of these talk shows (primarily women) believe that the "women's issues" raised on these shows constitute critical social, political, and economic concerns. In essence, female viewers may be allowing a media outlet to set an agenda for what should be most important to them. In a subsequent section of this chapter, we describe in more detail some possible ramifications of believing that "being a man trapped inside a woman's body" is one of the most critical issues facing contemporary women.

Cultivation Theory

This theory suggests that mass media consumption, with special reference to television viewing, "'cultivates' in us a distorted perception of the world we live in, making it seem more like television portrays it, than it is in real life" (Bittner, 1989, p. 386). It can be described as a blurring of reality and fantasy, of what life is really like and how it appears on television or in the movies (Signorelli & Morgan, 1988). Media scholar George Gerbner and his colleagues are among the most prominent researchers to use cultivation theory. For example, these researchers have specifically compared the social reality of violence and crime to media's depiction of it (Gerbner, Gross, Eleey, Jackson-Beeck, Jeffries-Fox, & Signorelli, 1977; Gerbner, Gross, Morgan, & Signorelli, 1980). Another media researcher used cultivation theory to discover adolescents' perceptions of values in proportion to their television viewing habits (Potter, 1990). In subsequent sections on the effects of television and film portrayals on men's and women's relationships, we illustrate this theory in more depth. For now, just remember this theory in connection with an example: Think about people who believe that romantic relationships are supposed to happen just like they happen in Hollywood movies, happy endings and all.

Your understanding of what makes mass communication different from other forms of communication, as well as basic knowledge of some theories of how media affect our lives, is critical to your comprehension of the information remaining in this chapter. As we explore various forms of media, think about ways that each medium affects you personally. Then consider how a particular medium affects your gender communication and your relationships.

COMMUNICATION ABOUT WOMEN AND MEN VIA ADVERTISING

Advertising is a huge industry. Estimates suggest that over $100 billion *per year* is spent by U.S. advertisers (Lysonski & Pollay, 1990). Researchers contend that advertising does not operate solely for the purpose of selling products to consumers. As media researchers Lysonski and Pollay point out, advertising "creates a pervasive and persuasive communication environment that sells a great deal more than just products. Through the use of imagery, the display of life-styles, and the exercise and reinforcement of values, advertisements are communicators of culturally defined concepts such as success, worth, love, sexuality, popularity, and normalcy" (p. 317). Do you think that gender and sex roles should be added to that list?

Female Depiction in Advertising

The programmatic research of two marketing professors, Alice Courtney and Thomas Whipple (1974, 1983; Whipple & Courtney, 1980, 1985), supports the claim that advertising has a major impact on individuals' views of sex roles in society. From the compiled results of numerous studies, Courtney and Whipple produced the following comprehensive list of female sex-role stereotypes that are common in advertising. Subsequent research has corroborated these findings (Bretl & Cantor, 1988; Craig, 1992b; Goldman, Heath, & Smith, 1991; Lovdal, 1989).

1. Women in isolation, particularly from other women
2. Women in sleepwear, underwear, and lingerie, more frequently than in professional clothing
3. Young girls portrayed as passive and in need of help
4. Women as kitchen and bathroom product representatives
5. Women appearing more than men in ads for personal hygiene products (e.g., deodorants, toothpaste)
6. An abundance of women serving men and boys
7. Medical advertisements depicting male physicians interacting with hysterical, hypochondriacal female patients
8. Women more often depicted in family- and home-oriented roles than in business roles
9. Young housewives shown performing household duties, whereas older men act as product representatives who give advice to housewives
10. Women portrayed as decorative, nonfunctioning entities
11. Fewer depictions of older women than older men
12. Fewer depictions of minority women, compared to depictions of minority men
13. Fewer women than men advertising expensive luxury products
14. Few women depicted actively engaged in sports
15. Ads overtly critical of feminist rights and issues

Lysonski and Pollay (1990) describe the portrayals of women in advertising as "an inaccurate reflection of reality and an unhealthy programming of youth" (p. 318). Their international study of consumers' perceptions of sexism in advertising is pervasive and revealing. Between the years 1985 and 1986, subjects in four countries—Denmark, Greece, New Zealand, and the United

States—responded to a survey assessing their attitudes toward sexist depictions of men and women in advertisements. Sample questions probed whether subjects believed that ads they were exposed to in their daily lives depicted men and women as they really are, if they portrayed men and women in real-life situations, if they indicated that women were dependent on men and were depicted as sex objects, and so forth. Three survey items assessed boycott intentions, that is, whether subjects would purchase products from companies using offensive sexist ads.

Lysonski and Pollay's study showed a "systematic shift in attitudes" (1990, p. 323) compared to results of a similar study conducted 10 years earlier (Lundstrom & Sciglimpaglia, 1977). Male and female subjects were significantly more critical of sexist portrayals of women in ads than their counterparts a decade earlier, with female subjects offering more criticism than males. This is a positive sign that attitudes toward sexist portrayals may be changing. However, while subjects were more critical of sexist ads, they were less likely to boycott the products of companies that used sexist ads—a result especially pronounced for U.S. subjects. The researchers could offer no reasonable explanation for the finding regarding boycotting intentions; they suggested that, even though sensitivity to sexist advertising has increased, it may not have increased to the point that it affects most people's buying behaviors.

Marketing executive Rena Bartos's (1983) study of television commercials supports other research findings regarding attitudes toward sexism in advertising. Female subjects in this study were identified by four categories: (1) the Stay-At-Home Housewife; (2) the Plan-To-Work Housewife; (3) the Just-A-Job Working Woman; and (4) the Career-Oriented Working Woman. Despite the differences implied by the categories, Bartos found more commonality in subjects' reactions to stereotypical sexist advertising than she expected. She contends that "portraying women as sex objects is particularly abhorrent to women. While they do not reject sensuality per se, there is a very fine line that needs to be drawn between showing that women want to be attractive to the men in their lives and the suggestion of sex-object exploitation" (p. 37). Bartos's results indicate that women respond more positively to contemporary commercials that depict women in real-life situations, as opposed to traditional ads that show women only in subordinate roles. Women who work in the home respond as favorably as career-oriented women to ads depicting the changing roles of women and men.

In accord with these trends, some manufacturers have changed their approach to advertising products aimed at female consumers. Laura Zinn (1991), an author for *Business Week* magazine, describes how ads for women's products have evolved, citing Maidenform lingerie ads and Nike's women's line as examples. Maidenform ads in the past had displayed the "Maidenform Woman," typically a young, beautiful, thin woman who turned up in strange places wearing only her bra and panties. In efforts to change with the times, Maidenform recently launched a series of ads which analysts have termed "politically correct." One such ad depicts a baby chick, a Barbie doll, a tomato, and a fox, with the caption "A helpful guide for those who still confuse women with various unrelated objects" (Zinn, 1991, p. 90). Since women in increasing numbers are making sports and exercise a greater part of their lives, Nike's ads have wisely reflected this trend. Nike has made a serious, laudable, and quite successful attempt to communicate to female consumers that the company understands them. According to the manager of Nike's women's division, a significantly higher percentage of Nike's profits now comes from the sale of women's products—directly attributable to the success of contemporary ads.

Nevertheless, there are still those maufacturers and advertisers who appear to be either ignoring what the public is saying about sexist ads or finding a slice of the market that likes their ads and buys their products. In a subsequent section, we reproduce for you an actual billboard advertisement and offer a framework for analysis. For now, just think about how many automobile ads use women to sell their products, with messages that often compare the woman's curves to the contours of the car. If the products represented in the ads continue to generate profits, then it is likely that the themes in ads will be slow to change, reminding us of the old phrase, "the more things change, the more they stay the same."

Male Depiction in Advertising

Research contrasts female depiction in ads with findings that men are typically portrayed as dominant, successful professionals in business settings or as engaged in fun activities in settings away from home (Courtney & Whipple, 1983; Craig, 1992a; Skelly & Lundstrom, 1981). However, other information points to a subtle change: Depictions of men have been broadened to include domestic settings in which men take care of children, prepare family meals, and clean house (Kanner, 1990; Richmond-Abbott, 1992). More prevalent now are ads in which men are portrayed as fathers who get the Vicks Vapo-rub for sick children or husbands who are teased for their inability to figure out how to do laundry or operate a microwave oven. However, in an article by *New York Magazine* staff reporter Bernice Kanner (1990), ad executives suggest that "male-bashing" ads are on the way out. Kanner points to changing societal roles; with more women working outside the home, domestic duties may be shared by wives and husbands. Kanner warns that "men have become too sophisticated as shoppers for advertisers to risk alienating them" (p. 20).

Media analyst Jennifer Nicholson, in a 1992 article in *Adbusters,* suggests that the societal roles of men and corresponding depictions in ads reflect a sort of male image schizophrenia. Nicholson explains: "By creating a variety of new male identities, advertisers gain access to a wider collection of pocketbooks. Whether the '90s man is actually changing is irrelevant—the point is to convince him that he's part of a market-driven trend" (p. 21). She cites varying depictions of men in television and print ads, such as businessmen with babies strapped to their backs, faceless men in Jockey underwear commercials and Calvin Klein cologne ads, and scantily clad men working out in Soloflex ads. The broader and more varied the depictions of men in advertisements, the more messages get conveyed that there are diverse nonstereotypical roles for men. What's your reaction to an ad in which a man is sexually objectified, as some would argue that male characters appearing in many Calvin Klein magazine ads are? Do you notice these more or in a different way than, for example, women's lingerie ads in magazines or on television? Have you become sensitized to sexually objectifying ads—for both men and women—so that you hardly notice them any more? Since sexually objectifying female ads don't seem to be going away, do you think it's a form of equality to sexually objectify men in ads?

Look at the billboard advertisement reproduced in Figure 4.1. Some of you might think that there's nothing inherently wrong or sexist about this advertisement. The ad is simply catching the eye of motorists in Dallas, Texas, and effectively selling a product. Granted, everyone has a right to her or his opinion regarding what is sexist and what is merely provocative. (Remember the discussion in Chapter 1 about the difference between something that is sexual versus sexist?) However, others of you may look at this ad and think to yourself, "Not another scantily clad woman selling beer!" Since the ad contains elements that could be interpreted as sexist, analyzing the ad might be an interesting exercise. Using the following set of questions, let's analyze this ad for its potentially sexist elements. Supply your own answers to the questions first; then we'll provide our perspective.

1. Who is the target audience for this product?
2. What is being sold here, beer? Sexuality? Leisure?
3. Would you say that there is anything unusual in the fact that only a woman appears in this ad?

FIGURE 4.1.

4. What is your interpretation of the clothing (or lack thereof) the woman is wearing?
5. Do you find anything sexist in her body position, meaning her prone position on the billboard?
6. What is your interpretation of the positioning of the beer bottle underneath the woman's body?
7. What is the meaning of the caption, "Tap into the cold, Dallas"?

It might be interesting to compare your answers with that of your classmates, particularly classmates of the opposite sex. A comparison like this will demonstrate to what extent judgments of sexism are subjective. Here's our interpretation of this advertisement. Since statistics show that more men than women are beer drinkers, we can safely assume that this ad is likely geared more for a male than a female target audience. Perhaps the argument could be made that, in isolation, this one ad isn't sexist. But what about the trend of many beer advertisers to display almost exclusively women, typically in revealing attire, draped or posed in various suggestive positions with oversized beer bottles? When men and women appear together in ads, note who is more often portrayed in a sexy, flirtational, vulnerable, and unclothed characterization. Most often female characters are used for this effect. One example may not strike you as sexist, but when time and time again you see women being used as objects to sell products—especially products geared to men—then a judgment that the practice is sexist is justified. Why not show just the cold beer bottle and the caption? Could it be that what is really being sold here is sexuality, not beer? Could the subconscious message to men be, "If you drink this brand of beer, you'll attract the attention of a woman who looks like this"? Or for the female viewers of this ad, the message could be, "If you look like this woman, you'll attract beer-drinking, fun-loving men."

We think this is a sexist ad for many reasons, the main one being that it represents yet another attempt on the part of advertisers to use a woman's sexuality for a profit. There are other aspects of the ad that could also be interpreted as sexist. For example, the vulnerable position of a woman (in a bathing suit) lying on her back conveys a sexual, submissive message. The fact that she is on top of a cold beer bottle suggests sexual imagery, if you want to go so far as to construct the neck of the beer bottle, intentionally placed underneath and between her legs, as a phallic symbol. Concerning the caption, one wonders if it is the beer that is to be tapped or the woman.

Now, possibly at this point you're disagreeing with us or wondering if we see sexism lurking at every turn. Granted, you don't have to assess the hidden or overtly sexist elements in every ad you see. And someone isn't likely to pull off this Dallas freeway to critique this billboard. But we encourage you to think about how you are bombarded by images of women in sexual poses being used to sell all kinds of products. Men are occasionally objectified in ads to sell products—which can be sexist as well—but much more often the sexual object is a woman. It's a good idea to stop at times and critically analyze what you're seeing in magazines or television commercials. What's being communicated about women and men when sexist ads appear with such regularity? How do these messages affect you—your own self-image and your expectations of the opposite sex? How do they affect your communication with the opposite sex?

The Voice of Authority in Television Commercials

A related area of research on sex roles and advertising surrounds the use of voiceovers in television commercials. Voiceovers for ads represent unseen authorities or product experts, who typically greet the viewer, introduce the product or service, and conclude the ad with emphatic praise or a final sales pitch (Marecek, Piliavin, Fitzsimmons, Krogh, Leader, & Trudell, 1978). Three studies conducted in the 1970s to investigate the use of men and women for television voiceovers produced almost the exact same results. Of the voiceovers for hundreds of television commercials analyzed in these studies, researchers reported that more than 93 percent of them used male voices, while only 6 to 7 percent used female voices (Culley & Bennett, 1976; Maracek et al., 1978; O'Donnell & O'Donnell, 1978). Results of a 1986 study conducted by the Screen Actors Guild indicated that women's voiceovers in television commercials have increased by only 2 percent since the 1970s (Kalish, 1988).

More women's voices can be heard as "unseen experts" in today's television ads. Media investigator David Kalish (1988) contends that "advertisers are slowly becoming more flexible in their choice of voice-over artists" (p. 30). Celebrity women with distinguishable voices, like Sally Kellerman, Lauren Bacall, and Kathleen Turner, have begun to do television commercial voiceovers. But an interesting common characteristic of these female voices emerges when you listen closely. The voices are low, deep, and husky, sort of a blend of masculine and feminine. While things are improving in the area of voiceovers, do you think that perhaps society is still at the point where women have to have somewhat masculine-sounding voices to carry credibility as product or service spokespersons?

The Effects of Sexist Advertising on Media Consumers

Results of studies on the effects of sexism in television advertising don't offer much good news for equality advocates. Media scholars Myers and Biocca (1992) investigated the relationship between television advertising/programming and young women's perceptions of their own bodies. What they found was that young women's body images are "elastic," meaning that they "fluctuate in response to media content that focuses on the presentation of the ideal body shape" (p. 108). Even very brief exposure to television images of ideal female bodies caused female subjects to think about the shape of their own bodies and to distort their views of themselves. Feminist media researchers Goldman, Heath, and Smith (1991) describe the harmful effects of stereotypical, idealized images in advertising on female consumers. They contend, "A growing proportion of female viewers have grown antagonistic to the uninterrupted procession of perfect, but unattainable looks that daily confront them. Women don't have to be feminists to feel oppressed by images of perfection and beauty that batter and bruise self-esteem" (p. 335).

Students of all ages explain that they are confused by images in the media; at times they see the consequences of this confusion reflected in their relationships and communication. Men wonder if women want to be treated as equals and professionals, as traditional helpmates and caregivers, or as sex kittens—since the media readily provide continuous, seemingly acceptable images of each. Many women try not to relate to men as though they were "macho" stereotypes. But then they wonder if men actually prefer such treatment, given that macho images of men still pervade many forms of media—from magazine ads depicting rugged cowboys smoking on horseback to television ads with Joe Piscopo pushing vitamin supplements after "pumping up." Women and men are coping with the mixed messages, ultimately making decisions as to what the reality will be for their lives and in their relationships, compared to what they see in mediated form.

One source of confusion is the cover pictures on women's magazines and the contradictory headlines or "teasers" that describe the magazine's contents. Voluptuous female models on the covers of *Cosmopolitan,* in tandem with headlines like "How to Create a Professional Image," send mixed signals to men and women alike. In ads found in newspapers, magazines, and other print sources, the images themselves set up a paradox that is only compounded when one reads the copy accompanying the ad (Jackson, 1991). An example of this is one magazine ad's depiction of a typical day in the life of a professional career woman. She's dressed in a business suit, briefcase in hand, but the copy says that she'd really like to be anywhere but at work; she's on the job, but actually thinking of her man. While the number of advertisements depicting women holding blue- and white-collar jobs has increased over the past decade, research reports that mixed signals still emerge from many of these ads (Sullivan & O'Connor, 1988).

A prime example of mixed-signal advertising can be found in a recent ad for a line of hosiery. The magazine ad depicts a professional woman sitting at her desk in an office. On the floor by her feet are the contents of an empty sack—an opened package of hose and two peaches. The ad draws your eye toward the skirt's hemline above her knees and to her legs. That's understandable, since the ad is for hosiery. However, the copy that accompanies the ad reads: "I went looking for peaches and came back with a pair. This time of the year. . . and he wanted his favorite peach desert, *right!* So off to the market I went. But instead of something mundane, I found something fabulous. [The copy then gives the name of the product and the manufacturer.] These new, shapely, very *silky* pantyhose, right there! And so affordable, I couldn't wait to put them on. And they felt so delicious. To heck with dessert, I made reservations" (Jackson, 1991, p. 2C). The ad sends mixed signals to many people, since the professional woman is depicted in her office, but she is thinking about preparing a man's dessert that evening rather than about her job. While she's a working woman, her thoughts and subsequent actions are relationally motivated. This has emerged as a repeated advertising image of women in the 1990s, one that, by some interpretations, pays lip service to the fact that many women work while insinuating that they are more relationship conscious than professional. This ad is only one example among hundreds that send mixed messages about the sexes.

Another example of mixed-signal advertising can be found in ads for a particular tobacco product that emerged during the heyday of the women's movement. While typically depicting youthful, attractive women doing fun, active things, these ads employ "liberation"-type language and motivation epitomized by the slogan "You've come a long way, baby!" This ad campaign has long been criticized by media scholars as well as feminists, who resent the fact that a tobacco company has virtually ignored women's health issues and has packaged this product as though it epitomized liberation, women's rights, and feminism. People in one state have recently become adamant about tobacco company messages. Kathy Harty, chief of the Minnesota Department of Public Health's smoking prevention program, describes a statewide ad campaign designed to get the message to women that they've been exploited too long by the tobacco industry. One particular television commercial from this organization depicts a billboard model coming to life, only to put her cigarette out on a balding ad executive's head. Harty believes that the ad campaign clearly communicates to women that they can do something about manipulative messages in ads ("Minnesota Ad Campaign," 1992).

Let's explore how some critics reacted to a recent ad produced by this tobacco company. The ad depicted a young, blue-eyed, blonde woman wearing jeans, a black leather motorcycle jacket, and a pink T-shirt with the statement "Sugar and spice and everything nice? Get real!" printed across the chest. One hand is in a pocket and the other is on her waist, holding the infamous cigarette. The copy in the upper left-hand corner reads, "Now's your chance to tell the world just how far you've come." When media educators and advertising experts were asked to assess the sexism in this particular ad, one female critic responded, "Just look at the real mixed messages there. She's got this pink shirt on that suggests innocence, and that's contradicted by the message on the shirt. And the black motorcycle jacket. . . . What is it that we're supposed to be here? Are we supposed to be tough or vulnerable, innocent or passionate?" A male critic responded, "I would think that that's a feminist ad. They're appealing to the modern-day woman. It's a brand oriented toward women." Another female analyst said, "I don't really think that's sexist. A lot of guys wear that color" (Jackson, 1991, pp. 1C 2C). Of these three responses, one critic thought the message was confusing and ambiguous, one thought it was profeminist, and one thought it wasn't sexist. In sum, it appears that mixed signals produce mixed reactions.

We've talked about the effects of sexism in advertising on critical consumers of media. It is possible for advertising to affect one's self-esteem and sex-role identity as well as one's expectations for the opposite sex and one's gender communication in relationships (Bretl & Cantor, 1988; Dambrot, Reep, & Bell, 1988). But what about the possible effects on people who have not yet developed the ability to critically analyze and selectively retain mediated information?

Studies continue to investigate the impact of certain elements in ads that accompany children's television programming. Some of these elements include the numbers of male characters and the roles they enact, the lack of positive female portrayals, and the predominant use of male voiceovers in television commercials. As cultivation theory suggests, these factors have the potential to reinforce for children conventional sex-role definitions, meaning that children may come to believe life is supposed to be like it is portrayed in commercials. Advertising may also influence how children develop an identity for themselves, relative to their own sex and gender, and how they come to expect certain behavior from women and men (Kolbe, 1991; Macklin & Kolbe, 1984; Schwartz & Markham, 1985).

COMMUNICATION ABOUT MEN AND WOMEN VIA TELEVISION PROGRAMMING

Television, as you well know, is a rapidly changing industry. A chicken-or-egg argument continues about whether the media merely reflect what is happening in society or actually create the issues and trends that then become reflected in society. Since there's no accurate way to test this—although media scholars keep trying—perhaps it's a bit of both. For example, one could argue that the economic pressures and changing life-styles of young professionals in the 1980s was captured and reflected in the hit series *thirtysomething*. One could also argue that the innovative, long-running comedy *I Love Lucy* influenced the dynamics of many American marriages. Media scholars supporting the latter view suggest that television programs may actually expand viewers' range of behaviors (Comstock, 1983; Frueh & McGhee, 1975; Larson, 1989). Yet another school of media thought contends that television programming, for the most part, neither reflects nor creates reality; rather, its exaggerated portrayals and overly dramatized situations are nowhere near the realities of most people's lives. In this view, television programs and other forms of media serve purely escapism and entertainment functions for consumers, as uses and gratifications theory suggests (Christ & Medoff, 1984; Rubin, 1986; Rubin, Perse, & Powell, 1985).

Reprinted by permission: Tribune Media Services.

Media expert Joseph Dominick (1993) estimates that, as of 1991, at least one television set was present in 99 percent of American households, with about 65 percent of homes having more than one set. By 1991, some 59 percent of American television viewing households were cable subscribers. Former chair of the Federal Communications Commission Newton Minow (1991) reports that average household television viewing increased from 2 hours per day in 1961 to over 7 hours per day in 1991. When you consider that the latter figure equals about 49 hours of TV watching per week, this activity amounts to more than the average person works (i.e., the 40-hour work week). Another way to examine the pervasiveness of television viewing in our lives is to track increases in the videocassette recorder (VCR) industry. Dominick indicates that by 1991, some 72 percent of American households owned VCRs. The VCR has diffused into American culture faster than any other mass communication technology in the past 25 years (Klopfenstein, Spears, & Ferguson, 1991). Videocassette recording has expanded television's impact by adding convenience to television viewing; consumers can "reschedule" the cable companies and networks by simply recording TV programming and watching the playback whenever convenient. With so much exposure to television programming, it seems reasonable that television's depiction of the sexes has an impact on the viewing audience.

Women and Men in Prime-Time Television Programming

To better understand depictions of the sexes in prime-time television programming, media researcher Marvin Moore (1992) conducted an extensive survey of family depictions in American prime-time television programming during the years 1947 to 1990. Moore analyzed 115 "successful family series," operationally defined as prime-time programs that aired for more than one season (p. 45). Ninety-four percent of these television families were white and two-thirds involved the traditional family profile of a married couple, with or without children.

Of particular interest to our discussion of gender, Moore discovered some trends regarding prime-time depictions of male and female family members. He found that men's roles were "exaggerated, with a large number of male single-parent portrayals and an emphasis on the family roles over work roles" (p. 58). Television sitcoms that exemplify this nontraditional male portrayal include past hit shows such as *The Courtship of Eddie's Father, Family Affair,* and *The Beverly Hillbillies* (Jed Clampett was a single father), and current shows such as *Full House* and *Empty Nest*. However, in *Empty Nest*, the male leading character is portrayed in his pediatric clinic as frequently as in his home. Moore points out that while such portrayals reflect positive roles for men, they may also create false images and distortions of reality. His main criticism of the portrayals of women and men in prime-time television families is this: While television programs have depicted men in nontraditional roles, communicating that men have the freedom to choose different paths for themselves without societal sanctions, women's changing roles in society have been largely ignored.

Moore found that mothers and wives in family series were rarely identified as having occupations. They were predominantly home-centered and supported by their male counterparts in the shows. Moore makes specific reference to *The Cosby Show*'s Claire Huxtable, who was a successful lawyer, but rarely referred to her job and was only occasionally depicted in legal settings. By the decade of the 1980s, the percentage of family profiles in TV shows that included a woman who held a job outside the home had increased considerably. However, many of these working women conducted business from their homes, as in *thirtysomething* and *Murder, She Wrote*. Moore describes this development as "a large change over presentations in earlier decades, but still a long step from the reality of family life in the 1980s" (p. 54).

Other studies of the depiction of contemporary women in prime-time television are concerned specifically with the portrayal of tension between a female character's personal life and her work (Atkin, 1991; Faludi, 1991; Japp, 1991; Vande Berg & Streckfuss, 1992). Media and gender researcher Phyllis Japp argues that working women's professionalism is rarely the focus of plot lines or crises for the characters. The typical emphases for these working women are their relationships with men and the tension created when they juggle work and these relationships. While this tension constitutes a reality for many contemporary women, the personal and relational elements in television characters' lives receive more emphasis, or "air time," than the professional, career-oriented elements. When a female character faces a crisis, the crisis is more often about a relationship, usually with a man, than a situation at work or a decision that involves her career. Japp cites multiple episodes of *Designing Women* as examples, stating that most often the main female characters are depicted sitting in their place of business discussing "clothing, food, relationships with men, and problems with children" rather than work-related, professional issues (p. 62). Japp concludes that "little cultural guidance exists for creating a credible, well-rounded image of a working woman, for such a character is necessarily a composite embodying cultural meanings of 'woman' and 'work,' concepts that have long been on opposite sides in American cultural mythology" (p. 50).

Japp developed four categories of working women's depictions in prime-time television; however, she believes that "none of the four successfully integrated work into woman's life or woman into the workplace" (p. 51). Category 1 is "Working Woman at Home," in which female TV characters have jobs outside the home, but their characters are primarily defined within the home and within their relationships to family members. Examples in this category include Angela, the advertising executive who hires a male housekeeper on *Who's the Boss?* and Claire Huxtable of *The Cosby Show*. Japp contends that these two female characters are given neither the "status of a serious working professional nor the dignity of a skilled homemaker" (p. 61). Thus she concludes that these kinds of depictions portray women as outsiders, in both the home and the workplace.

The sitcom *Designing Women* typifies Japp's second category, "Woman's Workplace in the Home." As in the first category, women are depicted primarily in the home, but the main distinction is that the home is also the workplace.

Again, most of the plots for these kinds of shows center around personal and relational themes, rarely reflecting work-related concerns. Japp argues that these shows dichotomize or widen the gap between women and work, because a plot line involving an actual work-related issue would be seen as contaminating the home environment.

"Displacement of Woman and Workplace: Work on the Run" is Japp's third category, a depiction which serves to separate images of women from their work and which "relocates both women and the workplace, attempting to neutralize the power of place to engender activities" (p. 63). Japp offers as an example the character of Maddie Hayes in *Moonlighting,* who was constantly on the run and often depicted in neutral, nonwork, nonhome settings. Perhaps the character of Maggie O'Connell in *Northern Exposure* matches this category, in that she is a pilot but is rarely depicted in work-related situations.

The final strategy is termed "Woman in the Workplace: Woman Displaced." This strategy is exemplified by *Cheers* and *LA Law,* in which female characters have been significantly integrated into the workplace. But, as Japp points out, "Gender eventually tends to overpower professional identity" (p. 65). Japp provides multiple examples of female characters who demonstrate more interest in their relationships with others, particularly men, than in their work. This trend led her to conclude that "little integration of woman and work is evident. With rare exceptions, television's working woman of the 1980s was a woman who just happened to be a worker rather than the worker who happened to be a woman" (p. 67). While these kinds of television portrayals may match some women's experiences by exposing similar dilemmas of work versus home, Japp points to the need for more positive, realistic portrayals of working women. Such portrayals would involve a variety of jobs, locales, types, and personalities of characters to emphasize women's professional development and contributions, rather than their personal lives.

Similar sentiments emerge from the work of communication researchers Vande Berg and Streckfuss (1992), who surveyed female characters in prime-time television. They concluded that "television continues to present working women as lacking the competitively achieved occupational hierarchical power and status of male workers" and that female characters are defined through "stereotypically domestic, expressive, and socio-emotional roles" (p. 205). One such portrayal can be found in the character of Rebecca in the long-running sitcom *Cheers.* When this character was first introduced as the new manager of the bar Cheers, she was portrayed as a strong, emotionally and socially aloof professional woman. But as episodes progressed, Rebecca was exposed as less than highly regarded by the parent company that purchased the bar and as incapable of sustaining a successful romantic relationship. In one episode, Rebecca can be heard declaring rejuvenated professional interest in the management of Cheers, only to abandon this plan to marry a billionaire. The character developed into someone who could be described as, both professionally and socially, a "wreck."

A television series too new to be included in the research of Moore, Japp, or Vande Berg and Streckfuss represents an interesting example of sex-role portrayal. *Sisters* centers around the lives of four very different sisters; all have feminine names that have been shortened into masculine names. The sisters and their mother are obviously entangled in each others' lives, representing a tight-knit, matriarchal centerpiece for the show. Alex is the well-to-do eldest sister whose main plot lines center around her extravagant tastes in fashion and furnishings, her complex relationship with her daughter and son-in-law, her entanglements with men, and her recovery from breast cancer. Georgie is "everybody's favorite wife and mom"—a part-time realtor who is raising two cherubic sons and whose husband had a nervous breakdown. Teddie is the proverbial "screw-up" sister, the one who constantly copes with alcoholism, a failed marriage, and several career attempts, the most recent one being a fashion designer. Frankie is the "unable-to-have-a-baby" workaholic; she has achieved several promotions at a male-dominated company and is trying to juggle a highly successful job, a problematic marriage to sister Teddie's former husband, and a new baby carried to term for her by sister Georgie.

This dramatic series seems to be one network's attempt at covering all angles of "modern womanhood"—from home-centeredness to a shared focus on home and work. But the one constant in the picture is an emphasis on home and the family relationships to go with it, no matter whose home or how dysfunctional those relationships may be. One perspective suggests that *Sisters* illustrates the complexity and diversity of women's lives. Another interpretation is that it communicates to the viewing public that women's home environs and relationships with men should hold primary importance, that jobs and careers should hold secondary importance. If you have seen this show, do you hold the perspective that it is a fair, current, realistic portrayal of women's complicated lives? Do you think the roles are exaggerated or "on target"?

Are there any depictions of the sexes on television that are breaking new ground? Research argues that a new, softer male character, a "reconstructed male," has emerged in recent television programming (Craig, 1992a, p. 8). However, this characterization is not a consequence of raised gender consciousness but has more to do with the "feminization" of prime time. This is a trend for prime-time programming to reflect the interests of female viewers who have departed from daytime television viewing to enter the work force. As media scholar Stephen Craig (1992a) explains, "The 'enlightened' gender portrayals of prime time are more the result of the economic motivations of the producers, networks, and advertisers to reach (and please) working women rather than any morally-driven social consciousness" (p. 8). No matter the motivation, expanded male depictions are proving popular with male and female viewers alike. Two highly successful sitcoms reliant upon this new trend of male depiction are *Home Improvement* and *Coach*. In both of these shows, the main character is a somewhat macho male, who, through situations and communication with others, often ends up the brunt of the show's joke. This characterization has been termed in research the "playful patriarch" (Traube, 1992). In the highly successful drama *thirtysomething,* the popular character of Gary offered another example of what Craig (1992a) refers to as the "feminized man," in that this character stayed at home full-time to care for his daughter while his wife pursued her career. These characters are neither buffoons nor wimps but are portrayed as likable men who struggle as they learn about themselves, how to communicate with the women in their lives, and how to be better parents.

One could argue that such programs as *Murphy Brown, Reasonable Doubts, Nurses, Dr. Quinn, Medicine Woman, Star Trek: The Next Generation,* and the more recent *Star Trek: Deep Space Nine* (even though the settings for the last three examples are historical and futuristic, respectively) are breaking some new ground for female characterization. While the plots of these shows often focus on the personal, relational lives of women, especially in the example of the presence of Murphy Brown's baby when compared with series in the past, a higher percentage of the action surrounds these female characters' working lives. In both *Star Trek* series, most of the women's roles are high-ranking officers, doctors, security specialists, engineers, scientists, and the like. Media analyst Minh Luong (1992) contends, "*Star Trek: The Next Generation* has broken new ground by introducing women as senior commanding officers, as well as casting women in traditionally male-dominated occupational roles" (p. 1). Interestingly enough, this program with its nontraditional female depiction and "enlightened" treatment of gender issues in occasional episodes has been documented as the number one show on television among 18- to 49-year-old male viewers (Svetkey, 1992). Some of the characters on the hit sitcom *Roseanne* could be seen as groundbreakers. Actors Sandra Bernhardt and Morgan Fairchild portrayed a lesbian couple in a few episodes to conclude one season of the show. The character of Roseanne Connor is a contradiction—a challenge to the social norm of femininity, a struggling, blue-collar worker, and a sarcastic yet devoted wife, mother, and sister (Rowe, 1990). Even though the majority of plot lines for *Roseanne* focus on family relationships and situations, the characters of Roseanne and husband Dan Connor seem to epitomize recession-op-pressed life in America; thus the necessity of work in these characters' lives seems to represent new TV "territory" (Mellencamp, 1992; Probyn, 1990).

Whether one tends to relate more to traditional portrayals or to the ground-breaking characterizations of the sexes, one implication from all of this information is that viewers' communication with relational partners, as well as attitudes about appropriate sex roles and behavior in relationships, may be influenced, in varying degrees, by sitcoms and television dramas. For example, many of our traditionally aged college students reluctantly admit that they watch *Beverly Hills 90210* (jokingly referred to as *Beverly Hills Whine 0210*) and *Melrose Place,* two of the Fox Network's more successful shows. They say that they really don't like these shows, but they watch them every week anyway. For some, following the antics of a pack of Beverly Hills high school kids or California yuppies is definitely escapist activity. For others, it's possible that the interaction and relationships among the characters may affect their expectations, or create some impression of how relationships ought to function and men and women ought to communicate. It's not outlandish to suggest that media—television, espe-cially—affect how people develop their value systems, how they learn sex roles, how they develop expectations for themselves and the opposite sex, and how they communicate to initiate, develop, and even terminate relationships.

The Influence of Social Issues Programming

The label "social issues programming" can be attached to the kind of prime-time informational program that tackles a social or political issue, such as reproductive rights or gays in the military. This type of television offering is nothing new in daytime fare; however, daytime discussions typically occur within an already established format, such as a talk show or local interview program with invited guests or panelists. A rather recent development challenges networks and cable companies to explore social issues not only via the "movie-of-the-week" format, but through extended prime-time evening talk shows, "town hall debates," informative panel discussions and forums, and the like. Of special interest for our purposes are these nonfictional programs that have the potential to inform and instruct the viewing public about gender issues.

One way to get a better understanding of social issues programming is through a recent program that aired on ABC. Anchor Peter Jennings hosted a program entitled *Men, Sex, and Rape,* which featured two panels of experts placed in the middle of a small auditorium—six female experts on one side of the stage, six male experts on the other side. The show's producers even divided the audience seating by sex to further dramatize how women and men tended to hold polarized opinions of the issues to be discussed. The male lineup included such experts as Warren Farrell, author of the book *Why Men Are the Way They Are,* John Leo, columnist for *Time* and other magazines, and well-known Florida attorney F. Lee Bailey. The female panel included such experts as Susan Faludi, author of *Backlash,* Naomi Wolf, author of *The Beauty Myth,* and Catharine MacKinnon, well-known feminist and attorney at the University of Michigan School of Law.

Here's the gist of the 90-minute program. After a brief introduction by Peter Jennings, the program cut to a brief video clip of a scantily clad woman entertaining a room full of men at what looked like a bachelor party. After a commercial break, Jennings asked panelists for their reactions to the tape. Their reactions included an insightful critique of the network's efforts to increase ratings by educating while at the same time titillating the viewing public. The program then continued with panelists' comments about both stranger and acquaintance rape, in terms of what the problems are, how men and women view rape and respond to rape education efforts differently, methods of education and prevention, as well as treatment for victims and rehabilitation efforts for rapists, legal issues, and so on. Exchanges between panelists occasionally turned to banter, as when one of the female panelists responded to Warren Farrell's defensive comments about men with something along the lines of, "You just don't get it, do you?" At several key points in the program, Jennings turned to audience members for prearranged comments on the subject or for personal stories about rape incidents.

Several other social issues programs have aired on various networks and cable channels. Not all these programs involve a panel-moderator-audience comment format as was used in *Men, Sex, and Rape.* Other programs present a host or hosts who introduce the topic and key issues related to it. Then, typically, the issues are exemplified by interviews with people who share their experiences. Here are a few programs of interest to the subject of gender communication:

1. In the late 1980s, a CBS program entitled *Of Macho and Men* dealt with the pressure that expectations about machismo place on men as well as with men's attempts to reform male-discriminatory legislation. This program also gave viewers a look at the men's movement by interviewing Robert Bly and showing footage from all-male gatherings, termed "Wild Man Weekends."

2. In 1990, ABC's *20/20* aired a segment in which cohost Hugh Downs investigated the men's movement. Downs explored the various strains of the movement, highlighting the mythopoeic strain stemming from the work of Robert Bly. Downs also attended a Wild Man Weekend, sharing some footage from the event with the viewing audience.

3. In the fall of 1991, shortly after the Clarence Thomas Senate confirmation hearings, ABC sponsored a Town Hall Debate. These programs are arranged as open forums, encouraging exchange between invited guests or experts and members of the audience. Ted Koppel usually hosts the programs, since the debates air through the vehicle of ABC's *Nightline*. This particular program featured a few of the (braver) senators from the Senate Judiciary Committee, who engaged in lively interaction with a highly critical audience.

4. In 1992, Linda Ellersby and Harry Hamlin cohosted a Lifetime cable program about sexual harassment in the workplace. This program aired less than a year after the Clarence Thomas Senate confirmation hearings.

5. Also in 1992, NBC's *Dateline*, a recent descendant of *20/20* and other network newsmagazines, produced a program on sex bias in educational contexts (the topic of a subsequent chapter in this text). Co-anchor Jane Pauley explored ways in which male and female students receive different treatment within American educational institutions.

Little has been written on the effects of this type of programming; however, two studies conducted to determine viewers' reactions to dramatizations of social issues produced results that are applicable. Mass communication researcher Andrea Press (1991b) conducted a study of working-class and middle-class women's reactions to an episode of the 1980s television drama *Cagney and Lacey* that dealt with abortion. Specifically, Press was interested in whether women's language and their own views about abortion were similar to or different from the language used and views expressed in the episode, as well as how female viewers became involved with the program. The particular episode focused on the concept of justice and reproductive rights. Press's results showed that this emphasis on justice and the language used to discuss it affected viewers, in that they talked more about justice and "principles of right and wrong by which abortion decisions might be evaluated" after viewing the program (p. 430). According to Press, "When the moral language adopted by television differs from that of viewers, television viewing influences viewers to adopt its terms" (p. 438). Press's study indicated that television programming could serve an educational function, if only to cause viewers to talk about an issue in a different way.

Communication researchers Wilson, Linz, Donnerstein, and Stipp (1992) examined the effects of viewing a television movie about acquaintance rape on attitudes about rape. They explored "whether exposure to this movie could serve an educational function by decreasing acceptance of rape myths and/or increasing the belief that date rape is a serious social problem" (p. 181). Overall, the results of the study indicated that the film served an educational function for viewers, with male and female viewers of varying ages (ranging from 18 to around 50) reporting altered perceptions about the problem of date rape after viewing the television movie. Specifically, after watching the program, viewers were less likely to place blame on female victims of date rape, more likely to perceive of women as being coerced into sexual activity, and more concerned about the seriousness of date rape as a societal problem than before viewing the movie.

What effects do social issues programs have on the American viewing public? Research has yet to fully investigate this type of television programming; however, student reactions to the *Men, Sex, and Rape* program offer some initial insights. When discussing this program in some of our classes only a few days after it aired, students indicated that the program educated them further on the topic and that it influenced some of their views. Students in gender communication classes found the setup of "male-female opposing forces" intriguing, as though the network wanted to communicate that men and women are really far apart on the issue of rape. This was mostly viewed as a dramatic effect for ratings purposes rather than a true symbolic representation of how men and

---

What If ?

What if one day you got a call from Ted Koppel, asking you to appear on a special edition of *Nightline* focusing on college-aged persons' views about media influence? Your first reaction would probably be to think that one of your friends was playing a trick on you. But, *what if* the call was real? Your next reaction would probably be to find out how much ABC would be paying you for the nationally televised imparting of your particular wisdom. (Do we know how college students think?!) *What* would you do next, *if* you had a few days to prepare for the show? You'd start thinking about music, maybe a little about video, maybe a little about radio. Then you might start taking inventory of your favorite television shows and movies. You might also think about your least favorite TV commercials. But let's say you stopped your thinking process right there. *What if,* on the program, Ted Koppel asked you, "What is the single most powerful effect that the media have on your life?" Or *what if* Ted asked you, "*What if* you were forced to give up one form of mass media that is currently prevalent in your life?" Which one could you give up? How would you answer Ted's questions? Ted probably won't be calling you any time soon, but it's fun and thought-provoking to imagine yourself in an "expert's" seat—talking intelligently about media.

women stand on the issue. Students indicated that the factual, emotional accounts by rape victims, followed by the panelists' responses, were the key eye-opening moments in the show.

It appears that social issues programming may accomplish the following things:

1. By utilizing an accessible medium—the home television set—these programs bring social issues into a forum that is likely to catch people's attention.
2. They have the potential to educate the public about social issues of increasing importance.
3. They may provide new ways to think about issues; that is, viewers may understand an issue in more depth when a televised source discusses it.
4. They may spark healthy dialogue about an issue after the program has aired. Students indicated that after viewing the ABC program on rape, they had discussions with their roommates, friends, and relational partners or spouses about the program and the problem.

However, these programs also may present only one side of an issue, reflecting biases or concerns of the reporters, the networks or cable companies, or perhaps even the commercial sponsors. Whether producers of social issues programs feel a responsibility to provide evenhanded treatments of issues, whether these programs actually affect people's attitudes and, more important, their behaviors, and the exact extent to which the programs influence women, men, and the communication between them represent provocative research challenges. If social issues programs prompt honest, open dialogue between men and women about issues affecting their lives, then their outcome is positive. Perhaps in the near future social issues programming will be added to a list that includes teachers, classes, and textbooks as vehicles for education about gender communication.

Men, Women, and Daytime Television

Daytime television has its own viewing audience that includes a mix of people—full-time homemakers, teenagers (watching late-afternoon programs), people who work part-time, college students (some of whom arrange their class schedules around their favorite soaps), people who work full-time jobs on shifts that allow them daytime viewing, and others who make use of VCRs to record their favorite programs to watch at leisure. In this section, we briefly discuss two formats of daytime programming—soap operas and talk shows—with special regard for what these programs may communicate *about* women and men.

The Sexes in Daytime Soap Operas

Daytime dramas have been popular television fare for decades. A few researchers have analyzed the functions that soap operas appear to serve in our society, the predominant roles men and women play on soaps, the kind of communication that occurs between characters, and the parallel between soap opera story development and real life (Allen, 1985; Brown, 1989; Carveth & Alexander, 1985; Cassata, Anderson, & Skill, 1980; Rubin, 1985). Before we go further in this discussion, let's address a popular misconception—that soap operas are watched exclusively by women. Daytime television programming has been, and still is to a great extent, targeted to the needs and emotional realities of women. This is understandable, given the statistic that over 67 percent of daytime viewers are women (1988 Nielsen Television Index, reported in Papazian, 1990). However, the stereotype that soap operas are viewed only by women is wholly inaccurate. A study of the viewing behaviors of college students revealed an audience that was predominantly female, yet it included a surprising number of faithful, male soap opera viewers (Lemish, 1985). Some of our male college students also reveal, albeit somewhat reluctantly, that they are regular watchers of particular soaps.

Gender and media expert Marlene Fine's (1981) research continues to affect subsequent efforts to understand the effects of soap opera viewing on media consumers. Fine investigated the kinds of relationships as well as the interactions that take place within relationships that are regularly portrayed on daytime soap operas. Because the settings for most soaps are small, incestuous communities, the "multiple layers of relationships" become difficult to untangle and analyze (p. 99). However, Fine developed an effective coding scheme to isolate five types of depicted relationships: family, friends, romantic, professionals, and strangers. Upon examining the regularities in the depictions of female and male characters, Fine discovered that women were most often portrayed in family settings, men and women were most often portrayed in romantic heterosexual relationships (no portrayals of romantic homosexual relationships existed at the time), and men were primarily depicted in professional settings. Fine concluded: "The general picture of soap opera relationships is one in which male-male relationships are professionally defined and female-female relationships are interpersonally defined. Men venture into the realm of intimate relationships almost solely through their encounters with women, and then generally through romantic involvements" (p. 101).

Fine determined that over 20 percent of the female-female and the male-female conversations in soap operas concerned romance, while only 3 percent of all male-male conversations focused on romance. In Chapters 5 and 6 we discuss how this pattern appears to be replicated in real-life approaches to communication by the sexes, as well as in the topics of discussion typically emerging in women's and men's conversations. However, another finding showed that the "dream world" of the soap opera depicts women and men involved in intimate attachments and revealing their most intimate feelings to each other. Fine contends that this does not mirror real life, in which traditional sex roles separate men and women and quite often intimate thoughts and feelings are expressed to same-sex friends rather than to a romantic relational partner.

How directly does soap opera viewing affect a person's life? Media researcher Ronald Compesi's (1980) subjects revealed that they used soap operas to help them solve real-life problems, just as they might consult an advice columnist. In another study which used cultivation theory as its base, consistent consumers of soap opera programming believed that there were more doctors, lawyers, and businessmen in the real world and that extramarital affairs, illegitimate children, divorces, and serious operations were more prevalent occurrences in real life than was actually the case (Buerkel-Rothfuss & Mayes, 1981). This led these communication researchers to conclude: "There appears to be an important relationship between what a person watches on daytime serials and what he or she believes to be true about those aspects of the 'real world' which tend to be portrayed with exaggerated frequency on soap operas" (p. 114).

Not only does soap opera viewing affect one's perceptions of reality, viewers may be prone to take cues from various forms of television programming about what to expect from members of the opposite sex as well as how to communicate with them. In *Television Culture* media scholar John Fiske discusses the contradiction between the depiction of male characters in soap operas and reality as follows:

> Women's view of masculinity, as evidenced in soap operas, differs markedly from that produced from the masculine audience. The "good" male in the daytime soaps is caring, nurturing, and verbal. He is prone to making comments like "I don't care about material wealth or professional success, all I care about is us and our relationship." He will talk about feelings and people and rarely express his masculinity in direct action. Of course, he is still decisive, he still has masculine power, but that power is given a "feminine" inflection. (1987, p. 186)

This kind of depiction, Fiske suggests, is offered to please the primarily female audience of the daytime soap opera; thus the soap opera man could be considered an economically derived creation. The problem then becomes one of separating reality from fantasy. If a woman expects all men to behave and communicate like male characters on soaps, it's fairly safe to say that she will likely encounter some disillusion in her life. While this may sound like an exaggeration or overstatement—the notion that someone would be so foolish as to assume that people will behave like television or movie characters—it's not all that outlandish. Probably more times than we'd like to believe, people compare their experiences and relationships to dramatic versions, often to become disillusioned when their own lives don't measure up.

Soap opera portrayals also have the potential to affect how people form expectations about sexual behavior (Cantor, 1987; Greenberg & D'Alessio, 1985). Several studies have found that sexual activity depicted on television has not decreased and that it seems to be a predominant activity for unmarried partners and within extramarital affairs. Even given the rising societal concern about contraception, AIDS, and other sexually transmitted diseases, discussions or actions in the plot lines that show a concern for (or even an awareness of) these issues are almost nonexistent in both daytime and prime-time serials (Lowry, 1989; Sapolsky & Tabarlet, 1991; Schrag, 1990). In attempts to caution or educate the public, a 1986 full-page newspaper ad purchased by the Planned Parenthood

Federation of America displayed the headline "They did it 9,000 times on television last year." The ad copy warned against viewing sex from a "Don't worry; be happy" mentality, one that stresses enjoyment without responsibility, pleasure without consequences. Do you think that television programs have a responsibility to educate the public or to depict characters acting responsibly on a variety of social issues? Or do you think that the public receives education in other forums, leaving television programming to provide an "escapist" function?

Daytime Talk Shows

From *Oprah* to *Donahue* to *Geraldo* to *Sally Jesse Raphael*—what do daytime talk shows communicate to modern women and men? Do these shows "teach" women and men how they are supposed to talk to each other? Do these talk shows set an agenda for the viewing public?

Feminist media critic Roseann Mandziuk (1991) addresses some of these concerns when she describes the daytime talk show as a "pervasive presence, a highly rated type of program, and a very competitive and profitable property for television syndication" (p. 1). While many daytime talk show hosts, guests, audience members, and home viewers are men, Mandziuk argues that "daytime television is the exclusive province of women viewers" (p. 5), creating a parallel in daytime-prime time and female-male dichotomies. Mandziuk contends that talk shows seriously delimit gender boundaries for several reasons: their informational nature; their authenticity or realness, leading to judgments of authority; their "hyper-intimacy" (p. 10); their lack of closure; and their agenda-setting ability.

Mandziuk contrasts the *informational nature* of soap operas with that of daytime talk shows. Soaps and TV ads offer viewers "a subtle form of instruction, cloaked in the guise of fiction" (p. 11). However, the talk show's informative, factual nature carries persuasive power. Since talk show hosts, guests, and audience members are real people discussing real problems, these shows embody a unique kind of *authenticity* and *authority*. The *intimate* nature of talk show programs also corresponds with the cultural stereotype that women are supposed to be sensitive, nurturing, and responsive. This intimacy is exemplified by host-guest-audience relationships, by the camera closeups of tearful guests who are commended for their brave, emotional displays while recounting personal narratives on national television, by the accessibility phone callers have to the shows, and by the occasional personal disclosure or reaction of the host. The talk show format also reinforces women's existence, thus "genderizing" this programming, according to Mandziuk. The spontaneity of discussion limited by interruptive commercial breaks mirrors the realities of women's multitask existence. And the fact that there's never enough *time* to give full treatment to any issue sends a message to women that "conversation is never finished" and that "there is always more to be learned, always another talk show to seek out for information on another day" (p. 13). The genderized aspects of daytime talk shows can be viewed as a comfortable "fit" between the realities of women's lives and the television programming they prefer. According to Mandziuk, the drawback to becoming too comfortable with this fit relates to an agenda-setting function that these programs can serve.

Mandziuk contends that daytime talk shows may actually be instructing women as to what they should worry about; in other words, the programs may serve an *agenda-setting* function. While some talk show topics may be deemed outlandish or trivial, such as a problem with a husband who likes to dress in women's lingerie or a girl who flirts with her sister's boyfriend, other topics may make some women wonder if they're *supposed* to be worried about these issues. A greater problem ensues when the larger, general public "ghettoizes" important issues, such as reproductive rights, sexual harassment, and child care, by labeling them "women's issues" rather than societal or human issues. As Mandziuk contends, "Precisely because they are talked about in the context of women's programming, issues which demand political solutions become personalized and hence are easily dismissed from being worthy of serious consideration as part of any public policy agenda" (p. 19).

Have you ever considered the instructive potential of daytime talk shows? Perhaps you recall talking about particular shows in your college classes or in conversations with friends, dates, or your spouse. Have your sex-role attitudes or knowledge of gender issues been influenced by one of these talk shows? The power of talk shows like *Oprah* and *Donahue* is just beginning to be explored in research. The more we know about this informative function of television programming, the more we can understand its effects on gender communication and on expectations the sexes form about each other.

GENDER-BENDING IN THE MOVIES

According to film scholar Thomas Doherty (1988), "American motion pictures today are not a mass medium" (p. 1). He contends that the film industry caters to one audience—teenagers. This may be accurate if you think of the film industry in terms of going to movie theaters to view films. But when you consider how much wider the market and corresponding audience is for film nowadays, with videotape rentals, pay-per-view services, and cable companies showing first-run movies within short times of their initial theatrical releases, then the argument could be made that film is much more of a "mass" medium than it used to be.

For our discussion in this section, we focus on a phenomenon in film that has stirred up a great deal of talk and controversy; not surprisingly, that phenomenon has to do with gender. Before we begin, we ask you to think about something: Have you seen any movies that have affected how you interact with the opposite sex? Was there a memorable movie that changed your views about women's and men's roles, or that changed one of your relationships?

For your textbook authors, one such movie was *Tootsie*, a movie that to this day conjures up confused but pleasant thoughts about sex roles. If you haven't seen this movie, here's a brief synopsis of the plot. Dustin Hoffman plays Michael, an actor who desperately wants work, but whose opportunities are limited because of his reputation as being difficult. When his agent tells Michael that no one will hire him, Michael sets out to prove him wrong by auditioning for a role on a popular soap opera. The twist is that the role is for a woman, so Michael auditions "in drag," as an actress named Dorothy Michaels. After landing the part, Michael encounters a number of sticky situations because of his hidden identity. The stickiest situation arises when Michael realizes that he's falling for Julie, another actress on the soap, played in the movie by Jessica Lange. As Michael/Dorothy and Julie become good friends, he is confronted with a problem: How can Michael admit the deception and still maintain his closeness with Julie?

One amazing aspect of this movie is how Dustin Hoffman's portrayal of Dorothy, through the character of Michael, became real to viewers. It became so real that when Michael revealed his true identity in one of the final scenes, audiences felt saddened because they were going to miss Dorothy. Another intriguing aspect of this movie was that it fulfilled a fantasy many people hold—to be able to walk in the opposite sex's shoes, see how they are treated, and to get to know an attractive member of the opposite sex without the hangups and pressures that often accompany romantic relationships. The possibility of taking one's newfound insight into the opposite sex and putting it to work in a relationship captivated viewers. As the character Michael so aptly summed up in one of his last lines of dialogue with Julie, "I was a better man with you as a woman than I ever was as a man. I've just got to learn to do it without the dress."

The film *Tootsie* frames the rest of our discussion nicely, because it exemplifies a theme or phenomenon in film that we alluded to at the beginning of this section. This theme is *gender-bending,* a term used specifically to refer to media depictions in which characters' actions belie or contradict what is expected of their sex. In other words, characters display attitudes and behaviors more stereotypically connected with the opposite sex. Given this description of gender-bending, are you thinking of a recent movie that epitomizes the concept? If you're thinking of *Thelma & Louise,* you're on the right track.

Thelma & Louise was a groundbreaking gender-bending film on many counts. It was an open-road, "buddy" film, but with female buddies on the road instead of male buddies (Glenn, 1992; Kroll, 1991; Perren, 1993). It depicted women doing "outlandish" things, behavior generally deemed more acceptable for men (especially male film characters) than women. One of the most laudable effects of this film was that it sparked a great deal of discussion. After it opened, not only were moviegoers talking about it, but film critics were having a field day. Reactions included comments like, "It told the downright truth," "It was like seeing my life played before my eyes," and "[It was] a butt-kicking feminist manifesto" (Schickel, 1991, p. 52). Positive and negative reactions to the movie came from women and men alike, although it's still debatable whether this film was meant by its creators to provoke such strong reactions from its audience. Whatever your viewpoint on *Thelma & Louise,* if you've seen the film, you probably *have* a viewpoint. We expect that few people came out of the theater saying, "What a cute, fun little movie!"

While violent images appeared in this film, critics maintain that they were nowhere near the level of violence depicted in such films as *Terminator 2, Robocop,* and *Total Recall,* a movie in which, as he shoots a woman in the head, Arnold Schwarzenegger says, "Consider that a divorce" (Schickel, 1991, p. 56). In *Thelma & Louise,* one person gets murdered and one store gets robbed. The film's violence sparked reaction not only because women were being violent, but because the targets of their violence were men. A film scholar at Berkeley, Carol Clover, contends that *Thelma & Louise* probed some deep, mysterious issues by examining "the distance between men and women, the desire for each sex to separate itself" (Clover, cited in Schickel, 1991, p. 56).

Besides the dominant images and "radical" behaviors of the main female characters, male characters in *Thelma & Louise* were portrayed in an atypical fashion for the movies. Well-known feminist Marilyn French, author of *The Woman's Room* (1977) and *The War Against Women* (1992), explains: "Most male characters in this film are unexceptional—a selfish, contemptuous husband, an uncommitted lover, a predatory rapist, a predatory truck driver. Two are unlikely—a sexy thief and a sympathetic police officer. All the men exploit the female heroes in some way" (p. 173). However, some responses to the film included claims of male-bashing, based on contentions that men were characterized in unrealistic, exaggerated portrayals and were repeatedly vanquished by the two women. One critic from the New York *Daily News* contended that the movie justified violence, crime, and drunken driving and was "degrading to men, with pathetic stereotypes of testosterone-crazed behavior" (Johnson, cited in Schickel, 1991, p. 52). Film researcher Robert Glenn (1992) suggests, "Feminists have perpetuated a behavioral definition of sexism that has been fictionalized and lampooned for more than a decade in films and television. *Thelma & Louise* effectively reconstructs these identifiable caricatures in order to paint an extremely unflattering portrait of men as insensitive and ignorant savages who treat women as functional objects to be used and manipulated" (p. 12). From this viewpoint, the caricatures or overdrawn images of men in the film were created in efforts to further highlight the victimization of the two female characters. A viewer may not have found these characterizations flattering or realistic, but the presence of these characters drove home the point behind screenwriter Callie Khouri's script (Rohter, 1991).

How can one of the questions this chapter explores—"What do the media communicate about the sexes?"—be answered regarding *Thelma & Louise*? What messages about women and men did audiences get from this movie? Some people view such scenes as the police officer being locked in the trunk of his patrol car or the trucker's rig being blown up as indications that women are winning some kind of war against male oppression, that they are retaliating against unacceptable male behavior in like fashion. However, while believing that the movie made a significant statement about relationships between men and women in the 1990s, some film critics and feminist scholars contend that *Thelma & Louise* was not a cinematic triumph for women's rights. They assert that the film depicts the desperation of women in modern times—women who counter the powerlessness they feel with some very isolated, extreme actions, but who, in the long run, are still out of power in a patriarchal system (Klawans,

1991; Leo, 1991; Shapiro, 1991). This theme is epitomized by the ending (which we won't give away for those readers who have yet to see the film).

If you have seen *Thelma & Louise,* what's your opinion of the gender-bending in the movie? When the female characters enacted stereotypical male behaviors, did you react differently than you react to male characters who act this way? Do the kinds of male-female relationships depicted in movies like *Thelma & Louise* match your personal reality? Is it your opinion that some of the male characters, such as the obnoxious truck driver or whimpering highway patrol officer, were exaggerated and stereotypical? What did the film convey to you about women's status in society?

Other movies with strong central female characters include *Jurassic Park, What's Love Got To Do With It?, A Few Good Men, Sister Act, Sleeping with the Enemy, Silence of the Lambs, V. I. Warshawski, Aliens, This Is My Life, Mortal Thoughts, Fried Green Tomatoes, A League of Their Own,* and *Lost in Yonkers* (Corliss, 1993; Glenn, 1992; Hocker Rushing, 1989). Can you think of some gender-bending movies that depict men in nonstereotypical roles? The early 1980s movie *Kramer vs. Kramer* is an example of a gender-bending film, in that the main male character is a father raising his son after his wife leaves the family. The father eventually has to fight for custody of his son upon the mother's return. He even gets fired because of time spent away from his job to tend to his young son. It's interesting that this is another movie that stars Dustin Hoffman, and again Hoffman's character expands what might be traditionally thought of as the male or husband role. Such movies as *Dad, Mr. Mom, Three Men and a Baby,* its sequel *Three Men and a Little Lady, Look Who's Talking,* its sequel *Look Who's Talking Too,* and *The Crying Game* are other examples of male gender-bending movies. Have these films, or others you might think of, expanded men's range of options in dramatic ways similar to what critics contend *Thelma & Louise* did for women?

History documents the power of the media to sweep change through a culture. Will *Thelma & Louise* and other gender-bending movies that are bound to explore these issues further make a significant impact on the decade of the 1990s? Predictions are tricky, but movies like *Thelma & Louise* challenge us to think further and deeper, and in ways that may be new to us. They challenge us to take inventory of our attitudes and expectations about women and men. They ask us to reconsider how we communicate with one another and how we derive pleasure out of our relationships.

THE POWER OF MUSIC TO INFLUENCE THE SEXES

On the June 29, 1992, cover of *Newsweek,* the angry face and pointing finger of a female rap artist appeared next to the caption: "Rap and Race: Beyond Sister Souljah—The New Politics of Pop Music." What prompted this kind of media exposure was the criticism Bill Clinton leveled at Sister Souljah at a Rainbow Coalition Leadership Summit held prior to the 1992 presidential election. Coming on the heels of the Los Angeles riots, the rap artist was quoted in the

Washington Post as saying, "If black people kill black people every day, why not take a week and kill white people?" (Sister Souljah, cited in Leland, 1992, p. 47). Clinton's response was, in effect, that one could reverse the terms "black" and "white" in Souljah's remark and assume that the quote came from a racist.

We recount this incident to illustrate just how powerful a force popular music has become in our culture and how pervasive its influence can be throughout your existence. You're probably acutely aware of the importance of music in your life, but we're going to consider the subtle, sometimes insidious effects that the portrayals of women and men in popular song lyrics and music videos may have on your self-identity as a man or woman, your gender communication, and your relationships with other people.

Sometimes when you listen to a song, you want to concentrate on the lyrics. You attend to the words from a more critical standpoint in this instance. But other times you simply like the rhythm, beat, and musical performance of the song, and so you tune out the lyrics. Have you ever read the lyrics to a particular song and said to yourself, "Oh, *that's* what they're saying"? What we're getting at here is that there are just about as many ways to process music as there are people who listen to it. But have you considered the possibility that music, specifically song lyrics depicting the sexes, may have more impact on you than you may realize?

In an article about how music listeners learn from song lyrics, mass communication researcher Roger Jon Desmond (1987) offers a few assumptions about the nature of lyrics. Lyrics are often redundant within songs, so that they form a "hook," or memorable strain, that runs through the listener's mind long after the song has played. (We all know that once we get hooked by a certain refrain of a song, it's really hard to get unhooked.) Given how many times songs are repeated in a typical radio day, listeners are likely to have lyrics reinforced in their memories. And, finally, lyrics can be compared to poetry, in that they are often symbolic and "not easily accessible to a casual listener" (p. 277).

Desmond then goes on to formulate an argument that song lyrics are generally not attended to by music listeners and that very little meaning is extracted from lyrics when they *are* attended to. He supports this argument by citing studies in which adolescent subjects reported attending most often to the beat of a song and least often to lyrics. He closes his essay with this suggestion: "While we may conclude that there is not much evidence for specific learning from lyrics, there may be an affirmative answer to questions about the pervasiveness of style in dress, image, and talk about lyrics among adolescent listeners" (p. 283).

There is merit in some of Desmond's conclusions; however, the methods used in the studies Desmond cites merely address the notion of media effect on a conscious, intentional level. For example, in most of these studies subjects were asked a range of questions regarding their opinions or attitudes about the importance of song lyrics. Asking for an opinion is quite different from measuring an actual effect; measuring an actual effect is a challenging methodological task.

Communication scholars Susan Butruille and Anita Taylor (1987) researched the portrayal of women in American popular music, primarily to detect sex-role stereotypes in lyrics. They found "three recurring images of women: The Ideal Woman/Madonna/Saint, the evil or fickle Witch/Sinner/Whore, and the victim (often dead)" (p. 180). Some of these images date back to early religious customs and beliefs about the sinful versus the virginal nature of woman. However, Butruille and Taylor concluded, "The images of women in popular American songs historically reflected the stereotypes created and perpetuated by masculine values in a male-dominated society. The images have continued through the twentieth century and into the present day. A number of researchers have confirmed the continuation of the three images" (p. 182).

Another study of the images of men and women in song lyrics was conducted by media researchers Freudiger and Almquist (1978). Although this study was done in the 1970s, it continues to offer insights into sex-role depictions in the song lyrics of three genres of popular music. These researchers viewed song lyrics as agents of socialization. They were mostly interested in determining what sex-role stereotypes would emerge from an examination of one year's worth of the top fifty hits on the *Billboard* country, soul, and easy listening charts. In a nutshell, Freudiger and Almquist found that women were more the focus of song lyrics across all three musical genres than men, and that they were most often positively portrayed with a stereotypical trait of supportiveness. In contrast, when men were mentioned in lyrics, their portrayals were more negative than positive, especially in country lyrics. Men's depictions in lyrics conformed more to a stereotype involving aggression, consistency, action, and confidence than women's depictions conformed to female stereotypes.

Popular culture researchers Harding and Nett (1984) contended that rock music provided the most derogatory, sexist images of women among all forms of popular music. However, recent opinion on this issue holds that rap music has overtaken rock as the most misogynistic form of music, in that rap often imposes old-fashioned attitudes on its lyrics (Leland, 1992). While current rap and hip-hop artists, such as Public Enemy, Ice Cube, Ice-T, and the adolescent group Kris Kross, are choosing to focus on racial and political issues and are attempting to show more positive images of relationships in their music, other rap artists have been notorious for their depictions of women as virtual sex slaves to men. Some of the lyrics by 2 Live Crew and N.W.A. (Niggaz With Attitude) depicting men as brutal terrorizers and users of women communicate skewed, nonrepresentative images that do nothing to improve relationships between the sexes.

While we can agree with the finding that listeners more readily attend to a song's beat than its lyrics—since students tell us the same thing—we can't help but wonder about subtle, less conscious effects of some messages within song lyrics, and how to measure those effects. Have you ever found yourself humming a tune or singing along with a song on the radio or on a favorite cassette tape, when you suddenly realize what the words really *are*? You may become acutely aware that what you're singing with or listening to isn't something you'd like to repeat in *any* company, especially mixed company.

Students in our gender communication classes complete a media assignment in which, first, they select from any form of mass media an example of gender depiction that they find interesting. Then they make a brief oral presentation about the example to the class. Finally, they write a short paper on the topic of gender depiction in media. Invariably, several students out of each class choose song lyrics to play for the class and analyze for the assignment. What is most interesting is when students select cuts from their own music collections—cuts that they didn't realize were sexist, stereotypical, and/or degrading until they worked on this class assignment.

For example, in recent semesters students have selected such songs as 2 Live Crew's "S & M" (sadism and masochism), Motley Crue's "Same Ole Situation," "Stone Cold Bush" by the Red Hot Chili Peppers, "Dopeman" by N.W.A. (Niggaz With Attitude), Bell Biv Devoe's "Do Me," and "Quickie" by Full Force. If you listen to any of these tunes, you might be surprised, even appalled, at the language and brutal imagery conveyed through the lyrics. Or maybe you won't have this reaction, because you believe that song lyrics get "tuned out" and thus have no real effect. Many times, students explain that they generally listen to a particular tape or CD without ever attending to what the lyrics convey. When they are *forced* to critically listen to the words, they often become quite serious and concerned about the effects of such messages on noncritical consumers. If they consider themselves critical consumers of mass media and even *they* don't consciously process the messages in the lyrics, then they begin to worry about the effects of such material on noncritical minds, that is, adolescents and children. Do you think that song lyrics should be taken seriously? Do you think it's possible to simply enjoy the music and the beat, without being affected by the message behind the music? Do you think sex-role attitudes and gender communication can actually be shaped or affected by the messages contained in song lyrics?

Sex Kittens and He-Men in Music Videos

What happens when negative messages of song lyrics become reinforced with visual images in music videos? As one researcher put it, "Music videos are more than a fad, more than fodder for spare hours and dollars of young consumers. They are pioneers in video expression, and the results of their reshaping of the form extend far beyond the TV set" (Aufderheide, 1986, p. 57). Since MTV aired in 1981 and quickly infiltrated approximately 22 million American households, the music video industry has skyrocketed (Sherman & Dominick, 1986). So have profits in the music industry—an industry that wasn't foundering, but that wasn't booming either, prior to the innovation of music video. Nowadays, the music video industry has sparked so much attention and has become such a vehicle for boosting recording sales, popular music artists reveal that they feel compelled to create and market videos to accompany their songs.

Several studies have been conducted to determine the extent of sex-role stereotyping in music videos (Peterson, 1987; Seidman, 1992; Sherman &

Dominick, 1986). Music video researcher Richard Vincent (1989) found that women are depicted in music videos predominantly as decorations and sex objects and that female artists were highly likely to portray themselves and other women in their videos in seductive clothing, with Tina Turner and Madonna heading up this list. Media specialists Brown and Campbell (1986) compared portrayals of black and white women and men in music videos airing on both MTV and *Video Soul,* a music video program broadcast by the Black Entertainment Television cable channel. Results of the study were interpreted as "subtle indications of persistent stereotypes of women as less active, less goal-directed, and less worthy of attention" (p. 101). The finding that women of both races were portrayed in professional settings significantly less often than both races of men has been corroborated by recent research (Seidman, 1992). White females were more often depicted as trying to gain the attention of a man who ignores them or in solitary activity, such as walking alone or riding in a car alone. Black women were more likely to be shown dancing, singing, or playing a musical instrument. Brown and Campbell conclude from their results, "White men, primarily by virtue of their greater numbers, are the center of attention and power and are more often aggressive and hostile than helpful and cooperative. Women and black people are rarely important enough to be a part of the foreground" (p. 104). Similar results were produced in a study by media researchers Sherman and Dominick (1986), who concluded, "Music television is a predominantly white and male world. Men outnumber women by two to one" (p. 84).

One can hardly discuss the topic of sex-role depiction and music video without exploring Madonna's impact on this area. While she remains a controversial figure, scholars and critics alike recognize her gender-bending efforts and significant impact on the recording and music video industries (Ayres, 1990; Brubach, 1985; Pareles, 1990). Communication researcher Madeline Keaveney (1991) contends that "Madonna has progressively blurred gender boundaries and strained gender conventions by challenging taboos and stereotypes that have restricted and sometimes oppressed women" (p. 1). Keaveney explored how Madonna expressed her opposition to traditional female sex roles and behavior via her music videos spanning the years 1984 through the controversial "Justify My Love" video in 1990. Most of Madonna's videos have been of the storytelling or concept variety, as opposed to performance videos. In these videos, Madonna has depicted independent, liberated, and sexually unconventional characters and "has pushed back the boundaries of what is considered appropriate feminine behavior" (Keaveney, 1991, p. 14).

However, Madonna critics suggest that her blatant sexuality, especially via music video portrayals and live performances, actually impedes the feminist crusade for equality (Sawyer, 1990). Questions surround the viability of female sexuality as a symbol of liberation and independence. Concern also exists over the messages that young viewers receive from Madonna's videos. Communication researchers Brown and Schultz (1990) investigated gender and race differences in how college students perceived two Madonna videos, "Papa Don't Preach" and "Open Your Heart." The results most germane to this discussion revealed that female and male subjects differed in their perceptions of Madonna and of the relationship depicted in the "Open Your Heart" video. First, unlike female students, male students conceived of Madonna as primarily a sex object, describing her by using language about her body and sexuality. Second, female students perceived a platonic relationship between Madonna and the young boy in the video, whereas male students perceived a sexual relationship. What's your opinion? Do you think that Madonna's music, performances, and videos embody feminist ideals or actually contradict them?

Concerning depictions of violence against the sexes in music videos, Sherman and Dominick (1986) found that close to 60 percent of the concept videos (as opposed to performance videos) contained violent episodes, mostly involving men as aggressors and also as victims. In this study, male characters were three times as likely as female characters to get hurt or killed in the music video. Another study of aggression in music video produced similar results (Kalis & Neuendorf, 1989). Thus it may be a misperception that women are almost always depicted in music videos as sex objects who alone suffer the violent outbursts of men.

Do music videos have an impact beyond that of song lyrics? As Desmond (1987) points out, "Music videos, with their capacity for both verbal and visual coding, and their tendency to dramatize the themes of lyrics, do add a potential for learning and arousal beyond the realm of music lyrics" (p. 282). While disagreement exists as to the exact added effects of visual images produced by music videos, there is considerable agreement that the combined visual and auditory channels have profound effects on memory and recall. And for some, this is a real concern when the lyrics and accompanying video images are sexist, racist, violent, and otherwise disturbing.

Music video is a pervasive medium, particularly in the lives of high school and traditionally aged college students. However, it is not as pervasive or intrusive into your day as music that you hear on the radio as you're driving to class or to work or that you turn on instantly when you walk in the door of your dorm room or home. Turning on the television and tuning in to music videos implies more conscious choice and more action than merely listening to background music. But think for a moment about the whole effect—the effect of combining visual images with musical sound, a beat, and lyrics. It is potentially a very powerful effect. Whether or not you actually watch every second of the average 3-minute music video or really attend to the lyrics in a song, you still receive the message. Somewhere your brain is processing the information, sometimes on a conscious level, most times on a subconscious level.

Do you think that taking in so many stereotypical, often sexist messages on both conscious and subconscious levels has some kind of effect on you? What do *you* think the effect is? Could music be a catalyst to people's actions? Think about how the music you listen to and watch in the form of music videos may affect your view of self, your attitudes about sex roles in society, the expectations you form especially of the opposite sex, and your gender communication within relationships.

CONCLUSION

You may not feel you have reached media expert status, but we suspect that you know more about the forms of media that surround you every day than you did before you read this chapter. When you think about the many media outlets and methods that have the potential to influence you, it's almost overwhelming. But rather than feeling overwhelmed by media influence, your knowledge can empower you to better understand the effects of media messages about the sexes. We hope that you not only have an increased knowledge about mass communication, but that you are able to more critically assess the role media play in your life. That critical assessment enables you to make thoughtful choices about just how much you will allow the media to affect you.

Think about whether you have some standards for romantic relationships between women and men, for example, and where those standards came from. Do your expectations reflect romance as portrayed in movies or between characters on television? When you think about communication between marital partners, do you think about your parents, your married friends, or married characters on soap operas or prime-time television shows? When you're feeling down, are there certain songs and musical artists that either help you feel your pain more fully or help raise your spirits? Have you ever watched TV characters go through some trauma, such as the death of a loved one, an angry exchange between friends, or the breakup of an important relationship, and then later used their reactions for experiences in your own life events? We encourage you to take more opportunities to consciously decipher media influence, particularly in reference to gender communication. The more you understand what's influencing you, the more ready you'll be to dive into new relationships or to strengthen your existing ones. That's where you're headed with your reading— into the adventures and perils of women and men in relationships.

Key Terms

mass communication
mediated communication
gatekeeper
critical consumption
hypodermic needle theory
direct-effects theory
uses and gratifications
  theory

agenda-setting theory
cultivation theory
voiceovers
mixed media messages
prime-time television
social issues programming
daytime television
soap operas

talk shows
ghettoization
gender-bending
song lyrics
hooks
music videos

Discussion Starters

1. On a piece of paper, list all forms of mass media we provided for you early in this chapter. Then rank order these media, with a 1 ranking indicating the form of media you use the most, 2 indicating the second most used form of media, and so on. After you've ranked the items on the list, review your ranks. You should have a fairly accurate profile of yourself as a media consumer. Do any of the ranks surprise you?

Is there a form of media that you believe you consume too much at present? Which one(s) and why?

2. When your favorite magazine arrives at your door, or when you decide to buy the newest edition of it at the store, don't plunge into it right away. Try an exercise first. Thumb through the magazine, paying special attention to the advertisements. How many ads depict members of your same sex? How many depict members of the opposite sex? Can you detect any trends or patterns regarding the ads in this magazine?

3. After doing question 2, select one ad in particular from the magazine—an ad that you think is the most provocative one in the entire issue. Take the ad and analyze it using the system we provided in this chapter. Do you see the ad in a different light after having analyzed it in this manner? What does the ad communicate about the sexes?

4. What's your favorite prime-time television show? Think of several reasons why this show is your favorite. Do your reasons have more to do with the characters, the setting and/or scenery, the plot lines, or something else? Now think about a prime-time television show that you watched and just hated. What was so irritating about that show? Are there any gender issues affecting your decision about most and least favorite TV shows?

5. After having read the section in this chapter about daytime talk shows, try to watch one or record one on videotape. If you don't have the necessary equipment, ask a friend to record a talk show for you. What's the particular issue being discussed on the talk show? Is the host of the talk show a man or a woman? Do you think the sex of the host makes a difference? Would an opposite-sex host have put a different spin on the topic of the particular show you watched? If so, why?

6. Assess your music collection. Whom do you listen to—predominantly artists of the same sex as you or of the opposite sex? If there's a pattern, why do you think the pattern exists? Then pick one album, CD, or cassette tape and play the cut that you are the least familiar with. Listen carefully and try to take in every word of the song lyric. Did you hear anything for the first time? Did you realize that this song was actually on this tape?

7. Think about the most sexist music video you've ever seen. What makes this video memorable to you? Was it sexist toward men, toward women, or both? How was the sexism conveyed in the video? Who was the artist in the video? What do you think the connection is between the artist and the sexism inherent in that artist's video?

References

ALLEN, R. C. (1985). *Speaking of soap operas*. Chapel Hill: University of North Carolina Press.

ATKIN, D. (1991). Sex in primetime television: 1979 versus 1989. *Journal of Broadcasting and Electronic Media, 35*, 517–523.

AUFDERHEIDE, P. (1986). Music videos: The look of sound. *Journal of Communication, 36*, 57–77.

AYRES, A. (1990, May 19). TV's in-vogue video vamp. *TV Guide*, pp. 20–22.

BARTOS, R. (1983). Women and advertising. *International Journal of Advertising, 2*, 33–45.

BITTNER, J. R. (1989). *Mass communication: An introduction* (5th ed.). Englewood Cliffs, NJ: Prentice-Hall.

BRETL, D. J., & CANTOR, J. (1988). The portrayal of men and women in U.S. television commercials: A recent content analysis and trends over 15 years. *Sex Roles, 18*, 595–609.

BROWN, J. D., & CAMPBELL, K. (1986). Race and gender in music videos: The same beat but a different drummer. *Journal of Communication, 36*, 94–106.

BROWN, J. D., & SCHULZ, L. (1990). The effects of race, gender, and fandom on audience interpretations of Madonna's music videos. *Journal of Communication, 40,* 88–102.

BROWN, M. E. (1989). Soap opera and women's culture: Politics and the popular. In K. Carter & C. Spitzack (Eds.), *Doing research on women's communication: Perspectives on theory and method.* Norwood, NJ: Ablex.

BRUBACH, H. (1985, August). Heavy petal: Women in rock. *Vogue,* pp. 328–331.

BUERKEL-ROTHFUSS, N. L., & MAYES, S. (1981). Soap opera viewing: The cultivation effect. *Journal of Communication, 31,* 108–115.

BUTRUILLE, S. G., & TAYLOR, A. (1987). Women in American popular song. In L. P. Stewart & S. Ting-toomey (Eds.), *Communication, gender, and sex roles in diverse interaction contexts* (pp. 179–188). Norwood, NJ: Ablex.

CANTOR, M. (1987). Popular culture and the portrayal of women. In B. Hess & M. M. Ferree (Eds.), *Analyzing gender: A handbook of social science research* (pp. 190–213). New York: Sage.

CARVETH, R., & ALEXANDER, A. (1985). Soap opera viewing motivations and the cultivation process. *Journal of Broadcasting and Electronic Media, 29,* 259–273.

CASSATA, M. B., ANDERSON, P. A., & SKILL, T. D. (1980). The older adult in daytime serial drama. *Journal of Communication, 30,* 48–49.

CATHCART, R., & GUMPERT, G. (1986). I am a camera: The mediated self. *Communication Quarterly, 34,* 89–102.

CHRIST, W. G., & MEDOFF, N. J. (1984). Affective state and the selective exposure to and use of television. *Journal of Broadcasting and Electronic Media, 28,* 51–63.

COMPESI, R. J. (1980). Gratifications of daytime TV serial viewers. *Journalism Quarterly, 57,* 155–158.

COMSTOCK, G. (1983). Television and American social institutions. In J. C. Wright & A. C. Huston (Eds.), *Children and television* (3rd ed.). Lexington, MA: Ginn Custom Publishers.

COMSTOCK, J., & STRZYZEWSKI, K. (1990). Interpersonal interaction on television: Family conflict and jealousy on prime-time. *Journal of Broadcasting and Electronic Media, 34,* 263–282.

CORLISS, R. (1993, April 5). A few good women. *Time,* pp. 58–59.

COURTNEY, A. E., & WHIPPLE, T. W. (1974). Women in TV commercials. *Journal of Communication, 24,* 110–118.

COURTNEY, A. E., & WHIPPLE, T. W. (1983). *Sex stereotyping in advertising.* Lexington, MA: Lexington Books.

CRAIG, R. S. (1992a, October). *Selling masculinities, selling femininities: Multiple genders and the economics of television.* Paper presented at the annual meeting of the Speech Communication Association, Chicago, IL.

CRAIG, R. S. (1992b). The effect of television day part on gender portrayals in television commercials: A content analysis. *Sex Roles, 26,* 197–211.

CULLEY, J. O., & BENNETT, R. (1976). Selling women, selling blacks. *Journal of Communication, 26,* 160–174.

DAMBROT, F. H., REEP, D. C., & BELL, D. (1988). Television sex roles in the 1980s: Do viewers' sex and sex role orientation change the picture? *Sex Roles, 19,* 387–401.

DESMOND, R. J. (1987). Adolescents and music lyrics: Implications of a cognitive perspective. *Communication Quarterly, 35,* 276–284.

DOHERTY, T. (1988). *Teenagers and teenpics: The juvenilization of American movies in the 50s.* Boston: Unwin Hyman.

DOMINICK, J. R. (1993). *The dynamics of mass communication* (4th ed). New York: McGraw-Hill.

FALUDI, S. (1991). *Backlash: The undeclared war against American women.* New York: Crown.

FINE, M. G. (1981). Soap opera conversations: The talk that binds. *Journal of Communication, 31,* 97–107.

FISKE, J. (1987). *Television culture.* New York: Methuen.

FRENCH, M. (1977). *The women's room.* New York: Jove/Harcourt Brace Jovanovich.

FRENCH, M. (1992). *The war against women.* New York: Summit Books.

FREUDIGER, P., & ALMQUIST, E. M. (1978). Male and female roles in the lyrics of three genres of contemporary music. *Sex Roles, 4,* 51–65.

FRUEH, T., & McGHEE, P. E. (1975). Traditional sex role development and amount of time spent watching television. *Developmental Psychology, 11,* 109.

GERBNER, G., GROSS, L., ELEEY, M. F., JACKSON-BEECK, M., JEFFRIES-FOX, S., & SIGNORELLI, N. (1977). TV violence profile no. 8: The highlights. *Journal of Communication, 27,* 171–180.

GERBNER, G., GROSS, L., MORGAN, M., & SIGNORELLI, N. (1980). The "mainstreaming" of America: Violence profile no. 11. *Journal of Communication, 30,* 10–29.

GLENN, R. J. III. (1992, November). *Echoes of feminism on the big screen: A fantasy theme analysis of "Thelma and Louise."* Paper presented at the annual meeting of the Speech Communication Association, Chicago, IL.

GOLDMAN, R., HEATH, D., & SMITH, S. L. (1991). Commodity feminism. *Critical Studies in Mass Communication, 8,* 333–351.

GREENBERG, B. S., & D'ALESSIO, D. (1985). Quantity and quality of sex in the soaps. *Journal of Broadcasting and Electronic Media, 29,* 309–321.

HARDING, D., & NETT, E. (1984). Women and rock music. *Atlantis, 10,* 60–77.

HOCKER RUSHING, J. (1989). Evolution of "The New Frontier" in *Alien* and *Aliens:* Patriarchal co-optation of the feminine archetype. *Quarterly Journal of Speech, 75,* 1–24.

JACKSON, K. (1991, September 14). Have you come a long way, baby? *The Dallas Morning News,* pp. 1–3C.

JAPP, P. M. (1991). Gender and work in the 1980s: Television's working women as displaced persons. *Women's Studies in Communication, 14,* 49–74.

JENSEN, K. B. (1987). Qualitative audience research: Toward an integrative approach to reception. *Critical Studies in Mass Communication, 4,* 21–36.

KALIS, P., & NEUENDORF, K. A. (1989). Aggressive cues prominence and gender participation in MTV. *Journalism Quarterly, 66,* 148–154.

KALISH, D. (1988, March). Which sex speaks louder? *Marketing & Media,* pp. 30–31.

KANNER, B. (1990, May 21). Big boys don't cry. *New York,* pp. 20–21.

KEAVENEY, M. M. (1991, February). *Women in the media: How the material girl justifies our love.* Paper presented at the annual meeting of the Western States Communication Association, Phoenix, AZ.

KLAWANS, S. (1991, June 24). Films: *Thelma & Louise. The Nation,* pp. 862–863.

KLOPFENSTEIN, B. C., SPEARS, S. C., & FERGUSON, D. A. (1991). VCR attitudes and behaviors by length of ownership. *Journal of Broadcasting and Electronic Media, 35,* 525–531.

KOLBE, R. H. (1991). Gender roles in children's television advertising: A longitudinal content analysis. *Current Issues in Advertising Research,* 196–205.

KROLL, J. (1991, June 24). Back on the road again. *Newsweek,* p. 67.

LARSON, M. (1989). Interaction between siblings in primetime television. *Journal of Broadcasting and Electronic Media, 33,* 305–315.

LELAND, J. (1992, June 29). Rap and race. *Newsweek,* pp. 47–52.

LEMISH, D. (1985). Soap opera viewing in college: A naturalistic inquiry. *Journal of Broadcasting & Electronic Media, 29,* 275–293.

LEO, J. (1991, June 10). Toxic feminism on the big screen. *U.S. News & World Report.* p. 20.

LINDLOF, T. R. (1987). *Natural audiences: Qualitative research of media uses and effects.* Norwood, NJ: Ablex.

LINDLOF, T. R. (1991). Qualitative study of media audiences. *Journal of Broadcasting and Electronic Media, 35,* 23–42.

LOVDAL, L. (1989). Sex role messages in television commercials: An update. *Sex Roles, 21,* 715–727.

LOWRY, D. T. (1989). Soap opera portrayals of sex, contraception, and sexually transmitted diseases. *Journal of Communication, 39,* 76–83.

LUNDSTROM, W. J., & SCIGLIMPAGLIA, D. (1977). Sex role portrayals in advertising. *Journal of Marketing, 41,* 72–78.

LUONG, M. A. (1992, October). *Star Trek: The Next Generation: Boldly forging empowered female characters.* Paper presented at the annual meeting of the Speech Communication Association, Chicago, IL.

LYSONSKI, S., & POLLAY, R. W. (1990). Advertising sexism is forgiven but not forgotten: Historical, cross-cultural and individual differences in criticism and purchase boycott intentions. *International Journal of Advertising, 9,* 317–329.

MACKLIN, M. C., & KOLBE, R. H. (1984). Sex role stereotyping in children's advertising: Current and past trends. *Journal of Advertising, 13,* 34–42.

MANDZIUK, R. (1991, February). *Cementing her sphere: Daytime talk and the television world of women.*

Paper presented at the annual meeting of the Western States Communication Association, Phoenix, AZ.

MARACEK, J., PILIAVIN, J. A., FITZSIMMONS, E., KROGH, E. C., LEADER, E., & TRUDELL, B. (1978). Women as TV experts: The voice of authority? *Journal of Communication, 28,* 159–168.

MELLENCAMP, P. (1992). *High anxiety: Catastrophe, scandal, age, and comedy.* Bloomington: Indiana University Press.

Minnesota Ad Campaign Targets Women Smokers. (1992, September 5). *Raleigh News and Observer,* p. 6A.

MINOW, N. N. (1991). Television: How far has it come in 30 years? *Vital Speeches, 57,* 121–125.

MOORE, M. L. (1992). The family as portrayed on prime-time television, 1947–1990: Structure and characteristics. *Sex Roles, 26,* 41–61.

MYERS, P. N., JR., & BIOCCA, R. A. (1992). The elastic body image: The effect of television advertising and programming on body image distortions in young women. *Journal of Communication, 42,* 108–133.

NICHOLSON, J. (1992, Summer/Fall). The advertiser's man. *Adbusters,* pp. 21–26.

NIELSEN MEDIA RESEARCH. (1988, November). *Nielsen Television Index national audience demographics report* (Vol. 1). Northbrook, IL: Author.

O'DONNELL, W. J., & O'DONNELL, K. J. (1978). Update: Sex-role messages in TV commercials. *Journal of Communication, 28,* 156–158.

PALMGREEN, P., & RAYBURN, J. D. II. (1985). A comparison of gratification models of media satisfaction. *Communication Monographs, 52,* 334–346.

PAPAZIAN, E. (Ed.) (1990). *TV dimensions '90.* New York: Media Dynamics.

PARELES, J. (1990, January 11). On the edge of the permissible: Madonna's evolving persona. *The New York Times,* pp. 11–12C.

PERREN, N. J. (1993, February). *Thelma & Louise: The drive toward feminine freedom.* Paper presented at the annual meeting of the Western States Communication Association, Albuquerque, NM.

PETERSON, E. E. (1987). Media consumption and girls who want to have fun. *Critical Studies in Mass Communication, 4,* 37–50.

PLANNED PARENTHOOD FEDERATION OF AMERICA. (1986, November 25). They did it 9,000 times on television last year. *Washington Post,* p. A18.

POTTER, W. J. (1990). Adolescents' perceptions of the primary values of television programming. *Journalism Quarterly, 67,* 843–851.

PRESS, A. L. (1991a). *Women watching television: Gender, class, and generation in the American television experience.* Philadelphia: University of Pennsylvania Press.

PRESS, A. L. (1991b). Working-class women in a middle-class world: The impact of television on modes of reasoning about abortion. *Critical Studies in Mass Communication, 8,* 421–441.

PROBYN, E. (1990). New traditionalism and post-feminism: TV does the home. *Screen, 31,* 147–159.

RAYBURN, J. D., PALMGREEN, P., & ACKER, T. (1984). Media gratifications and choosing a morning news program. *Journalism Quarterly, 61,* 149–156.

RICHMOND-ABBOTT, M. (1992). *Masculine and feminine: Gender roles over the life cycle* (2nd ed.). New York: McGraw-Hill.

ROHTER, L. (1991, June 5). The third woman of *Thelma & Louise. New York Times,* pp. C21, C24.

ROSENTHAL, P. (1992, May 22). Lighten up Dan; it's only a television show. *Raleigh News and Observer,* p. 6D.

ROWE, K. (1990). Roseanne: Unruly woman as domestic goddess. *Screen, 31,* 408–419.

RUBIN, A. M. (1985). Uses of daytime television soap operas by college students. *Journal of Broadcasting and Electronic Media, 29,* 241–258.

RUBIN, A. M. (1986). Uses and gratifications. In J. BRYANT & D. ZILLMANN (Eds)., *Perspectives on media effects.* Hillsdale, NJ: Lawrence Erlbaum Associates.

RUBIN, A. M., PERSE, E. M., & POWELL, R. A. (1985). Loneliness, parasocial interaction, and local television viewing. *Human Communication Research, 12,* 155–180.

SAPOLSKY, B. S., & TABARLET, J. O. (1991). Sex in primetime television: 1979 versus 1989. *Journal of Broadcasting and Electronic Media, 35,* 505–516.

SAWYER, F. (1990, December 13). ABC News *Nightline.*

SCHICKEL, R. (1991, June 24). Gender bender. *Time,* pp. 52–56.

SCHRAG, R. L. (1990). *Taming the wild tube: A family's guide to television and video.* Chapel Hill: University of North Carolina Press.

SCHWARTZ, L. A., & MARKHAM, W. T. (1985). Sex stereotyping in children's toy advertisements. *Sex Roles, 12,* 157–170.

SEIDMAN, S. A. (1992). An investigation of sex-role stereotyping in music videos. *Journal of Broadcasting and Electronic Media, 36,* 209–216.

SHAPIRO, L. (1991, June 17). Women who kill too much. *Newsweek,* pp. 52–56.

SHERMAN, B. L., & DOMINICK, J. R. (1986). Violence and sex in music videos: TV and rock and roll. *Journal of Communication, 36,* 79–93.

SIGNORELLI, N., & MORGAN, M. (1988). *Cultivation analysis.* Newbury Park, CA: Sage.

SKELLY, G. U., & LUNDSTROM, W. J. (1981). Male sex roles in magazine advertising, 1959–1979. *Journal of Communication, 31,* 52–57.

SULLIVAN, G. L., & O'CONNOR, P. J. (1988). Women's role portrayals in magazine advertising: 1958–1983. *Sex Roles, 18,* 181–189.

SVETKEY, B. (1992, March 6). "Star" struck. *Entertainment Weekly,* p. 20.

TRAUBE, E. (1992). *Dreaming identities: Class, gender, and generation in 1980s Hollywood movies.* Boulder, CO: Westview Press.

TUCHMAN, G. (1979). Women's depiction by the mass media. *Signs, 4,* 528–542.

VANDE BERG, L. R., & STRECKFUSS, D. (1992). Prime-time television's portrayal of women and the world of work: A demographic profile. *Journal of Broadcasting and Electronic Media, 36,* 195–208.

VINCENT, R. C. (1989). Clio's consciousness raised? Portrayal of women in rock videos, re-examined. *Journalism Quarterly, 66,* 155–160.

WHIPPLE, T. W., & COURTNEY, A. E. (1980). How to portray women in TV commercials. *Journal of Advertising Research, 20,* 53–59.

WHIPPLE, T. W., & COURTNEY, A. E. (1985). Female role portrayals in advertising and communication effectiveness: A review. *Journal of Advertising, 14,* 4–8.

WILSON, B. J., LINZ, D., DONNERSTEIN, E., & STIPP, H. (1992). The impact of social issue television programming on attitudes toward rape. *Human Communication Research, 19,* 179–208.

ZINN, L. (1991, November 4). This Bud's for you. No, not you—her. *Business Week,* pp. 86–87.

PART THREE

Let's Talk: Initiating and Developing Relationships

Disclaimers, Derogatives, and Discussion: Functions and Styles of Talk for Women and Men

So you've read the first two parts of this book. Are you getting a handle on gender communication at this point? In this part of the text, for the next three chapters, we ask you to think about how your knowledge of gender communication applies to various relationships in your life. Are your current relationships—friendships, family connections, dating and romantic relationships—running as smoothly as you'd like? Is your gender communication within those relationships as effective as you want it to be?

CASE STUDY

"So, what do you want to do tonight?"

"I thought maybe we'd just stay here at my place and talk. We haven't seen much of each other this week."

"Well, is something wrong? Do we need to talk about something?"

"No; nothing's wrong. I just thought we'd spend a quiet evening together, just talking."

Can you label the sex of the speakers in this conversation? Granted, we may be playing into some stereotypes here, but students generally recognize this conversation as being very typical at the beginning stages of dating relationships. It seems as though just about all of us have had a conversation like this in our relational history. And usually it's the woman who wants to stay home and talk, while the man worries that "let's talk" signals that something is wrong in the relationship.

If you're a man reading this text, do you ever wonder why women seem to want to talk more than do anything else? Wondering something like this may lead you to believe that women talk considerably more than men—that they're chatterboxes. If you're a woman, do you often wonder why it seems that men just do not want to talk as much about things? Wondering something like this may lead you to the false assumption that men can't talk their way out of a paper bag. (Research presented later in this chapter explains how both of these conclusions are myths.)

Reread the conversation that opened this case study. What's going on in these four simple statements? While the exchange seems fairly innocuous and common, we contend that volumes are going on. This conversation represents a fundamental, patterned difference in how women and men *use conversation*. Read on to learn what we mean by *uses* of conversation.

OVERVIEW

In Part Two we explored the kinds of influences that affect your choices—choices about self, communication, and others. We focused on communication *about* the sexes. This third part of the text examines gender communication that facilitates the initiation and development of relationships—communication *between* the sexes. In Part Four we address gender communication within certain relational contexts: at school, at work, with friends, and within serious, committed romantic relationships.

But before you start thinking about communication within specific kinds of relationships that you may have, it might be wise to more fully understand why you communicate. Do women and men communicate for similar purposes or to accomplish similar goals? Once we've explored that question, we'll examine some language usage differences exposed in research as being sex- and gender-connected. We'll look at specific differences in the ways that men and women use language to form the structure of their communication. Then an exploration of *how* gender communication operates in the basic coming together, staying to-gether, and possibly coming apart of relationships between men and women will make more sense. Here are some of the ideas we explore with you in the next pages:

- Women's and men's varying approaches to conversation
- The balance between relational and content functions of communication
- How interpersonal motives affect communication within relationships
- Three levels of conversational depth
- Qualities of the voice that differ for men and women
- Language usages that communicate tentativeness versus assertiveness and dominance
- How the sexes use color terms, profanity, and sexual slang
- Conversation management by women and men

INTRODUCTION

Before reading further into this chapter, it might be wise to take an inventory of your current relationships. A configuration of concentric circles is a helpful tool in assessing relational situations as well as the communication that charac-

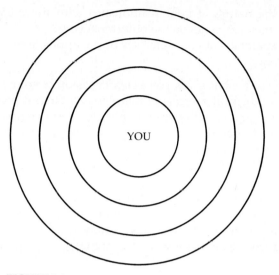

FIGURE 5.1.

terizes those relationships. Because concentric circles can greatly clarify even the most complicated of things, we've included Figure 5.1 for your use. You can either fill in the circles here or copy this figure onto your own paper to use as you wish.

Note that "You" are in the core of the circles, so the easiest way to use the circles is to work from the inner ring outward. Now, who is (or are) the person(s) closest to you? Is there one person you consider to be your best friend? The closest person to you could be a family member. On the first ring away from the core, fill in the name or names of persons with whom you have the closest relationship(s). Now think about the second ring: Who are you close to, but not as close to as those on the first ring? Write those names (or maybe labels for a group of people, like "coworkers" or "my sisters and brothers") on this ring. Continue this process, going further out with the concentric circles as you consider your range of relationships. When you've filled in all of the circles—and you may need to add a few rings to the figure—sit back and look at what you wrote.

Analyze your relational concentric circles for a moment, using these questions:

1. Were you readily able to enter on the first ring the name or names of persons closest to you? If not, why not?
2. What kind of relationships are represented on the first, most intimate ring—friendships, family members, dating partners, or a spouse?
3. When you supplied names for the second ring, what made the difference between inserting these names on the second ring versus the first?
4. As you moved further away from the core circle, what was the basis for deciding where to insert people's names?

5. What is the nature of your relationship with the person (or persons) whose name(s) appears on the outermost ring?
6. Do more members of your same sex or the opposite sex appear throughout the rings?

Maybe this exercise has given you a clearer vision of your current relational involvement. It's a helpful exercise in many ways. First, it provides a graphic representation of your connection to other people. If you've never thought about levels of closeness to people in your life, it's an interesting discovery process. Second, and of prime importance for our purposes, it challenges you to analyze your relationships according to sex. For example, if you are female and you find that more relationships with women appear on the inner rings, you may want to spend some time thinking about why that is. If you are male and, for example, your inner rings depict relationships with women while your outer rings depict relationships with men (or vice versa), you may want to analyze what makes some types of relationships closer, more intimate, and more satisfying than others.

A final benefit from this exercise, again central to our purposes, relates to communication. Probably the single variable most affecting your choice of where to put people in the diagram is communication—both the frequency and quality of your communication with the people in these relationships. It's highly likely that the person you communicate with most and best shows up on the first ring of the concentric circles arrangement. It's also likely that the frequency and quality of your interaction changes (and probably diminishes) as you move further out from the core. Was anyone on the line between circles 2 and 3, for example? Is there anyone you'd like to move into a more intimate circle? How will you accomplish this? Your communication with that person will probably have to change. It might involve something as simple as communicating with her or him more often, but probably the nature or quality of your communication with that person needs to change as well. (In Chapter 7 we discuss more fully this process of moving someone from one ring to another within your relational structure.)

Now that we've energized your thinking about the topic of communicating within relationships, let's explore some information that will help you understand how men and women approach the communication that is necessary for relationships to function.

APPROACHES TO COMMUNICATION

Experience and research tell us that men and women often have difficulty communicating with each other. This difficulty isn't some great "mystery of the universe," but it does seem puzzling at times, so examining why it exists is worthwhile. From our own research and that of others, we've recently developed a supposition to help explain why gender communication is so complex. But first let's backtrack for a moment to explore the research of some communication theorists in the late 1960s, which forms the basis for our supposition.

An Axiom of Communication

Three communication scholars in the 1960s developed a set of axioms or basic rules about how human communication operates. Paul Watzlawick, Janet Helmick Beavin, and Don Jackson (1967) formulated an axiom contending that "Every communication has a content and a relationship aspect such that the latter classifies the former and is therefore a metacommunication" (p. 54). The content aspect of communication is what is actually said or the information that is imparted from one communicator to another. The relational aspect of the message is termed *metacommunication* (communication about communication) because it tells the receiver how the message should be interpreted and it communicates something about the nature of the relationship between the interactants. For example, saying a simple "hello" to someone in a warm, friendly tone of voice conveys a sense of friendship and familiarity, whereas a hollow, perfunctory tone may indicate that the relationship between two people is more formal and impersonal. Tone of voice, in this case, serves as metacommunication; that is, it indicates how the message should be interpreted and gives clues about the interactants' relationship. The content element is generally conveyed through verbal communication, while the relational element primarily takes the form of nonverbal communication (although it can be conveyed through verbal communication, too). Watzlawick, Beavin, and Jackson suggested that rarely do interactants deliberately define the nature and state of their relationship; thus the relational elements of messages are usually conveyed in subtle, unspoken, and unconscious ways.

For example, the basic content or information of a message can be worded two ways, so that the way the message is said defines the relationships quite differently. Compare the following statements:

"Turning your paper in on time is important if you expect a good grade."

"You'd better make your paper deadline this time or you'll blow your shot at an A."

These two statements contain basically the same message, but two different relationships are implied. The first statement would likely be said by an authority figure of some sort who has a fairly formal relationship with the listener, such as a teacher communicating an assignment to his or her students. The second message takes a more casual, informal tone, implying that the relationship between the speaker and listener is a more intimate one, possibly a close friendship or family relationship.

Even the simplest of exchanges has a relational and a content dimension. For example, if a complete stranger walked toward you on the sidewalk, made eye contact with you, and said, "Hi; how's it going?" you might reply with some minimal greeting like, "Okay, thanks." But if someone you knew was walking down the hallway at school and the same greeting was extended, you might answer with the same wording, but your response would probably sound and look different from the exchange with the stranger. In both of these simple interactions, the content of the message is a basic greeting, but the relational aspect signals that there is a difference in the relationship between you and the stranger versus you and the school acquaintance. The relational dimension signals how the content of the message is to be interpreted, given the relationship between the interactants.

Neither element of communication is more important than the other. Watzlawick, Beavin, and Jackson believed that healthier relationships involved a balance of the content and relational aspects of talk. To these researchers, a "sick" relationship could be characterized by communication that focuses too heavily on the relational dimension, so that even the simplest messages become interpreted as "statements" about the relationship. Likewise, relationships in which communication has degenerated into a mere information exchange rather than "clueing" one another as to the state of the relationship could also be termed sick (p. 53).

Women, Men, and the Relational versus Content Approach to Talk

Extending Watzlawick, Beavin, and Jackson's relational and content axiom of communication, we contend that a fundamental difference exists in what women and men believe to be the function or purpose of conversation. Granted, we are generalizing here and we know that there are exceptions to this contention. But for now, suspend your concerns to see if there's a ring of truth or a match with your experience to what we're saying. We begin by talking through this perspective, offering explanations in the form of anecdotes. In the next section we present some research and theory that offer initial support for this perspective.

We believe that men approach conversation more with the intent of imparting information (the content aspect) than to convey cues about the relationship (the relational aspect). In contrast, women view conversation as functioning more as an indication of relationship than as a mechanism for imparting information. This does not mean that every time a man speaks, he is conveying information only; on the contrary, *every* message carries content and relational meanings. This also does not mean that women communicate only relationally, without ever exchanging any real information. What it does mean is that men may use communication primarily for information exchange rather than for relationship development. The development of male friendships comes more often in the form of *doing* rather than *talking*. Women like to *do* as well as *talk*, but they often reveal that their relationship maintenance with other women is more frequently accomplished through conversation than just by doing things together. This

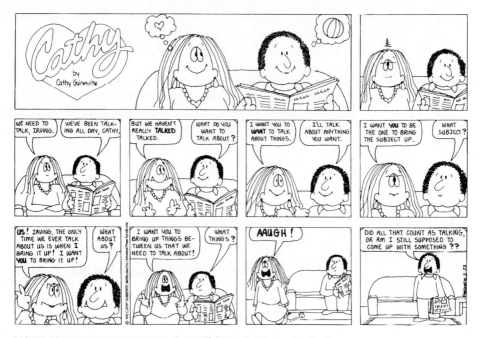

represents a fundamental sex difference before women and men even meet, and it may set us up for conflict when we communicate in opposite-sex relationships.

Remember the conversation cited in the opening case study? Here are a few more examples to illustrate this supposition, which we term the relational versus content approach to communication. (These examples are drawn from actual accounts generated by students and friends.) One of our colleagues, upon hearing an explanation of the relational versus content approach, said, "Is this like, when the other morning my wife and I woke up before we had to actually get up, and she said, 'Let's just lie here and talk,' and I didn't have anything to talk *about?*" In a similar account, a friend explained that a man she'd been seeing gave her the "silent treatment" one evening when they had decided to spend some time at her house rather than going out. She asked him a couple of times if anything was wrong and he politely replied, "No," but he continued to be quiet. In frustration, she finally accused him of holding something back and making her feel like he didn't care about her, or else they would be talking with one another. His response was that he just didn't have anything to say, but that obviously he must care about her because, "After all, I'm *here* aren't I?"

One of our students, after hearing a class explanation on this topic of conversational sex differences, recalled a recent argument he'd had with his partner: "We'd been talking about something that happened a few nights before and it led to an argument. When I felt that I'd explained my side of the story sufficiently and that we'd argued enough, I simply said, 'There's nothing more to say. End of discussion.' This made her furious and I couldn't figure out why. She wanted to continue talking about the incident, my side of it, her side of it, what the argument meant about our relationship, and I just wanted the conversation *over.*"

Another example generated by some married friends depicts an exchange between spouses. See if you can spot relational and content approaches operating here. Both spouses work full-time jobs; on this particular day, the wife had arrived home just before the husband did and the conversation proceeded as follows:

WIFE: Hi honey; how was your day?
HUSBAND: Fine.
(Long pause.)
W: Well, did anything interesting happen at work today?
H: Nope; just the same old same old.
(Long pause.)
W: Well, what about that deal you were going to talk to Bob about? Did you guys talk?
H: Yeah, we talked, but nothing much came out of it.
(Silence.)

Let's analyze this brief, fairly ordinary conversation. The wife's three verbalizations were in the form of questions designed to draw the husband into a conversation; the husband's verbalizations were brief responses to his wife's queries. Research indicates that it is typically the woman in a male-female dyad who initiates conversation and keeps it going (Fishman, 1983). The husband didn't seem to be making any attempt to extend the conversation. If the wife hadn't continued to ask questions, it's likely that the conversation would have ended after the first question-and-answer sequence. The information imparted (content element) was logical; the questions received appropriate answers. However, the relational elements may speak volumes. Depending on the relational history of this couple, along with how the words were said and other nonverbal cues such as facial expressions and eye contact (or the lack of it), a couple of interpretations are plausible. One is that this is just a typical, ritualistic conversation between couples at the end of a long, tiring workday. Basic information is exchanged, and there is no real need for relationship maintenance or relational work in this particular conversation. Another interpretation is that the husband wants to maintain and strengthen his relationship with his wife, but he simply doesn't prefer to do this kind of maintenance during the first 10 minutes at home after a tiring day at work. Yet another interpretation might be that there is a real communication problem in this relationship, whether the couple acknowledges it or not. It might be that the wife's attempts at conversation signal her need for relationship involvement and that her husband's thwarting of her efforts signals a lack of relationship engagement on his part. This couple probably needs to discuss when and how they are going to do relationship maintenance, so that they can reach a compromise.

This example illustrates men's and women's different views on the uses or functions of conversation. Many times women want to talk just to reinforce the fact that a relationship exists and that the relationship is important. What is actually being said is usually less important than the fact that a conversation is taking place. Conversely, men generally approach conversation from a functional standpoint. A conversation functions as a means of exchanging information or content, not as some reinforcement that a relationship is intact.

Another example of how the relational versus content approach operates was generated by one of our students. He stated that his telephone conversations with male friends are radically different from phone conversations with female friends. According to Rob, when a male friend calls, "it's usually to discuss what's happening, when we're going to do something, and where we're going to meet. The conversation is quick and to the point." But, Rob explained, "When my girlfriend or female friends call, I know that the conversation's going to take a while. We have to catch up with each other, find out how the other is doing, what happened that day, and so on. I don't really prefer one type of conversation over another; it's just that the conversations are really different. If a male friend called me up just to chat, I'd think it was really strange."

Rob's experience was met with agreement by both female and male students in class that day. Most of the male students indicated that they didn't have many "shoot the breeze" conversations with male friends, either in person or on the phone. Usually, man-to-man conversations had a reason or a point to them; that is, "There was something to say." The female students found this hilarious, in that their woman-to-woman conversations were so different from those the men were describing. One woman remarked, "If a female friend called me up and, without any explanation, she was really quick and to the point with me—like Rob said his guy friends did—I'd wonder what was wrong or I'd think she was really being rude." Male students and friends have asserted that they call male friends from time to time, just to talk and catch up on one anothers' lives. When probed further, the men reveal that these calls are usually long-distance, to male friends whom they haven't seen or talked to recently. So while there's nothing wrong with men calling other men just to chat, they don't seem to do it as often as many women do.

No wonder some men think women talk on and on about nothing. No wonder women often think that men's relationships (and sometimes men themselves) are superficial. What's going on here? It's not that women are chatterboxes who have nothing better to do than idly carry on long, pointless conversations with everyone they meet. It's not that women are so generally insecure that they need relational reinforcement every time they talk to someone. And it's not that men are such clods that they can't manage even a simple conversation to save their souls. It's not that they're relationally aloof, that they don't need relationship reinforcement, or that they avoid conversation to keep others guessing. What's going on here is that it appears that, in general, women and men get their "relational goodies" in dramatically different ways. They use communication for different purposes. What does the research say about this?

Research on Relational and Content Approaches to Communication

Research and theory generally support the notion that men and women approach conversation from different functional points of view. However, some of the terminology and research approaches vary across disciplines. We review some of the more prominent research in this area, and then offer a synopsis of our own investigations into the relational versus content perspective.

Human Development Theory

Going back to Carol Gilligan's (1982) explanation of human development (explored in Chapter 2), recall that Gilligan views female development almost entirely within the context of relationships. Gender-role identity development includes the ability or inability to identify with the primary caregiver—usually the mother. As a female child develops, she identifies with the mother figure; thus her identity is steeped in her relationship with the mother from the start. A male child, on the other hand, must develop his identity separately from an identification with the mother figure. According to this theory, then, the sense of development via relationships is not as innately ingrained for male children as it is for female children. Regarding Gilligan's perspective, communication researchers Wood and Lenze (1991) suggest that for women, "people are not considered as separate or separated individuals, but interdependent within web-like contexts of multiple human relationships. Thus, distance or separation from others tends to be threatening to female identity in the same way that close connections to others jeopardize male identity" (p. 5).

Gilligan's theory has an interesting connection to the relational versus content approach to talk. It suggests that the very way men and women develop from infancy might set up an eventual difference between the sexes. Women's identity develops out of connectedness and affiliation, whereas men's develops from a sense of independence and separation. It follows, then, that women would use conversation as a vehicle of relationship development in a way that is not preferable or possibly natural for men.

Instrumental and Expressive Orientations

Classic research by sociologists Parsons and Bales (1955) and Bakan (1966) described clusters of traits and interest patterns commonly linked to masculinity and femininity. The masculine or instrumental traits include a "me against the world" view of self, along with concerns about self-protection, self-assertion, and self-expansion. Feminine or expressive traits include a communal view of self, that is, being at one with the world, along with affective, nurturing concerns about others and an expressive sense of emotion. These male and female innate qualities, according to Parsons and Bales, allowed for traditional, natural, and functional sex roles within traditional societies. The instrumental-expressive dichotomy has been used within a few disciplines to describe men's and women's communication patterns, with special emphasis on how androgynous individuals (high instrumental and high expressive) are perceived on a range of communication variables (Ickes, 1981; Myers & Gonda, 1983; Schrader, 1992; Shapiro & Shapiro, 1985).

Interpersonal Communication Motives Research

Interpersonal communication researchers have recently taken more interest in the purposes of talk, specifically in persons' motives for engaging in conversation. Rubin, Perse, and Barbato (1988) propose that while interpersonal communication research has been thorough in its examination of *how* interaction occurs, it has been less pervasive in its attempts to understand *why* people choose to interact—their interpersonal motives. Thus Rubin et al. conducted a study with a primary goal of discovering a possible relationship between gender and interpersonal communication motives. More than 500 subjects ranging in age from 12 to 91 years completed the Interpersonal Communication Motives (ICM) scale developed by the researchers. In essence, the scale tapped whether subjects communicated with other people for such purposes as wanting to be included by others, extending and receiving affection, for simple relaxation purposes, to meet one's needs for companionship, or to control situations and people (among other purposes, totaling 15 in all).

Rubin et al. (1988) detected a significant sex difference from the results of their study. Female subjects reported that they were "more likely to talk to others for pleasure, to express affection, to seek inclusion, and to relax" (p. 621). Men in this study reported communicating more to exert control over a situation than to express affection or seek inclusion from others. Results from this study seem to support the contention that, in many cases, men's and women's motives or purposes for engaging in conversation differ.

Report Talk versus Rapport Talk

In her book *You Just Don't Understand,* sociolinguist Deborah Tannen (1990) describes male and female talk in ways that parallel the relational versus content supposition. She terms the female style "rapport-talk" and the male style "report-talk" (p. 77). Rapport-talk is most women's "way of establishing connections and negotiating relationships. For most men, talk is primarily a means to preserve independence and negotiate and maintain status. . . . This is done by exhibiting knowledge and skill, and by holding center stage through verbal performance such as story-telling, joking, or imparting information" (p. 77). Tannen offers several illustrations of this conversational sex difference, one being a "Blondie" comic strip in which Blondie is frustrated by Dagwood's reading the newspaper over breakfast, instead of talking to her. One difference in this information and the relational versus content approach is that Tannen's ideas describe the kind of talk women and men typically engage in rather than the sexes' views of the functions of talk. The relational versus content perspective deals with *why* men and women communicate; Tannen deals more with *how* they talk, but the ideas are similar enough to support one another.

Conversational Intimacy

In an effort to gauge the level of intimacy or depth inherent in typical conversations, sociologists Davidson and Duberman (1982) investigated communication patterns in same-sex friendships. Rather than distinguishing talk as intimate and nonintimate, Davidson and Duberman developed three levels: (1) The *topical* level involved discussions of topics "which are external to the individuals and the dyadic relationship," such as politics and work (p. 813). (2) The *relational* level consisted of "exchanges between the two people in terms of the friendship" (p. 813). (3) The *personal* level represented the most intimate form of communication, or talk that focused on private and personal feelings and thoughts. Subjects in the study provided detailed accounts of usual conversations with a same-sex person identified as a best friend. These accounts were analyzed in two ways: for the number of times a level was represented in the talk and by which level of communication a subject viewed as primary or most emphasized.

Results indicated that women related twice as many personal accounts and three times as many relational accounts of communication with their female best friends than men participating in this study. However, when assessing which form of communication was considered primary or most important to these female subjects, Davidson and Duberman discovered that equal numbers of women deemed each of the three levels to be primary and important. In contrast, male subjects reported relating to their male best friends usually on a topical, external level, which was also considered to be the primary or most important level of communication. A final result of the study was that men generally talked less than women about interrelationships, or the relationships between themselves and their best friends.

Videotaped Conversation Research

We want to discuss the initial results of our own studies that have begun to systematically test our supposition; this research is preliminary and ongoing, so findings must be interpreted tentatively. We conducted two videotaped conversation studies to see if subjects would assign different purposes or reasons for why the interactants in the tapes were engaged in conversation. Both studies involved scripted, videotaped conversations (written and enacted by undergraduate students enrolled in a gender communication class) between two opposite-sex classmates. At various points for both studies, the researcher/facilitator would stop the tape during breaks in the conversation and ask subjects to complete certain items on a questionnaire. Granted, this isn't the same as determining why interactants themselves engage in conversation, but we believed that this would be one way of initially investigating the relational versus content approach.

For the first study, a group of seventy-three undergraduate subjects (51 percent male; 49 percent female) used the questionnaire to record their responses to a videotape we entitled "Acquaintances." The taped conversation took place in a classroom before class had started, and it entailed a male student recognizing a female classmate as someone from a previous class. They slowly remembered each other and the past class, discussed problems they were having in the current class, and ended the conversation with the female student agreeing to lend her class notes to the male student.

When asked "What do you think the purpose of this conversation is?" a dramatically higher percentage of female (42 percent) than male respondents (16 percent) indicated relational purposes for the conversation. Female subjects reported such purposes as "to become friends rather than just acquaintances," "he was really trying to get to know her better," and "to introduce something larger, perhaps a date or to study together for a test." Male subjects who perceived relational elements in the conversation revealed such purposes as "to get to know each other better" and "acknowledging that she is alive and feeling her vibes, to see if he's got a shot."

Only 58 percent of the female subjects compared to 84 percent of the males ascribed an exchange of content or other purposes to the conversation, offering comments such as "simply acknowledging that they remember each other from another class" and "idle chatter." One interpretation for subjects connecting more content-based purposes to the conversation than relational purposes may relate to the fact that the male character initiated the conversation with the female character in the videotape. Perhaps male and female subjects alike just didn't expect that a man would attempt a conversation for relationship purposes in that setting and with someone he barely knew. Or perhaps the finding is more related to the artificiality of having watched a staged, videotaped conversation; it may have been a stretch for some viewers to interpret relational purposes from such a setup. They may have simply keyed on what was being said, rather than looking beyond the words to find relational cues.

For the second video study, a group of eighty-four undergraduate subjects (56 percent male; 44 percent female) participated in the same procedure, but in response to a videotape entitled "Just Friends." The same before-class setting was used, but the topic of conversation and the relationship of the interactants were altered. The script involved a female student telling a male friend about a club she'd been to and about a party that she was going to with some friends that coming weekend. The conversation ended just before class started, with the guy deciding to go to the party with the female student and her friends.

Of the female responses, 56 percent suggested purposes of a relational nature, revealed in such comments as "They're establishing 'extra interest' at this point" and "It seems like they're trying to get to see each other outside of class, as maybe more than just friends." Only 22 percent of the female subjects saw a content purpose to the conversation, revealed by the comment "She's just sharing information with him and letting him know that she has plans for the weekend." Another 22 percent of the female subjects found other purposes for the conversation, such as "killing time before class."

The results for male subjects' responses weren't quite so clear-cut. Forty-one percent of the male subjects responded with content purposes for the conversation, revealed by comments like "She's telling him about a party" and "They're catching up on what they've been doing." But another 35 percent of the male subjects saw a relational purpose to the conversation, revealed in comments like "They're trying to 'pick up' each other," "The woman wants to spend more time with the dude," and "They're flirting so they can 'hook up' this weekend." Twenty-four percent of the male subjects found other purposes for the conversation, such as "passing time."

More data need to be collected before definitive conclusions can be drawn from this kind of "eavesdropper" study. Both of these studies suggest more women than men interpret a relational purpose or function when overhearing an opposite-sex conversation, but the results are too preliminary for anything but conjecture at this point. We plan to extend this study to include male and female perceptions of same-sex conversations as well as more subjects' reactions to videotaped conversations.

What's Preferable—Relational or Content Communication?

The answer to that question is that neither approach to communication is necessarily preferable. Remember that in every message—no matter how brief or trivial—both content and relational elements exist. The difference seems to lie in a person's view of the function or purpose of a given message. In Chapter 2 we discussed gender transcendence and an androgynous gender-role identity, and throughout this text we encourage you to expand your choices of behavior into a more fully developed repertoire of communicative options. It follows that, while we are interested in learning more about male and female approaches to talk, we are motivated by the goal of developing an integrated or balanced approach derived from the best attributes of both. This approach recognizes that there are certain times, situations, and people that require different kinds of communication. The skill comes in learning which communicative approach is best, given the dictates of the situation. Let's return to one of our earlier examples for clarification.

In the opening case study conversation, the couple who provided this account were both enrolled in one of our gender communication classes. Simone and Malcolm explained that they were both frustrated with the exchange, but for different reasons. Simone felt that Malcolm either was beginning to care less for her or was irritated with her for insisting that they stay home and talk. Malcolm became concerned that Simone's insistence at conversation was a signal that "trouble was coming." He accepted her explanation that everything was all right but remained uncomfortable at the prospect of having to talk when he really didn't have anything to say. How could this situation have gone more smoothly?

To review the basic theme of this text, being a personally effective gender communicator means that one develops a wide range of communication options, learns how to analyze a situation, selects the most appropriate behavior for the situation, performs that communicative behavior with skill, and evaluates the results of this process. With that model in mind, let's reconstruct the couple's conversation. If both individuals had broadened their communication reper- toires to include options that the prevailing thinking currently attaches exclu- sively to one sex or the other, they could have selected the best option for the situation rather than defaulting into sex-typed messages and reactions. More specifically, if Simone realized that conversation meant relationship develop- ment to her, she could have "clued" Malcolm to that fact, so that he would understand her reasons for wanting to talk. As is, he had to either read her mind or default into a stereotypical male reaction of "talk equals trouble." (As we said in the values section of Chapter 1, talking about it makes it better.) Malcolm needs to expand his communication repertoire to understand that talking can be relationship development, not just an idle way to fill time or a signal that something is wrong. Relationship maintenance can be accomplished by doing things or just being together, but talk conveys certain relational cues that action cannot.

Another way to rewrite this scenario is to increase Simone's behavioral repertoire so that she is comfortable with doing things, or doing nothing in particular, and possibly with the absence of talk, as forms of relationship development. It may be possible that she can discover how Malcolm feels about her less by what he says than by just being with him and from the things he does. Malcolm can discuss with Simone his discomfort with talk that seems forced and unnatural, or with having a conversation when there is no real issue at hand. A more successful, effective approach here would be to respond with the best option for the situation, regardless of sex-role expectations, thereby avoiding sex stereotypes that lead to aggravation and separation.

The ideal would be for relational and content purposes to be stressed when the situation deems one approach more effective than the other. In this manner, men could strengthen their male friendships over the phone rather than relying primarily on action to indicate friendship. The male co-author of your text and one of his best friends, Eric, are doing exactly that. They regularly call each other on the phone as a means of simply staying in touch, not necessarily because they have some information to convey. Likewise, more women could realize that many of their relationships with men—relationships of all types and levels of intimacy—will not be developed primarily through talk. Women might become more comfortable in approaching conversation with men on more of a content-exchange basis, rather than expecting to learn through the conversation how men feel about them or how men view the relationship. The ideal would be for us to respond to each other in the most effective manner possible, unencumbered by what is expected or stereotypical for persons of our sex.

Thus far in this chapter we've explored what women and men bring to a relationship, specifically in terms of their views of the purpose of communica- tion. This can be seen as the *why* we talk; now let's focus in the next half of this chapter on *how* we talk. As we delve into this topic, keep the personal effectiveness, non–sex-stereotypical goal in mind. When we draw a contrast between how men and women use language, think about why that contrast currently exists, how communication and relationships could be improved if the behaviors weren't identified with a particular gender, and ways that we can diminish the polarization of the sexes.

LANGUAGE USAGE AMONG WOMEN AND MEN

We began this chapter by exploring some sex differences in approaches to communication—the "why" we communicate. Now we need to discuss the ways in which language is used in communication *between* women and men—the "how" we communicate. The information presented in this section is divided into three parts, vocal properties and linguistic constructions, word selection, and conversation management. For some topics, the research has produced contradictory results regarding linguistic patterns of the sexes, but a general, unsettling trend is for the research to label the feminine patterns as weaker, passive, and less commanding of respect when compared to masculine styles. Some sources of information view linguistic sex differences as being profound enough as to form "genderlects," variations of dialects indicative of men's and women's speech patterns (Cameron, 1985, p. 29).

Vocal Properties and Linguistic Constructions

Vocal properties are aspects of the production of sound that are related to the physiological voice-producing mechanism in humans. Some researchers argue that these properties are biologically determined; others believe that the differences are more influenced by social norms than by physiological attributes. We use the heading *linguistic constructions* to refer to choices people make when they communicate, such as using tag questions, hedges, and disclaimers. More specifically, linguistic constructions reflect speech patterns or habits, but they do not relate to specific word selections.

Pitch

The pitch of a human voice can be defined as the highness or lowness of a particular sound as air causes the vocal chords to vibrate. It is a generally accepted belief that physiological structures related to voice production are configured so that women produce higher pitched sounds, while men produce lower pitched sounds. Thus women's speaking voices tend to be higher in pitch than men's—a conclusion that is probably nothing new to you. But scholarly evidence, especially in the area of singing voices, has uprooted some notions about physiological sex differences and voice production. Current thinking suggests that sex differences in voice production have more to do with social interpretations than with physiology alone (Brownmiller, 1984; Graddol & Swann, 1989; Steinem, 1983).

Gender scholar Dale Spender (1985) believes that pitch can be seen "as an index for the measurement of women's language inferiority" (p. 38). Spender draws from research which indicates that women and men have equal abilities to produce high pitches, but men have been socialized not to use the higher pitches for fear of sounding feminine. If this were not the case, what would be the cause for men's ability to flip their voices into a falsetto (an extremely high-pitched singing voice)? Research has discovered that men actually have a greater range of pitches at their disposal than women, but they choose not to use these "feminine" pitches (Brend, 1975; Henley, 1977; Kramer, 1977; Pfeiffer, 1985).

The so-called high-pitched female whine has drawn longstanding societal criticism, in comparison to the low, rumbling, melodic tones that men are able to produce (McGonnell-Ginet, 1983). In a patriarchal society such as ours, men's lower pitched voices are viewed as being more credible and persuasive than women's, leading to what Cameron (1985) terms "a widespread prejudice against women's voices" (p. 54). Recall in Chapter 4 our discussion of the fact that men significantly outnumber women in the production of voiceovers for television and radio commercials. Women who possess lower than average-pitched voices have begun to make it into the voiceover ranks. But women who possess typically higher pitched, feminine voices most often portray silly, dependent, helpless women in commercials.

Men who possess higher pitched voices are often ridiculed for being effeminate. Their "feminine" voices detract from their credibility and dynamism, unless another physical or personality attribute somehow overpowers judgments made because of the feminine voice. (Mike Tyson, former heavyweight boxing champion, is one example of this.) However, women whose voices are lower than the expected pitch norm are not generally derided for possessing "masculine" voices. Women whose voices generate comparisons to men have supposedly received a compliment rather than an insult. Spender (1985) asserts, "It is not a mystery why men choose not to speak in the high pitched tones which are available to them in a society which links low pitch and masculinity, and high pitch and femininity; males who did produce high pitched utterances would be venturing into that negative realm and violating the gender demarcation lines. They would be ridiculed—as many adolescents whose voices have been late in breaking could testify" (p. 39).

Indications of Tentativeness

There are several ways that humans indicate tentativeness in their communication. One of these involves a property of the voice, while the others involve linguistic constructions. Well-known language and gender scholar Robin Lakoff suggested in the 1970s that these linguistic forms offer a way that "a speaker can avoid committing himself [herself], and thereby avoid coming into conflict with the addressee" (1975, pp. 16–17). The problem is, according to Lakoff and other scholars, women use far more tentative constructions and vocal properties in their communication than men. The tentative means of expression undermines the messages that women convey, making them appear uncertain, insecure, unstable, incompetent, and not to be taken seriously (Graddol & Swann, 1989; Lakoff, 1975; McConnell-Ginet, 1983).

One vocal property that indicates tentativeness is *intonation*, described by sociolinguist McConnell-Ginet (1983) as "the tune to which we set the text of our talk" (p. 70). Research has produced contradictory findings on whether the use of statements ending in a rising intonation (typically associated with asking questions) is more indicative of a female style than a male style. Lakoff (1975) contended that the rising intonation pattern was unique to English-speaking women, with the effect being the seeking of confirmation from others. An example of rising intonation can be found in a simple exchange such as the question, "What's for dinner tonight?" followed by the answer, "Spaghetti?" The intonation turns the statement or answer into a question, as if to say, "Is that okay with you?"

Not long after Lakoff (1975) labeled tentative vocal properties and constructions elements within "women's language" (p. 53), research conducted by language and education expert Carole Edelsky (1979) refuted Lakoff's findings. Edelsky's study of intonation patterns of male and female speakers indicated that the interpretation of a rising intonation depended on the context in which it was used. In certain contexts within her research, female subjects used the rising intonation pattern more than men. But in other contexts, no patterns of sex differences emerged. Contradictory findings produced by research led feminist scholar Julia Penelope (1990) to conclude the following: "Women are said to use . . . structures that are servile and submissive ('polite'), tentative, uncertain, emotionally exaggerated, and self-demeaning. These alleged traits represent a stereotype of how women talk, *not* the way we do talk" (pp. xxii–xxiii).

A linguistic construction related to intonation, which some research views as indicative of feminine uncertainty, is the *tag question* (Fishman, 1980; McMillan, Clifton, McGrath, & Gale, 1977; Zimmerman & West, 1975). Lakoff (1975) described the tag question as being "midway between an outright statement and a yes-no question: it is less assertive than the former, but more confident than the latter" (p. 15). An example of a tag question would be, "This is a really beautiful day, don't you think?" Rather than asserting an opinion in the form of a statement about the day, the speaker attaches the question onto the end of the statement. The primary use of the tag question is to seek agreement or a response from a listener, or, as Lakoff suggested, to serve as an "apology for making an assertion at all" (p. 54). Lakoff attributed the use of tag questions to a general lack of assertiveness or confidence about what one is saying, a usage that her research indicated was more related to a female style than a male style. While Lakoff assigned certain linguistic practices to certain sexes, she was also perturbed by the tendency of people to "form judgments about other people on the basis of superficial linguistic behavior that may have nothing to do with inner character, but has been imposed upon the speaker" (p. 17).

Other research investigating Lakoff's claims found no evidence that tag questions occurred more in female speech than in male speech or that tag questions necessarily functioned to indicate uncertainty or tentativeness (Baumann, 1979; Dubois & Crouch, 1975; Holmes, 1990). Tag questions may operate as genuine requests or to "forestall opposition" (Dubois & Crouch, 1975, p. 292). As

Spender (1985) points out, it is inappropriate to view tag questions as always indicating hesitancy, as evidenced by her example "'You won't do that again, *will you?*'" (p. 9).

Another linguistic construction generally interpreted to indicate tentativeness and stereotypically associated with women's speech is the reliance on such devices as *qualifiers, hedges, disclaimers, intensifiers,* and *compound* versus *simple requests.* Lakoff (1975) claimed that women's speech incorporated more of these constructions, indicating women's general uncertainty and inability to "vouch for the accuracy of the statement" (p. 53). Qualifying terms include *well, you know, kind of, sort of, really, perhaps, possibly, maybe,* and *of course.* Hedging devices include such terms as *I think/believe/feel, I guess, I mean,* and *I wonder* (Holmes, 1990; Lakoff, 1975; Spender, 1985). Disclaimers are typically longer forms of hedges which act as prefaces or defense mechanisms when one is unsure or doubtful of what one is about to say (Beach & Dunning, 1982; Bell, Zahn, & Hopper, 1984; Bradley, 1981; Hewitt & Stokes, 1975). Disclaimers generally weaken or soften the effect of a message. Examples of disclaimers include such statements as "I know this is a dumb question, but. . ." and "I may be wrong here, but I think that. . .." (Researchers label some of these devices qualifiers and others hedges or disclaimers; thus examples we provide here may not correspond to discrete categories.) Compound requests typically involve a negative construction and are the longer, more complex requests for action or assistance more characteristic of women's speech than men's, according to Lakoff (1975). The question "Won't you please come with me tonight?" is a compound request, compared with the simple or direct construction "Come with me tonight." Again, compound requests signal tentativeness or that "the speaker is not committed as with a simple declarative or affirmative" (Lakoff, 1975, p. 19).

Documentation of intensifiers by language scholars dates back as far as 1922 when linguist Otto Jespersen studied women's use of exaggeration, specifically in the form of the term *vastly.* His studies led him to conclude that women are much more prone to hyperbole in their communication than men. Lakoff (1975) focused on the word *so,* claiming that women use such constructions as "I like him *so* much" (p. 55) more than men. Penelope (1990) adds *so much, such,* and *quite* as ways of signaling a feeling level or intensifying what one is saying (p. xxii).

Two linguists, Janet Holmes (1990), who studied male and female speech patterns in New Zealand, and Deborah Cameron (1985), who studied tentativeness in the speech patterns of London natives, as well as researchers in the United States, have concluded that sex-typed interpretations of a range of linguistic devices, including qualifiers, hedges, disclaimers, intensifiers, and compound requests, must be made within the given context in which the communication occurs (Bradley, 1981; Kramarae, 1982; Mulac & Lundell, 1986; O'Barr & Atkins, 1980; Ragan, 1989; Sayers & Sherblom, 1987).

Holmes (1990) discovered, for example, that men and women were equally likely to use tentative linguistic devices, depending on the needs or mandates of the particular situation. Female subjects in her study demonstrated regular uses of tentative communication when in the presence of men, but less often when with other women. Cameron (1985) found that male subjects exhibited tentative communication when placed in certain roles, such as facilitators of group interaction. Male and female subjects alike in O'Barr and Atkins's (1980) study of courtroom communication used the entire range of features constituting what Lakoff (1975) called "women's language" with equal frequency, with the exception of tag questions.

We grant that an overabundance of tentative forms of expression in one's communication can be interpreted as a sign of uncertainty and insecurity. But there may also be positive, affiliative uses of tentative language; these kinds of expressions need not be identified with one sex or the other. For example, a manager holding a higher status position within an organization might use disclaimers or hedges in an attempt to even out a status differential, to foster a sense of camaraderie among staff members, and to show herself or himself as open to suggestion and ideas from employees. While research suggests that women use more forms of tentativeness in their communication, other research indicates that both sexes may actually use tentative forms of expression at certain times and in a variety of contexts to convey affiliation and to facilitate interaction with others. As an example, a male friend explains that he often uses compound requests, tag questions, and disclaimers when dealing with a range of people— coworkers, subordinates, friends, and so on—to convey a nondogmatic, supportive, and less dominant attitude to others. It's a good idea to use caution, to consider the context, and to avoid stereotypes when interpreting tentative communication.

Word Selection

The discussion in this section has to do with men's and women's preferences in their choice of words. The most interesting information surrounds the use of color terms, profanity, and sexual slang.

Color Language

In one episode of *Designing Women*, Julia Sugarbaker, one of the main female characters, and a man she had begun to date reported to Julia's coworkers the results of their shopping expedition. The male character explained that he had tried to talk Julia into buying a "mauve" suit that had a figure-enhancing "peplum." Later, Julia's female cohorts suggested that the man was probably homosexual, based on two key words he had mentioned, mauve and peplum— terms that they insisted no heterosexual man would use (or be able to define). (How many of you reading this are wondering, "Just what *is* a peplum?") We use this example for two purposes: (1) to emphasize what we said earlier in this text, that a man who exhibits what society deems "feminine" behavior is often demeaned and accused of being homosexual, an unfortunate trend often highlighted in media; and (2) to dramatize the research conducted on women, men, and the language of color.

Very little is written about this topic, but most often "colorful" language is relegated to women's realm. Lakoff (1975) contended, "Women make far more precise discriminations in naming colors than do men; words like beige, ecru, aquamarine, lavender, and so on are unremarkable in a woman's active vocabulary, but absent from that of most men" (pp. 8–9). One of our friends remarked recently that she gave her husband a nice "dusty plum" shirt for his birthday. Ask yourself if you've ever heard a man describe something as being "dusty plum." Probably not, but do you wonder why that is so? Research provides few explanations of why women tend to use more discrepant categories for colors than men. One explanation relates to the tendency for more men than women to be color blind. But this doesn't seem to have much practical value if, in your experience, men who aren't color blind don't tend to use many variations of color terms. Another explanation is simply that the whole topic of color may be more important to women than to men, given that women have traditionally been more closely linked with home decoration and fashion. In this view, women have developed microdistinctions between colors and the words to go with them out of necessity.

Lakoff (1975) asserted that men relegate colors to the realm of the "unworldly," which they equate with a woman's realm. She argued that "since women are not expected to make decisions on important matters, such as what kind of job to hold, they are relegated the noncrucial decisions, . . . whether to name a color 'lavender' or 'mauve'" (p. 9). In *Basic Color Terms* sociologists Berlin and Kay (1969) explain that designations of color are closely connected to one's culture. As a final note, some students believe that the trend for women to use more color terms than men is changing among persons of their generation. They assert that as more men and women enter professions stereotypically associated with the opposite sex, such as men entering interior and fashion design fields, terminology tendencies will continue to change. Do you agree with this prediction?

Profanity and Sexual Slang

We talked in Chapter 3 about sexual terms that are used to refer to the sexes in a derogatory fashion, but what about profanity and sexual slang in interpersonal communication? Are there sex-typed tendencies for these kinds of language usage? Even in the 1990s, is it more acceptable for men than women to say shit, damn, hell, son of a bitch, and other colorful metaphors and profane terms?

Use of profanity has long been considered a man's behavior (if it's considered *anyone's* behavior), thus the conventional reference to "cursing like a sailor." Lakoff (1975) contended that women's language encouraged them to remain "little ladies" (p. 11). A woman violates this ladylike demeanor if she uses an overabundance of slang or profanity. In support of this argument, Lakoff offered two versions of the same statement, asking readers to label them as being spoken by a man or a woman. The statements were: "Oh dear, you've put the peanut butter in the refrigerator again," and "Shit, you've put the peanut butter in the refrigerator again" (p. 10). Lakoff believed that the gender labeling of these statements would be obvious, despite the fact that more women were feeling comfortable using profanity as a result of the women's movement occurring at the time. However, she also anticipated that most of "Middle America" would still flinch and disapprove of female cursing (p. 10). If profanity made one's opinions more forceful and believable, but such usages were unacceptable for women, then the acceptance of their use of profanity only enhanced men's position of strength, according to Lakoff.

A fascinating study of male and female college students' uses of profane and hostile language was conducted in 1978 by a gender linguist named Constance Staley. A most interesting perceptual discrepancy emerged from Staley's data. Female subjects held the perception that men used profanity and hostile language to a much *greater* degree than male subjects indicated they did. In contrast, male subjects thought that women used *far less* profanity than female subjects reported actually using. So, even during a liberated decade like the 1970s when women experimented with profanity, they still placed profanity and "rough talk" predominantly into a male domain. At the same time, men expected women to talk like ladies, not sailors.

In a classic article concerning the use of sexual language, linguist Otto Jespersen (1922) wrote that "women in all countries are shy of mentioning certain parts of the human body and certain natural functions by the direct and often rude denominations which men, especially young men, prefer when among themselves" (p. 245). According to Jespersen, women's distaste for blunt, graphic terminology leads them to develop euphemisms which then become more common usages in everyday language. In this way, Jespersen believed that "women exercise a great and universal influence on linguistic development through their instinctive shrinking from coarse and gross expressions" (p. 246).

You might argue that a lot has changed since Jespersen's research in the 1920s. But has it really changed all that much? Are women really that much freer to use sexual language that is typically reserved for men? Research published in 1990 by gender and language expert Julia Penelope specifically addressed forms of language she termed "the slang of sexual slurs" (p. 46). Penelope concluded (with significant resentment) that it appears to be unacceptable even in our modern society for women to use sexual slang or to hear it used. Men are permitted to use such language, but with one restraint: "They rarely exhibit the full range of it in the company of women" (p. 46).

An interesting sex difference emerged from gender researcher Rinck Simkins's (1982) study of preferred language in discussions of male and female genitalia and sexual intercourse. Both female and male undergraduates reported that in mixed company they would use more formal, clinical terminology for genitalia and intercourse. However, when in the company of same-sex friends, men were more likely to use sexual slang while women still preferred the more formal terminology.

One of the problems people face when they have discussions about sex—with a dating or marital partner, with their children, with *anyone*—is that the language describing body parts and sexual activity is either completely clinical or "gutter" (Potorti, 1992). In other words, it's sometimes hard to talk frankly about sex-related topics, even though those kinds of discussions are important, because the embarrassing choices are (1) to use awkward medical-book terminology that may not be understandable to both speaker and listener; (2) to use "gutter terms" or graphic slang which may be offensive and is likely to demean the very topic you are discussing; or (3) to keep the discussion vague, by using inferences rather than specific language, thus risking misunderstanding. If people in general, and women in specific, have difficulty expressing themselves on sexual topics, it's somewhat understandable when you consider the language that currently exists for our use. In Chapter 9 we discuss some strategies for communicators who may find themselves engaged in such kinds of discussions.

Women and Men in Conversation

The final element within this discussion of how language is used in gender communication relates to the basic structure of ordinary conversation. Have you ever considered how conversation is organized or how it gets "managed"? The elements that make conversations appear to be organized are typically subsumed in research under the heading "conversation management." If you were to read about conversation management in other sources, you might see descriptions of the following: conversation initiation and maintenance; talkativeness; turn-taking; topic control and gossip; interruptions and overlaps; question asking versus answering; and the use of pauses and silence. Most of these areas would probably be discussed in terms of the contradictory research findings produced by studies that have attempted to isolate sex differences.

We choose a different approach to this topic, one that examines conversational management from the standpoint of research on two divergent types of interactions or "floors." We draw information for this section primarily from the work of Carole Edelsky, an educator and scholar who became interested in male and female communication styles within groups. In an article entitled "Who's Got the Floor?" Edelsky (1981) describes her participation in a series of university committee meetings in which two very different types of discussions occurred (Floor 1 and Floor 2). Edelsky became fascinated by sex differences that emerged in these committee meetings, in relation to aspects of conversation management, for example, turn-taking, topic control, interruptions or overlaps, and talk time (which she termed "floor holding"). Let's first review some definitions of these terms, then describe how they function in conversation.

Conversation Management Terminology

Conversation typically occurs in *turns,* meaning that one speaker takes a turn, then another, and so on, such that interaction is socially organized (Sacks, Schegloff, & Jefferson, 1978). A speaker's interjection into a conversation is her or his "turn at talk." *Topic control* is fairly self-explanatory; it occurs when a speaker initiates a topic and works to see that that topic continues to be the focal point of discussion. Part of that work involves fending off *interruptions,* defined by West and Zimmerman (1983) as "violations of speakers' turns at talk," and *overlaps,* defined as "simultaneous speech initiated by a next speaker just as a current speaker arrives at a possible turn-transition place" (pp. 103–104). The range of interpretations of interruptions and overlaps includes the following: they indicate disrespect and restrict a speaker's rights, they serve as devices to control the topic, and they indicate an attitude of dominance and authority (Marche & Peterson, 1993). *Talk time,* sometimes referred to as *air time* or *verbosity,* refers to how long a speaker takes to accomplish one turn at talk (Eakins & Eakins, 1976; Edelsky, 1981).

Edelsky's Floor 1

A Floor 1 interaction is described by Edelsky as "the usual orderly, one-at-a-time type of floor" (p. 384), characterized by "monologues, single-party control and hierarchical interaction where turn takers stand out from non-turn takers and floors are won or lost" (p. 416). Certain speakers (usually men, if the group is mixed sex) dominate discussion by imposing a hierarchical or status-based order to turns at talk; taking longer turns at talk; offering more statements than questions; interrupting other speakers; and using vocal devices to ward off interruptions to their own talk. Conversation exemplifies competition rather than cooperation. In Edelsky's experience with Floor 1 discussions, men's turns were four times as long as women's turns. Noted feminist Gloria

---

What If ?

What if you could be a fly on the wall, eavesdropping on a conversation between a group of women or men? Have you ever wondered what an all-opposite-sex discussion sounds like? If you're a female reader, *what if* you were able to be a fly on the wall in the men's locker room, to overhear a group of guys talking about women? Think for a moment about what that conversation would be like, in terms of the language that would be used, the topics that would be discussed, and the signs of male competitiveness that would be evident from the "flow" of the conversation. If you're a male reader, *what if* you were invisible and sat in on a conversation between a group of female friends over happy hour? Do you suspect that they'd talk more about their jobs or the men in their lives? Recent research indicates that conversation looks and sounds quite different for all-female versus all-male groups of people. Would a difference be noticeable to you, and would it make you uncomfortable? Would you find women's conversation to be disorganized and chaotic, or more fun and free-flowing than a typical conversation among men? Think about those times when you may have overheard a conversation between two or more people of the opposite sex. Were there elements to the way the conversation was conducted that surprised you? It's interesting to think about these experiences, or to imagine *what* your reactions would be *if* you were that fly on the wall.

Steinem (1983) calls this behavior a "policing of the subject matter of conversation" (p. 179).

Floor 1 discussions do not necessarily occur only within group settings; two people might have a Floor 1 conversation. For example, think about a conversation you may have had in which you became very aware that "conversational rules" were operating. Such a conversation might have arisen between you and your employer over an issue at work, or between you and a friend who comes to you for a favor, or between you and a parent, sibling, or spouse. Several things affect how the conversation will go, such as the nature or sensitivity of the topic being discussed, any status differentials between the participants, or the history of interaction between the two people. Later we discuss sex as one of the variables that has the potential to affect how a conversation will go. In a Floor 1 conversation, the tone or shape of the conversation is likely to be dominated by one person's interaction style. If your boss speaks in declaratives rather than with language that invites response, if she or he indicates that interruptions or overlaps are not welcome, if his or her talk consists of minimonologues rather than even exchanges—all aspects of conversation management—then those tendencies may configure the conversation into the Floor 1 type or profile.

Edelsky's Floor 2

Floor 2 interactions are characterized by cooperation rather than competition. Cooperation is evidenced by simultaneous talk, or "free-for-alls" as Edelsky termed them, the "joint building of an answer to a question," and by "collaboration on developing ideas" (p. 391). Floor 2 discussions may also contain a good deal of laughter, as well as flows of turn-taking and overlapping talk, indicative of members being "on the same wave length" (p. 391). In Edelsky's experience with Floor 2 discussions, participation was more balanced for the sexes, with men participating significantly less than they did in Floor 1 discussions and women participating more. Steinem (1983) contends that the "rotating style of talk and leadership" that emerges in a discussion of the Floor 2 variety is a predominant characteristic of women-only group discussions (p. 183).

Think of other conversations you've participated in that fit Edelsky's description of Floor 2. It may be that, on another day about another topic, the same employer you considered an exemplar of Floor 1 interactions will converse with you in a manner indicative of a Floor 2 variation. Have you been in conversations in which the rules and organizing, managing structures seem to be left outside the door? Such conversations might appear to an eavesdropper to be completely incoherent. As a personal example, your female co-author's conversations with her mother almost without exception take the form of Edelsky's Floor 2, to the amazement of her father. The two get teased for "going from Los Angeles to Seattle via Dallas," but the pattern of conversation makes perfect sense to them. Such a conversation is full of give and take, riddled with interruptions and overlapping talk, sporadic in its constant topic switching, and almost mystical in how the interactants finish each others' thoughts and sentences. This kind of discussion—a Floor 2 discussion—accomplishes its goals and has structure and management properties within it, but it just doesn't seem to match many people's versions of an "orderly" conversation.

Floor Comparisons

Edelsky explains that both types of floors may arise within a single discussion, but the main distinguishing characteristic is that Floor 1 develops singly, while Floor 2 develops jointly. It is important to understand that Edelsky contrasts the two floors by the *style* of interaction that emerges, not by what gets accomplished during each type of discussion. For example, Edelsky does not conclude that Floor 1 discussions are more conducive to getting tasks accomplished, while Floor 2's make interactants feel more positively toward one another. Edelsky reports that almost all of her meetings began socially, with joking, idle chitchat, and refreshments. What signaled the type of floor were who spoke first and how he or she spoke, the topics discussed in the first series of turns, the composition of the particular group (in terms of who was present and who was absent), and so on. These characteristics define a floor as well as move a group from one kind of floor to the other.

Conversational Management and the Sexes

The research on conversational management styles of men and women has produced such contradictory findings that presenting them one by one in this chapter would likely irritate more than enlighten. Another indictment of the conversation management research is that most of it is based on only one format for interaction—the "one-at-a-time" format that equates to Edelsky's Floor 1—as the model by which standards are determined and sex differences are measured. Many women and men alike have come to expect that a mixed-sex discussion will take the format of a Floor 1, with masculine individuals dominating the conversation, controlling what gets talked about and by whom. Edelsky sums up this faulty expectation: "One-at-a-time is not a conversational universal, nor is it essential for the communication of messages. Moreover, the unquestioning adoption of this premise causes researchers to see more-than-one-at-a-time as degenerate, a breakdown, or something requiring repair" (p. 397). She argues that researchers should question what conditions must exist for the sexes to interact as equals, rather than to question how the sexes demonstrate a power differential in one format of interaction.

Edelsky discovered some sex-related trends among her research findings. Women in the study tended to participate more and experience more satisfaction from Floor 2 than Floor 1 conversations because these informal, cooperative discussions provided "both a cover of 'anonymity' for assertive language use and a comfortable backdrop against which women can display a fuller range of language ability" (p. 416). As language and gender scholar Pamela Fishman

(1983) put it, women in cooperative conversations don't have to accomplish the "conversational shitwork" that they typically do in competitive conversations (p. 99). In Edelsky's research, men talked less in Floor 2 discussions than they did in Floor 1's, but they still talked at a rate even with women in Floor 2's. Their participation did not appear to be hampered by the cooperative, free-flowing style. Edelsky also made no mention of a higher level of satisfaction from male subjects participating in Floor 1 versus Floor 2 discussions. Edelsky concludes that men can benefit from the "high-involvement, synergistic, solidarity-building interaction" characteristics of Floor 2 discussions (p. 417). Women and men alike could certainly benefit from the knowledge that they can indeed experience satisfying, power-equalizing interactions—an experience that many would probably welcome.

To conclude this section on conversational management, we encourage you to think about some of the more recent discussions you've been in and to assess your involvement in them. Did you display communication behaviors stereotypically connected to your sex and gender? Do you think that such dominant behaviors as interrupting and controlling the topic are necessarily male or masculine conversational devices? Is it "just like a woman" to wait for her turn at talk, rather than speak up and offer her input? Are the sexes somehow limited by such designations of "appropriate" behavior? What happens when the conversational expectations of women and men are violated? Consider the kind of condemnation a man who never speaks up might receive. What might be the response to a woman who interrupts others' comments and changes the topic, without the use of a disclaimer? It's fairly safe to say that the sex typing that may accompany conversational style is as debilitating as other forms of sex and gender stereotyping. Even to the point of expecting conversations to take certain forms because of women and men involved in them, gender stereotyping gets in the way of successful, effective gender communication.

CONCLUSION

We've given you a lot to think about in this chapter for one main reason—so that you'll more fully consider how communication occurs *between* women and men. Studying how it occurs empowers you to apply this information when you go about the business of initiating and developing all sorts of relationships. Knowing what you now know about varying approaches to communication, how would you describe your own approach, relative to that of someone of the opposite sex? Consider whether you typically approach communication as serving more of a relational or a content function, or whether you select an approach based on the needs or demands of the situation. Think about a special person—a past love, someone you're currently seeing, your spouse, or your best friend. How would you describe this person's style and approach to conversation? If it is significantly different from your own style, perhaps you find the contrast workable. But is it possible that the difference in your very purposes for having conversations has caused you significant relational problems?

Consider also your preferences for the management of conversation. Are you equally comfortable in Floor 1 and Floor 2 interactions? If you have set rules about things like interrupting and turn-taking in conversations, where did those rules come from? What happens if someone, perhaps someone who's on an inner ring of your relational concentric circles, has a set of rules vastly different from yours? It is well worth the energy to think about these things, especially if you feel that your current relational profile could use some improving. And this knowledge is critical as you prepare to initiate new relationships. In the next chapter we build on the ideas in this chapter as we explore ways that women and men use gender communication to initiate relationships.

Key Terms

communication axiom	personal level of talk	compound requests
relational dimension	genderlects	simple requests
content dimension	vocal properties	word selection
human development theory	pitch	profanity
gender-role identity	tentativeness	sexual slang
interpersonal communication motives	intonation	conversation management
	linguistic constructions	floors
rapport-talk	tag questions	turn-taking
report-talk	qualifiers	topic control
topical level of talk	hedges	interruptions
relational level of talk	disclaimers	overlaps
	intensifiers	talk time

Discussion Starters

1. Think of two people—a woman and a man—whose communication styles most closely (or stereotypically) correspond to the relational versus content approach model presented in this chapter. What are the most marked aspects of each person's communication that make them stand out in your mind as examples?

2. Have you ever considered the notion of motives for talking with other people? In casual conversation, how do interpersonal motives operate between women and men? When you meet someone new, for instance, what are several possible motives you might have for engaging in conversation with this person?

3. Imagine that you are talking to the most special, most important person in your life right now. That person might be a spouse, family member, best friend, lover, dating partner, boss. Now review the information in this chapter about the topical, relational, and personal levels of intimacy. Which level would you say most characterizes your communication with your special person? Are you happy with that level, or do you feel a need to change it?

4. Research has concluded that many stylistic properties of women's speech cause them to communicate tentativeness and powerlessness. Do you agree with the research on this topic? Why do you think this conclusion has been reached, when women's communication tends to be affiliative, supportive, other-oriented, and nurturing?

What would cause communication like that to be devalued in our society? How can you help change the "devaluing" into a "valuing" process?

5. If you are a female reader, assess your own style of communication. How often do you communicate in questions? Research suggests that women use questions as means of attempting to ensure that they'll get a response. Does this explanation apply to you? Do you have a lot of tag questions, hedges, and disclaimers in your communication? Are you more likely to be interrupted while speaking than to interrupt someone else? If so, do you believe that these elements weaken your effect or make you appear tentative or powerless? Why or why not?

6. If you are a male reader, assess your own style of communication. How often do you communicate in statements rather than questions? Research suggests that men use statements as a means of controlling a conversation and to further establish their sense of importance in the world. Do you agree with the research findings? Is this style typical of you? Do you use many tag questions, hedges, and disclaimers in your communication? Do you generally interrupt people more than they interrupt you? If not, why not?

References

BAKAN, D. (1966). *The duality of human existence.* Chicago: McNally.

BAUMANN, M. (1979). Two features of "women's speech"? In B. L. Dubois & I. Crouch (Eds.), *The sociology of the languages of American women* (pp. 33–40). San Antonio, TX: Trinity University Press.

BEACH, W. A., & DUNNING, D. G. (1982). Pre-indexing and conversational organization. *Quarterly Journal of Speech, 67,* 170–185.

BELL, R. A., ZAHN, C. J., & HOPPER, R. (1984). Disclaiming: A test of two competing views. *Communication Quarterly, 32,* 28–36.

BERLIN, B., & KAY, P. (1969). *Basic color terms: Their universality and evolution.* Berkeley: University of California Press.

BRADLEY, P. H. (1981). The folk-linguistics of women's speech: An empirical examination. *Communication Monographs, 48,* 73–90.

BREND, R. (1975). Male-female intonation patterns in American English. In B. Thorne & N. Henley (Eds.), *Language and sex: Difference and dominance* (pp. 84–87). Rowley, MA: Newbury House.

BROWNMILLER, S. (1984). *Femininity.* New York: Simon & Schuster.

CAMERON, D. (1985). *Feminism and linguistic theory.* New York: St. Martin's Press.

DAVIDSON, L. R., & DUBERMAN, L. (1982). Friendship: Communication and interactional patterns in same-sex dyads. *Sex Roles, 8,* 809–822.

DUBOIS, B. L., & CROUCH, I. (1975). The question of tag questions in women's speech: They don't really use more of them, do they? *Language in Society, 4,* 289–294.

EAKINS, B., & EAKINS, G. (1976). Verbal turn-taking and exchanges in faculty dialogue. In B. L. Dubois & I. Crouch (Eds.), *The sociology of the languages of American women* (pp. 53–62). San Antonio, TX: Trinity University Press.

EDELSKY, C. (1979). Question intonation and sex roles. *Language in Society, 8,* 15–32.

EDELSKY, C. (1981). Who's got the floor? *Language in Society, 10,* 383–421.

FISHMAN, P. M. (1980). Conversational insecurity. In H. Giles, W. P. Robinson, & P. M. Smith (Eds.), *Language: Social psychological perspectives* (pp. 127–132). New York: Pergamon Press.

FISHMAN, P. M. (1983). Interaction: The work women do. In B. Thorne, C. Kramarae, & N. Henley (Eds.), *Language, gender, and society* (pp. 89–101). Rowley, MA: Newbury House.

GILLIGAN, C. (1982). *In a different voice.* Cambridge, MA: Harvard University Press.

GRADDOL, D., & SWANN, J. (1989). *Gender voices.* Cambridge, MA: Basil Blackwell.

HENLEY, N. M. (1977). *Body politics: Power, sex, and nonverbal communication.* Englewood Cliffs, NJ: Prentice-Hall.

HEWITT, J. P., & STOKES, R. (1975). Disclaimers. *American Sociological Review, 40,* 1–11.

HOLMES, J. (1990). Hedges and boosters in women's and men's speech. *Language and Communication, 10,* 185–205.

ICKES, W. (1981). Sex role influences in dyadic interaction: A theoretical model. In C. Mayo & N. M. Henley (Eds.), *Gender and nonverbal behavior* (pp. 95–128). New York: Springer-Verlag.

JESPERSEN, O. (1922). *Language: Its nature, development, and origin.* New York: Holt.

KRAMARAE, C. (1982). Gender: How she speaks. In E. Bouchard Ryan & H. Giles (Eds.), *Attitudes toward language variation: Social and applied contexts* (pp. 84–98). London: Edward Arnold.

KRAMER, C. (1977). Perceptions of female and male speech. *Language and Speech, 20,* 151–161.

LAKOFF, R. (1975). *Language and woman's place.* New York: Harper & Row.

MARCHE, T. A., & PETERSON, C. (1993). The development and sex-related use of interruption behavior. *Human Communication Research, 19,* 388–408.

MCCONNELL-GINET, S. (1983). Intonation in a man's world. In B. Thorne, C. Kramarae, & N. Henley (Eds.), *Language, gender, and society* (pp. 69–88). Rowley, MA: Newbury House.

MCMILLAN, J. R., CLIFTON, A. K., MCGRATH, D., & GALE, W. S. (1977). Women's language: Uncertainty or interpersonal sensitivity and emotionality? *Sex Roles, 3,* 545–559.

MULAC, A., & LUNDELL, T. L. (1986). Linguistic contributors to the gender-linked language effect. *Journal of Language and Social Psychology, 5,* 81–101.

MYERS, A. M., & GONDA, G. (1983). Utility of the masculine-feminine construct: Comparison of traditional and androgyny approaches. *Journal of Personality and Social Psychology, 43,* 514–523.

O'BARR, W. M., & ATKINS, B. K. (1980). "Women's language" or "powerless language"? In S. McConnell-Ginet, R. Borker, & N. Furman (Eds.), *Women and language in literature and society* (pp. 93–110). New York: Praeger.

PARSONS, T., & BALES, R. F. (1955). *Family, socialization, and interaction processes.* New York: Free Press of Glencoe.

PENELOPE, J. (1990). *Speaking freely: Unlearning the lies of the fathers' tongues.* New York: Pergamon Press.

PFEIFFER, J. (1985). Girl talk, boy talk. *Science, 85,* 58–63.

POTORTI, P. (1992). Personal communication, October.

RAGAN, S. L. (1989). Communication between the sexes: A consideration of sex differences in adult communication. In J. F. Nussbaum (Ed.), *Life-span communication: Normative processes* (pp. 179–193). Hillsdale, NJ: Lawrence Erlbaum Associates.

RUBIN, R. B., PERSE, E. M., & BARBATO, C. A. (1988). Conceptualization and measurement of interpersonal communication motives. *Human Communication Research, 14,* 602–628.

SACKS, H., SCHEGLOFF, E. A., & JEFFERSON, G. (1978). A simplest systematics for the organization of turn taking for conversation. In J. Schenkein (Ed.), *Studies in the organization of conversational interaction* (pp. 7–55). New York: Academic Press.

SAYERS, F., & SHERBLOM, J. (1987). Qualification in male language as influenced by age and gender of conversational partner. *Communication Research Reports, 4,* 88–92.

SCHRADER, D. (1992, November). *Instrumental and expressive orientations to interaction and judgments of communicator acceptability: The effects of interaction goals.* Paper presented at the annual meeting of the Speech Communication Association, Chicago, IL.

SHAPIRO, J., & SHAPIRO, D. H. (1985). A "control" model of psychological health: Relation to "traditional" and "liberated" sex-role stereotypes. *Sex Roles, 12,* 433–447.

SIMKINS, R. (1982). Male and female sexual vocabulary in different interpersonal contexts. *Journal of Sex Research, 18,* 160–172.

SPENDER, D. (1985). *Man made language* (2nd ed.). London: Routledge & Kegan Paul.

STALEY, C. (1982). Sex related differences in the style of children's language. *Journal of Psycholinguistic Research, 11,* 141–152.

STEINEM, G. (1983). *Outrageous acts and everyday rebellions.* New York: Signet Books.

TANNEN, D. (1990). *You just don't understand.* New York: William Morrow.

WATZLAWICK, P., BEAVIN, J. H., & JACKSON, D. D. (1967). *Pragmatics of human communication.* New York: W. W. Norton.

WEST, C., & ZIMMERMAN, D. H. (1983). Small insults: A study of interruptions in cross-sex conversations between unacquainted persons. In B. Thorne, C. Kramarae, & N. Henley (Eds.), *Language, gender, and society* (pp. 102–117). Rowley, MA: Newbury House.

WOOD, J. T., & LENZE, L. F. (1991). Gender and the development of self: Inclusive pedagogy in interpersonal communication. *Women's Studies in Communication, 14,* 1–23.

ZIMMERMAN, D. H., & WEST, C. (1975). Sex roles, interruptions, and silences in conversation. In B. Thorne & N. Henley (Eds.), *Language and sex: Difference and dominance* (pp. 105–129). Rowley, MA: Newbury House.

CHAPTER 6

Turning Potential into Reality: Women, Men, and Relationships

Now that you've read Chapters 1 through 5, why should you read this chapter? Not because you have nothing else to do this Saturday night, but because we guess that you, like most people, are intrigued by the incredible range of potential relationships out there. The question is, how do you make those relationships *happen?* This chapter looks at exactly that—the process of turning relationship potential into reality. First, here's a case study to get your mind in gear.

CASE STUDY

A classroom exercise used at the University of Denver, as well as in other communication departments across the country, provokes some interesting reactions in students. At about midterm, after students have begun to know each other better, we have a class discussion on attraction and its effect on communication between men and women. In the course of that discussion, we do this exercise. Everyone in the room is asked to stand up and clear the chairs out of the way. We introduce the exercise by saying: "We all must make choices in initiating relationships. This exercise makes that process of choice obvious for everyone."

We give the students a series of instructions, the first being: "Go place your hand on the shoulder of the person in this room whom you have known the longest." Students do this fairly readily, even if they have just met someone and report "knowing" him or her for only 5 minutes. The second instruction is: "Go place your hand on the shoulder of the person in this room with whom you spend the most time." Students shrug, look a little uneasy, and do it. We ask the students to look around and see who is partnered with whom and if chains of people have formed. The third instruction is: "Go place your hand on the shoulder of the person you think is most similar to you in attitudes, beliefs, and values." For some students this is a little harder, but they do it. The fourth instruction is: "Go place your hand on the shoulder of the person you most believe you could gain or learn something from and tell her or him what that is." For some students this instruction requires no new action because they stay with the same person from the time before. The final instruction is: "Go place your hand on the shoulder of the person you see as a winner and tell him or her why." This is the set of instructions we use most often, but other instructions can be added for specific instructional purposes.

This exercise causes discomfort on some level for everyone, because it forces people to choose, to be chosen, or to not be chosen. Afterward, we talk with the class about what all those choices feel like. Then we talk about the basis of choice or who chooses whom and why. It always comes down to one thing—not physical appearance, not "opposites attract"—just *information*. Students choose students they *know the most about*. The initiation of relationships depends more on information than on other things, even physical appearance—no matter what the media and the fashion industry would have you believe.

OVERVIEW

Before getting into the specifics of this chapter, we want to clarify our use of the terms relationship, relationship initiation, and relational partner. The word *relationship* gets tossed around about as much as the word *communication:* Friendships, platonic relationships (which some people prefer as a term for opposite-sex friendships), romantic relationships, dating relationships, work relationships, marital relationships, premarital relationships, extramarital relationships, parent-child relationships, and teacher-student relationships are all types of relationships that are important in our lives. These relational labels, as well as their characteristics, overlap all because, for example, we'd like to think that some marital relationships are also romantic relationships! When we use the word *relationship* in our gender communication classes, students typically think of dating or romantic relationships rather than other kinds. For our purposes in this text, we discuss some elements that pertain to all kinds of relationships. Then there are those elements that are more relevant to dating or romantic relationships than to other types, so we are specific in those instances.

We use the term *relationship initiation* to mean the beginning stages of relationship development—from the first thought about having one to actually stepping into the action. When we use the term *relational partner* in those instances where we refer specifically to dating relationships, it is not with the permanence implied by the term *marital partner*. It is simply a means of identifying the two people in a relationship.

Have you ever considered relationship initiation from the standpoint of choosing and being chosen? We bet not, because it's a fairly unusual way to approach it. Since we anticipate questions about this approach, we offer an explanation early in this chapter for the role of choice in the relational arena. Then we frame our discussion around a three-stage model of relationship initiation. Here are some specifics that you'll be reading about in the pages that follow:

- Barriers or roadblocks to relationship initiation
- Choosing relationships, as well as being chosen for them
- How information about yourself and others plays a significant role in initiating relationships
- The effects of attraction on relationship initiation and development
- Ways to assess your own level of interest in a potential relational partner, as well as her or his level of interest in you
- How to start conversations and show that you like someone through sensitive communication
- Factors that influence the decision to continue in a relationship

As you read this chapter, think about strategies you currently use to begin relationships, strategies you have seen others use, and what factors have contributed to success or failure. It really is possible to become more successful at initiating relationships and responding to people who initiate relationships with you. Thus the main goal of this chapter is to offer ways for you to become more relationally effective by understanding the choices available to you.

INTRODUCTION

Sometimes, in spite of our best efforts, relationships just don't go well. Things seem to pop up that get in the way of a successful beginning to a relationship. One way of becoming a more personally effective communicator is to examine why things go wrong. What *does* get in the way of a good relationship, and what do you do about it? The following are some relational "roadblocks" that may or may not be familiar to you. By understanding these roadblocks, maybe you can avoid them the next time you choose to initiate a relationship or when someone chooses to initiate a relationship with you.

Roadblock 1: High Expectations

In Chapter 4 we discussed the impact of the media on our behavior. MTV, movies, and television shows frequently set us up for a rude awakening. The media depict attractive, beautiful people engaged in seemingly carefree, highly physical romantic relationships. Life just isn't like that, but many students want the dating relationships they see in the media—sexy, passionate, and lots of fun. The media rarely show these relationships 6 months later, as they have developed over time, nor do they typically depict the work necessary to make relationships successful. Women may fantasize about the "perfect" man who is a combination of strength and sensitivity. Men may fantasize about the "perfect" woman who looks great and who embodies a blend of ambition and traditional family values. But we know that nobody's perfect, so sometimes when we set high expectations for others and our relationships, we are really setting ourselves up for a fall.

Roadblock 2: "This Should Be Easy"

You know now that communication isn't a natural thing that you can do successfully just because you've been communicating all your life. So why do we sometimes think that it ought to be so easy to just relax and talk to someone? Why, in reality, is communication so difficult in relationships—especially in really important relationships? Effective communication isn't easy, and the more that you have riding on the success of your relationship, the more difficult communication seems to be. Navigating the communication waters in a relationship can be tough but not necessarily overwhelming. If you go into a relationship with the expectation that communication will be or ought to be easy, you may be setting up a roadblock to relational success (Grove, 1991).

Roadblock 3: Fear of Failure

We talked in Chapter 1 about your relational "batting average" and the fact that no one can be successful all the time. But how many people do you know who are so afraid of failure—failure to initiate and keep a relationship going—that they don't even try to make friends? Failure is part of the relational process, however painful it might be. And even though it is a cliché, we do learn from failure. Sometimes when we are at our most exasperated, beaten-down state from relationships gone awry, that's when we look up and see that new person walking into the room.

Roadblock 4: "If I Just Relax, a Good Relationship Will Find Me"

It does seem that the more we want something, the harder it is to get. The more we try to make friends, the less friendly people seem to become. And there are those times when you aren't thinking about dating anyone, when you least expect to meet someone wonderful, and—bingo—Ms. or Mr. Right (or Right Now) comes into the picture. There's no outguessing this process, but you may be setting yourself up for some lonely times if you merely wait and expect friendship or romance to find you. A proactive, balanced approach—introspection, planning, patience, communication skill development, and maybe a bit of faith—is likely to generate far better results than just "waiting for something to happen."

Notice that this information isn't geared to only one sex. Traditional thinking is that men are the proactors, that they are responsible for initiating dating or romantic relationships with women. Research shows that among college-aged people, men still solicit almost all of the dates, even though they grow tired of the asking (Berger, 1988). Many women of all ages agree that it's perfectly fine for a woman to initiate a date (and a relationship) with a man, yet few of them will actually ask men out. This is evidence of what can be called the "tension" of mixed messages. If a woman accepts the traditional thinking, then she's supposed to wait around and hope that a relationship will find her.

Doesn't this seem like a lousy use of time? Many women are discovering that they can be proactive and make relationships happen in their lives just as readily as men can.

Roadblock 5: The "Bozo Pill"

Some people get really tongue-tied when they talk to someone they are attracted to and interested in. Nothing seems to work, weird sentences come out of their mouths, they break into a sweat, and things generally go from bad to worse. Men and women who are articulate in every other situation suddenly get an attack of the "Bozo's" when faced with an attractive person. Sometimes they can't even remember their own names to introduce themselves. Has this ever happened to you? What did you do about it at the time? What *should* you have done? The "Bozo's" probably happen to all of us at one time or another. Experience and a concentrated effort to expand and apply one's communication repertoire can lessen the likelihood of this happening.

Roadblock 6: "It Has to Happen Now!"

As in the line Carrie Fisher wrote for the movie *Postcards from the Edge,* "Instant gratification takes too long." Some people express a desire to have a "remote control for relationships," so that they can zip and zap, getting what they want when they want it. Probably all of us could use a bigger dose of patience in our relationships. Solid, successful relationships of all kinds take time to develop. Wanting too much too soon (and sometimes getting it) can be a big problem. Not taking the time to nurture a relationship, not allowing it to develop at its own pace, can sabotage a potentially wonderful relationship before it has had its chance. In Chapter 7 we discuss strategies for accelerating as well as slowing down a relationship.

Roadblock 7: Giving Up Too Much Just to Have a Dating Relationship

University residence hall managers and advisers describe a problem they see regularly: Some students (more often female than male) are too willing to compromise themselves sexually or in other ways in order to get a dating relationship started. Are women more prone than men to want dating or romantic relationships, or is this just a stereotype? It may be that women and men place equal importance on romantic relationships, but again that tension of mixed messages mentioned in roadblock 4 comes into play, especially for women. Women often feel a tension between the traditional message that they should have a man in their lives to be fulfilled and the modern messages related to careerism and independence. (Remember the simple difference in connotation between a male who is a bachelor and a female who is a spinster or an old maid, which we discussed in Chapter 3?) Sometimes women and men alike feel that having a boyfriend or girlfriend, dating someone, or being married signals to everyone else that they are okay, adult, and to be taken seriously. Sometimes this desire for acceptance causes people to do things that they really don't want to do. The confusion generated by mixed messages is understandable, but no one should have to bend to pressure or be motivated by the desire to impress another person or to achieve some form of social status.

Do any of these roadblocks to beginning relationships sound familiar to you? What keeps you from making effective relational choices sometimes? What keeps you from being chosen for relationships as often as you would like? Think about how you'd answer these questions, as you continue to read about relationship initiation.

CHOOSING AND BEING CHOSEN: A DIFFERENT WAY OF LOOKING AT RELATIONSHIPS

Rather than hoping or believing that if you wait long enough or experiment enough, the perfect friend, dating partner, or mate will find his or her way to you, the following is a potentially more proactive (rather than reactive) strategy. We propose that relationship initiation and development are based on choice—*choosing* and *being chosen*. You clearly can't have close personal relationships with everyone, so you must choose. Perhaps, in your life you have chosen to be close to only a few people, family members and one or two close friends, for example. Other people may choose to have a wider circle of friends, acquaintances, and dating partners. Choosing relationships requires mental, physical, and emotional activity. On the flip side, it is very flattering to be chosen and can be very painful not to be.

Have you ever considered relationships from a choosing and being chosen perspective? Do you think that this choice business takes all the fun out of friendships and the romance out of dating? Do you believe that fate—epitomized by the expression "If it's meant to be, it will be"—guides your relational destiny? The proactive approach presented here may be a different way for you to look at relationships, because it puts you in charge of your relational life; you neither wait for something to happen nor blame something or someone if it doesn't. A proactive approach may increase your opportunity to turn relational potential into reality.

STAGES OF RELATIONSHIP INITIATION

This discussion is framed around a three-stage process of relationship initiation first proposed by communication researchers McCroskey, Larson, and Knapp (1971) and augmented by the work of communication researchers Cushman, Valentinsen, and Dietrich (1982). All of these scholars were intrigued with this idea of choosing and being chosen. In an attempt to blend these compatible research perspectives, we have crafted labels corresponding to each stage. As we explore each stage, increase your insight by comparing your own relational history with the information.

Stage 1: Finding Approachables and Being Approachable

Ever see that bumper sticker "So many men, so little time"? In your lifetime, you have the potential to initiate and develop hundreds of relationships. And particularly while you're in college, whether you begin right out of high school or start your college career later in life, this period constitutes prime time for experiencing various kinds of relationships. Stage 1 of relationship initiation is characterized by watching people and being watched. Research on this stage provides a substantial amount of insight into what leads up to a first conversation.

When men and women scan a crowd, what do they look for? What catches the eye and sparks the imagination? We like to ask our male and female students, separately, what they look for, not just in terms of physical appearance. The sexes' responses are amazingly similar. Both sexes seem to look for people who are physically appealing (but not so exceptionally gorgeous that they are unapproachable), who look "nice" (usually that means nonthreatening, well-groomed, etc.), who show an appropriate degree of self-confidence, who smile a lot and have a good sense of humor, who aren't too afraid or too macho to show interest, and who will impress their parents and friends. A recent *Ebony* magazine cited the following attributes as important in the attraction process: appearing approachable, increasing an "intrigue factor" (meaning that you project yourself as an interesting and captivating person), dressing to enhance not entice, not getting "lost in the crowd," strengthening your conversational skills, being assertive, exuding confidence, combining independence with a "touch of vulnerability," staying in good physical shape, having a good sense of humor, and being positive about life in general (Turner, 1990, pp. 27–28, 30). It's interesting that neither our students' list nor the *Ebony* list contains comments about being "Joe Stud" or looking like Cindy Crawford.

The Role of Information in Relationship Initiation

Before you take any action based on the qualities you perceive about a person, there's some knowledge that would be helpful—knowledge about yourself, about relationships and gender communication, and about the other person. Instead of knowledge, we call this *information.* Remember in the opening case study of this chapter when we said that information was critical to the process of initiating relationships? Since it is so critical, we focus first on the role of information in Stage 1 of relationship initiation.

Recall our previous discussions in this text about uncertainty. In brief review, communication researchers have detected that one of the primary things a person wants to do upon meeting someone new is to reduce uncertainty about him or her (Berger & Calabrese, 1975; Berger & Douglas, 1981; Douglas, 1990). We want to know: What would this person be like in a friendship or romantic relationship with me? On meeting some people you may make a decision in only a few seconds that relationship potential just isn't there. With others you decide just as quickly that further interaction is desirable. And while you're making those decisions, the other person is likely doing the same about you. Reducing uncertainty by gaining information enables *choice*—the choice you will make about whether or not to initiate a relationship with someone, as well as the choice that someone else will make about you.

How exactly do people reduce their uncertainty? Communication scholars Berger and Calabrese (1975) describe three general strategies for reducing uncertainty, all of which are based on information. The strategies are progressive, meaning that people usually start with the first and progress through the other two. Anywhere along the line, however, you can choose to break off the search for information if you deem it too risky because of possible rejection or if you discover something that leads you to think the relationship will not be rewarding.

First, people engage in *passive strategies.* You do this when you just watch people without them knowing it. You may watch people in different contexts, noting what they do, how they respond, and what kind of personality they possess. If you are thinking about making friends with someone, you may watch to see who that person hangs with. The more observations you make, the more

What If?

What if every day were Sadie Hawkins Day? Have you ever been to a Sadie Hawkins Dance, sometimes called a Backwards Dance, where the women ask the men out, purchase the tickets to the dance, pick the men up, and escort them to and from the dance? The name Sadie Hawkins comes from the old comic strip "Lil' Abner," in which on one day of the year, the women would chase the men through the town of Dogpatch. If a woman caught up to a man and touched him, her "prize" was that she got to marry him. We won't go that far, but *what if* you had grown up in a society abiding by the protocol that women did all of the calling, asking, paying, escorting, soliciting of physical favors, and decision making, in terms of whether to continue and deepen the relationship? Some men respond immediately: "Hey, that'd be great!" Some women argue that this list merely reflects their current relational responsibilities with their male partners. Other women feel that this arrangement would be a mixed blessing. On the one hand, it would represent a kind of proactive relational control that many women are not accustomed to. But it also places them in the path of rejection. Some men are relieved by the notion: *"What if* I didn't have to do all the initiating any more?" Other men realize that the change might take away some of the power and control they feel when they guide a relationship on its way. No matter the consequences, it would be interesting to try a Sadie Hawkins-type of arrangement for longer than one day or one dance. *What if* we tried a Sadie Hawkins month, just to see how women and men would respond? Do you think it would shake up how the sexes view each other? *What* would be the worst thing that could happen, *if* we changed our expectations of one another?

information you gain. Since the more direct methods of gaining information involve risk and heighten uncertainty, most of us go with the passive noninvolvement strategies first.

The second category of strategies encompasses *active strategies*. An active strategy requires more action than mere observation, but it typically involves a third party or another indirect means of gaining information. The most obvious tactic is to ask other people about someone: What is the person like? What does he or she do? Who are the person's friends? Is the person involved with someone at the time? In sociologists Knox and Wilson's (1981) study of the dating behaviors of college students, female and male subjects alike reported that they learned about their current dating partner through a third party.

As another active strategy, you can also stage situations to gain information about how another person responds. Haven't you seen (or arranged) situations where one friend sets up another friend who's interested in someone? For example, Brian asks a female friend, Katie, to start a conversation with Cindy— the woman he's becoming increasingly interested in as the night progresses. He asks Katie to find out if Cindy's dating someone (and how seriously), what Cindy's like, and so on. In other words, "Check her out for me, will you?" If this active strategy works for Brian, he may have an opening to more directly get information about Cindy.

That more direct method is referred to as an *interactive strategy,* one that involves asking the "interesting party" direct questions or engaging her or him in conversation, either one on one or in a group. This strategy is considered the most risky, and it takes self-confidence and nerve for most of us, but it seems to be the most reliable, straightforward, and time-efficient method of getting information. And it's unwise to assume that interactive strategies are for men's use only; women as well as men can actively seek to get to know someone and can make the first move toward getting a relationship started.

Sources of Information. Gaining information about yourself and someone else empowers you to behave effectively in given situations. But if you don't know anything about the other person, how can you be effective? What sources of information are available to you?

Interpersonal communication researchers Miller and Steinberg (1975) describe three levels of information that people use to make decisions and predictions about others. They start most generally with the *cultural level* of information; this includes sex, race, regionality, nationality, and so forth. Commonalities in these areas are sources of basic information, but your information-seeking process shouldn't stop there. Remember in Chapter 1 when we discussed the value of treating persons like individuals, not like stereotypes? If you stop with only cultural information about someone, you run the risk of communicating based on stereotypes.

The next type of information Miller and Steinberg describe is on a *sociological level*. This pushes further than cultural commonalities to more individual, specific experiences. For example, even though you may not know other students on a personal level, you can talk to them about classes and campus events because you share a common experience—college. If you are a windsurfer, you can easily strike up a conversation with another windsurfer as you share a very common, specific experience. However, just as with the cultural level, stopping at this level of information can also lead to communication based on stereotypes.

The third level of information is the *psychological level.* This is specific information about a person that you can learn only through interaction. As relationships develop, people expect you to interact with them based on what you know of them as an individual. Miller and Steinberg's theory suggests that you may not be able to do that right away, but it is useful to begin as soon as possible. For example, have you ever been in a class where the professor treated you like "just another student"? (Or worse, like a number?) Have you ever felt like another person was relating to you based simply on the fact that you were, for example, an African-American, particularly when that person assumes you'll be interested in a conversation about Spike Lee simply because Lee is also African-American? If you are male, have you ever been treated as "just another man" by a woman you were interested in? If you are female, have you ever had the experience of feeling like a guy is looking for a date, any date, and you just happen to be there? If you have had experiences like these, then you know what it is like to be talked to based on cultural or sociological information rather than on information that makes you a unique human being.

Information to Know about Yourself. What do you need to know about yourself as a potential friend or relational partner, so that you will make the best choices and be chosen more often? The information revolves around three areas—needs, goals, and self-image.

We all have relational *needs,* ranging from the superficial to the spiritually profound. In this short section, we can't describe all the things people need each other for, but we can present a system that is helpful to the process of understanding your own needs more fully. The more you understand your own needs, the easier it will be to get them met.

A number of years ago, interpersonal researcher William Schutz (1960) described three basic interpersonal needs of all human beings: inclusion, affection, and control. Schutz defined *inclusion* as the need to be around people and to be included in the activities of others. A person with high inclusion needs wants to spend a lot of time with people, wants to be part of social groups, and has a strong need for friendships. A person with low inclusion needs is more comfortable spending time alone. *Affection* is defined as the need for relationships that are emotionally and physically close and personal. A person with high affection needs wants to develop intimate relationships that are characterized by sharing private thoughts, feelings, and experiences, and by expressing feelings of closeness. A person with low affection needs does not see this kind of intimacy or closeness as important or desirable. *Control* is defined as decision making in a relationship. A person with high control needs may want to get other people to do what he or she wants them to do in a relationship. A person with low control needs is fairly comfortable with being controlled, that is, having someone else make relational decisions for her or him.

Before going any further, let's focus on some thoughts you may be having. As we discussed in Chapter 2, evidence indicates that women, on the whole, are biologically more nurturing. However, it is unwise to infer from this assumption that women have higher affection needs than men. Conversely, just because men currently hold the higher status and power positions in our society, it's unwise to assume that men necessarily have higher control needs than women. It just isn't that simple. Inflicting stereotypes based on biology or socialization at the point of initiating a relationship can stop it dead in its tracks.

How does Schutz's system of needs most directly connect with relationship initiation? Needs are the primary motivators for relational behavior. People have different levels of needs, as well as ways of getting needs met. While this may strike you as obvious or oversimplistic, needs fulfillment has a significant impact on the successful initiation of a relationship and on your satisfaction with the relationship once it's up and running. For example, if one person in a relationship has high affection needs and the other has low affection needs, that combination will likely lead to some conflict and dissatisfaction over unmet needs. And what happens when two high controllers couple up? (Get out of the way.) The point is that it helps to first understand what *you* need in terms of inclusion, affection, and control, before you try to find someone with compatible needs or before you attempt to understand the unique needs profile of a person you're interested in.

The second area of information about yourself that is closely related to needs is *goals*. Needs tend to be subconscious, though we can become more aware of them. Goals, on the other hand, tend to be conscious and purposeful. The clearer you are about what your goals are for any relationship, the more likely it is that your relationships and your goals will match. Perhaps your first goal is just to *have* a friendship or dating relationship with someone. The question connected to this goal becomes, where am I likely to get this goal met, in terms of meeting someone? The next set of goals pertains to initiating a relationship. These goals might be as simple in the beginning as wanting companionship, someone to show you some attention, someone to talk things over with, someone who will impress your friends and parents, and the like. These initial goals are likely to change once the relationship actually begins and as it develops, as you each find and express various needs.

Even though this section focuses on information about yourself, you know that just thinking about your own goals is not enough. A singleminded effort to get your own goals met in a relationship is usually a doomed approach. If you consider the other person's goals in the relationship, you increase your chances of forming some sort of compatible match. Since the other person is also looking to fulfill relational goals, you need to try to discover what those goals are, as well as the role you could play in helping someone meet her or his relational goals.

How does gender affect the notion of goals in dating or romantic relationships, for example? Stereotypically, men's goal in dating or romantic relationships is sex. The stereotypical goal for women is to talk about feelings and to "get close." A man and a woman can watch the same conversation occur between two other people and the man might conclude that something sexual is going on, while the woman is more likely to conclude that the couple merely wants to get to know each other better. As stereotypes go, neither is particularly accurate, but there may be at least some basis in reality for both.

Social psychologists Townsend and Levy (1990) conducted two studies to explore the possibility of sex differences in tendencies to select a partner—tendencies that might be affected by preferences for physical attractiveness and goals regarding sexual activity. The most revealing gender-based results of their research were as follows:

> Potential partners' physical attractiveness appears to operate differently for men and women in terms of partners' acceptability. In both studies, if male subjects did not find a woman sufficiently physically attractive to be desirable as a sex partner, then they did not find her sufficiently attractive for any other type of relationship—not even for coffee and conversation. If a potential partner was acceptable for dating, a serious relationship, and marriage, then female subjects might be willing to have sex with him. (p. 385)

Results like these may make you question if there isn't some measure of truth behind a stereotype. While we certainly don't believe that all men set for themselves the goal of having romantic, sexual relationships with highly attractive women only, enough of Townsend and Levy's subjects responded this way to support a significant goal difference between male and female subjects in their studies. Attaining a sexual relationship was a more pertinent goal for male subjects; female subjects preferred some level of commitment before indicating a willingness to have sex.

Note that Townsend and Levy's research doesn't attach value judgments to the tendency for their subjects to have differing goals for relationships. A difference in goals does not mean that one person's goals are necessarily preferable to another's. It is probable that you will encounter a difference in goals somewhere down your relational path. Maybe that difference will be gender based or maybe it will have more to do with individuals' personalities and value systems. The main point about relational goals is that it is wise, when initiating a relationship of any kind, to attempt to discover what the other person's relational goals are, in comparison with your own. Doing this will allow you to make a more informed choice about relationship potential.

The last topic in this section on self-information is *self-image*. How do you see yourself? How do you communicate your self-image to others, particularly those persons with whom you'd like to have a relationship? Do you project an androgynous, masculine, or feminine image?

Researchers have studied the process of presenting one's self to "the public" (Goffman, 1959; Tedeschi, 1981). Noted scholar and social critic Erving Goffman views people as always being involved in staging dramas that let them display their self-images and project their definitions of situations. Like a stage actor, the social actor presents to other people a character in the hopes that it will be accepted. Do you consciously present an image of yourself to other people? Having gone this far through this text and in this class, we might guess that you have an increasing awareness of the number of times you project your image to someone else. You project it regularly, but the question is the degree to which you are consciously aware of what you are projecting.

Two factors are critical to an understanding of how the self-image affects relationship initiation and development—consistency and confidence. The *consistency* of your self-image has to do with conveying a clear, constant image of yourself to others. Understanding your self-image and consistently projecting that image to people will help to reduce uncertainty, both for yourself and for others. We don't mean that you should find an image and stick with it until you die. In fact, there will be times when you may experiment because you don't know exactly what you want your image to be. For example, you might try being the class clown rather than someone who offers serious input in class discussions. If you decide that this isn't the "real you," you might go a different route with the image you choose to project. However, inconsistency drives most people crazy. Think about professors you've had who are laid-back and easygoing in the classroom until the day they hand back your first graded paper or exam, when they turn into the "Terminator." Or think about the woman who believes her fiancé is the most open-minded man in the world until after the wedding, when she realizes she's married "Al Bundy."

Specific to gender communication, think about times you've felt burned by someone who projected a totally different image of himself or herself to you than was really "true." Maybe this person portrayed his or her notion of the ideal masculine man or feminine woman in the hopes of attracting you. When you discover this inconsistency, it's not only confusing; it can be maddening, possibly even abusive. Have you ever fallen into the trap of pretending to be some image of an ideal, or someone you *thought* you were supposed to be as a woman or a man, instead of the person you really *are*? Projecting false images is hard work, and it is quite unsatisfying. What do you do if someone falls in love with your false image?

The second aspect pertaining to self-image is *confidence*. While it takes time to understand which image works best for you and to develop confidence in it, confidence does have an amazing effect. At times people will say, "It wasn't that this person was so good-looking, but he [she] just had an air of confidence that was really attractive." As we alluded to earlier in this chapter, it is common to hold a degree of uncertainty about relationships and how to communicate effectively within them. But uncertainty has the potential to cut into your confidence level, so that you avoid initiating relationships or lessen the likelihood that a relationship will be initiated with you. Without the trial and error that is inherent in any kind of relationship, it's hard to learn about yourself and others, which is a primary way to gain confidence and to strengthen your self-image.

The Role of Attraction in Relationship Initiation

What *is* attraction? Here are a few responses to that question proffered by students: "lust," "a sort of chemistry between you and another person," "wanting to have sexual intercourse with another person," "liking someone— not just physically, but for personality traits." You can see from these responses that some people apply the term to platonic friendships, in which you might be attracted to someone in a nonphysical or nonsexual basis, while others correlate attraction with sexual interest. And there are other complications associated with attraction. If you realize that you are physically attracted to someone, then, given more information, you become attracted to other aspects of the person as well, should both of these reactions be termed *attraction?* Or perhaps in cases of friendship you are attracted to someone's personality or intelligence. If we labeled all of these processes *attraction*, it would get really confusing. In this chapter we've chosen to discuss attraction in terms of the physical and sexual reactions we have to certain people. We don't use the term *attraction* here to describe general liking between friends. When we talk about other attractive elements that might cause you to initiate a relationship with someone, we call this *interest* (to be discussed in the next section). The terms *attraction* and *interest* are often used interchangeably in casual conversation, but for our purposes here, let's keep them distinct.

Before we delve further into this discussion of attraction, we want to share an experience with you. We discuss sexual attraction and relationship initiation between heterosexual men and women a good deal in this chapter, primarily because heterosexual relationships match more of our readers' experiences. However, we have probably learned more about the nature of attraction and how it functions in relationship initiation from our homosexual friends and colleagues than from other sources. A gay male friend taught a profound lesson when he simply posed a hypothetical situation to the female co-author of this text. His question was, "If someone came up to you and said, 'You must now be sexually attracted to women; you have no other choice in life,' could you do it?" Her reaction was no, she could not change her basic instincts as to what she found sexually attractive. The friend then explained that being attracted to other men wasn't a choice for him either, it was just something that *was* and always had been. For many people, attraction is primal and instinctual—not based on cognitive processing. It's not our purpose in this text to get into a discussion about whether homosexuality is innate or a matter of choice. Our purpose is simply to cause readers to consider the same question our gay friend posed, so that they more fully understand the nature of sexual attraction beyond mere application to heterosexual relationships.

While there are as many variations on the definition of attraction as there are people attracted to one another, one thing everyone seems to agree on is this: When you're sexually attracted, you know it (quickly); when you're not, you know you're not. We like to call the personal reaction to sexual attraction the "internal toilet flush." When you see someone and almost instantly register that physical jolt of attraction, it's as though something rushed inside you from your head to your toes.

While initial attraction to a dating partner or potential spouse is usually based on a response to someone's physical appearance, attraction can reflect deeper aspects and can also be fickle. For example, a woman who is initially attracted to a man's looks may, given more information (say, he starts talking), find herself saying "What did I ever find attractive in him?" Or, for another example, a man may not be particularly attracted to a woman physically at first, but over time and given more information, her looks become incredibly attractive. Then he may find himself wondering, "Did her looks change somehow, or is it just how I *see* her now?" Attraction remains a fascinating subject, but one that's difficult to nail down because of its individual and changeable nature.

Nonverbal Cues, Physical Appearance, and Attraction. You look at others; they look at you. So let's briefly explore this looking business. In a large number of social situations, the opening gambit in attraction is "the look." Here is a stereotypical setup. A male looks at a target female who notices his glance. If she wants to encourage him, she will glance back, then look down. A few seconds later, she'll look again to see if he is still looking. Usually it is the male who maintains the greater degree of eye contact, with the female looking just often enough to indicate an interest. As the opportunity presents itself, the male will do a quick body scan. We said that this scene was stereotypical, so this is certainly not the way it *has* to be.

A few years ago, Nancy (a friend of one of this book's co-authors) liked to have some fun with the eye contact game when she went to clubs with friends. If she happened to approach and pass a guy in a club, she would turn to glance back at him just about the same time he was turning around to check out the rear view. She would meet his eyes, then drop her gaze to a few inches below his belt buckle, then look back at his eyes. Most guys were very confused by this approach, but it was truly fascinating to watch the reactions!

Sometimes people do some odd things to be attractive. Men, at times, will do what humorist Dave Barry (1991) calls "guy" behavior. In a newspaper column he described a scene in Washington, D.C., in which two guys who were driving nice cars reached a point "where their two lanes were supposed to merge. But neither one would yield, so they very slowly—we are talking maybe one mile per hour—DROVE INTO EACH OTHER" (p. 7C). Barry then asks: "Why do guys do these things?" This is his answer:

> One possible explanation is that they believe women are impressed. In fact, however, most women have the opposite reaction to macho behavior. You rarely hear women say things like, "Norm, when that vending machine failed to give you a Three Musketeers bar and you punched it so hard that you broke your hand and we had to go to the hospital instead of to my best friend's daughter's wedding, I became so filled with lust for you that I nearly tore off all my clothes right there in the emergency room." No, women are far more likely to say: "Norm, you have the brains of an Odor Eater."*

You would probably agree that our culture places too much importance on physical appearance, especially on female beauty. As we discussed in Chapter 4, many movies, advertisements, television programs, music videos, and the

*"Road Warriors," *The Miami Herald,* Tropic Magazine, 1991, p. 7.

like, overtly or subtly communicate to both men and women that their looks are what attract others to them, so they should work on their looks day and night. The competition related to appearance and attractiveness creates a significant pressure in people's lives. In a study conducted across social classes and races, health educators Dornbusch, Gross, Duncan, and Ritter (1987) found that the majority of their adult female subjects wished they were thinner. The pressure to be beautiful affects the lives of even very young children, evidenced by a recent study which found that a high percentage of fourth-grade girls were on diets and were overly concerned with their weight (Mellin, Scully, & Irwin, 1986).

In her best-selling book *The Beauty Myth,* Naomi Wolf (1991) describes how physical fitness facilities, diet product manufacturers and diet services, producers of self-help books and programs, health and beauty aids manufacturers, the plastic surgery industry, and countless others capitalize on the pressure society places, particularly on women, to be beautiful. We've all seen or read about some of the negative side effects of an overemphasis on physical appearance, such as the damage that breast implants and silicone injections can do to a person's body, or eating disorders, which have reached almost epidemic proportions in our society. One survey of college students nationwide found that approximately 20 percent of the women and more than 4 percent of the men had developed eating disorders, out of a hyperconcern with thinness (Hesse-Biber, 1989).

But a deeper problem relates to *why* heterosexual women, in particular, buy into the notion of working hard to be beautiful—not because it will enhance their self-esteem but primarily because it will make them attractive to men. We're not saying that a concern about one's physical appearance is necessarily a negative thing, because some of the efforts to enhance one's physical condition are positively motivated. And we're not saying that heterosexual women should not be concerned about their attractiveness to men, because that's some of the reality. But we argue that it shouldn't be the complete reality. An emphasis on impressing others that outweighs the desire to build one's own self-esteem and confidence, to please oneself as well as others, is out of balance and can be a destructive way to live life.

Are the sexes different in terms of how much importance they place on physical appearance? Social psychologist Alan Feingold (1990) conducted a meta-analysis on the subject of gender differences in the effects of attraction on establishing romantic relationships. Briefly, a meta-analysis is an effective technique that allows a researcher to compile, compare, and contrast findings on a given topic across various studies and research methods. In Feingold's meta-analysis, the notion that men value physical attractiveness more than women do when deciding to initiate and develop heterosexual romantic relationships was explored across approximately fifty studies of five different types. His categories of studies were (1) questionnaires tapping mate preferences; (2) content analyses of personal ads; (3) studies correlating judgments of physical attractiveness with popularity; (4) studies measuring the amount of attraction between persons in actual conversations; and (5) experiments in which subjects rated the physical attractiveness of a stranger depicted in a photograph or videotape. In this thorough meta-analysis, Feingold found significant sex differences across all five categories of studies. Evidence emerged in all categories to indicate that men value physical attractiveness more than women when approaching heterosexual romantic relationships. The trend was more pronounced in some studies than in others.

What can you make of this significant sex difference? How does it affect you when it comes to initiating relationships and having them initiated with you? Just the knowledge that women and men tend to look for and be attracted to different things is empowering. If a woman finds a man's emphasis on looks frustrating, what are her options? She can set her frustrations aside and use the realization to her advantage by concentrating on her looks when trying to attract a man. Or, probably a better option, she can find a male relational partner whose emphasis on the standards for physical attractiveness match her own.

How is this information empowering to men? This may be a bit obvious, but if you are male and you know that women generally place less emphasis on physical characteristics than other qualities (personality, intelligence, kindness and sensitivity, sense of humor, etc.), then it would be to your advantage to work on developing these qualities rather than concentrating much of your energy on how you look. Women are often baffled by men's competitiveness and vanity about looks, being fit, physical signs of aging, and so forth. They are baffled because they know that most women put less pressure on men to look good than men put on women. A conclusion reached by many women is that men are concerned about appearance more out of a need to impress other *men* than a need to impress women.

Another interesting point on this topic of physical attractiveness is that you may see someone you deem attractive but not be attracted to that person for a variety of reasons, including availability, personality aspects, and intelligence factors. The research of social psychologists Bar-Tal and Saxe (1976) produced a fascinating observation of human behavior, which has come to be known as the Matching Hypothesis. Their research indicates that while you may appreciate the appearance of someone who is stunningly good looking, you usually have relationships with (and even marry) people you feel are similar in attractiveness to you. An average looking man may appreciate the physical appearance of a very good-looking woman, but he will be unlikely to act on that judgment. He is more likely to be attracted to a woman whom he believes holds a level of attractiveness that is similar to his own. Thus the lesson that could be learned here is that we need to appear physically in a way that is in line with how we see ourselves and in line with the kind of people we want to attract. Physical appearance is important, but it is only one determinant of attraction.

Actually, the research says that if you are looking for a satisfying relationship, a judgment of communicative competence outweighs physical appearance in determinations of how satisfying a relationship will be. Communication researchers Zakahi and Duran (1984) investigated the effects of perceptions of communication competence and physical attractiveness on judgments of communication satisfaction within a relationship. They found that only 5 percent of subjects' judgments of relational satisfaction were related to physical appearance, while 32 percent were related to communicative competence. From these findings they conclude that "although physical attractiveness may be the primary predictor of initial interaction, it does not appear to be as important as communication skills once the relationship is underway" (p. 56). So, in the long run, it is more important to work on your competence (or personal effectiveness) in gender communication than your physical appearance.

Proximity. People can be attracted to someone they've never met and will likely never meet. This is idol worship, the kind of attraction one might feel for movie stars or sports celebrities. Realistically, we are more likely to be attracted to someone if we perceive that there are opportunities to be around that person. Research has shown that *proximity is the single most influential variable in attraction* (Bersheid, 1985). Proximity is the physical distance between you and someone else, the amount of time you spend physically near that person, and also how easily you can gain access to her or him.

Have you ever heard the old saying, "There's one right person in the world for you"? If you believe this, did ever wonder why that "right" person probably went to the same school as you? Why wasn't she or he born in Calcutta? For another example, have you ever been involved in a long-distance romantic relationship? If you have, then you know firsthand the effects of proximity and the importance of being able to gain access to your relational partner. Simply put, it's hard (and fairly self-defeating) to maintain your attraction for a person if you cannot be around him or her.

So proximity can increase or decrease your opportunity for attraction—that's simple enough. Now it's a matter of turning this to your advantage. Have you ever stationed yourself in the hallway so that a certain special person will walk by and maybe you'll get a chance to talk? Ever take up a dangerous sport or a crazy hobby, just because a certain person participates in that activity? This translates into the "just-happened-to-run-into-you-at-the-gym" approach. If you have done any of these things, then you've been putting proximity to work for

DRABBLE reprinted by permission of UFS, Inc.

you, so that you can make more informed choices about initiating relationships.

The Role of Interest in Relationship Initiation

Here, this term is used as an extension of attraction, referring to intriguing qualities about a person that you find appealing, other than physical appearance. These qualities usually take time and involvement to discover, whereas proximity and physical appearance can be accomplished with minimal investment. Interest variables require more information—information about you that a potential friend or relational partner seeks to learn and information that you seek about that person.

Reciprocity of Liking. This term sounds sort of fancy, but basically it means that you are likely to be more interested in someone who likes you than someone who seems neutral or indifferent toward you or doesn't like you at all. If this sounds fairly commonsensical, think again. Sometimes you may find yourself liking someone because he or she doesn't seem to respond to your attempts at friendship or, on a romantic level, she or he won't give you the time of day. This is the old "chase" or "challenge" trap. We call it a trap because most often it's a poor use of time and energy to try to initiate a relationship with someone who just isn't interested. On occasion, you may have a positive outcome to such a challenge, but more times than not it causes the ego to deflate rather than inflate.

If you are choosing to initiate a relationship with someone, how do you convey your interest? Do you express curiosity about the other person's background, opinions, and so on? Do you compliment her or him, or show a concern for his or her well-being? For example, assume that you've been introduced to someone a couple of times in social settings. With each occasion, you come to believe more and more that the person could become a really good friend. How do you convey your interest in developing a friendship with this person? Is it common for you to ask the person about herself or himself, including questions about hometown, occupation, or hobbies? Are you more likely to talk about yourself or about nonthreatening topics, such as the weather or sports, rather than ask the other person questions? Maybe your pattern is more connected to doing mutual activities with another person until the proximity and shared activity just seem to develop into friendship. There's no right way to show interest in developing a relationship with someone It's quite an individual process, but it might be worth your time to put some thought into how you show interest in another person. Perhaps you've never realized that you have a pattern, or maybe you'd like more friends but are discovering that how you go about making new friends is somehow faulty or needs changing.

On the being-chosen flip side, is it typical of you to be unaware when someone really does like you? How do you detect that someone is interested, either on a friendship or romantic level? No matter the type of relationship being initiated, interest is usually conveyed through nonverbal channels. After all, few people are likely to walk up and say, "Hey; I like you; let's start a relationship." If people like each other and are interested in getting to know each other better, they will probably begin by increasing their proximity to each other, both in terms of how often they see each other and how close they physically get when interacting. Other cues of liking, or "immediacy" as nonverbal scholar Albert Mehrabian (1981) termed it, will be present as well, including increased eye contact and head nodding, more direct body position and forward body lean, more animated facial expression, increased touch, increased conversational time, and even the use of more variation in vocal expression. But get ready for yet another sex difference.

Mehrabian (1981) discovered that men tend to display indirect nonverbal cues (turned-out body positions, less eye contact, etc.) even with people they really like. Women display some indirect cues when interacting with less-liked individuals, but with people they like they use far more nonverbal immediacy indicators than do men. In relationship initiation contexts, this finding has led some people to claim that women are transparent, especially heterosexual women when they are romantically attracted to men. In many instances, this is frustrating for women who, due to the lack of men's nonverbal immediacy cues, cannot detect their effect on men. As we've said at other points in this chapter, this information can be empowering for you. For example, if a man wonders whether a woman is attracted and interested in him, the research indicates that it is highly likely that her feelings will be conveyed through nonverbal channels. Granted, you can't always accurately interpret someone's nonverbal signals, but a man might want to be attuned to or "clue in" to a woman's nonverbal behavior if he thinks interest is developing. In some ways, it's harder for women to detect interest from men's nonverbal communication, since, as the research suggests, men tend not to alter their nonverbal or outward behavior according to their internal emotional states. Women's options include (1) on the reactive side, waiting for an obvious overture of a man's attention, such as being asked out or asked to dance, or (2) on the proactive side, asking the man out or to dance, thus judging his interest by his reaction to the invitation.

Similarity of Attitudes, Beliefs, and Values. Perhaps you have heard the cliché "opposites attract." Probably more accurate is the notion that opposites attract but they typically don't last. Research indicates that under most circumstances you will generally be more interested in someone who holds attitudes, beliefs, and values similar to yours than to someone's whose attitudes (and especially values) are quite different (Lydon, Jamieson, & Zanna, 1988; McCroskey, Richmond, & Daly, 1975). For example, some people may be interested in those who are radically different from them—mainly because the differences are intriguing. But often these relationships don't last because, over time, the initial intrigue fades and the differences become obstacles, sometimes insurmountable.

Generally, when you look around a room you gravitate toward people you think are like you. For example, some years ago, Phil (one of your text's co-authors) accepted a position at a new university. Early in his first semester, the college held a reception for new faculty. Upon arriving at the reception, Phil and his wife, Judy, looked around, saw another couple who appeared to be of the same age and dressed similarly, and made a beeline toward them. The other couple had exactly the same thought and it turned out that the four became very good friends. The point of this example is that given a choice, we tend to move toward people we see as being similar to ourselves. This illustrates the "Birds of a feather flock together" cliché. But the flip side is also true—"Flocking together makes birds of a feather." You may have noticed that some people begin to look alike and talk alike after a period of time, in that they may have similar haircuts, clothes, facial expressions, ways of labeling things or expressing themselves, and so on. So how do you turn this information into a strategy—both for choosing and being chosen?

It's a good idea to place yourself in the company of people who are similar to you and to learn the extent of those similarities. For example, if you hold an attitude that bar or club scenes are great opportunities for socializing with interesting people, you are more likely to find someone with similar attitudes if you look in a bar or club than elsewhere. If your religious values are such that you believe attending church is important, then your chances of finding some-one with similar values and beliefs are greater in a church setting than other places. If you believe that political action is important, for instance, then raising this topic with someone in a conversation, rather than talking about other topics, might give you some important information. This information might form the basis for a decision to initiate a relationship with the person. It may not be the case that you intend to initiate a friendship or romantic relationship upon first encountering someone, even if you find yourself interested in or attracted to her or him. However, if you are on a committee with him or her at work or if you do a class project with that person, attitudes, values, and beliefs might surface from extended contact with the person; this can inform your relational decision making as well. When you are in the company of someone whom you believe to be similar to you, emphasize those similarities. Nine times out of ten, it will be to your benefit to let someone know that you see things the same way she or he does.

In summary, remember that the three factors in our discussion of Stage 1—information, attraction, and interest—are things over which you have some control. Granted, some aspects of physical appearance aren't alterable, even given the advances of modern technology. Some of us will always be "vertically challenged." But a great deal about your appearance, as well as how you communicate information, attraction, and interest, can become empowering strategies that will turn your relationship potential into reality.

Stage 2: Approaching and Interacting

There is no clear-cut line between the first and second stages; each merely has some identifying characteristics. Stage 2 consists of the opening interactions of a relationship. Each person has made the initial choice in favor of the other person and each has indicated a willingness to begin to interact. In this stage, people expend a good deal of energy trying to get the other person to think well of them. Here are a few strategies that help accomplish this.

Conversation Starters

Everyone laughs at the old pickup lines of the 1960s and 1970s: "What's your sign?" "Haven't I seen you somewhere before?" and "What's a nice girl like you doing in a place like this?" In fact, a book from the year 1970 entitled *How to Pick Up Girls!* offered a list of opening lines that "guaranteed" men success with women. Here are a few of the more laughable ones: "You're Miss Ohio aren't you? I saw your picture in the paper yesterday." "Do you have change for a ten?" "What kind of dog is that? He's great looking." "Here, let me carry that for you. I wouldn't want you to strain that lovely body of yours." "Are you a model?" "Please pass the ketchup." "Didn't I meet you in Istanbul?" (Weber, 1970, pp. 72–78).

Opening lines can be funny to think and talk about, but they can reduce the art and skill of effective communication to a gimmick. We're not advocating the development of a set stock of lines that can be used for all situations and people. Packaged opening lines are inconsistent with the principles underlying the receiver orientation to communication because they generally ignore the process of adapting one's communication to the situation and the receiver of the message. So why would someone use a line on someone else? The first reason relates to laziness. It is simply easier for some people to use lines rather than come up with unique, creative approaches that match a person and a situation. The receiver orientation calls for more work than simply tossing out a tired, overused line to someone. The second reason relates to nervousness. It's tough to approach somebody new for that first conversation, especially if you are attracted to the person. Many times people resort to stock phrases and trite beginnings to just get the ball rolling. Because of this second point, we also grant that lines, or conversational openers, may be useful at times.

Opening lines should be intended as conversation starters, not necessarily as efforts to "pick up" or "hit on" someone. It's wise to assume that a positive response is just that—a positive *initial* response—not an automatic indication of attraction and interest. Conversational beginnings that reflect a thoughtful, sincere attempt at interaction can serve as icebreakers between you and someone you are interested in. Maybe you know some things to say that have received relatively positive responses in past conversations. If you define lines in this way, then they can become part of an effective communication repertoire. But are conversation starters more associated with male behavior than female?

Gender psychologists Kleinke, Meeker, and Staneski (1986) found that over 90 percent of their subjects believed it was just as appropriate for a woman to open a conversation with a man as the reverse. In this study, college students generated examples of conversation starters that they had heard and/or used, including things that men might say to women and vice versa. Then the researchers surveyed over 250 college students' preferences for these openers, divided into general and situation-specific categories. Here are the five most preferred general openers (in descending order) for men who initiate conversation: (1) "Hi." (2) "Hi. My name is ___." (3) "I feel a little embarrassed about this, but I'd like to meet you." (4) "That's a very pretty (sweater, dress, etc.) you have on." (5) "You have really nice (hair, eyes, etc.)."

Do you see how these are really just common ways to get someone talking, rather than suggestive, manipulative lines that make the other person feel uncomfortable or set up? The five least preferred general openers (with the very least preferred listed first) from this study were: (1) "Is that really your hair?" (2) "You remind me of a woman I used to date." (3) "Your place or mine?" (Some things *never* change.) (4) "I'm easy. Are you?" (5) "Isn't it cold? Let's make some body heat."

The results for openers that women might use on men are as follows. Top five most preferred openers: (1) "Since we're both sitting alone, would you care to join me?" (2) "Hi." (3) "I'm having trouble getting my car started. Will you give me a hand?" (4) "I don't have anybody to introduce me, but I'd really like to get to know you." (5) "Can you give me directions to (anywhere)?" Top five least preferred openers: (1) "Didn't we meet in a previous life?" (2) "It's been a long time since I had a boyfriend." (3) "Hey baby, you've got a gorgeous chassis. Mind if I look under the hood?" (We're *not* kidding.) (4) "I'm easy. Are you?" (5) "What's your sign?"

Studies by Kleinke et al. revealed that both women and men tended to agree that "cute, flippant" conversational openings were less effective than direct or nonthreatening, innocuous ones (p. 596). How this information is put to use, like other topics covered in this chapter, is left to your discretion. If the thought of using a premeditated conversation starter on someone sounds fake, forced, or downright ridiculous to you, then you probably couldn't do this to initiate a conversation anyway. But if some of the openers we've cited here from the recent research didn't strike you as lines at all, then maybe you can find this information useful.

Affinity-Seeking

Wanting people to like us is a basic human instinct referred to in research as "affinity-seeking." Interpersonal communication researchers Bell and Daly (1984) define affinity-seeking as "the active social-communicative process by which individuals attempt to get others to like and to feel positive about them" (p. 91). You may seek affinity with someone else simply because you want to be liked or out of a motivation to seek some sort of reward or kindness.

Communication researchers Richmond, Gorham, and Furio (1987) asked male and female college students to indicate how likely they would be to use a variety of affinity-seeking strategies when wanting to get to know someone better—someone whom they might want to date. Female subjects in the study preferred such affinity-seeking strategies as asking questions in order to elicit disclosure from the other person, listening intently and paying close attention to the other person's responses, allowing the other person to control the conversation and future activities, and generally showing empathy and sensitivity to someone's concerns. Male subjects preferred such affinity-seeking strategies as actively communicating to make the other person feel important and to validate the other's self-concept, putting themselves in positions to be included in future events, presenting a positive, interesting image of themselves to the other person, and taking charge of conversations and planning future activities. On all but three possible strategies, female and male subjects responded significantly differently in terms of how likely they were to employ various strategies. At first glance, the results of the study appeared to "characterize females as reactive and other-oriented and males as proactive and self-oriented" (p. 344).

However, Richmond et al. used caution in their interpretation of sex differences. They found it hard to conclude whether the main difference was a female focus on other persons and a male focus on the self, or if the difference had more to do with female reactivity and male proactivity. For example, one of the most preferred strategies for male subjects was to confirm the other person's self-concept—a strategy that is quite other-directed. However, the way the self-concept was confirmed, via overt communication that the other person was important, differed from how female subjects indicated other-orientation. The women were more likely to draw the other person out by using questions and by offering supportive responses to the person's answers. Both strategies indicate a concern for another person; the difference pertains to proactive versus reactive communication.

We believe that this research is useful if you are interested in getting a relationship off the ground. An understanding of what men and women might do to be liked is empowering. Sometimes a woman might interpret a man's proactive communication as a signal of self-absorption. That might be a correct interpretation in a given situation, but his style or strategy might really indicate a desire to be liked rather than to be the focus of attention. A woman's reactive, responsive style might be interpreted by a man as timidity or as a lack of confidence, when, in reality, the woman is employing a commonly used affinity-seeking strategy. Her style may have nothing to do with her level of confidence.

As we suggested in connection with other research that has highlighted sex differences, knowledge of sex differences empowers people to overcome their differences and to avoid mistrust and divisiveness. Developing a full range of affinity-seeking strategies can make a person a more personally effective communicator, friend, and relational partner. Well-rounded, flexible individuals develop the ability to respond with the best affinity-seeking strategy for the situation, independent of one's sex.

Rhetorical Sensitivity

On the subject of how you might present yourself to be liked by others, another interesting theory has applicability to gender communication. Communication researcher Roderick Hart and his colleagues describe three types of communicators (Hart & Burks, 1972; Hart, Carlson, & Eadie, 1980). While no one fits one type 100 percent of the time, the three categories offer valuable insight into how people communicate and how you might alter your own style to be more effective.

The first type is termed the *noble self*. Persons with this communication style tend to stick to their own ideals with little variation and adjustment to others. They do and say things the way they want to do and say them and, in many instances, they care very little about what other people might think—the complete reverse of the receiver-oriented communicator. These individuals may attempt to justify their unpopular actions by saying "I'm just being true to myself" or "I'm just being honest." Perhaps you know people like this. While this style can be strong and useful, it causes conflict a good deal of the time and can be problematic for a person who seeks to initiate relationships.

At the other end of the spectrum are people who Hart et al. term *rhetorical reflectors*. These individuals mold themselves to other people's wishes in virtually every circumstance. They adapt to anyone, say whatever they think the other person wants to hear, and rarely push their own viewpoint. This represents adopting a receiver orientation to a debilitating extreme. These individuals generally communicate out of a lack of self-confidence or for manipulative purposes; that is, they adapt in order to get what they want.

The third style—one that combines the best of the first two—is called *rhetorical sensitivity*. Individuals possessing this communicator style combine a concern for themselves with a concern for others and the situation. Hart and colleagues identified the following five characteristics of the rhetorically sensitive individual:

1. *Acceptance of personal complexity*, meaning an understanding that each person is a composite of many selves with many sides to the personality. An example might be avoiding being shocked or reacting with condemnation when someone communicates in what you might consider an "uncharacteristic" manner. A person with this first characteristic realizes that people are complex and unpredictable; sensitivity and flexibility make one more comfortable in dealing with the complexity and unpredictability.
2. *Avoidance of rigidity in communicating with others*, demonstrating flexibility and a lack of dogmatism. A person without this characteristic might, for example, exhibit a tendency to hold to a position, to defend a particular stance, and to refuse to consider alternatives.
3. *Interaction consciousness* evidenced by balancing self-interest with another person's interests during conversation. Have you ever known people who couldn't hold a conversation unless the conversation was about themselves? This third characteristic emphasizes the benefits of showing an other-interest, balanced by a healthy self-interest.
4. *Awareness of appropriate communication for a given situation*—an ability to "scope out" a situation and respond accordingly. Some people tend to communicate the same way no matter who they're with, what the topic of conversation is, and where the conversation is taking place. These aren't generally the people who win awards for their excellent commu-

nication skills! It's important to develop enough "savvy" to be able to respond to differing demands of different situations.

5. *Realization that an idea can be communicated in many different ways* combined with an ability to adapt one's message to a particular person in a particular situation. You probably realize that there's no one "perfect" way to say something. For example, an apology can be communicated in various ways: nonverbally by doing some gesture for someone to indicate regret, blurting out an apology when next you see the injured party, sending a note of apology, or engaging the person in a conversation about the event in general. Selecting a mode of communication depends on careful analysis of the situation, the topic or issue at hand, and the persons involved.

These five characteristics of rhetorical sensitivity should sound familiar to you, because they are another way of stating some of the principles inherent in the personal effectiveness model of gender communication. The description of the rhetorically sensitive communicator offers worthwhile options, especially if your goal is to increase the chances of a relationship continuing.

Clearly, there are many factors that influence the relationship initiation process. We have reviewed three important aspects in this section pertaining to Stage 2, the approaching and interacting stage: conversation starters, affinity-seeking, and rhetorical sensitivity. These factors contain some highly useful strategies that benefit the relational decision-making process. Now let's move on to the third and final stage of relationship initiation.

Stage 3: The Decision to Continue

In the third phase in the initiation of relationships, information has been gathered, initial attraction and interest have occurred, and first conversations have been successful enough to make you feel that there is real relationship potential with someone. Now you look for information and communication behavior that will suggest to you that the relationship has longer term potential. By longer term potential, we don't mean that you will decide whether every relationship will be a "friend for life" or will end up in marriage or some other form of commitment. We simply mean that you will come to the point when you decide whether or not to move any relationship—platonic, romantic, and so on—into a deeper phase with longer lasting effects. While many different ideas could be presented in this section, we focus on two that are most central to this stage, social exchange theory and listening to confirm.

Social Exchange Theory

During Stage 3 of relationship initiation, the question "Am I getting what I want out of this relationship?" becomes a major factor. It's highly likely that you and the other person in your relationship are both asking this question. Not only that; you're both comparing what you're getting out of the relationship with what you think the other person is getting out of it.

In 1959, a social science researcher named George Homans proposed an interpersonal theory of social exchange. Homans viewed interpersonal interaction from an economic perspective, proposing that one could view relationships as deals or bargains in which parties compared the costs likely to be incurred (e.g., time, money, effort) with the rewards likely to be received (companionship, heightened self-esteem, acceptance, etc.). One might offer assistance in exchange for gratitude, friendship in exchange for conversation, love in exchange for security, and sex in exchange for affection. According to this theory, one is more likely to stay in relationships that minimize costs and maximize rewards.

Feminist scholars have been critical of social exchange theory as a cogent explanation of why relationships continue. One basis for this criticism stems from the view that different standards apply to men and women as to what counts as "costs" and "rewards." In our society, women often feel significant pressure to be in a dating or romantic relationship or a marriage, since for centuries women's relationships with men have legitimized their existence. Even though these notions are changing, some women still believe that any relationship—no matter how destructive or "costly"—is better than no relationship at all. Examples of costly relationships might include one which tears down the self-esteem of one or both partners, one that involves verbal, emotional, and/or physical abuse, or one that seems to be going nowhere, representing a costly time investment for one or both partners. For women in such relationships, the reward of just having a man in one's life outweighs the costs or toll the relationship may take.

Another criticism maintains that social exchange theory actually ascribes greater male power in relationships. Social psychologists Thibaut and Kelley (1959) proposed that whoever brings more resources to the relationship has greater influence over its development, thus experiencing the rewards of decision-making abilities and power. As feminist psychologists Unger and Crawford (1991) explain, men more often than women bring resources such as money, education, and prestige to relationships—resources that are more highly valued in our society than emotional nurturance, for example. This places the man in the power position, which implies that he holds sole right to financial decision making. A problem occurs, according to Unger and Crawford, when "the money he brings in also gives him the right to make other important decisions that have nothing to do with money" (p. 372). "Important decisions" could include such things as making decisions about the future of the relationship, deciding whether vacations or trips will be taken and where, even to such an extent as deciding who the woman is allowed to socialize with or have as friends. Another problem occurs when a woman actually does bring more earning power to a relationship. Because of remnant societal attitudes about sex roles, the woman's resource contribution may not necessarily identify her as the powerholder and decision maker.

For example, Herschel and Carol are dating and Herschel has a job; Carol doesn't have a job but is a full-time college student. Social exchange theory would say that because Herschel makes the money that finances the couple's dates, he holds the greater power in the relationship. What if the situation were reversed? If Carol held the full-time job while Herschel attended college and if she paid for their social excursions, would you be as likely to assign the greater power to her in the relationship?

Family researchers Steil and Weltman (1991) report that equal resources contributed to a relationship do not necessarily result in a shared balance of power. In a society where being a provider and earning an income is valued more highly than nurturing children, a man's income will be more highly valued since he is living up to the "provider" expectation. A woman's income, even if it is roughly equal to or more than a man's, may be seen as undermining the provider image of the man and as proof that the woman is distracted from her duties as homemaker and child-care giver.

We find merit in the substantial criticism of social exchange theory, but we believe that the criticisms have actually increased the practical value of the theory, when it comes to making a decision to continue a relationship. The criticisms can cause people to take a longer look at what they deem to be the rewards and costs of any romantic relationship or friendship. Then they can compare their own cost and reward criteria to another person's, and to that of society in general. For example, do you believe that the reward of being in a romantic relationship outweighs the cost of being in a bad one? Does your relational history include a string of unrewarding, unbalanced, possibly even abusive relationships? Setting your own terms for costs and rewards will help you determine what exchange must be present in order for you to continue in relationships.

Sometimes the best way to discover cost and reward information about one another is to simply talk about it, to simply ask one another, "What's important to you in this relationship?" We realize that having a discussion like this may not seem normal or comfortable for you at the beginning stages of relationships. But one way or another, at some time or another, you will want to ask some important questions. For example, if you value a great deal of time to yourself, will the cost of sacrificing some time alone be balanced by the reward of doing things with your friend, date, or spouse? If the other person does not value time alone in the same way you do, that may cause problems. How will you negotiate the difference? More generally, how will each of you react if relational rewards aren't being realized or the costs are running too high? It's wise to discover how people view these kinds of issues, so that you can negotiate ways to bring the costs and rewards into balance.

Listening to Confirm

Since we are major proponents of the receiver orientation to communication, it's no surprise that we believe that listening ability more significantly controls the direction of a relationship than speaking ability. But here we refer to a special kind of listening—not just listening in general. One of the most important aspects of relationship initiation and the decision to continue is the skill of listening to confirm someone else's self-concept (Cissna & Keating, 1979; Lifshitz & Shulman, 1983).

Have you ever said something to someone whose lack of response made you feel like you were completely invisible? Or maybe the person responded by offering her or his own ideas, never acknowledging yours. In situations like these, you may very quickly decide that the relationship potential with the person is zero. On a more positive note, have you ever found yourself talking more and about more personal things to someone, only to stop and wonder how you got that deeply into the conversation? Have you ever felt like an exchange with someone was really balanced and that it confirmed who both of you are as people? In both positive and negative circumstances, the quality of the listening most likely brought about the result.

Communication scholar Evelyn Sieburg (1969) describes some basic aspects of listening to confirm, including (1) directly acknowledging another person's communication and responding to it verbally and nonverbally; (2) giving a supportive response by expressing understanding and reassurance; (3) clarifying the content and/or feelings expressed in the other's message by asking questions, paraphrasing what the other person said, or encouraging more communication; and (4) expressing positive feelings that communicate support and confirmation of the other person. Confirming, supportive listening is a powerful motivator in the decision to continue a relationship. If you can accomplish this, the other person is very likely to make the decision to stick with the relationship. If the other person can listen to you in a confirming, supportive manner, then you will be more likely to want that relationship to continue since you believe that your very basic idea of yourself is being accepted.

An interesting related topic is the purported difference between the listening behaviors of men and women. Deborah Tannen (1990), a sociolinguist whose work we've cited at other points in this text, explains that women tend to listen differently and for different reasons than men. Tannen describes women's listening as being aimed at confirming both the other person and the relationship between the speaker and the listener. Women tend to process the information, but they really tune in to the emotional level of the other person. They empathize, sympathize, and let the other person disclose whatever seems important at the time. Research indicates that men listen more for the informational than the emotional aspects of a message. Many men would rather talk, explain, and advise than listen, because listening signals a feminine, dependent, and subordinate position in conversation (Booth-Butterfield, 1984; Tannen, 1990).

Communication researcher Melanie Booth-Butterfield (1984) concludes from her studies that women and men "learn to listen for different purposes and have different listening goals. The primary contrast appears in task versus interpersonal understanding; males tend to hear the facts while females are more aware of the mood of the communication" (p. 39). An interesting parallel emerges between confirmatory listening patterns of the sexes and the relational versus content approaches to communication, discussed in Chapter 5. While the information for both listening patterns and approaches to communication does not elevate one form over another, we contend that one form of listening is more critical to the decision to continue a relationship. The kind of listening that is required to confirm someone else's sense of self, not merely to "take in the facts," is a significant factor in the potential of a relationship. Adding this ability to your communication repertoire will enhance your personal effectiveness and relational success.

CONCLUSION

The topics explored in this chapter represent a significant challenge for most of us—the challenge of turning relationship potential into reality. The challenge involves communicating effectively so that we make wise relationship choices and so that we are chosen as friends, dating partners, colleagues, and spouses. Information, attraction, and interest play significant roles in the beginning stages of getting to know other people and being known by them. Once you've deemed someone "approachable," then such communication variables as conversation starters, affinity-seeking strategies, and rhetorical sensitivity become critical to getting a new relationship off the ground. Understanding the costs and rewards inherent in relationships as well as developing your ability to listen to confirm someone's self-concept become increasingly important as you make the decision to continue a relationship. The more you understand about relationships, the more you can take charge of your relational future and optimize your chances for successful, satisfying relationships. And it is in those kinds of relationships where we really "test the waters" of gender communication—over time and with change, trial, error, and second chances.

Key Terms

relationship	goals	reciprocity of liking
relationship initiation	self-image	attitude similarity
relational partner	inclusion	conversation starters
platonic relationships	affection	affinity-seeking
approachables	control	rhetorical sensitivity
uncertainty reduction	consistency	noble self
passive strategies	confidence	rhetorical reflectors
active strategies	attraction	social exchange theory
interactive strategies	physical appearance	costs
cultural information	meta-analysis	rewards
sociological information	Matching Hypothesis	listening to confirm
psychological information	proximity	
needs	interest	

Discussion Starters

1. Some people believe that the initiation of a dating or romantic relationship should be "men's work." Do you think women should be able to initiate dating relationships in the same ways men do? If you believe that they can, and you are a woman, have you

ever initiated a relationship with a man? If you are a man who has been "chosen" by a woman, how did you feel when she initiated a relationship with you?

2. Think about the role of information in the initiation of relationships. What information do you use to make decisions about people when initiating a friendship? Do you need different kinds of information when initiating a dating relationship versus a friendship with someone? What information about yourself as a potential relational partner do you think is most important? What's the most important information to learn about someone else as a potential relational partner?

3. What are some of the most unusual and/or funny examples you have seen of men trying to be attractive by appearing too masculine? Of women trying to appear too feminine? Do think there is such a thing as too masculine or feminine?

4. Do women and men have different goals in initiating relationships? What do you think men see as major relationship goals, for men and then for women? What do you think women see as major relationship goals, for women and then for men? If your lists reveal discrepancies, think about why you believe that men and women view relationship initiation differently.

5. We've noticed that some students present a particular image of themselves in classes, but we imagine that they are really different than that image when they are with their friends. Do you personally choose an image you want to project in class and then actually project it? Have you ever tried to purposefully alter the image you convey? Do you project one image to the same sex and another to the opposite sex?

6. Make your own list of useful conversation starters. What is the best conversational opening you have ever heard? Was it directed at you, or did you open a conversation with someone else? Why was the opening successful or unsuccessful? Can men and women become equally skilled at starting conversations?

7. Recall a time when you or a close friend was at the point of deciding whether to continue or put a halt to a relationship that was trying to get off the ground—the third stage of relationship initiation discussed in this chapter. Do you recall what factors made the difference or helped you make your decision? Did you (or your friend) make a wise decision at the time? If not, what do you wish had been done differently?

References

BARRY, D. (1991, February 3). What makes guys do that weird macho stuff? *Miami Herald*, p. 7.

BAR-TAL, D., & SAXE, L. (1976). Perceptions of similarity and dissimilarity of attractive couples and individuals. *Journal of Personality and Social Psychology, 33,* 772–781.

BELL, R. A., & DALY, J. A. (1984). The affinity-seeking function of communication. *Communication Monographs, 51,* 93–114.

BERGER, C. R. (1988). Planning, affect, and social action generation. In R. L. Donohew, H. Sypher, & E. T. Higgins (Eds.), *Communication, social cognition and affect* (pp. 93–116). Hillsdale, NJ: Lawrence Erlbaum Associates.

BERGER, C. R., & CALABRESE, R. J. (1975). Some explorations in initial interaction and beyond. Toward a developmental theory of interpersonal communication. *Human Communication Research, 1,* 99–112.

BERGER, C. R., & DOUGLAS, W. (1981). Studies in interpersonal epistemology: III. Anticipated interaction, self-monitoring, and observational context selection. *Communication Monographs, 48,* 183–196.

BERSHEID, E. (1985). Interpersonal attraction. In G. Lindzey & E. Aronson (Eds.), *Handbook of social psychology* (3rd ed.). New York: Random House.

BOOTH-BUTTERFIELD, M. (1984). She hears . . . he hears: What they hear and why. *Personnel Journal,* *44,* 36–42.

CISSNA, K. N. L., & KEATING, S. (1979). Speech communication antecedents of perceived confirmation. *Western Journal of Speech Communication, 43,* 48–60.

CUSHMAN, D. P., VALENTINSEN, B., & DIETRICH, D. (1982). A rules theory of interpersonal relationships. In F. E. X. Dance (Ed.), *Human communication theory* (pp. 90–120). New York: Harper & Row.

DORNBUSCH, S. M., GROSS, R. T., DUNCAN, P. D., & RITTER, P. L. (1987). Stanford studies of adolescence using the National Health Examination Survey. In R. M. Lerner & T. T. Foch (Eds.), *Biological-psychosocial interactions in early adolescence* (pp. 189–205). Hillsdale, NJ: Lawrence Erlbaum Associates.

DOUGLAS, W. (1990). Uncertainty, information-seeking, and liking during initial interaction. *Western Journal of Speech Communication, 54,* 66–81.

FEINGOLD, A. (1990). Gender differences in effects of physical attractiveness on romantic attraction: A comparison across five research paradigms. *Journal of Personality and Social Psychology, 59,* 981–993.

GOFFMAN, E. (1959). *The presentation of self in everyday life.* Garden City, NY: Doubleday.

GROVE, T. G. (1991). *Dyadic interaction: Choice and change in conversations and relationships.* Dubuque, IA: Wm. C. Brown.

HART, R. P., & BURKS, D. M. (1972). Rhetorical sensitivity and social interaction. *Speech Monographs, 39,* 75–91.

HART, R. P., CARLSON, R. E., & EADIE, W. F. (1980). Attitudes toward communication and the assessment of rhetorical sensitivity. *Communication Monographs, 47,* 1–22.

HESSE-BIBER, S. (1989). Eating patterns and disorders in a college population: Are college women's eating problems a new phenomenon? *Sex Roles, 20,* 71–89.

HOMANS, G. C. (1959). *Social behavior: Its elementary forms.* New York: Harcourt, Brace & World.

KLEINKE, C. L., MEEKER, F. B., & STANESKI, R. A. (1986). Preference for opening lines: Comparing ratings by men and women. *Sex Roles, 15,* 585–600.

KNOX, D., & WILSON, K. (1981). Dating behaviors of university students. *Family Relations, 30,* 255–258.

LIFSHITZ, P., & SHULMAN, G. M. (1983). The effect of perceived similarity/dissimilarity on confirmation/disconfirmation behaviors: Reciprocity or compensation? *Communication Quarterly, 31,* 85–94.

LYDON, J. E., JAMIESON, D. W., & ZANNA, M. (1988). Interpersonal similarity and the social and intellectual dimensions of first impressions. *Social Cognition, 6,* 269–286.

MCCROSKEY, J. C., LARSON, C. E., & KNAPP, M. L. (1971). *An introduction to interpersonal communication.* Englewood Cliffs, NJ: Prentice-Hall.

MCCROSKEY, J. C., RICHMOND, V. P., & DALY, J. A. (1975). The development of perceived homophily in interpersonal communication. *Human Communication Research, 1,* 323–332.

MEHRABIAN, A. (1981). *Silent messages: Implicit communication of emotions and attitudes.* Belmont, CA: Wadsworth.

MELLIN, L. M., SCULLY, S., & IRWIN, C. E. (1986, October). *Disordered eating characteristics in preadolescent girls.* Paper presented at the American Dietetic Annual Meeting, Las Vegas, NV. Cited in Hesse-Biber, S. (1989). Eating patterns and disorders in a college population: Are college women's eating problems a new phenomenon? *Sex Roles, 20,* 71–89.

MILLER, G. R., & STEINBERG, M. (1975). *Between people: A new analysis of interpersonal communication.* Palo Alto, CA: Science Research Associates.

RICHMOND, V. P., GORHAM, J. S., & FURIO, B. J. (1987). Affinity-seeking communication in collegiate female-male relationships. *Communication Quarterly, 35,* 334–348.

SCHUTZ, W. (1960). *FIRO: A three-dimensional theory of interpersonal behavior.* New York: Holt, Rinehart & Winston.

SIEBURG, E. (1969). *Dysfunctional communication and interpersonal responsiveness in small groups.* Unpublished doctoral dissertation, University of Denver, Denver, CO.

STEIL, J. M., & WELTMAN, K. (1991). Marital inequality: The importance of resources, personal attributes, and social norms on career valuing and the allocation of domestic responsibilities. *Sex Roles, 24,* 161–179.

TANNEN, D. (1990). *You just don't understand: Women and men in conversation.* New York: William Morrow.

TEDESCHI, J. T. (Ed.) (1981). *Impression management theory and social psychology.* New York: Academic Press.

THIBAUT, J. W., & KELLEY, H. H. (1959). *The social psychology of groups.* New York: John Wiley & Sons.

TOWNSEND, J. M., & LEVY, G. D. (1990). Effects of potential partners' costume and physical attractiveness on sexuality and partner selection. *Journal of Psychology, 124,* 371–389.

TURNER, R. D. (1990, October). How to attract the opposite sex. *Ebony,* pp. 27–28, 30.

UNGER, R., & CRAWFORD, M. (1991). *Women and gender: A feminist psychology.* New York: McGraw-Hill.

WEBER, E. (1970). *How to pick up girls!* New York: Bantam Books.

WOLF, N. (1991). *The beauty myth.* New York: William Morrow.

ZAKAHI, W. R., & DURAN, R. L. (1984). Attraction, communicative competence, and communication satisfaction. *Communication Research Reports, 1,* 54–57.

CHAPTER 7

We Have a Relationship, So What Do We Do Now? Relationship Development and Change

Well, you've gotten this far in the book, and you've made it past the beginning stages of at least one friendship or dating relationship. Now that you are in the middle of the book and maybe in the middle of a relationship, it's time to take a good, long look at what to do next.

CASE STUDY

In our gender communication classes, we sometimes ask our students not about their relationships but about the relationships of their friends. Some questions we ask them are these: When you look at your friends' relationships, can you tell which ones will make it and which ones won't? Can you tell which friendships will survive, which romantic relationships will work, or which roommates will get along? Which relationships will develop? Which will stagnate? The answer is usually "yes," they can tell. When asked how they can tell, most students shrug and say something like, "I just can." And most students are right, they can tell. But they do not know why. Do you know why?

Take a look around at your own friends, their relationships with you, and their relationships with each other. Think for a moment about relationships you have seen in the past. If you're a male reader, can you tell which of your male friends is better at keeping a relationship going? What makes one friend better at this than another? Do your male friends seem to take as much responsibility for the development of a relationship as your female friends? Do your male friends even think about relationships (either same sex or opposite sex) as needing development? If you are a female reader, can you tell which of the relationships you observe will work? Does it seem to you that your female friends take more responsibility for the development of their relationships—both friendships and romantic relationships—than your male friends? If some of your female friends are better at it than others, what makes the difference?

213

How relationships get developed and changed and who takes responsibility for these tasks are questions not many of our students have thought much about. However, understanding the answers to these questions and, more importantly, knowledge of the differences in how women and men deal with these relational issues are critical to long-term personal effectiveness in gender communication. If you've ever been in a relationship and wondered "How can I make this better?" this chapter is for you. If you have never wondered that, maybe it's time to start.

OVERVIEW

Chapter 5 explored gender differences in approaches to communication and Chapter 6 focused on the process of initiating a relationship. In these two chapters, we explored information that would help you understand the relational process and suggested ideas for how to become more personally effective. Initiating a relationship, making a new friend, falling in love, and other relationship beginnings are great experiences. When it works, it is an exhilarating feeling. However, as you well know, these feelings will change. The euphoria will diminish and will likely be replaced by strong feelings of caring and commitment. Evolution of feelings is a natural part of relationship change and development.

Perhaps you have seen this happen. People fall in love, roommates find they are very compatible, and two people discover they can work well together. People in each of these relationship types can experience the initial excitement of finding someone who generates those strong, happy feelings. But it is also possible that in each relationship type, those initial feelings diminish and things move into the "warm glow" phase. People react differently to this change. Some may miss the excitement, think that the relationship is over, and start looking for someone new. Others hang in there knowing that the relationship will continue to develop. Why do some people stay and others leave? The stereotypical claim is that men have "commitmentphobia." Do you think men are more likely to leave, while women are more likely to stay?

Perhaps, too, you have looked at all the divorces and relationship failures around you and wondered, "Why has this happened?" Perhaps your friends have come to you (or you've gone to friends) and said something like, "I just can't figure this relationship out; nothing I do seems to work." For our male readers, how many times have you gone to your male friends to talk about relationship problems? If you fit the stereotype, you probably haven't done this very much. If you are a woman, how many conversations like this have you had with your female friends? Do you think women have more conversations like this than men? It is tough to succeed at relationships. Evidence of failure is everywhere. And some of your relationships are going to be failures; although painful, that's to be expected. However, we want to help you increase your relational success ratio. Increasing your personal effectiveness related to moving a relationship to new levels contributes a great deal to long-term relational satisfaction. Understanding this process, understanding how gender communication affects the process, and understanding what to add to your repertoire of communication behaviors are the basic goals of this chapter.

When you get to the point in a new relationship where the initial exhilaration has started to diminish, and you've decided (at least for yourself) that you are going to stick with this particular relationship, you have entered the main part of the relationship development process. If you look at this process as you might look at the development of a speech, the introduction is over and you are now "in the body." Success in the relationship "body" takes a different combination of knowledge and skill than what was required to get the relationship started. It's interesting to discover whether this combination works differently for women and men. In order to do that, this chapter will explore:

- Personal communication skills in relationship development, including self-disclosure, empathy, listening, and nonverbal expressiveness and sensitivity
- Sex and gender differences related to these skills
- Movement and change in relationships
- The stages of relationship development and deterioration
- Dysfunctional beliefs about relationship development
- Stabilizing a relationship (keeping it at the level you want)
- Strategies for changing a relationship
- How influence and conflict pose challenges to relationships

INTRODUCTION

At the beginning of Chapter 5 we asked you to analyze your relationships by using a configuration of concentric circles. Turn back to those circles now. Do you want to move any names more toward the inner ring? Are there any you would like to move further away? Should any new names be added to the circles? These relationships can be friendships, dating relationships, and so on; just put the names into the circles in the spot you think appropriate. Have any relationships ended? Now reanalyze the circles using these questions:

1. Is there a pattern to any of the movement? Are there more people you want to move closer than move away? Why?
2. Are the relationships that you would like to move from one circle to another same-sex or opposite-sex relationships? Are they friendships, dating relationships, work relationships?
3. Think for a moment about relationships that have ended. Where are they in the circles?
4. What kinds of relationships have ended, same-sex or opposite-sex relationships? Were they friendships, dating relationships, marriage?

5. Is there any commonality or pattern behind why these relationships ended?

As in Chapter 5, we hope this exercise helps you visualize two important aspects of relationship awareness—desired change and an understanding of why it's over. After relationships become established, they may stabilize in one level or another. Sometimes this may work for you, sometimes not. Out of this natural tendency for relationships to reach a level and stay there come two questions: How do you effectively stabilize a relationship at the level you want? How do you change the level when change is what you want?

In beginning to answer these questions, an examination of a relationship that has ended can provide some insight. Maybe one of your relationships ended because one or both of you wanted to change the level, but you couldn't agree on a new level. Did it end because one person saw no possibility for change and the relationship just no longer met her or his needs or did it end just out of neglect? Look at these questions again in light of gender communication. Which relationships tend to be the ones you would like to change, same-sex or other-sex? Who seems to take responsibility for relationship change—women or men?

These questions should get you thinking about how relationships stay alive, how they change, and how you can become more personally effective in guiding a relationship to a level that is comfortable for you and for another person. The goal of this chapter is to review some of the communication skills and processes that contribute to relationship development. To move toward this goal, we have organized this chapter into three major sections. The first section is a review of values; the second introduces four personal communication skills that are essential to relational change and development. Research suggests that women and men tend to approach these skills from different directions. For example, men's listening behaviors and patterns are generally somewhat different from women's. Women self-disclose in different ways and for different reasons than men. Thus if you want to communicate more effectively with each sex and develop more satisfying relationships, a knowledge of the sex differences in these critical communication variables will help you do just that. The final section in the chapter is a discussion of how you might use the values and communication skills to actually move a relationship from one level to another.

A QUICK REVIEW OF THE VALUE OF "VALUES"

Before we get into our discussion of personal skills and relationship development, let's do a quick review of something we discussed in Chapter 1. We talked in Chapter 1 about success and effectiveness in gender communication and in relationships. As we said many times, we want to help you increase your success ratio and the point of each chapter is to explore options and skills that will allow you to develop more successful communication strategies. Success means different things to different people, so we described the values necessary for effective gender communication. Let's briefly review these values, since the decisions you make about how to apply the skills we discuss in this chapter and the decisions you make about changing a relationship could be guided by them. Throughout the text, we have suggested that combining masculine and feminine approaches and communication styles is our preferred goal for your personal effectiveness development. These values reflect that preference.

Value 1: Equality of Power. This value refers to an equitable distribution of power or control in any relationship. Individuals should try to achieve and maintain a balance of influence, control, or power in their relationships. Again, men and women approach the dimension of power differently and have different means of exerting influence in a relationship. How do those differences affect relationship development? In this chapter we talk more specifically about how influence relates to relationship change.

Value 2: Talking about It Makes It Better. The ability to talk over issues is absolutely critical to success. The willingness to sit down and talk about the relationship, each other's feelings, and possible solutions to problems are critical to personal effectiveness. The stereotype (and the research cited in Chapter 6) holds that women are much more willing to do this than men. Is this true for you or your friends? Does someone need to change, and if so, how? Since each person contributes to changing a relationship, both men and women need to examine their own ability and willingness to talk about how the relationship is going. Ideas in this chapter build on this basic belief.

Value 3: Confirmation and Acceptance. In developing effective relationships, the ability to communicate confirmation and acceptance is highly useful to long-term effectiveness. One of the greatest sources of satisfaction and pleasure in a relationship is the feeling of being truly accepted for oneself and having one's self-image confirmed. Unfortunate cultural stereotypes suggest that men need to have their egos stroked and that it is the woman's job to do that. But members of each sex want respect and acceptance. How is this acceptance communicated? It is generally communicated through a combination of confirmation, empathy, and listening. Confirmation was discussed in Chapter 6; empathy and listening are described more fully in the next section of this chapter.

Value 4: Freedom of Choice. When we talk about the ability to direct the course of a relationship, we include the possibility that you may want to influence or persuade another person, a notion somewhat related to Value 2. Many of our communication efforts are designed to get people to do what we want. However, the freedom to choose to accept or decline influence is important to long-term relational satisfaction. This may not be easy, as there may be times when you want desperately to change something in the relationship. The fundamental right each person has to choose her or his own way is one that should not be abridged. How do you set up a relationship that strikes the right balance between freedom of choice and change?

Value 5: Treating Another Person as an Individual. Stereotyping is difficult to avoid. However, in the development of an effective relationship, knowledge of and appreciation for the other person as an individual is critical to success. But knowledge of the other is not enough; the additional necessary step is to communicate with that person, *using* the knowledge.

Value 6: Being Open-Minded and Willing to Change. Personal growth and development are part of life. If you expect other people to be open to your suggestions for relational change, perhaps you should be open to theirs. Relationships are filled with compromise and adaptation. A key decision in many relationships is the degree to which each person is willing to change. That is a decision only you can make.

These values serve a number of different purposes. As you work on becoming more personally effective, these values are a great set of decision guidelines to help you determine where you want to go in the relationship. They also suggest how and when to use the skills we describe later. Inappropriately used, these skills can hurt relationships more than they help. Finally, since these are values your authors hold personally, they also guide our choice of information and suggestions in this chapter.

PERSONAL COMMUNICATION SKILLS FOR WOMEN AND MEN IN DEVELOPING RELATIONSHIPS

Our main interest here is in increasing your knowledge about relationship development and the movement from one level of a relationship to another. In this first section, we focus on personal communication skills that can help stabilize a relationship or move it to a different level. While there are literally dozens of communication variables that can affect the outcome of a relationship, we have selected four that are most central to the relationship development process. In describing self-disclosure, empathy, listening, and nonverbal expressiveness and sensitivity, we explore some traditional sex differences and how members of each sex might expand their communication behavior repertoire to become more personally effective.

Self-Disclosure and the Sexes

You probably know by now that it's hard to make effective decisions or act effectively toward another person without accurate and useful information. Women and men both need information, but each sex asks for, gives, and emphasizes different kinds of information. Here we examine the disclosure process, what sex or gender differences are present, and how members of each sex can expand their ability to effectively disclose useful information so that relationships are developed and enhanced.

While many definitions of self-disclosure exist, most are similar to one offered by interpersonal communication researchers Judy Pearson and Brian Spitzberg (1990). They define self-disclosure as "communication in which a person voluntarily and intentionally tells another person accurate information about himself or herself that the other person is unlikely to know or find out from another source" (p. 142). This definition reinforces our earlier focus on the importance of information and uncertainty reduction in initiating a relationship. Continued disclosure is also central to relationship development and change.

The conventional wisdom is that women like to self-disclose more than men, especially about relationships. Women are stereotypically seen as more willing to convey information about themselves to others. Conversely, men are stereotyped as "strong, silent types." Interestingly enough, these stereotypes are supported by some of the disclosure research. For example, interpersonal communication researchers Greenblatt, Hasenauer, and Friemuth (1980) reported that women disclosed more and received more disclosure than men. They also found that men disclosed more often and more openly to women than to other men. Specifically, in terms of the depth and breadth of information the participants share with one another, female-female relationships have been ranked first in several studies, followed by male-female relationships, with male-male relationships rated lowest on degree of intimacy and amount of disclosure (Derlega, Winstead, Wong, & Hunter, 1985; Henley, 1986; Ickes, 1985). Winstead (1986), a gender researcher, suggests that these trends may reflect a self-fulfilling prophecy, in that some people consciously or unconsciously live up to the sexual stereotypes.

Why are women considered better people to disclose to? Women are usually seen as more supportive and responsive (and as better listeners), which encourages others to open up to them. Thus they are more likely to be the targets of others' disclosure. Interpersonal communication researchers Petronio, Martin, and Littlefield (1984) found that women more than men feel it important that the receiver of disclosure "be discreet, trustworthy, sincere, liked, respected, a good listener, warm, and open" (p. 270). In addition, these researchers reported that women feel more strongly than men that it is important for a discloser to feel accepted, to be willing to disclose in an honest and frank manner without being anxious, and to not be provoked into giving information. When you think about yourself as a "target" of disclosure, it may be helpful to consider how you respond to someone's disclosure. For example, if you are listening to a "strong, silent type" man's disclosure, what type of response style might match his particular needs? Both sexes may need to adjust their response style to more fully match the needs of the sender, since this is an integral part of the receiver orientation to communication.

For several reasons, men often have difficulty disclosing to other men. Psychologist Sidney Jourard (1971) described the effect of this on men's health in a book chapter entitled "The Lethal Aspects of the Male Role." Jourard's research determined that men who have difficulty expressing their feelings also had higher levels of stress-related diseases than did men who were able to disclose more fully. Nondisclosure affects not only relational health but personal health as well. Bottled-up feelings literally do eat away at you. Since the stereotypical masculine role implies that men don't disclose to other men, this causes men to rely more on women as outlets for disclosure. Men are generally open only with lovers and other women, according to research. As Snell, Miller, and Belk (1988) contend, "Men, it seems, are dependent upon women listeners for emotional self-expression" (p. 69). In self-disclosing conversations, men may express uncertainties, vulnerabilities, and weaknesses that would rarely be disclosed to another man. As a result, many men use women as the targets of emotional disclosure since it is unlikely that they will find a male partner with whom to share these issues.

Do men use women to get a regenerative jolt to recharge their batteries? Who do men seek to talk over important things, their female friends? If you are a female reader, would you say that in your conversations with men the amount

---

What If?

What if men were rewarded socially for being able to express their feelings? *What if,* in addition to making decisions and having physical strength, men also easily admitted their weaknesses and uncertainties and talked about their relationships? *What if* actors like John Wayne, Clint Eastwood, Wesley Snipes, and Kevin Costner were models of emotional expression, and people admired them for it? This country would probably be a different place. As it is, there are only a few contexts in which many men feel safe in disclosing or revealing their emotions. One is the athletic context; the other is war. Think about it: The rules for male emotional expression change in athletic competition or under the stress of combat. In these situations, men's masculinity is sort of a given, meaning that it isn't called into question. Being emotional in these settings doesn't put one's masculinity at risk; in fact, shows of emotion are somewhat expected. Sometimes men reveal their emotions in such settings as funerals or when their children are born. But even in these situations, men may feel that showing emotion makes them vulnerable or is a threat to perceptions of them as masculine. *What if* men didn't have to worry about perceptions of their emotional displays? Would male friendships be different if this were the case? How would male-female relationships change? If you are male, imagine how *you* and your relationships would be different. Would you be pleased about the opportunity to express yourself or would you resist it? What would be the advantages and disadvantages to you? If you are female, how would you react to this change in men? Would it help your relationships with them? Imagine *What* life might be like, *if* men were positively reinforced for expressing their emotions.

and level of disclosure for each of you is equal? If not, which way is the scale tipped? For either sex, do you find yourself falling into the stereotypical disclosure patterns?

There are reasons for the differences in men and women regarding disclosure. There is social pressure on both sexes regarding the appropriateness of disclosure. One study found that women were judged more positively when disclosing more information, as it is attributed to their high degree of affiliation and supportiveness. Men were rated as *less* competent by both men and women when showing a high level of disclosure (Jones & Bruner, 1984). That's not good news. In other research, a man who hid his fears was judged more appealing to some women than a man who was more emotionally forthright (Zillman, Weaver, Mundorf, & Aust, 1986). Women are reinforced for disclosing, which encourages more disclosure. The opposite seems to be the case for men; they receive more negative reinforcement, especially from peers, so disclosure lessens. Do women generally react supportively when a man discloses personal information, especially if it has to do with fears and uncertainties, or do they think him "less of a man" because of what he said? How do men typically react when a male friend discloses fears and uncertainties? Perhaps both men and women need to look at how supportive and responsive they are to men's disclosure, since responses can either encourage or discourage the sharing of personal information.

Beyond socialization, why else do men keep their thoughts to themselves? Here's one explanation: Some men use inexpressiveness as a means of maintaining power and control (what we refer to as the "Clint Eastwood effect") (Rosenfeld, 1979). Giving information is seen by some men as giving up control. However, if you think back to the values for relationships section, you'll recall one that emphasized the equality of control. This implies that disclosure also needs to be equally balanced between the partners in a relationship, including friendships, romantic relationships, marriages, and working relationships with peers. But some men say "We don't tell women (or anyone) things because we don't want them to worry." Many people, especially women, see that as a fear of intimacy and as a move to increase relational distance.

The content of disclosure is also important to relational development and there are clear differences between the sexes on what might be defined as disclosure (Derlega, Durham, Gockel, & Sholis, 1981). Some men may think they are disclosing when they talk about work. After all, for many men, that's what is most important in their lives. Women tend to talk about the self when expressing feelings about people or personal issues. Gender scholar Barbara Bate (1988) suggests that each sex gives "information that the sender considers essential to intimacy and the receiver finds pointless" (p. 186).

Following up this point on the relationship between intimacy and disclosure, reporter Carole Tavris (1992) makes the case that in present-day relationships, the feminine language has become the dominant one. She contends that women appear to "be better than men at intimacy because intimacy is defined as what women do; talk, express feelings, disclose personal concerns. Intimacy is rarely defined as sharing activities, being helpful, doing useful work, or enjoying companionable silence. Because of this bias, men rarely get credit for the kinds of loving actions that are more typical of them" (p. 100). Perhaps men disclose themselves partially through what they do with their partner. Does disclosure need to be based in words? Perhaps some men who have difficulty disclosing with words attempt to disclose through actions. While this may be an overgeneralization, if certain forms of disclosure are important to your relational partner or friend, perhaps they should be important to *you*.

But there is more to an understanding of disclosure differences than one's sex. Research shows that gender-role socialization influences both the ability to disclose and the perception of the appropriateness of disclosure (Derlega, Durham, Gockel, & Sholis, 1981; Jourard, 1971; Sollie & Fischer, 1985; Stokes, Fuehrer, & Childs, 1980). Psychologists Stephens and Harrison (1985) identified the feminine communication style as characterized by emotional sensitivity, sympathy, and consideration. Men tend to preserve a masculine image, disclose more about their own strengths (such as professional or athletic successes), and use a dominant, assertive, and aggressive communication style. Given that, whom would you rather disclose to? Men who adhere to a strong, masculine gender role not only disclose less than androgynous men and women but are much less likely to be targets of others' disclosure (Greenblatt et al., 1980). If a man is interested in information to use in developing effective relationships, then the masculine gender role may inhibit that goal.

A number of researchers suggest that a positive combination of femininity and masculinity contributes to a person's ability and willingness to form satisfying relationships. Studies identify androgynous people as being more flexible and adaptable, which allows for a potentially broader range of encounters, a higher level of self-disclosure, and a decreasing potential for loneliness (Bem & Lenney, 1976; Lavine & Lombardo, 1984; Wheeless & Lashbrook, 1987; Wheeless, Zakahi, & Chan, 1988). Thus it appears that it is not just your sex but how you play out your gender role that makes a difference.

So what does all this mean? Here's what it could mean to you:

1. There are differences in the way men and women (and feminine, androgynous, and masculine individuals) give and receive disclosure.
2. Each sex needs to understand its own general tendencies in giving and receiving disclosure, as well as the tendencies of the other sex. Knowledge of these tendencies may help you compensate for them.
3. Each sex needs to understand what constitutes disclosure for the other and to react in a manner that supports the disclosure and the discloser.
4. This understanding can help each person expand his or her disclosing repertoire.
5. Effective use of self-disclosure is central to the relationship acceleration or movement from one stage to another.

Progress on these five points is important to the development and growth of any relationship. Now let's turn to more detail on how you might respond to someone's self-disclosure.

The Big "E": Empathy

Understanding and responding effectively to another person is critical to long-term relational effectiveness. You probably value people who seem to understand you and likely want to increase the amount of contact you have with them. Most researchers view this type of deep understanding as *empathy*. While you have probably studied this concept in another class, it is important to review it here, since there are significant sex and gender differences in expressions of empathy and because empathy serves as a basic building block to relationship development.

Empathy is a difficult concept to define; it is not our purpose here to review all the suggested definitions. However, we do need a basic understanding of the concept to begin our discussion. Interpersonal communication researchers Stiff, Dillard, Somera, Kim, and Sleight (1988) described three relevant dimensions of empathy: *perspective-taking*, a cognitive ability to adopt the viewpoint of the other person; *emotional contagion*, an emotional response experienced by one person in parallel to the other person; and *empathic concern*, a sympathetic and altruistic concern for the other person (p. 199). Empathy seems to be a concept (and skill) that expresses a full understanding of and concern for the other individual in both cognitive (content) and emotional/relational dimensions of the relationship. Communication researcher Mark Redmond (1985) added a critical point to this discussion. He pointed out in his research that it is not enough to be empathic; the other person must perceive you as having empathy. It does you no good to have empathy if the other person never finds out.

How do women and men show empathy in relationships? It's unwise to assume that members of the opposite sex see the world in the same way you do. Nor can you assume that someone of the opposite sex will express empathy in the same way you do. While this may be somewhat obvious, it does suggest that it takes conscious effort to create an empathic understanding with another person. The stereotype suggests that women are more empathic than men. This is based partly on listening behavior and partly on emotional response. It may be a stereotype that women express more empathy, but is the stereotype based in truth?

Research seems to be mixed as to differences, according to both gender and sex. Some research found no significant differences between the sexes related to empathic ability (Brehm, Powell, & Coke, 1984). Other research focused on gender differences rather than sex. For us, this is most interesting as it relates to androgyny. Psychologist Sandra Bem (1975) found that traditionally feminine participants demonstrated more apparent empathy than less traditional women, because traditionally feminine women are socialized to exhibit supportive responses. In later research, Fong and Borders (1985) found that androgynous individuals were more empathic, regardless of sex. An important part of the movement toward more androgynous communication behavior is the expansion of your abilities to both feel and express empathy for another person.

As you increase in personal effectiveness and move to a more androgynous communication style, empathy is a fundamental skill to add to your communication repertoire. The expression of empathy can do much to strengthen and deepen a relationship. Interpersonal communication researchers Pearson and Spitzberg (1990) identify communication behaviors that express empathy, including inviting additional comments from someone who is disclosing, identifying areas of agreement, providing clear verbal responses, and providing affirming feedback. As you contemplate the movement between stages in a relationship, empathy will play a significant role. Empathy is a building block for intimacy and for trust between people. But even more generally important, empathy helps to deepen a relationship, to move it from one stage to another. In general, both men and women tend to trust someone of either sex who can effectively demonstrate empathy. People will more likely disclose to a person of either sex who can effectively demonstrate an empathic response.

Are You Listening?

Listening is closely related to empathy. We explored some aspects of listening in Chapter 6, so we don't repeat that material here. However, we do want to spend a little more time describing sex differences in listening behavior. Listening, like empathy, enhances disclosure, increases trust, and decreases psychological distance between people. Listening and responding to disclosure are obviously important in encouraging or discouraging further disclosure. However, just as in disclosure, women and men differ in listening patterns. These differences can help or hurt relationship maintenance and development.

In her book *You Just Don't Understand*, Deborah Tannen (1990) discusses gender differences in listening. Men and women seem to have very different styles, with men again focusing on the content of what is said and women on the relationship between the interactants. For example, during situations where someone is disclosing a personal problem or issue, men seem to listen for solutions and to give advice to "solve the problem." This may or may not be what the speaker wants. Women, on the other hand, tend to listen to reflect understanding and support for the other person. As you might guess, this behavior makes both sexes feel more understood. This basic difference also leads to a difference in the amount of effort each sex puts into listening. Men tend to tune out things they can't solve right away or wonder why they should even listen if there isn't a problem to solve. Women tend to become more involved and connected to the speaker and see listening as something important to do for the other person.

This difference can lead to frustration between the sexes. Tannen describes a number of different situations. For example, if a man uses male listening behavior with a woman and begins to offer immediate solutions to a concern she is expressing, she may feel that he is dismissing and trivializing those concerns. Men tend to listen to solve problems, not to express support. A woman may react to this rush to a solution by dismissing him as "someone who just doesn't understand." If she rejects the solutions proposed, the man in fact may feel misunderstood. After all, he was just trying to help.

As we look at expanding one's repertoire of communication behaviors, men may need to pay closer attention to listening and the nonverbal cues that support listening. One suggestion is for men to make more listening noises such as "uh-huh," "yeah," and other encouragers so that the other person feels listened to. It's also a good idea to find out what the other person in a conversation wants—advice or just an ear—so that one knows how to listen in a particular situation.

Listening is also related to power (Tannen, 1990). Men tend to use talk to establish status, whereas women use listening to empower others. If men do see things as "one-up, one-down" in listening, then careful listening can be seen as a loss of power and control (e.g., "If I hop to what she says, then I'm subordinate."). This is a real issue for some men (Warshaw, 1992). However, if each sex holds the same value that we expressed at the beginning of this chapter, that of equality of power, then listening can be used to support and strengthen the closeness of a relationship. It does not need to be a source of power differences.

One last point on listening has to do with the correlation between the amount of listening and the amount of talk. After all, most us prefer not to do both at the same time. If you are a man and happen to be in a mixed-sex group, who does most of the talking? How much do you really listen to the women in the group? Communication researcher Elizabeth Aries (1982) reports that men do not listen effectively in these situations, since the talk may not be focused on single issues or since some men believe that listening isn't as powerful as talking. In Aries's research, men generally failed to respond when women tried to initiate conversations. Yet men who initiated talk with women were nearly always successful in eliciting responses. A direct response to another person that demonstrates effective listening can be the beginning of empathic feelings, support for each person's self-concept, and an opportunity for a deeper, closer relationship.

As in disclosure, an awareness of the different styles of listening behavior can do much to increase the likelihood that you will apply the appropriate listening behavior to match your (and the other person's) intent in the situation. As members of each sex develop an awareness of their own tendencies and an understanding of the other's tendencies in listening, then listening can be used effectively to generate the kind of relationship both people want.

Nonverbal Communication Expressiveness and Sensitivity

An integral component of the receiver orientation to communication, as well as one of the most useful skills in demonstrating empathy and effective listening, is nonverbal communication expressiveness and sensitivity. Behavioral scientist Albert Mehrabian (1970) first described these skills in terms of nonverbal "immediacy." Immediacy is indicated by increased eye contact, closer proximity, greater touching, more direct body orientation, more facial expressive responses, and the like. Generally, as one person in a relationship uses more immediate and direct nonverbal communication, the other person feels support and is more likely to value the interaction and the relationship.

However, an overuse of these behaviors can make the other person uncomfortable, as though someone was concentrating too much on being "responsively correct" to the point that she or he wasn't really listening. Communication researchers Sabatelli and Rubin (1986) define nonverbal expressiveness as "an individual's spontaneous tendency to accurately communicate his or her emotional state to others via nonverbal channels" (p. 121). Note the word *spontaneous*. Results from their study indicate that those people who display nonverbal information in an automatic and uncensored manner create more favorable impressions on others. They also found, interestingly enough, that even negative uninhibited nonverbal responses result in more attractive perceptions of a person than awkward and censored nonverbal signals. It's hard to work on your nonverbal expressiveness, so that it will appear natural and unrehearsed to others—that's almost a contradiction in terms. But what we mean here is that becoming more nonverbally expressive and sensitive doesn't come naturally for many of us; we have to learn which skills work and when to use them, and then practice their use. (Remember the levels of unconscious and conscious competence from Chapter 1?) With enough practice and positive reinforcement from others, your nonverbal sensitivity and expressiveness can become a more natural element of your communication repertoire.

Would it surprise you to learn that women tend to be more nonverbally sensitive and expressive than men? We suspect not, since you probably know by now that women's behaviors, both verbal and nonverbal, tend to emphasize their connection to and affiliation with others. Again, it's not that women value relationships more than men, but that women more actively communicate the importance of relationships by utilizing verbal and nonverbal channels.

Here are some sex differences in nonverbal communication suggested by research; see if they match your experience. In general, men tend to talk at angles to each other and don't look directly at each other; that is, men use more signals of power and are less immediate in conversations with other men. Women, in conversations with other women and with men, are more likely to face people physically and look directly at others (Ellyson, Dovidio, & Fehr, 1981; Hall, 1984; Mulac, Studley, Wiemann, & Bradac, 1987; Tannen, 1990). Part of the explanation for this difference in behavior relates to the basic idea that a person in a subordinate position usually makes more eye contact than a person in a dominant position (Hickson & Stacks, 1993). Beyond that explanation, women appear to be more comfortable with greater levels of eye contact than men. Other research on sex differences in nonverbal communication suggests that women display more general immediacy behaviors than men, such as forward lean, direct body orientation, head nodding, smiling, and touching (Deutsch, LeBaron, & Fryer, 1987; Fugita, Harper, & Wiens, 1980; Jones, 1986).

Spending some time watching other people and comparing their use of immediate nonverbal cues to your own might cause you to become more self-aware. Do you think it would improve your relationships if you were more nonverbally expressive and sensitive? It also might be a good idea to think about how you would react to a man who uses a higher degree of immediacy cues than the average. At what point might the use of these cues make you uncomfortable? If both members of any kind of relationship are interested in developing an effective relationship, then attention to nonverbal cues and their use will play a significant role.

Now we move beyond personal development of skills and look to relationship change. Effective use of the four skills we just discussed—self-disclosure, empathy, listening, and nonverbal expressiveness and sensitivity—will likely lead to greater feelings of closeness and less psychological distance between persons in a relationship. When certain relational issues arise that cause you to make decisions (sometimes referred to as "decision points"), these basic communication skills can do much to help you implement effective choices and become more personally effective. These four skills can also serve as "relationship accelerators," meaning that when they are used well, they can accelerate the movement between stages in a relationship. In the next section of this chapter, we consider accelerators and the concept of relational movement more fully.

MOVEMENT FROM ONE RELATIONAL LEVEL TO ANOTHER: PROPELLING A RELATIONSHIP

It seems that everyone wants relationship satisfaction and will work hard to achieve it. Literary critic Kenneth Burke (1966) went so far as to define humans as "rotten with perfection" (p. 7). We've always liked that definition, as it speaks to why each of us strives for something better. This striving is rarely more clear than in our efforts to build relationships. Each of us has a strong motivation for the "perfect" relationship but may not have the knowledge and skill to effectively advance in that direction. The previous section of this chapter described some of the central communication skills necessary to translate your motivation into effective behavior. This section of the chapter provides insight into how one uses those skills to move or propel a relationship to a different level (sometimes higher, sometimes lower).

Change versus Stability in Relationship Stages

You probably face countless decision points in relationships. These decisions range from the abstract (e.g., Where is this relationship going? Where do I want it to go?) to those made on the spur of the moment (e.g., you have an opportunity to ask a coworker to have a cup of coffee with you, opening up the possibility of a friendship, rather than just a professional relationship). These decision points are exciting and they offer many possibilities. Recognizing them and making the best decisions are central elements in effective long-term relational success. Relationships involve growth; the relationship life cycle implies movement—either forward or backward. But is it possible to communicate so that you influence the movement? For example, have you ever felt dissatisfied with a relationship and wanted to move it to a deeper level? Are there strategies you could follow to accelerate or decelerate the rate of change in a relationship? Are there differences between men and women regarding movement? While we cannot cover all possible strategies and ideas, we believe that the concept of movement between stages of a relationship (described in this section) is important to personal effectiveness in gender communication.

Relational Stages

Most researchers agree that relationships go through relatively identifiable stages. You may have studied these stages in another course; however, we review one set of stages here for two reasons. First, relationship development is the point of this chapter and reviewing these stages gives each of us the same point of reference. Second, women and men seem to play different roles in the movement between stages. Understanding these differences can make each sex more effective in propelling a relationship along.

One of the most frequently cited sets of stages was described first by Mark Knapp (1978) in his book *Social Intercourse: From Greeting to Goodbye*. In the beginning of this book, Knapp asks some interesting questions—questions that are worth exploration.

> (1) Are there regular and systematic patterns of communication that suggest stages on the road to an intimate relationship? Are there similar patterns and stages that characterize the deterioration of relationships? (2) Can we identify communication strategies that attract and repel us at various stages in a relationship? Specifically, how do people talk to each other when they are building, maintaining, or tearing down a relationship? (3) What are these mysterious forces that propel us in and out of relationships? And what determines how fast or slow a relationship progresses or dissolves? (p. 4)

These questions are highly useful guides as we attempt to make sense of the relationship change process for ourselves. Knowledge of the stages of relationships is an example of "forewarned is forearmed." If you know what to expect, if you know what happens at each stage of the relationship, if you know what sex differences exist, and if you have the knowledge and skill to help move a relationship from stage to stage, you will have achieved real progress on the road to increased personal effectiveness in gender communication.

Let's review Knapp's identification of the stages of relationship development. We refer back to them in later chapters (particularly the chapters on friendship, romance, and marriage). Knapp identified five stages of "coming together" in a relationship: *initiating*, those first decisions about attraction and the initial decisions to continue the relationship; *experimenting*, the stage of uncertainty reduction (somewhat akin to the sniffing ritual in animals); *intensi-*

fying, the first real stage of intimacy, which includes more disclosure and a greater awareness of the process of the relationship; *integrating,* where attitudes become more similar and the level of "coupleness" increases; and *bonding,* a public ritual that announces to the world that commitments have been contracted.

Have you noticed these stages before? If you think about it, you will be able to recognize these stages in your own and in other people's relationships. Awareness is the first step to controlling the movement between stages.

Knapp also describes five stages of "coming apart." While we are not focusing our attention on relationship disintegration, an awareness of each stage may help you recognize them, should you find yourself in them. The five stages are *circumscribing,* where certain topics are not discussed but are ignored or talked around (circumscribed); *differentiating,* where differences between the two people become the focus of attention; *stagnating,* where people have almost given up hope that the relationship can be worked out; *avoiding,* where partners actively seek to close the communication channels; and *termination.* These stages contained within relational "coming together" and "coming apart" describe the pattern of a relationship from greeting to good-bye.

Relational Movement and Change

Not all relationships follow all stages, and the questions become what can you expect and what can you do to control the movement between stages and levels. To illustrate, imagine that you have a superficial friendship with someone at work. Up to now, your relationship with this person has consisted of conversation necessary to get the job done and not much else. However, you decide that a more personal friendship with this person is possible. By making that decision, you have exercised some control over the direction of the relationship. You've decided to "accelerate the rate of change" and move the relationship from one stage to another. The question becomes, how is this best done? Each of us has faced decisions like this and asked the same questions: Do I want to turn this acquaintance into a friend? This friendship into something deeper? This romantic relationship *back* to a friendship?

As a beginning in understanding the concept of relational movement, we return to Knapp's (1978) work, specifically his description of some principles of movement from stage to stage within a relationship.

1. Movement is generally systematic and sequential. It is rare to skip stages, as one stage usually prompts the next. Knapp doesn't say that all relationships go through all stages. A relationship may go from intensifying to differentiating without the intervening stages. While little research exists on which sex is more likely to initiate the movement between stages, neither person in the relationship should feel like it is the other person's job to initiate change.
2. Movement can occur in a forward or backward motion. In fact, movement may be back and forth among the stages as a relationship evolves, changes, and develops.

3. Movement is always to a new place; this is an important lesson to learn. You can never go back to the way things were. Even if a couple revisits previous stages, their experience will be colored by their previous interaction.

These are interesting and useful points that describe what happens as people move through various stages over the course of a relationship. In the next section of this chapter, we consider more specifically some strategies that may make the movement from one stage to another easier and more effective. The strategies may help you accelerate the rate of change in the relationship so that you can reach the level you seek more quickly.

What Gets Changed?

Can you really change a person within a relationship? Consider this folk wisdom: "Never go into a relationship with the idea that you can change the other person." It seems, however, that a number of our students, female students in particular, have precisely that goal in mind—"I'll be able to change him." It's probably more realistic to believe that each person can change only himself or herself within the relationship, not someone else. So, if you can't change the other person, are you the only thing that's changing? Does anything else change? The answer appears to be, "Yes; the *relationship* changes." In her book *The Ship That Sailed into the Living Room*, Sonja Johnson (1991) presents an insightful view which suggests that the relationship is a third entity, separate from the two people involved. Johnson describes the "relation Ship" as a large object between the two people—not either person—but something that comes with its own expectations and rules. For example, people in relationships are supposed to do things like "work on the relationship." Johnson says the Ship virtually "shouts" orders at the two people in it.

This is a useful perspective. What does it mean to get into a relationship? When you say to someone, "We have a relationship," do patterns of expectations arise almost automatically? Are the expectations the same for men and women? Can the female member of the relationship say as easily as the male, "I'm going out to get a beer; see you later." While this is a superficial example, we would guess that many relation Ships come with different expectations for men and for women, different expectations regarding control, emotions, amount of time spent together, quality of communication, basic treatment of each other, and so forth.

In Chapter 6, we discussed Miller and Steinberg's (1975) levels of information in relationships. As we mentioned, initial stages of a relationship are usually based on sociological rather than psychological information about the other person. But here is a critical point: The relationship begins to develop its own patterns based on sociological information, such as the person goes to the same school, *not* based on personal knowledge of the other person. The patterns get set up before you even get to know the other person. By the time you want to make the relationship truly yours, you have to change some patterns that were established before you knew what you wanted. So Johnson's perspective—that it is the relationship that deserves to be examined and possibly changed—sheds light on two important and helpful factors: each relationship comes with its own built-in patterns of expectations; and change and movement need to focus on the patterns in the *relationship,* not the *individuals.*

The insight Johnson provides suggests a focal point for change. Interpersonal communication researchers Shea and Pearson (1986) add to this insight by suggesting that you need to consider whether your goal for a particular change is one of compliance (a content goal, such as getting the other person to agree with you on where to go for a vacation), an effect on the relationship (an interpersonal goal, such as getting another person to like you more), or an effect on the partner's self-image (an identity management goal, such as helping the other person feel better about herself or himself). A careful consideration of goals can help you achieve the desired result and avoid results that are inadvertent and off the mark. Along this line, communication researcher Joseph Ayres (1983) found a clear connection between relationship goals and the strategy selected to achieve the goals. Clarity of relational and personal goals are critical in selecting an effective strategy.

We find it interesting to talk with our students about problems they encounter in attempts to move a relationship from one stage to another. Many students seem to hold a number of inappropriate, unrealistic beliefs about how relationships change and work, such as the ones listed below. These beliefs seem to be so widespread that researchers have been able to identify patterns in them. Psychologists Eidelson and Epstein (1982, pp. 716–720) worked out a system of what they termed "dysfunctional relationship beliefs," the five most common being:

1. "Disagreement is destructive." Have you ever heard the idea that "if you really loved me, we would never fight"? Disagreement can be very healthy for a relationship.
2. "Partners cannot change." People can and do change. Relationships can change.
3. "Mindreading is expected." This belief is epitomized by the statement, "If you really loved me, you would know what I'm thinking (needing, wanting, etc.)." Expecting someone to read your mind or automatically know what you want is unrealistic.
4. "Sexual perfection." This one seems to be propagated by television, which presents images of wonderful sex that everyone seems to have. Shouldn't your life be like that?
5. "The sexes are different." This one is a cultural stereotype which leads to the conclusion that it is virtually impossible to understand someone of the other sex. How many times have you heard men say something like, "Women; you just can't figure them out," or women say, "I never will understand men and their need for competition"?

This is an interesting list of dysfunctional beliefs about relationships. Is there anything on the list that you have seen in yourself or in others? Do you think one sex has more of these expectations than the other? Unrealistic beliefs have derailed many relationships, and getting past them is a step to becoming more effective in moving a relationship from one stage to another.

Relational Stability

We include this section on relationship stability for one reason. In our discussions related to relationship change, we want to make sure you realize that relationships don't always have to change. In fact, in many instances, relationships stabilize at one level or another (Shea & Pearson, 1986). People seek comfort in the familiar and in relationships from which consistent benefits can be drawn. Change usually comes about when one person or the other feels that the relationship no longer meets his or her needs and that some change may be necessary. If the relationship has a long history, it will be more difficult to change. For example, if you have recently moved away from home to go to college, what has been your experience when you have gone home and talked to old friends? Did they treat you as they used to treat you, in spite of the fact you probably changed a lot since you left? Relationships, once they get a momentum going, can be difficult to change. That's why we suggest that each person be aware of how the relationship begins, since the patterns developed in the beginning are the ones that are likely to continue. The longer the patterns have been in place, the more difficult they will be to change.

What do you do if you want to stabilize a relationship where it is? In an attempt to address this question, Ayres (1983) identified three primary strategies that can be used to stabilize relationships. First, individuals who want to stabilize a relationship at a particular level should avoid bringing up topics that might alter the level. Maybe you have experienced something like this or felt like, "If I bring this up, I know it will change everything." For example, a man who wishes to keep a relationship at a friendship level probably shouldn't ask the other person for a date. A woman who is in a new romantic relationship may want to avoid bringing up previous romantic relationships out of concern that the information would damage the present one. In reference to the second strategy, Ayres found that equity or balance in areas like the amount of time, amount of control, and level of emotional commitment in the relationship were critical. If the relationship got out of balance, it became less stable. For example, you may have found yourself in a relationship where you feel you are putting more time and energy into the relationship than the other person. At that point you may question the other person's commitment and the relationship might be headed for conflict. The third strategy involves individuals usually having at least one direct discussion of relational goals—a discussion which clarifies the relationship in each person's eyes. This clarification will likely reinforce the stability of a relationship. For example, if one person in a cross-sex, heterosexual friendship senses that the other person might want to move to a dating or romantic status, an honest discussion of that possibility, including advantages and disadvantages, might be wise. If the decision is *not* to change the relationship, then the discussion will have helped to stabilize the friendship.

Do men and women approach strategies for relational stability similarly? Interpersonal communication researchers Baxter and Wilmot (1983) explored this question and found that women tend to be more relationally oriented and thus more likely to discuss their relationships. Remember the value "Talking about it makes it better"? Baxter and Wilmot's research suggests that direct conversations about the desired level of the relationship is important to the relationship's stability, but that women may be more inclined than men to make these conversations happen. We realize that it may be awkward to sit down with a friend and say "Let's talk over our relationship and where we want it to go." But it is possible, and sometimes necessary, if both individuals wish to maintain and stabilize the relationship.

Strategies for Relationship Change and Movement

What can be done to propel a relationship from one level to another? Are women and men likely to use similar or different strategies? As you read this material, consider your own relationships (friendships, classmates, coworkers, romantic relationships, etc.) and think specifically about how you might more effectively achieve your goals regarding relational movement.

A study conducted by interpersonal communication researcher James Tolhuizen (1988) investigated communication strategies used to change casual dating relationships into serious dating relationships. While his research focused on dating relationships, the strategies he identified are applicable to most other contexts. These strategies include the following (listed in descending order of use): (1) increased amount of contact; (2) relationship negotiation (i.e., direct discussion about the relationship, feelings in the relationship, and the future); (3) social support and assistance (e.g., asking for advice, information, and support from others in attempts to intensify a relationship); (4) increased rewards; (5) direct definitional bid (e.g., "Here's what I think we should do with this relationship"); (6) accepting a direct definitional bid; (7) tokens of affection; (8) personalized communication through verbal expressions of affection; (9) suggestive actions (i.e., flirting); (10) nonverbal expressions of affection; (11) social enmeshment (e.g., "I want you to meet my family"); (12) changing or improving one's personal appearance; (13) increased sexual intimacy; and (14) adapting self-presentation (i.e., altering how you communicate yourself to others). While this is a rather lengthy list, we include it because you probably will recognize at least some of the strategies as familiar.

With regard for men's and women's use of these strategies, Tolhuizen found that men reported using direct definitional bids (e.g., "Let's have this kind of relationship") and verbal expressions of affection more than women. Women reported using the strategies of relationship negotiation and accepting a definitional bid. Tolhuizen contends that "these results depict males as being more direct and more willing to explicitly express feelings of affection, and females as being less direct, more responsive, and more concerned with the relationship" (p. 5). In subsequent research, Tolhuizen (1992) found that women and men relied on the same types of strategies as previously reported, but women reported using more strategies, in general, and more active than passive strategies. Perhaps this information on strategies will begin to answer questions you might have about relational change. We suggest that you monitor your own behavior and look for these strategies in your friendships with women and men. See if you employ any of these strategies in attempts to move relationships from one level to another.

In similar research predating Tolhuizen, psychologists Falbo and Peplau (1980) investigated relational movement strategies from the viewpoint of directness and simultaneous use. The most interesting aspect of this research for our purposes was their attention to gender rather than sex. Corresponding to categories from the Bem Sex Role Inventory (described in Chapter 2), masculine and androgynous subjects reported reliance primarily on multiple and direct strategies to escalate or intensify relationships, since these individuals typically saw themselves in power positions. Feminine and undifferentiated subjects used single and indirect strategies, since they were more likely to anticipate or expect another person to turn them down. These results revealed that the self-concept of the individual was critical in the type of strategy selected. In other words, your selection of a movement strategy is related to how you, as a communicator, define yourself. We have repeatedly suggested in this text that the effective communicator takes on androgynous characteristics, with the ability to use feminine or masculine communication behaviors depending on the mandates of the situation. This research seems to indicate that androgynous individuals might be generally more self-confident and thus can use more direct strategies for changing a relationship.

This section focused on some strategies that might be followed if you want to affect the rate of change in a relationship. Space doesn't allow for the inclusion of all possible strategies for change, so if you don't recognize in this material your own ways of bringing about change in a relationship, don't be concerned. Changing a relationship can be as unique as the people within the relationship; however, this information may have given you some choices you

"Reprinted with special permission of North America Syndicate."

hadn't previously considered. Relational change is possible, and the ability to accomplish effective change takes sensitivity to sex differences and to your own and others' tendencies. The change process, however, is not without its downside.

Possibilities and Problems Connected to Relational Change

The cliché "Nothing worthwhile ever comes easy" seems to apply to relational change as well as to many other things. Relationships of all kinds are wonderful and exhilarating, but, unfortunately, they are hardly ever simple. Two of the more complicated elements of relational change warrant discussion here: influence and conflict.

Influence in the Process of Relational Change

Mutual influence seems to be an inevitable part of relationships between coworkers, friends, classmates, family members, and romantic partners. Given that basic belief, you don't have to look too far to see attempts at influence gone awry. People get divorced, are fired from jobs, and lose friends because of attempts to influence that backfire. Have you ever resented someone's ill-conceived efforts to influence you to do something? Continuing with Johnson's (1991) "relation Ship" perspective described earlier, a central aspect of relational change is the influence each person has over the quality and level of the relationship. While most people in a relationship do want to influence each other, Johnson suggests that the focus of influence should not be on the *other person*, but on the *relationship*. This is a subtle but very helpful distinction. The question is not "How can I get *you* to change?" but "How are *we* going to change the relationship so it becomes what we want it to be?" And when things go wrong, the best approach is "How can we change the *relationship* so things go better?" Using this perspective, each person may have to alter some behavior in the relationship to achieve the quality that both desire.

Early research questions asked: "Which sex is more persuadable or easily influenced—women or men? Who gives in more easily?" Beginning in the 1950s, attitude change studies began to conclude that women are more persuadable than men (Janis & Field, 1959). However, in a later study psychologists Sistrunk and McDavid (1971) expanded the approach to understanding persuadability and the sexes. They measured women's and men's persuadability according to whether a stimulus topic was typically feminine, typically masculine, or gender neutral. The results indicated a connection between the gender-relatedness of a topic and a subject's sex. Specifically, men were more persuaded to conform when the topic was feminine, while women conformed more on masculine topics. No sex differences emerged for gender-neutral topics. What this suggests is that men and women seem to show independence in areas they are familiar with, but they conform to other people in topics that are unfamiliar to them. This research did not detect an overall difference in the basic persuadability of the sexes.

Perhaps each sex is basically equally persuadable. This point of view supports the value we stated in the beginning of this chapter regarding openness to change. Not only does the possibility exist that each sex is equally persuadable, but each sex might find it valuable to *be* equally persuadable. If one person isn't always trying to influence the other person, and the other person doesn't feel like she or he is always being influenced or controlled, the relationship will likely be more balanced and successful, in both the short and the long run.

What does this section on influence mean to you, personally? First, it's probably not a good idea to hold any assumptions about who is or is not persuadable in a relationship. It seems to depend far more on the individual than the individual's sex or gender. Second, it's wise to focus on how the pattern of the relationship can change, not on how the other person should change. A pattern is easier to change than a person, because you can work together on changing relational patterns.

Learning to Manage Conflict

In spite of one's best efforts, change isn't always easy. In any relationship, especially when change is an issue, conflict is a likely outcome. It is not our purpose here to review the substantial amount of material on conflict management and resolution; a good interpersonal communication text can do that for you. Our purpose is to discuss conflict as it relates to problems you might face in relational movement. It's probable that you will face conflict in your relationships—especially the more intimate ones—so it helps to learn how to deal with it.

Based on your experience, who is more likely to start a conflict? Who is more likely to suggest a solution? Who is more likely to focus on the relationship than on the particular topic of disagreement? Identified sex differences in conflict resolution are few, and they both fit and contradict the usual stereotypes. Interpersonal communication researcher Frost (1980) asserts that women have been socialized into avoidance as a conflict resolution pattern. This relates to women's stereotypical inclination to be affiliative and supportive and to avoid creating or escalating situations in which negativity and disconfirmation are the outcomes. However, another communication study found no support "for the perspective that women more than men prefer conflict styles requiring concern for relationships or cooperativeness" (Shockley-Zalabak & Morley, 1984, p. 31).

Psychologists Jones and Pittman (1980) discuss the presence of patterns in how people present themselves in conflict situations. For example, you may know people who cause conflict when they want someone to do something because they use ingratiation strategies (i.e., trying to get on someone's good side, better known as "sucking up"). They will be really nice and very likable, and you just don't want to disappoint them by saying no. Or you may know people who use anger as their main tactic. They will rant and rave until the other person gives up. Identifying the pattern that you typically follow and the pattern of the other person in a relationship can enhance your ability to resolve conflict, to reduce the likelihood that conflict will arise and escalate, and to preserve the level of relationship.

In addition to the discovery of patterns, one's goals for a relationship affect the conflict within it. Interpersonal communication researcher Rusbult (1987) found that greater commitment to a relationship was related to active, constructive strategies in working on conflict. In essence, this means that the more you care, the more important it is to work conflicts out in a positive, supportive, and fair manner. Research on self-disclosure cited previously in this chapter suggests that men are less likely than women to express or initiate active relational strategies; thus men may be less likely to promote positive outcomes from conflict. But this doesn't mean that women alone should carry the burden of bringing up the problems and resolving the conflict. It would appear that if a relationship is to succeed, members of both sexes need to learn how to initiate conflict resolution strategies and be willing to act.

We emphasize in this section that change in the stage or level of a relationship rarely occurs without some influence, and attempts at influence sometimes lead to conflict. It is advisable, as people make decisions regarding relational change, for both sexes to be open to the possibility of personal change. Women and men alike should be willing to initiate relational movement, to accept and to offer attempts at influence, and to be committed to working out potential conflicts.

CONCLUSION

To borrow Sonja Johnson's term, the "relation Ships" that sail into your life can change you in powerful and significant ways. Friendships, work relationships, romantic relationships, and marriages can all have a significant impact on you. This chapter has explored the other side of that process—your influence on the development of your relationships. A consistent theme in this text has been the acquisition of awareness—awareness of how various factors (e.g., biology, sociology, language, and media) influence you and influence your choices, awareness of how you can gain control over or manage those influences, and, in this part of the text, awareness of how you can influence the development of relationships.

Becoming more personally effective in creating the type of relationships you desire is a worthwhile, important goal. In this chapter we discussed four skills that are central to developing a relationship—self-disclosure, empathy, listening, and nonverbal expressiveness and sensitivity. Understanding how these skills are associated with moving a relationship from one level to another and understanding women's and men's tendencies in relational change can give you greater insight into how positive change might be brought about. The final section of this text connects these concepts to some specific contexts in your life—friendships, romance, family life, work, and education. Effective gender communication in these contexts involves an application of the concepts described in the chapters you have just read.

Key Terms

relationship development
self-disclosure
socialization
intimacy
empathy
perspective-taking
emotional contagion
empathic concern
listening
nonverbal expressiveness
nonverbal sensitivity
immediacy
relational movement and
  change

accelerators and
  decelerators
stages of relationships
initiating
experimenting
intensifying
integrating
bonding
relationship deterioration
circumscribing
differentiating
stagnating
avoiding
terminating

relation Ships
compliance
identity management
dysfunctional
  relationship beliefs
relational stability
movement strategies
influence
persuadability
conflict
ingratiation

Discussion Starters

1. How do people signal that they want to change the level of the relationship? Do men and women use different signals? Are the signals usually nonverbal in nature? Do people ever say to you "I'd like to change our relationship"? Have you ever said that to someone?

2. What strategies have you used to change the level of a relationship? How do your strategies compare with those we describe in this chapter?

3. Do you know men who share more than the average amount of personal information? What are some reactions to these men? Are they the same or different from the reactions women get when they share more than average?

4. Let's say that two men are driving somewhere. The drive will take about 2 hours. The two men are pretty good friends. One of them pulls out a book on cassette tape and suggests that they listen to it on the way. What do you think of this? Do women react any differently to this situation than men?

5. Is it possible to change someone? If not, how do people change? Where does the motivation for personal change come from? Is it possible to change the relationship without working on changing the people involved?

6. What seems to be the basis of most male-female conflict you have witnessed or participated in? Are there sex and gender differences in the source of conflict? Are there differences in the way conflict is resolved? What is the usual male strategy? The usual female strategy?

7. Think about whether or not you believe that there is such a thing as "women's

intuition." If you believe it exists, how might you account for this phenomenon? Is there a "men's intuition"? What is the relationship of intuition to communication, both verbal and nonverbal?

References

ARIES, E. (1982). Verbal and nonverbal behavior in single-sex and mixed-sex groups: Are traditional sex roles changing? *Psychological Reports, 51,* 127–134.

AYRES, J. (1983). Strategies to maintain relationships: Their identification and perceived usage. *Communication Quarterly, 31,* 62–67.

BATE, B. (1988). *Communication and the sexes.* Prospect Heights, IL: Waveland Press.

BAXTER, L. A., & WILMOT, W. W. (1983). Communication characteristics of relationships with differential growth rates. *Communication Monographs, 50,* 264–272.

BEM, S. (1975). The measurement of psychological androgyny. *Journal of Consulting and Clinical Psychology, 42,* 155–162.

BEM, S. L., & LENNEY, E. (1976). Sex typing and the avoidance of cross sex behaviors. *Journal of Personality and Social Psychology, 33,* 48–54.

BREHM, S. S., POWELL, L., & COKE, J. S. (1984). The effects of empathic instructions upon donating behavior: Sex differences in young children. *Sex Roles, 10,* 415–416.

BURKE, K. (1966). *Language as symbolic action: Essays on life, literature, and method.* Berkeley: University of California Press.

DERLEGA, V. J., DURHAM, B., GOCKEL, B., & SHOLIS, D. (1981). Sex differences in self-disclosure: Effects of topic content, friendship, and partner's sex. *Sex Roles, 7,* 433–447.

DERLEGA, V. J., WINSTEAD, B. A., WONG, P., & HUNTER, S. (1985). Gender effects in initial encounters: A case where men exceed women in disclosure. *Journal of Social and Personal Relationships, 2,* 25–44.

DEUTSCH, F. M., LEBARON, D., & FRYER, M. M. (1987). What is in a smile? *Psychology of Women Quarterly, 11,* 341–352.

EIDELSON, S., & EPSTEIN, D. (1982). Development of a measure of dysfunctional relationships beliefs. *Journal of Consulting and Clinical Psychology, 50,* 715–720.

ELLYSON, S. L., DOVIDIO, J. F., & FEHR, B. J. (1981). Visual behavior and dominance in women and men. In C. Mayo & N. M. Henley (Eds.), *Gender and nonverbal behavior* (pp. 63–94). New York: Springer-Verlag.

FALBO, T., & PEPLAU, L. A. (1980). Power strategies in intimate relationships. *Journal of Personality and Social Psychology, 38,* 618–628.

FONG, M. L., & BORDERS, L. D. (1985). Effects of sex role orientation and gender on counseling skills training. *Journal of Counseling Psychology, 32,* 104–110.

FROST, J. (1980). The influence of female and male communication styles on conflict strategies: Problem areas. *Communication Research and Broadcasting, 3,* 126–136.

FUGITA, B. N., HARPER, R. G., & WIENS, A. N. (1980). Encoding and decoding of nonverbal emotional messages: Sex differences in spontaneous and enacted expressions *Journal of Nonverbal Behavior, 4,* 131–145.

GREENBLATT, L., HASENAUER, J. E., & FRIEMUTH, V. (1980). Psychological sex type and androgyny in the study of communication variables. *Human Communication Research, 6,* 117–129.

HALL, J. A. (1984). *Nonverbal sex differences: Communication accuracy and expressive style.* Baltimore: Johns Hopkins University Press.

HENLEY, N. (1986). *Body politics: Power, sex, and nonverbal communication.* New York: Touchstone Press.

HICKSON, M. I., & STACKS, D. W. (1993). *Nonverbal communication: Studies and applications* (3rd ed.). Dubuque, IA: Wm. C. Brown.

ICKES, W. (1985). *Compatible and incompatible relationships.* New York: Springer-Verlag.

JANIS, I. L., & FIELD, P. B. (1959). Sex differences and personality factors related to persuasibility. In I. L. Janis (Ed.), *Personality and persuasibility.* New Haven: Yale University Press.

JOHNSON, S. (1991). *The ship that sailed into the living room: Sex and intimacy reconsidered.* Estancia, NM: Wildfire Books.

JONES, E. E., & PITTMAN, T. S. (1980). Toward a general theory of strategic self-presentation. In J. Suls (Ed.), *Psychological perspective on the self.* Hillsdale, NJ: Lawrence Erlbaum Associates.

JONES, S. E. (1986). Sex differences in touch communication. *Western Journal of Speech Communication, 50,* 227–241.

JONES, T. S., & BRUNER, C. C. (1984). The effect of self-disclosure and sex on perceptions of interpersonal communication competence. *Women's Studies in Communication, 7,* 23–37.

JOURARD, S. (1971). *The transparent self.* Princeton, NJ: Van Nostrand.

KNAPP, M. (1978). *Social intercourse: From greeting to goodbye.* Boston: Allyn and Bacon.

LAVINE, L. O., & LOMBARDO, J. P. (1984). Self-disclosure: Intimate and nonintimate disclosures to parents and best friends as a function of Bem sex-role category. *Sex Roles, 11,* 735–744.

MEHRABIAN, A. (1970). A semantic space for nonverbal behavior. *Journal of Counseling and Clinical Psychology, 35,* 248–257.

MILLER, G. R., & STEINBERG, M. (1975). *Between people: A new analysis of interpersonal communication.* Palo Alto, CA: Science Research Associates.

MULAC, A., STUDLEY, L. B., WIEMANN, J. M., & BRADAC, J. J. (1987). Male/female gaze in same-sex and mixed-sex dyads. *Human Communication Research, 13,* 323–343.

PEARSON, J. C., & SPITZBERG, B. H. (1990). *Interpersonal communication: Concepts, components, and contexts* (2nd ed.). Dubuque, IA: Wm. C. Brown.

PETRONIO, S., MARTIN, J., & LITTLEFIELD, R. (1984). Prerequisite conditions for self-disclosing: A gender issue. *Communication Monographs, 51,* 268–272.

REDMOND, M. (1985). The relationship between perceived communication competence and perceived empathy. *Communication Monographs, 52,* 377–382.

ROSENFELD, L. B. (1979). Self-disclosure avoidance: Why I am afraid to tell you who I am. *Communication Monographs, 46,* 63–74.

RUSBULT, C. E. (1987). Responses to dissatisfaction in close relationships: The exit-voice-loyalty-neglect model. In D. Perlman & S. Duck (Eds.), *Intimate relationships* (pp. 209–237). Newbury Park, CA: Sage.

SABATELLI, R. M., & RUBIN, M. (1986). Nonverbal expressiveness and physical attractiveness as determiners of interpersonal perception. *Journal of Nonverbal Behavior, 10,* 120–133.

SHEA, C., & PEARSON, J. (1986). The effects of relationship type, partner intent, and gender on the selection of relationship maintenance strategies. *Communication Monographs, 53,* 352–363.

SHOCKLEY-ZALABAK, P. S., & MORLEY, D. D. (1984). Sex differences in conflict style preferences. *Communication Research Reports, 1,* 28–32.

SISTRUNK, F., & McDAVID, J. W. (1971). Sex variables in conforming behavior. *Journal of Personality and Social Psychology, 17,* 200–207.

SNELL, W. E., MILLER, R. S., & BELK, S. S. (1988). Development of the emotional self-disclosure scale. *Sex Roles, 18,* 59–73.

SOLLIE, D. L., & FISCHER, J. L. (1985). Sex-role orientation, intimacy of topic, and target person differences in self-disclosure among women. *Sex Roles, 12,* 917–929.

STEPHENS, T. D., & HARRISON, T. M. (1985). Gender, sex-role identity, and communication style: A Q-sort analysis of behavioral differences. *Communication Research Reports, 2,* 53–61.

STIFF, J. B., DILLARD, J. P., SOMERA, L., KIM, H., & SLEIGHT, C. (1988). Empathy, communication, and prosocial behavior. *Communication Monographs, 55,* 198–213.

STOKES, J., FUEHRER, A., & CHILDS, L. (1980). Gender differences in self-disclosure to various target persons. *Journal of Counseling Psychology, 27,* 192–198.

TANNEN, D. (1990). *You just don't understand.* New York: William Morrow.

TAVRIS, C. (1992, February). The man/woman thing: Moving from anger to intimacy. *Mademoiselle,* pp. 98–101, 135.

TOLHUIZEN, J. H. (1988, November). *Intensification strategies in dating relationships: Identification, structure and an examination of the personality correlates of strategy preferences.* Paper presented at the annual meeting of the Speech Communication Association, New Orleans, LA.

TOLHUIZEN, J. H. (1992, November). *The association of relational factors to intensification strategy use.* Paper presented at the annual meeting of the Speech Communication Association, Chicago, IL.

WARSHAW, R. (1992, August). Why won't he listen?!!!! *New Woman*, pp. 67–70.

WHEELESS, V. E., & LASHBROOK, W. B. (1987). Style. In J. C. McCroskey & J. Daly (Eds.), *Personality and interpersonal communication* (pp. 243–277). Beverly Hills, CA: Sage.

WHEELESS, V. E., ZAKAHI, W. R., & CHAN, M. B. (1988). A test of self-disclosure based on perceptions of a target's sex and gender orientation. *Communication Quarterly, 36,* 109–121.

WINSTEAD, B. A. (1986). Sex differences in same-sex friendships. In V. Derlega and B. A. Winstead (Eds.), *Friendship and social interaction.* New York: Springer-Verlag.

ZILLMAN, D., WEAVER, J. B., MUNDORF, N., & AUST, C. F. (1986). Effects of opposite-gender companion's affect to horror on distress, delight, and attraction. *Journal of Personality and Social Psychology, 51,* 586–595.

PART FOUR

The Contexts for Our Relationships: Personal Effectiveness in Action

So You Want to Be Friends? Gender Communication in Same-Sex and Cross-Sex Friendships

"*In good times, in bad times, I'll be at your side for ever more, that's what friends are for. . . .*" Do these song lyrics make you wonder if you have friends who'll always be "at your side"? When you read this chapter, take a long inventory of your involvement in friendship, then decide if you like what you see. If you think your friendship situation could use a little work, this chapter's for you. If you're comfortable with the quality and quantity of friendship in your life, this chapter's *still* for you.

CASE STUDY

Maybe things are changing. This case study describes an experience of the male co-author of this text. When Phil was in high school and college, the prevailing attitude among most guys (men) was that girls (women) were basically for one thing and that wasn't friendship. Phil was in a fraternity during college, and while it was a valuable experience, his friendships with fraternity brothers didn't do much to change his general stereotype of women. Women were "things" to be pursued and most of his conversations with buddies revolved around real, imagined, or partial conquests. Few of Phil's friends had any female friends, a situation that could be considered somewhat typical for men in the late 1960s.

Have things changed in the past two decades? Now Phil is the father of three sons, aged 13, 17, and 21. Each is unique, but each has something in his life that is very unlike Phil's experience at that age. Here's a recent event to illustrate the difference. One night, a gang of Phil's sons and their buddies—which included both female and male friends—descended on the home front, probably for the purposes of checking out the refrigerator. No one in the group was a "couple"; they were just groups of friends who were out having a good time together. Phil's sons have had female friends pretty much all of their lives. While they have their share of male friends through sports and school activities, they also have female friends developed through shared class experiences, activities, and sports. These boys, as well as their male friends, don't seem to attach "sex object" definitions to women—particularly their female friends. There appears to be a more natural, personal acceptance of individuals as individuals, regardless of sex. As a father, Phil appreciates the kinds of friendships his sons have and, frankly, wishes it had been that way when he was their age.

This is an example of one person's experience, not exactly enough to draw conclusions. Have things changed? Is there a greater possibility of having rewarding friendships with members of the opposite sex? Perhaps you, as a reader, can do some research to see if Phil's experience matches that of other people of his age. If you have the opportunity, talk with a baby boomer and ask if he or she has observed changes in the patterns of male-female friendships. We bet you'll find the answer is "yes." Evidence from our own experience and from that of our students indicates that things have definitely changed for the better.

OVERVIEW

In previous chapters we focused on helping you more fully understand the gender-related influences on your communication behavior. We encourage you to consider using this information to make more informed choices regarding your gender communication behavior, so as to enhance your overall effectiveness. Now we explore another necessary element in the overall picture. Each relationship you have occurs within some type of context. Each context has its own norms, patterns, and tendencies that influence the communication behavior within it. Understanding these influences can help you communicate more effectively within each particular context. In this final section of the text, we devote chapters to the contexts of friendship, romance, marriages and families, education, and work.

The first context we examine is a familiar one—friendships. Aristotle described a friend as "a single soul who resides in two bodies." Friends of both sexes are important to our overall satisfaction with life. Many of you may have no trouble with friends of your same sex, but what about cross-sex friendship? Is it possible to be friends with someone of the opposite sex? Or is female-male friendship just a prelude to something more intimate? The movie *When Harry Met Sally* asked that question. The movie's answer was, "yes and no." Harry and Sally became friends, but the friendship did lead them to become lovers and the dramatic tension of the movie was reflected in the questions "Will they?" and "What happens after they do?" This type of plot line has been carried out in countless television sitcoms as well, revealing society's general attitude toward cross-sex friendship. However, is this the inevitable outcome for all male-female friendships? Of course not, though perhaps you have heard people advocate limited or no friendships with the opposite sex, just because of that possibility.

Clearly, limiting one's friends to 50 percent of the population is a bad move. As much as female friends are important to a woman and male friends to a man, friendships with the opposite sex have their place and their own importance. Many of the concepts related to gender communication that you've been studying in this text and in your course are critical to the development and maintenance of friendships. Thus it is the purpose of this chapter to explore the aspects of communication knowledge and skill that will lead to increased personal effectiveness in the specific contexts of same-sex and cross-sex friendship. The discussion in this chapter is consistent with what we've said throughout the text—that both sexes can expand their repertoire of communication behaviors to become more effective in gender communication. In an area as central to our mental health and our general satisfaction in life as the quality of our friendships, each sex can learn much from the other as to how to increase that quality. An increased range of behaviors, an orientation to the receiver (the friend), and increased personal effectiveness can all lead to greater satisfaction, fewer conflicts, and deeper friendships.

In this chapter, as is true of each of the contextual chapters, some current issues related to the context are described. Then we suggest what might be done to improve your chances for increasing communication effectiveness within the context. Specific topics include:

- Changing patterns of friendship
- The friendship socialization process
- Issues and possibilities in same-sex friendship
- Intimacy and disclosure in male-male versus female-female friendship
- Increasing your ability to develop meaningful friendships with women and men
- What enhances and detracts from satisfying cross-sex friendships

INTRODUCTION

It wasn't too many years ago that friendship was seen as an almost exclusively male prerogative. People believed that women apparently just did not have the same friendship bonding capacity that men did. From ancient Greece and the story of Damon and Pythias, to more modern comments such as one from Simone de Beauvior, who felt that "women's feelings rarely rise to genuine friendships" (Brenton, 1975, p. 142), the belief has persisted that women cannot experience the same quality of friendship men can. Look up the word "friend" in a thesaurus or dictionary. One thesaurus lists six examples of friendships—all male (Morehead, 1985). Author Lionel Tiger (1969), in a well-known book about the male experience, maintained that men, not women, have a strong predilection to form deep, enduring same-sex bonds. Men have faced common hazards over evolutionary history; these common hazards and pressures have attributed to men a capacity for close friendships that women cannot duplicate (Wright, 1982). Do you agree with these researchers and writers?

A different perspective has developed since about 1970. The past two decades have brought about a distinct shift in thinking regarding the qualities of same-sex and cross-sex friendship. A commonly accepted belief has emerged in the past few years that women actually have a greater capacity for developing strong, supportive friendships than men. As we discussed in Chapter 7, women have the ability to achieve more intimacy through increased self-disclosure and through the sharing of emotions. Men are criticized for lacking the ability to disclose themselves effectively and to form truly open relationships with other men. It almost appears that the accepted standard for "correctness" in friendships has shifted from male superiority to female superiority. This is an overgeneralization, but it seems to reflect the perspectives and research on this topic.

Are we then insinuating that women's friendships are to be emulated, to be held up as the model for men to follow in their friendships? Not really, because we believe that each sex can learn from the other. Women and men can develop greater appreciation for and understanding of the qualities of the friendship style of the opposite sex. This appreciation and understanding will likely lead to better friendships.

How is friendship defined? Not easily, apparently. Back in the 1970s, social science researcher John Reisman (1979) spoke of the difficulty of defining friendship. He described a friend as "someone who likes and wishes to do well by someone else and who believes those feelings and good intentions are reciprocated" (p. 108). Although this may not sound like a very profound definition, it is representative of others we have read and seems to express the central characteristics of friendship.

Reisman also makes the point that "viable friendships, like all significant relationships, are ongoing communicative achievements, requiring interactively developed expressive and interpretive practices" (p. 101). He suggests that friendships must develop effective communication patterns to be successful. But he also acknowledges that this is not easy, as he contrasts friendships with other social relationships, such as marriages, business partnerships, and family ties. Each of these relationships is embedded within social structures that reinforce them. For example, married couples live together (at least, most of them do) and have fairly constant contact, people maintain relationships with colleagues during the workday, and families form the most basic tie of all. We're not saying that these relationships maintain themselves without any effort, but they do involve a social structure that is conducive for relationship maintenance. This is not the case with friendship; friends have to set up social structures—a weekly bowling night or study session, a pattern of telephoning, "happy hours," and so on—as vehicles of relationship maintenance. If someone takes friendship for granted, assuming that this form of relationship does not require as much attention and maintenance as other types, that person could find herself or himself friendless.

Remember the discussion in Chapter 2 of the impact of socialization on your attitudes regarding gender and on your communication behavior? A point here echoes that information: An awareness of how you are influenced can give you more control over that influence. Your friendship patterns have had years of reinforcement from society; thus the socialization process affects your views about friendship, as well as how you approach friendship development and maintenance. As we discuss later in the chapter, clear sex differences exist in that socialization. Society suggests different patterns for male-male friendships, female-female, and cross-sex friendships. You act the way you do with friends because, to a large extent, society and your family have conditioned you to act that way. Understanding that conditioning may help you change some of those patterns.

Research has described how society extends its influence to teaching children how to be friends. Reisman (1990) found that, beginning at about age 7, boys form extended friendship networks with other boys while girls cluster into exclusive same-sex friendship dyads. In those dyads, girls acquire the social skills of communicating their feelings and being nurturing. In contrast, boys learn to follow rules and to get along with groups of people, even those they do not like. In different degree, this tendency remains into adulthood. Women tend to form small, intimate groups while men tend to form clubs and societies with hierarchical structures (Diamond & Karlen, 1980).

Reisman (1990) also examined self-disclosure and the changing patterns of friendship through the formative years. He found that male adolescents reported that they disclosed about the same amount of information with friends of either sex, but female adolescents reported less self-disclosure with boys than with other girls. This appears to change as persons leave their teen years. Young male adults reported higher levels of self-disclosure with the opposite sex than with their same sex. Young female adults reported similar levels of disclosure with both males and females. Does this correlate with your experience? Has your disclosure and friendship pattern changed since you were a teenager? Have you shifted some of your disclosure to the opposite sex? Has your pattern of friendships changed as you have moved into early adulthood?

Another point related to friendship socialization concerns the type of communication environment in which a person is raised. Research by two developmental psychologists, Park and Waters (1989), found that children who were raised in a secure environment were able to establish more compatible and less dominant relationships and were more able to listen than children raised in other environments. This points to two ideas: (1) A secure family environment is highly beneficial to children and this environment will have a profound, positive effect on friendships. (2) Secure external environments are conducive to friendship. If the social environment that surrounds the friendship is unsafe or nonsupportive, then the relationship may never be formed or is likely to suffer. Thus both the family environment and the social environment significantly influence how an individual approaches and develops friend-ships.

We presented this consideration of changes in friendship patterns, difficul-ties in definitions, and socialization for two reasons. First, we want you to become more aware of how your own friendship patterns have been influenced throughout your life and how they may influence you. Second, we sought to offer a brief explanation for the divergent approaches each sex brings to communication and friendships. Again, this understanding is empowering, in that you can exert more control over an influence once you are aware of its existence.

COMMUNICATION IN SAME-SEX FRIENDSHIPS: FROM BUTCH AND SUNDANCE TO THELMA AND LOUISE

Chapter 5 pointed out that women and men approach communication differ-ently and these differences affect how relationships develop. The same point seems to be true regarding friendships; there are differences in all three possible combinations—male-male, female-female, and female-male. What women want and get from their female friends appears to be different from what men want and get from their male friends, and both differ from what each sex wants and gets from opposite-sex friends. In this section of the chapter, we focus on same-sex friendships, operating from an assumption that understanding gender differences can lead to improved friendships.

Male-Male Friendship: Issues and Possibilities

As we said in the introduction to this chapter, friendships between men seem to have evolved from the standard of "true" friendship to something that both male and female writers have begun to critique in recent decades. Part of this critique extends to mild teasing about male bonding activities. In this section we review some ideas around the value found in male-male friendships, then explore issues of intimacy and disclosure.

What Do Men Get from Friendships with Other Men?

We ask our male readers, why do you form friendships with other men? If you follow the typical pattern, you form them so that you have *something to do* and *someone to do it with*. Research has shown that while men and women typically have similar numbers of friends and spend similar amounts of time with friends, men's friendships with other men serve very different purposes than women's friendships with other women (Caldwell & Peplau, 1982). Men's friendships begin with, are sustained by, and sometimes dissolve over activities and doing things together (Brehm, 1985; Farr, 1988; Rawlins, 1992). In studying friendship, sociologists in the 1970s found that men value doing things together more than having someone to talk to (Crawford, 1977; Weiss & Lowenthal, 1977).

Through these shared experiences and activities, men are able to develop feelings of closeness and to express their commonality with male friends. In essence, activities create a vehicle for male friendship development and maintenance. Think of the "war stories" or "fishing tales" that maybe your father, uncle, or grandfather tells. Usually these kinds of stories include details about experiences with male friends. While they might not readily admit it or talk about it, shared conquests (or defeats) in battle or sports are significant male bonding events for men.

As you are no doubt aware, women generally base their friendships not around activities but around conversation and an exchange of thoughts and feelings (Brehm, 1985). We talk more about female-female friendships in a subsequent section, but we allude to the basic contrast here to bring it to your attention. Think about friendships between men that you know. Were most of these male friendships initiated through an activity, such as a sport, drinking beer, hunting, working on cars? Is most of the time with male friends spent in these kinds of activities? Has a friendship ended because one of the men lost interest in the activity that bonded them together?

Men also form group friendships through participation on teams, memberships in clubs and fraternities, involvement with work or study groups, and the like. These organized friendships centered around group activities give men a sense of belonging (Strikwerda & May, 1992). Many men place great emphasis on "the group" and being "one of the guys." Each of us feels a need to belong, but for some, the belonging has a price. This sense of belonging is so important to some men that they sometimes place being a team player above their own self-respect to the point of humiliation. Various club initiation rites are good examples of this. The fraternity initiation ritual that the male co-author of this text went through was difficult and sometimes humiliating, but it was required to join. The need to belong, to be accepted in a group of other men, can hold a great deal of control over a man's behavior.

In addition to activities and belongingness, some men form friendships to get ahead in the professional world. Psychologist Suzanna Rose (1985) explored what she referred to as the "homosocial norm" of seeking social enjoyment through the company of the same sex. A homosocial norm is the societal pressure that encourages men to seek out other men for friendship. Rose suggests that since men control the power and rewards in the society, men value friendship with other men more than with women because a man can attain more social and economic rewards from other men. This isn't as manipulative a motivation as it seems at first glance. It doesn't mean that men necessarily form friendships with other men for the sole purpose of furthering their own achievement, although, granted, for some men this is the primary motivation. A more accurate explanation is that often, in forming friendships with other men, men look beyond mere commonality and the opportunity to share activities to consider other, possibly lucrative, benefits of friendship. What do you think of this contention? Do you know men who use male friendships for personal gain? Do you view this approach as a "use" or an "abuse"?

Communication researchers Hickson and Stacks (1989) report that when men meet for the first time, they are likely to disregard physical appearance and begin with a mutual attempt to determine the major interests of the other man. Hickson and Stacks also found that if a man is not interested in sports, the possibility of a relationship is lessened for many men. In the business world, if another man cannot help you get ahead, the possibility of a friendship may likewise decrease—not disappear, but it may decrease. These three motivations—doing things together, using friendships to get ahead, and needing to belong—go a long way in explaining friendships between men.

Closeness and Intimacy in Male-Male Friendship

Feelings of closeness are important in any friendship (Rawlins, 1992). How do men become "close"? If you are a man reading this, would you say that shared activities bring you close to your male friends? Most men would like to have close male friends, but the issue of closeness or intimacy is the one most commonly highlighted as a problem in male-male friendship.

Levinson (1978), a popular author on men's friendships, concluded from interviews with forty men that "most men do not have an intimate male friend of the kind they recall fondly from boyhood or youth. Close friendships with a man or woman is rarely experienced by the American male" (p. 335). A friendship author with a similar viewpoint comments, "To say that men have no intimate friends seems on the surface too harsh. . . . But the data indicate that it is not far from the truth. . . . Their relationships with other men are superficial, even shallow" (Pogrebin, 1987, p. 253). Feminist author Alice Walker (1989) has one of her characters (Mr. Hal) make the following remarks:

> Life is so very different when you have a good friend. I've seen people without special friends, close friends. Other men, especially. For some reason men don't often make and keep friends. This is a real tragedy, I think, because in a way, without a tight male friend, you never really are able to see yourself. That is because part of shaping ourselves is done by others; and a lot of our shaping comes from that one close friend who is something like us. (p. 114)

This is a rather sad commentary on male-male friendship. Do men cringe at the thought of intimacy with other men? It appears so, but why?

Gender researchers Strikwerda and May (1992) offer this explanation: "Men in America are clearly stymied in pursuing intimacy with other males because of fears involving their sexuality, especially culturally inbred homophobia. . . . The taboo against males touching, except in firm public handshake, continues these teenage prohibitions" (p. 118). Students confirm this point. Many of the men in our classes admit that they have a good deal of difficulty with intimacy, especially in the form of hugging or otherwise expressing affection for a male friend.

The group nature of many male friendships also works against intimacy and closeness and can actually be a way of avoiding intimacy for some men. Strikwerda and May (1992) explored the role of the group, describing male friendship as comradeship. Comrades tend not to reflect on their relationship;

they are more bound to each other because of "groupness," not individual concern. Strikwerda and May suggest, "What passes for intimate male bonding is really the deep loyalty of comradeship, which is based on so little information about the person to whom one is loyal that it is quite fragile and likely to change" (p. 114). Feminist scholar Mary Daly (1978) contrasts comradeship and male friendship with sisterhood and female friendship. Comradeship, because of its lack of reflection, can have destructive consequences. She gives examples of mob-type behavior in males and the involvement of fraternities in college rapes. Daly contends that "male bonding/comradeship requires the stunting of individuality" (p. 379). Because of the fragile nature of comrade relationships, a writer for *Esquire* magazine termed male-male friendships "serial friendships" (Bing, 1989, p. 51).

For many men, male friends are important but replaceable. Communication scholars Davidson and Duberman (1982) suggest that even if some level of intimacy is achieved, society doesn't accept it very well. If a man manages to have a true emotional attachment to another man, a lot of subtle pressures are placed on him to eliminate it. These researchers contend that "for many men, maintaining one's lawn is more important than maintaining one's friendships" (p. 811).

Regarding male intimacy (or the lack thereof), a man might say, "But what about the experience of just sitting at a bar, drinking a beer, and just 'BS-ing'? At the end of the evening, you shake hands and head out. Isn't that closeness? I really enjoy those times." Granted, those can be close, good times, but do they actually create intimacy? Wright (1982) suggests that many people think so. In describing male-male friendships, he finds that "for the most part the characteristics of loyalty, fellow feeling, and concern for the other's interests have been stressed much more heavily than intimacy in male friendships. Moreover, the presence of these characteristics has been thought to make male friendship superior to female friendship" (p. 110). Reisman (1990) echoes this sentiment. He concedes that women develop a feeling of closeness to one another by talking but contends that men gain an equally intimate feeling by sharing activities. Results of a study conducted by communication researchers Caldwell and Peplau (1982) indicated that many men thought their friendships with other men were intimate; these men felt just as close and satisfied in their male friendships as women did with their female friends.

Disclosure in Men's Friendships

In addition to differences in the way same-sex friends accomplish intimacy, differences also exist in both the amount and type of disclosure exchanged between same-sex friends. Research generally concludes that men are less self-disclosive in their same-sex friendships than women (Clark & Reis, 1988; Fox, Gibbs, & Auerbach, 1985; Hacker, 1981; Reis, 1984). As we described in Chapter 7, disclosure is a building block of intimacy.

Wright (1982) explored the relationship between disclosure and the development of friendship. He found that pairs of minimally acquainted same-sex subjects made a better start toward becoming friends if one of them revealed a highly intimate personal detail than if she or he revealed only nonintimate things. This was true for both men and women. However, here's a revealing point from the study: It was necessary to solicit *half again* as many male subjects to obtain the number necessary to complete the experiment because so many men refused to follow instructions that led them into intimate self-disclosure. In Wright's words, "Men who disclosed intimate things about themselves became better friends if they ever overcame their reluctance to engage in intimate self-disclosures. None of the women in the experiment showed a similar reluctance to disclose intimate items of information" (p. 8). Perhaps the message to men about disclosure is—"Try it, you'll like it."

Some authorities go so far as to say that men avoid disclosure in their friendships because some topics are "too feminine" for male conversation. Author of *The New Male* Herb Goldberg (1979) contends that many men view the following topics as too feminine and thus to be avoided in men's conversations: emotional expression, giving in to pain, asking for help, paying too much attention to diet, self-care, dependency, touching, and alcohol abstinence. But Goldberg actually believes that the avoidance of this type of personal topic is destructive to men.

Perhaps men don't disclose as much as women because men's style of conversation does not suggest disclosure. In an examination of this notion, Haas and Sherman (1982) concluded that talking about sports may be more appropriate in an excited pattern of conversations—one that contains stylistic devices more commonly associated with men's communication, such as topic dominance and the use of interruptions. In contrast, discussions in female same-sex friendships of topics such as family and other relationships may typically occur in a more reflective, supportive mode that has been identified with women's style (Thorne & Henley, 1975). This information directly relates to the relational versus content approaches to talk, a topic that we explored in Chapter 5. Since evidence is beginning to indicate that men tend to approach conversation more from a content function and less from a relational function, the lack of disclosure in order to increase closeness in a friendship may be related to a perception of what purpose talk serves. Next time you watch television, compare characters' conversations in such shows as *Coach* and *Designing Women*. Do the amounts, topics, and styles of self-disclosure among male characters differ from that of female characters?

Thus far it appears that men may not be as capable as women when it comes to disclosure in a same-sex friendship; most folk wisdom would agree. However, some research suggests that preference, not capability, is responsible for the difference. Reisman's (1990) male subjects described their same-sex friendships as being as high in disclosure as female subjects described theirs. In addition, he found that male college students believed that they have the capability of disclosing at the same high level as women. Perhaps males may *prefer* not to be as disclosing with their male friends as they are with their female friends, dating partners, or spouses. The purposes of friendship for men and the social pressures men face explain at least part of it.

Men's studies researcher James Doyle (1989) addresses this issue:

> Why should men—granted, some men more than others—hold back their feelings, create false appearances about how they feel, or withhold their real emotions from the very individuals who they openly call their best male friends, their buddies? One possible answer lies in the proscriptive norm that most males in our society subscribe to—under no circumstances let down your emotional guard in the company of other men. To do so would more than likely get one branded as an emotional weakling, a sissy, or the latest in unkind cuts delivered to a man these days, a wimp. (p. 252)

Some men equate disclosure with vulnerability—the belief that if a man discloses his thoughts and feelings, to women or to other men, he has put himself in a one down, powerless position. Since powerlessness is undesirable, actions linked to powerlessness are to be avoided, even at the cost of closeness in friendship (Lombardo & Lavine, 1981).

So we are left with two conflicting lines of thought regarding intimacy and disclosure. On the one hand, sources claim that male-male friendships are deficient due to a lack of intimacy derived through personal disclosure. On the other hand, some argue that the type of closeness men achieve through activities is just as legitimate and beneficial as any other type of closeness. Perhaps we could suggest a combination of perspectives. Intimacy in male-male friendships requires the sharing of activities and experiences but may be enhanced by disclosure of personal information and treatment of the other person as a unique, irreplaceable individual.

If you are a male reader, how do you react to these lines of thought? For the men, do you have male friendships that are characterized by the three things we just mentioned? Would you use the word "intimate" to describe a close friendship with another man, or does that word conjure up a meaning too close to sexual intimacy, striking a possible homophobic reaction in you? Concerning disclosure, what topics do you avoid in your friendships with other men? What would happen if you tried to talk over some of these topics with close male friends? Could there be a consequence to the friendship if you don't bring them up? Are your male friends unique, or are they "replaceable"? Giving thought to the questions of intimacy and disclosure in male friendships may lead to some changes in the way these friendships develop. It may also cause men to think about the quality of their friendships with other men. We ask similar questions of female readers at the close of the next section.

Female-Female Friendship: Issues and Possibilities

Many women attest to the fact that since the earliest days they can remember as girls, same-sex friendships have been sustaining, highly significant forces in their lives. However, until only recently, little research specific to female friendship was available. This absence was noted a few years ago when psychologists Block and Greenberg (1985) wrote: "It is rare to read of the electricity that suffuses female friendship, of the feelings women develop for one another that intensify their existence. Friendship remains a vast, fertile area of women's lives that is unexplored" (p. 1). More academic and popular attention has been paid in recent years; feminist scholars and researchers have described friendships between women with far more detail and insight than we can recount here (Arliss & Borisoff, 1993; Block & Greenberg, 1985; Briles, 1987; Eichenbaum & Orbach, 1988; Gibbs-Candy, Troll, & Levy, 1981; Johnson, 1991).

The women's movement has given more status to friendships between women and has emphasized their value. Psychologists Eichenbaum and Orbach (1988) state that it wasn't until the 1970s that the significance of women's friendship was recognized by general society. While somewhat overgeneralized, it seemed that up until that time, friendships between women had to be interspersed between relationships with men and family commitments. The increased attention to women's friendships not only coincides with changing perceptions of their importance; it coincides with the changing roles of women in general society. Friendship between women, once viewed as well down on the priority list for most women, has "moved up." Let's explore some of the more prominent features, both positive and negative, that characterize female-female friendship.

What Do Women Get from Friendships with Other Women?

Well-known author and gender researcher Shere Hite (1989) conducted an intense study of women and their relationships. She reports that approximately 95 percent of single women and 87 percent of married women in her study described their same-sex friendships as "some of the happiest, most fulfilling parts of their lives" (p. 457). Many women feel that their friendships with other women are more intimate, rewarding, and accepting than their relationships with men (Basow, 1986; Fitzpatrick & Bochner, 1981). Eichenbaum and Orbach (1988) state that "connectedness, attachment, affiliation, and selflessness have been and still are largely the foundations of women's experience" (p. 11). They also suggest that an individual woman "creates and maintains a sense of self through her connections with others. Women live in a network of relationships and know themselves through these relationships" (p. 179). Block and Greenberg (1985) describe women's friendships as having an atmosphere of discovery and delight. To paraphrase one of their passages, men fix things, women fix each other.

Women also appear to develop friendships that function on multiple levels, as opposed to many male friendships that operate around one activity or issue. Carol Gilligan (1982), in her discussion of friendships, characterizes female friendships as developing an intertwined series of obligations and responsibilities which draws the participants into a friendship that bonds at multiple levels. Women focus on the individuals involved in the friendship and the pattern of interconnectedness between them. This pattern encourages mutual support, emotional sharing, and increased acceptance (Rawlins, 1992).

Closeness and Intimacy in Women's Friendships

Regarding female friendship, author Pamela Sattran (1989) believes that "today's friendships between women are no longer stand-ins for family, but may be the most intimate, profound, and most durable relationships in our lives" (p. 159). Other friendship research indicates that women value and desire relationships that emphasize intimacy, emotional sharing, and the discussion of personal problems (Brehm, 1992; Caldwell & Peplau, 1982; Lyness, 1978). Weiss and Lowenthal (1977) found that female friends tend to emphasize reciprocity, as exemplified by helping behaviors, emotional support, and confiding in one another. The intimacy characteristic of female friendship is typified by the tendency for female friends to interact in a face-to-face configuration, whereas male friends tend to position themselves side-by-side (Wright, 1982). Friendship researcher William Rawlins (1993) suggests that women have a greater intimacy competence. This stems from the tendency for women to embrace the intimacy challenge and to learn how to communicate closeness with female friends quickly.

While verbal communication is most often linked in research to the creation of intimacy in female friendship, nonverbal communication may actually be more relevant. Since research documents women's greater nonverbal sensitivity, it follows that female friends rely on nonverbal cues to respond to people, events, or other stimuli and to communicate attitudes, feelings, and emotions. Female subjects in Davidson and Duberman's (1982) study relied heavily on nonverbal communication, including touching, eye contact, smiling, and posturing, for both the sending of information and the interpretation of a female friend's communication. One of their subjects revealed, "My friend has certain gestures, like grimacing, raising her eyebrows, or touching me lightly, to communicate with me on a nonverbal level. We often read each other's minds. Sometimes we just look at each other and start laughing and know why" (p. 818).

As a similar example, the female co-author of your textbook and her best friend, Claire, developed a special nonverbal signal while in graduate school together. When one wanted to "clue" the other about something interesting going on or about someone who deserved notice, they would alert each other nonverbally, in a manner more subtle than saying, "Hey, look at *that.*" One friend would make direct eye contact with the other, then dart the eyes back and forth from the friend to the stimulus. The eye behavior indicated the direction and location of what the other was supposed to notice. We don't mean to insinuate by these examples that men don't develop nonverbal signals with their buddies, but it does seem that women are notorious for developing complete and very private signal systems with their close friends. Tapping the signal system heightens the intimacy of the friendship.

Intimacy appears, then, to be a powerful dimension in women's friendships. This power can create some difficulties. Block and Greenberg (1985) point to the nature of intimacy—one of the most positive values of women's friendships—as a contributing factor to the problems women face in friendships. Here's their description of the downside of intimacy:

> Because women are so often uninhibited about sharing their genuine feelings and concerns with each other, they are often able to move beyond competitive barriers. Women offer support for each other during their worst times as well as their best; they will admit weaknesses and faults to each other and will share defeats as well as victories. In short, women dare to be vulnerable with each other. And this vulnerability brings with it the joy and pain of intimacy. Like mother-daughter relationships, female friendships are seldom bland. They are intensely loving, sustaining, and supportive; when they have gone amiss, they are envious, deceitful, and treacherous. Intimacy, it appears, breeds intensity of feelings. (p. 3)

The intensity of the feelings may lead to a related issue between women—competitiveness. When you think about competitiveness, you might first think of it as a prime descriptor of how men approach the world. Competitiveness still drives many men's communication and behavior, but it has become a recent descriptor of women's behavior. In their book entitled *Between Women: Love, Envy, and Competition in Women's Friendships*, Eichenbaum and Orbach (1988) report that "according to popular culture, women don't trust each other, women don't work well for other women, and women are inherently in competition for the available men" (p. 2). They describe the envy and competition between women as follows: "[Women] find themselves acutely aware of the successes and achievements of other women. Women gauge and measure themselves in relation to friends, coworkers, neighbors. How does she manage a job, a relationship, and children? How does she manage to keep herself looking so well and fit when I feel exhausted?" (p. 11). In *Woman to Woman: From Sabotage to Support*, Briles (1987) speaks even more emphatically about this issue. She believes that women's competitive sabotage of each other is the single most significant problem in female friendship.

Women's relationships with men may create or heighten competitiveness between women and can interfere with female friendship. Wright (1982) suggests that "if two women have made arrangements to get together and one of them subsequently has an opportunity to get together with a man, the women's date is automatically cancelled" (p. 3). While the situation may have changed since that was written, some women do operate on the premise that a friendship with another woman generally takes second place to any relationship with a man, particularly a romantic relationship. Many of our students verify this.

We believe that the competitiveness issue, as well as other descriptions of the dynamics within female friendship, are changing and thus opening up possibilities for increased intimacy. But maybe we're just being optimistic. It seems, however, that as more women enter the work force and attain higher achievement and greater recognition, they focus more attention on their jobs and place more value on coworker relationships, especially those with female coworkers. This change affects their tendencies to only talk about men, families, and relationship issues; many professional women talk long and hard about their jobs and careers.

What does your experience tell you about this issue? Do you see more women today, maybe as compared to when you were in high school, acknowledging the importance of female friendships and honoring their commitments to those relationships? Or does the friend who is ready to "cancel the female plans at the drop of a male hat" still predominate? For male readers, do women you know view friendships with other women as more important than friendships with men?

The changing role of women in society has brought changes and pressures to friendships between women. Eichenbaum and Orbach (1988) claim that today, based on changing roles, enormous misunderstandings can exist between women. They describe problems as "messy uncomfortable bits one wishes would just disappear, the hurt, the envy, the competition, the unexpressed anger, the feelings of betrayal, and the experience of abandonment" (p. 11). As the perceived value of women's friendships increases, so do the pressures. Intimacy is a value and a goal, though it may not be as easy to achieve. Let us turn to disclosure, and its relationship to intimacy.

Disclosure in Women's Friendships

How important is disclosure to same-sex friendships? Reisman (1990) points out that individuals of both sexes who rate their friendships low in disclosure also tend to rate them low in closeness and satisfaction. Since friendships between women are usually characterized by greater intimacy, this implies a greater amount of disclosure in these relationships than in male-male friendships. Research bears this out by concluding that, in general, women are more intimate or self-disclosing in their same-sex friendships than men (Clark & Reis, 1988; Fox, Gibbs, & Auerbach, 1985; Hacker, 1981; Reis, 1984).

Davidson and Duberman's (1982) content levels were discussed in Chapter 6, but let's briefly review them here for their pertinence to the context of same-sex friendship. In this research, three content levels of communication were investigated: a *topical* level in which discussion focuses on topics that are external to the individuals and the dyadic relationship; a *relational* level in which discussion focuses on the relationship between the two interactants; and a *personal* level involving discussion about one's feelings, thoughts, and private life. The results of the study indicated that female subjects discussed twice as many personal topics and three times the relational topics when compared to male subjects. Male subjects believed the topical level to be most important in their communication.

In an earlier but related study, Crawford (1977) reported that women were more than twice as likely as men to be able to name a close friend with whom they could disclose, other than their spouse. The women in Crawford's sample stressed that trust and having someone to talk with were most important in their friendships, while men spoke of having someone to do something with.

Beyond the amount of disclosure, greater intimacy also implies possible differences in what gets talked about and how. Social scientists Aries and Johnson (1983) found what you might expect concerning women's disclosure. Female subjects talked primarily about personal and family matters, in greater depth and with more detail than male subjects. This sex difference appeared to remain constant throughout most subjects' lives. In an analysis of conversational topic differences between same-sex friendships, communication researchers Haas and Sherman (1982) found the following:

> Women's talk tended to focus on family, relationship problems, men, health, pregnancy and menstruation, food, things they've read, movies, television, clothing. . . . Men talked more about women, sex, money, news, sports, hunting, and fishing. The most frequently talked about topic for either sex was the other sex. Men also were less likely to report that they spoke "frequently" about topics than women. (p. 341)

For our readers who are women, do these research findings reflect your experience with female friendship? Do you choose female friends because of the potential for being able to share feelings? Do you think your communication pattern with female friends has changed over time? As we said at a number of places in this text, information is the key to understanding the other person. Disclosure is the primary vehicle through which information is shared and the use of disclosure has a clear impact on same-sex friendships. We ask you to examine the degree of disclosure you allow or seek in your same-sex friendships.

What If?

What if there were no sex or gender differences in friendship? *What if* same-sex and cross-sex friendships had exactly the same range of possibilities? *What if* male friends met together for the simple joy of sharing a conversation about their relationships with other people? *What if* female friends just went bowling and never really engaged in much conversation? *What if* (and here's a big *if*) the romantic or sexual expectation exempted from heterosexual, same-sex friendship was also exempted from perceptions of cross-sex friendship? What difference would this make? Would both sexes be better off? If so, how so? In this text, we advocate the expansion of one's repertoire of communication behaviors and the development of a more androgynous, sex-blended approach to communication. We view this as a goal to enhance someone's personal effectiveness. Should another goal be the reduction or removal of differences related to friendships? If not, why not? What do these differences preserve about friendship? *What if* one's sex or gender had no bearing at all on one's friendships?

Same-sex friendships for both men and women offer unique problems and potentials. Our goal in this section has been to provide you with the major issues in each type of same-sex friendship and to suggest ways to increase your friendship satisfaction potential. Same-sex friendships are important to each of us, but so are cross-sex friendships. Let's turn our attention to the issues surrounding these sometimes troubling, but often fulfilling friendships.

CROSS-SEX FRIENDSHIP: COULD HARRY AND SALLY HAVE BEEN "JUST FRIENDS"?

For some people, "friends of the opposite sex" is an oxymoron (kind of like "military intelligence"). As we mentioned in the opening case study for this chapter, the tendency for contemporary young people to "travel in herds," that is, the frequent socializing in groups of same- and opposite-sex friends, just doesn't match the experience of persons in older generations. Just a few decades ago, young men and women socialized together only as dates, rarely if ever as friends. That may be why it seems so difficult to explain to grandparents that the statement "We're just friends" is reality, not an evasive answer to their questions.

You've probably heard that Michael Bolton tune with the chorus of "How can we be lovers if we can't be friends?" This lyric suggests that a successful love affair, dating relationship, or marriage must be based on friendship. We've all heard folk wisdom (often in the form of advice that wasn't asked for) which cautioned us to like each other on a friendship level before loving each other on some other level. Granted, there's merit in that advice, but there's also merit in keeping a male-female relationship at the friendship level. In cross-sex heterosexual friendships, the constant pressure or expectation is to move the relationship beyond friendship into romance. Why can't people let cross-sex friendships alone? Why do people wonder about female-male friendship, as though it weren't valid or "normal," or as though it were a mere pretense for an underlying romantic or sexual motivation?

Rawlins (1993) suggests that society actively works to create static for cross-sex friendships. You've probably heard someone say about a cross-sex friendship, "Oh yeah, their relationship is completely platonic (wink, wink, nudge, nudge)." People frequently use the word "platonic" to describe a friendship that they suspect is something else altogether! Another problem is that we have few ready role models or prototypes of cross-sex friendships; each couple seems to make up their own rules as they go. So if you've had some problems in this context, you aren't alone.

As with other aspects of friendship that we've discussed, society is slowly changing its expectations and notions about the appropriateness of cross-sex friendship. While research from the 1970s suggested that both women and men preferred and actually had more same-sex friendships than cross-sex friendships, the experiences of modern students challenge those findings (Booth & Hess, 1974; Larwood & Wood, 1977). Anecdotal evidence from our students and our own friends suggests that both sexes are seeking better friendships with the opposite sex. As more and more women enter various walks of life (business, politics, education, etc.), effective friendships are increasingly necessary and probable. In this section of the chapter, we first explore some of the negative aspects or things that get in the way of cross-sex friendship. Then we end on a more positive note by discussing some benefits of this form of friendship.

What Gets in the Way of Cross-Sex Friendships?

Many of us have experienced the joys that cross-sex friendships can provide, but we also know that these kinds of friendships come with their own unique complexity. Let's examine three issues that are likely to pose problems in cross-sex friendships. We are back to our "forewarned is forearmed" perspective here, meaning that a knowledge of potential problems may help you avoid them.

Perceptual Issues

Research indicates that men perceive a distinct difference between same-sex and cross-sex friendships, generally related to the purposes such relationships serve (Phillips & Metzger, 1976; Wright, 1982). Men tend to view different types of friendships as serving particular needs. Women, on the other hand, tend to evaluate each of their relationships independently, without any sweeping generalizations related to sex or gender. They view relationships more holistically, meaning that one individual may fulfill friendship needs on many levels.

A related issue is the attitude that a woman and man bring to a cross-sex friendship. Wright (1982) describes folk wisdom which suggests that friendships between and with women are not only different from, but inferior to, those between men. We alluded to this folklore earlier in this chapter, but at the base of it is the suggestion that men form stronger friendships through sports, the rigors of war, the stress of work, and so on—opportunities that women just don't have. An overwhelming majority of Wright's male subjects, when asked about the comparative quality of men's and women's friendships, initially responded that they had not given the matter any thought. Perhaps one of the first things each sex may need to bring to the friendship is a realization that each may be approaching it with different attitudes.

Perceptual differences also extend to views of intimacy. According to research, men appear to have at least two different conceptualizations of intimacy in cross-sex friendships (Komarovsky, 1976; Rands & Levinger, 1979). First, men have greater emotional dependence than women on cross-sex friendships. As we reported in an earlier section of this chapter, men typically avoid emotional intimacy with other men; thus they often seek it with women. In contrast, some women think men are insufficient to meet their emotional needs and, as a result, they create strong bonds with other women (Chodorow, 1976; Gilligan, 1982). This can lead to problems of balance in cross-sex friendships. If a man views the relationship as an outlet for meeting his emotional needs but the woman sees it as unable to do so for her, then the friendship might be headed for problems.

The second perceptual difference of intimacy relates to sexuality. Men apparently find it more difficult than women to develop cross-sex friendships free of romantic involvement and sexual activity (Rawlins, 1993). They also tend to form cross-sex friendships more out of sexual motivation, whereas women's motives are more often platonic (Lipman-Blumen, 1976; Rose, 1985). In some ways, this attitude is a remnant of past generations, when relationships with women were said to be for one thing—and that one thing was not friendship. Gender scholars Rubin, Peplau, and Hill (1980) found that men were more likely to believe in the romantic ideology of relationships and more likely to perceive a potential for romance than women. Perhaps because of this, men are more likely to view both men's and women's behaviors in a sexualized manner. In other words, men sometimes see sexual overtones when they are not present and spend more time wondering "where this will go" than women (Abbey, 1982). In Rose's (1985) study, female subjects frequently reported that their belief that men's motives were sexual made them mistrustful of male friendship overtures and unwilling to establish friendships with men. The perceived sexual motivation led to suspicion and hesitancy.

While other perceptual differences exist, these two—perceptions of the satisfaction of emotional needs and of the possibility of romance and sexual activity—probably create the greatest potential for difficulty in cross-sex friendships. However, perceptual differences aren't the only source of problems.

Social Issues

Cross-sex friendships face a unique set of social pressures and judgments. Social perceptions range from "It shouldn't happen at all," to "You must be fooling around," to "Sure, we can be friends." However, it is clear that cross-sex friendships do not have a strong base of social support and approval. Communication researchers Bell and Healey (1992) report that it has long been acknowledged that friends look to the images, norms, and rules of society as they attempt to make sense of their connection and understand their rights, privileges, and obligations. But what images of effective cross-sex friendship exist in this society—Harry and Sally?

Bell and Healey describe how difficult it is for two individuals to initiate a relationship in the absence of a prototype or model. Do you know of any prototypes of successful cross-sex friendships? If you do, what would you say makes these friendships successful? We suspect that no clear prototype exists in this culture for successful cross-sex friendships; the successful ones become so because the individuals involved have worked to create their own definition of success.

Few role models exist because society places clear limits on what it approves in cross-sex friendships. Rawlins (1993) discusses the perception that cross-sex friendships are socially "deviant." He describes three somewhat socially approved contexts for cross-sex friendships: "(1) between males and females who work together; (2) between non-married men and women, since 'friendship' can be viewed as a euphemism for dating and hence, a stage in the 'natural' progression to publicly acknowledge romance and possibly marriage; and (3) if sanctioned by one or both friends' spouse(s) or romantic partner(s)" (p. 61). Concerning this "deviance" theme, the author of *Friends and Lovers*, Robert Brain (1976), believes:

> We have been brought up as "dirty old men," assuming the worst when two men are constantly and devotedly together or when a boy and girl travel together as friends—if they share the same bedroom or tent, they must be lovers. We have imbued friendly relations with a smear of sexuality, so that frank enjoyment of a friend for his or her sake is becoming well-nigh impossible. (p. 26)

Rawlins (1993) contends that "in a frustrating cultural setting, cross-sex friends must orchestrate social perceptions of their relationship as well as develop a shared private definition" (p. 61). This statement offers a clear description of the unique problems faced by cross-sex friends. Together with the lack of a prototype, the issues of public and private definitions contribute to a less-than-solid base for the development of the relationship. These issues lead Rawlins to say that managing a cross-sex friendship requires "conscious supervision" (p. 62). He advocates that cross-sex friends should openly and continually discuss relational definitions.

Interpersonal Issues

A third source of difficulties in cross-sex friendships arises from interpersonal issues between the sexes, beginning with the presence of tension in a friendship. Any interpersonal relationship will experience strain to some degree or another. Wright (1982) researched strain within cross-sex friendships and found that women were less inclined to develop strong friendships with people with whom they have difficulty getting along. Men, in contrast, were more likely to form friendships (particularly with other men) under circumstances of potential conflict. In addition, when meaningful cross-sex friendships became strained or tense, women were more likely than men to either terminate the relationship or become less good friends. Men indicated that they usually

NANCY reprinted by permission of UFS, Inc.

ignored and worked around sources of strain while pursuing unstrained aspects of the friendships. Understandably, working around relational tension or strain is easier to do if doing things together is more the focus of your relationship than talking.

In related research, gender scholars Martin and Nivens (1987) found that women in cross-sex friendships tended to internalize and blame themselves for relational failures, while externalizing or crediting others for relational success. Men tended to do the reverse. This is a significant difference, one that relates to how women and men are socialized with regard to relationships. Whether the relationship is friendly, romantic, or professional, women are often socialized to place relationships (especially with men) at the center of their lives and to assume that relational problems are their fault. The female co-author of this text clearly remembers her grandmother instructing her to "not let the sun go down on your anger." "Apologize and make the relationship right again, even if it's not your fault," she used to say. Does this advice strike you as appropriate?

In general, men are not socialized to place as much importance (or assume blame for problems) on their relationships with women; thus they do not typically look inward for the source of a problem. This difference in approach to strain and tension in cross-sex friendships can at the minimum cause misunderstanding; it can also lead to greater difficulties within the friendship, even to possible termination. Think about how you view strain or tension within your cross-sex friendships. Do you typically assume the blame when something goes wrong in the relationship, or do you externalize the blame? How do you cope with stress or conflict that arises in cross-sex friendships?

A second potential area of interpersonal problems relates to the expression of feelings. We've mentioned this topic before, but there's another twist we'd like you to be aware of. One issue in cross-sex friendships is the *recognition* of feelings. Research indicates that men seem to have a harder time recognizing the feelings of another person, particularly if the other person is female (Rubin, 1983). Men tend to have less capacity for the reciprocity of feelings, that is, the ability to assume or role-take another person's feelings. This can become a real problem for male-female friendships, one that is compounded when men don't realize that they have trouble recognizing the feelings of women. In trends emerging from related research, men and women reported similar levels of intimacy and emotional recognition with their friends. But in role-play situations, women were judged to display higher levels of emotional recognition, evidenced by such behaviors as more affectionate touch, expressions of empathy, and feedback after disclosure (Buhrke & Fuqua, 1987; Caldwell & Peplau, 1982; Davidson & Duberman, 1982). Differences in the recognition of feelings can create problems for cross sex friends if an imbalance is perceived in the amount of emotional support one derives from the relationship.

A final interpersonal issue we raise is not research-based, but stems from our own experience, corroborated by numerous experiences our students describe. There is a form of communication unique among men that tends to backfire when men use it with women. In a gender communication class a few semesters back, this phenomenon received the label "jocular sparring." Here's how it typically works: A guy will see one of his buddies and greet him by saying, "Man, you look *terrible* today; where'd you get that shirt, off somebody who died?! And your hair, geez—put a hat on that shit." This harmless teasing between male friends can be directly translated into "I like you; you're my buddy." It's a less threatening way for men to communicate liking and affection for one another. Now we realize that this is generalizing a bit, but women don't typically talk this way with their female friends. If a woman greeted a female friend by saying, "Hey, you look like death warmed over today—what happened?! That outfit looks like it's been through the wringer and your hair looks like the cat's been chewing on it," the female friend would likely get her feelings hurt, get mad, or wonder what in the world got into her friend.

Intrafriendship teasing, or jocular sparring, just doesn't seem to work the same way with women as it does with men. What happens when a guy teases a female friend, assuming that she'll react the way his male friends do? For example, consider what's likely to happen if a guy greets a female friend by saying, "Not getting enough sleep lately? Your eyes look like you've been on a four-day drunk. And that outfit—did you get dressed in the dark?!" More often than not, the woman will not take the teasing lightly. She might act as though she is tossing off the comments, when in fact the teasing is probably causing her discomfort because it introduces an element of uncertainty into the relationship. (We hope you're nodding your head while you're reading this, because most people find a high level of correspondence between this information and their own experiences.)

Now, this doesn't mean that women don't have a sense of humor or that they're fragile creatures who can't take teasing among friends. In fact, after a friendship foundation has been established and with greater understanding of the communication styles of one another, women can often take jocular sparring (and dish it right back) in the friendly spirit intended. It's not that women can't or don't engage in teasing with both their male and female friends, but they tend not to prefer it as a form of indicating closeness or affection. When women do engage in teasing, it just seems to be communicated differently and with a different effect (sometimes negative) than when men do jocular sparring. If this sounds all too familiar and descriptive of your own experience with friends, then perhaps you will want to reassess this form of communication. Jocular sparring has the potential either to hurt or to engender a sense of playfulness and closeness in a relationship; if you desire the positive outcome, it's wise for friends to negotiate the use of this kind of communication.

These three areas—perceptual, social, and interpersonal issues—are not the only potential problems facing a cross-sex friendship, but they seem to be the most common. If you become aware of these potential problems, you might be able to understand why the other person is responding in a particular way, and what you might do to keep these issues from having too negative an impact on the friendship. Now that we've explored some of the more difficult aspects of cross-sex friendship, we turn our attention to topics that enhance effectiveness.

What Enhances Cross-Sex Friendships?

Each of us needs friends, and one of the benefits of the changes over past decades is the increased potential for satisfying friendships between men and women. Author Pamela Sattran (1989) believes that men and women are much more likely now to establish solid, long-lasting, platonic friendships than they were in the past. Research published in the mid-1980s indicated that approximately 18 percent of the American population reported having close friends of the opposite sex (Davis, 1985). We project that this figure is low compared to the experiences of people in the 1990s. While many students, both male and female, are aware of some of the problems we just discussed, they also report a desire for more and better friendships with the opposite sex. In this final section of the chapter, let's explore some strategies one might follow to increase the chance that a cross-sex friendship will develop successfully.

Defining the Relationship

One of the values we described in Chapter 1, "Talking about it makes it better," is one that we keep coming back to. Within the context of cross-sex, heterosexual friendship, it's particularly pertinent that friends define their relationship by addressing the question "Are we just friends or is this leading to something else?" While we hope that cross-sex friendship will become so commonplace that people won't suspect the relationship of being something else, we grant that society hasn't evolved to a position of complete tolerance on this issue. The sexual dynamic between women and men is still an undercurrent, so getting past that issue or negotiating the nature of the relationship is necessary for the friendship to grow.

Rawlins (1993) insightfully describes how the "friends versus lovers" decision generates three combinations of trajectories in cross-sex friendships, as follows: (1) a person interested in "friendship as not romance" meets another person interested in "friendship as not romance"; (2) "friendship as not friendship (that is, looking for romance)" meets another "friendship as not friendship"; and (3) "friendship as not romance" meets "friendship as not friendship" (pp. 59–60). In these possible combinations, two people described by either (1) or (2) are unlikely to run into too many problems. Two people in situation (1) will usually follow the normal pattern of a cross sex friendship with its attendant gender issues. Two people in situation (2) will follow the pattern of using friendship as a prelude to a romantic relationship. However, the people involved in situation (3) will need to confront the differing expectations each has for the relationship.

No matter which of the three combinations apply in a given cross-sex friendship, a mutually shared definition of the friendship is critical to long-term success. Sometimes this is relatively easy to accomplish, because circumstances (e.g., professional ethics, marital status, value discrepancies, age differences) lead to a conscious decision to be friends. In other instances, say, in situation (3) where the goals for the relationship differ for the two individuals, the decision will not be made so easily. These situations in particular will benefit from a discussion devoted to "Where is this relationship headed?" "State-of-the-relationship" conversations may need to take place more than once if one or both friends change their minds about intentions. Keeping each other informed about relational intentions is critical to the success of cross-sex friendships.

"Where is this relationship headed?" is a question that applies to same-sex friends as well, given that it does occur that one person in a same-sex friendship may want to move the relationship to sexual intimacy. The same suggestions apply here as well; clarity of intentions, open communication, and a willingness to reach a mutually agreed-upon friendship definition are important to long-term relationship success.

Cross-Sex Friends as Romantic Advisers

One benefit of cross-sex friendship relates to getting firsthand information about the opposite sex. We've spoken about the curiosity women and men have about each other. That curiosity is a natural diversion, but when it turns into perplexity because one relational partner cannot understand the other, then we feel like we need help. Who better to turn to than an opposite-sex friend?

Men frequently ask their female friends to help them understand women; often they just seek support, empathy, maybe even sympathy. This applies to the guy who is frustrated over his lack of success in the "dating market," to the man who wants female insight into his dating relationships, to the married man who seeks advice about his relationship with his wife, possibly from one of her friends. At times, women remain a mystery to men; thus men often feel that a female friend, more than a male friend, can help them understand women. As some research that we reviewed in the male-male friendship section indicates, men may not want to disclose their problems, insecurities, or concerns to other men for fear of appearing weak or vulnerable. Thus men often find female friends to be valuable confidantes (Buhrke & Fuqua, 1987; Doyle, 1989). Likewise, women who are puzzled or troubled by some situation involving romantic entanglements with men (or the lack thereof) can find their male friends a source of support, strength, and insight.

Of course, like anything else, this advice-giving, lend-an-ear function of cross-sex friendships has its abuses as well as its benefits. For example, if your sole purpose for having an opposite-sex friend is to seek counsel on your romantic relationships, that may be seen by your friend as unfair treatment. As we said earlier, friendships need special kinds of maintenance. Using someone merely as a source of support, a guidance counselor, a spokesperson for all men or all women, or a captive audience for your relational problems could be considered a selfish, abusive way to conduct a friendship. What if your friend needs your ear sometime? What if your friend becomes unwilling to "be there for you," simply because the friendship ended up being too one-sided? These important issues warrant sensitive discussion and negotiation between cross-sex friends (not to mention same-sex friends). If you don't talk about possible abuses of the friendship, or of any relationship for that matter, you might wind up with one less friend.

Sexual Activity between "Just Friends"

Thus far in this section we have been operating under the implicit assumption that cross-sex friendships are platonic; that is, they do not include sexual activity. Our unspoken dividing line has been that as soon as two friends begin to have sexual relations, the relationship moves from friendship to some other level. Whatever level that might be, it is not "just" a friendship any longer so won't be discussed in this chapter. Perhaps it is time to question that assumption.

Is a physical relationship a logical extension of the intimacy that two people can develop? If a strong friendship includes deep sharing at the psychological level, what about the physical level? If that happens, is the relationship no longer a friendship? We are not suggesting that definitive answers exist to these questions. We raise the point to start you thinking about the qualities of a cross-sex friendship and what it should or shouldn't include. Here's a related question our students ask with regularity: Is it possible to go back to being "just friends" after being lovers? Of course the possibility exists, but it may take some careful conversations about intentions and needs before it becomes a reality. Early in this chapter we referred to Reisman's (1979) claim that friendship is an ill-defined concept in this society. The question of sexual relations in a friendship further complicates the concept. Since this is one of those areas where no clear guidelines exist, we can only repeat our earlier advice—talk it over.

The Future for Cross-Sex Friendship

Friendship between men and women has changed. We wonder where these changes will lead, and so we close this chapter with one thought on the direction and future of friendship between the sexes. Buhrke and Fuqua (1987) concluded the following from their research:

> Given that [our research found] women wanted more contact with men, wanted to be closer to men, and wanted more balance in their relationships with men than they did with women, one could conclude that women more highly value their relationships with men and wish to better those relationships. However, women were already more satisfied with the frequency of contact, closeness, and balance in their relationships with women. Thus it seems women want more from their relationships with men and make efforts to improve the quality of those relationships so that they are more similar to their relationships with women. (p. 349)

This is an interesting thought—that women want better relationships with men, but want them to become more like their friendships with other women. Perhaps men would like their cross-sex friendships to become more like their same-sex friendships. We suggest that neither goal is particularly realistic. It may not be a good idea to force cross-sex friendships into the mold of the familiar same-sex friendship. Men and women can develop more effective cross-sex friendships by learning to incorporate the patterns of the opposite sex into their communication repertoire and by treating each friendship as a unique entity. The process takes thought, sensitivity, and a willingness to learn and change.

CONCLUSION

This chapter began with the suggestion that the type and quality of same-sex and cross-sex friendships may be changing. Optimistically, we believe this to be true. Men are seeking closer ties and greater depth to their friendships with other men. Women are seeking even closer ties with other women by confronting some of the issues that may separate them. Both sexes are learning to relate more effectively to each other. We encourage and applaud these efforts.

Each type of friendship has unique communication issues and potentials. In this chapter we examined some of the more critical issues that enhance friendship, as well as some that detract from it. We believe that through an analysis of the issues, an exploration of the options, and the important ability to talk with a friend about the friendship, each of you can increase your personal effectiveness in this important communication context.

Key Terms

contexts	homophobia	sexuality
same-sex friendship	comradeship	social issues
cross-sex friendship	disclosure	prototypes
friendship	topical content level	interpersonal issues
socialization	relational content level	interpersonal strain
male bonding	personal content level	reciprocity of feelings
homosocial norms	competitiveness	role-taking
closeness	platonic relationship	jocular sparring
intimacy	perceptual issues	relational definitions

Discussion Starters

1. In your experience, how do most male friendships seem to form? What brings the friends together? Is this different from the circumstances that bring female friends together?
2. Some researchers propose that the intimacy men achieve through doing things together is of the same quality as the intimacy achieved by women through conversation. Do you believe that men and women are equally capable of forming intimate relationships? Intimate same-sex friendships? Intimate cross-sex friendships? How are women and men different, in terms of accomplishing intimacy in their relationships? How are they similar?
3. Earlier in the chapter we referred to competitiveness between women. Have you seen this happening in women's friendships? Are you competitive for grades in your

college classes? Are you more competitive with female classmates or male classmates? What are the benefits and the hazards of being competitive?

4. Is it possible to achieve power equity in cross-sex friendships? Does one person or the other need to "take the lead"? How can this be discussed within the relationship? What happens if both friends are leaders?

5. Think about the issue of sexual activity in cross-sex friendships. How is the issue dealt with in most of the cross-sex friendships you know? In your own cross-sex friendships? Is the issue discussed openly, hinted at, or avoided?

6. If you had to write down on a piece of paper the name of the opposite-sex person with whom you've had the best platonic relationship or friendship, whose name would come to mind first? What factors about the friendship or the person caused you to think of him or her?

7. What do you think are the biggest obstacles to effective cross-sex friendships? What do you think it will take to improve friendships between women and men? Which sex would have to change most and why? What would the ideal cross-sex friendship look like?

References

ABBEY, A. (1982). Sex differences in attributions for friendly behavior: Do males misperceive females' friendliness? *Journal of Personality and Social Psychology, 42,* 830–838.

ARIES, E. J., & JOHNSON, F. L. (1983). Close friendship in adulthood: Conversational content between same-sex friends. *Sex Roles, 9,* 1183–1196.

ARLISS, L. P., & BORISOFF, D. J. (1993). *Women and men communicating: Challenges and changes.* Fort Worth, TX: Harcourt Brace Jovanovich.

BASOW, S. (1986). *Sex role stereotypes: Traditions and alternatives.* Monterey, CA: Brooks/Cole.

BELL, R. A., & HEALEY, J. G. (1992). Idiomatic communication and interpersonal solidarity in friends' relational cultures. *Human Communication Research, 18,* 307–335.

BING, S. (1989, August). No man is an isthmus. *Esquire,* pp. 51–53.

BLOCK, J. D., & GREENBERG, D. (1985). *Women and friendship.* New York: Franklin Watts.

BOOTH, A., & HESS, E. (1974). Cross-sex friendship. *Journal of Marriage and the Family, 36,* 38–47.

BRAIN, R. (1976). *Friends and lovers.* New York: Basic Books.

BREHM, S. (1992). *Intimate relationships.* New York: McGraw-Hill.

BRENTON, M. (1975). *Friendship.* Briarcliff Manor, NY: Stein and Day.

BRILES, J. (1987). *Woman to woman: From sabotage to support.* Far Hills, NJ: New Horizon Press.

BUHRKE, R. A., & FUQUA, D. R. (1987). Sex differences in same- and cross-sex supportive relationships. *Sex Roles, 17,* 339–351.

CALDWELL, M. A., & PEPLAU, L. A. (1982). Sex differences in same-sex friendships. *Sex Roles, 8,* 721–732.

CHODOROW, H. (1976). Oedipal asymmetries and heterosexual knots. *Social Problems, 23,* 454–468.

CLARK, M., & REIS, H. T. (1988). Interpersonal processes in close relationships. *Annual Review of Psychology, 39,* 609–672.

CRAWFORD, M. (1977). What is a friend? *New Society, 42,* 116–117.

DALY, M. (1978). *Gyn/ecology.* Boston: Beacon Press.

DAVIDSON, L. R., & DUBERMAN, L. (1982). Friendship: Communication and interactional patterns in same-sex dyads. *Sex Roles, 8,* 809–822.

DAVIS, K. E. (1985, February). Near and dear: Friendship and love compared. *Psychology Today,* pp. 24–28, 30.

DIAMOND, M., & KARLEN, A. (1980). *Sexual decisions.* Boston: Little, Brown.

DOYLE, J. A. (1989). *The male experience* (2nd ed.). Dubuque, IA: Wm. C. Brown.

EICHENBAUM, L., & ORBACH, S. (1988). *Between women: Love, envy, and competition in women's friendships.* New York: Viking.

FARR, K. (1988). Dominance bonding through the good old boys sociability group. *Sex Roles, 18*, 259–277.

FITZPATRICK, M. A., & BOCHNER, A. (1981). Perspectives on self and other: Male-female differences in perceptions of communication behavior. *Sex Roles, 7*, 523–535.

FOX, M., GIBBS, M., & AUERBACH, D. (1985). Age and gender dimensions of friendship. *Psychology of Women Quarterly, 9*, 489–501.

GIBBS-CANDY, S., TROLL, L. E., & LEVY, S. G. (1981). A developmental exploration of friendship functions in women. *Psychology of Women Quarterly, 5*, 456–472.

GILLIGAN, C. (1982). *In a different voice*. Cambridge, MA: Harvard University Press.

GOLDBERG, H. (1979). *The new male: From self-destruction to self-care*. New York: Signet.

HAAS, A., & SHERMAN, M. (1982). Reported topics of conversation among same-sex adults. *Communication Quarterly, 30*, 332–342.

HACKER, H. (1981). Blabbermouths and clams: Sex differences in self-disclosure in same-sex and cross-sex friendship dyads. *Psychology of Women Quarterly, 5*, 385–401.

HICKSON, M. I., & STACKS, D. W. (1989). *Nonverbal communication: Studies and applications* (2nd ed.). Dubuque, IA: Wm. C. Brown.

HITE, S. (1989). *Women and love*. New York: St. Martin's Press.

JOHNSON, S. (1991). *The ship that sailed into the living room: Sex and intimacy reconsidered*. Estancia, NM: Wildfire Books.

KOMAROVSKY, M. (1976). *Dilemmas of masculinity: A study of college youth*. New York: Norton.

LARWOOD, L., & WOOD, M. M. (1977). *Women in management*. Lexington, MA: Lexington Books.

LEVINSON, D. J. (1978). *The seasons of a man's life*. New York: Alfred A. Knopf.

LIPMAN-BLUMEN, J. (1976). Toward a homosocial theory of sex roles: An explanation of the sex segregation of social institutions. In M. M. Blaxall & B. Reagan (Eds.), *Women and the workplace* (pp. 15–22). Chicago: University of Chicago Press.

LOMBARDO, J., & LAVINE, L. (1981). Sex-role stereotyping and patterns of self-disclosure. *Sex Roles, 7*, 403–411.

LYNESS, J. F. (1978). Styles of relationships among unmarried men and women. *Sociological Abstracts, 26*, 1249.

MARTIN, V., & NIVENS, M. K. (1987). The attributional response of males and females to noncontingent feedback. *Sex Roles, 16*, 453–462.

MOREHEAD, P. D. (1985). *Roget's college thesaurus in dictionary form*. New York: Signet.

PARK, K. A., & WATERS, E. (1989). Security of attachment and preschool friendships. *Child Development, 60*, 1076–1080.

PHILLIPS, G. M., & METZGER, N. J. (1976). *Intimate communication*. Boston: Allyn and Bacon.

POGREBIN, L. C. (1987). *Among friends*. New York: McGraw-Hill.

RANDS, M., & LEVINGER, G. (1979). Implicit theories of relationship: An intergenerational student. *Journal of Personality and Social Psychology, 37*, 645–661.

RAWLINS, W. K. (1992). *Friendship matters: Communication, dialectics, and the life course*. Hawthorne, NY: Aldine de Gruyter.

RAWLINS, W. K. (1993). Communication in cross-sex friendships. In L. P. Arliss & D. J. Borisoff (Eds.), *Women and men communicating: Challenges and changes* (pp. 51–70). Fort Worth, TX: Harcourt Brace Jovanovich.

REIS, H. T. (1984). Social interaction and well-being. In S. Duck (Ed.), *Repairing personal relationships*. London: Academic Press.

REISMAN, J. J. (1979). *Anatomy of friendships*. New York: Irvington.

REISMAN, J. J. (1990). Intimacy in same-sex friendships. *Sex Roles, 23*, 65–81.

ROSE, S. M. (1985). Same- and cross-sex friendships and the psychology of homosociality. *Sex Roles, 12*, 63–74.

RUBIN, L. B. (1983). *Intimate strangers: Men and women together*. New York: Harper & Row.

RUBIN, Z., PEPLAU, L. A., & HILL, C. T. (1980). Loving and leaving: Sex differences in romantic attachments. *Sex Roles, 6*, 821–835.

SATTRAN, P. R. (1989, November). The evolution of women's friendships. *Working Woman*, pp. 158–160, 190.

STRIKWERDA, R. A., & MAY, L. (1992). Male friendships and intimacy, *Hypatia, 7*, 110–123.

THORNE, B., & HENLEY, N. (Eds.) (1975). *Language and sex: Difference and dominance.* Rowley, MA: Newbury House.

TIGER, L. (1969). *Men in groups.* New York: Random House.

WALKER, A. (1989). *The temple of my familiar.* San Diego: Harcourt Brace Jovanovich.

WEISS, L., & LOWENTHAL, M. (1977). Life course perspectives on friendship. In M. Lowenthal, M. Thurnher, & D. Chiriboga (Eds.), *Four stages of life.* San Francisco: Jossey-Bass.

WRIGHT, P. (1982). Men's friendships, women's friendships, and the alleged inferiority of the latter. *Sex Roles, 8,* 1–19.

CHAPTER 9

Romance, Love, and Sex: Gender Communication beyond Friendship

You'll *probably agree that this chapter has the most interesting, eye-catching title in this text.* Anyone with a pulse is probably interested in such subjects as romance, love, and sex. Read the case study first, to see how some people talk about this topic.

CASE STUDY

"You know one thing that really bothers me? Men still have to pick up the phone to 'make the call.'" Cliff complained in class one day about something he doesn't see changing, that it is *still* the man's responsibility to pick up the phone, to put his ego on the line, and call for a date. Bonnie countered with, "Wait a second, you don't know what it's like to wait by the phone, hoping for a call. That's really hard, too." This led Nicole to chime in, "Hey, if you don't like waiting for a guy to call you, call him. I know lots of women who call men for dates. I've called a few myself." At this point, an informal class poll was taken and the results showed that the traditional model was still very much in evidence. Few men receive calls for dates from women (even though they'd *like* to); few women actually call men for dates (even though they know they *can*). Men feel the responsibility to do the calling, and while some women do take the initiative, most are uncomfortable with it.

As the class discussion continued, Bonnie asked, "Men say they'll call, but then they never do. Why say it if you don't intend to do it?" Jawarren responded with, "It's tough. We don't always know whether we're going to call or not. So, saying 'I'll call you' is one way to be polite when you meet someone." Freelance author Steven Hollandsworth (1991) wrote an article about this topic based on his experience, in which he stated, "It's no wonder women think 'I'll call you' means 'Good-bye forever'" (p. 130). According to Hollandsworth, "I'll call you" is a symbolic way of stating that a man enjoyed a first meeting, but actually calling is something else altogether. While the guy might feel bad at the time for saying it, a few days later he finds it hard to pick up the phone and call. Hollandsworth contends that women don't face the same pressure: "You [women] never have to call men. You never have to say 'I'll call you.'

And I'll bet that's exactly the way you want it. . . . I'd love for the tables to be turned so that a woman meets me and then has to decide whether it's worth going through all the trouble of calling me. I'd love it if all I had to do was wait for the phone to ring" (p. 130). How does this compare to your experience? For the men reading this, do you identify with Hollandsworth's views? Would you really like to wait by the phone? If you are a woman reading this, what do you think of the author's explanation? Would you rather be the one who calls or the one who gets called? If you are an older nontraditional student, do you think the same stereotypical roles for romantic relationships are in place for men and women in your age group, compared to traditionally aged college students?

Research we review in this chapter supports the idea that things haven't changed much in the area of romantic relationships. While women report feeling free to assume more active, initiating roles in platonic friendships, it is still a predominant belief that taking initiative in dating relationships is a male activity (Buhrke & Fuqua, 1987; Green & Sandos, 1983; McKinney, 1987). So it seems that, despite changes in many areas of male-female relationships, romantic relationships cling to some old patterns. Do you think things have changed, in terms of female and male roles in dating or romantic relationships? If not, then should they? If you think things should change, what might you do to help bring about the change?

OVERVIEW

Part Four of the text focuses on gender communication corresponding to contexts within which relationships are initiated, developed, maintained, and sometimes terminated. One of these contexts which greatly affects our lives is the romantic relationship context. Hollywood movies would have us believe that romantic relationships happen almost by magic, as though we all know what it takes to make them happen and how to keep them going. Movies throughout the years have also shown us various faces of pain when romantic relationships have gone awry. Given the idealized, overdrawn images in our heads, it may sometimes come as a shock, or at least a rude awakening, when a real romantic relationship produces a different reality. Romance brings its own unique communication and challenges to men and women who venture into this realm. But even in the midst of a breakup, when the relationship seems doomed and we wonder why we ever wandered into such uncharted territory, we'd probably say that we'd do it all over again if given the chance. Humans are innately romantic creatures, if you connect romance to a desire to be loved and accepted by another human being. Some offer less evidence of their romantic natures than others, but for many of us, the opportunity for romance and love is one of life's greatest experiences.

What kinds of gender issues and communication make this relational context so special and unique? That's exactly the focus of this chapter, through these topics:

- The difficulty in choosing language to describe a romantic relationship
- Achieving a balance between autonomy and connection
- How relational partners cope with attempts to change one another or the relationship
- Women's and men's fears of commitment
- Ways that men and women test each other and the romantic relationship
- The sexes and relationship termination
- Attitudes and communication about sexual activity in a romantic relationship
- Communication, sex or gender, and the crime of date rape

INTRODUCTION

Romance, love, and sex are wonderful, confusing, and challenging dimensions of relationships. Few things motivate individuals more strongly than the emotions that surround love and sex. And because such strong emotions are tapped in romantic relationships, the communication within them is critical and complex. As a beginning example of this complexity, consider the terms that are used to describe the nature of a romantic relationship and the two people in it. For heterosexual couples, the term *girlfriend* is still the most common usage of traditionally aged male students, but *boyfriend* seems to be on the decline in use by their female counterparts. Instead, these women often say "the guy I'm dating" or less often, "a man I'm seeing." Homosexual couples face the naming problem as well, if not to a more difficult degree. Most often they refer to one another as *partners*, a term that heterosexual couples have begun to co-opt, because it communicates the sense of equality and cooperativeness inherent in a partnership. Older adults especially cringe when they refer to a romantic involvement, understandably so when the choices seem juvenile to them (as in boyfriend and girlfriend), ambiguous and nondescript (e.g., my "friend"), too personal (as in "lovers"), or clinical (as in "significant other," a term widely used in the 1970s).

Gender researcher Laurie Arliss (1993) believes that there is a gap in our language when it comes to terms for relationships that are more than "just friends" but are not marital (and perhaps not likely to be). We've seen a number of people stumble in introductions. A newspaper editorial once gave this example: "I'd like you to meet my . . . uh. . . ." Sadly enough, the English language hasn't progressed much past calling these relationships "uh," so for the purposes of this chapter, we use the term *relational partner* to refer to members of romantic relationships. We believe that this term is the best option around. It sounds a bit clinical, but to a lesser degree than *significant other.* The more this term works its way into common usage, the more people will be able to connect it with the kind of relationship it describes. We use the term *romantic relationship* in reference to dating relationships, more long-term, committed relationships (where the term *dating* doesn't seem to fit), and nonmarital relationships that include sexual activity. One quick note: We don't mean to insinuate that marital relationships are somehow not romantic because we don't discuss this form of relationship until Chapter 10. The "romantic relationship" designation here is just to keep things simple and clear.

A romantic relationship is a powerful force in one's life. Social psychologist Caryl Avery (1989) states, "Given one wish in life, most people would wish to be loved—to be able to reveal themselves entirely to another human being and be embraced, caressed, by that acceptance" (p. 27). The strength of this wish seems to cause our culture to be highly romantic (Arliss, 1993). Children learn of romance through such stories and movies as *Beauty and the Beast, Aladdin,* and other legends of princes and princesses. In Chapter 4 we described some of the media images of romance and relationships. By this point in your life you've seen and read countless stories of passionate, engulfing, magical love between, typically, very attractive people. These images and legends you grew up with may have formed powerful, albeit unrealistic models for romantic relationships. Such images lead our culture to assert pressure on finding, "winning," and "keeping" a desirable partner. Arliss (1993) contends that a realization of the great contrast between the myth and the reality of romantic relationships may lead to a high degree of frustration, disillusionment, and even violence.

The pressure to find a relational partner also results in misperceptions and outright silly ideas, one of the most prevalent being the "drunk with love" aspect. That wonderful, dizzying feeling of falling in love is like no other. But many people almost get addicted to this feeling and want it to go on indefinitely. If the feeling fades away or changes into something else (as it often does), they drop the relationship and seek the same feeling from someone else. This addiction, like any other, is unhealthy. Author Lesley Dormen (1990) examined this issue from a health (both personal and physical) point of view. She suggests that "healthy lovers know that there's a world of difference between falling in love and being in love. They don't mistake dizziness for love's beginning any more than they assume calm is love's end," and they don't have a "dreary and predictable two-part tale—exciting romance followed by the bland 'working out' required by a relationship" (p. 310).

There is a host of issues that could be discussed regarding this topic. We've selected what we consider to be the most pertinent gender-related issues to present to you. Admittedly, we tend to explore the issues related to romance more from a heterosexual than a homosexual or bisexual relationship context. This decision is based primarily on the trend for more of our students (and, likely, our readers) to be heterosexual than homosexual or bisexual. The decision does not stem from a prejudicial stance since, as you've probably detected in other places in your reading of this text, we consider homosexuality, bisexuality, and heterosexuality to be equally viable personal orientations. As you're reading this information, do what we've asked you to do before—put yourself and your experiences into your reading. Compare the research and ideas to your own views about romantic relationships and your own experiences. Maybe you'll find that your approach is "on the money." Or maybe you'll find some things you want to do differently.

ISSUES AFFECTING ROMANTIC RELATIONSHIPS

In comparison to friendships, romantic relationships engender a different set of issues, perhaps more aptly described as "tensions" within a relationship. By tensions, we don't mean to imply the negative connotation you might normally associate with the word. Romantic relationship tensions arise from the decision making a couple faces, not necessarily because of the individuals in the relationship. The tensions are usually framed in questions related to "Should I [we] do this or should we do that?" and "Should our relationship be this or that?" These tensions are not unique to romantic relationships, but they seem to intensify with the context.

Communication researcher Daena Goldsmith (1990) describes five types of tensions that come into play as a relationship moves into the romantic stage: (1) whether to get involved and get to know the other person on this level; (2) whether or not to date others, especially if the relationship is a long-distance one; (3) trade-offs with other priorities, such as spending time with one's friends; (4) whether or not one person's will should be imposed on the other (such as "I wish you wouldn't drink"); and (5) the degree of commitment. Respondents in Goldsmith's study found these tensions to be unpleasant experiences. Some resolved them by going totally one way (complete submersion into the relationship) or the other (breaking the relationship off altogether). Most people tried to find a middle ground, although it can be difficult for two people to find the same middle ground. Sometimes women tend to take one side or end of an issue while men take the other. Identifying these issues or tensions in your own relationships may give you the opportunity to talk about them with your partner.

Communication researchers Bell and Buerkel-Rothfuss (1990) also describe a number of relational issues or tensions. They cast their list in the form of

ROSE IS ROSE reprinted by permission of UFS, Inc.

alternatives that include (1) honesty versus the protection of feelings ("Should I tell you everything I think and feel about you?"); (2) self-disclosure versus privacy ("Should I tell you my secrets?"); (3) personal autonomy versus interdependence ("How often can I pursue my own interests?"); (4) integration versus differentiation ("How alike do we need to become in our attitudes, values, and beliefs?"); (5) reciprocity versus generosity ("Do I do things for you because I care about you or do I expect something in return?"); (6) commitment versus voluntarism ("Do I do things with you because I have to or because I want to?"); and (7) novelty versus predictability ("How unpredictable should I be to keep the interest going?"). Again, these are issues that couples are likely to face. Talking about them may make resolving them easier, or it may lead to two people deciding that they just aren't suited for each other. The earlier these issues are talked about, the sooner a wise decision can be made. From these two long lists, as well as our own thoughts, we have extracted the following issues or tensions to describe in more detail: autonomy, acceptance, expressions of love, levels of commitment, testing a relationship, and ending a relationship.

Autonomy versus Connection

One of the most difficult issues to confront is the degree of autonomy each person will have within a relationship (Duck, 1988). In the early stages of romance, the tendency is to spend as much time together as possible. This creates a sense that your life together almost operates in a vacuum, sheltered from the outside world. Have you ever experienced such immersion in a relationship that you realize you haven't seen a newspaper or heard a news broadcast for days? The country could be at war and you wouldn't know it, nor would you particularly care? After a period like this, the rest of life usually intrudes and begins to whittle time away from one person or the other in a relationship. It is at this point that a couple may experience the tension created by issues of separation and independence.

Goldsmith (1990) suggests, "Each of us wants the support and companionship that come from connection with others, yet we simultaneously want independence, privacy, an individual identity" (p. 538). Interpersonal communication researcher William Rawlins (1982) makes this issue even more complicated when he describes the freedom to be independent and to be dependent as moving to different levels within the relationship at different points in time. At one point, the issue for a couple might be time spent in independent activities versus time spent together. At another point in the relationship, autonomy and connection might be dealt with more abstractly in terms of identity and commitment (e.g., "Who am I? What am I doing here?"). As an issue rises and falls, an individual will feel needs in both directions at different points in time.

Relationship researcher Leslie Baxter (1988) contends that individuals in romantic relationships are faced with working out the details of autonomy and connection, including negotiating the freedoms outside the relationship and the rights and responsibilities within it. One might view this as an integral part of love; as Dormen (1990) suggests, "The constant tension between individuality and fusion is love" (p. 271). How do couples manage the transition from constant togetherness that often typifies the beginning stages of romantic relationships to a more balanced blend of togetherness and separateness? How can relational partners enjoy a necessary autonomy while avoiding the possible hurt or rejection the other person might feel when the first clues of separateness arise? How do you avoid the possibility that issues surrounding independence don't degenerate into power struggles? Conventional wisdom in romantic relationships says that self-interest should become secondary to other-interest, that romantic relationships are supposed to be demonstrations of unconditional love. But you know as well as we do that conventional wisdom doesn't always match reality.

Let's work through a real-life example so as to better understand this first issue or tension in romantic relationships. Mary and Don met, fell in love, and spent a significant amount of time together (an understatement). Then they had the first major "crisis" in their relationship. Mary had a longstanding interest in the theater, so she auditioned for a play and was awarded a part. Rehearsals were scheduled for six nights a week for five weeks. When Don learned of this, he hit the roof. "That's too much time! You're putting a *play* ahead of me? You're putting your interests ahead of our relationship?" Don wanted Mary to quit the play. Mary felt that she would be giving up one of her real interests for the sake of the relationship, and this led to some serious concerns. Would Don try to control all of her activities? Would he always insist that she put the relationship above everything else, that she check things with Don before making decisions? On the other hand, Don felt that he needed reassurance from Mary that she was committed to the relationship. Don reacted to Mary's taking a part in the play because he thought she didn't really care about him. Don had been dumped before; he was truly afraid for the relationship and didn't want to lose Mary or the closeness they had enjoyed. The ending to this story is that the couple was able to work out this tension through heart-to-heart conversation (and Mary stayed in the play). One relational partner offered reassurance that the relationship was important, and the other agreed to ask questions and talk a situation out next time before jumping to angry conclusions. Both realized that the negotiation of time spent apart versus time spent together required honest, loving communication so that the insecurities or actions of the other person wouldn't be a dividing point.

Have you experienced a situation like this? Have you seen your friends go through it? What did you or they do to work it out? Since this balance between personal freedom and shared activities is one of the single toughest issues in a relationship, talking it out isn't easy. It's particularly problematic in the initial stages of romantic relationships, when both people want to spend all their time together and conflict is the last thing you want. So when a time-consuming activity such as a play comes up, or even when the "first night out without you" arises, a relational partner is likely to feel a degree of betrayal or have problems dealing with the contrast from doing everything together. To keep the relationship alive, relational partners might benefit from an honest, open, nondefensive conversation about the amount of time they expect to spend together versus time spent apart. Talking about this issue or tension won't necessarily ensure a perfect balance or protect the relationship from having this problem again, but it will allow partners to know each other better and it will open the door for discussions if the problem arises again.

The notion that women are more likely to have problems with men's assertion of independence in romantic relationships than the reverse may be more a myth than a reality. As more women pursue career goals, as they continue to explore the range of options open to them, and as they enjoy the fulfilling companionship of friendships with other women, it is likely that women's dependence on men has lessened. This doesn't mean that romantic relationships aren't as important to women as they once were; it simply means there is more competition for women's attention than existed in the past. The change in a romantic relationship from doing everything together to doing some things with other people or alone and the discomfort in going along with the change don't appear to be sex-typed issues.

Acceptance versus Change

Consider this stereotypical belief in romantic relationships: "I can change this person. I know she [he] has faults, but I can fix those faults." This is such a part of relational folklore that, even though your friends will warn you that you can't change a person, deep down inside you might be saying, "I'll be the exception; I'll be the one to do it." Family communication expert Kathleen Galvin (1993) describes this phenomenon in relation to the early stages of marriage. She contends that "in the beginning, couples frequently make allowances for behavior that isn't quite acceptable because new spouses focus on what they are getting, and differences seem enhancing. Later, differences become annoying and call out for resolution" (p. 95).

How do you feel when you know another person wants to change you or change the relationship? The tendency is to resist the person's attempt or to view it as one person's power play designed to exert control over another. Consider an example. Anthony and Amy were in the middle of the powerful, exhilarating emotions that exist in a romantic relationship. But the intense romantic feelings subsided a bit for Amy before they did for Anthony. She didn't care for Anthony any less, but she just wasn't so caught up in the "emotional rush." Anthony was really bothered by this change in Amy; he tried several ways to recreate the initial level of feeling. Amy didn't want to and really couldn't change her feelings. The more Anthony pushed to get things back to the way they had been, the more Amy resisted; she soon began to resent Anthony's pressure. It wasn't until Anthony stopped putting on the pressure and relaxed enough to accept the change in Amy that Amy regained some of her positive feelings about the relationship. They didn't return to the early phase, but the relationship attained a new level of closeness.

The importance of acceptance in this type of relationship can hardly be overemphasized. Having complete confidence in another person is a great feeling, and it's quite disconcerting when your confidence in the other person is lacking. One of life's paradoxes is that real change in people seems to be possible only when a person feels completely secure and accepted in a relationship. It seems that each of us wants to be accepted for who we are. It is within that acceptance that we can change to please ourselves and to improve the relationship.

Expressions of Love

One of the clearest expressions of a desire to move a relationship to a more intimate level is saying the words "I love you." These words can bring a reaction of intense pleasure—or a nervous response like "What do you mean by that?" A consistent theme throughout this text is the need to verbalize intentions, desires, and goals with your relational partner, including the expression of love.

The statement itself has many different meanings. Back in the 1950s, a communication researcher named Meerloo (1952) offered this truly memorable description of the range of meanings for "I love you":

> Sometimes it means: I desire you or I want you sexually. It may mean: I hope you love me or I hope that I will be able to love you. Often it means: It may be that a love relationship can develop between us or even I hate you. Often it is a wish for emotional exchange: I want your admiration in exchange for mine or I give my love in exchange for some passion or I want to feel cozy and at home with you or I admire some of your qualities. A declaration of love is mostly a request. I desire you or I want you to gratify me, or I want your protection or I want to be intimate with you or I want to exploit your loveliness. ... "I love you,"—wish, desire, submission, conquest; it is never the word itself that tells the real meaning here. (pp. 83–84)

Who is likely to express love and under what circumstances? Contrary to romance novels, movies, and stereotypes that tend to cast women as the first to say "I love you," research has shown otherwise. Communication researcher William Owen (1987) found that men were more often the initiators of a declaration of love, a critical communication event in a romantic relationship. Owen offered the following reasons for this tendency: (1) it is a way to coerce commitment from women; (2) men are less able than women to withhold their expressions of love when they feel love; (3) women are more capable of discriminating between love and related emotions; and (4) women wait until they hear the phrase from men because they often play a reactive rather than active (or proactive) role in a romantic relationship.

Does your experience or that of your friends match this research finding? If you've ever been (or are currently) in a romantic relationship that involves love, who said the "dreaded" three words first—the woman or the man?

Another difficult issue surrounds the concern of whether or not you'll hear the statement "I love you, too," in response to a declaration of love. Not having the sentiment reciprocated may signal an imbalance of emotion or level of commitment in a relationship, which may in turn signal relational "troubled waters." Once someone has expressed love, who do you think is more likely to repeat the expression, men or women? Is it someone's place to offer reassurances of love in a relationship?

Levels of Commitment

Commitment involves the decision to stay in a relationship, but it also implies a coordinated view of the future of the relationship. In many ways, being in a relationship is largely a coordination problem—a meshing of the language, gestures, and habits of daily life, primarily through attentiveness, courtesy, and a mutual desire to make the relationship work. Research findings suggest that such variables as anticipated duration of the relationship (short-term versus long-term), sex roles enacted by the partners, and the level and quality of disclosure within the relationship interact to influence the outcome of a relationship (Cline & Musolf, 1985; Kenrick, Sadalla, Groth, & Trost, 1990). If participants have different views of one variable or another (e.g., the woman sees the relationship as short-term while the man sees it as long-term or vice versa), this difference may affect other variables and work against relational success.

Commitment also represents a level of seriousness about one's relational partner. It indicates a deeper level of regard, possibly even intimacy, in the relationship. What are some factors related to the decision to commit? Sometimes a trial or crisis causes people to make the decision to commit to each other. Here's a real-life example (with altered names) taken from some friends' experience. Frederick and Jacquie had been "going together" for about three years and were considering marriage. As it turned out, Frederick met another woman and had a brief affair with her. This affair, however, involved not just sex but some strong emotions. Because of Fred's feelings for Jacquie, he told her about his affair. As you well might imagine, this event precipitated a crisis in Jacquie and Fred's relationship. After a number of hours of very emotional discussion, Fred and Jacquie decided that they wanted to stay together. For Fred, if he wasn't going to leave Jacquie for this other woman, he wasn't going to leave her for anyone. Jacquie couldn't imagine a more stressful crisis and decided that if they could get through this one, they could get through anything. The crisis resulted in a strong commitment to each other and an ongoing, successful relationship.

The stereotype surrounding this issue suggests that women are more willing to commit to a relationship than men. Jacquie and Fred's situation fit the stereotype; however, research indicates that women and men today are having equal trouble with the commitment issue. Social psychologist Maxine Schnall (1981) calls this condition "commitmentphobia," defined as "a social disease characterized by fear of the opposite sex, inability to establish long-term intimate relationships, unsatisfying sexual encounters and loneliness" (p. 37). She contends that commitmentphobia was "first noticed among men in the 1970s" but has "spread to the female population" (p. 37).

One reason for this trend is similar to one we described in the section on autonomy versus connection. More options mean greater flexibility and more complex decision making (Baber & Monaghan, 1988; Duck, 1988; Galvin, 1993). Some of you reading this text and taking a gender class may be nontraditional students who married at a young age and are now returning to college to start or complete a degree at a later point in life. For traditionally aged students, it used to be fairly commonplace for college-educated men and women to marry in the last year of college or upon graduation. While this still happens, it happens less frequently than in the past. It may be a strange thing to think about now, but only a few decades ago it was quite common for couples to marry upon graduation from high school. For many people, getting married at age 17 or 18 is unthinkable today. Granted, teenagers still marry, but with nowhere near the frequency of past generations. According to Galvin (1993), "A sharp increase in age at first marriage has occurred over the last three decades—from 20 for women and 23 for men in 1955 to 24 for women and 26 for men in 1988" (p. 87).

Nowadays, increasing numbers of women and men alike seem to be postponing commitment and marriage or opting not to marry at all, either to help advance a career or merely for reasons of personal growth. Some people simply feel that they aren't personally stable enough or just aren't ready for a serious involvement with another person. Others believe that marriage and the fidelity and commitment that accompany it are unrealistic. Schnall (1981) connects this under-35 generational trend to a variety of societal shifts, for example, the carryover into personal relationships of competitive, self-interested values typically associated with the marketplace, the disillusionment brought on by rising divorce rates in recent decades, and economic pressures that have turned people more toward their jobs than toward one another. Another explanation surrounds health and sexuality, meaning that an enhanced knowledge of health risks related to sexual activity may be heightening the isolation. While you might think that the fear of health risks associated with sexual promiscuity would only lead to a greater incidence of committed, monogamous relationships, it also has a converse effect—people choose abstinence or celibacy, immerse themselves in their jobs, and become even more fearful of connecting with another person.

We certainly aren't suggesting that you have an affair or fabricate some means of testing the level of commitment in your relationship. With enough trust in one another, maybe a relationship won't have to be tested. But trusting your relational partner involves some risk—risk that the person may violate your trust and your commitment. Partners have to communicate to decide if the trust and the risk are worth it. It's complicated and, like many other things we've discussed in this text, there are no quick fixes or magic formulas for success.

Secret Tests of a Relationship

We have discussed the notion of a test or crisis that may arise to challenge the level of commitment in a romantic relationship. Not all relationships involve testing, and, as you might guess, most people do not sit down with their partners and say "Okay, it's time to test the relationship." Instead, people may generally give their partners covert tests of commitment and trust, termed *secret tests* by communication researchers Leslie Baxter and William Wilmot (1984). They provide the following seven categories of tests an individual uses to determine the feelings of the other person:

1. *Endurance.* If a partner puts up with "costly" behavior like being criticized or receiving inconvenient requests, then one can assume a commitment to the relationship.
2. *Indirect suggestion.* This includes hints of increased intimacy, such as flirting, to see if the partner responds in kind.
3. *Public presentation.* One partner introduces the other as "my girlfriend/boyfriend" (in Baxter and Wilmot's terms) to see how the other reacts to that label.
4. *Separation.* Two people separate for a while to see if the relationship can take it, although it is not clear which cliché holds most often—"absence makes the heart grow fonder" or "absence makes the heart go wander."
5. *Third-party questioning.* One partner asks his or her friends to find out the other person's feelings.
6. *Triangle tests.* This involves using someone else to make the partner jealous or setting up a situation to see if a partner would give in to temptation.

Baxter and Wilmot (1984) found that women were more likely to use secret tests than men. This finding was most pronounced for separation and triangle tests, leading the researchers to suggest that "the use of tests by females more than by males may reflect their greater relationship monitoring. . . . It is through secret tests that females monitor a relationship's pulse" (p. 197). Similar conclusions about women's behavior in romantic relationships were noted by gender researcher Letitia Peplau (1983). She found that women were more pragmatic in their approaches to courtship and were more likely to analyze or monitor the development of their relationships. In a study conducted by communication scholars Honeycutt, Cantrill, and Greene (1989), women were deemed more attentive to the relational process than men. Women in this study also employed a wider range of actions than men to engage in, test, escalate, and deescalate a romantic relationship.

Bell and Buerkel-Rothfuss (1990) further investigated secret tests; however, they uncovered little support for the argument that women are more active monitors during courtship than men. In fact, they found that "males were more likely to describe their tests as deliberate ones than were females and were more likely to believe that they had acquired a better understanding of their relationships" (p. 79). Bell and Buerkel-Rothfuss also indicated that some people set up tests that their partners cannot fail, particularly in relationships with romantic potential. Thus the research evidence is contradictory on the sexes' use of "secret tests" in romantic relationships. Perhaps testing a relationship has more to do with personality and possibly relational history (meaning a person's relational track record) than with sex or gender. What's your experience with tests in a relationship? Can you recall a time when a relational partner tested your level of involvement? Have you tested someone's commitment or interest level in you? If so, what was the outcome?

Ending a Relationship

We realize that a discussion of this topic can be a downer, but you're probably realistic and experienced enough to know that not all relationships make it. While we may enter a romantic relationship with a "forever and ever" vision in mind, relationships often don't work out as we first imagined. Thus it's wise to consider some effective communication strategies for ending romantic relationships.

Breakups can cause stress and anguish for both persons involved—the understatement of the year! Relational breakups may be better understood by applying social exchange theory (Banks, Altendorf, Greene, & Cody, 1987; Roloff, 1981). If partners see the costs of the relationship as beginning to outweigh its rewards, then the problem may be discussed, the relationship may be terminated, or both. Communication researcher Michael Roloff (1981) contends, "If relationship problems cannot be negotiated over time, a person is likely to dissolve the relationship and eventually enter into another, more rewarding one" (p. 20).

Michael Cody (1982), an interpersonal communication scholar interested in relationship disengagement, identified the following general categories of strategies: *behavioral deescalation,* defined as the avoidance of a relational partner without offering a justification for the behavior; *negative identity management,* which typically is a rude explanation of the desire to end the relationship, one that blames the partner and ignores her or his feelings; *justification,* an in-depth explanation of a partner's reasons for ending the relationship; *deescalation,* an explanation of what will possibly be gained by changing the relationship, one that implies a future relationship of some sort; and *positive tone,* showing concern for the feelings of the partner (the "dumpee"), thus ending the relationship on a somewhat positive note.

Leslie Baxter (1982), a prolific researcher in the area of relationship initiation and termination, offers some insight into how a relational partner chooses to disengage. She contends, "Both relationship closeness and perceived cause of the relationship demise affect the disengager's use of termination strategies" (p. 241). Such issues as what prompted the breakup, the duration of the relationship, how intense the relationship had become, and especially the partners' expectations for future contact affect how one approaches terminating a romantic relationship.

Who is more likely to take the step toward ending a relationship? Communication researchers Rubin, Peplau, and Hill (1981) report that men more often initiate relationships while women more often terminate them. (Maybe this is why so many country and western tunes depict a male "jilted lover.") Findings also indicate that women tend to foresee a breakup sooner than men, but men tend to be more deeply affected by the breakup. This last result is particularly interesting, given the stereotype that suggests that women are more interested in relationships, their self-esteem has a more direct connection to the success of their relationships than men's self-esteem, and that they suffer more than men when a relationship ends. Possibly the stereotype relates more to the difference in the ways men and women express themselves regarding relationships than to an actual value placed on relationships in general.

As we saw in the chapter on friendship, women usually deal with things and make sense of their world by talking. Conversely, men typically deal with things by distracting themselves with activities or by withdrawing and isolating themselves until the situation is resolved. When men do choose to talk out a relational issue such as a breakup, the conversation is typically not as long, deep, detailed, and emotionally displayed as a woman's conversation on the subject. Think about how female friends will talk to each other for hours, either face to face or over the phone, about a relationship. They'll explore what happened, what was said, how it was said, how it made the woman feel, what she thinks she'll do next, and so on. The male equivalent of the breakup aftermath might look like this: A guy learns about his buddy's breakup. He consoles his friend by saying, "Hey, forget about her, man. She's not worth it. Let's go shoot some hoop and have a few beers. I guarantee you'll feel better." This is an overgeneralized example to expose the contrast, but does it sound familiar?

You may be wondering, is there a "personally effective" way to end a romantic relationship? Romantic relationships are so situation- and person-specific that advising an optimum termination strategy would be unwise. However, as we've said time and again, to communicate is better than to not communicate (recall the value "Talking about it makes it better"). From our own experiences and those shared by our students, the worst relationship ending is the "Dear John letter" or it's equivalent, the "silent treatment." Even a screaming match, while traumatic, doesn't seem to carry the same sting of noncommunication or one-sided communication. Being told it's over with no explanation is painful; it leaves no chance for negotiation, no opportunity for the one who gets "terminated" to express her or his feelings. Many people would rather talk it out—even argue it out—than be shut out and left to wonder what went wrong. The wondering will likely plunge a person's self-esteem to a new low in rapid fashion.

So, to conclude this section on relational conclusions, the receiver orientation to communication implies that women and men would do well to think through their breakups, to consider what strategy is best to use—given the person who will be on the receiving end of the upsetting information—and to communicate as sensitively and clearly as possible. Not only is it probable that that kind of communication will lessen the blow to the other person, but it will also keep the "terminator" from feeling like a louse, a "schmuck," or a downright terrible person for hurting someone and communicating poorly.

These tensions in romantic relationships are by no means *all* of the issues relational partners may have to face, but they represent some of the more prominent, common, and troublesome ones examined by research. One remaining issue connected to women and men involved in romantic relationships surrounds the presence of sexual activity—more specifically, how gender communication plays a significant role in a relationship that becomes a sexual one.

GENDER ISSUES SURROUNDING SEXUAL ACTIVITY

At some point in a romantic relationship, the issue of sexual activity will probably make itself known. Then the question becomes—"What do we do about it?" There are a number of answers ranging from "absolutely nothing" to "absolute passion." We're not making any assumptions as to how the question should be answered, for obvious reasons. More important to us is the communication of a clear and mutually agreed-upon decision on the course to take. Sexual activity is an awkward topic to talk about with another person; it may be an especially uncomfortable topic to discuss with your relational partner. It's difficult, in what might be the heat of building passion, to stop and talk about the advisability of advanced sexual activity. Yet you know there are many reasons for doing so, not the least of which is the threat of AIDS and other sexually transmitted diseases (STDs). This section of the chapter focuses on understanding variant attitudes about sexual activity, talking about sex with a relational partner, and developing a broader repertoire of communication behavior in dealing with sexually problematic situations.

Attitudes toward Sexual Activity

In the 1970s, coming off the "free love" tone of the 1960s, sexual decision making was a prominent issue. It still is, though perhaps not for the same reasons. The following commentary by newspaper columnist Ellen Goodman (1979) expressed a particularly thoughtful point of view about sexual decision making at the time, but one that speaks wisdom for current generations:

> There is often a sexual aura between people who genuinely like each other. But there may be a thousand reasons not to turn it into a romance. And reasons make the difference between the urge and the act. I find it sometimes amusing and sometimes sad that we attribute so much more power to the sexual urge than to our own restraint, or to our wider choices. If caution is just as predictable as attraction, friendship may be as valuable an alternative as love. We surely have wider options than segregation or sex. (p. 10A)

In considering your options, it may be helpful to know what some research says about the sexes' attitudes toward sexual activity. Sex-role researcher Antonia Abbey (1982) conducted a study of female and male perceptions of sexual interest. In this study, opposite-sex dyads conversed for 5 minutes while hidden male and female subjects observed the interaction. Results indicated that, in comparison to female observers, male observers more often perceived female friendliness as seduction, made more judgments that female interactants were promiscuous, and frequently reported being sexually attracted to female interactants. Male observers also rated male interactants' behavior as sexual in nature, whereas female observers did not perceive as much sexuality in male subjects' behavior. From these results, Abbey concluded that "men are more likely to perceive the world in sexual terms and to make sexual judgments than women are" (p. 830).

In a study sponsored by the Medical Research Institute of San Francisco, Barbara Critchlow Leigh (1989) explored sex-role stereotypes which suggest that people differ in their reasons for engaging in sexual activity. A random sample of 844 individuals, 76 percent of whom described themselves as heterosexual, 24 percent as homosexual or bisexual, were asked to rate the importance of a variety of reasons for having and avoiding sexual activity. Differences emerged between female and male subjects as well as between sexual orientations. With regard for reasons to have sex, male subjects placed more importance on pleasure, pleasing one's partner, and relieving tension than did female subjects. Women in the study rated the expression of emotional closeness as a more important reason or motivation for having sex than did male subjects. Male-female differences emerging in Leigh's study were consistent across sexual orientations. Gay male subjects reported similar reasons for engaging in sexual activity as did heterosexual men, while lesbians connected sexual activity as closely to love and emotional involvement as did heterosexual women. With regard to reasons to avoid sexual activity, female subjects gave high ratings to such reasons as fear of pregnancy, lack of interest in the partner, and a general lack of enjoyment in sexual acts. Male subjects rated the fear of AIDS and a fear of rejection more highly than did female subjects. These findings led Leigh to conclude the following:

> Men attached more importance than women to sexual pleasure, conquest, and the relief of sexual tension as reasons for sex, while women saw emotional closeness as more important than did men. These sex differences appeared in both heterosexuals and homosexuals, lending credence to the notion that men's and women's motivations for sex are different, no matter what the sex of their partners. (p. 205)

Other research has produced consistent findings regarding sexual orientation and motives for engaging in sexual activity (Basow, 1992; Bell & Weinberg, 1978; Peplau, 1981; Peplau & Gordon, 1983).

In a similar survey about college students' motives and sexual activity, researchers posed this question: "For you, is an emotional involvement a prerequisite for participating in sexual intercourse?" (Carroll, Volk, & Hyde, 1985, p. 135). Results indicated that 85 percent of female subjects in the study, as compared to 40 percent of the male subjects, responded "always" or "most of the time"; 15 percent of the women responded either "sometimes" or "never," compared to 60 percent of the men. The most frequent response from women in this study to the question "What would be your primary reason for refusing to have sexual intercourse with someone?" was "not enough love/commit-ment" (p. 135). The most frequent answer provided by men was "never neglect an opportunity," meaning that they would never refuse to have intercourse (p. 135).

Corroborating findings emerged from a study by gender psychologist Bernard Whitley (1988). He asked college students: "What was your most important reason for having sexual intercourse on the most recent occasion?" (p. 623). In his study, 45 percent of the female subjects compared to 21 percent of the male subjects indicated that love and emotional fulfillment were their primary reasons for engaging in sexual activities. In contrast, 38 percent of the men compared to only 10 percent of the women indicated lust or pleasure reasons. Furthermore, the biological sex of Whitley's subjects was a better predictor of reasons for engaging in sexual activity than psychological gender. In other words, a subject who was androgynous tended to have similar reasons for having sexual intercourse as persons of his or her same sex. The results of these studies and others (DeLamater, 1987; DeLamater & MacCorquodale, 1979; DeLucia, 1987; Hatfield, 1983; Hite, 1976) are epitomized in Leigh's (1989) comment that research findings are "consistent with the notion that the expression of love is a more important motivator of sexual activity in women than in men" (p. 200).

These contemporary research findings suggest male-female differences in both the perception of sexual interest and the motivations for having and

What If?

What if you lived in a country where romantic or dating relationships didn't exist, where the only legally recognized, societally sanctioned relationship between a man and a woman was marriage? *What if* communication about sexual activity, even the use of language to describe sexual genitalia and behavior, was strictly forbidden and constituted a punishable offense in your society? *What if* only husbands were allowed to initiate sexual activity with their wives, and wives who expressed sexual enjoyment ran the risk of being divorced by their husbands, or worse? Given the standards we've become accustomed to in the United States, it's fairly obvious that most of us would not want to live in such a society. You probably realize that this scenario isn't fantasy; there are foreign countries in which relationships between young men and women are not allowed, where marriages are prearranged, where sexual communication of any sort is taboo or even illegal, and where the sexual freedom of men far exceeds that of women. *What if* our sexual, relational rights in this country were suddenly taken away? How would your life be different?

avoiding sexual activity. What can be made of these results? Do the researchers' findings match your experience or the experiences of your friends? Is it your perception that men tend to read more sexuality into things, while women attribute other causes or motivations for what they see? Or do you think that the difference is more a stereotype than a reality? One thing seems obvious to us: Stereotypes or not, given findings that reveal potential differences in women's and men's approaches to sexual activity in their relationships, it seems to be even more critical for relational partners to communicate openly and honestly about sex.

When Women and Men Talk about Sex

Talking about sexual activity represents a proactive approach to what can be a critical turning point in a relationship, although it may be seen by some as taking the romance out of the act or the situation. Some research suggests that the woman's role in sexual "game-playing" has traditionally been to hint or subtly, nonverbally convey to the man whether or not she is sexually interested. Then the man is supposed to "catch the clue" and either abstain from or initiate sexual involvement (Anderson, Schultz, & Staley, 1987; Grauerholz & Serpe, 1985; McCormick & Jesser, 1983; Perper & Weis, 1987). Could it be that this hinting and guessing game in the name of preserving romance causes more problems than it's worth?

A survey by sociologists Knox and Wilson (1981) of the dating and sexual behaviors of more than 300 college students asked: "What do university men and women do to encourage their partners to become more sexually intimate?" (p. 257). One-third of the female and one-fourth of the male subjects responded that they preferred to "be open about sexual desires and expectations" (p. 257). Less direct methods of expressing sexual expectations included "creating an atmosphere" for sexual intimacy, "expressing love," "moving closer to" a partner, and "hinting" (p. 257). These findings suggest that direct, open discussion of sexual activity isn't a first option for many people, but it's becoming a viable option as opposed to the guessing games that can cause misunderstanding. Honest communication appears to be preferable to trying to read each others' minds (and nonverbal cues), expecting sexual activity to be like it is portrayed on television or in the movies, or "taking the plunge" only to discover that one's haste was a real mistake—one that may cost a relationship.

But just how do you approach the topic of sex with someone you're involved with or dating? When we say "approach the topic of sex," we mean having a conversation about sexual activity in a relationship—no matter your views on whether sexual activity outside of marriage is wrong in general, inadvisable for you and a partner, or something that might occur in your relationship. This also involves discussing topics related to sexual activity, such as birth control, monogamy versus multiple partners, and views about protection from sexually transmitted diseases, especially AIDS (Edgar & Fitzpatrick, 1988). But even if you believe that this kind of discussion is important, it doesn't necessarily make the actual talking over of sexual issues any easier. Many of us were raised with the belief that honest discussion about sexual acts was somehow improper, particularly in mixed company. Communication researchers Anderson, Schultz, and Staley (1987) explored some of the issues involved when a woman must become assertive in a sexual situation. They discuss how women are not usually taught or encouraged to talk about sex or to use sexual words in normal conversation; thus their societal conditioning may work against them when they confront the need to be assertive. But they contend that initiating a conversation about sexual activity with one's partner isn't a role expected of one sex more than the other. In other words, it is equally appropriate for the female or the male partner to initiate a discussion of this kind.

Another problem is that our language doesn't provide much help; in fact, it often works against honest, serious discussion (Potorti, 1992). What language can you use in a frank discussion with your partner about sex? Your options are (1) to use clinical, scientific terms, such as "You believe that sexual intercourse and oral sex should be postponed until marriage, but heavy petting of clothed genitalia is okay?"; (2) to use euphemisms that may sound immature or condescending, such as "When I get close to you, my 'thing' reacts"; or (3) to use "gutter" terms for sexual acts and body parts, examples of which you're probably well aware. Many of us are uncomfortable using clinical terms, thinking we'll come off sounding like we're quoting the latest anatomy textbook. Euphemisms can bring about such embarrassment or laughter that the discussion becomes distracted or off-track. Gutter terms don't represent an option that many of us are comfortable with either; they can make sexual activity sound crude and unappealing rather than the way one partner wants it to sound to another. There's no perfect way to talk to a partner about sex and, for now at least, there appears to be no way around the language problems. We encourage you to acknowledge the language limitations with your partner, maybe even to have a good laugh, and then to make the best of it as you work your way through an honest discussion about sexual activity. Defects in the language don't have to become an excuse for avoiding a discussion about sex.

Personal Rights and Sexual Activity

When sexual expectations and desires in a romantic situation differ, when one person's acceptable level of intimacy conflicts with another's so that personal rights are violated, sometimes the damaging consequence is date rape. Date rape (also referred to as friendship or acquaintance rape) is a critical topic in many contexts, especially college campuses. After years of being ignored, attention is now being paid to this very serious societal problem. While a few victims of date rape are male, typically connected with homosexual rape, the victims are predominantly female; thus most of the literature refers to the rapist as "he" and the victim as "she." We will be consistent with this language, given your understanding that date rape victims can be male and that date rape can be homosexual as well as heterosexual victimization. This section of the chapter focuses on how date rape might happen and what might be done to avoid it, from a communication standpoint.

Researchers from the Project on the Status and Education of Women, sponsored by the Association of American Colleges, Jean O'Gorman Hughes and Bernice R. Sandler (1987), describe date rape as "forced, unwanted intercourse with a person you know. It is a violation of your body and your trust" (p. 1). Hughes and Sandler report estimates that more than 90 percent of all rapes go unreported; of those that are reported, about 60 percent of victims know well or are acquainted with the person who raped them. Other information suggests that most women are raped by persons they know and that only one in five rapes are committed by strangers (Gibbs, 1991). In a recent national survey conducted for *Time* magazine, approximately 20 percent of female respondents reported that they had been in a situation with a man where they said no to sexual advances but ended up having sex anyway (Yankelovich Clancy Shulman, 1991). Some of these respondents may have changed their minds, deciding to agree to the sexual activity, but the implication in the survey was that most of them did not consent to sexual intercourse.

Mary Koss, a Kent State University professor, surveyed 7,000 students across 32 American college campuses (Koss, reported in Sweet, 1985). The results of her survey are as follows: (1) One out of every twelve men responding to the survey revealed that they had tried or had actually succeeded in forcing a woman to have sexual intercourse. (2) None of the men who admitted such behavior would call themselves rapists. (3) One in eight women responding to the survey revealed that they were victims of rape. (4) Only a little over half of these rape victims actually called their experiences rape; the other victims revealed a difficulty in acknowledging that their experiences were rapes. This gives you further indication of the magnitude of the problem.

What factors lead to or cause date rape to occur? Hughes and Sandler (1987) explain that no one cause can be ascribed; they contend that "acquaintance rape is not simply a crime of passion, or merely a result of miscommunication. It is, instead, often an attempt to assert power and anger" (p. 2). Some key elements common to the problem include socialization, miscommunication, and changing sexual standards, but Hughes and Sandler emphasize that none of these key elements is in itself, or collectively, a justification for the crime of rape. Regarding socialization, society teaches men to be aggressive and competitive, while women are conditioned to be submissive and to go along, as we explored in Chapter 2. Men are reinforced for expressing and exploring their sexuality, whereas women are often discouraged from having sexual feelings, especially from expressing their sexual desires and openly discussing the limits they want to place on sexual activity. When transferred into a sexual scenario, these stereotypical sex roles resulting from socialization can lead to a power struggle, and the struggle may turn into violence.

Of special interest to our study of gender communication is the miscommunication aspect of Hughes and Sandler's key elements. Many women and men are becoming educated about the problem of date rape. As a result, men are learning not to let their own desires color their interpretation of a woman's nonconsent to sexual activity. And women are learning how important it is to be as clear as possible with their sexual intentions and communication. Given Abbey's (1982) research indicating that men are likely to read sexual intent into a woman's friendly behavior, being clear with one's verbal and nonverbal communication becomes even more important. Some men have been taught— either directly or from subtle media messages—to try to turn a woman's "no" into a "yes." However, many men are "unlearning" that outdated information; they are learning to interpret a woman's "no" as actually meaning "no." Granted, some women still give mixed messages about sexual activity, saying "no" when their actions say "yes," or feigning resistance to sexual overtures in an effort to tease a man they want to have sex with (Muehlenhard & Hollabaugh, 1988). Women may also send mixed signals for fear that, if they agree to sex too easily, they'll be seen as "loose" or "slutty." They may even avoid discussing sex for the same reason, worried that a frank discussion of sexual decisions will make them appear too overt about sex or as though they have "been around." As Hughes and Sandler advocate, the best approach for women is to say "no" when they mean "no" and "yes" when they mean "yes"—that is, to avoid game playing and pretense in a romantic or sexual situation. For men, their advice is to take a woman's "no" at face value, assuming that "no" really does mean "no"—no questions asked or disagreement voiced. Any actions beyond the woman's "no" are sexual violations, and intercourse without agreement or consent is rape. This may seem like an overstatement to you, but everything you've learned about gender communication and personal effectiveness from this text applies with even more urgency to this situation of negotiating sexual waters with a relational partner. The principles behind the receiver orientation to communication, as well as the necessity of expanding one's repertoire of communication to enable alternatives for confronting different situations, are highly applicable and useful in sexual contexts.

Several researchers contend that sexual standards have loosened in past decades and that this factor may contribute to the crime of date rape (Hughes & Sandler, 1987; Koss & Leonard, 1984; Malamuth, Haber, & Feshbach, 1980). Changing sexual standards may lead some college-aged men to expect sex from women, almost as a given or a reward for having dated someone a few times. Some men believe that they are entitled to sex when they have spent money on a date, that somehow sex and money are an even exchange. A man may even believe that if a woman is sexually active by reputation, she will willingly have sex with anyone, including him. Perhaps when faced with the realization that sex isn't an eventuality to a date, a man may become enraged or despondent, turning that rage onto the woman. Changing sexual standards may contribute to the problem, but they don't work to explain or justify date rape.

As we indicated earlier, none of these elements—socialization, miscommunication, changing standards—is itself a reasonable cause or a justification for date rape. There is no justification for date rape, since it is a violation of a person's basic human rights. As Hughes and Sandler explain, "Rape is violence.

It strikes at the heart of the personal relationship between a man and a woman, how they treat each other, and how they respect each other's wishes" (p. 2). Respect for another's wishes is key; respect is a critical element that open sexual communication helps to protect and that date rape violates. It is highly advisable for partners in romantic relationships to engage in clear communication of their sexual desires, attitudes, and expectations; both need to be ready to abide by the wishes of the person who wants to slow down, stop, or not start at all.

Hughes and Sandler offer useful guidelines to help minimize the possibility of date rape. Their advice is designed with the female reader in mind; however, men need to understand these points, being aware that these behaviors may not come easily for some women. Some of their suggestions are as follows:

1. Examine your feelings about sex.
2. Set sexual limits for yourself and your partner or date.
3. Decide early if you would like to have sex. (Communicate your decision clearly and firmly.)
4. Do not give mixed messages; be alert to other unconscious messages you may be giving.
5. Be forceful and firm; don't worry about being polite.
6. Be independent and aware, meaning that you can have input on dates as to where you'd like to go, what you think is appropriate, and so on.
7. Do not do anything you do not want to just to avoid a scene or unpleasantness.
8. Be aware of specific situations in which you do not feel relaxed or in charge.
9. If things start to get out of hand, protest loudly, leave, or go for help.
10. Realize that drugs and alcohol are often present in date rape situations. (adapted from Hughes & Sandler, 1987, p. 3)

One should not get the perception that Hughes and Sandler believe that date rape is up to women to prevent or avoid; they encourage men to carefully examine their own behavior, suggesting that "real men accept the responsibility to not harm another person" (p. 4). Their advice for men includes the following:

1. Rape is a crime of violence; it is illegal. It is *never* okay to force yourself on a woman, even if she teases you, dresses provocatively, leads you on, is under the influence of a substance, or if you've had sex with her before or know of someone who has.
2. Communicate your sexual desires honestly and as early as possible.
3. If you have any doubts about what your partner/date wants, stop, ask, and clarify her answer.
4. If you think you are getting mixed messages, ask your partner/date what she wants. If she is unsure of what she wants, back off and try to talk about it.
5. Do not assume that a desire for affection is the same as a desire for sexual intercourse.

6. You may not be able to control your *desires*, but you can control your *actions*.
7. Your own intoxication or high is not a legal excuse or a defense to an accusation of rape. Sober or not, you are responsible for your actions.
8. Not having sex on a date—not "scoring"—doesn't mean you are not a "real man." (adapted from Hughes & Sandler, 1987, p. 4)

Obviously, each sex needs to become more aware of the problem. Men need to understand what date rape is, how it occurs, and that they are responsible for their own behavior. Women need to be aware of what date rape is, how it occurs, and what they can do to lessen the likelihood of it happening to them. As Hughes and Sandler explain, date rape is "a problem that concerns all men and all women because it deals with the basic issue of the ways in which men and women relate to each other" (p. 7).

CONCLUSION

Romance, sex, love, acceptance, autonomy, change, monogamy, commitment, respect—these are just some of the integral issues within a romantic relationship. While issues surrounding romance aren't particularly easy to write or talk about, they're easier to talk about than to negotiate in an actual relationship. Your own experience, the experiences of your friends, and what we've described in this chapter are enough to reemphasize for you the considerable complexities inherent in romantic relationships. It may sound simple, for example, to read about negotiating a balance between one's sense of independence apart from the relationship and the time spent together. However, when you actually confront that first discussion and witness the hurt as a result of one partner's assertion of independence, that's a much harder, more complex "tension" to manage. It's easy to give lip service to the "I love you for what you are; I'll never want to change you" attitude, but what happens when you really, honestly think that your way is better? It seems, though, that even an understanding of the complexity involved in these kinds of relationships isn't enough to scare us away from romance. When it's going well, when it's "right," hardly anything is comparable.

As we advocated in earlier chapters, we continue to suggest that communicating is preferable to *not* communicating. Most of us function better with information, rather than feeling we've been "cut out of the loop," and romantic partners need just as much information as family members, coworkers, or friends. It's fairly safe to say that an expanded communication repertoire and a willingness to openly communicate in a non–sex-role stereotypical fashion with one's partner or date is a more successful way to approach romantic relationships than the reverse. This approach doesn't mean that you'll be successful every time, because you know that there are no guarantees, especially in the romantic context. But, given the chances that your relationship success ratio could improve, it's probably well worth it to attempt to expand the range of your gender communication in this unique context.

Key Terms

romantic relationship	commitmentphobia	sexually transmitted
relational partner	promiscuity	diseases (STDs)
significant other	monogamy	game playing
tensions	secret tests	date or acquaintance rape
autonomy	abstinence	socialization
connection	celibacy	miscommunication
acceptance	relationship monitoring	sexual standards
change	relationship termination	
commitment	sexual activity	

Discussion Starters

1. Consider the language that is used to refer to special people in our lives. How did you refer to the person in your first romantic relationship, like the first boy or girl you really liked in a different way from the rest? How did those references change as you grew up and experienced different types of relationships? Do you think there is a weakness in our language when it comes to references for relational partners? Does the term *relational partner* work for you, or can you suggest a better term?

2. Think of an example—in your own life or the life of someone close to you—that epitomizes the "tension" of autonomy versus connection. If you are married, was it difficult when you and your spouse experienced that first rift of independence? Did it happen while you were dating, or after you got married? Have you seen this issue arise for other married couples? How did they handle it? How did you and your spouse handle it? Do you think this issue is more easily negotiated among marital partners or persons who are only steadily dating?

3. Review the information in this chapter on "commitmentphobia." Did this information change your views regarding commitment and the sexes? Is it your current opinion that men are generally more fearful of commitment in a romantic relationship than women, or the reverse, or neither? Could it be that commitmentphobia has more to do with personality variables and family background, for instance, than with sex or gender?

4. Think of a time when someone tested you or your relationship. Was the test a major event or crisis, such as unfaithfulness or dishonesty? Or was it more of a "secret test," the more subtle way of finding out how your partner feels about you, as we described in this chapter? How did you respond to the test?

5. Imagine that you are currently in a romantic relationship. (If you *are* in one, just use your own relationship for the example.) The relationship has the usual ups and downs, but generally things are going fairly well. Now imagine that your relational partner is breaking up with you—it's terrible, we know, but it might be wise to think about this. How would you prefer that your partner terminate the relationship? Do you prefer an impersonal phone call or letter, so that you don't have the embarrassment of losing face or getting upset? Would you prefer a rational, open, face-to-face discussion about the breakup? Or a shouting match, so that each person could express

his or her views and emotions without restraint? How do you respond to the old "I still want to be friends" line? What's the best way for bad news to be communicated to you?

6. Do you think that "negotiating the sexual waters" with a relational partner is a difficult communication challenge? If so, why is it that women and men may have difficulty openly discussing sexual activity in their relationship? What are the barriers to a successful discussion of this kind? If you don't think that this sort of communication is problematic, how have you avoided the difficulty?

References

ABBEY, A. (1982). Sex differences in attributions for friendly behavior: Do males misperceive females' friendliness? *Journal of Personality and Social Psychology, 42,* 830–838.

ANDERSON, J., SCHULTZ, B., & STALEY, C. C. (1987). Training in argumentativeness: New hope for nonassertive women. *Women's Studies in Communication, 10,* 58–66.

ARLISS, L. P. (1993). When myths endure and realities change: Communication in romantic relationships. In L. P. Arliss & D. J. Borisoff (Eds.), *Women and men communicating: Challenges and changes* (pp. 71–85). Fort Worth, TX: Harcourt Brace Jovanovich.

AVERY, C. S. (1989, May). How do you build intimacy? *Psychology Today,* pp. 27–31.

BABER, K. M., & MONAGHAN, P. (1988). College women's career and motherhood expectations: New options, old dilemmas. *Sex Roles, 19,* 189–203.

BANKS, S., ALTENDORF, D., GREENE, J., & CODY, M. (1987). An examination of relationship disengagement: Perceptions, breakup strategies and outcomes. *Western Journal of Speech Communication, 51,* 19–41.

BASOW, S. A. (1992). *Gender: Stereotypes and roles* (3rd ed.). Pacific Grove, CA: Brooks/Cole.

BAXTER, L. A. (1982). Strategies for ending relationships: Two studies. *Western Journal of Speech Communication, 46,* 223–241.

BAXTER, L. A. (1988). A dialectical perspective on communication strategies in relationship development. In S. Duck (Ed.), *Handbook of personal relationships: Theory, research and interventions* (pp. 257–273). New York: John Wiley & Sons.

BAXTER, L. A., & WILMOT, W. W. (1984). "Secret tests": Social strategies for acquiring information about the state of the relationship. *Human Communication Research, 11,* 171–201.

BELL, A. P., & WEINBERG, M. S. (1978). *Homosexualities: A study of diversity among men and women.* New York: Simon & Schuster.

BELL, R. A., & BUERKEL-ROTHFUSS, N. L. (1990). S(he) loves me, s(he) loves me not: Predictors of relational information-seeking in courtship and beyond. *Communication Quarterly, 38,* 64–82.

BURIRKE, R. A., & FUQUA, D. R. (1987). Sex differences in same- and cross-sex supportive relationships. *Sex Roles, 17,* 339–351.

CARROLL, J. L., VOLK, K. D., & HYDE, J. S. (1985). Differences between males and females in motives for engaging in sexual intercourse. *Archives of Sexual Behavior, 14,* 131–139.

CLINE, R. J., & MUSOLF, K. E. (1985). Disclosure as social exchange: Anticipated length of relationship, sex roles, and disclosure intimacy. *Western Journal of Speech Communication, 49,* 43–56.

CODY, M. (1982). A typology of disengagement strategies and an examination of the role intimacy, reactions to inequity and relational problems play in strategy selection. *Communication Monographs, 49,* 148–170.

DELAMATER, J. (1987). Gender differences in sexual scenarios. In K. Kelly (Ed.), *Females, males, and sexuality.* Albany, NY: SUNY Press.

DELAMATER, J., & MACCORQUODALE, P. (1979). *Premarital sexuality: Attitudes, relationships, behaviors.* Madison: University of Wisconsin Press.

DELUCIA, J. L. (1987). Gender role identity and dating behavior: What is the relationship? *Sex Roles, 17,* 153–161.

DORMEN, L. (1990, October). Healthy love: How nineties couples create it. *Glamour,* pp. 270–271, 310–311.

DUCK, S. (1988). *Relating to others.* Chicago: Dorsey Press.

EDGAR, T., & FITZPATRICK, M. A. (1988). Compliance-gaining in relational interaction: When your life depends on it. *Southern Speech Communication Journal, 53,* 385–405.

GALVIN, K. (1993). First marriage families: Gender and communication. In L. P. Arliss & D. J. Borisoff (Eds.), *Women and men communicating: Challenges and changes* (pp. 86–101). Fort Worth, TX: Harcourt Brace Jovanovich.

GIBBS, N. (1991, June 3). When is it rape? *Time,* pp. 48–54.

GOLDSMITH, D. (1990). A dialectic perspective on the expression of autonomy and connection in romantic relationships. *Western Journal of Speech Communication, 54,* 537–556.

GOODMAN, E. (1979, May 20). Mork and Mindy are just pals. *The Utica Observer Dispatch,* p. 9A.

GRAUERHOLZ, E., & SERPE, R. T. (1985). Initiation and response: The dynamics of sexual interaction. *Sex Roles, 12,* 1041–1059.

GREEN, S. K., & SANDOS, P. (1983). Perceptions of male and female initiators of relationships. *Sex Roles, 9,* 619–638.

HATFIELD, E. (1983). What do women and men want from love and sex? In E. R. Allgeier & N. B. McCormick (Eds.), *Changing boundaries: Gender roles and sexual behavior.* Palo Alto, CA: Mayfield.

HITE, S. (1976). *The Hite report.* New York: Macmillan.

HOLLANDSWORTH, S. (1991, September). Why I didn't call. *Madamoiselle,* p. 130.

HONEYCUTT, J. M., CANTRILL, J. G., & GREENE, R. W. (1989). Memory structures for relational escalation: A cognitive test of the sequencing of relational actions and stages. *Human Communication Research, 16,* 62–90.

HUGHES, J. O., & SANDLER, B. R. (1987). *"Friends" raping friends: Could it happen to you?* Project on the Status and Education of Women. Washington, DC: Association of American Colleges.

KENRICK, D. T., SADALLA, E. K., GROTH, G., & TROST, M. R. (1990). Courtship: Qualifying the parental investment model. *Journal of Personality, 58,* 97–115.

KNOX, D., & WILSON, K. (1981). Dating behaviors of university students. *Family Relations, 30,* 255–258.

KOSS, M. F., & LEONARD, K. E. (1984). Sexually aggressive men: Empirical findings and theoretical implications. In N. M. Malamuth & E. Donnerstein (Eds.), *Pornography and sexual aggression* (pp. 213–232). Orlando, FL: Academic Press.

LEIGH, B.C. (1989). Reasons for having and avoiding sex: Gender, sexual orientation, and relationship to sexual behavior. *Journal of Sex Research, 26,* 199–209.

MALAMUTH, N. M., HABER, S., & FESHBACH, S. (1980). Testing hypotheses regarding rape: Exposure to sexual violence, sex differences, and the "normality" of rapists. *Journal of Research in Personality, 14,* 121–137.

MCCORMICK, N. B., & JESSER, J. C. (1983). The courtship game: Power in the sexual encounter. In E. R. Allgeier & N. B. McCormick (Eds.), *Changing boundaries: Gender roles and sexual behavior* (pp. 64–86). Palo Alto, CA: Mayfield.

MCKINNEY, K. (1987). Age and gender differences in college students' attitudes toward women: A replication and extension. *Sex Roles, 17,* 353–358.

MEERLOO, J. A. (1952). *Conversation and communication.* New York: International Universities Press.

MUEHLENHARD, C. L., & HOLLABAUGH, L. C. (1988). Do women sometimes say no when they mean yes? The prevalence and correlates of women's token resistance to sex. *Journal of Personality and Social Psychology, 54,* 872–879.

OWEN, W. F. (1987). The verbal expression of love by women and men as a critical communication event in personal relationships. *Women's Studies in Communication, 10,* 15–24.

PEPLAU, L. A. (1981). What homosexuals want in relationships. *Psychology Today, 15,* 28–37.

PEPLAU, L. A. (1983). Roles and gender. In H. H. Kelley (Ed.), *Close relationships.* San Francisco: W. H. Freeman.

PEPLAU, L. A., & GORDON, S. L. (1983). The intimate relationships of lesbians and gay men. In E. R. Allgeier & N. B. McCormick (Eds.), *Changing boundaries: Gender roles and sexual behavior.* Palo Alto, CA: Mayfield.

PERPER, T., & WEIS, D. L. (1987). Proceptive and rejective strategies of U.S. and Canadian college women. *Journal of Sex Research, 23,* 455–480.

POTORTI, P. (1992, October). Guest lecture, North Carolina State University, Raleigh.

RAWLINS, W. (1982). Negotiating close friendship: The dialectic of conjunctive freedom. *Human Communication Research, 9,* 255–266.

ROLOFF, M. E. (1981). *Interpersonal communication: The exchange approach.* Beverly Hills, CA: Sage.

RUBIN, A. M., PEPLAU, L. A., & HILL, C. T. (1981). Loving and leaving: Sex differences in romantic attachments. *Sex Roles, 7,* 821–835.

SCHNALL, M. (1981, May). Commitmentphobia. *Savvy,* pp. 37–41.

SWEET, E. (1985, October). Date rape: The story of an epidemic and those who deny it. *Ms. Magazine,* p. 56.

WHITLEY, B. E., JR. (1988). The relation of gender-role orientation to sexual experience among college students. *Sex Roles, 19,* 619–638.

YANKELOVICH CLANCY SHULMAN. (1991, June 3). Would you classify the following as rape or not? *Time,* p. 50.

CHAPTER 10

And They Lived Happily Ever After . . . :
Gender Communication in Marital and Family Contexts

Marriage and families—here are two complicated topics! Complicated, fascinating, maddening, sometimes profound—marriage and families form the primary relationships of your life. Imagine that you have an acute awareness of marital and family relationships, a keen sense of gender similarities and differences, and an excitement and enthusiasm to make these relationships successful. Doesn't that sound useful? That's what this chapter is about.

CASE STUDY

Beth and Tom got married last summer. They had been going together for about three years, and during that time they shared interests in backpacking, water sports, and gourmet coffee. Beth is employed as a public relations director for a city museum, and Tom manages a retail paint store. Both are self-assured, independent people with ambitions of moving up in their careers. They don't consider themselves "liberated," but both have an unquestioned acceptance of the need for gender equality in the workplace.

After they got married, Beth found herself coming home from work to Tom, who was reading the paper and watching the news while waiting for dinner to be cooked. And Beth found herself cooking it! Pretty soon Tom was watching football on the weekends, fixing the car, and not helping with the housework. Beth was doing the cooking and cleaning along with her full-time career. One day it hit Beth: "I'm turning into my mother! And Tom's helping!"

Beth and Tom's situation is not at all unusual. In spite of tremendous gains in many areas of life, work, recreation, education, and even politics, tradition seems to hold fast within most marriages. The pull of traditional role expectations has a powerful influence on many marriages. People who consider themselves highly liberated often undergo a metamorphosis when married. Many individuals are met head-on by a large dose of old-fashioned reality. The philosopher Goethe foresaw Tom and Beth's situation aptly when he said, "Love is an ideal thing; marriage is a real thing." And with that reality comes all the excess baggage of a first family, with its role models. As Tom said at one point, "I understand that things are supposed to be different in today's relationships, but still I can't help feeling that husbands are supposed to do some things and wives something else. Maybe I was born 100 years too late."

Was he? Or were Beth and Tom responding more to a complicated series of conflicting messages: "Be liberated." "Look out for number 1." "Put your spouse's needs first." "You can have it all." "Be a man." These and many similar contradictory messages make it very difficult to know what to do. What is a marriage supposed to be? What kind of gender communication makes marriage go more smoothly? What are families supposed to be like? How are the changes in gender roles to be handled? Like Tom and Beth, you may find yourself in a marriage or family and notice that you're acting just like your parents, doing some of the things you swore you'd never do. If this or the fear of this sounds familiar, read on. This chapter focuses on how effective gender communication will help increase the success of your marital and family relationships.

OVERVIEW

In a way, you are very fortunate, for you can choose many things in this life. For example, you chose to take this class and read this book. But you couldn't choose the family into which you were born. Your first family had a great deal to do with creating who you are now, and you in turn have an opportunity to participate in the creation of another family. What kind of family might you create (traditional or not), and how will you go about this challenging task? For better or worse, your first family had a powerful effect on the person you are today. But what about your next family? You can choose your mate; you can choose how to communicate with him or her. You can choose some aspects of your next family, such as the number of children you might have, where you will live, and what kind of life-style you will have. You can also choose to learn techniques and strategies that will make communication more effective in that family. You can choose to establish communication patterns in your marriage and family that are more likely to lead to increased satisfaction, commitment, and stability.

Throughout this book we attempt to increase your awareness of the gender influences on your communication. As we have said many times, it's important to understand yourself and your communication behavior more fully. We want you to understand both sexes' communication tendencies more completely. By gaining this understanding, you will be more aware of how you are influenced by gender, and, in turn, how you can gain more control over your communication behavior as you become more personally effective.

Such awareness and understanding are crucial to gender communication within a marriage and family. Probably nothing has a stronger influence on the kind of person you are than your family. No single relationship is likely to be more important than the one with your spouse. Certainly few responsibilities are greater than raising children. Yet so many people go into marriage and parenthood with little more than romantic dreams and good intentions. They feel that if and when they find the right person, they will live happily ever after. That may happen in fairy tales, but not too often in real life. Here is what Carl Rogers had to say about contemporary marriages:

> Though modern marriage is a tremendous laboratory, its members are often utterly without preparation for the partnership function. How much agony and remorse and failure could have been avoided if there had been at least some rudimentary learning before they entered the partnership. (Quoted in Buscaglia, 1986, p. 28)

All the good intentions and dreams of happily ever after, without some of the awareness, understanding, and strategies we are discussing, can lead to shattered dreams, broken lives, and a fruitless reliving of past relationships.

We're not saying that the traditions of this society regarding marriage and the family are wrong. But they can be restrictive, and often they reinforce negative aspects of traditional gender roles. In complicated times, as these clearly are, simplistic, vague notions of marriage are inadequate. Effective marital and family relationships take significant amounts of time and energy. As all of us have seen so pointedly time and time again, successful relationships don't just happen—they are created.

Since literally hundreds of books and thousands of articles representing many different perspectives on communication within a marriage and/or the family have been written, we cannot possibly hope to review them all. Our focus is on gender communication, how it is shaped, and how it shapes you within the particularly powerful contexts of marriage and family. As we continue this chapter we concentrate on:

- Describing the changing face of marriage and family
- Developing effective communication patterns within this context
- Understanding the role of power and empowerment in marriage and families
- Moving toward intimacy through effective gender communication

INTRODUCTION

Do you think you will get married? Will you have a family? An informal class survey might indicate your classmates' intentions. Ask the ones who say "no" to getting married how they feel about making that opinion public. Do they feel shy about expressing it? A little defensive? Like they aren't doing the "right" thing? There is a very strong cultural push to be married and to raise a family. As we describe in this chapter, that pressure seems to be increasing. Some statistics say that in spite of the alternatives to marriage (living together, remaining single, communal living, etc.) between 90 and 95 percent of all Americans will get married (Fitzpatrick, 1988). Yet other statistics, reported from new U. S. Census Bureau figures, note that almost one in four U.S. adults have not yet strolled down the aisle into matrimony. These census statistics indicate that people are waiting longer to get married, but they are likely to eventually marry.

These numbers only tell part of the story. What other trends are there in marriage and family? Our culture has held the nuclear family as the ideal for quite a long time. This is the family of June and Ward Cleaver—working father, housewife mother, and two or more school-aged children. In 1955 this model represented 60 percent of all families; now it represents 7 percent (Otto, 1988, cited in Galvin & Brommel, 1991). This change has had a profound effect on this nation's children. Otto reports some disturbing statistics on these effects. Based on 1985 statistics, he estimates that of every 100 children born today:

12 are born out of wedlock

41 are born to parents who divorce before the child is age 18

5 are born to parents who separate

2 will experience the death of a parent before they reach age 18

41 will reach age 18 without such incidents (p. 7)

Population statistics show profound changes over the past 20 years in areas such as the number of women in the work force, the number of divorces, the number of children living with only one parent, the number of alternative life-style arrangements (being single, communal living, etc.), the number of same-sex households, and the ethnic composition of American families. This increased diversity has had a significant impact on American family life (Richmond-Abbott, 1992). Let's look more closely at just one part of those statistics and discuss it in light of sex differences and the effects of traditional gender roles.

There are more women than ever in the work force. However, most women seem to become employed for economic rather than career reasons. Dual-earner marriages (where both partners work out of economic necessity) outnumber dual-career marriages (where both partners work primarily for personal satisfaction) ten to one. These dual-earner marriages tend to be more traditional in their gender roles at home. Family researcher Yogev (1987) found that despite the nontraditional behavior of a dual-career couple, marital satisfaction in these relationships is often related to the perception that spouses fit sex- or gender-role stereotypes. A significant percentage of both husbands and wives report more satisfaction if the husband is seen as more intelligent, competent, and of higher professional status than his wife. In these marriages, husbands tend to be poor at expressing themselves and at nurturing, and often they do not sufficiently acknowledge and support working wives (Fitzpatrick & Indvik, 1982). Again, in spite of changes, it appears that the traditional model is still exerting a strong pull over today's marriages and families.

This societal pressure led author Gerri Hirshey (1989) to describe what she calls the "tyranny of the couple." Not only is marriage still "in"; it is hip, the thing to do. She calls it "commitment obsession" (p. 49). Couples argue that they are doing what comes naturally, two by two. But, she says that this attitude is hard on singles. Couples become so self-involved, so centered on each other, that single friends are just left out. She refers to a 1986 *Newsweek* article that said a single woman over 40 was as likely to get killed by a terrorist as she was to get married. (The data were in error, as pointed out by Susan Faludi, 1992.) Hirshey goes on to make a joke of the situation, as in "Question: How does a single woman get rid of roaches in her apartment? Answer: She asks them for a commitment" (p. 49). After a period in the 1970s when other life-styles became acceptable alternatives to marriage, the culture now seems to be struggling back to the traditional model. "Lifestyle apologists defend retro tendencies under the rubric of 'The New Traditionalism'" (Hirshey, 1989, p. 53). Divorce rates have leveled off and even dropped in some areas. Hirshey sees a "widening gulf between the haves and have nots, and a creeping conservatism in social options" (p. 53). It's all wrapped up in one question: "So how come you're still single?"

This strong pressure toward "coupleness" comes at a time when the basic nuclear family makes up only a small percentage of U.S. households. The chances are better than 50-50 that you will find yourself, at one point in your life, living alone, divorced, and/or as a stepparent. This tension between the reality of relationships and the culture's increasingly intense desire to impose the goal of coupleness can be demoralizing.

At the same time that there is increasing pressure to be coupled, society has also removed some of the reasons for staying together in a marriage that once kept many couples married. Thirty years ago, there was a strong social norm that prohibited breakups, a divorce was legally difficult to obtain, and divorced people were viewed negatively by almost everyone. This clearly has changed. One small piece of evidence of this change was contained in the marriage vows of a televised wedding. The presiding minister, in performing the ceremony, uttered the line ". . . as long as you both shall *love*," using the word *love* rather than the traditional *line*. This shift of just one letter creates an entirely different set of expectations.

In the absence of external forces keeping the relationship together, couples have looked inward for relationship justification, for appreciation and companionship, and for emotional gratification. Marriage researchers Fitzpatrick and Badinski (1985) report that as more pressure is placed on internal factors, couples watch the "pulse of the relationship" and "such pulse watching leads to increased insecurity" (p. 704). This increased introspection can cause increased uncertainty, which may lead to less stability. The sexual stereotype suggests that the female partner will be the one who worries more about the relationship. However, as we describe shortly, this isn't always the case. Analysis through

What If?

What if everyone had to start from scratch? *What if,* one morning, everyone forgot all they had ever learned about sex roles in marital relationships and in parenting? *What if* we had to create it all again? This is an interesting thought. Obviously, this won't happen, but think for a while about what might be created in place of what exists. How would you structure patterns in relationships? How would you design power and decision-making patterns in families? What would you design as sex-role education for children? What instructions would you give parents? Spend some time discussing this with members of your own sex and of the other sex. What agreement do you find? What are some areas of disagreement? What is important? What is trivial? Think of the possibilities; think of the problems. *What if* everyone had to start from scratch?

introspection may be increasing, but that doesn't appear to lead necessarily to less satisfaction (Turner, 1990).

Given the possibility that you will enter a long-term relationship such as a marriage, what does it take to succeed? How can you increase your chances of reaping the benefits and avoiding the pitfalls? We certainly don't have all the answers, but we would like to explore some research, share some stories we have heard, and describe the experiences we have personally participated in, regarding both marriage and family relationships. Of the many communication and gender variables to consider, we have chosen to focus on three and apply each to marriage and to family communication. First, we examine the role of *communication patterns* in these two types of relationships. Effective communication patterns support positive interactions and outcomes in each context. Second, in keeping with a theme we have discussed throughout this text, we discuss the role of *power and empowerment* in communication. Last, we revisit the concept of *intimacy* as it relates to interaction and the development of closeness.

MARRIAGE AND GENDER COMMUNICATION

The face of marriage in the United States constantly changes. Various population statistics report change in the average age people get married; change in the longevity of marriages; alterations in the chances of divorce; increasing complexity with long-distance relationships; changes in sex-role expectations; increases in dual-career and dual-earner relationships; and fluctuations in economic factors that impinge on a couple once they say "I do." Since many of our readers are likely to get married (if they haven't already done so), we can safely assume that most of you want your marriage to succeed not only in length of time but in the quality of its communication and the satisfaction you derive from it.

It is not our goal here to review all of the material available on the subject of marital communication. Instead, we explore three points that provide a focus for discussing gender and sex roles in marriage, a springboard for learning about improving marital communication, and a means of developing a wider repertoire of communication behaviors for both sexes that leads to greater personal effectiveness.

Patterns in Marriage

First of all, just what are patterns? Pearson (1989) defines patterns as "predictable and manageable sets of behaviors that are unique to the family and are distinctive from any one family member's own actions" (p. 34). Every relationship develops its own patterns. Most of the time these patterns seem to develop on their own, formed by general societal rules and norms or by the individual's needs and desires. For the most part, people in relationships don't sit down together and say, "Let's work out our pattern of communication." You've probably noticed, however, that in more than one place in this text we have advocated exactly that. We believe that "talking about it makes it better" and that couples need to hold periodic conversations about aspects of their relationship. The sooner in the relationship this is done, the more likely it is that the patterns will be formed purposefully rather than by accident. Talking about your relationship may seem forced and contrived at the onset, but persevere with patience and enthusiasm.

Why Examine Patterns?

In the previous section of this chapter, we referred to research that suggested increased introspection could lead to increased uncertainty. And as we discussed at other points in this text, individuals who feel uncertain about their relationship will do whatever they can to reduce that uncertainty. One clear way to reduce uncertainty is to develop routine communication (Berger & Calabrese, 1975). Routines help lend predictability to a situation, and the predictability breeds security. Perhaps this explains, to an extent, why some people seem to prefer the more traditional view of marriage—it is more predictable.

Security through predictability, however, can be achieved through means beyond jumping on the traditional marriage bandwagon. As you might guess, it involves developing patterns for your own relationship that support the kind of communication and relationship you want to achieve and maintain. Moreover, it involves time, energy, and a desire for a successful marriage. We're reminded of a couple, Diane and Ken, who are nearing their golden anniversary. From the time of their honeymoon, into diapers, and through their children's teen years, Ken and Diane have had a weekly date. Sometimes it has been simply a cup of tea late at night after the chores are done and the kids are in bed; sometimes it's planning and working together on a household project; other dates might actually involve a weekend getaway for just the two of them. What is important is that these weekly dates are as regular as clockwork. Ken and

Diane take the time to establish priorities in their relationship. They talk and listen to each other. Sometimes the discussions are heated, and sometimes they are tender. But they always happen. These weekly dates have become a predictable pattern for both Diane and Ken, one that has created a strong sense of security and reduced a great degree of uncertainty in their longstanding marriage.

One researcher wanted to know if sex differences exist regarding uncertainty in marriages. Communication scholar Lynn Turner (1990) hypothesized that women, because they think more about relationships, would report higher levels of uncertainty in a marriage, whereas men, who traditionally spend less time thinking about relationships, would report more satisfaction. The research showed the opposite. Women reported a slightly higher level of satisfaction with the relationship than the men did. It would appear that sex differences in uncertainty do not have a differential effect on the perception of the relationship. The important point seems to be the ability to consciously talk about the relationship.

The Relationship of Patterns to Reported Satisfaction

Assuming you are convinced of the need to talk about and develop your own communication patterns with your marriage partner, what kind of patterns do communication researchers say you might try to develop? Dainton, Stafford, and McNeilis (1992) explored the question of what kinds of routine patterns of behavior were related to satisfaction. They found that sharing tasks (such as housework); keeping everyday interactions pleasant and positive; maintaining a high mutual level of self-disclosure and assurances of worth and love; and sharing time together are important to satisfaction and to relationship maintenance. In similar research, psychologists Yogev and Brett (1985) found that both husbands and wives report greater marital satisfaction when they share home and child-rearing responsibilities equally. These research results do not fit the traditional model of marriages in that they suggest a higher level of involvement of men in the relationship through increased disclosure, the sharing of responsibilities, and positive relational comments.

In other research, happily married couples appear to be more flexible in their communication patterns with each other than they are with other people. Their patterns with each other are more relaxed, open, friendly, dramatic, and attentive (Honeycutt, Wilson, & Parker, 1982). They listen more; they talk less. Certainly, these are important ingredients in a satisfactory relationship. According to Lauer and Lauer (1985), 350 couples who claimed to be satisfied with their marriages tended to find mutual satisfaction in and agreed with such statements as "my spouse is my best friend"; "I like my spouse as a person"; "marriage is a long-term commitment"; "marriage is sacred"; "we agree on aims and goals"; "my spouse has grown more interesting"; and "I want the relationship to succeed" (p. 5). Although statements like these are usually thought to stem from the female partner, it is clear that both partners need to believe and state them equally. It's not an exaggeration to say that without healthy communication patterns that include some kind of regular talking about each other and the relationship (including subjects like those in the preceding statements), this kind of mutual satisfaction would simply not exist.

And for many couples, perhaps it doesn't exist. Communication scholar Mary Anne Fitzpatrick (1988) observed that researchers have consistently found low correlations between husbands' and wives' judgments of marital satisfaction. Perhaps the two people in the marriage experience it differently because satisfaction, like a successful marriage, is never guaranteed (Bernard, 1972). However, statements like those listed above can lead to increased clarity of feelings of satisfaction. Achieving satisfaction in a relationship is an ongoing process, for in most relationships each partner has a personal agenda to ensure satisfaction. For instance, satisfaction, at least for some women, is related to their ability to meet and exceed the role expectations expressed to them by their spouses (Petronio, 1982). And it would probably be safe to say that at least an equal number of women would find little if any satisfaction with this kind of a marriage pattern. As we described elsewhere, both sexes tend to report more satisfaction in marriages where equality is the pattern. Communicating in a way that allows each partner to share their basis of satisfaction appears to be helpful. The factors that bring you satisfaction must be talked about with your partner, for few of us are mind readers. The ability to talk it over, and to adapt messages to your partner's individual beliefs and needs, not only fits with a value we mentioned in this text (treat the other person as an individual) but leads to greater reported marital satisfaction (deTurck & Miller, 1986).

Research shows that satisfied couples also score high in mutual trust, and they work to reciprocate that trust, since nonreciprocated trust is often a good indicator of a failing marriage (Honeycutt, Wilson, & Parker, 1982). Often trust is taken for granted, especially during the early stages of a relationship. With starry eyes, and usually little experience in causing each other pain, trust tends to be automatic. Rarely is it even talked about. But as the honeymoon ends and days turn into years, something happens, especially if the subject of trust is just taken for granted and never talked about. Little by little trust is broken; it's not reciprocated or nurtured and soon the security of a once strong relationship becomes a failed-marriage statistic.

Problems in Patterns

There are some potential problems associated with the conscious development of communication patterns. Many times the communication patterns can remain unexamined over a period of time. Author Sonya Johnson (1991) suggests that people who say their relationship is good usually won't look at it carefully, won't see all the major and minor frustrations. She contends that "the longer they have been together, the more built-up pressure there is, the more terrified they are of breakup, and therefore the more resistance they have to seeing themselves truthfully" (p. 74). Sometimes it takes courage to sit down and carefully examine the patterns within a relationship. Research presented in Chapter 5 suggests that women are more likely to initiate this analysis. If the woman does feel the need to do this, she may find it difficult to bring it to the attention of her partner. There's no magic answer for this dilemma, but it is possible that a little technique called "I'm listening" will assist you. This useful technique proceeds as follows: The partner who feels a need to bring up an uncomfortable topic can ask his or her partner to simply listen. The partner's only response throughout must be "I'm listening," with little physical response other than nodding the head. As the partner pauses in talking, the listening partner can say "I'm listening" in an encouraging tone. When the partner initiating the encounter feels that she or he is through talking, they switch places. The key point here, especially with difficult topics, is that you often just need your partner to simply hear you out, while encouraging you to continue talking. Usually by the time both people have had a chance to openly share in a problem or concern, fear, anger, and frustration are reduced, and, if needed, a more level-headed, caring conversation can take place.

Psychologist Caryl Avery (1989) suggests that a comparison of other people's communication styles to your own can also lead to problems: "There is a tendency to idealize others and compare their 'perfect' relationship to our own" (p. 29). People may feel satisfied with what they have to the extent that it exceeds their expectations of handy comparisons. Given the wide range of relationship types and styles, you may need to be careful about adopting the behavior of role models.

In addition to problems created by idealizing external models, gender scholar Carol Gilligan (1981) spoke of internal (to the relationship) misunderstandings as a factor that interferes with effective communication patterns:

> What a man will see as care and respect, a woman may experience as neglect. What she sees as care and concern, he may see as interference with his autonomy. A woman who sees herself as loving may discover that her man views her as manipulative, castrating, and out of control. Women consider failure to respond as a serious moral problem. A man who sees himself as caring may be surprised to find that his woman finds him cold and unresponsive. (p. 64)

As this quote suggests, it is highly important to develop a shared perception of the communication intentions of each person and to recognize that significant sex differences may exist in these perceptions.

Communication patterns in marriages are important, and the longer they are in existence, the harder they are to change. That is why it is critical to establish the patterns early and evaluate them regularly. In spite of your best efforts, at times problems may occur. Establishing, evaluating, and changing patterns within a relationship can be painful, but as the saying goes, "no pain, no gain." And aren't growth and progress toward a better relationship goals that couples should strive for?

Power and Control in Marriage

No matter how effectively you establish equitable patterns, one fact of any marriage is the reality of differences. Yet many people believe these differences will not lead to conflict or problems. In Chapter 7 when we referred to the dysfunctional relationship beliefs described by Eidelson and Epstein (1982), we included two that apply here: disagreement is destructive and partners cannot change. The first of these two is sometimes manifested in the belief that "we'll never fight, we love each other too much." When the first fight does come, the relationship is perceived as having failed, and it's home to mom. The second belief is evidenced when one or both partners say to themselves, "He [She] won't change, what's the use? I'm out of here." In either case, the relationship is in jeopardy. Communication researchers Metts and Cupach (1990) investigated the connection between these dysfunctional beliefs and destructive problem-solving responses in couples' relationships. Their research showed a positive correlation between such beliefs and ineffective problem-solving behaviors.

While not all relationship problems can be solved by communication, many can. We advocate developing a pattern in which relationship issues involving change and control can be worked out. In *The Intimate Enemy: How to Fight Fair in Love and Marriage,* Bach and Wyden (1968) described ways to "fight fair." Some of our students have difficulty with this idea, thinking that learning how to fight will just cause more fighting. But that's not been our experience. Since disagreements are bound to happen, it makes sense to develop communication patterns that support chances for a mutually satisfying resolution to an issue. A pattern that Phil (the male co-author of this text) and his partner developed regarding heated disagreements (as suggested by Bach & Wyden, 1968) is to disallow "carpetbagging," meaning that you don't allow old wounds or past arguments to resurface. During the early stages of their marriage they mutually agreed (established a pattern) to discuss only the matter at hand when in the throes of an argument. If the topic of discussion is money, neither partner is allowed to bring up unrelated frustrations that happen to come to mind at the time. For them, this pattern has been an effective one for encouraging fair fighting. When one topic is resolved or run into the ground, they mutually agree to get on with their lives or to get into another issue.

A related issue that appears to be central to long-term relationship effectiveness is the pattern of control. In keeping with the values described in Chapter 1, equality of control in a marriage seems to be the most effective pattern for both people. In virtually all instances, it seems that shared decision making is a benefit. Research in this area is beginning to support the value of equitable, shared decision making, documenting a positive correlation between equality of decision making and satisfaction (Ting-Toomey, 1984; Yogev & Brett, 1985). Conversely, a lack of equitable decision making is related to low satisfaction. Wives, more than husbands, feel distress when the relationship is inequitable (Ragolin & Hansen, 1985). Thus research suggests that equality of control can lead to greater satisfaction and can enhance overall decision making. Perhaps this is an idea whose time has come.

Let's continue with the discussion of equality of control. Shared control in a marriage is more likely to occur when the norms (the patterns) are egalitarian and when the husband's level of competence is perceived to be the same as the wife's (Nye, 1982). This is related to education in that the more educated both spouses are, the more egalitarian the authority tends to be between them (Gottman, Markman, & Notarius, 1970). Developing this equality seems to involve three dimensions: integrity (respecting each other), reciprocity (what is good for one is good for the other), and flexibility (both partners are able to adapt to shifts in conditions) (Bate & Memmott, 1984). Equality won't happen, according to Gilligan (1981), until both the man and the woman transcend traditional roles. Women, according to Gilligan, must understand their own needs before they understand those of others: "Until a woman, in any relationship, can give up saying that she has no needs and desires or that they are not important and that all she wants to do is what the other person wants, she is bound to be resentful and there are bound to be problems in a relationship" (p. 64). The corollary for men appears to be to take some of the focus off personal needs and attend to balancing the needs of both people. Balance in a relationship may be acquired as well as given. It seems that as the traditional man moves away from attempting to exert control, and the traditional woman moves away from acquiescence or indirect methods of control, both people are able to discover greater satisfaction and effectiveness.

Dominance, a variable related to control, has long been part of the marital relationship with tradition dictating that men usually maintain the dominant role. Like so many aspects of marriage, this appears to be changing as well. One interesting point about dominance is the distinction between it and domineeringness. Domineeringness is the willingness to assert one's own wishes, while dominance occurs in a marriage when one partner asserts a controlling power over the other person (Rogers & Millar, 1979). Dominance can also be described by one person's "one-up statement" being followed by the other person's "one-down" statement. If Amy says, "Let's go to lunch," and Stephen responds, "Okay," Amy is in the dominating position. However, if Stephen had responded with, "Okay, but first I want to finish watching this video," he would have been exhibiting domineeringness (the willingness to exert his point of view). The interesting part of the research that relates to our value of equality of power is that statements of domineeringness decrease the other person's dominance. However, research shows that high domineeringness in both sexes is inversely related to marital satisfaction (Rogers & Millar, 1979). Domineeringness appears to be related to assertiveness. The judicious use of domineeringness may help keep one person or the other from being too dominant. If both partners are sensitive to the balance of dominance, then the stage may be set for a more equitable relationship.

In addition to being related to dominance, control has also been related to the concept of "ownership." Johnson (1991) talks about this as a potential source of conflict in a relationship. She contends that in marriage people attempt to own each other—body, time, attention, talents, energy, loyalty. According to Johnson, the concept of ownership underlies all (or most of) the interactions, puzzles, and muddles of relationships. She gives an example that may sound familiar to many of you. Couples generally need to negotiate their time, so that they make time for each other and for themselves. In Johnson's case, she and her partner were both writers who worked at home, so they had 24 hours per day to negotiate. Sometimes couples will use ownership as a means of control: "You owe me this much time." If you are married, how much of your partner's

time do you own? How much is hers or his? How much of your partner's time do you give him or her permission to use?

Our last point in this section on power and control relates to how individuals approach the issue of control in conflict. We have talked of the reality of conflict in marriage, but are there sex differences in approaches to conflict? Communication researchers Burggraf and Sillars (1987) reported that sex differences were barely apparent in marital conflict. In a similar vein, Fitzpatrick (1988) reported that conflict style was more related to marital type than sex. Three types were identified: (1) *traditionals*, who have high levels of interdependence, a willingness to engage in conflict, and conventional ideas of marriage; (2) *independents*, who emphasize autonomy and sharing, engage in conflict, and reject traditional ideas of marriage; and (3) *separates*, who express a need for autonomy and their own space and show little willingness to engage in conflict. In spite of some research that offers little support for sex differences in style of conflict, other research contends that men and women approach conflict differently. Interpersonal communication researcher Ritter (1989) suggests that husbands often argue to win, whereas wives argue to get approval from the other person. In addition, communication researcher Krueger (1986) found that women believe control over the conflict process is just as important as men's control over the content of the argument. These differences in approach are useful in understanding how each sex views the conflict process and how each might attempt to control the relationship.

Issues of power and control in personal and relationship change will continue to be difficult challenges for both men and women. Acquiring the ability to share power and implementing strategies to empower others constitute a significant shift in communication patterns for many people. Unresolved, these issues can become barriers to a common relationship goal, the achievement of intimacy and satisfaction.

Intimacy and Relationship Satisfaction in Marriage

Everyone wants to live happily ever after, and everyone wants to enter into a relationship that is intimate and satisfying. If developing this type of relationship is the goal, then it is probably useful to examine what research and married people report about the strategies that help reach this goal.

Intimacy

Realizing that the term *intimacy* can mean different things to different people, psychologists Waring, Tillman, Frelick, Russell, and Weisz (1980) asked the question, "What does intimacy mean to you?" to a wide variety of individuals. The answers were organized around four themes: (1) sharing private thoughts, dreams, and beliefs; (2) sexuality, with an emphasis on affection and commitment; (3) having a personal sense of identity; and (4) absence of anger, resentment, and criticism. In similar research, social psychologist Feldman (1979) found that intimacy involved the characteristics of (1) a close, personal, and usually affectionate relationship; (2) detailed and in-depth knowledge of the other; and (3) sexual relations. Gender scholar Laurie Arliss (1993) describes the contemporary expectation that couples create a union with emotional connectedness at its core. She contends that spouses are supposed to be best friends as well as serve a variety of pragmatic roles (e.g., maintaining a household).

Sex differences in approaches to intimacy are clearly present in marriages. Feldman (1982) suggests that traditional sex-role conditioning has a negative impact on marital intimacy and encourages male inexpressiveness and nagging by women. In a similar point of view, Fitzpatrick and Indvik (1982) report:

> The husbands in our sample perceived themselves as rarely nurturant, passive, or dependent, always dominant and task-oriented, and generally incapable of discussing or expressing their feelings. Consequently, it falls to the wives in these relationships to maintain some level of expressivity. . . . [W]hen wives cannot or refuse to be expressive, the relationship suffers. Wives may be said to bear the burden of expressivity in their marital relationships. (p. 696)

These sex differences, and one sex's lack of awareness of the other sex's tendencies, are likely to lead to diminished intimacy. Research indicates that wives are more likely to use a range of affective or emotional responses and greater emotional expressiveness than husbands (Notarius & Johnson, 1982). Wives tend also to be more expressive and affectionate than husbands (Thompson & Walker, 1989). Not only are differences present, but men are sometimes confused and mystified by what women want in terms of intimacy (McGoldrick, 1989). There also appears to be a lack of direct conversation about the differences, with women being more likely to talk about them than men (Rubin, 1984; Shimanoff, 1985). Some differences in intimacy can be attributed to different perceptions of disclosure. Rubin (1984) also found that women may fail to recognize their husband's comments as self-disclosure, since men may feel intimacy just being in physical proximity with their wives. Physical closeness, however, does not replace clear information.

We describe some aspects of the traditional model of marriage to prepare you for these questions: Will you be bound by these traditions? Does this research reflect the way it has to be? In Chapter 6 we explored in some detail sex differences related to disclosure, and we suggested that each sex broaden its range of disclosive behaviors. This becomes even more important in a marriage. Levels of intimacy and satisfaction are linked to effective disclosure.

To achieve an increased level of satisfaction, balanced definitions of intimacy are very helpful. These balanced definitions are expressed through what Galvin and Brommel (1991) call "relational currencies." These are agreed-upon ways of conveying affection, information, caring, and other relational variables. The key is the mutual definition of the currency. For example, if the husband thinks he is expressing affection through an activity like tuning his wife's car, but she doesn't see that act as affectionate, then these two have not yet achieved a mutual agreement on defining the currency of affection.

Developing definitions of relational currency and recognizing the role of open expression of thoughts and feelings are important parts of the perception of satisfaction. Communication scholar Barbara Montgomery (1981) found that satisfying marital communication requires four things: openness though mutual self-disclosure, confirmation and acceptance, transactional management, and situational adaptability. This view is supported by Pearson and Spitzberg (1990), who found four stages in developing an effective relationship: sharing self, affirming the other, becoming one, and transcending one.

Increasing the amount of information sharing can do more than increase understanding and intimacy. It can also have a significant impact on the level of commitment to the relationship. Family researcher Mary Lund (1985) defines commitment as "an attitude about continuing a relationship that is strengthened by a person's own acts of investing time, effort, and resources in the relationship" (p. 4). The more a person has invested in the relationship, and the more the investment is shared through relational currency, the less likely she or he is to leave it. The investment itself continues and becomes a barrier to reducing commitment in the relationship. In some ways, commitment is related more to investment than to rewards. Lund contends that commitment is predicted from a combination of satisfaction, investments in a relationship, and poor prospects for alternative relationships. If men and women follow the traditional relational roles, then men are less likely to invest and thus less likely to commit.

These variables appear to be intertwined. Sharing information and disclosing feelings not only increase understanding but lead to the development of a greater commitment to the relationship and increased feelings of satisfaction. However, we can't say that "more is always better" when it comes to sharing information. For example, communication researchers Sillars, Folwell, Hill, Maki, Hurst, and Casano (1992) investigated the extent to which communication produced greater understanding in a relationship. Sometimes a couple's best efforts to communicate only reinforce the misunderstandings. Discussions about the patterns of intimacy, about the currency of the relationship, and the limitations of sex roles can help avoid the misunderstandings these researchers identified.

Satisfaction

Most people would say that love is the basis for satisfaction. Yet, as we discussed in Chapter 9, love is difficult to define. Communication researchers Marston, Hecht, and Robers (1986) investigated the subjective experience of romantic love and discovered six different levels:

1. Collaborative love, characterized by feelings of increased energy, inten-
   sified emotional response, and reciprocal support
2. Active love, characterized by feelings of strength and doing things
   together
3. Secure love, manifested in a strong feeling of security and discussion of
   intimate topics
4. Intuitive love, experienced, though not expressed verbally
5. Committed love, being together and planning the future
6. Traditional romantic love

A couple experiencing love, when each is experiencing a different kind, may
have trouble attaining the satisfaction they desire. Even if a couple is
experiencing the same type of love, research shows that both love and
satisfaction are likely to decline in the first two years of marriage (Huston,
McHale, & Crouter, 1986). Maintaining a level of satisfaction is not easy.

Communication researchers Vangelisti and Huston (1992) also investigated
the relationship between satisfaction and love. While not conclusive, their
findings are interesting. This research correlated eight factors: assessment of
leisure time, division of household labor, communication with partner, influence
in making decisions, sexual relationship, time spent with partner, contact with
friends, and the couple's financial situation. Results showed that during the first
year of marriage, wives' satisfaction focused on the amount of time they had to
do things as a couple and the amount of time they spent with friends. In the
second year, however, wives' focus changed. In that year, wives who were
satisfied with the quality of communication and the nature of the sexual
relationship were more satisfied overall. In the third year, wives' emphasis again
moved to the quality of communication, to the division of household labor, and
to influence in decision making. For husbands, none of the eight indicators were
associated with satisfaction in the first year of marriage. In the second year,
satisfaction with relational influence and the quality of communication were
associated with husbands' overall satisfaction.

Vangelisti and Huston (1992) also compared these factors to expressions of love.
For women, none of the eight factors was significantly associated with feelings
of love in the first year of marriage. During the second year, wives who were
more satisfied with the way they had been spending their free time were
significantly more in love with their husbands. In the third year, wives who were
more satisfied with their sexual relationship tended to report stronger feelings
of love. For husbands in the first year of marriage, those satisfied with the sexual
relationship were significantly more in love with their wives. None of the eight
factors correlated in the second year. In the third year, husbands' satisfaction
with finances was negatively associated with love (the more I like the money,
the less I like you), and sexual relations were marginally associated with love.
While it may be a little difficult to sort out these findings, one clear outcome of the
research is the changing basis for relationship satisfaction. What brought satisfaction one year did not necessarily bring it the next. This suggests that couples
need to be attuned to and talk about the bases for their relational satisfaction.

We have covered only a small part of the available information on the topic of marriage. Our focus has been on the creation of effective communication patterns, developing into communication behaviors those patterns that increase the equality of power within the relationship and increase the opportunities for intimacy. In the next section of the chapter, we apply these three factors to an examination of gender communication in the family.

FAMILY COMMUNICATION

In the early 1970s Virginia Satir (1972) wrote a book called *Peoplemaking*. In her introduction she said the family is the "factory" where the person is made. "You, the adults, are the *people makers*" (p. 3). This is an interesting perspective, in that families do create *people* and not just *children*. The family structure continues to shape and mold an adult throughout her or his life. As humans, we are never finished being made. Given the centrality of the family to definitions of self, and given the power of the family to socialize people, it seems highly appropriate that we examine this context as it affects gender communication. Gender is important for at least two reasons. First, the gender-role identity of the individuals who begin the family will guide (even govern) a large part of the communication that takes place within the family. Second, the family has the ability to influence the gender-role identity of the children it raises. The family has the power to reinforce the status quo regarding gender-role identity, or it can use that power to give the people it makes a broader, more complete view of how to be a boy or girl, woman or man.

Patterns in Families

The family has long been viewed as a "system" by researchers concerned with family communication. Satir (1988) has a nice analogy that may help you picture a family as a system. She described the family as a mobile. Picture the kind of mobile that hangs over a child's crib, but instead of animals on it, picture the members of the family. As events (such as leaving for college, contracting an illness, getting a new job, losing a job) touch one member of the family, they will affect everyone else. But unlike a mobile, members of a family can create their own change, create their own reverberations through the system. This view of communication is generally known as the "pragmatic" approach, so named and described by communication theorists Watzlawick, Beavin, and Jackson (1967). They argue that any given communication behavior is simply a reaction to particular interactive situations and that understanding one person in a family or one communication act is possible only by understanding the system or pattern in which the act takes place. Communication behaviors, in this view, are the result not of people but of other communication behaviors. The pragmatic researcher believes that identification of recurrent patterns will effectively explain what is happening within a system like a family (Trenholm, 1991). Since

"Reprinted with special permission of North America Syndicate."

patterns of communication describe what is happening within a family, gaining control of the patterns of communication within a family may help make the kind of people and kind of satisfaction you may be looking for.

Here's an example. It's 8:30 on a Saturday morning, and 6-year-old Matt knocks on his parents' bedroom door, hears a "Come on in," and runs into the room. He's greeted with smiles and hugs and snuggles with his mom and dad for a while; they all chat and then everyone gets up. This brief example speaks volumes about the interaction within the family. Matt knows it is okay to go into the bedroom with permission, and he knows he will probably be warmly welcomed. Physical expressions of affection are appropriate, as is talking with mom and dad. We don't know how realistic this example is to you, but we can assure you that it is real. What kind of child is being made here?

As we talk about "making people," we turn our attention to the role of the family communication patterns in sex-role development. Are men and women born with sex and gender differences, or are the sexes socialized into these differences? Communication researchers Arntson and Turner (1987) found that research had generated little evidence to support a theory of innate difference. Indeed, some researchers regard sex role as a completely social construction (Rogers & Walsh, 1982; Sherif, 1982). Arnston and Turner go on to say that "since sex role development begins at an early age, . . . it follows that the family is the preeminent agency for socializing children" (p. 305).

Extensive research describes the family's role in the socialization of children. Our place here is not to review all that research but to point out some of the more significant aspects of it as it relates to gender communication. As you might guess, families with traditional sex-role behaviors tend to develop children who stereotype the sexes (Repetti, 1984). Conversely, extensive interaction between father and child is associated with the development of androgyny in children (Lavine & Lombardo, 1984). The children in Lavine and Lombardo's study showed an ability to shift between typically masculine and feminine behavior based on the needs of the situation. They were developing a broader communication repertoire.

The ability of children to develop a broad range of skills appears to be partially dependent on the parents' ability to model these behaviors. Author Alvin Poussaint (1986) described recent changes in this way:

> A new movement has spawned that has been pushing American men and women closer to the acceptance of androgynous fatherhood—men who take a significant share of nurturing responsibilities for children and the home. . . . This often requires that they give up old-fashioned ideas about so-called manliness, "who wears the pants in the family," and what constitutes "women's work" as opposed to "men's work." (p. 9)

If children are to be socialized with a broader view of sex roles, perhaps both the father and the mother may need to give up some of the traditional sex-role expectations in their parenting. In some cases this may be as difficult for the mother as it is for the father.

Research on patterns of interaction between parents and children shows communication behavior differences between fathers and mothers and differences based on the sex of the child. For example, communication researchers Bellinger and Gleason (1982) found that fathers and mothers do not speak the same way to each of their children. Differences were found in both the amount and content of talk, with the mother reflecting the traditional maternal role. Researchers Buerkel-Rothfuss, Covert, Keith, and Nelson (1986) found that parents do not speak the same way to daughters and sons. Sons are spoken to in a more active manner with the content focused around the activities of the son. Daughters are generally spoken to in softer tones, with more emphasis on thoughts and feelings. Sociologists Golinkoff and Ames (1979) found that both mothers and fathers took more conversational turns with sons than with daughters, but had longer conversations with daughters. In an interesting study of timing within the socialization process, child development researchers Fagot and Hagan (1991) found little differentiation in the socialization of 18-month-old children, whereas they found a great deal of differentiation in the socialization of 5-year-old boys and girls. If you are interested in guiding the sex-role socialization of your children, then it may be helpful to closely examine the communication patterns developed not only from parent to parent but from child to child.

One way to examine this pattern is suggested by communication scholars Beebe and Masterson (1986). They describe the difference between person-centered and position-centered patterns of communication in a family. Position-centered patterns focus on the relatively "stable position" a person holds in the family. Each person has his or her job, and they do it. Person-centered families place a high value on the individuality of each member. It appears that the person-centered approach encourages androgynous communication and the ability to behave flexibly in various social situations. As Galvin and Brommel (1991) state: "A key point in this process would be that the parents view each child as naturally fitting somewhere within the broad range of gender communication patterns, rather than pressuring the child to fit the parents' own gender ideal" (p. 122).

The traditional family model holds that men are more position than person centered. This stance (explained further by research we describe shortly) has had an impact on the male role in the family. Men have traditionally been less involved in parenting than women and they can be involved fathers only if it does not jeopardize their role as breadwinner (Lamb, Pleck, & Levine, 1987). Sociologists Harris and Morgan (1991) describe this traditional approach in more detail. They argue:

> Contemporary American norms encourage paternal involvement but there is no single model fathers should follow. . . . The traditional paternal role is the instrumental role as breadwinner. This role identifies some paternal responsibilities for training and discipline, but father-child relationships need not be close or companionate. . . . Fathers are seldom negatively sanctioned if they spend little time with their children because of long work hours or frequent travel. (p. 532)

Some people are beginning to notice the impact of the father's absence on children. Psychologist Chris Bacorn (1992) makes a strong argument for the increased role of fathers in parenting:

> There are men who spend time with their children, men who are covering for all those absentee fathers. . . . [F]athers who quietly help with homework, baths, laundry and grocery shopping. Fathers who read to their children, drive them to ballet lessons, who cheer at soccer games. . . . These are the real men of America, the ones holding society together. . . . If fathers were to spend more time with their children, it just might have an effect on the future of marriage and divorce. Not only do many boys lack a sense of how a man should behave; many girls don't know either, having little exposure themselves to healthy male-female relationships. With their fathers around, many young women might come to expect more than the myth that a man's chief purpose on earth is to impregnate them and then disappear. (p. 13)

If it is a goal to reduce sex-stereotyped behavior, then perhaps more equitable involvement on the part of both parents will lead to less traditionally sex-stereotyped attitudes about male and female roles.

In Chapter 1 we defined gender as being constructed and it appears to be constructed, at least in part, through the family. The ideal gender role can be created, and the family has a tremendous opportunity to create it effectively.

Power and Control in Families

Back in the 1960s, psychologist Robert White (1965) wrote an article entitled "The Experience of Efficacy in Schizophrenia." In this article White pondered the roots of mental illness, specifically forms of schizophrenia. Among other ideas, White came to the conclusion that some aspects of schizophrenia could be traced back to early childhood and to early language development. He noted that one symptom of schizophrenia is the belief on the part of the patients that their efforts do not matter. Schizophrenics tend to see no relationship between their actions and any effect in the outside world. White was interested in how this belief might have originated. The conclusion he came to was that infants need to develop the connection early in life between their own actions and an effect in their outside world. If an infant cried, something should happen—the infant should be picked up, held, changed, fed, or in some way responded to to meet its needs. Not attending to an infant's needs, thereby neglecting the establishment of a necessary link, might be related to schizophrenia. White believed that the first 6 months were critical for the infant; this was the time the infant began to believe that he or she could affect the surrounding world, could mold it to meet needs, and could begin to feel a sense of power. White believed that a child could not be "spoiled" before 6 months of age; after that, some tempering was in order to avoid creating an overindulged child.

What does all this mean and what does it have to do with power? In different families, it could mean a number of things. It could mean that a couple's children use language to influence the world around them, that they see that their efforts to influence others through spoken language will have some effect. Perhaps some children are allowed to change their parents' minds occasionally. Children brought up like this know that they will not always get what they want, but they know that it is worth the effort to ask. In addition, they become able to transfer this ability to situations outside the family. White's approach embodies one of the values we describe in this text—that of empowerment. A person (in this case, a child) can develop a more positive view of herself or himself through positive reinforcement and effective use of communication. As this develops, the child begins to feel that he or she has greater control or influence over situations, greater responsibility, and eventually greater power.

Empowering someone else (especially a child) requires that someone give up power. In traditional families, this may be difficult to do. Arliss (1993) suggests that "parenting tends to emphasize traditionally feminine behaviors, such as nurturing, sensitivity, and awareness of emotions; masculine traits such as dominance, competitiveness, and aggressiveness may not be a part of the typical parenting skills repertoire" (p. 93). Since power struggles are a central theme in human existence, power and control may be a difficult issue in a family (Simon, 1982). Family communication scholars Galvin and Brommel (1991) devote a chapter of their family communication text to the issue of power within the family. Their book is filled with examples of people who attempt to get power through indirect and devious ways. We expect each of you knows examples of a parent who held power through fear, who used guilt to get his or her way, who played helpless so that the other person would do things for her or him, or who intimidated. It is beyond the scope of this text to fully explore all the issues around the use of power within a family, but we found one power distinction that applies here. Steiner (1978, cited in Galvin & Brommel, 1991) described two types of power, gentle power and control power. Here is the distinction between the two: "Gentle power sends the message: 'I can give you what I feel and think. You can understand it and you can compare and decide.' This makes people powerful. Ideally, to use communication effectively to counteract the negative aspects of power, there can be no power plays between the persons involved" (Galvin & Brommel, 1991, p. 151). Control power, on the other hand, suggests that "I can't let you decide; I will decide for you." At

various times, either type of power may be appropriate. The key is understanding when.

As you think about the patterns of power you might develop in your current
or future family, we suggest that consideration be given to the role of control
and power within the family system. One aspect to consider is traditional sex
roles regarding the power and control. It may be useful for both parents to
examine their own behavior and to consider ways to expand their range of
effective communication in this area. The failure to do so can have negative
effects on the individuals within the system.

Intimacy in Families

Much of the literature in this area concerns itself with how communication
within the family system serves to bring the members together or pull them
apart as the family moves through the various phases of development. An
analytical model developed by family scholars Olsen, Sprenkle, and Russell
(1979) attempts to explain family communication via three primary variables:
cohesion, adaptability, and communication.

Family cohesion is one of those variables that can add up to too much of a
good thing. Too little cohesion leaves family members feeling alone, discon-
nected, and alienated. Too much cohesion draws a family so tightly together that
it develops an "us against them" mentality and the members' individual growth
is restricted. In Chapter 9 we discussed the tension between personal autonomy
and connectedness in a romantic relationship. This tension is present in families
as well. The key, in a family as in a romantic relationship, is finding a balance
between connection and independence. For a family this is a continual struggle,
because the changing events in a family, no matter what type, bring new issues
and feelings that pull one way or the other between the two poles. With many
men viewing independence and self-reliance as important parts of their self-image
within the family, and many women seeing themselves as more home and child(ren)
oriented, traditional families may have a built-in disagreement over the appropriate level of cohesion and, by extension, the degree of intimacy within the
family (Arliss, 1993). Of the range of topics that might be covered in a discussion
of intimacy, we examine two central points—nonverbal communication and
self-disclosure. The nonverbal communication patterns of a family reveal much
about the family structure and about the feelings of the members (Hickson &
Stacks, 1989).

Nonverbal Communication: Time

One of the parental rallying cries of the 1980s was "quality time" with
children. Economic and work pressures helped push parents away from a great
deal of contact with their children. We know of some parents who leave for
work before the kids get up and return from work after they have gone to bed
in the evening. As fathers, in particular, move from the traditional model to a
more involved role in the family, they experience stress as a result of attempts
to schedule working time around couple time, combined with the demands of

being a parent (Cooper, Chassin, & Zeiss, 1985). But the pressures and the desire for a career also have an impact on the amount of time mothers spend with their children and with their spouse (Arliss, 1993). The onset of parenthood can put so much pressure on time that it may be the greatest single challenge faced by married couples as they make the transition to parenthood (LaRossa, 1983).

Few things substitute for time spent as a family. Giving someone time, especially when it is a scarce commodity, is a measure of consideration and respect (Hickson & Stacks, 1989). When a spouse or parent chooses to spend time with the other spouse or the children, this sends a message about priorities within the family. However, at the same time, any one individual in the family can't let the family totally control his or her time. As children grow, the need for personal time increases, and adjustments may be needed.

If a family has a conversation about its own communication patterns, one topic that could be discussed is the type and amount of time spent together. Some families make a point of having dinner together a specified number of evenings a week. Others set aside family evenings. There are many different patterns of time within families, and not everyone will get the amount of time desired. But as a factor in the intimacy of the family, time needs consideration.

Nonverbal Communication: Touch

Another indication of the amount of intimacy is the degree of physical affection present in the patterns of interaction. A wide range of sources speak to the role touch plays in infant care (Lamb, 1982; Montagu, 1971). Other studies describe the role of touch in relationship bonding (Andersen & Sull, 1985; Jones, 1986; Nguyen, Heslin, & Nguyen, 1976). Touch is clearly a powerful factor in the development of any relationship. Research suggests that fathers and mothers touch children for different reasons. Fathers seem to touch more in play, while mothers touch for caretaking (Lamb, 1977). In research on the amount of touch that occurs between different family relationships, the least amount of touch occurred between fathers and sons (Jourard & Rubin, 1968).

Some years ago we came across two letters in the advice columns in newspapers. The first talked of a father who had trouble touching his infant son because he said he "couldn't kiss a guy." The other talked of a father who played roughly with his sons until they cried in pain. Both could be considered examples of inappropriate patterns of touch within a family. Some men, perhaps as an extension of homophobia, may fear physical contact with their sons. Clearly, we do not believe this is an effective pattern for fathers and sons. One of this text's co-authors, Phil, has continued an uninterrupted pattern of physical affection with his sons, even through their teenage years. The pattern appears to have had a positive influence on their development.

Given the force of this variable, and given the clear danger of abuse and violence, it is valuable to examine the pattern of touch within a given family. If you grew up in a two-parent family, how much physical affection is evident between your parents? What sex differences seem to exist between your father and mother? What are the patterns of touch present between each parent and each child? How does physical affection support cohesion in your family? We suggest that you consider the role of touch and its effect on the level of intimacy in your family.

Self-Disclosure

The second area related to intimacy is disclosure. Family intimacy is demonstrated through a number of means, not the least of which is shared understanding and knowledge. The primary means of sharing understanding and knowledge is through disclosure. We defined disclosure earlier and also discussed disclosure within friendships and romantic relationships. However, in the context of the family, disclosure takes on some additional factors. For example, self-disclosure has long been considered a skill for fostering intimate communication within families (Gilbert, 1976; Jourard, 1971). Historical patterns of disclosure in families reveal sex differences and tend to work against increased intimacy with the father. Children of both sexes tend to self-disclose more to their mothers than fathers, and mothers receive more information from children than do fathers (Pearson, 1989).

The value of positiveness and supportiveness within the family communication pattern was discussed earlier. Obviously, not all disclosure can or should be positive. However, as Gilbert (1976) points out, the impact of negative disclosure has to be weighed carefully. Gilbert describes the "curvilinear" relationship between disclosure and satisfaction. In a relationship, feelings of satisfaction increase up to a point as disclosure increases, then increased disclosure may lead to decreased satisfaction. Gilbert strongly suggests that working toward ever-increasing levels of disclosure won't always have a positive effect. Care needs to be taken in developing the family pattern for the amount of both positive and negative disclosure. The traditional role suggests that positive disclosure and interaction are generated by the mother while negative and sanctioning communication comes from the father ("Just wait till your father gets home!").

In developing the disclosure pattern, time becomes an important factor. It is difficult enough for two people to find time for personal communication. How does a mother or father of four find time for disclosure with each child and with his or her spouse? How much time is the optimum? Where does the time come from?

We are suggesting that you, in developing your family communication patterns, consider the way with which nonverbal communication and self-disclosure are dealt. Each has an impact on the quality of communication; each does not develop easily. Awareness of the tendencies of each sex toward certain kinds of communication behavior may help inform the patterns you develop. This awareness also may lead to an increased range of behaviors on the part of both the man and the woman as parents.

CONCLUSION

Gender communication within marriages and families is complicated by a wide range of sociological, biological, linguistic, and relational factors. Success in these relationships is never guaranteed, but the chances for success can be increased by broadening the range of communication behaviors that you bring to these contexts.

Of particular interest are the patterns of communication that develop within the context of marriage and families. Effective patterns may lead to greater success and increased feelings of satisfaction. Ineffective patterns may lead to any number of destructive possibilities. If we, as a society, are to improve the functioning of these two critical contexts, we need to understand the role of gender communication. As we have said elsewhere in this text, as individuals acquire a broader range of communication behaviors that allows for gender-blended communication, perhaps we will move in that direction.

Key Terms

traditional model	dual career	peoplemaking
commitment	tyranny	systems
marriage	coupleness	person-centered
family	routine	position-centered
communication	communication	gentle power
patterns	dysfunctional beliefs	control power
power	egalitarian	cohesion
empowerment	dominance	adaptability
intimacy	domineeringness	self-disclosure
dual earner	ownership	

Discussion Starters

1. Do you find that college-aged people are embracing the traditional model of marital relationships? Or do you find that students are continuing to seek alternative relationship styles? What is affecting their choices?
2. What is the most effective pattern of communication you have seen in a marriage? What made it effective? Did the two people develop this consciously or did the pattern tend to evolve out of trial and error?
3. How should decisions be made in a marriage or a similarly committed relationship? Should each decision be a 50-50 proposition? Should different partners take the lead on different things? How are these decisions to be negotiated?
4. How can feelings of intimacy be maintained over a long period of time? Is it even possible? Should a relationship expect to go through periods of time of less intimacy?
5. If the traditional nuclear family represents only 7 percent of all current families, why does the culture seem to hold so strongly to this model? Are there advantages to it? Should society continue to hold this up as a model, or should other models attain equal validity?
6. Is it possible to raise children who have the ability to draw from both traditional sex roles for their behavior? How could this be done? Is it desirable to do so?
7. How important is self-esteem in the development of children? Think about the kinds of communication patterns in a family that lead to higher levels of self-esteem.
8. What are the patterns of communication within a family that promote feelings of intimacy? What are the problems faced by single-parent families in developing feelings of intimacy?

References

ANDERSEN, P. A., & SULL, K. K. (1985). Out of touch, out of reach: Predispositions as predictors of interpersonal distance. *Western Journal of Speech Communication, 49,* 57–72.

ARLISS, L. P. (1993). First marriage families: Gender and communication. In L. P. Arliss & D. J. Borisoff (Eds.), *Women and men communicating: Challenges and changes* (pp. 86–101). Fort Worth, TX: Harcourt Brace Jovanovich.

ARNTSON, P., & TURNER, L. (1987). Sex role socialization: Children's enactments of their parents' behaviors in a regulative and interpersonal context. *Western Journal of Speech Communication, 51,* 304–316.

AVERY, C. S. (1989, May). How do you build intimacy? *Psychology Today,* pp. 27–31.

BACH, G. R., & WYDEN, P. (1968). *The intimate enemy: How to fight fair in love and marriage.* New York: Avon Books.

BACORN, C. N. (1992, December 7). Dear dads: Save your sons. *Newsweek,* p. 13.

BATE, B., & MEMMOTT, J. (1984, March). *Three principles for dual career marriages.* Unpublished manuscript, Northern Illinois University, De Kalb, IL.

BEEBE, S. T., & MASTERSON, J. T. (1986). *Family talk: Interpersonal communication in the family.* New York: Random House.

BELLINGER, D. C., & GLEASON, J. B. (1982). Sex differences in parental directives to young children. *Sex Roles, 8,* 1123–1139.

BERGER, C., & CALABRESE, R. J. (1975). Some explorations in initial interaction and beyond: Toward a developmental theory of interpersonal communication. *Human Communication Research, 1,* 99–112.

BERNARD, J. (1972). *The future of marriage.* New York: World.

BUERKEL-ROTHFUSS, N. L., COVERT, A. M., KEITH, J., & NELSON, C. (1986, November). *Early adolescent and parental communication patterns.* Paper presented at the annual meeting of the Speech Communication Association, Chicago, IL.

BURGGRAF, C. S., & SILLARS, A. L. (1987). A critical examination of sex differences in marital communication. *Communication Monographs, 54,* 276–294.

BUSCAGLIA, L. F. (1986). *Loving each other: The challenge of human relationships.* New York: Fawcett/Columbine.

COOPER, K., CHASSIN, L., & ZEISS, A. (1985). The relation of sex-role self-concept and sex-role attitudes to the marital satisfaction and personal adjustment of dual-worker couples with preschool children. *Sex Roles, 12,* 227–241.

DAINTON, M., STAFFORD, L., & MCNEILIS, K. S. (1992, November). *The maintenance of relationships through the use of routine behaviors.* Paper presented at the annual meeting of the Speech Communication Association, Chicago, IL.

DETURCK, M., & MILLER, G. (1986). The effects of husbands' and wives' social cognition on their marital adjustment, conjugal power, and self-esteem. *Journal of Marriage and the Family, 48,* 714–724.

EIDELSON, S., & EPSTEIN, D. (1982). Development of a measure of dysfunctional relationships beliefs. *Journal of Consulting and Clinical Psychology, 50,* 715–720.

FAGOT, B. I., & HAGAN, R. (1991). Observations of parent reactions to sex-stereotyped behaviors: Age and sex differences. *Child Development, 62,* 617–628.

FALUDI, S. (1992). *Backlash: The undeclared war against American women.* New York: Crown.

FELDMAN, L. B. (1979). Marital conflict and marital intimacy: An integrative psychodynamic-behavioral systemic model. *Family Process, 18,* 69–78.

FELDMAN, L. B. (1982). Sex roles and family dynamics. In F. Walsh (Ed.), *Normal family processes* (pp. 345–382). New York: Guilford Press.

FITZPATRICK, M. A. (1988). *Between husbands and wives: Communication in marriage.* Newbury Park, CA: Sage.

FITZPATRICK, M. A., & BADINSKI, D. (1985). All in the family: Communication in kin relationships. In M. L. Knapp & G. R. Miller (Eds.), *Handbook of interpersonal communication* (pp. 687–736). Beverly Hills, CA: Sage.

FITZPATRICK, M. A., & INDVIK, J. (1982). The instrumental and expression domains of marital communication. *Human Communication Research, 8,* 195–213.

GALVIN, K. M., & BROMMEL, B. J. (1991). *Family communication: Cohesion and change* (3rd ed.). New York: Harper Collins.

GILBERT, S. (1976). Self-disclosure, intimacy, and communication in families. *Family Coordinator, 25,* 221–229.

GILLIGAN, C. (1981, December). Are women more moral than men? *Ms. Magazine,* pp. 63–65.

GOLINKOFF, R. M., & AMES, G. J. (1979). A comparison of fathers' and mothers' speech with their young children. *Child Development, 50,* 28–32.

GOTTMAN, J., MARKMAN, H., & NOTARIUS, C. (1970). The typology of marital conflict. *Journal of Marriage and the Family, 6,* 192–203.

HARRIS, J. M., & MORGAN, S. P. (1991). Fathers, sons, and daughters: Differential paternal involvement in parenting. *Journal of Marriage and the Family, 53,* 531–544.

HICKSON, M. I., & STACKS, D. W. (1989). *Nonverbal communication: Studies and applications* (2nd ed.). Dubuque, IA: Wm. C. Brown.

HIRSHEY, G. (1989, March/April). Coupledom über Alles: Tyranny of the couples. *Utne Reader,* pp. 48–55. Originally published in *The Washington Post Magazine,* February 14, 1988.

HONEYCUTT, J. M., WILSON, C., & PARKER, C. (1982). Effects of sex and degrees of happiness on perceived styles of communicating in and out of the marital relationship. *Journal of Marriage and Family Counseling, 44,* 395–496.

HUSTON, T. L., McHALE, S., & CROUTER, A. (1986). When the honeymoon's over: Changes in the marriage relationship over the first year. In R. Gilmour & S. Duck (Eds.), *The emerging field of personal relationships* (pp. 109–132). Hillsdale, NJ: Lawrence Erlbaum Associates.

JOHNSON, S. (1991). *The ship that sailed into the living room.* Estancia, NM: Wildfire Books.

JONES, S. E. (1986). Sex differences in tactile communication. *Western Journal of Speech Communication, 50,* 227–249.

JOURARD, S. M. (1971). *The transparent self.* New York: Van Nostrand Reinhold.

JOURARD, S. M., & RUBIN, J. E. (1968). Self-disclosure and touching: A study of two modes of interpersonal encounter and their interrelation. *Journal of Humanistic Psychology, 8,* 39–48.

KRUEGER, D. L. (1986). Communication strategies and patterns in dual career couples. *Southern Speech Communication Journal, 15,* 164–173.

LAMB, M. E. (1977). The development of mother-infant and father-infant attachments in the second year of life. *Developmental Psychology, 13,* 637–646.

LAMB, M. E. (1982). Early contact and maternal-infant bonding: One decade later. *Pediatrics, 70,* 763–768.

LAMB, M. E., PLECK, J. H., & LEVINE, J. A. (1987). Effects of increased paternal involvement on fathers and mothers. In C. Lewis & M. O'Brien (Eds.), *Researching fatherhood* (pp. 109–125). London: Sage.

LAROSSA, R. (1983). The transition to parenthood and the social reality of time. *Journal of Marriage and the Family, 45,* 579–589.

LAUER, J., & LAUER, R. (1985, June). Marriages made to last. *Psychology Today,* pp. 19, 22–26.

LAVINE, L. O., & LOMBARDO, J. P. (1984). Self-disclosure: Intimate and nonintimate disclosures to parents and best friends as a function of Bem sex-role category. *Sex Roles, 11,* 735–744.

LUND, M. (1985). The development of investment and commitment scales for predicting continuity of personal relationships. *Journal of Social and Personal Relationships, 2,* 3–23.

MARSTON, P. J., HECHT, M. L., & ROBERS, T. (1986, February). *What is this thing called love? The subjective experience and communication of romantic love.* Paper presented at the annual meeting of the Western Speech Communication Association, Tucson, AZ.

McGOLDRICK, M. (1989). The joining of families through marriage: The new couple. In G. Carter & M. McGoldrick (Eds.), *The changing family life cycle* (2nd ed., pp. 200–226). Boston: Allyn and Bacon.

METTS, S., & CUPACH, W. R. (1990). The influence of relationship beliefs and problem solving responses on satisfaction in romantic relationships. *Human Communication Research, 17,* 170–185.

MONTAGU, A. (1971). *Touching: The human significance of the skin.* New York: Perennial Library.

MONTGOMERY, B. M. (1981). The form and function of quality communication in marriage. *Family Relations, 30,* 21–29.

NGUYEN, T., HESLIN, R., & NGUYEN, M. L. (1976). The meaning of touch: Sex and marital differences. *Representative Research in Social Psychology, 7,* 13–18.

NOTARIUS, C., & JOHNSON, J. (1982). Emotional expression in husbands and wives. *Journal of Marriage and the Family, 44,* 483–490.

NYE, F. I. (1982). *Family relationships: Rewards and costs.* Beverly Hills, CA: Sage.

OLSEN, D., SPRENKLE, D., & RUSSELL, C. (1979). Circumplex model of marital and family systems: Cohesion and adaptability dimensions, family types, and clinical applications. *Family Process, 18,* 3–23.

OTTO, H. (1988). America's youth: A changing profile. *Family Relations, 37,* 385–391.

PEARSON, J. C. (1989). *Communication in the family.* New York: Harper Collins.

PEARSON, J. C., & SPITZBERG, B. H. (1990). *Interpersonal communication: Concepts, components, and contexts* (2nd ed.). Dubuque, IA: Wm. C. Brown.

PETRONIO, S. S. (1982). The effect of interpersonal communication on women's family role satisfaction. *Western Journal of Speech Communication, 46,* 208–222.

POUSSAINT, A. F. (1986). Introduction. In B. Cosby, *Fatherhood* (pp. 1–11). New York: Berkley Books.

RAGOLIN, V. C., & HANSEN, J. C. (1985). The impact of equity or egalitarianism on dual-career couples. *Family Therapy, 2,* 151–162.

REPETTI, R. L. (1984). Determinants of children's sex-stereotyping: Parental sex-role traits and television viewing. *Personality and Social Psychology Bulletin, 10,* 457–468.

RICHMOND-ABBOTT, M. (1992). *Masculine and feminine: Gender roles over the life cycle.* New York: McGraw-Hill.

RITTER, M. (1989, September 17). She was a woman, he was a man—and they fought. *Milwaukee Journal,* p. 6G.

ROGERS, L., & WALSH, J. (1982). Shortcomings of the psychomedical research on John Money and co-workers in sex differences in behavior: Social and political implications. *Sex Roles, 8,* 269–281.

ROGERS, L. E., & MILLAR, F. E. (1979). Domineeringness and dominance: A transactional view. *Human Communication Research, 5,* 238–246.

RUBIN, L. B. (1984). *Intimate strangers: Men and women together.* New York: Harper & Row.

SATIR, V. (1972). *Peoplemaking.* Palo Alto, CA: Science and Behavior Books.

SATIR, V. (1988). *The new peoplemaking.* Mountain View, CA: Science and Behavior Books.

SHERIF, C. W. (1982). Needed concepts in the study of gender identity. *Psychology of Women Quarterly, 6,* 375–398.

SHIMANOFF, S. B. (1985). Rules governing the verbal expression of emotions between married couples. *Western Journal of Speech Communication, 49,* 85–100.

SILLARS, A. L., FOLWELL, A. L., HILL, K. L., MAKI, B. K., HURST, A. P., & CASANO, R. A. (1992, November). *Levels of understanding in marital relationships.* Paper presented at the annual meeting of the Speech Communication Association, Chicago, IL.

SIMON, R. (1982). Reflections on the one-way mirror: An interview with Jay Haley, Part II. *Family Therapy Network, 6,* 32–36.

STEINER, C. (1978, March). *Problems of power.* Lecture delivered at the National Group Leaders Conference, Chicago, IL.

THOMPSON, L., & WALKER, H. (1989). Gender in families: Women and men in marriage, work, and parenthood. *Journal of Marriage and the Family, 51,* 845–871.

TING-TOOMEY, S. (1984). Perceived decision-making power and marital adjustment. *Communication Research Reports, 1,* 15–20.

TRENHOLM, S. (1991). *Human communication theory* (2nd ed.). Englewood Cliffs, NJ: Prentice Hall.

TURNER, L. (1990). The relationship between communication and marital uncertainty: Is "her" marriage different from "his" marriage? *Women's Studies in Communication, 13,* 57–83.

VANGELISTI, A. L., & HUSTON, T. L. (1992, November). *Maintaining marital satisfaction and love.* Paper presented at the annual meeting of the Speech Communication Association, Chicago, IL.

WARING, E., TILLMAN, M., FRELICK, L., RUSSELL, L., & WEISZ, G. (1980). Concepts of intimacy in the general population. *Journal of Nervous and Mental Disease, 168,* 471–474.

WATZLAWICK, P., BEAVIN, J. H., & JACKSON, D. D. (1967). *Pragmatics of human communication.* New York: W. W. Norton.

WHITE, R. (1965). The experience of efficacy in schizophrenia. *Psychiatry*, 28, 199–221.

YOGEV, S. (1987). Marital satisfaction and sex role perceptions among dual-earner couples. *Journal of Social and Personal Relationships, 4,* 35–46.

YOGEV, S., & BRETT, J. M. (1985). Patterns of work and family involvement among single and dual earner couples. *Journal of Applied Psychology, 70,* 754–768.

CHAPTER 11

Talking Shop: Gender Communication in the Workplace

It should be easy for you to work up the energy to read this chapter, since it deals with the world of work—a topic that's sure to be of interest to you. The information given here affects many students' lives, because so many of you are already working full-time or part-time jobs while slaving away at a college career. Take your textbook with you to work, to read on your break.

CASE STUDY

Monique's situation was by no means unique, but it was rare enough that neither Monique nor the company she worked for had run up against this kind of problem before. Here's a bit of the history of this situation. Right after college graduation Monique landed a job as an entry-level manager at a medium-sized company. She was hired by Jack, her supervisor, and has worked for this company for a little over a year. During this time she has come to trust Jack's advice, to value the mentoring relationship that they have developed, and to appreciate the opportunities he has given her to excel on the job.

Near the close of a meeting in which Monique and Jack were planning sales strategy for the upcoming fiscal year, Jack began to turn the conversation to more personal topics. He asked Monique if she was dating anyone, if she was sexually involved with anyone at the time, if she thought her work went more smoothly when her sex life was running smoothly, and so forth. Jack and Monique had always maintained a fairly friendly, informal working relationship, so at first Monique hesitatingly offered minimal responses and basically laughed off Jack's questions, until they became too personal and began to make her feel uncomfortable. When Jack seemed to push for sexual information, Monique covered her discomfort by saying something like, "Well, I think, on *that* note, we should end our meeting because customers are waiting, sales are out there to be made, ha, ha, ha. . . ." Monique left the meeting and made her way back to her office, knowing that something very wrong had just happened. But she couldn't make sense out of it, or out of what she was feeling.

In subsequent encounters Jack continued to put out signals of romantic interest in Monique. While he didn't say anything as direct as he had said in their meeting, he got closer to Monique when talking to her; occasionally he would touch her arm or put his arm around her shoulders and praise the good job she was doing. At one point in a meeting with several other managers, Jack leaned over to Monique, put his arm around the back of her chair, and whispered a comment to her about a colleague's ideas. Monique became very bothered about the turn her relationship with Jack was taking. She'd always thought Jack a somewhat attractive man, but he was at least 20 years her senior and he was married—happily, so she thought.

Finally, over lunch one day, Monique told two of her coworkers about her problem with Jack. She explained that it was the first time anything personal or sexual had been communicated to her by a boss; it bothered her to think that maybe Jack had been looking at her all along in a sexual way, rather than as a professional and a colleague. She wondered if Jack's actions constituted sexual harassment. Monique's coworkers didn't exactly offer what you'd call a "textbook" empathic response. They began teasing Monique about her boss having a crush on her, and they said she ought to be flattered that someone like Jack—someone of such status in the company—had taken an interest in her. Monique should take it as a compliment, they advised. But Monique didn't feel complimented.

As a man reading this case study, would you say that you'd agree with Monique's colleagues? If Monique was attracted to Jack, should she go for it? Would that further her career? If you could put yourself in Monique's shoes, think about how you would feel if your boss was attracted to you. Would you feel flattered? Disillusioned? Betrayed? You probably don't think that Jack's behavior was particularly professional, but was it understandable, given his attraction to Monique? Think about your own opinion of romantic liaisons on the job; think about the possibility of such a situation happening to you. Consider the positive things that might come out of such a relationship, and then consider the negatives.

Women reading this case study will likely not have mixed opinions of Jack's behavior. While you might understand Jack's attraction to a sharp, young, professional woman like Monique, probably few would condone his behavior. Sexual harassment is a complicated problem. As an example of just one of its complications, try to make sense out of the contradiction of women labeling Jack's behavior sexual harassment while men might call it flattery or "basic human attraction." The dynamics between women and men in the workplace are complex; some of those complexities are examined in this chapter.

OVERVIEW

Part Four is devoted to how communication occurs between men and women in various contexts of our lives. Thus far we've examined gender communication within the contexts of friendships and romantic or dating relationships. We've explored how relationships within families involve unique communicative elements. Let's now turn our attention to how gender communication occurs within occupational or workplace settings.

Some of you who are reading this text may have quit a full-time job and gone back to school to finish your college degree or to begin one. For others, work experience may consist of full-time summer jobs or part-time jobs during the year to supplement your income while you're in school. For still others of you who have put yourselves through college, your experience has been one of juggling full-time school and a full-time job. If you fit this last description, you know that "personal life" becomes a virtual thing of the past. No matter what your job experience has been or will be, we give you some things to think about in this chapter regarding men and women communicating on the job. Some specific topics regarding workplace communication include:

- How sexual stereotypes can impede the likelihood of getting hired
- The pros and cons of employment quota systems
- How relational versus content approaches to communication apply to job interviewing
- Verbal and nonverbal indications of sex bias in job interviews
- Detecting and responding to unethical job interview questions
- Men's and women's advancement on the job
- The presence of a glass ceiling for female professionals
- Managerial communication of women and men
- The problem of sexual harassment in the workplace

INTRODUCTION

For many of us, our work is our livelihood, our most time-consuming activity. Work can be a rewarding experience or a real downer on the self-esteem. Sometimes how we feel about our jobs or our work productivity is how we feel about ourselves. Your textbook authors don't advocate that position (even though we've felt this way about work at times), because that's giving work too much power over other important things in life. But we recognize that the reality for many people is, if work goes well, life goes better and is more enjoyable; if work is "the pits," then life can feel "pitiful" as well.

When asked what makes their jobs enjoyable, many working persons—men and women alike—admit that their relationships with people they work with are the real payoffs in a job (McCallister & Gaymon, 1989). There's a fairly healthy list of things that make a job worthwhile and rewarding, like the satisfaction of getting an important sale, making a client happy, receiving a raise or a promotion, watching a student learn a new idea, or healing someone's mental, physical, or spiritual pain. However, many people readily contend that coworkers make the most significant difference between job satisfaction and dissatisfaction.

Coworker relationships are important; they're also dependent on effective communication for development and maintenance. After reading this far in the text, you've probably realized, first, just how complicated communication is and, second, how it becomes more complicated when affected by gender. When you add the connection between work and security or livelihood, plus status and power—variables more present in the workplace than perhaps any other context—you've compounded the complexity once again. Effective communication on the job is possible and many professional people learn to do it quite well. As we've said throughout this text, the key is avoiding a rigid style of communication that ignores the context of the situation. Again, the best approach is an expanded repertoire of communication behaviors from which to choose, given the dictates of the occupational context.

Just how complicated is communication between male and female coworkers? Before we address that question, think about your own work experience— whether that experience involved a full-time position of rank within a corporate giant or occasional baby-sitting for the neighbors' kids. Think about the people you worked with in one particular job, just to keep it simple. How was your communication different with these people, compared to communication you've had with non–work-related friends, dates, a spouse, or other family members? Think of the most memorable person you worked with at that job and what made her or him memorable. Was that person your boss, a coworker on the same level as you, or a subordinate? Was that person the same sex as you or opposite? Now think of the most dramatic or memorable instance in which poor communication occurred during this job; think about who was involved and how the situation was resolved (if it was resolved). What variable was most responsible for how the miscommunication arose—a status difference, a simple misunderstanding, a power struggle, something to do with sex or gender?

We're not suggesting that a gender or sex element is at the center of every ineffective communication situation at work; in fact, stressful workplace communication is quite often related to things other than a male-female dynamic. However, a good number of problems in the workplace that appear to be power- or status-based are really problems between the sexes. We address some of those problems via research that has studied them, with the intent of increasing your awareness before your next stint in the working world, or so that you can apply your increased insight to your current job. We also explore what the research says about female, male, and androgynous approaches to management, in terms of how varying styles are received in organizational contexts.

What is the likelihood that you will be working with members of both sexes in your next job? Granted, it depends on the job. But generally speaking, if you're a woman, your chances of working with male bosses and coworkers are very good. If you're a man, your chances of having female bosses and coworkers are greater than they used to be. Your chances of having female subordinates are as good as they've always been, according to recent statistics.

In 1991 the U.S. Department of Labor examined employment profile data from 94 Fortune 500 corporations to assess women's and minorities' gains in the work force. The results indicated that women represent roughly 37 percent and minorities represent 15 percent of employees at these companies. Across all levels of management, including first-line supervisors, about 17 percent of these positions are held by women, 6 percent are held by minority employees. At management levels of assistant vice president and higher, roughly 7 percent of these positions are held by women, under 3 percent are held by minorities. These figures are supplemented by those of Korn/Ferry International, an executive search firm, which surveyed 1000 of the largest companies in the nation. Within the overall labor force, women's representation rose from 43 percent in 1981 to 46 percent in 1991; across management positions, the representation rose from 27 percent to 41 percent. At the senior executive level, the figure rose from 1 percent in 1981 to 3 percent in 1991.

It is beyond the parameters of our discussion in this chapter to interpret trends in work-force statistics, nor do we want to attempt to assess the impact of working women on American society. We do want to explore some possible explanations for the fact that in 10 years, female senior management representation has increased by only two percentage points. Also examined is how the increased presence of women in the workplace is affecting professional communication and the dynamics between the sexes, particularly at the management level. However, before tackling these "on the job" issues, it's a good idea to understand how being female or male may come into play in the process of getting a job.

GETTING THAT ALL-IMPORTANT JOB

Gender bias may impede you from getting a chance at a job. Often you don't know that this has happened; you believe your résumé simply didn't elicit a response from an organization. We explore how this kind of treatment may occur in some employment contexts. Then we discuss some sex-related issues regarding the employment interview—the "foot in the door" conversation where some basic knowledge of sex differences and gender communication may help you on your way toward the job you desire.

Sex Stereotyping and Hiring Practices

Remember when we said several chapters ago that being treated like a stereotype rather than an individual is degrading? If you happen to learn that some form of sex stereotyping or bias has created a barrier between you and a job you want, it's extremely frustrating and demoralizing. But aren't there laws to prevent sex discrimination in hiring practices? Laws do exist to protect equal employment opportunities for all citizens; note the usual designation on applications and job notifications that an organization is an "Equal Opportunity

Employer." However, such laws are difficult to enforce, in that hiring decisions may be explained and justified in a number of ways to indicate an absence of bias. In many hiring situations, firms need demonstrate only that they considered a range of candidates of varying profiles and backgrounds for a position, not that their final decision was necessarily free from bias.

Research in the early 1980s offered some evidence of sex bias in the hiring or interviewing practices of national companies. Management researchers McIntyre, Mohberg, and Posner (1980) submitted unsolicited "dummy" résumés and cover letters to companies in order to examine trends in responses. The résumés described persons with equal qualifications, but they were varied by sex. They found that male applicants were far more likely to receive responses than female applicants. However, recent research indicates that qualifications are now more likely to counteract sex biases in interview opportunities and hiring practices than in the past (Graves & Powell, 1988).

We'd like to take a guess at what you may be thinking about right now, as you read these last paragraphs. Is the dreaded "Q-word" crossing your mind— "Q" for quota system? Our students, particularly male students, often enter into a heated discussion about how unfair they believe quota systems to be. One of our former students recently argued, "Quota systems keep the best people from getting a job. The person who has the toughest time getting a job these days is the white male." Some immediate responses he heard across the classroom echoed the sentiment, "Well, it's about time," meaning that white males have had employment (and other) privilege for so long, it's only fair they feel the isolation and discrimination others have felt for a long time.

In the quota argument, advocates tend to oversimplify their opponents' position on this complicated issue. Before making a judgment as to whether the use of a quota system within a particular organization is fair or appropriate, one has to consider the contextual and historical variables connected to the organization. The argument can also degenerate into "tit for tat" or a "what goes around, comes around" mentality. These positions don't seem to advance the cause of equality; they create more divisiveness between sexes and races than they create equal opportunity.

There are some good arguments in favor of quota systems. If employment opportunities are dominated by persons of one profile and exclusionary to other persons, then the system feeds on itself and protects itself from change. How can a qualified person who happens to not fit the profile ever get a chance? The pressure to enact some form of quota-based hiring may create opportunities for equally qualified persons to get a chance at employment, when without that pressure they would never have had the chance to show that they are qualified. On the other hand, we sympathize with the frustration a quota system presents to qualified persons who feel they are denied employment simply because they are the wrong sex, color, nationality, sexual orientation, ethnicity, whatever. Many times if an informal quota system is operating in a hiring decision, applicants will be hard-pressed to discover its existence. Often you don't know who was hired; all you're told is that that person wasn't you.

The controversy over hiring quotas exemplifies something suggested throughout this book—that society places too much importance on sex or gender, for starters, and not enough on the individuality or uniqueness of a person. Perhaps we are at the point when we can only look forward to a society in which equal opportunities abound for persons to become educated, to gain access to means of self-improvement, and to achieve the kind of employment that they desire.

Gender Issues and the Job Interview

Let's assume that you've gotten past any kind of sex bias in the hirer's process of weeding out résumés and that a quota system isn't in operation for a particular opening. Let's assume the best of all possible situations, which also happens to be quite typical—that you got an interview because you are qualified and the company or institution is interested in you. Are there any insights regarding communication about and between women and men that would assist you with your interviewing process? Some of the following insights are things you already know from having read the previous chapters of this text, but maybe you haven't thought far enough to apply the information to such a context as a job interview. Other insights come from research into this topic, so we want you to be aware of this research in order to better your chances of getting hired (or at least of having a positive interview experience).

Approaches to Talk

What application to the job interview can you make of the information in Chapter 5 about relational versus content approaches to communication? First, a caution: Don't take the relational versus content idea too far by assuming that a person's sex delineates his or her preferred functions of communication. Research suggests a tendency for men to view conversation as functioning to impart content or information and women to view it as relationship maintenance or as a means of establishing connections with others. Since this is a trend that is beginning to emerge in research, it would be unwise to automatically assume that an interviewer or prospective employer will value one approach more than another simply because of her or his sex. Rather, you can use this information to better understand yourself and your own approach to communication, and maybe it can help you read clues from an interviewer.

For example, an appropriate goal for a job interview may be to enhance your chances of being hired by communicating who you are and establishing some sense of relationship between yourself and the interviewer. But that may just as well be an inappropriate goal for the situation. What if the interviewer is straightforward, informative and factual in approach, terse in tone, and rushed for time? What if that interviewer behavior comes from a woman, someone you expected to take a very different approach to the interview? This example may be stretching things a bit, but more often than we imagine, an interview (or at least part of an interview) will go contrary to expectations.

Imagine how you might feel if you were the applicant in such an experience. Conversely, have you ever been to a job interview in which all the person interviewing you seemed to want to do was "chitchat" and get to know you, as opposed to discussing the particulars of the job? If you went in expecting lots of information, you may be frustrated with what you aren't told or with what you have to pry out of the interviewer by asking repeated questions.

As we've suggested before, a well-developed communication repertoire, good listening skills, an alertness to nonverbal cues, and an ability to be flexible in your communication style will increase the likelihood of success in the interview context (as well as most other contexts for communication). It's wise to survey yourself and your goals for an interview and to understand your own preferences regarding approaches to talk before you enter the situation. You need not expect a sex-typed approach to surface from the interviewer, but you will be able to detect the use of a relational or content approach and align your behavior with that of the interviewer.

Being Taken Seriously

Unfortunately, this issue applies more to female than male candidates for jobs. We're not insinuating that men never have to worry about being taken seriously when they interview for jobs. Men do have to exert energy to create the right, positive impression on a potential employer. These pressures are especially real for traditionally aged college graduates who face credibility and inexperience issues with potential employers (termed the "young whippersnapper" judgment). However, there are generally more question marks about female applicants, meaning that the opportunity exists for greater sex-based suspicions on the part of many employers regarding female potential employees than male at this point in societal evolution. Women in the work force are nothing new, but their presence is noted in a different way than a man's. The old expectation still exists that men work out of necessity—to be breadwinners and because that's *just what men do*. The counterpart expectation for women is that they work for distraction, merely supplementing a man's work and income, as an interim activity before they "settle down," get married, and have children, or to prove to themselves and others that they can vitally contribute (sort of the "testing ground" reason to work), and so forth. The alternative explanations for why women work are far more numerous than the simple possibility that they work for the same reasons as men.

Nonverbal Indications of Sex Bias

Nonverbal communication is critical in a job interviewing situation; the nonverbal often carries more of the true message than the verbal communication (Hickson & Stacks, 1993). But just how are sex-role expectations revealed nonverbally during a job interview? A dead giveaway (or at least a fairly reliable nonverbal signal that a sex stereotype is in operation) resides in the opening greeting, especially the handshake. Often men and women alike appear awkward when shaking hands with a woman. (It's particularly irritating when a woman is on the receiving end of a bad handshake from another woman, who should know better.) This situation is improving; people are learning, but women still get the "cold fish," cup the fingers, half handshake (the one that translates into "You sweet, frail thing; I couldn't possibly grasp your whole hand because it'd fall right off"). A potential employer may have no intention of conveying negative impressions regarding a female applicant's credibility; the person just has a lousy handshake or has never learned the importance of a firm one. Nonetheless, it should raise the eyebrows of a female applicant when the handshake extended to her is less firm or confidence-inducing than one extended to a male applicant or colleague. This can be a subtle indication of a sex-based value system that is tolerated within the organization.

Besides the handshake in an interview, sex-role attitudes may be subtly communicated by nonverbal indications of general disinterest, such as a facial expression accompanied by a lack of eye contact, which communicates that you're just not being taken seriously for the position. If the interviewer seems unprepared, rushes through the interview, or accepts interruptions from associates or phone calls, these actions can send direct signals that the candidate is not a serious contender. Sex bias may be exhibited in interviews with male and female candidates alike. Granted, you can't always tell whether the behavior has to do with your sex, your qualifications, some idiosyncratic reaction on the part of the interviewer, or some other variable totally unrelated to you and your interview. It's important to take in as many nonverbal cues as possible and apply caution when interpreting the cues.

Verbal Indications of Sex Bias

Another way that sex-role stereotypes are evidenced in job interviews has to do with the interviewer questioning process. If a potential employer holds some doubt as to whether a person of your sex is serious about a job or is capable of handling the job, the interviewer might reveal these doubts by asking leading questions. Leading questions are designed to trap the interviewee into a forced response or into a no-win situation. They often take the form of a posed hypothetical situation followed by a question as to what the applicant would do. For example, when men apply for jobs in a currently female-dominated field such as nursing, they may receive leading questions that translate into doubts about their nurturing abilities. Or a woman applying for a position in a male dominated office might get this leading question: "What would you do if a male colleague disagreed with one of your ideas and started to argue with you in front of your coworkers? Would you be able to handle that?"

Sex bias may be communicated overtly in a job interview when applicants are asked unethical and illegal questions. It is illegal for a potential employer to ask an applicant about his or her marital status, parental status, or sexual orientation, among other things. Most employers know this, so most avoid this area. But if they want this kind of information before making a hiring decision, they can use covert means or be very indirect in how they approach these subjects during a job interview. By covert means, we refer to tactics of checking out a person's background, learning information in roundabout ways from

What If?

What if you've landed that big job interview you've been wanting for months. You really want this job; this is the "plum" your sights have been set on since you first heard about the position and sent in an application. *What if,* during the interview, the potential employer asks you an unethical, illegal question? *What if* the interviewer asks about your sexual orientation? *What if* the interviewer merely expresses a "company opinion" that married people, married men especially, are considered better risks in the company than single people, especially single women? How will you respond if you're a single woman? A single man? Remember that this is a job *you really want* (or at least *thought* you really wanted). Have your opinions of the job and the company changed because of the interviewer's unethical behavior? Or perhaps you don't consider the comment about marital status to be unethical. *What if* you respond in disagreement with the interviewer's company opinion about married people and responsibility? *What if* you disagree but choose not to voice that disagreement in hopes of increasing your chances of being hired? Have you "copped out" or done the smart thing?

former employers, and the like. With regard for indirect approaches, here's an example to clarify.

The female co-author of your textbook experienced an awkward situation some years back. During a segment of a job interview with the second ranking member of the organization, the subject of transition was raised. The interviewer said something to the effect of how moving from one job and one state to another was typically stressful, and even more stressful if one had a spouse and children who were uprooted in the process. After making this statement, he stopped talking, made direct eye contact, and waited for her response. Even though she knew what information he was after, she wanted the job, so her reply revealed her current marital and parental status.

Another example involves a woman who was put in an awkward position not as much by her interviewers, as occurred in the first example, but by a person who joined the group for lunch. The woman was interviewing for a prestigious position within the organization, so you can imagine her surprise and dismay when the lunch guest, a relative of one of the interviewers, began quizzing her about her private life. He asked whether she was married, had she ever been married, did she have any plans to be married, did she have or want to have children, and so forth. What was quite unfortunate, and what almost caused the woman to turn down the job offer, was that the hiring body made no attempt to stop the unethical behavior on the part of the lunch guest. It was as though they knew they weren't liable or at fault since the questions weren't coming from them, so they let the information be tapped by a secondary source. The woman stammered, hesitated, and somehow managed to avoid answering the man's intrusive, unethical questions.

The first example is fairly typical of the way an employer might attempt to obtain information when questions cannot be asked directly. This strategy throws off an applicant who knows that such aspects of private life should not be discussed, but who wants to communicate smoothly, wants the job, and doesn't want to insinuate that any impropriety has occurred on the interviewer's part. In this example, hindsight caused the applicant to think, "I wish I hadn't fallen into that trap; I could have simply agreed with him by saying 'Yes, transition can be quite stressful.' " In the second example, the woman diffused the situation, choosing not to respond to the unethical questions. Indeed, there are ways to communicate effectively to indicate to an employer that you know what's going on and you're not going to play along. But you don't have to be contentious or cause the interviewer to lose face. The options of simple agreement or diffusion are nonconfrontational responses, but they communicate an awareness of what's happening. Another option is to respond to the question with a question, as though you didn't understand what the interviewer was getting at. Certainly another option is to use more confrontational, educative responses, but you have to weigh the risks of such tactics (like not getting the job). The main thing to think about is whether you want to work for a company whose interviewers would use strategies like these, as the woman in the second example had to do. When verbal and nonverbal indications of sex bias surface in a job interview, it increases the likelihood that sex-biased behavior and attitudes will be in evidence on the job.

Granted, the example conversation might have occurred with a male applicant and this particular male interviewer. But the sex bias lies in how the applicant's response is interpreted. Since an applicant doesn't know how a response will be interpreted, it's an unfair advantage for the interviewer. For instance, if a female applicant indicates that she is single and has no children, that information is likely to raise doubts about her stability and long-term connection to the company—the old "she might quit to get married and pregnant" stereotype. If a move or a lot of travel is involved in a job, an applicant's response that she has a husband and children may raise suspicions that she isn't serious about the job or that she will be resistant to traveling. If a male applicant is single and childless, his status won't typically raise similar suspicions. It's almost humorous to think of an employer saying, "He's a hiring risk because he's single; he might leave the company to get married and raise kids." The expectation, thus the sex bias, is that a woman's connection to a man weighs more in her professional decisions than a man's connection to a woman.

When Working Women Walk, Talk, and Look Like Men

The basic message behind the "dress for success" slogan is obvious: You need to dress well and exude confidence in an interview, you need to appear attractive (physically and in terms of personality), and you need to dress in a manner consistent with (or a bit more formal than) the employees who work where you are interviewing. For male job candidates, the dress for success advice generally works well, but it's not so straightforward for female candidates.

As communication researchers Borisoff and Merrill (1992) explain, "Women are encouraged not to dress in too feminine a manner; perhaps the perception is

CATHY COPYRIGHT 1991 UNIVERSAL PRESS SYNDICATE. Reprinted with permission. All rights reserved.

that such apparel would be too frivolous for the workplace. So they, too, must dress like men—but not so much like men that they risk being evaluated as masculine" (p. 71). These researchers describe the double bind that women experience and the challenge they face when they must strike some acceptable balance between femininity and masculinity in order to be taken seriously. If a female job applicant is perceived as masculine—by downplaying her appearance, dressing in too masculine a manner, or communicating too assertively, which is interpreted as masculine by some employers—she may incite homophobic reactions from interviewers or may be labeled a "headstrong feminist" (with all the negative connotations of the "f-word"). If she is perceived as feminine, she may not be seen as credible or capable of handling the job. If a woman is also highly physically attractive, her looks may be a deterrent to her getting a job, since female beauty often accompanies a perceived lack of intelligence. Another suspicion that accompanies high physical attractiveness for a woman is that she will cause more problems on the job than she is worth, in terms of "being a distraction" or inciting male interest. If you think these statements are ridiculous, imagine them in the reverse. Would a male job applicant be likely to lose credibility or be deemed not right for the job because he was perceived as masculine in an interview? Would a handsome man be denied a job because he might be unintelligent or too distracting to his female coworkers?

Women have reacted in some interesting ways to the realization of this double bind. During the 1970s when American society witnessed a significant increase in women working outside the home, female applicants who wished to be accepted into the male-dominated work force dressed like smaller versions of men, as their self-help books advocated. They wore dark, pin-striped suits, with skirts instead of pants and bows at the neck instead of ties. They wore wing-tipped pumps and carried leather briefcases, because heaven help a woman who showed up in a professional setting carrying a purse! They kept their jewelry, perfume, and makeup to a bare minimum, generally in attempts to play down the fact that they were women vying for the same positions as men. They did everything they could to be taken seriously. What happened?

In some instances, women gained some ground on the "being taken seriously" front. But in large part women's emulation of men didn't work. What women have learned since then is that when they attempt to emulate men—their dress, their verbal displays of aggressiveness and competitiveness, even their joking behaviors—they aren't received in the same favorable manner as men. Women are recognizing that while the emulation of men is usually an unsuccessful strategy, it may also cause a woman to lose her own identity as a professional (Fine, Johnson, Ryan, & Lutfiyya, 1987). Thus, since the 1970s, women have continued to find ways of creating their own paths and making their own voices heard within the world of work. The most obvious evidence of this can be found in many women's fashion magazines. When the fashion industry saw the opportunity to capitalize on the professional woman's dilemma, it responded with "middle ground" professional clothing. Now it is quite common to see working women in dress that combines traditional, conservative lines with softer materials and a wide range of colors.

But while the area of professional dress has broadened women's choices and provided some relief to the double bind, other areas haven't kept pace. Sex-role stereotypes are still alive and the double bind is still active for women who attempt to attain positions within the work force. As organizational communication scholar Linda Putnam (1983) contends, "Women function as representatives of their sex while simultaneously trying to liberate themselves from the negative aspects of their stereotype. As aspiring executives they are told to behave assertively and independently while being criticized for becoming parodies of men" (p. 39). The best rule of thumb that we can offer female and male students regarding job interviewing should sound quite familiar to you by now: Develop your communicative repertoire as fully as possible, employing masculine and feminine behaviors that can be effectively used given the demands of the interview situation and the particulars of the job and the company. For female readers, you might want to consider the possibility that society is in the middle of a shift or change regarding what is appropriate female professional demeanor. In some settings, communicating confidently and assertively in a job interview will be perceived positively. In other settings and with other interviewers, sex-role stereotypes may be operating, in that the same behavior may be viewed as masculine and therefore inappropriate coming from a female applicant (Borisoff & Merrill, 1992). For male readers, you might want to think about the possibility that some of the behaviors stereotypically labeled feminine—like verbal and nonverbal affiliative, supportive behaviors—may be highly valued by an interviewer, so it would be to your advantage to work these behaviors into how you present yourself in an interview. The personal effectiveness approach is by no means a prescription for success, but it can enhance your success ratio in professional as well as personal situations.

ON THE JOB AND MOVING UP

There's a wealth of information about communicating effectively on the job, about management styles, and about gender differences among professionals.

So much information exists that it can be confusing to weed out the helpful and accurate from the popular, often overly simplistic advice books on the subject. What we attempt to do in this section of the chapter is to give you the main themes of gender communication on the job, relying on research that has been conducted recently on the topic. Our goal is to hit the high points, with specific focus on two areas: sex-related concerns regarding advancement in an organization, including information about the glass ceiling; and management styles of women and men.

Male and Female Advancement within an Organization

Refer back to the statistics from the Department of Labor and the Korn/Ferry studies cited in the introduction to this chapter. A rough glance at this information might lead you to conclude that the work force is becoming more equitable, since the numbers indicate that women are steadily increasing their presence in the work force. But a more careful inspection will reveal something that has been written and talked about a great deal in recent years—the fact that women are just not achieving the higher, more responsible, and more rewarding ranks within the work arena. It appears that men and women are being hired with more equal frequency than in times past, but greater numbers of men than women are moving up into leadership positions. What factors are connected to this trend?

The Glass Ceiling

So much has been written using the "glass ceiling" phrase, that we expect you've heard the term before. To review, or if you are unfamiliar with the reference, here's a brief explanation and some background on the glass ceiling. In the mid-1980s a group of researchers based at an organization called the Center for Creative Leadership began a 3-year study entitled the Executive Women Project (Morrison, White, & Van Velsor, 1987). The term *glass ceiling* stems from a metaphor for working women who operate in "glass houses," whose behavior is not only scrutinized by individuals on every level of the organization, but whose success or failure might affect the status of working women everywhere (Kanter, 1977). Professional women who look upstairs, see the possibilities, and are repelled by a transparent barrier have seen the "glass ceiling." Lead researchers on the project, Morrison et al., describe the glass ceiling as follows: "Many women have paid their dues, even a premium, for a chance at a top position, only to find a glass ceiling between them and their goal. The glass ceiling is not simply a barrier for an individual, based on the person's inability to handle a higher-level job. Rather the glass ceiling applies to women as a group who are kept from advancing higher *because they are women*" (p. 13). Out of their extensive investigation of executives in the top 100 companies of those designated Fortune 500, these researchers placed the barrier for women at "just short of the general manager position" (p. 13).

Former Secretary of Labor Lynn Martin, in the Department of Labor's *Report on the Glass Ceiling Initiative* (1991), issued the following challenge: "The glass ceiling, where it exists, hinders not only individuals but society as a whole. It effectively cuts our pool of potential corporate leaders by eliminating over one-half of our population. If our end game is to compete successfully in today's global market, then we have to unleash the full potential of the American work force. The time has come to tear down, to dismantle the 'Glass Ceiling'" (p. 2). The Labor Bureau's study tracked nine Fortune 500 companies in order to understand the barriers to advancement for women and minorities and to assist corporations in determining strategies for eliminating the barriers.

The findings of the Glass Ceiling Initiative led Secretary Martin to place the ceiling at a lower level within the company than originally thought by Morrison et al. (1987). Martin contended that "attitudinal and organizational barriers are an indication that the progress of minorities and women in corporate America is affected by more than qualifications and career choices" (p. 4). Some of the factors contributing to the barrier for female and minority advancement include (1) corporate lack of attention to equal-opportunity principles, such as monitoring the progress and development, as well as compensation patterns, for all employees; (2) discriminatory placement patterns; (3) inadequate recordkeeping; (4) internal recruitment practices that maintained white male–dominated networks; and (5) lack of EEO (Equal Employment Opportunity) involvement in the hiring processes for mid- and upper-level management positions. When instances of barrier-building were detected within the companies, Labor Bureau investigators worked with corporate management, suggesting ways to correct the situation to allow for more female and minority advancement.

Explanations for Barriers

Other explanations for the discrepant advancement of female and male professionals have been suggested. Educational psychologist Dianne Horgan (1990) contends that, beyond external barriers to advancement, women often face internal barriers; that is, they communicate and behave in ways that hold them back from advancement. Some of these behaviors include deemphasizing and trivializing successes by attributing them to luck or circumstance rather than to ability, emphasizing failures rather than promoting successes, and accepting and perpetuating sex-typed language that widens the sexes' credibility gap.

But as gender communication researchers Nadler and Nadler (1987) point out, "The condemnation of women for their communication patterns seems inappropriate, as it would be like blaming the victim for being abused" (p. 130). While some internal factors may play a role in convincing women that they aren't "management material," the external factors are more devastating and actually reinforce the internal doubts that many women hold. As organizational communication researchers Stewart and Clarke-Kudless (1993) explain, "Women have not reached the top of the corporate hierarchy in part because of the sex-role stereotype held by many corporate decision makers that women do not have the personality characteristics necessary for top leadership roles" (p. 150). This points to the stereotypical judgment that because women are naturally affiliative and nurturing, they cannot make tough decisions that might disappoint others and they aren't assertive decision makers, opting not to make decisions out of a fear of "rocking the boat." (We discuss in more detail these perceptions of female leadership in a subsequent section on management ability and gender.) Whether one locates the problem internally, externally, or both, the glass ceiling for women still remains intact.

Nadler and Nadler (1987) suggest a dual approach to combating the problem. The first step isn't immediately gratifying, in that it calls for societal change. These authors contend that organizations must actively ensure that male and female employees' careers are developed with equal attention. They also encourage teachers, parents, and academic advisers or mentors to work with children at early ages to eliminate negative sex-role stereotypes *where they begin.* The second approach to change lies within the woman's own behavior. Nadler and Nadler suggest that women rely on those skills stereotypically related to their sex, but which most women possess and which are generally perceived positively in work settings. These skills include active and empathic listening, open communication styles, verbal and writing abilities, and nonverbal sensitivity. A final suggestion to women is to plan their careers well in advance and to proactively seek the advancement of their careers, rather than waiting for a superior to notice and reward their accomplishments. When women do advance within organizations, they again face perceptions that their behavior is "nontraditional" or "not the norm," distinctions which pose special challenges.

Women and Men in Management

Communication researchers, organizational behavior experts, and gender scholars alike have focused attention for decades on how the sexes approach management, leadership, conflict resolution, and decision making. They have attempted to separate the myth from the fact, surrounding the perception that men—and their stereotypical masculine traits of aggressiveness and competitiveness—make better managers. We offer you a capsule of some of the more provocative research into the topic of perceived management styles, beginning with a 1970s study cited with regularity in this literature. Then we address the self-reported and actual managerial behaviors of women and men in organizational contexts.

How Are Male and Female Managers Perceived?

In 1979, researchers Baird and Bradley examined employees' perceptions of the communication styles of their male and female managers. Employees also evaluated their level of satisfaction with their jobs. Results of the study indicated that employees were generally more satisfied with their jobs when they felt they had direct access to a manager who would communicate openly with them.

Employees also indicated that they believed female managers were more sensitive to their needs and more likely to openly communicate with them about problems on the job. Conversely, employees believed that male managers were more likely to resort to traditional power strategies as means of handling problems, rather than discussing them in an open manner. Results of a more recent study support Baird and Bradley's finding; that is, interpersonal communication skills were perceived as more valuable than other managerial attributes (Fine, Johnson, & Foss, 1991).

This information is inconsistent with the long-held attitude that, as communication scholars Berryman-Fink and Eman Wheeless (1987) point out, men "possess such stereotypically masculine characteristics as aggressiveness and competitiveness, are more capable, more acceptable, and preferred for management positions" (p. 85). Berryman-Fink and Eman Wheeless conducted a study to examine whether male and female employees held different attitudes regarding women in general, women as managers, and the communication competencies of women versus men in management. Female employees participating in the study held women in higher regard than male employees, viewed female managers in a more positive light, and believed that female managers were communicatively competent. Male employees evaluated the communication and management of female managers negatively in this study. This finding pointed to a concern discussed by the authors, a concern about the mediating effects of sex and gender when a female manager is being evaluated.

This study also exposed the problems with traditional, male-oriented management approaches that are based on military and team-sports models and that emphasize such aspects as competitiveness (balanced by a sense of teamwork), aggressiveness, risk taking, strategizing, and adhering to the chain of command. In organizations dominated by male management styles, female management styles will be "deficient" (Berryman-Fink & Eman Wheeless, 1987, p. 91). When women attempt to emulate the management behaviors of their male counterparts, they perpetuate the male-oriented system and are often devalued for this behavior, too. (This finding echoes some of the things we talked about in the earlier section on job interviewing.) What is most interesting from the Berryman-Fink and Eman Wheeless study was female employees' positive perceptions about female managers, especially that they were competent communicators. The authors conclude the following from this finding:

> Thus, as more women enter management spheres, the male-oriented management model is likely to give way to a flexible style that integrates traditional female behaviors and skills with traditional male behaviors. Management trends already are evolving to combine task-oriented skills (traditionally masculine) with people-oriented skills (traditionally feminine) to meet the demands of a changing work force and competitive marketplace. (p. 91)

Did you notice the reference to "flexible style" in that quotation? We follow up on the notion of a flexible management style in a subsequent section of this chapter. But for now the question is, if perceptions exist that women and men manage differently, what's the reality?

How Do Men and Women Communicate as Managers?

Attempts to expand the research design and to corroborate perception-based findings, particularly Baird and Bradley's (1979), have produced consistent results. Organizational communication scholars Rossi and Wolensensky (1983) and Rossi and Todd-Mancillas (1987) examined the communicative behavior of managers, rather than employees' perceptions of their behavior. These studies found that female managers, with both female and male employees, were more likely to resolve problems within the organization through open discussion and supportive communication, whereas male managers were more likely to use organizational protocol and power strategies. All these findings support the notion of the relational versus content approach to communication. Generally speaking, female managers approached situations out of a people-centered, relationship-based motivation, using open, supportive discussion as a means of solving a problem. Male managers typically used power strategies and structural or organizational protocol, such as engaging an organizational policy as a means of solving a problem. The latter approach places more emphasis on the task of resolving the problem rather than on the relationship between the manager, the employee, and the organization where both work.

One of the more distinctive differences in the management styles of men and women surrounds listening versus talking. Business researcher Josephowitz (1980) found that female managers were accessible and receptive to employees at about twice the rate of male managers. This study indicated that female managers communicated receptiveness by listening to the concerns of employees rather than offering them advice or attempting to solve their problems too quickly, before the real problem or deeper issue was revealed.

Another difference that receives a good deal of attention is the ability to resolve conflict within an organization—an ability in which men are believed to "have the edge" because of their stereotypical competitiveness and aggressiveness traits. Gender communication research Barbara Gayle (1991) investigated the conflict management styles of 1990s managers and discovered "no general predisposition for women in organizations to be any less controlling or more compromising than their male counterparts" (p. 165). Female managers did not report using more cooperative or nurturing strategies to resolve conflict; male managers did not report using more competitive or forceful strategies. Gayle asserted that managers operated more from a context-of-the-organization base than a sex-defined base, meaning that the culture of the organization affected their managerial responses more than being female or male.

Can Effective Managers Have It Both Ways?

As mentioned earlier, research and popular literature on the subject of gender and management currently call for a blended style, one that draws upon both masculine and feminine strengths in communication and leadership (Berryman-Fink & Eman Wheeless, 1987). This represents a move away from the traditional, male-oriented management style, in attempts to correspond to less traditional, less hierarchically based, flatter, and more decentralized organizations that face global competition in the 1990s.

As reporter Jaclyn Fierman (1990) contends, "What were once labeled women's weaknesses and cited as reasons they were ill suited for top jobs are suddenly the very traits *male* executives are expected to wear on their sleeves" (p. 115). In support of her contention, Fierman quotes Tom Peters, co-author of the best-selling management treatise *In Search of Excellence*, who suggests, "Gone are the days of women succeeding by learning to play men's games. Instead the time has come for men on the move to learn to play women's games" (p. 115).

The strongest proponent of the blended management approach has been Alice Sargent, author of a book entitled *The Androgynous Manager* (1981). Androgynous management "calls for a synthesis, a blending of the best of two existing polarities. . . . [It] embraces instrumental and expressive behavior, vicarious and direct achievement styles, collaboration and confrontation behavior, a proactive and reactive style, and compliance- and alliance-producing skills" (Sargent, 1983, pp. 71, 73). Sargent argues that men and women alike have suffered the consequences of a masculine management style, citing men's stress and related health problems as their negative consequences. However, while health problems caused by job stress are serious, it is possible that the negative consequences for women who adopt masculine management styles are more broadly based. Stress levels and health are affected, but women also face negative evaluations on the job, being denied raises and advancement opportunities and being isolated by coworkers.

Some of Sargent's ideas about androgynous management are provocative, such as the blending of linear, systematic problem solving with intuitive approaches, the balancing of competition and collaboration, and the ability to deal with power as well as with emotion. Sargent contends that "men need more than power and competitiveness to have a full repertoire of effective behavior. They need to learn to express and deal with emotions other than anger and frustration. They need to engage less in joking and jockeying to establish a position and more in sharing and nurturing to build a team" (1983, p. 73). Sargent's suggestion about an expanded repertoire of behavior corresponds nicely to the personal effectiveness approach.

However, you might want to exercise some caution regarding the androgynous management style. This may surprise you, since we are such advocates of androgyny and gender blending throughout this text. In most other contexts, an androgynous approach stemming from a well-developed communication repertoire seems to elicit the most positive responses from others. The problem is that, in the corporate setting, exhibiting behaviors that many people stereotypically associate with the opposite sex has the potential to backfire (Bate, 1988). For example, a male manager who reacts emotionally to bad news at work may be labeled the "corporate wimp," rather than being valued for his honest reaction. A female manager who aggressively communicates her views to her colleagues may be labeled the "corporate bitch." Sometimes, when a female manager uses stereotypically feminine behaviors, she receives negative reactions as well. Things are changing and female managers are still finding their way in the male-dominated corporate arena, so a simple prescription of androgyny at this point in the evolution doesn't really suffice.

No matter what jobs men and women hold—from front-line workers to middle managers to CEOs—they will most likely face some form of complication related to sex and gender. Right now, the sexes seem to be trying to figure each other out, trying to decide what kind of woman or man they want to be on the job, and trying to communicate effectively and be received positively. All this "trying" represents the current struggle in the workplace, but this struggle is manifested most dramatically by the problem of sexual harassment—the subject of the final section of this chapter.

THE PROBLEM OF SEXUAL HARASSMENT IN THE WORKPLACE

Just reading this heading may make you want to jump to the end of this chapter. As difficult as this topic is to think about, we bet you'll agree that it's an extremely important area for discussion. If you've ever experienced the problem firsthand, no further justification of the significance of the topic is necessary. If you've never experienced it firsthand, you're probably aware enough of the world around you to know that sexual harassment in the workplace is a topic on everyone's minds, as well it should be. But don't get the idea that sexual harassment is a recent phenomenon, one that only gained attention in the 1990s because of Anita Hill's sexual harassment allegations that emerged during the Clarence Thomas confirmation hearings or because of the Navy "Tailhook" scandal. In the 1970s, feminists coined the label "sexual harassment" for the behavior, but one can imagine that as long as men and women have worked together in many diverse settings, sexual harassment has occurred. (Notice that we didn't say, "and as long as they continue to work together, sexual harassment will still occur.") Many corporations, universities, and other types of organizations have had sexual harassment policies in place for years. Those organizations that haven't are probably busy drafting them now.

Before immersing ourselves in this discussion, let's consider a few cautions. First, women and men working together doesn't necessarily mean that sexual harassment is bound to happen. It's more likely that it will happen in a mixed-sex workplace than in a setting involving only same-sex workers, but sexually harassing behavior is not a "given" in the world of work. Second, most sexual harassment that is reported and researched involves heterosexual men and women; however, incidences of same-sex, homosexual harassment occur also. This phenomenon receives less study because of the infrequency of reported occurrence, but one shouldn't assume that it does not occur. Third, most reports and statistics about sexual harassment occurring within companies and institutions (such as universities) reflect a male-harasser, female-target profile (Fitzgerald et al., 1988; Leonard, Carroll, Hankins, Maidon, Potorti, & Rogers, 1989; Reilly, Lott, Caldwell, & DeLuca, 1992; Rubin & Borgers, 1990; Terpstra, 1989). Instances of female sexual harassment of men do occur; however, since the overwhelming majority of incidences of harassment involve female targets, our discussion focuses on this problem.

Perhaps many of you will have to jog your memories to recall the dramatic events that were played out on national television in the fall of 1991. For others of you, the images of Anita Hill claiming that she was sexually harassed by now Justice Clarence Thomas, who called his confirmation hearing a "high-tech lynching," will be etched into your memories for a long time. No matter whom you believed, no matter what your reaction was to this event, the Hill-Thomas situation had at least one profoundly positive effect—it opened a floodgate of discussion on the problem of sexual harassment. The topic had been researched by communication scholars and business leaders alike for at least two decades prior to this event, but the hearings generated a flurry of discussion, debate, and research unparalleled in previous years.

Exactly what *is* sexual harassment? The definition is fairly straightforward; however, the interpretation of what behaviors constitute sexual harassment is much more complicated and is the basis of many problems. Let's track back in time a bit, before a definition or conceptualization was available. Title VII, the Civil Rights Act of 1964, protected citizens from discrimination based on a variety of factors, one of which is sex. In essence, this law made sexual harassment illegal. With the passage of Title IX in 1972, educational institutions were mandated by law to avoid sex discrimination (Wood, 1992). But as you can well imagine, instances of sexual harassment continued despite the legislation. In 1980, the Equal Employment Opportunity Commission (EEOC) produced a set of guidelines containing the following definition of sexual harassment:

> Unwelcomed sexual advances, requests for sexual favors, and other verbal or physical conduct of a sexual nature constitute sexual harassment when (1) submission to such conduct is made either explicitly or implicitly a term or condition of an individual's employment, (2) submission to or rejection of such conduct by an individual is used as the basis for employment decisions affecting such individual, or (3) such conduct has the intention or effect of unreasonably interfering with an individual's work performance or of creating an intimidating, hostile, or offensive working environment. (EEOC Guidelines, 1980)

Until this time, most documented cases of sexual harassment were of the "quid pro quo" type: "Have sex with me or you'll lose your job." In 1986, a U.S. Supreme Court decision acted on the third clause in the EEOC definition, the "hostile climate" aspect, extending and legitimizing complaints of sexual harassment beyond the quid pro quo variation (*Meritor Savings Bank v. Vinson*, cited in Paetzold & O'Leary-Kelly, 1993). The most recent legal accomplishment came in the form of passage of the 1991 Civil Rights Act, which enabled sexually harassed individuals to sue organizations for both punitive and compensatory damages (Clair, 1992; Wood, 1992).

Even with definitions and legal history, sexual harassment remains difficult to characterize and prove legally. There are several issues regarding this topic to address in the remaining pages of this chapter: (1) A determination that sexual harassment has occurred is rooted in something we have discussed throughout this text—the receiver orientation to communication. A judgment of sexual harassment lies within the receiver of the communication; this judgment is not formed out of the sender's intentions. (2) Sexual harassment is an offense based on power, not on sex—just as rape is a crime of violence, not of passion. (3) Targets or victims have a range of personal, interpersonal, professional, and legal responses to sexual harassment.

The Receiver of Sexually Harassing Communication

We trust that you know the principles of the receiver orientation to communication backward and forward by now. Sexually harassing communication exemplifies the receiver orientation so well, in fact, that we used a harassment example to illustrate the orientation in Chapter 1. It boils down to this: When someone believes that communication directed to her or him is sexually harassing, that perception carries more weight than the sender's intentions. The sender may have meant his or her comments as a joke, a compliment, or simple teasing among friendly coworkers. Or the sender may have been trying to "get a rise" out of the target or "put out a feeler," just to see what the response would be. If there's a bottom line in sexual harassment, it's that the receiver's interpretation of the communication negates (or at least counters) the effects of the sender's intention.

Let's make this more personal. Say that two coworkers at a local company meet to discuss a project. The man is the woman's boss, and they have worked together at the company for about a year. As the discussion winds down, the man says, "Well, it's gonna get rough, but we've got to get this project rolling." The female employee responds, "We'll treat it as a challenge; the rougher, the better" to which the boss replies, "Yeah; I thought you were the kind of woman who likes it really *rough.*" If this example makes you chuckle, that's somewhat understandable, given that you're reading an artificial conversation on a page. But would it surprise you to know that this exact conversation occurred to a female friend of one of your text's co-authors? Others of you reading this example won't chuckle at all, because you interpret this seemingly simple exchange to be typical of sexually harassing communication.

Let's push this argument even further, adding further realism. When we use this example or similar ones in our classes, students immediately question, "What's wrong with *that?* He's just trying to be funny, to make a simple joke out of something she said. There's nothing sexual, nothing harassing in *that.* If she thinks that's harassment, then she has no sense of humor or she takes things *way* too seriously." (Did you say something like this to yourself when you first read the statements?) Granted, you have to factor into the female employee's interpretation of her boss's last comment several pieces of information: the nonverbal behaviors that accompanied the man's words (e.g., tone of voice, facial expression, touch), her history of interacting with him, her knowledge of his personality and how he communicates, her own understanding of sexual harassment, the climate or culture of the organizational setting, and so forth. Once these aspects have been factored in, the female employee in the situation can decide if her boss's comment constituted sexual harassment. *One* comment alone can constitute sexual harassment, if a receiver or target believes it to be.

This points to one of the main problems surrounding sexual harassment: What is deemed sexual harassment by one person (target) may not be taken as harassment by another. There are no magical rules that emerge or buzzers that sound when sexual harassment occurs. The boss could really have intended his final comment as a humorous way to close a stressful meeting. Nothing sexual could have been in the mind of the sender. But if his words caused the receiver or target to feel uncomfortable, if the comment was unwarranted or unwelcome, if she perceives that talk like that taints her work environment, then sexual harassment has occurred, according to the third aspect of the EEOC definition— the "hostile environment" aspect.

We cannot stress this point enough, because it seems that many people "just don't get it"—men and women alike. But in talking with students, we've learned they desperately *want* to "get it," especially before they land career-type jobs. If what you believe to be a simple compliment designed to make a coworker feel good, for example, was taken by that coworker as too personal, as an inappropriate entrance of sexuality into a professional setting, or as an unwelcome advance or invasion of some sort, then your coworker has a right to claim sexual harassment. Proving it or obtaining legal recourse may be a struggle, but the person has grounds. You can believe that your co-worker was paranoid and insecure, was out to get you, was an oddball, or held hatred for your sex. You can find a variety of explanations as to why your compliment was misinterpreted. But, given the tense climate surrounding this issue within organizations, some action toward you could be taken, such as a simple reprimand from a superior. This is extreme, and rarely does an employee push a harassment claim over one isolated, relatively benign incident. But the point is the same: The employee has grounds no matter how benign or seemingly innocent the incident.

If this information seems harsh or outlandish, go back and review the EEOC's definition of sexual harassment, especially point 3. The receiver of your "compliment" could claim that you communicated to her or him as a woman or man first, in a personal or sexual sense, rather than as a professional coworker. Even one instance of this kind of communication could create for some people a sense of a hostile or uncomfortable work environment.

These extreme examples are to help readers see that since even the most simple, inane, off-the-top-of-your-head comment can be taken in a way other than you intended, that kind of communication in the workplace is inadvisable.

People make comments to the effect that "Nothing's funny any more" or "Men just don't know *what* to say at work around women any more; they're walking on eggshells." Our reaction to this is that it is an opportunity for everyone on the job to learn some skillful, sensitive communication. If events or information have caused people to be more careful with how they communicate, that's a positive outcome. If something like the threat of being sued for sexual harassment causes women and men alike to think about the effects of their words and actions on others, then perhaps that is the impetus some people need to learn to communicate in a more equity-based manner in the workplace.

Sexual Harassment Is Power Play

Many people hold a misperception that sexual harassment is about sex. What the research reveals is that it is about power, not sex (Berryman-Fink, 1993; Jones, 1983; Konsky, Kang, & Woods, 1992; Norment, 1992). Sexually harassing communication is designed to put the target in a one-down position or to emphasize the harasser's status or power over another person. Many instances of sexual harassment occur between individuals who function within clearly drawn power lines, in relationships of boss-employer, teacher-student, doctor-patient, lawyer-client, and the like. However, recent evidence shows that peer harassment—sexually harassing communication between persons of equal status, power, and/or rank—is a disturbingly prevalent phenomenon, especially on college campuses (Hughes & Sandler, 1988; Ivy, 1993; McKinney, 1990). The problem of peer harassment is examined in Chapter 12.

Another characteristic of sexual harassment is that harassing incidents often occur within a well-established, trusting relationship between two people (Taylor & Conrad, 1992). Harassment can be an abuse of a mentor relationship, one in which the person with less power trusts, confides in, and looks up to the higher power person, as was illustrated in the opening case study to this chapter. Some targets of harassment have described a "grooming process" in which the harasser (who desires a sexual connection) slowly develops a professional, possibly friendship relationship with the target, winning her or his trust and admiration before extending the relationship into a sexual arena. Many believe this type of power abuse to be the most devastating to a target's self-esteem, confidence, and professional development.

Some attempts to understand why sexual harassment occurs link the behavior with male reactions to women's increasing presence in the work force. As women infiltrate organizations and institutions that were once considered exclusively male domains, men's reactions vary. On the positive side, some men may be genuinely supportive of women's achievement in the workplace and may even express relief that they have someone to talk to on a professional level, other than just men. However, some may express pleasure over women's workplace presence for the wrong reasons. An attitude like this is epitomized by a statement such as, "It's good to have women around the office because it gives a man something pretty to look at while he's working." On the negative side, men's reactions to professional women range from mild intimidation to feelings of being threatened to covert and overt displays of anger. Even though men still control a majority of the power positions, as described in the introduction to this chapter, many working men are likely to feel threatened in some way, or at least are likely to react with uncertainty at the presence of female coworkers. One way to outpower a female coworker, to "put her in her place," so to speak, is to treat her and address her as a woman first, and as a coworker, professional, and colleague second (or last). The same tenet about treating someone like an individual rather than a stereotype applies to the work area. If a male coworker wants to demean or outpower a female coworker, either as a vent for his anger or to incite a reaction on the woman's part, he will treat her like a sex object or like a helpless, incapable female who deserves disrespect, sexual joking, teasing, and worse.

Other explanations for the incidences of sexual harassment involve simple awkwardness, a lack of experience, and poor communication skill. In some instances, the reason for the harassing communication is ignorance—a person just simply did not know that sexual, personal communication on the job or in certain relationships is generally a carefully negotiated activity, if it is tolerated at all. Ignorance cannot be your excuse if you've read this chapter. We encourage you to keep informed about this topic so as to reduce the likelihood that your communication will be misinterpreted as harassing. The best advice that the research gives on this point is to communicate professionally, not personally and certainly not sexually, with all coworkers—subordinates, peers, and superiors. Sexual innuendo, disseminating sexual material, sexist language and jokes, excessive compliments about appearance rather than professional performance, questions about private life, requests for social contact, invasive, unwelcomed nonverbal behaviors—anything of this sort generally *has no place at work.*

Target Responses to Sexual Harassment

Responses to sexual harassment are as numerous as the persons who have experienced it, but we attempt to review some of the more common responses—personal, professional, and legal—that have been reported in research and literature on this subject.

The first issue is knowing when to call something sexual harassment, which sounds simpler than it really is. Research indicates that one of the more common reactions to sexual harassment is a reluctance to call it harassment (Fitzgerald & Ormerod, 1991; Kenig & Ryan, 1986; Konrad & Gutek, 1986). A target or victim of sexual harassment is likely to doubt or deny that the event occurred as she or he remembers it. In essence, there is a sense of "What just happened? Was that comment what I think it was? Did I hear that right, or am I imagining things?" Since sexual harassment is power play, the intentional harasser means to cause the target doubt, discomfort, loss of face, and any other one-down reactions that he or she can cause. When a target becomes befuddled or embarrassed over a comment or touch, for example, then the harasser's power play has had its intended effect. If you have been a victim of sexual harassment, or if you have the unfortunate experience of becoming one, realize that questioning the reality of the situation and your feelings of embarrassment or discomfort are common, understandable, justifiable reactions to being the target of a power play. Also realize that you have an empowering right to label the behavior or treatment "sexual harassment."

Another quite common, understandable response is for the target to blame herself or himself (Hughes & Sandler, 1986). Evidence of this comes from targets' typical negative self-messages: "If I'd only seen it coming," "I should have let him know that I wouldn't go for that sort of talk," and "Did I do something wrong? Did I encourage this person, or somehow give off clues that it was okay to talk to me like that?" It is not uncommon for a target to replay the event later, wondering in hindsight if another response would have been preferable (the old "I should have said . . ." dilemma). The main point here is that in most instances the target has not behaved or communicated in a way that invites sexual harassment. That's like saying a victim deserves punishment. Few would argue that victims of sexual harassment "asked for" the treatment they received.

However—and this is a big "however"—there are certain behaviors, both verbal and nonverbal, that an employee may enact which increase the possibility that she or he will become a target of sexual harassment (Cummings Jacobs, 1993). For example, a female employee who wears unprofessionally short skirts, extremely high heels, overdone makeup and hair, and flashy jewelry may find it difficult to avoid the "sex object" label. Understand that this is not a "blame the victim" stance; we're not saying that a woman who maintains this appearance at work deserves to be harassed. We're saying that a woman who presents herself in an unprofessional, sexual manner in the workplace is "playing with fire." She doesn't deserve unprofessional treatment, but she is increasing the likelihood that she'll be taken any way but seriously.

Likewise, when women try to "play with the big boys"—say by responding to sexual, off-color, or otherwise inappropriate jokes by attempting to "top" them with even dirtier jokes—it usually backfires on them. Earlier in this chapter we described what happened to women who tried to dress and behave like their male counterparts at work—emulation didn't work. Women often face double binds at work; they're damned when they act like women and damned when they act like men. The same applies to the topic of sexual harassment. When women try to diffuse an incident by responding passively and letting it go, they usually suffer great personal loss of self-esteem, confidence, and comfort on the job. They also become fearful of a future encounter with the harasser. When they respond aggressively, perhaps as a man would when in a power-down position, the response usually gets them labeled "office bitch" (when they protest) or "office slut" (when they accept or join in the joke).

Maybe you're wondering—"What can you do if you're a target of sexual harassment?" Research suggests responses on personal, professional, and legal levels. Sociologist James Gruber (1989) developed a four-part typology of personal responses to sexual harassment. Ranging from least assertive to most assertive, these responses are avoidance, defusion, negotiation, and confrontation. Given the discomfort level of the target, it's understandable that the most commonly used tactics or responses from a target to a harasser are to avoid or ignore the harassment (sometimes to the point of quitting one's job) or to defuse the situation (Cammaert, 1985). Many times female targets report defusion tactics, such as simply "laughing off a comment," "acting as though I didn't understand what was said," or "stumbling out a 'thank you' to a compliment that I didn't really appreciate and just walking away."

Some targets react more assertively to the situation by negotiating with the harasser, in the form of directly requesting that the behavior stop. A negotiating response might be "I think that kind of talk is inappropriate and it makes me uncomfortable, so I'd appreciate it if you would stop talking to me like that." Another tactic is to confront the harasser, typically by issuing an ultimatum such as "I'd appreciate it if you'd keep your distance and stop asking me personal questions. If you don't, I'll have to talk to the boss about it." Organizational communication researcher Shereen Bingham (1991) suggests that "more frequent and effective use of interpersonal communication for dealing with sexual harassment may improve relationships between men and women at work and reduce costs to organizations due to sexual harassment problems" (p. 110). It is more likely that assertive tactics will be used when the relationship is a close one with a longer history, one in which trust was set up and then violated, rather than when the harasser is a mere acquaintance. However, avoidance and defusion tactics are still common recourse when a closer, long-term coworker communicates inappropriately. Keep in mind that there are no "right" or "wrong" reactions; an assertive response to sexual harassment is not necessarily a wiser or better strategy than avoidance or defusion.

But, and this is a really important point, if you are a victim of sexual harassment, if you even just *think* that you may have been harassed, *tell someone.* It's critical to tell someone—a friend, family member, or coworker—what happened, what you interpret from the incident, how it made you feel, how you currently feel about yourself, your job, the harasser, and so on. Keeping it bottled up is an immediate, understandable reaction. Research documents a characteristic time lag for acting upon one's harassment experience due to the victim's feelings of helplessness and shame and because, for many victims, it takes time to realize that sexual harassment has actually occurred (Taylor & Conrad, 1992) People who have researched and experienced sexual harassment understand why it goes untalked about and unreported; they deem it understandable that Anita Hill waited 10 years to allege sexual harassment (whether they believe her allegations or not) (Foss & Rogers, 1992).

Internalizing a harassing experience won't help you if you have been victimized. Telling someone also allows a victim to gain another person's perspective on the situation, as well as creating documentation that can be used for possible professional and legal action in the future (Booth-Butterfield, 1986; Jones, 1983). We're not laying a guilt trip by saying that every victim should report sexual harassment to her or his superior (or to a person of authority if it occurs outside a work setting), because the decision to come forward and accuse someone by reporting an incident is an extremely personal one. There are always costs of such action—personal and sometimes professional costs (even though the law and workplace policies are doing a better job of protecting whistleblowers). But it's important to tell someone if you've been victimized. If you're the person someone speaks to about a sexually harassing experience, then your knowledge of the dynamics of such situations and of gender communication in general will be of tremendous value to you and to the other person in a conversation like this.

One last word of caution from experience and research regarding telling someone about a harassing experience: *Be careful whom you select to talk to.* This will either sound strange to you or eerily familiar, but remember the discussion in Chapter 7 about sex differences in listening and responding? Recall the information about how men often react to women's communication by problem solving, rather than responding empathically to what women are feeling. If you are a female victim of sexual harassment—at work, school, wherever—think long and hard before deciding that the first person you'll tell is your husband, boyfriend, or father. We're not suggesting that you shouldn't tell one of these persons, but that it is wise to apply the principles of the receiver orientation here. Consider what this man's reaction will likely be to your sexual harassment experience. If you do decide to confide in him, think a good deal about *how* you will tell him. You may have heard stories like we have, of men who "took on" women's harassment problems by confronting the harasser (often violently) or by going to the woman's boss, actions that only exacerbated the situation. It may be more empowering to fight your own harassment battle, with as many sources of support as possible *behind* you. This strategy may do more to repair your self-esteem, as well as enhance your respectability in the eyes of a boss or your coworkers, should you choose to report the harassment.

After you have told someone about the incident, it is wise to form a strategy for how you will respond to and deal with the situation on a professional level. If, for example, the harassment comes from a professor, how will you interact with that professor if you're in his or her class the rest of the semester? Will you drop the class, become withdrawn so as to endure the class, speak to the professor and possibly risk your grade, or will you take the first step in the grievance procedures most universities and colleges have developed, which typically is to inform the head of the professor's department?

If the harasser is a coworker, what will be your response? Again, there's no "right" answer, no magic response that wipes away the injury or affront you feel, but it's wise to put some thought to your future behavior, especially if you are concerned that the harassment may continue or if you anticipate future contact with the harasser. Your first action might logically be to consult an employee handbook for organizational policies and procedures regarding sexual harassment. However, you may have the rude awakening that your organization does not have such a document or hasn't developed a policy. In that case, your options are more limited because of likely ignorance among your organization's leaders and because there are no set, tested policies that address the problem. Your best hope is that the harasser's supervisor will take your complaint seriously and will take action to stop the behavior from recurring. If the harasser *is* the boss, then your next course of action is to file a complaint with the EEOC, starting legal action against the harasser and the organization.

Legal recourse for victims of sexual harassment is costly, time-consuming, and without guarantee of a desired outcome. But as more and more charges are filed, the issue continues to be taken more seriously, the laws and organizational policies are strengthened, and more victims are compensated. In the year following the Hill-Thomas testimony, the EEOC received 10,522 complaints of sexual harassment, compared with 6,883 filings in the fiscal year of 1991 ("Did America 'Get It'?" 1992). There are other indications that organizations are taking more seriously the prospect of litigation over charges of sexual harassment. A 1992 *Working Woman* magazine survey showed that among Fortune 500 companies, 81 percent reported having training programs dealing with sexual harassment. That figure compares to only 60 percent in a similar survey conducted in 1988 (Sandroff, 1992).

Whether we want to believe it or not, sexual harassment is a reality in the workplace—not in all workplaces, but in more than you'd imagine. Sometimes it arises out of ignorance, sometimes out of sincere intentions to get acquainted or to compliment, and many times out of a desire to embarrass or outpower another individual. Most of the time it comes from men and is aimed at women, but it does happen in the reverse and between same-sex individuals. If there is a bottom line to this discussion—a rule of thumb to leave you with—it's this: Intrusively personal, sexual communication of any sort has no place at work. It's best to avoid it unless, and *only* unless, you have negotiated these "dangerous waters" with persons at work and you all feel *completely* comfortable with this kind of communication. But, as a caution, there are very few of us who feel completely comfortable with this kind of communication with all of our coworkers, across all situations, at all times.

CONCLUSION

This chapter of the text has presented some of the more prominent issues challenging working women and men. We've tried to explore this particular context with students in mind, considering the situations and concerns that may arise when students launch or restart their careers. We've examined what the research says about sex effects in hiring practices, job interviewing, on-the-job communication, advancement opportunities, and management style. You've also been given an introduction to the topic of sexual harassment. Are you now magically equipped with a solution for every problem and a strategy for overcoming every obstacle you encounter at work? Will you be able to confront sex bias and gender-related communication perplexities with skill and ease? The answers are "probably not" to the first question, and "we hope so" to the second one.

Again, when it comes to gender communication, to the unique and complex dynamics of communication between women and men, there are no magical formulas, no sure-fire remedies, no easy answers. By ridding one's professional communication of stereotypes and personal or sexual forms of communication that are inappropriate in the workplace and by assuming a flexible, non–sex-specific communicative style with colleagues and superiors, you have gone a long way toward projecting a professional, successful image of yourself at work.

Key Terms

sexual stereotyping	unethical questions	grooming process
equal employment	double bind	avoidance
opportunity	barrier detection	defusion
quota system	hierarchy	negotiation
relational approach	management style	confrontation
content approach	global competition	assertive tactics
credibility	sexual harassment	interpersonal
leading questions	quid pro quo	strategies
hypothetical questions	hostile environment	

Discussion Starters

1. What do you know or what have you read about quota systems as part of hiring practices for some organizations? Have you formed an opinion about the use of a quota system? Think about your own profile—your sex, gender, race, and so on. Are you a person who would benefit from a quota system? What are some possible abuses of quota systems?

2. Think of a time you interviewed for a job you really wanted. It could be any kind of job—paper route, baby sitter, part-time waiter. Now imagine yourself in that interview, but as a member of the opposite sex. Would the person who interviewed you treat you any differently? If so, how so? Do you think your sex had anything to do with your getting or not getting that job?

3. Some people claim that sexual dynamics between women and men will always impede successful working relationships between them; that is, sexual tension taints the workplace and undermines professional relationships. Do you agree with this opinion? Have you ever been so attracted to someone in a job that it negatively affected your ability to work? How can an attraction like this be overcome? Should it be?

4. Think of a person who holds a position of power and authority in her or his job. This person might be one of your parents, your doctor, someone you've worked for—anyone with authority. What is the sex of that person? If that person is male, do you think he'd have as much power and respect in his job if he were female? Would he have to change his communication style or the way he dealt with coworkers, subordinates, and clients if he were female? If the person is female, what kinds of barriers or challenges has she faced as she achieved that position of respectability?

5. In this chapter, we discussed the double bind for women in management. We described how they are "damned if they do" act like men, and "damned if they don't" act like men (i.e., if they act like women). Do you think this double bind is real for working women? Have you ever experienced it, or know of a woman who has faced this kind of challenge in her job? Is there a corresponding double bind for male managers? What's an option out of the double bind?

6. From the fairly extensive discussion of sexual harassment in this chapter, think of something you learned, something that you did not know before reading this chapter, regarding harassment. For example, did you know that sexual harassment was about power, not sex? Were there any points that we raised in the sexual harassment section with which you disagree?

7. Whether you are male or female, think about how you would react if you were sexually harassed on the job. (Perhaps some of you have experienced it. If so, how did you react?) Do you imagine you'd respond by avoiding or ignoring the situation, or will you use some tactic of interpersonal communication with the harasser? What would be the possible range of risks of confronting the harasser, if he or she is your boss? A coworker? A subordinate?

References

BAIRD, J. E., & BRADLEY, P. H. (1979). Styles of management and communication: A comparative study of men and women. *Communication Monographs, 46,* 101–111.

BATE, B. (1988). *Communication and the sexes.* New York: Harper & Row.

BERRYMAN-FINK, C. (1993). Preventing sexual harassment through male-female communication training. In G. L. Kreps (Ed.), *Sexual harassment: Communication implications.* Cresskill, NJ: Hampton Press.

BERRYMAN-FINK, C., & EMAN WHEELESS, V. (1987). Male and female perceptions of women as managers. In L. P. Stewart & S. Ting-Toomey (Eds.), *Communication, gender, and sex roles in diverse interaction contexts* (pp. 85–95). Norwood, NJ: Ablex.

BINGHAM, S. G. (1991). Communication strategies for managing sexual harassment in organizations: Understanding message options and their effects. *Journal of Applied Communication, 19,* 88–115.

BOOTH-BUTTERFIELD, M. (1986). Recognizing and communicating in harassment-prone organizational climates. *Women's Studies in Communication, 9,* 42–51.

BORISOFF, D., & MERRILL, L. (1992). *The power to communicate: Gender differences as barriers* (2nd ed.). Prospect Heights, IL: Waveland Press.

CAMMAERT, L. P. (1985). How widespread is sexual harassment on campus? *International Journal of Women's Studies, 8,* 388–397.

CLAIR, R. P. (1992, November). *A critique of institutional discourse employed by the "Big Ten" universities to address sexual harassment.* Paper presented at the annual meeting of the Speech Communication Association, Chicago, IL.

CUMMINGS JACOBS, C. (1993, February). *Giving students a corporate picture: Sexual harassment in the workplace.* Paper presented at the annual meeting of the Western States Communication Association, Albuquerque, NM.

Did America "get it"? (1992, December 28). *Newsweek,* pp. 20–22.

FIERMAN, J. (1990, December 17). Do women manage differently? *Fortune,* pp. 115–117.

FINE, M. G., JOHNSON, F. L., & FOSS, K. A. (1991). Student perceptions of gender in managerial communication. *Women's Studies in Communication, 14,* 24–48.

FINE, M. G., JOHNSON, F. L., RYAN, M. S., & LUTHYYA, M. N. (1987). Ethical issues in defining and evaluating women's communication in the workplace. In L. P. Stewart & S. Ting-Toomey (Eds.), *Communication, gender, and sex roles in diverse interaction contexts* (pp. 105–118). Norwood, NJ: Ablex.

FITZGERALD, L. F., & ORMEROD, A. L. (1991). Perceptions of sexual harassment: The influence of gender and academic context. *Psychology of Women Quarterly, 15,* 281–294.

FITZGERALD, L. F., SHULLMAN, S. L., BAILEY, N., RICHARDS, M., SWECKER, J., GOLD, Y., ORMEROD, M., & WEITZMAN, L. (1988). The incidence and dimensions of sexual harassment in academia and the workplace. *Journal of Vocational Behavior, 32,* 152–175.

FOSS, K. A., & ROGERS, R. A. (1992, February). *Observations on the Clarence Thomas–Anita Hill hearings: Through the lens of gender.* Paper presented at the annual meeting of the Western States Communication Association, Boise, ID.

GAYLE, B. M. (1991). Sex equity in workplace conflict management. *Journal of Applied Communication Research, 19,* 152–169.

GRAVES, L., & POWELL, G. N. (1988). An investigation of sex discrimination in recruiters' evaluations of actual applicants. *Journal of Applied Psychology, 73,* 63–73.

GRUBER, J. E. (1989). How women handle sexual harassment: A literature review. *Sociology and Social Research, 74,* 3–7.

HICKSON, M. I., & STACKS, D. W. (1993). *Nonverbal communication: Studies and applications* (3rd ed.). Dubuque, IA: Wm. C. Brown.

HORGAN, D. (1990, November/December). Why women sometimes talk themselves out of success and how managers can help. *Performance & Instruction,* pp. 20–22.

HUGHES, J. O., & SANDLER, B. R. (1986). *In case of sexual harassment: A guide for women students.* A publication of the Project on the Status and Education of Women. Washington, DC: Association of American Colleges.

HUGHES, J. O., & SANDLER, B. R. (1988). *Peer harassment: Hassles for women on campus.* A publication of the Project on the Status and Education of Women. Washington, DC: Association of American Colleges.

IVY, D. K. (1993, February). *When the power lines aren't clearly drawn: A survey of peer sexual harassment.* Paper presented at the annual meeting of the Western States Communication Association, Albuquerque, NM.

JONES, T. S. (1983). Sexual harassment in the organization. In J. J. Pilotta (Ed.), *Women in organizations: Barriers and breakthroughs* (pp. 23–37). Prospect Heights, IL: Waveland Press.

JOSEPHOWITZ, N. (1980). Management of men and women: Closed vs. open doors. *Harvard Business Review, 58*(5), 56–62.

KANTER, R. M. (1977). *Men and women of the corporation.* New York: Basic Books.

KENIG, S., & RYAN, J. (1986). Sex differences in levels of tolerance and attribution of blame for sexual harassment on a university campus. *Sex Roles, 15,* 535–549.

KONRAD, A. M., & GUTEK, B. A. (1986). Impact of work experiences on attitudes toward sexual harassment. *Administrative Science Quarterly, 31,* 422–438.

KONSKY, C., KANG, J., & WOODS, A. M. (1992, November). *Communication strategies in instances of work place sexual harassment.* Paper presented at the annual meeting of the Speech Communication Association, Chicago, IL.

KORN/FERRY INTERNATIONAL & JOHN E. ANDERSON GRADUATE SCHOOL OF MANAGEMENT, UCLA. (1990). *Executive profile 1990: A survey of corporate leaders.* Los Angeles: University of California Press.

LEONARD, R., CARROLL, L., HANKINS, G. A., MAIDON, C. H., POTORTI, P. F., & ROGERS, J. M. (1989). *Sexual harassment at North Carolina State University.* Unpublished manuscript.

MARTIN, L. (1991). *A report on the glass ceiling initiative.* Washington, DC: U.S. Department of Labor.

MCCALLISTER, L., & GAYMON, D. L. (1989). Male and female managers in the 21st century: Will there be a difference? In C. M. Long & C. A. Friedley (Eds.), *Beyond boundaries: Sex and gender diversity in communication* (pp. 209–229). Fairfax, VA: George Mason University Press.

MCINTYRE, S., MOHBERG, D. J., & POSNER, B. Z. (1980). Preferential treatment in preselection decisions according to sex and race. *Academy of Management Journal, 23,* 738–749.

MCKINNEY, K. (1990). Sexual harassment of university faculty by colleagues and students. *Sex Roles, 23,* 421–438.

MORRISON, A. M., WHITE, R. P., & VAN VELSOR, E. (1987). *Breaking the glass ceiling: Can women reach the top of America's largest corporations?* Reading, MA: Addison-Wesley.

NADLER, J. K., & NADLER, L. B. (1987). Communication, gender and intraorganizational negotiation ability. In L. P. Stewart & S. Ting-Toomey (Eds.), *Communication, gender, and sex roles in diverse interaction contexts* (pp. 119–134). Norwood, NJ: Ablex.

NORMENT, L. (1992, January). Black men, black women, and sexual harassment. *Ebony,* pp. 118, 120, 122.

PAETZOLD, R. L., & O'LEARY-KELLY, A. M. (1993). Organizational communication and the legal dimension of hostile work environment sexual harassment. In G. L. Kreps (Ed.), *Sexual harassment: Communication implications.* Cresskill, NJ: Hampton Press.

PUTNAM, L. L. (1983). Lady you're trapped: Breaking out of conflict cycles. In J. J. Pilotta (Ed.), *Women in organizations: Barriers and breakthroughs* (pp. 39–53). Prospect Heights, IL: Waveland Press.

REILLY, M. E., LOTT, B., CALDWELL, D., & DELUCA, L. (1992). Tolerance for sexual harassment related to self-reported sexual victimization. *Gender & Society, 6,* 122–138.

ROSSI, A. M., & TODD-MANCILLAS, W. R. (1987). Male/female differences in managing conflicts. In L. P. Stewart & S. Ting-Toomey (Eds.), *Communication, gender, and sex roles in diverse interaction contexts* (pp. 96–104). Norwood, NJ: Ablex.

ROSSI, A. M., & WOLENSENSKY, B. (1983). Women in management: Different strategies for handling problematic communication interactions with subordinates. In *Proceedings of the 1983 American Business Communication Association International Conference* (pp. 79–83). Houston: American Business Communication Association.

RUBIN, L. J., & BORGERS, S. B. (1990). Sexual harassment in universities during the 1980s. *Sex Roles, 23,* 397–411.

SANDROFF, R. (1992, June). Sexual harassment: The inside story. *Working Woman,* pp. 47–51, 78.

SARGENT, A. G. (1981). *The androgynous manager.* New York: AMACOM.

SARGENT, A. G. (1983, April). Women and men working together: Toward androgyny. *Training and Development Journal,* pp. 71–76.

STEWART, L. P., & CLARKE-KUDLESS, D. (1993). Communication in corporate settings. In L. P. Arliss & D. J. Borisoff (Eds.), *Women and men communicating: Challenges and changes* (pp. 142–152). Fort Worth, TX: Harcourt Brace Jovanovich.

TAYLOR, B., & CONRAD, C. (1992). Narratives of sexual harassment: Organizational dimensions. *Journal of Applied Communication, 20,* 401–418.

TERPSTRA, D. E. (1989, March). Who gets sexually harassed? *Personnel Administrator,* pp. 84–88, 111.

WOOD, J. T. (1992). Telling our stories: Narratives as a basis for theorizing sexual harassment. *Journal of Applied Communication, 20,* 349–362.

CHAPTER 12

At the Head of the Class: Gender Communication in Educational Settings

W*e couldn't let you finish a textbook on gender communication* without a gentle reminder of what brought you to this text in the first place—your education. Your "sex" education, including your view of women's and men's roles in society and your communication with your own sex and the opposite sex, is an ongoing process. This education began quite early, as the case study illustrates.

CASE STUDY

Ruth found herself at a crossroads—one of those amazing points in life where you know that you're about to make the kind of decisions that change your life forever. Only a few years before reaching this intersection, Ruth had celebrated the fruits of her hard labor by achieving tenure and promotion at a major research university. As she was nearing the end of her thirties, Ruth enjoyed life's circumstances, as they had played out. She was a single, successful, career woman—a dynamic classroom teacher, a published researcher, and a valued member of her department. While Ruth typically spent more time on work than anything else, she still managed to maintain meaningful relationships with friends and family members.

In her thirty-ninth and fortieth years of life, Ruth married a wonderful man, gave birth to a child, and became an integral part of a family that extended to her husband's 15-year-old son by a previous marriage. Needless to say, life changed drastically for Ruth, and it has been changing ever since. In a very short period of time, Ruth went from what could be termed an independent, single, nonconventional life-style to one that is interdependent and more conventional. (Although to meet Ruth is to know that she approaches very few things in a conventional manner.) While she carried over the values, beliefs, and attitudes central to her identity into her "new life," obviously she confronted new experiences on a daily basis. One of the things she neither anticipated nor could have planned for in such a rapid turn of events was having to find creative ways of communicating nonstereotypical sex roles to daughter Angela—something in which she and her husband believed strongly.

As parents, Ruth and her husband agreed to be especially careful with the reading material Angela was exposed to. They attempted to shield Angela from such stereotypically depicted characters as "Dick," who leaves for work every morning, and "Jane," who waves goodbye to him as she's washing the breakfast dishes, and from the male-hero–female-damsel-in-distress dichotomy within many children's fairy tales. They exposed Angela to such nursery rhymes as "Jack and Jill Be Nimble," "The Old Couple Who Lived in a Shoe," and "Mr. and Ms. Pumpkin Eater," written by Doug Larche, better known as *Father Gander* (1985). They hoped that their attention to media stereotypes would give their daughter a broader vision of gender roles.

Ruth was recounting to some of us (her faculty colleagues) a recent experience with Angela. One day when Angela arrived home from preschool, she ran up to Ruth yelling "Cinderella, Cinderella; I want to hear about Cinderella." It seems that several children at Angela's preschool had been talking about Cinderella, making Angela curious because she didn't know who Cinderella was. To Ruth, it wasn't just that her daughter wanted to hear a story about a sweet, innocent, somewhat abused girl whose life is transformed by a handsome prince; this story also extolled the evils of stepmothers—another of Ruth's roles in her newly formed family. Ruth's protectiveness of Angela's reading material and knowledge about sex roles in society was being undermined, in a way, by Angela's early schooling experiences.

This incident dramatizes how something as seemingly innocuous as a children's fairy tale can act as an agent of sex-role socialization. What's your reaction to this case study? Is it one of irritation over an insinuation that something sexist might exist in the story of Cinderella? Or are you wondering about the possible effects that children's literature you were exposed to throughout your early years of education had on you? It's likely that one story alone didn't shape your entire perspective on the sexes. But what about a repeated theme that emerges in many fairy tales? Have you ever considered what those early stories may have taught you or led you to expect?

OVERVIEW

As a result of reading the four previous contextual chapters, you have no doubt become aware of how gender and sex affect one's communication and the communication one receives from others in each of these contexts. You probably remember the importance of context within the personal effectiveness approach, the notion that the effective communicator analyzes the situation, including the setting, the topic, and the persons in the situation, selects the best communication from a widely developed repertoire, enacts the communication with skill, and then assesses the result. But did you ever consider that the personal effectiveness model might apply to communication within classrooms, as well as it does to other contexts?

In this final chapter we examine communication in educational settings, primarily classrooms, in which teacher-student and student-student interaction has the potential to be affected by sex and gender. Specifically, this chapter explores:

- Children's nursery rhymes and fairy tales as agents of early gender-role socialization
- Textbooks and other educational literature that contribute to children's ideas about gender
- How teacher and student expectations based on sex and gender are formed and how they have the potential to affect classroom interaction and student learning
- Factors that contribute to the "chilly classroom climate" for women
- How textbooks and male and female communication styles affect the classroom
- Teacher classroom behaviors that are sex and gender linked
- The problem of peer sexual harassment on college campuses

INTRODUCTION

As you began to grow and develop, your ideas about your own sex and gender began to form. There were many influences or agents of socialization who shaped those ideas. The primary socializing agents were your parents, siblings and family members, friends, and exposure to various forms of media. This list of influences or socializers should also include your teachers—those individuals who gave you a formal education and from whom you learned some important, informal lessons about men, women, and how they function with one another. The information in this chapter challenges you to examine the effects of your experiences in educational settings—from preschool or kindergarten days to your college career—on your gender-role identity and your gender communication.

Do you view educational institutions as havens of equality, as places where such aspects of human diversity as gender and race are left outside the ivy-covered walls? While some of us who've made education our careers would like to think so and while we believe that educational institutions may be more sensitive to diversity issues than the world at large, no institution is exempt from various forms of discrimination. In this chapter, we examine the likelihood that subtle forms of sexism are lurking in the halls of education. The philosophy or belief that all persons are entitled to a formal education, ranging from preschool to college, is central to the functioning of educational institutions. However, educators also realize that individuals within the institutions do not arrive on the front steps as "blank slates." Everyone comes to the institution with sets of values, beliefs, attitudes, experiences, and behaviors that make them unique. Educators encourage that diversity, since working through differences is a direct route to higher learning and discovery. But sometimes, in subtle and not-so-subtle ways, you may get the feeling that your own brand of diversity is not as welcome or celebrated as someone else's.

Thus the educational institutions in your experience have contributed to the shaping of who you are, in regard to your biological sex and your psychosocial gender. They have informed you as to what being female or male means and how masculinity and feminity are manifested behaviorally, within their own cultural confinements. They have also affected how you have learned to communicate with members of your own sex and the opposite sex. How have educational institutions accomplished these feats? We explore the various methods in the pages that follow. Some may strike you as being so subtle that they couldn't possibly produce an effect, as in the case of children's nursery rhymes, fairy tales, and other forms of literature. Others may seem so blatant and realistic that you find your educational experience being discussed and matched in every paragraph. No matter how you react, it's important to explore the possible contributions of your education and your educators to your attitudes and communication behaviors with women and men. Let's begin at one of the earliest points in your lifelong learning process.

CHILDREN'S LITERATURE AND SEX-ROLE SOCIALIZATION

When we think back to childhood, many experiences come to mind—some good, some maybe not so good. Do your fonder memories include the stories that were read to you by a parent before you went to sleep, or stories you read with a teacher and classmates as part of your early education? Can you remember imagining yourself as one of the characters of a particular story? Did you ever want to be the prince who finds Cinderella's glass slipper or Gretel, who saves her brother by pushing the witch into the oven? Maybe it seems silly to think about these things now, but it's possible that who you are as an adult—your view of self, others, relationships, and communication within those relationships—has been affected in some way by the early lessons you received from children's literature at home and at school. In this section of the chapter, we focus on the potential sex-role socialization function of children's literature, from nursery rhymes and fairy tales to children's textbooks and readers.

Fairy Tales, Nursery Rhymes, and Sex Roles

JACK AND JILL BE NIMBLE
Jack be nimble, Jack be quick,
Jack jump over the candlestick!
Jill be nimble, jump it too,
If Jack can do it, so can you!*

*Source: Copyright © Girls Incorporated of Greater Santa Barbara. Reprinted with permission of Advocacy Press, P.O. Box 236, Santa Barbara, CA 93102. Not to be duplicated in any other form.

THE OLD COUPLE WHO LIVED IN A SHOE
There was an old couple who lived in a shoe,
They had so many children they didn't know what to do.
So they gave them some broth and some good whole wheat bread,
And kissed them all sweetly and sent them to bed.
There's only one issue I don't understand
If they didn't want so many why didn't they plan?*

Have you ever heard these versions of two well-known nursery rhymes? These represent one author's attempts to "ungenderize" traditional children's nursery rhymes. As we mentioned in the opening case study, Doug Larche (aka Father Gander) published a book of rewritten nursery rhymes that attempted to alter the adherence to sex-stereotypical portrayals of male and female characters. Another author, Jack Zipes (1986), edited a volume of fairy tales and critical essays about fairy tales written from feminist, non–sex-stereotypical perspectives. Do these efforts seem like a stretch to you, meaning that people are trying to find harm in the most innocent places? Students sometimes balk at the introduction of forms of children's literature as possible contributors to sex-role stereotyping and gender bias. Have you ever thought that the earliest stories and nursery rhymes you were exposed to had an effect on your expectations and communication behavior, especially with members of the opposite sex?

Suspend any doubts or disbelief for just a moment to consider the potential effects of reading or having read to you numbers of stories with the same basic plot—one that represented to you the kind of romance, excitement, and fulfill- ment possible for men and women. The young, beautiful girl, helpless or abandoned, encounters a series of obstacles (events or people) that place her in jeopardy. Enter the young, handsome, usually wealthy prince or king who rescues and marries the girl. This basic theme serves as the plot, with minor deviations, for such fairy tales as *Cinderella, Snow White and the Seven Dwarfs, Sleeping Beauty, Goldilocks and the Three Bears, Little Red Riding Hood,* and *Rapunzel,* to name only a few of the better known tales from folk culture. The basic attributes of female leading characters in such tales include beauty, innocence, passivity, patience (since they often have to wait a long time for the "prince to come"), dependence, and self-sacrifice. Male characters as rescuers have to be handsome, independent, brave, strong, action-oriented, successful, romantic, and kindhearted (for the most part). Does our characterization seem overdrawn to you? Are the characters' descriptors sex specific, meaning that they reflect stereotypical male and female traits? What's the potential effect of this depiction?

Feminist scholars have focused on the effects of stereotypical sexist portray- als in fairy tales on children's socialization. Marcia Lieberman (1986) believes, with specific regard for the effects on girls, that "an analysis of those fairy tales that children actually read indicates that they serve to acculturate women to traditional social roles" (p. 185). She goes further to suggest that "millions of women must surely have formed their psycho-sexual self-concepts, and their ideas of what they could or could not accomplish, what sort of behavior would be rewarded, and of the nature of reward itself, in part from their favorite fairy tales. These stories have been made the repositories of the dreams, hopes, and fantasies of generations of girls" (p. 187). Karen Rowe (1986) discusses the relationship between fantasy and reality, in that storybook characters and relationships may become a standard of how life is "supposed to be." She explains, "Subconsciously, women may transfer from fairy tales into real life cultural norms which exalt passivity, dependency, and self-sacrifice as a female's cardinal virtues. In short, fairy tales perpetuate the patriarchal status quo by making female subordination seem a romantically desirable, indeed an inescapable fate" (p. 209). Although not the focus of Rowe's or Lieberman's analysis, male consumers of such fiction may form standards for their own behavior, as well as for the behavior of women in relationships, based on idealized characterizations.

To get more concrete with these scholars' claims, let's think about the story of Cinderella, the beautiful girl who was abandoned after her father's death and terrorized and subjugated by her evil stepmother and two stepsisters. She is relegated to a virtual slave existence, until her crying is heard by a benevolent fairy godmother who sends her to the prince's ball. Everyone in the land knows that the handsome prince is searching for a wife, so all of the eligible women are decked out and positioned at the ball in order to win the prince's favor. You know how the story turns out: Cinderella "steals the show," loses her slipper as she exits the ball, and causes the prince to search for her. He is reunited with Cinderella because of her tiny, feminine shoe size, after which he punishes her stepfamily and triumphantly marries Cinderella.

Both Rowe and Lieberman draw some themes from this tale and others. First, the main characters must be physically attractive to be worthy of romance. Is this telling young children that good looks are essential to happiness and getting what you want out of life? Do only beautiful people deserve to find love and romance? The second theme is one of competition; that is, the heroine must often compete with other women for the attention and affection of the hero. The message here runs counter to the female tendency to cooperate rather than compete to accomplish one's goals; what might that communicate to young girls? And third, rewards for stereotypically sex-linked behavior include romance, marriage, often wealth, and a life that is "happy ever after." This may reinforce a message, especially for female children, that the ultimate goal is to marry a wonderful man who will protect you and make your life completely happy. There's nothing wrong with this goal, but is it the only appropriate goal? Could it communicate too much importance on having a relationship, especially on getting married, rather than exploring a range of options for fulfillment? Since even among modern women, many describe the pressure they feel to be in a relationship and especially to find a husband, one wonders where those thoughts originated.

To counter the possible effects of stereotypes conveyed via fairy tales, one school is using the literature as an opportunity to teach students to think critically. Teachers at the Longfellow School in Teaneck, New Jersey, indulge students by reading *Cinderella* in class, but the reading is followed by questions designed to elicit students' insights into the characterizations and plot. "Will Cinderella be happy after she and the prince are married?" and "Wouldn't it be better if Cinderella had wanted other things to make her happy?" are typical questions posed to get students thinking beyond the "happily ever after" ending (Sunstein Hymowitz, 1991).

Before you conclude that this examination of traditional fairy tales is gender paranoia or an affront to folk history, consider some adult variations on the themes. Why do you think so many people worldwide tuned in to the marriage ceremony of Prince Charles and Lady Diana? Many viewers were caught up in the romantic events—the beautiful, innocent girl swept off her feet by a modern-day prince, the stately, elegant ceremony, the romantic exit in a horse-drawn carriage. The prince and princess roles seemed fairly clear at that time, but the world has also watched the fracturing of its fairy tale as the couple's royal relationship has disintegrated. For another example, consider why romance novels constitute such a huge and profitable industry. Could it be that romance novels are mere extensions of the romantic themes we learned first as children reading fairy tales? Even though life is seldom like the fairy tales, do we still want to believe that relationships can be like that? Do we hold these idealized images of women, men, and romantic love as some sort of standard for how relationships really ought to be? What happens to people when the ideal and the reality don't intersect? Karen Rowe's (1986) perspective on this issue is illuminating:

> Precisely this close relationship between fantasy and reality, art and life, explains why romantic tales have in the past and continue in the present to influence so significantly female expectations of their role in patriarchal cultures. Even in the "liberated" twentieth century, many women internalize romantic patterns from ancient tales. Although conscious that all men are not princes and some are unconvertible beasts and that she isn't a princess, even in disguise, still the female dreams of that "fabulous man." But as long as modern women continue to tailor their aspirations and capabilities to conform with romantic paradigms, they will live with deceptions, disillusionments, and/or ambivalences. (p. 222)

Maybe you're wondering, "What's this have to do with me?" Have you ever thought that maybe these early, idealized images of what men and women were supposed to be for one another have set up some unattainable standards for your adult life? For example, think about a man who grew up believing in his role as provider and protector, led to think that his superior strength and independence were characteristics that would win women to him, characteristics that would allow him to rescue the fairer sex. What happens when he confronts a liberated, 1990s woman? She may not need rescuing or protecting; she may be stronger and more independent than he is or than he expected, so what happens to his version of "ideal"? What if this man, with these same characteristics, comes to a conscious realization somewhere along the line that he's gay? Consider the outcome for a woman who believes that some dashing, princelike figure on a white steed will come charging up to rescue her from life's unpleasant circumstances. What happens when women expect princelike qualities, when they form expectations of men that are too high and all-encompassing for virtually any man to fulfill? What happens when the "prince" turns into the "beast," an abusive wife-batterer? One thing you rarely get to see in fairy tales is what happens *after* the marriage ceremony; "happily ever after" is generally the closing line.

Obviously, many people cope with the incongruencies of life and fantasy. Most people don't live their lives in complete frustration because relationships don't mirror the movies or romance novels or childhood fairy tales. We learn—sometimes the hard way—that perfect people and perfect relationships aren't possible, or particularly interesting for that matter. We come to learn that the imperfections and the struggles are more worth our interest and energy than something we could call "ideal." But should we have to work to dismiss the early images? Could the early stories we're exposed to as children better prepare us for the realities we will soon encounter? Could the female and male characters represent more positive, balanced, realistic images of persons we'll likely deal with as we age and mature? What fairy tales could you write for your future children?

Gender Depiction in Textbooks and Literature
for Schoolchildren

Two main sources of gender bias exist within children's textbooks and supplemental educational literature: the numbers of depictions of and references to men versus women and stereotypical role portrayals of male and female characters. According to instructional communication scholar Pamela Cooper, male characters, figures, pictures, and references to authors still greatly outnumber those of females in current public school textbooks. The discrepancies "present negative images of females and reinforce sex-role stereotypical behavior" (Cooper, 1993, p. 124). As evidence of sexist role portrayals, Cooper cites various examples from textbooks for such content areas as science, economics, mathematics, and history. She describes a speech communication text which offers such hypothetical applications of communication skills as a woman making an announcement in a PTA meeting while a man argues a case in court.

Regarding supplemental children's literature in the schools, Cooper (1993) contends that "numerical disparities and stereotyped behavior patterns and characteristics reflected in children's literature teach girls to undervalue themselves and teach boys to believe that they must always be stereotypically masculine" (p. 125). In her study of award-winning children's books, Cooper (1991b) found that between the years of 1967 and 1987, a mere fourteen of ninety-seven books depicted female characters who worked outside the home. According to research, the old "Dick and Jane" breadwinner-housewife images and sex-typed behaviors are alive and well in children's literature (Cooper, 1987b; Heintz, 1987; Peterson & Lach, 1990, White, 1986). These images reinforce stereotypes that many children see operating in their own worlds. But they may also offer false images that are inconsistent with reality. Think of the impact of what a child reads in school, how that reading material can shape a child's vision of what is "right," acceptable, or "normal" in life. What if, for example, a child grows up in a single-parent household in which the parent must hold down multiple jobs just to make ends meet? How can this child compare "Dick and Jane" portrayals to her or his own existence? How "normal" does life look in comparison to what is being read?

Some alternative reading materials are being produced to widen the range of experience for schoolchildren; however, wading through the bureaucracy to gain acceptance in school systems can be a time-consuming task. One such book is *My Daddy Is a Nurse*, a supplemental reader for elementary grades that depicts alternative career paths and roles for men and women. Educational researchers Tetenbaum and Pearson (1989) would likely applaud such expanded role depiction in children's literature, since they concluded their article on gender and storybook characters by stating, "One would wish that the authors of children's stories would begin to depart from the gender-linked behavior of their characters. Narrow role definitions have been postulated to impede healthy emotional adjustment" (p. 393). In some cases, however, books with modern depictions of alternative life-styles may not be the kind of reading material that some schools prefer for their kids. One such book is *Daddy's Roommate* by Michael Willhoite. This book has stirred up a great deal of controversy across the country, since it is about a young boy whose parents divorce because the father is gay. Its intention is to teach young children how to cope with having a homosexual parent or parents. One passage from the book explains, "Mommy says Daddy and Frank are gay. At first I didn't know what that meant. So she explained it. Being gay is just one more kind of love. And love is the best kind of happiness. Daddy and his roommate are very happy together. And I'm happy too!" (Willhoite, quoted in Seese, 1992, p. 1B).

Can you imagine what your reaction would have been to some of these contemporary books when you were in grade school? What would have been your mother's or father's reaction? Some of you who are nontraditional college students may have already dealt with such controversies while raising your own children. What reading material have you used to educate your children about the roles of the sexes in society? For the traditionally aged students, those yet to raise children, how do you think you will approach this issue when you have kids? It's important to consider the kinds of subtle messages you may pass on to future generations, either by what you allow your children to read or by how you react to what they read in school. We're not insinuating that there's a "correct" message, but that some kind of message is likely to be sent and received, just as there are subtle messages in the programs children watch on television.

EDUCATIONAL EXPECTATIONS AND GENDER BIAS IN THE CLASSROOM

Even though educational institutions hold up as a goal inclusion and equality for all students, the smallest denominator within an educational institution is the individual. Teachers, like other human beings, come to the educational setting with their own sets of beliefs, values, attitudes, opinions, experiences, and expectations. Within that set are their viewpoints on sex and gender. Here we use both terms *sex* and *gender* because attitudes generally go beyond mere biology, or sex. Attitudes apply to such things as one's view of appropriate roles for women and men in society, what is deemed masculine and feminine behavior, and how sexual orientation affects the picture—that is, components of *gender*, as we have used the term throughout this text. So no one begins with a clean slate; we all approach situations and contexts with imprints of our experiences. However, when teachers and students allow their imprints to form rigid expectations about the behavior and aptitude of the sexes, gender bias may be the result. In subsequent sections we describe a variety of ways in which expectations manifest themselves in classrooms and other educational settings. Before we do that, let's get a basic understanding of how expectations form and how they can create an atmosphere of gender bias in an educational context.

Did you ever sit in a classroom and feel like the teacher had formed an expectation about you before you even had a chance to open your mouth? Did you feel, in high school for example, that a teacher labeled you a jock, bad girl, or nerd and then treated you differently based on that label? Ever felt like you were deemed a C student in a class, and that no matter how hard you tried or what you said or did, you were going to get a C in that class? These things point to the impact of expectations on achievement and enjoyment in a classroom setting, but how does gender fit into the expectations picture?

If you're a male reader, have you ever experienced treatment or communication from a female college professor that conveyed to you a different expectation, merely because you were male? You might have picked up an attitude like, "You are a man, so you'll think like a man and probably be a chauvinist or a potential harasser. You probably won't take to this material as well as the women." Maybe you picked up on an attitude that communicated you were more highly valued as a student than the female students in the class, simply because you were male. Or what about with teachers of your same sex? Have you ever felt that a male professor expected you to agree or comply with his terms, simply because of some male camaraderie expectation? Or have you felt that a male professor expected more of you than your female counterparts? For the female readers, can you think of a male professor who held expectations of how women were going to approach his course content and how they were going to achieve in the class, in comparison to the male students? Think about a more obvious example; think about the lone female student in an engineering class full of male students and taught by a male professor. Gender or sex bias might not necessarily exist in that classroom, but then again, it might. Conversely, have you ever felt that a female professor expected you to agree with her information and views, just because of some "sisterhood" standard? What happened when you voiced a dissenting opinion or interpretation? These are just a few hypothetical examples of how teacher expectations can affect your involvement, appreciation, and achievement in a class.

Student expectations also play a role in this process. The male co-author of your text has occasionally sensed in communication classes that female and male students alike entered his classroom with a "Show me" attitude, simply because he was male and the expectation was that communication is more of a woman's field than a man's. In gender communication classes, in particular, he occasionally senses an attitude from students that translates into, "So what would *you* know about sex discrimination? You're a man in a man's world." Likewise, the female co-author of your text has occasionally felt like students held her up to more scrutiny in the classroom, as if they were saying, "So, show me what you know, woman"—more so than her male colleagues were likely to encounter. Sometimes envy is experienced when female teachers would like to have what they perceive to be male teachers' "instant credibility."

Research across public school grade levels has explored a range of teacher and student expectations stemming from a number of characteristics, including expected aptitude to grasp content, general intelligence, sex or gender, social class, age, reading ability, race, and personality attributes, to name just a few (Brophy, 1983; Cooper & Good, 1983; Dusek & Joseph, 1983). Educational researchers Dusek and Joseph (1983) conducted a meta-analysis of studies examining a common set of teacher expectancies, in order to isolate the "types of information teachers use in forming expectancies for students' academic potential" (p. 328). Of particular interest to us were their results regarding student gender. Among sixteen studies of the effect of gender expectations on student academic performance, measured in terms of grades on essays, work habits, expected future grades, and expected test performance, the results were mixed and contradictory. This led Dusek and Joseph to conclude that "student gender is not a basis of teacher expectancies for general academic performance" (p. 331). However, among fourteen studies measuring expectancies for social and personality development, female students were expected to outperform their male counterparts. The researchers thus concluded that teacher expecta-tions related to sex and gender may have more to do with classroom demeanor than with actual academic achievement.

However, educational researchers Benz, Pfeiffer, and Newman's (1981) results varied with previous studies of gender expectations. Teachers in grades one through twelve read descriptions of male, female, high-achieving male and female students, and low-achieving male and female students. They then assigned each description a masculine, feminine, androgynous, or undifferenti-ated label (based on scores from the Bem Sex Role Inventory). Results showed that across male and female teachers and across grade levels, teachers more often expected high-achieving students to be masculine or androgynous and low-achieving students to be feminine or undifferentiated, regardless of student sex. Benz et al. concluded that "if teachers expect girls to be feminine and boys to be masculine, the results clearly show what playing the roles can mean in terms of academic behavior" (p. 298).

A more contemporary study conducted by communication researchers Lawrence Nadler and Marjorie Keeshan Nadler (1990) focused on college students' perceptions of their own and their instructors' classroom behavior, as a means of examining how expectations get translated into behaviors. Their study was motivated by prior research suggesting that college classrooms are largely masculine domains in which male students exhibit dominant behaviors (Brophy, 1985; Hall & Sandler, 1982; Spender, 1983). Nadler and Nadler's results indicated that students brought expectations regarding the behaviors of female and male instructors into class with them. Specifically, "male instructors were depicted as more dominant . . . while female instructors were viewed as more supportive than their male counterparts" (p. 60). However, these expectations of teacher behavior did not vary according to the sex of the student. Nadler and Nadler report that "students did not believe they were treated differently by instructors based on sex and reported few differences in their own class-related communication behavior" (p. 60). The researchers conclude, "Clearly, percep-tions of sex-related differences in patterns of classroom communication in the college setting exist. Awareness of the nature and impact of the sex-related communication patterns is a necessary condition for beneficially altering these practices in the college classroom" (p. 3). Knowing that gender-biased expectations may possibly emerge in a classroom is useful information, but just what are these "practices" to which research refers? Just how do instructors and students communicate a sense of sex and gender bias via their classroom behavior?

GENDER COMMUNICATION AND THE COLLEGE CLASSROOM

Throughout this text we have discussed our values related to gender communication. As classroom teachers, we are highly concerned with how gender differences manifest themselves within the educational context. Although it is not easy (and perhaps not possible) to describe the "ideal" in all aspects of gender communication, the classroom may be a special case. It does seem possible, at least partly, to describe the ideal gender communication within the average college classroom. Communication opportunities in this context would be equally available to each student; each student would have equal access to the education available. The suggestion has been made that learning in the classroom is mediated through the communication process and if communication is biased, then the educational opportunities each student receives may be biased as well (Cooper, 1991a).

Years ago it was clear that this ideal of equality for men and women was not achieved in the average college classroom. From the 1950s into the 1970s men and women were given very different opportunities regarding their education. For example, one of your co-authors overheard a male professor in 1973 say, "Women are not capable of teaching at the college level and should not be admitted to doctoral programs." Certain fields (e.g., engineering and accounting) were completely male domains. Women were guided to elementary school teaching, nursing, and home economics. A standard joke of that time period (and you still hear it some today) was that "girls go to college to get their MRS. degree."

College Classrooms of the 1990s

How much has changed in the past few decades? How close are we to the ideal of equality in the classroom? As a student, do you believe that women and men have equal opportunities to communicate in the average college classroom? That they receive similar treatment from professors? That they have equal access to careers? Research suggests that men and women do not have the same experience in the classroom (Belenky, Clinchy, Goldberger, & Tarule, 1986; Cooper, 1993; Gilligan, 1982). This difference has a profound impact on the educational experiences of women and men. What occurs within classrooms that contributes to this trend? In the next several pages, we address that question by reviewing research on sex and gender differences in the classroom. We explore such topics as campus climate, sexism in textbooks, student participation, teacher-to-student interaction, effects of the identified differences, and suggested changes that may bring classroom communication closer to the ideal. As this research is discussed, we challenge you to determine if the research findings reflect the reality of your academic life.

The "Chill" in Higher Education

Instructional scholars believe that higher education is still strongly influenced by the "dominant intellectual ethos of our time," that is, the male majority (Cooper, 1993, p. 122). Education and communication expert Pamela Cooper contends that "an enormous amount of differential treatment, with regard to both the academic and social climate for women still exists in some form at all institutions" (p. 123). Some of these differences occur, if for no other reason, because only about 28 percent of college professors in the 1990s are women (Cooper, 1993).

Differences in the communication behavior of women and men in college classrooms and differences in the manner in which college professors communicate with male and female students are so pronounced that they have given rise to the term "chilly climate" as a descriptor for academic settings (Hall & Sandler, 1982, 1984; Sandler & Hall, 1986). Educational researchers Hall and Sandler describe the difficulties women face in the average college classroom—difficulties their male counterparts do not face. These difficulties are based on differences in the communication behavior of men and women and in the way each sex is communicated to by instructors. In other chapters in this text, especially the contextual chapters, we described the potential influences on your communication behavior that exist within the context. We then suggested communication options that will enable you to increase your chances of communicating effectively within the context. The same process applies to educational settings. An understanding of the influences members of each sex face in the college classroom can help create a communication climate that supports the educational needs of everyone.

Sex Bias in Textbooks

One influence on communication behavior of students is the textbooks used in courses. While it is beyond the parameters of this chapter to catalog all of the examples of male-female differences in texts, we do want to point out enough examples of differential treatment so that you become more adept at spotting them. Textbooks are excellent examples of subtle but pervasive sex bias and sex-role stereotyping. For example, science texts include approximately three times as many pictures of men as women and adult women are almost never presented in scientific roles (Nilsen, 1987). Educational researcher Balzer (1989) states, "If women do not see women in science, if their teachers are 95 percent men, and if textbooks are predominantly male, they won't go into science unless they're specifically out to break down those barriers" (p. 33). In these science texts, men control the action and women watch the action; boys perform experiments, girls clean up. Communication textbooks are not to immune sex-stereotyped behavior. Communication scholar Jo Sprague (1975) reported that most public speaking texts feature speeches only by men. Cooper (1993) concludes that "despite the adoption of nonsexist guidelines during the past decade, textbook publishers have made relatively few changes to increase the viability of females and decrease the stereotyping of males and females. . . . 'Nonbiased' material is sometimes added to the center or end of a text, without any attempt to integrate it into the overall format of the rest of the book" (p. 125).

As you move through your college career, it might be interesting to examine your textbooks for evidence of sex or gender bias. Which sex is represented more frequently in examples and/or illustrations within a text? Does a text treat both sexes equally in discussing applications of the material or careers? Does it offer other ways of thinking than what might be considered the traditional male pattern? Does it use nonsexist language, meaning that *he* and *she* both appear as personal pronouns? Reading textbooks with these questions in mind may help point out examples where the ideal we discussed earlier is still not being met.

Male and Female Students' Classroom Participation

In the ideal college classroom, members of both sexes participate with about the same frequency, ask similar amounts and types of questions, and actively engage in their own learning. Research, however, suggests that this is not the case; currently, student participation is far from "ideal" with respect to sex-based behavior. Some of the research on sex differences dates back to the 1960s and 1970s. For example, in 1968 education and gender scholar Goldberg found that when given identical essays, evaluators gave the essay a higher grade when it was attributed to a man than to a woman. In research related directly to classroom communication, Sternglanz and Lyberger-Ficek (1977) found that men more often dominated class discussions, while women were less verbally aggressive.

Interest in these kinds of differences accelerated throughout the 1980s. Communication and gender scholars Treichler and Kramarae (1983) contend that women and men literally do have different cultures, and thus different interaction patterns. These patterns lead women and men to experience the classroom differently. However, Hall and Sandler (1982, 1984) conclude that patterns of classroom participation contribute to the "chilly climate" for women in higher education. Research they reviewed on communication within college classrooms found the following: (1) men talk more than women, (2) men talk for longer periods and take more turns at speaking, (3) men exert more control over the topic of conversation, (4) men interrupt women much more frequently than women interrupt men, and (5) men's interruptions of women more often introduce trivial or inappropriately personal comments that bring the women's discussion to an end or change its focus. Hall and Sandler conclude that women are not given the same opportunity as men to express themselves in the average college classroom.

Research on the teaching process has found that most classrooms tend to favor a traditionally male approach to learning and devalue or disconfirm a traditionally female approach (Treichler & Kramarae, 1983; Wood & Lenze, 1991). Cooper (1993) describes the conventional model of classroom interaction as emphasizing "objectivity, separateness, competitiveness, and hierarchical structure," which she contends are more indicative of male characteristics than female (p. 122). Communication researchers Wood and Lenze summarize research results on this issue as follows:

> In most classrooms, asserting self is more rewarded than waiting one's turn, individual achievement is valued more highly than collaborative efforts, talking is encouraged more than listening, presenting new ideas is emphasized whereas responding to and synthesizing classmates' ideas is not, competition is stressed more than cooperation, and advancing firm conclusions is more highly regarded than holding tentative ones. (p. 17)

Based on this research, most classrooms appear to follow the male pattern of communication. Does this match your experiences in college classes?

Three dimensions of classroom communication have received research attention, as they relate to sex bias: initiation, discipline, and dominance (Cooper, 1993). In terms of who initiates interactions in class, research indicates that male students initiate more interactions with teachers and these interactions generally last longer than those of female students (Brophy, 1985; Hall & Sandler, 1982). Research results on classroom discipline parallel findings for initiation. Coinciding with a higher incidence of male participation in classrooms, male students are more often the target of a teacher's discipline than female students (Brophy, 1985). However, this trend may be counterbalanced by what other research has found. In a study of the relationship between academic achievement and teacher praise, researchers discovered that low-achieving and high-achieving male students alike received more praise than high-achieving female students (Parsons, Heller, & Kaczala, 1980).

Regarding dominant classroom participation, research shows that men interrupt professors and other students significantly more often than women, particularly in female-taught classes (Brooks, 1982). Sandler and Hall (1986) indicate that some of the more typically male verbal behaviors, such as talking longer than women, taking more turns at talk, controlling the topic of discussion, and interrupting and overlapping others' speech, are abundant in classrooms as well as other contexts. Conversely, female students use stereotypical feminine linguistic patterns (described in Chapter 5) in classrooms, such as hesitations, tag questions, excessive qualifiers, and generally deferential patterns of speech that decrease their dominance. Male students are more likely not only to dominate classroom talk but also to control such nonverbal aspects such as physical space (Sandler & Hall, 1986; Thorne, 1979). Overall, research on student participation in classrooms presents an extensive list of differences between the sexes. As we suggested earlier, it's to your advantage to use these research findings as a means of examining your own communication patterns, as well as those of classmates.

Teacher-to-Student Classroom Interaction

In addition to the communication patterns of students within a classroom, research has also identified differential communication behavior some faculty accord male and female students that goes beyond surface classroom verbal contributions. In her analysis of classroom communication patterns, Cooper (1993) found that teachers tend to use sexist language, call on male students more often, and ask male students more complex questions than female students. Other research indicates that male students are perceived as being more fun to teach than female students and that male students are given more opportunities to interact with the teacher (Sadker & Sadker, 1985), more time to talk (Keegan, 1989), and longer explanations about class assignments and procedures (Cooper, 1993).

In their analysis of the "chilly climate" for women in university settings, Hall and Sandler (1982) describe a number of areas of differential behavior. Their findings begin with the fact that most faculty are men and faculty tend to affirm students of their own sex more than students of the other sex. This simple difference may lead to different levels of confirmation and support. Hall and Sandler identify the following behaviors that represent differential treatment of men and women in the classroom:

1. Ignoring female students while recognizing male students
2. Calling directly on male students but not on female students
3. Calling male students by name more often than female students
4. Addressing the class as if no women were present (e.g., "When you were a boy . . .")
5. Working toward a fuller answer to a question by probing or coaching male students for additional information
6. Waiting longer for men than for women to answer a question
7. Interrupting female students and allowing them to be interrupted by classmates
8. Asking women lower order, more simplistic questions
9. Responding more extensively to men's comments than to women's
10. Making seemingly helpful comments which imply that women are not as competent as men
11. Phrasing classroom examples in a way that reinforces stereotypical negative views of women's psychological traits
12. Using classroom examples that reflect stereotyped ideas about men's and women's social and professional roles
13. Using the generic "he" to represent both men and women
14. Reacting to comments or questions articulated in a "feminine style" as inherently of less value than those stated in a "masculine style"

15. Making eye contact more often with men than with women
16. Nodding and gesturing more often in response to men's questions and comments than women's
17. Changing vocal tone to indicate a more serious treatment of men's comments
18. Assuming a posture of attentiveness when men speak, but the opposite when women make comments
19. Habitually choosing locations within classrooms that are near male students
20. Excluding women from course-related activities
21. Grouping students according to sex
22. Allowing women to be physically "squeezed out" from viewing laboratory assignments
23. Favoring men as student assistants (pp. 7–9)

This is quite an extensive and detailed list. However, research shows that many students experience at least some of the differential treatment described here.

Other research suggests that the sex of a professor makes a difference in the interaction patterns of students. Research in the 1970s found that when an instructor is male, male students participate at a rate three times more frequent than female students. Educational researchers Karp and Yoels (1977) found that in male-taught classes, male students were much more likely to be directly questioned by the professor and twice as likely as female students to respond to a comment. In female-taught classes, however, professors were equally likely to directly question male and female students, and participation by students of both sexes was found to be more nearly equal. Subsequent studies support these findings, in that classes taught by women had more student input, more teacher and student questions, more feedback, and more overall student interaction (Macke, Richardson, & Cook, 1980). Female professors were also less direct in reprimands and less likely to confront students directly; rather they corrected students in such a way as to avoid the appearance of authority (Richardson, Cook, & Macke, 1981).

However, other findings are contradictory. Education and gender researchers Boersma, Gay, Jones, Morrison, and Remick (1981) reported that male students made proportionally more comments than females in female-taught classes, yet in male-taught classes female students were involved in proportionally more interactions. Communication researchers Pearson and West (1991) found that male instructors received more questions than female instructors from students, and that male students asked more questions than female students in the classes of male instructors. Nadler and Nadler (1990), in exploring sex differences in students' perceptions of instructors' classroom communication behavior, found that male students did not report receiving more supportive behaviors and female students did not indicate receiving more dominant behaviors from instructors of the opposite sex. In this study, male and female students alike did not believe that they were treated differently by instructors of different sexes; they reported few differences in their own classroom communication behavior. Even though research findings reveal different trends, it appears that the sex of the professor may have at least some influence over the interaction patterns that emerge within a classroom. Again, if you are enrolled in courses taught by both women and men, compare the research findings to experiences in your classes.

Differential treatment works both ways; research indicates that male and female students treat female faculty differently than male faculty (Ryan, 1989). However, students who perceive that their male teachers are sexists generally dislike those teachers and describe their classes as less supportive and less innovative than those taught by nonsexist teachers (Cooper, 1993; Rosenfeld & Jarrard, 1986). Thus it would appear that nonsexist professors of either sex are rated more positively than sexist professors. As one might guess, communication researchers Rosenfeld and Jarrard found that sexism in the classroom is primarily something exhibited by men. In their research, Rosenfeld and Jarrard found that student coping behaviors such as withdrawing or hiding feelings were used only in classes taught by men. Are these patterns you observe in your classes?

Effects of Educational Sexism on Students

Cooper (1993) considered the effects of sex bias on students' self-confidence (as related to self-concept development), curriculum choices, and occupational choices. Interpersonal theorists suggest that the manner in which something is communicated to a person has an impact on his or her self-concept. For example, educational researchers Leonard and Sigall (1989) found that over the four-year span of college, women's grades, career goals, and self-esteem decline more than men's. Educational psychologist Lenney's (1977) investigation revealed that women's self-confidence is negatively influenced when a classroom task is not appropriate for women, the information on the task is ambiguous, and the task is evaluated by others. This is the usual pattern of most college classrooms—one that appears to negatively affect women's self-confidence.

In addition to effects on self-confidence, sex bias also affects students' choices related to learning and curriculum. According to Hall and Sandler (1982), these effects include (1) students dropping or avoiding certain classes, (2) minimizing one's relationship with the faculty, (3) diminished career aspirations related to certain fields of study, and (4) a general undermining of self-confidence because of suggestions that certain areas within college curricula are too difficult or are inappropriate for members of one's sex. More specifically, studies show that male students are far more likely to major in math, science, engineering, and other areas that rely on problem-solving ability, while female students typically shy away from these areas (Goldman, 1987; Lawrenz & Welch, 1983). Some of this trend may have to do with factors of biology and sociology, as we discussed in Chapter 2. However, recent research indicates that curriculum choice may be more related to how students are advised and reinforced than to some innate tendency or natural ability (Hall & Sandler, 1984). Unfortunately, some of the advice and reinforcement students receive from faculty advisers at some universities is sex biased.

Because of choices related to curriculum, the effects then extend to occupational choices. Sex bias first affects the probability that women will stay in school. Earle, Roach, and Fraser (1987) found that women drop out partly because of school practices that depress and devalue women's overall achievement. Another effect regards career choices. Hall and Sandler (1984) report that "counselors and academic advisors alike may overtly or subtly discourage many women by counseling students in accord with stereotypical ideas of 'male' and 'female' majors and careers" (p. 7). Advisers may also communicate bias by "suggesting that men broaden their academic focus to give them greater flexibility in the job market, but neglecting to do so for women" (Hall & Sandler, 1984, p. 7).

Differential sex-biased communication behaviors appear to be present in a variety of educational settings, especially in classrooms. Some negative effects have been identified by researchers, but remember that we began this section with a description of "how things used to be." Has the educational climate changed for women and men? If so, in what ways?

Changing the Educational Climate for Women and Men

Gender scholar Barbara Bate (1988) reports that colleges are the most masculine of learning environments but qualifies this point in two ways: "(1) Women now outnumber men in the number of students enrolled for credit in college courses and (2) students of either sex can now study engineering, or physical therapy, ceramics or accounting, if the requirements for admission have been met" (pp. 141–142). Bate also describes the changing mix of the average college classroom by noting that more and more nontraditional students (particularly women) are returning to college and enrolling in courses with high income potential in business and technical areas. These changes are evidenced by a greater balance in the numbers of men and women in traditionally male college majors. For example, at the university of one of your textbook co-authors, the number of women in the accounting program (one of the university's most rigorous and highly rated programs) has increased from approximately 10 percent in 1980 to approximately 50 percent in 1992. The nontraditional student will continue to exert a strong influence on the average college classroom. As the demographics of the average university begin to reflect the demographics of the society at large, more changes are expected.

These kinds of changes, however, are not happening very quickly. In interviews with a number of higher education professionals, education researcher Lippert-Martin (1992) found mixed messages as to the degree to which the educational climate has changed over the past decade. Those interviewed generally shared a consensus that the climate has not changed very much, except for small pockets of improvement, over the past decade. Change has come to some parts of higher education—sometimes brought on by women's studies programs, sometimes by institutional purpose.

How do we change the system? The male-as-norm conception of educational purposes, of students, of teachers, of curricula, of pedagogy—indeed of the profession of education—must be closely examined (Leach & Davies, 1990). Cooper (1993) suggests gathering more information about the diversity of the female experience, reconceptualizing the curricula, and infusing alternative approaches into the curriculum. She also describes the value of a perspective in education that focuses on personal knowledge, empowerment, diversity, and change. However, gender communication scholar Eric Peterson (1991) found that when a department consciously tried to incorporate gender balance in the curriculum, student response was mixed. Efforts to affect the climate for women and men included revising courses to include material on sex and gender diversity, incorporating into course content some significant works of female scholars rather than relying totally or primarily on male contributions, and acknowledging alternative ways of knowing and conducting educational inquiry. Some students found these changes interesting and valuable; others found them too oriented toward women or confusing as to the application to their lives. How would you respond if your department undertook a conscious effort to become more sex and gender sensitive?

The most applicable suggestions to you as a student are those that focus on classroom dynamics. The following suggestions were adapted from lists written primarily for faculty members, as a means of increasing the chances that their classes would reach the ideal we described at the beginning of this section. Perhaps you might find yourself in a position to help these behaviors occur more frequently.

1. Engage in interaction patterns during the first few weeks of classes that draw women into discussions.
2. Design and enforce course policy statements which make it clear that biased comments and behavior are inappropriate for the classroom.
3. Incorporate the institution's policy on classroom climate and sex bias into one's teaching.
4. Make a specific effort to call directly on female as well as male students.
5. Use terminology that includes both women and men.
6. Respond to male and female students in similar ways when they make comparable contributions in class.
7. Intervene when communication patterns develop among students that may shut out women.
8. Give male and female students an equal amount of time to respond after asking a question.
9. Give female and male students the same opportunity to ask for and receive detailed instructions about the requirements for an assignment.
10. When talking about occupations or professions in class discussion, use language that does not reinforce limited views of male and female role and career choices.

11. Avoid placing professional women in a special category, such as "female doctor."
12. Use the same tone of voice when responding to both male and female students.
13. Eliminate sexist materials from course readings and information.
14. Include items about classroom climate and sex bias on student evaluations.

This lengthy list serves as an effective way to analyze and guide potential areas for change. But the list does not exhaust the possible suggestions. Wood and Lenze (1991) describe the gender-sensitive classroom as one that includes "balanced content that highlights the strengths of traditionally masculine and feminine . . . inclinations," texts that "acknowledge and value both women's and men's concerns about interpersonal communication," and an educational climate "that equally values the interaction style women tend to learn . . . but also advances important social goals such as cooperation, effective listening, and being open minded" (pp. 16–17). They then provide strategies for creating or enhancing gender sensitivity in the classroom. As a student, note the presence or absence of these strategies in courses you take. Examples include content that overemphasizes, neglects, devalues, or misrepresents the concerns generally associated with one sex; an emphasis on traditional productivity and power approaches to leadership, approaches that are typically associated with masculinity; and the neglect of such issues as relationships and empowerment, which are typically associated with femininity (Kanter, 1977; McCall & Lombardo, 1983; Sadker & Sadker, 1985).

Integrating different communication styles and reducing the chilly climate in education will not be easy. Different students see different dimensions of the problem; some see no problem at all. If an individual class or an entire university undertakes a discussion of classroom climate and sex bias, it's probably necessary for everyone to realize that "just because it didn't happen to you doesn't mean it didn't happen." Male and female students, as well as faculty and administration, need to be sensitive to sex and gender differences that may exist within the hallowed halls of the university.

Again, as in the other contextual chapters of this text, we are not suggesting that one sex's style is more valuable or appropriate than another. The key is the awareness of the influences on your communication behavior within the context—in this case, the context of the classroom. Treichler and Kramarae (1983) state the problem: Should men adopt women's style or should women adopt men's? Or should both exist side by side? These scholars believe that the two can and need to exist, not just side by side but in an integrated fashion, so that both men and women will have the ability to use the traditional style of the other sex. In this manner, both sexes can work to meet the ideal of equality we described at the beginning of this section. One final topic warrants discussion in this chapter; it relates to sex bias and a discriminatory educational climate—possibly at their worst.

PEER SEXUAL HARASSMENT AMONG COLLEGE STUDENTS

Regarding sexual harassment, Gloria Steinem (1983) remarked, "A few years ago this was just called life" (p. 149). We discussed sexual harassment in detail in Chapter 11, but in this chapter we examine a specific form of harassment that has a pervasive effect on college students' lives—peer sexual harassment. As you know from reading the previous chapter, the pattern of sexual harassment most often reported and documented in research involves a male harasser and a female victim or target in a superior-subordinate relationship, for example, boss-employee, doctor-patient, or teacher-student. You also now know that the most difficult interpretation of the definition of sexual harassment pertains to the third clause in the Equal Employment Opportunity Commission's guidelines, the "hostile climate" clause (Paetzold & O'Leary-Kelly, 1993). Are you aware that many academic institutions have expanded the EEOC definition to reflect their profiles, including the insertion of the word "learning," as in "hostile working/learning environment"?

What people are beginning to realize is that the working or learning environment is greatly affected by one's relationships with one's peers, possibly even more than relationships with superiors. Yet more attention is paid to abuses of power relationships when the status or power differential is clearly defined, even institutionalized. What about power abuses within relationships in which no clear power lines exist? What about power plays between peers, such as classmates or coworkers?

The Problem of Peer Sexual Harassment

Research has made us aware that sexual harassment, just like rape and sexual assault, has much more to do with power than with sex (Berryman-Fink, 1993; Konsky, Kang, & Woods, 1992; Norment, 1992). However, it appears that we may need to expand our view of power. As educational researcher Katherine McKinney (1990a) contends, "Most researchers in the area of sexual harassment have assumed that harassment occurs only when the offender has more formal or position power than the harasser. Recently, it has been recognized that other types of power can be used by the offender including ascribed power (e.g., gender) and informal power (engaging in anonymous forms of harassment)" (p. 135).

A few studies have investigated forms of sexual harassment other than that which occurs within overt power relationships, that is, superior-subordinate sexual harassment (Grauerholz, 1989; Lafontaine & Tredeau, 1986; Littler-Bishop, Seidler-Feller, & Opaluch, 1982; Maypole, 1986; McKinney, 1990a). Sexual harassment between persons of equal status, such as coworkers, classmates, or social acquaintances, has been termed *peer sexual harassment* and that which is directed from someone of lower status to someone of higher status has been termed *contrapower harassment*. Benson (1984) coined the latter term after

---

What If?

What if you were sitting in class one day and someone asked to borrow your notes to study for an upcoming test? After you politely reply that you can't lend your notes because you need them for your own studying, *what if* the person becomes agitated and starts to argue with you, insisting that you are smart enough to pass the test, so your notes might as well help someone else? What's your response? Most students would probably feel complimented by the insinuation of being a good student, but they'd probably still deny the person access to their notes (since good students, almost by definition, usually review their notes several times before an exam). *What if*, at that point, the person started to get angry and *personal*? *What* would you do *if* the person called you a sexist, derogatory name and announced to your classmates that the reason you wouldn't share your notes with a friend was because you were sexually frustrated or because you were suffering from PMS? Has the person crossed the line from harassment to sexual harassment? When you read this account, what sex did you insert into the role of the person asking the favor, the harasser? What sex did you imagine the other student to be? Think about why you attached those sexes to the roles, and then think about *what* you would do *if* this actually happened to you. It doesn't matter if you're female or male; this or something similar (or worse) could happen to you. *What* would be your reaction *if* you were the target of peer sexual harassment?

---

conducting research which revealed that "women in positions of authority within a university or a business can be subjected to harassment by men who occupy formally less powerful positions within those institutions" (p. 518). The studies of peer sexual harassment to date have detected a dramatic, often surprising prevalence of the behavior among coworkers and classmates.

Compared to studies of superior-subordinate sexual harassment, little research has been conducted on harassment at the peer level. To date, the most comprehensive analysis of the problem of peer sexual harassment on college campuses was written by Hughes and Sandler (1988) from the Project on the Status and Education of Women, sponsored by the Association of American Colleges. Hughes and Sandler explain, "There is a darker side to campus life, often unnoticed. If acknowledged, it is too often brushed off as 'normal' behavior. This darker side is peer harassment, particularly the harassment of female students by male students" (p. 1). The range of behaviors Hughes and Sandler include in the concept of peer harassment starts with "teasing, sexual innuendos, and bullying of a sexist nature, both physical and verbal" and ends with "sexual aggression" (p. 1). (They use the term "sexual aggression" because of the belief that rape should be a category by itself.)

How prevalent is peer sexual harassment among college students? Hughes and Sandler explain that only a few colleges and universities have surveyed their students regarding the problem. They cite 1986 Cornell University statistics indicating that 78 percent of female respondents had received sexist comments and 68 percent had received unwelcome sexual attention from their male peers.

At MIT, 92 percent of the women and 57 percent of the men reported having been targets of at least one form of sexual harassment, not necessarily peer harassment. They also make reference to studies documenting "widespread harassment of women students by fraternity members" (p. 2).

Factors Contributing to Sexually Harassing Behavior between Peers

Why peer sexual harassment occurs has been the subject of a few authors' speculation. Hughes and Sandler (1988) suggest that socialization, anger, power, control, and group belongingness are possible contributing factors in male-directed sexual harassment. Since many men are socialized in our society to be dominant and to expect submissiveness from women, when they encounter independence, competitiveness, and assertiveness in women, they may become angry. That anger may translate into power enactments, such as sexual harassment or worse. Some men may react with general anger directed toward feminism, which some deem the root of many problems in society.

Beyond general anger at women's independence, a man may feel anger and resentment based on sexual frustration. When a man is rejected sexually, he may react by lashing out at the woman who rejected him or at other women. Many harassers, Hughes and Sandler (1988) explain, suffer from insecurity and poor self-esteem; thus they try to control other people as a means of appearing strong. Hughes and Sandler call this the "bully syndrome" (p. 7). Another factor relates to a group effect, or peer pressure, many men experience. Hughes and Sandler explain, "A desire to be 'one of the boys' and be accepted can explain some men's behavior, especially in groups. Participating in harassing activities becomes a way to bond with other men, a way to prove oneself" (p. 7). Other external factors affecting male proclivity to harass include the use of alcohol and drugs, the pervasiveness and availability of pornography and media violence directed at women, and plain old ignorance. In discussions about this topic with students, the issue of intentionality is raised in connection with harassers who simply do not know that their behavior is inappropriate or that it could be construed as harassment. Regarding the causes of the behavior, it is important to note that Hughes and Sandler, as well as other scholars who offer explanations, talk about *explaining* sexually harassing behavior, not *justifying* it.

A Recent Campus Survey on Peer Sexual Harassment

Given the limited information and the seriousness of the problem, a survey project was conducted at the campus of one of your co-authors as an initial attempt to understand how peer sexual harassment affects college students' lives (Ivy, 1993). The survey was designed to reveal three areas of information: (1) students' personal experiences with peer sexual harassment; (2) what students knew about other people's experiences with peer sexual harassment; and (3) students' opinions as to whether peer sexual harassment was a problem on college campuses. The cover page contained a description of peer sexual harassment, derived primarily from the EEOC's definition and Hughes and Sandler's (1988) information. Peer sexual harassment and the corresponding range of behaviors were explained in the following instructions to subjects:

> If you're unsure as to actions that constitute peer harassment, then think of it this way: one individual attempts, through any form of verbal and/or nonverbal behavior, usually of a sexual or especially personal nature, to gain an advantage over another person or to place the other person in a one-down or compromising position. Generally, the recipient of such messages or actions feels uncomfortable or senses that the behavior is inappropriate. However, often it is difficult for the person to label that behavior "harassment."
>
> Don't limit your thinking about harassment to overt instances, such as someone trying to secure a date with a classmate by threatening to spread rumors across campus about him/her. This is clearly an example of peer sexual harassment, but the range of harassing behaviors is more extensive than this. Any behavior that a target/victim deems unwelcome and inappropriate may constitute harassment—including excessive compliments about personal appearance and dress; sexual jokes, questions, comments, and innuendo; invasions of personal space; and inappropriate touch.

Of the 316 students who completed the survey, half were female and half were male, with an average age of 21 years. Among the female subjects, 71 percent reported they had been a victim or target of peer sexual harassment; 29 percent indicated they had not. Of the male subjects, 22 percent indicated they had been a target while 78 percent had not. The disparity in these figures may serve as a symbol of how far apart women's and men's understanding and experiences are on the issue of sexual harassment.

Women's indications of frequency of harassment ranged from an isolated incident to over 200 times over the course of the college career. Other responses included "daily," "frequently," and "2 to 3 times per week." Male subjects indicated a frequency of harassment from an isolated incident up to 50 times and offered no verbal responses other than "several." Ninety-nine percent of the harassers of women were men. The harassers of male subjects were primarily women; however, more incidences of homosexual harassment were reported by male subjects than by female subjects. The primary profiles of harassers were classmates, casual acquaintances, coworkers, and friends. The most frequent settings in which harassment occurred included classrooms, work settings, and social events. Most of the harassment involved a combination of verbal and nonverbal communication, including such behaviors as comments related to personal appearance, violations of personal space, and unwanted touching.

In the survey, when victims or targets were asked to briefly describe one harassing incident, the responses were startling, to put it mildly. The range of offenses described by subjects include isolated nonverbal behaviors such as staring or ogling one's body or stalking someone in a parking lot, to sexual remarks such as suggestive comments, repeated personal compliments, and jokes about sexual activity, up to a dramatic, tragic account of a beating and date rape in a male student's dorm room. There were multiple instances of sexual harassment that accelerated into date rape.

About two-thirds of the students responding to the survey reported that they knew of someone who had been a target of peer sexual harassment; 90 percent of the identified victims were women. When asked, "Do you think that peer sexual harassment is a problem on college campuses?" 87 percent of the female and 75 percent of the male students said "yes."

Below this last question was a space labeled "Comments" in which many subjects offered an opinion on the problem of peer sexual harassment. In general, women's comments reflected their belief that this was a serious problem, even if it had never happened to them. Several male responses echoed those sentiments, adding that it was probably more of a problem for women than men, meaning that women were more likely than men to experience it. However, a troubling and repeated response emerged among the men's comments. Several comments revealed a "blame the victim" attitude, as though they believed women were at fault for somehow inducing the harassment or for "making too big a deal out of nothing." The literature supports this trend; that is, women take the problem of sexual harassment more seriously than men (McKinney, 1990b; Powell, 1983). However, the tendency to disregard the seriousness of the problem, tossing it off as a "woman's problem," was a disconcerting result, to say the least.

Another theme emergent from subjects' comments was the confusion produced by differing perceptions of what behaviors constitute peer sexual harassment. In particular, some of the male students seemed to want a clear-cut, concrete definition, epitomized by one male student's comment, "Guys just need to know what it *is*, what guys say or do that girls take the wrong way. If you tell a guy what that is, he'll know not to do it." The problem is that it just isn't that simple; spoken communication and actions may be interpreted differently by different women.

One final theme emerging from this survey is noteworthy. Many subjects who had experienced sexual harassment were unwilling to use that label for their experiences. One female student remarked, "You become numb to it." This involves becoming so accustomed to getting whistled at, to hearing lewd comments about your appearance and sexuality from male onlookers, to being the butt of sexual jokes, to expecting men's sexual urges to get mildly out of hand, that one is reluctant to attach the label of sexual harassment to the behavior. A correlation can be made to a child who grows up in an abusive home. If abusive behavior is what someone has come to expect, he or she may not know that the behavior is aberrant and undeserved or to give it a label as strong as "abuse." Research on various forms of sexual harassment documents a common tendency for victims to be reluctant to label their abuse as sexual harassment (Fitzgerald & Ormerod, 1991; Hughes & Sandler, 1988; Kenig & Ryan, 1986; Konrad & Gutek, 1986). But what we're finding out is that assigning the label to the behavior is extremely empowering, especially for women. The victim in some ways is vindicated by the knowledge that what happened has a label. The label also provides the legitimacy that comes with naming: the behavior is illegal; other people have experienced it; and, in almost all instances, it's not the victim's fault. Calling the behavior sexual harassment isn't creating something that isn't there; it isn't talking someone into believing that something that happened is worse than it really is—it's an act of empowerment. It's a way to get sexual harassment "out of the closet" and into the light where it can be examined, understood, and maybe someday eradicated.

What's your reaction to this information about peer sexual harassment in educational settings? Do you think that female college students, in particular, have become used to "boys will be boys" behavior? Do they consider being made to feel uncomfortable merely part of college life? Do you think, as some of our male survey respondents indicated, that college women contribute to the problem, that they send mixed signals to men? Is it hard to know when to call someone's behavior sexual harassment rather than simple kidding around, flirtation, or the "usual treatment"? These are important issues surrounding a tough problem. And it appears that men and women have somewhat different views of the problem, although most agree that it is a problem. There are no simple solutions, except maybe one that research suggests and that students in our study echo: Treat classmates and coworkers—your peers—as individuals worthy of respect; keep personal and sexual verbal and nonverbal communication out of your interaction until you're *completely* sure that your actions or words will be received in a positive manner (and even then it's risky). No one deserves to be treated like an object or a stereotype, so the best approach is to communicate based on that belief.

On the receiver's end, what if the behavior of a classmate or coworker has made you feel uncomfortable and you wonder if it's sexual harassment? A couple of strategies are advisable. First, reread the information in this chapter and in Chapter 11. Then talk to someone about what happened; this will help you understand what happened to you and help you decide what action you want to take, if any. In some cases, a peer harasser may not know that he or she has done you wrong; harassers may simply be ignorant of the effects of their communication on others. In other cases, peer harassers know exactly what they are doing. A target may decide that educating the harasser is worth it, or maybe not. The least helpful things a target can do are blame the entire event on herself or himself, remain silent about the event (not even telling a close friend or family member), and, in some ways, perpetuate the problem.

CONCLUSION

This wraps up the final part of the text on gender communication within specific kinds of relationships and within certain contexts. Intuitively, you know that something said among family members may be interpreted differently by a friend, a romantic partner, a classmate, or a coworker. But intuition, or what some people like to call "common sense," isn't common to everyone. Some people don't realize the power of a context to affect a message. After reading these contextual chapters, we expect that you aren't one of these people. We expect that the importance of context in gender communication has been reinforced for you in the last several pages of this text.

Learning all you can learn about communication in educational settings, as well as about how gender communication operates in other contexts and in various types of relationships, will take you a long way toward personal effectiveness as a communicator. Practicing what you've learned, talking with women and men about what you know, making mistakes but being wise enough to stare down those mistakes, learn from them, and avoid repeating them, puts you even closer to the personal effectiveness goal. Becoming an effective communicator in a world complicated by gender, for starters, is an incredible challenge. We think you're up to it.

Key Terms

nursery rhymes	classroom interaction	ascribed power
fairy tales	initiation	informal power
gender-role socialization	discipline	superior-subordinate
diversity	dominance	sexual harassment
blank slates	career aspirations	contrapower
romance novels	curriculum choice	harassment
educational expectations	peer sexual harassment	bully syndrome
differential treatment	hostile learning climate	
chilly campus climate	power plays	

Discussion Starters

1. Think about your favorite fairy tale. Maybe it's a Disney tale or a favorite story a parent read to you when you were young. Now analyze the main characters. Was the female main character the center of the story? How would you describe her character, both her appearance and her personality? Does her character represent feminine stereotypes? How would you describe her male counterpart, the main male character in the story? Is he as stereotypically drawn as the female main character? What interpretations did you make of the story as a child? Do you have different interpretations now, as an adult? Why or why not?

2. If you believe in gender equity that women and men should have equal opportunities and be treated equally in our society—and if you see negative aspects of gender stereotyping around you, then how will you communicate your attitudes to your future children? If you already have children, how have you confronted this issue with them? Have you thought about the nursery rhymes, storybooks, and fairy tales you will expose your children to? Have you thought about how you might discuss sex roles with a child?

3. This chapter discussed some of the effects of teacher expectations on students' learning and academic achievement. Can you think of a time, either in school or in college, when you became acutely aware that one of your teachers held certain expectations of you? Were the expectations positive or negative, such as an instructor expecting you to excel or fail? Were the expectations in any way related to your sex or your

gender? How did the realization that those expectations were operating make you feel? Did the realization affect how well you learned in that class?

4. Take some of the specific "chilly" behaviors mentioned in this chapter and see if you detect them in operation in your college classes. For example, when your instructor raises a question in a class discussion, watch to see if male hands go up first and if more men than women are called on to speak. Do any of your teachers seem to direct more complex questions to male students and then "coach" them through the answers, in a different way than they do female students?

5. How do students in your classes add to a "chilly classroom climate" for other students? Are there certain expectations and resulting behaviors that make women feel like second-class citizens in your classes? If so, what are some ways that classmates or peers can counter the chill? How can female students be made to feel more accepted and encouraged in collegiate contexts?

6. Think about the problem of peer sexual harassment on your home campus. Have you encountered any harassing experiences in college classrooms? College social events? Do you know of other people who believe that they have been sexually harassed by a peer? Have friends told you of sexually harassing experiences yet been reluctant to attach the label to the behavior? Knowing what you now know about the problem, will you respond to peer sexual harassment—either directed at you or at a friend—any differently? If so, how so? If not, why not?

References

BALZER, J. (1989, November). Chem text photos discourage women. *NEA Today*, p. 33.

BATE, B. (1988). *Communication and the sexes.* New York: Harper & Row.

BELENKY, M., CLINCHY, B., GOLDBERGER, N., & TARULE, J. (1986). *Women's ways of knowing.* New York: Basic Books.

BENSON, K. (1984). Comment on Crocker's "An analysis of university definitions of sexual harassment." *Signs, 9,* 516–519.

BENZ, C., PFEIFFER, I., & NEWMAN, I. (1981). Sex role expectations of classroom teachers, grades 1–12. *American Educational Research Journal, 18,* 289–302.

BERRYMAN-FINK, C. (1993). Preventing sexual harassment through male-female communication training. In G. L. Kreps (Ed.), *Sexual harassment: Communication implications.* Cresskill, NJ: Hampton Press.

BOERSMA, P., GAY, D., JONES, R., MORRISON, L., & REMICK, H. (1981). Sex differences in college student-teacher interactions: Fact or fantasy? *Sex Roles, 7,* 775–784.

BROOKS, V. (1982). Sex differences in student dominance behavior in female and male professors' classrooms. *Sex Roles, 8,* 683–690.

BROPHY, J. E. (1983). Research on the self-fulfilling prophecy and teacher expectations. *Journal of Educational Psychology, 75,* 631–661.

BROPHY, J. E. (1985). Interactions of male and female students with male and female teachers. In L. C. Wilkinson & C. B. Marrett (Eds.), *Gender influence in classroom interaction* (pp. 115–142). Orlando, FL: Academic Press.

COOPER, P. J. (1987a, November). *In or out of the pumpkin shell: Sex role differentiation in classroom interaction.* Paper presented at the annual meeting of the Speech Communication Association, Boston, MA.

COOPER, P. J. (1987b). Sex role stereotypes of stepparents in children's literature. In L. P. Stewart & S. Ting-Toomey (Eds.), *Communication, gender, and sex roles in diverse interaction contexts* (pp. 61–82). Norwood, NJ: Ablex.

COOPER, P. J. (1991a). *Speech communication for the classroom teacher* (4th ed.). Scottsdale, AZ: Gorsuch-Scarisbrick.

COOPER, P. J. (1991b). *Women and power in the Caldecott and Newbery winners.* Paper presented at the annual meeting of the Central States Communication Association, Chicago, IL.

COOPER, P. J. (1993). Communication and gender in the classroom. In L. P. Arliss & D. J. Borisoff (Eds.), *Women and men communicating: Challenges and changes* (pp. 122–141). Fort Worth, TX: Harcourt Brace Jovanovich.

COOPER, H., & GOOD, T. (1983). *Pygmalion grows up: Studies in the expectation communication process.* New York: Longman.

DUSEK, J. B., & JOSEPH, G. (1983). The bases of teacher expectancies: A meta-analysis. *Journal of Educational Psychology, 75,* 327–346.

EARLE, J., ROACH, V., & FRASER, K. (1987). *Female dropouts: A new perspective.* Alexandria, VA: National Association of State Boards of Education.

FITZGERALD, L. F., & ORMEROD, A. L. (1991). Perceptions of sexual harassment: The influence of gender and academic context. *Psychology of Women Quarterly, 15,* 281–294.

GILLIGAN, C. (1982). *In a different voice.* Cambridge, MA: Harvard University Press.

GOLDBERG, P. (1968). Are women prejudiced against women? *Transaction, 6,* 28.

GOLDMAN, D. (1987, August 2). Girls and math: Is biology really destiny? *New York Times Educational Life,* pp. 42–46.

GRAUERHOLZ, E. (1989). Sexual harassment of women professors by students: Exploring the dynamics of power, authority, and gender in a university setting. *Sex Roles, 21,* 789–801.

HALL, R. M., & SANDLER, B. R. (1982). *The classroom climate: A chilly one for women?* Washington, DC: Project on the Status and Education of Women, Association of American Colleges.

HALL, R. M., & SANDLER, B. R. (1984). *Out of the classroom: A chilly campus climate for women?* Washington, DC: Project on the Status and Education of Women, Association of American Colleges.

HEINTZ, K. E. (1987). An examination of sex and occupational-role presentations of female characters in children's picture books. *Women's Studies in Communication, 11,* 67–78.

HUGHES, J. O., & SANDLER, B. R. (1988). *Peer harassment: Hassles for women on campus.* Washington, DC: Project on the Status and Education of Women, Association of American Colleges.

IVY, D. K. (1993, February). *When the power lines aren't clearly drawn: A survey of peer sexual harassment.* Paper presented at the annual meeting of the Western States Communication Association, Albuquerque, NM.

KANTER, R. M. (1977). *Men and women of the corporation.* New York: Basic Books.

KARP, D. A., & YOELS, W. C. (1977). The college classroom: Some observations on the meanings of student participation. *Sociology and Social Research, 60,* 421–439.

KEEGAN, P. (1989, August 6). Playing favorites. *New York Times,* p. 26A.

KENIG, S., & RYAN, J. (1986). Sex differences in levels of tolerance and attribution of blame for sexual harassment on a university campus. *Sex Roles, 15,* 535–549.

KONRAD, A. M., & GUTEK, B. A. (1986). Impact of work experiences on attitudes toward sexual harassment. *Administrative Science Quarterly, 31,* 422–438.

KONSKY, C., KANG, J., & WOODS, A. M. (1992, November). *Communication strategies in instances of work place sexual harassment.* Paper presented at the annual meeting of the Speech Communication Association, Chicago, IL.

LAFONTAINE, E., & TREDEAU, L. (1986). The frequency, sources, and correlates of sexual harassment among women in traditional male occupations. *Sex Roles, 15,* 433–442.

LARCHE, D. (1985). *Father Gander.* Santa Barbara, CA: Advocacy Press.

LAWRENZ, F. P., & WELCH, W. W. (1983). Student perceptions of science classes taught by males and females. *Journal of Research in Science Teaching, 20,* 655–662.

LEACH, M., & DAVIES, B. (1990). Crossing the boundaries: Educational thought and gender equity. *Educational Theory, 40,* 321–332.

LENNEY, E. (1977). Women's self-confidence in achievement settings. *Psychological Bulletin, 84,* 1–13.

LEONARD, M. M., & SIGALL, B. A. (1989). Empowering women student leaders: A leadership development model. In C. S. Pearson, D. L. Shavlik, & J. B. Touchton (Eds.), *Educating the majority: Women challenge tradition in higher education* (pp. 230–249). New York: ACE/Macmillan.

LIEBERMAN, M. K. (1986). "Some day my prince will come": Female acculturation through the fairy tale. In J. Zipes (Ed.), *Don't bet on the prince: Contemporary feminist fairy tales in North America and England* (pp. 185–200). New York: Methuen.

LIPPERT-MARTIN, K. (1992). On campus with women. *AAC Newsletter, 21,* 1–10.

LITTLER-BISHOP, S., SEIDLER-FELLER, D., & OPALUCH, R. (1982). Sexual harassment in the workplace as a function of initiator's status: The case of airline personnel. *Journal of Social Issues, 38,* 137–148.

MACKE, A. S., RICHARDSON, L. W., & COOK, J. (1980). *Sex-typed teaching styles of university professors and student reactions.* Columbus: Ohio State University Research Foundation.

MAYPOLE, D. E. (1986, January–February). Sexual harassment of social workers at work: Injustice within? *Social Work,* pp. 29–34.

McCALL, M. W., JR., & LOMBARDO, M. M. (1983, February). What makes a top executive? *Psychology Today,* pp. 26–31.

McKINNEY, K. (1990a). Sexual harassment of university faculty by colleagues and students. *Sex Roles, 23,* 421–438.

McKINNEY, K. (1990b). Attitudes toward sexual harassment and perceptions of blame: Views of male and female graduate students. *Free Inquiry in Creative Sociology, 18,* 73–76.

NADLER, L. B., & NADLER, M. K. (1990). Perceptions of sex differences in classroom communication. *Women's Studies in Communication, 13,* 46–65.

NILSEN, A. P. (1987). Three decades of sexism in school science materials. *School Library Journal, 33,* 117–122.

NORMENT, L. (1992, January). Black men, black women, and sexual harassment. *Ebony,* pp. 118, 120, 122.

PAETZOLD, R. L., & O'LEARY-KELLY, A. M. (1993). Organizational communication and the legal dimension of hostile work environment sexual harassment. In G. L. Kreps (Ed.), *Sexual harassment: Communication implications.* Cresskill, NJ: Hampton Press.

PARSONS, J. E., HELLER, K. A., & KACZALA, C. (1980). The effects of teachers' expectancies and attributions on students' expectancies for success in mathematics. In D. McGuigan (Ed.), *Women's lives: New theory, research, and policy* (pp. 373–380). Ann Arbor: University of Michigan Center for Continuing Education of Women.

PEARSON, J. C., & WEST, R. (1991). An initial investigation of the effects of gender on student questions in the classroom: Developing a descriptive base. *Communication Education, 40,* 22–32.

PETERSON, E. E. (1991). Moving toward a gender balanced curriculum in basic speech communication courses. *Communication Education, 40,* 60–72.

PETERSON, S., & LACH, M. (1990). Gender stereotypes in children's books: Their prevalence and influence on cognitive and affective development. *Gender and Education, 2,* 185–197.

POWELL, G. N. (1983). Definition of sexual harassment and sexual attention experienced. *Journal of Psychology, 113,* 113–117.

RICHARDSON, L. W., COOK, J., & MACKE, A. S. (1981). Classroom management strategies of male and female university professors. In L. Richardson & V. Taylor (Eds.), *Issues in sex, gender, and society.* Lexington, MA: D. C. Heath.

ROSENFELD, L. B., & JARRARD, M. W. (1986). Student coping mechanisms in sexist and nonsexist professors' classes. *Communication Education, 35,* 157–162.

ROWE, K. E. (1986). Feminism and fairy tales. In J. Zipes (Ed.), *Don't bet on the prince: Contemporary feminist fairy tales in North America and England* (pp. 209–226). New York: Methuen.

RYAN, M. (1989). Classroom and contexts: The challenge of feminist pedagogy. *Feminist Teacher, 4,* 39–42.

SADKER, M., & SADKER, D. (1985, March). Sexism in the schoolroom of the '80's. *Psychology Today,* pp. 54–57.

SANDLER, B. R., & HALL, R. M. (1986). *The campus climate revisited: Chilly for women faculty, administrators, and graduate students.* Washington, DC: Project on the Status and Education of Women, Association of American Colleges.

SEESE, D. (1992, July 24). Kids' book about gay father sets town abuzz. (Raleigh) *News and Observer,* pp. 1B, 5B.

SPENDER, D. (1983). Telling it how it is: Language and gender in the classroom. In M. Marland (Ed.), *Sex differentiation and schooling* (pp. 98–116). London: Heinemann Educational Books.

SPRAGUE, J. (1975). The reduction of sexism in speech communication education. *Speech Teacher, 24,* 37–45.

STEINEM, G. (1983). *Outrageous acts and everyday rebellions.* New York: Holt, Rinehart & Winston.

STERNGLANZ, S. H., & LYBERGER-FICEK, S. (1977). Sex differences in student-teacher interactions in the college classroom. *Sex Roles, 3,* 345–352.

SUNSTEIN HYMOWITZ, K. (1991, August 19, 26). Babar the racist. *The New Republic,* pp. 12–13.

TETENBAUM, T. J., & PEARSON, J. (1989). The voices in children's literature: The impact of gender on the moral decisions of storybook characters. *Sex Roles, 20,* 381–395.

THORNE, B. (1979). *Claiming verbal space: Women, speech, and language in college classrooms.* Paper presented at the Conference on Educational Environments and the Undergraduate Woman, Wellesley College, Wellesley, MA.

TREICHLER, P. A., & KRAMARAE, C. (1983). Women's talk in the ivory tower. *Communication Quarterly, 31,* 118–132.

WHITE, H. (1986). Damsels in distress: Dependency themes in fiction for children and adolescents. *Adolescence, 21,* 251–256.

WOOD, J. T., & LENZE, L. F. (1991). Strategies to enhance gender sensitivity in communication education. *Communication Education, 40,* 16–21.

ZIPES, J. (1986). *Don't bet on the prince: Contemporary feminist fairy tales in North America and England.* New York: Methuen.

Name Index

Subject Index

Aggression, 47–50
Anatomical sex differences, 40
Androgyny:
  in children, 320
  defined, 58–62
  and management style, 351–352
  and relationship change, 234
  and self-disclosure, 222
  and teacher expectations, 378
Attraction, 191–196

Bem Sex-Role Inventory (BSRI), 61, 234, 378
Brain functioning, 52

Chauvinism, 12
Cognitive abilities, 51–52, 52–54
Cognitive development theory, 56–57
Communication:
  axiom of, 151–152
  competence, 21–23, 77, 195–196, 349
  process of, 14–15
  receiver orientation to, 16–19, 96, 200,
    288–289, 295
  relational vs. content approaches to, 150,
    152–155, 160–161, 207, 339–340, 350
  repertoire, 21, 60, 345, 351, 320
  report vs. rapport, 157
  routine, 309
Confirmation:
  definition of, 27
  in educational contexts, 383
  in listening behavior, 206–207
Conversation:
  intimacy levels of, 158
  management, 169–173
  starters, 200–201
Cycles, 50–52

Daytime television talk shows, 128–129
Decentering, 25–26

Educational contexts:
  chilly climate in, 380, 381, 383, 386–388
  sex/gender bias in, 376–379, 380–381,
    385–386
  student participation in, 381–383
  teacher-student interaction in, 383–385
Empathy, 223–224
Employment interviews:
  sex/gender bias in, 337–344
  unethical questions in, 341–343
Empowerment:
  definition of, 13–14,
  in educational contexts, 387–388
  in families, 323–324
  and listening, 225
  and nonsexist language, 98–99
  in relationship initiation, 195, 198, 202
  and sexual harassment, 393–394
  versus power, 13–14
Equal opportunity, 337–338
Expressive orientation, 58, 156

Feminism, 11–13
Friendship:
  cross-sex, 261–270
  definition of, 248
  female-female, 255–261
  impact of socialization on, 249–250
  male-male, 250–255
  and sexual activity, 261, 263–264, 267, 269

Gender:
  communication, 4–6
  definition of, 7–8